CYBERSPACE
IN PEACE
AND WAR

TRANSFORMING WAR

Paul J. Springer, editor

To ensure success, the conduct of war requires rapid and effective adaptation to changing circumstances. While every conflict involves a degree of flexibility and innovation, there are certain changes that have occurred throughout history that stand out because they fundamentally altered the conduct of warfare. The most prominent of these changes have been labeled "Revolutions in Military Affairs" (RMAs). These so-called revolutions include technological innovations as well as entirely new approaches to strategy. Revolutionary ideas in military theory, doctrine, and operations have also permanently changed the methods, means, and objectives of warfare.

This series examines fundamental transformations that have occurred in warfare. It places particular emphasis upon RMAs to examine how the development of a new idea or device can alter not only the conduct of wars but their effect upon participants, supporters, and uninvolved parties. The unifying concept of the series is not geographical or temporal; rather, it is the notion of change in conflict and its subsequent impact. This has allowed the incorporation of a wide variety of scholars, approaches, disciplines, and conclusions to be brought under the umbrella of the series. The works include biographies, examinations of transformative events, and analyses of key technological innovations that provide a greater understanding of how and why modern conflict is carried out, and how it may change the battlefields of the future.

CYBERSPACE

IN PEACE

AND WAR

MARTIN C. LIBICKI

NAVAL INSTITUTE PRESS
ANNAPOLIS, MARYLAND

This book has been brought to publication with the generous assistance of Marguerite and Gerry Lenfest.

Naval Institute Press
291 Wood Road
Annapolis, MD 21402

Library of Congress Cataloging-in-Publication Data
Names: Libicki, Martin C., author.
Title: Cyberspace in peace and war / Martin C. Libicki.
Description: Annapolis, Maryland : Naval Institute Press, [2016] | Includes
    bibliographical references and index.
Identifiers: LCCN 2016031363 (print) | LCCN 2016035110 (ebook) | ISBN
    9781682470329 (hardcover : alk. paper) | ISBN 9781682470336 (ePub) | ISBN
    9781682470336 (ePDF) | ISBN 9781682470336 (mobi)
Subjects: LCSH: Cyberspace operations (Military science) |
    Cyberspace—Government policy. | Cyberspace—Security measures. |
    Cyberterrorism—Prevention.
Classification: LCC U163 .L519 2016 (print) | LCC U163 (ebook) | DDC
    355.3/43—dc23
LC record available at https://lccn.loc.gov/2016031363

♾ Print editions meet the requirements of ANSI/NISO z39.48-1992 (Permanence of Paper).
Printed in the United States of America.

24 23 22 21 20 19 18 17 16   9 8 7 6 5 4 3 2 1
First printing

Contents

PART II. POLICIES

PART IV. STRATEGIES

PART V. NORMS

Illustrations

Acronyms and Abbreviations

AES	advanced encryption standard
APT	advanced persistent threat
ASLR	address space layout randomization
ATM	asynchronous transfer mode
BDA	battle damage assessment
BGP	Border Gateway Protocol
BIOS	basic input-output system
C^{4}ISR	command, control, computers, communications, intelligence, surveillance, and reconnaissance
C^{4}ISRTA	C^{4}ISR and target acquisition
CDMA	code-division multiple access
CEO	chief executive officer
CERT	Computer Emergency Readiness Team
CIA	Central Intelligence Agency
CISO	chief information security officer
CNCI	Comprehensive National Cybersecurity Initiative
CPU	central processing unit
CYBERCOM	Cyber Command
DDOS	distributed denial-of-service (attack)
DEFCON	defense condition
DHS	Department of Homeland Security
DNS	Domain Name System
DoD	Department of Defense
EMCE	economically motivated cyberespionage
EW	electronic warfare
FBI	Federal Bureau of Investigation
GAO	Government Accountability Office
GDP	gross domestic product
GGE	Group of Government Experts
HTML	hypertext markup language
HTTPS	hypertext transfer protocol–secure
IADS	integrated air defense system
IAEA	International Atomic Energy Agency
IANA	Internet Assigned Numbers Authority
ICANN	Internet Corporation for Assigned Names and Numbers
INEW	integrated network and electronic warfare
INFOCON	information (operations) condition
iOS	iPhone Operating System
IP	Internet protocol
IRS	Internal Revenue Service
ISIL	Islamic State of Iraq and the Levant
ISP	Internet service provider
ITU	International Telecommunication Union
JMEM	Joint Munitions Effectiveness Manual
LOAC	law of armed conflict

MAD	mutual assured destruction
MFA	multi-factor authentication
NATO	North Atlantic Treaty Organization
NHTSA	National Highway Traffic Safety Administration
NIPR	Non-classified Internet Protocol Router
NIST	National Institute of Standards and Technology
NSA	National Security Agency
NTP	network time protocol
NTSB	National Transportation Safety Board
OPM	Office of Personnel Management
OPSEC	operational security
PAL	permissive action link
PC	personal computer
PCCIP	Presidential Commission on Critical Infrastructure Protection
PDF	Portable Document Format
PIN	personal identification number
PLA	People's Liberation Army
PLC	programmable logic controller
R&D	research and development
RF	radio frequency
rpm	revolutions per minute
SCADA	supervisory control and data acquisition
SIPR	Secret Internet Protocol Router
SQL	Structured Query Language
SSL	Secure Sockets Layer
STEM	science, technology, engineering, and mathematics
STRATCOM	Strategic Command
sysadmin	systems administrator
TCP/IP	transmission control protocol/Internet protocol
TMI	Three Mile Island
TSA	Transportation Security Administration
UAV	unmanned aerial vehicle
UN	United Nations
US-CERT	U.S. Computer Emergency Readiness Team
USB	universal serial bus
VPN	virtual private network
WTO	World Trade Organization

Introduction

In 1991, the Vice Chairman of the Joint Chiefs of Staff asked Al Bernstein, my boss at the National Defense University, to produce a report contemplating the world of 2025. I was assigned the technology portion to write. My sense of things to come was that the information technology revolution would continue to change conventional warfare dramatically. I envisioned a battlefield filled with sensors from which huge flows of data across a network would be fused to generate real-time information on enemy targets, which could then be struck with missiles and other precision munitions.

Perhaps not so coincidentally, in 1993, the National Defense University started to hire faculty to teach in its newly established school of information warfare studies (which operated from 1994 to 1996). The faculty also had a notion of future warfare—one nowhere close to my perspective, which they deprecated as kinetic and hence so "20th century." In the future, they claimed, people would wage war noiselessly, without violence, destruction, gunpowder, shot, or shell. They would just attack their foes' computer systems, thereby disarming them. That seemed far-fetched. Moore's Law implied that the amount of information doubled every year. Waging war against something that doubled every year and hoping for success seemed absurd. Even if one could succeed this year, the job would be twice as hard next year—and twice as hard as *that* a year or so later.

But they insisted, and because they insisted, I ended up writing a small monograph, *What Is Information Warfare.*[1] Its take on cyberwar was quite skeptical. Then, as now, it was hard to conclude that cyberwar was going to trump every other form of warfare. I was confident that the threat from cyberspace could be contained, in part because I believed that people, aware of the threat, would not willy-nilly connect critical systems (such as those that supply electric power) to the Internet. In this, I was wrong; for instance, there were next to no articles on cybersecurity in the late 1990s in trade journals such as *Electrical World*. People made decisions that were poor for cybersecurity because they did not worry about cybersecurity.

Then, as now, cyberwar and various forms of malicious mischief in cyberspace cannot be ignored; they are a real problem. Yet when facing a problem such as the threat from cyberspace, it pays to be serious but not desperate.[2] Desperate people do desperate things, and sometimes their desperation repels other people from doing anything at all. The problems of cyberspace require sustained attention but nothing close to panic. The world is not going to end if the problem is not addressed. There *will* be costs, but life will find a way to go on.

Although people have been writing about computer security since the 1960s, it would have been difficult to get into cyberwar much earlier than the early 1990s.[3] Before then, much about information war was highly classified (it was linked with strategic deception). More important, popular global networking was scarce before 1992. True, there was the Cuckoo's Egg incident in 1987 and, before that, in 1983, an entertaining little film called *War Games* in which a teenager hacks through the (presumably fictional) modem bank connected to the nation's nuclear command and control.[4] But cyberspace as a medium of cyberwar largely had to wait until 1992, when the National Science Foundation declared that people no longer needed to conform to "acceptable use policies" to get on the Internet.[5] That essentially opened the Internet up to everybody, for better or for worse.

Fast forward to just after September 11, 2001, when I found myself listening to a lecture from a prominent cyberwar expert discussing the threat from cyberspace. He spoke of a fourteen-year-old who had managed to hack into the controls of the Roosevelt Dam and was a hair's breadth from being able to take over the controls and flood large portions of southern Arizona. The story was passed around Washington, D.C., as a case of why the United States should increase its vigilance against hackers. But such stories rarely made it outside the Beltway—until the *Washington Post* picked it up, thereby bringing it to nationwide attention and hence to Arizona, whereupon those who actually operated the Roosevelt Dam saw the story.[6] They wrote to the *Washington Post* admitting that although someone did get into the system, the systems in question were those that automated office work and matters such as billing and administration. But the hacker was not even in that system very long, and he never got anywhere close to the controls (and he was twenty-seven, not fourteen).[7]

There is a lesson here. Very important people believe the threat from cyberspace is something the United States must take very, very seriously. In June 2012, Secretary of Defense Leon Panetta said he was "very concerned about the potential in cyberspace of being able to cripple our power grid, to be able to cripple our government systems, to be able to cripple our financial systems, and then to virtually paralyze this country—and as far as I'm concerned that represents a potential for another Pearl Harbor." In 2011, Admiral Michael Mullen, Chairman of the Joint Chiefs of Staff, said, "The biggest single existential threat that's out there is cyber."[8] Federal Bureau of Investigation (FBI) director Robert Mueller said early in 2012 that "threats from cyberespionage, computer crime, and attacks on critical infrastructure will surpass terrorism as the number-one threat facing the United States."[9] In March 2013, James Clapper, the director of national intelligence, named cyberattacks—with the potential for state or nonstate actors to manipulate U.S. computer systems and thereby corrupt, disrupt, or destroy critical infrastructure—as the greatest short-term threat to national security.[10] Early in 2013, the secretary of the Department of Homeland Security (DHS) announced that she believed a "cyber 9/11" could happen "imminently."[11] In late 2014, Admiral Michael Rogers, commander of U.S. Cyber Command (CYBERCOM), testified that "there are nation-states and groups out there that have the capability . . . to shut down, forestall our ability to operate our basic infrastructure, whether it's generating power across this nation, whether it's moving water and fuel."[12] The fear was extant outside the Beltway as well; a survey of security professionals (admittedly, a self-interested source) in 2013 found that "79 percent believe that there will be some sort of large-scale attack on the information technology powering some element of the U.S.'s infrastructure—and utilities and financial institutions were the most likely targets."[13]

While that has not come to pass, there are indeed threats in cyberspace. If your information is on a network connected to the Internet and is of interest to large foreign countries (that need not be any larger or more powerful than Spain), such information is probably in their possession.[14] The fact that (putatively) Chinese hackers could break into the U.S. Office of Personnel Management (OPM), security clearance contractor USIS, health insurers Anthem and Premera, and United and American Airlines (although perhaps resulting in only a partial compromise) raises the question of whether there were any organizations with useful data they did *not* hack.[15]

As Shawn Henry, former head of the FBI's cybercrime unit, has observed, "There are two types of organizations—those that know they are under attack from cyberspace and those that don't know they're under attack from cyberspace."[16] It has also become apparent that not all threats in cyberspace come from overseas; if even half the material Edward Snowden provided to the media is correct, the National Security Agency has gotten into an impressive number of systems. And the ability to penetrate a network often implies the ability to muck with it, at least for a while. Furthermore, if the United States has yet to experience a major cyberattack, it may be in large part because many of the world's best hacker organizations are parts of the governments of U.S. allies (for instance, Unit 8200 is a division of Israel's Defense Force) or have yet to conclude that a major cyberattack on the United States is in their interest (for example, Russia or China). In the latter case, we can only guess whether it is within their capabilities. And mid-size potential cyber powers (such as Iran and North Korea) have discovered the value of having cyberwar capabilities comparatively late vis-à-vis the larger players; they may not yet have reached their full potential. All we can say is that no one has died as a direct result of hacking—and while this should put scare stories in their place, it hardly justifies complacency (after all, no one has died from an intercontinental ballistic missile strike, either). Cyberwar is clearly worth understanding.

All this calls for a text to make readers more intelligent consumers of the news, more intelligent users of technical advice, and more intelligent critics of the decisions that countries make with respect to the threat from cyberspace. This is *not* a technical treatment of cybersecurity. If there is a virus on your network, if your router is not working, if your systems are misconfigured, seek help elsewhere. But for those who ask what their country should do about cyberespionage or how countries should integrate cyberspace into their threat planning or cyberwar into their war planning, then read on. The goal is to help you integrate how you think about cyberwar into other elements of national power, including military power.

We start with foundational material. Whereas a deep knowledge of atomic physics is not necessary to hold your own in discussion about nuclear strategy, being conversant in cyberwar is helped by some understanding of what happens in a computer; such knowledge helps illustrate the art of the possible.

The next section deals with policy. How does the exploitation of faults in computers put the systems that use them at risk? What national policies should be adopted to manage this risk without undue cost in terms of economic outlays, privacy, or other values?

The third section deals with operations, specifically the potential military use of cyberwar and some considerations for its command and control. In other words, here we put the "war" into "cyberwar"—or, more precisely, put the "cyberwar" into "war."

The last section deals with strategy, the art of integrating cyberwar and peace in cyberspace into the broad approaches that countries use to manage their relationships with other countries. It discusses the potential of strategic cyberwar, deterrence strategies, escalation management, brandishing, signaling, narratives, international law, and negotiations.

CHAPTER 1
Emblematic Attacks

Those who follow the news are having an increasingly difficult time avoiding stories associated with intrusions into other people's computer systems. Nevertheless, because the history of these intrusions—even limited to those that hit the news—is long and well populated with many examples, it may help in understanding the topic to take up a quick review of the more emblematic attacks. Table 1.1 is the author's list of top cybersecurity incidents (and non-incidents) grouped by type. This variegated list was selected not necessarily for the severity of the incidents but for their impact on the consciousness of the public and policymakers and for the lessons that might be drawn from them.

The rest of the chapter will concentrate on three particular types of cybersecurity incidents: the advanced persistent threat (APT) form of cyberespionage, distributed denial-of-service (DDOS), or flooding, attacks, and destructive cyberattacks. The first category, the APT, covers most of what state intelligence agencies do—spying—but can also be used as an entry point for later cyberattacks. DDOS attacks, the second category, are meant to disrupt; they constitute a lesser form of cyberattack. Destructive attacks, the third category, are rare; even so, the concept of "destruction" has to be stretched to include wiping the hard drive of computers (which can often then be restored to factory conditions).

But first, a brief run-down of the incidents in the "other" category of table 1.1 will be useful—partially because they raised consciousness, and mostly because the techniques used or demonstrated in those shed light on how the other three types of incidents work.

CYBERCRIME AND OTHER SYSTEM INTRUSIONS

Although the techniques of cybercrime are similar to those of cyberwar, crime—however expensive it can sometimes get—is not war, nor is war necessarily cybercrime grown unacceptably large.[1]

The *Cuckoo's Egg* incident involved state-sponsored cyberespionage on sensitive but unclassified U.S. Department of Energy laboratory systems. It probably would have gone undetected but for the efforts of Clifford Stoll, who noticed a tiny discrepancy between computer time used and computer time charged and assiduously tracked the discrepancy to its source, despite FBI indifference (at least that attitude has changed).

The 1988 *Morris Worm* resulted from an experiment to understand how an infection could spread across the entire Internet (which, in 1988, was much smaller than the Internet today). One parameter in the code was set incorrectly, infecting 10 percent of the Internet.[2]

The 1991 *Michelangelo* virus was one of many viruses that spread from floppy disk to computer to floppy disk. It was notable for two reasons: first, the agitation produced by the rumor that millions of computers would become inoperable on the great artist's birthday, and second, a demonstration

TABLE 1.1 INTRUSIONS OF NOTE IN CYBERSPACE

INTRUSION	VICTIM	YEAR	TYPE
Titan Rain	Energy/atomic laboratories	2005	APT
Snooping Dragon	Free Tibet movement	2009	APT
F-35	Lockheed-Martin	2009	APT
Google Aurora	Google	2010	APT
Night Dragon, Shady Rat	Various U.S. companies	2011	APT
RSA	RSA (cybersecurity company)	2011	APT
Flame	Islamic nations	2012	APT
People's Liberation Army indictments	Chinese intrusions in western Pennsylvania	2014	APT
Office of Personnel Management hack	Records of government employees	2015	APT
Mafia Boy	E-commerce sites	2000	DDOS
Estonia	Estonia's links to Internet	2007	DDOS
Georgia	Georgia's link to Internet	2008	DDOS
Iran vs. Banks	Major U.S. banks	2012	DDOS
Spamhaus	Spamhaus (anti-spam organization)	2013	DDOS
Github	Great Firewall circumvention	2015	DDOS
DHS Aurora	Oil Pump (from the Alaska pipeline)	2007	Destruction
Stuxnet	Iran's nuclear centrifuges	2010	Destruction
Aramco/RasGas	Energy facilities	2012	Destruction
Las Vegas Sands	Gambling establishments	2014	Destruction
Sony	Sony Pictures Entertainment	2014	Destruction
Operation Orchard	Syrian air defenses	2007	Disruption
Libyan surface-to-air missiles	Libyan air defenses	2011	Disruption
Cuckoo's Egg	Energy/atomic laboratories	1987	Other
Morris Worm	The Internet as a whole	1988	Other
Michelangelo	PC users in general	1991	Other
Citibank	Citibank	1995	Crime
Eligible Receiver	U.S. DoD exercise	1997	Other
Solar Sunrise	U.S. DoD unclassified Internet	1998	Other
Moonlight Maze	U.S. DoD unclassified Internet	1998	Other
Serbian Deposits	Milosevic accounts in Greece	1999	Other
I Love You Virus	PC users in general	2000	Other
Code Red	PC users in general	2001	Other
EP-3 Hainan	Websites in the United States and China	2001	Other
Southern Brazil	Electrical generation capacity in Brazil	2007	Other
Buckshot Yankee	U.S. DoD classified Internet	2008	Other
Heartland	Heartland Payment Systems	2008	Crime
Snowden	National Security Agency	2013	Other
Heartbleed	E-commerce sites	2013	Other
Target	Target customers	2013	Crime
JPMorgan Chase	J.P. Morgan Chase customers	2014	Crime
Russo-Ukraine War	Russia and Ukraine	2014	Other

that any computer that could be infected could also be trashed to the point that a complete rewriting and reformatting would be necessary.

The 1995 *Citibank* hack was the first notable large-scale cybercrime. The hackers managed to transfer $10 million from various accounts but could only remove $400,000 from Citibank accounts before they were caught.[3] Two lessons were that all this theoretical musing about cybercrime was real and that removing money from the banking system can be difficult.[4]

Eligible Receiver was a Department of Defense (DoD) exercise undertaken to demonstrate that hackers could disrupt major military operations without using particularly special techniques. Not only was confusion sown within a simulated wartime Pacific Command, but also the hackers made a convincing argument that they could take down electric power in Oahu. Some people in the Pentagon took the results seriously, but many had to have repeated lessons.[5]

Solar Sunrise was an actual intrusion in 1998 into the Pentagon's computers as DoD was preparing a series of strikes on Iraq's air defense systems, which had radar-painted U.S. aircraft protecting Kurdish refugees.[6] Officials initially feared that Solar Sunrise was the work of the Iraqis. Later investigation showed that these intrusions were carried out by two California teenagers working under the tutelage of a young Israeli. Two ostensibly contradictory lessons can be drawn from that episode: that the fears of state-level cyberattacks as an asymmetric response to U.S. military operations were exaggerated, and that mere teenagers could make such mischief.

The same year, a similar, stealthier attack dubbed *Moonlight Maze* was carried out against Pentagon computers. Patient tracing of the attack's path led investigators to Moscow. After an initially promising dialogue, the Russians suddenly refused to help chase down the perpetrators or to allow U.S. investigators to do so, suggesting that what at first looked like random hackers may well have been the state security apparatus.

The unwillingness of the United States in 1999 during the Kosovo campaign to attack Greek banks where Serbian leader *Slobodan Milosevic* supposedly kept his money is a good example of an incident that did not happen.[7] The lesson here was the sensitivity of lawyers and Treasury officials to attacks on the international banking system. An attack on a bank account is an attack on the bank's memory. Its obligation to repay the customer for the money it borrowed, which is what a deposit is, does not go away; it just becomes harder to determine.

The 2000 *I Love You* virus infected millions of users of Microsoft's Outlook e-mail system. It was another demonstration of the power of malware and was said to cost billions of dollars in lost time and remediation (an estimate that, if true, had to assume that everyone affected was totally immobilized for days).[8]

The *EP-3/Hainan* confrontation in May 2001 between a U.S. Navy spy plane and a Chinese jet was echoed by an exchange of web defacements by each side's partisans.[9] This incident gave rise to the impression that China would wage low-level attacks on the United States through the use of proxies that allowed China deniability. It took a dozen years before that misimpression was corrected.

The 2001 *Code Red* worm was a rapidly propagating piece of malware strong enough to make people question whether the Internet could survive in its present form much longer.[10] Code Red, however, was only the beginning of a wave of worms; it was followed by NIMDA, MyDoom, SoBig, Slammer, and MSBlaster. Each version seemed more virulent than the previous one, and they kept coming until Microsoft issued Windows XP Service Pack 2 in August 2004.

A story circulated in 2007 via a Central Intelligence Agency (CIA) presentation and a 2009 CBS news report claimed that hackers had caused a power outage in *southern Brazil*.[11] The Brazilians countered that while the power outage was real, the cause was an accumulation of soot in the power plant smokestacks for which the company was fined several million dollars.[12]

Buckshot Yankee was the name given to the remediation effort to eradicate a worm (Agent.BTZ) that had worked its way into DoD's air-gapped secret Internet protocol router network (SIPRnet).[13] Indications are that the malware was transferred via a universal serial bus (USB) stick to a computer on the SIPRnet and from there to many other machines. The two lessons were that air-gapped systems could be infected and that configuration management—knowing the inventory and state of all machines on the network—was complex and difficult.[14]

Heartland Payment Systems, part of the hidden infrastructure of finance, provides credit, debit, and prepaid card services to small and medium-sized businesses. In 2008, an American cyber-criminal managed to steal upward of 150 million credit card numbers from them. That huge number should have been a wake-up call but apparently was not enough of one until the Target hack in 2013.

In the spring of 2013, a defense contractor working at the National Security Agency (NSA), *Edward Snowden*, leveraged his position as a systems administrator to take millions of files detailing all manner of the NSA's cyberespionage activities. Although not strictly speaking a hacking attack on computers (but a serious espionage crime nonetheless), it unmasked years of NSA activity, forcing the agency to rework its tools to recover its access to the world's networks. Many echoes from this revelation are described below.[15]

Later in 2013, researchers at Google and Finnish firm Codenomicon discovered that a piece of commonly used code within the secure sockets layer (SSL)—a standard method of securing e-commerce transactions—had a vulnerability, *Heartbleed*, that allowed hackers to extract passwords from systems running the code.[16] Once the flaw was revealed to the world, adroit system administrators quickly patched their systems. Unfortunately, some hackers managed to replicate the flaw and torment the systems of dilatory ones.

The 2013 Christmas season presented *Target*, the giant retailer, with the revelation that hackers had stolen information from tens of millions of credit cards.[17] This information was sold into the black market and used to burn new credit cards, which led to charges showing up on the accounts of unsuspecting customers. Banks subsequently had to issue new cards and were left on the hook for hundreds of millions of dollars of fraudulent transactions. Normally, credit card transactions are encrypted except for a brief interval during which they are processed in the cash register. Malware in the cash register (notably, Windows XP machines) ensured that a record of that interval was faithfully captured. The subsequent dismissal of Target's chief executive officer (CEO), albeit also for an ill-advised expansion into Canada, provided the wake-up call that company boards finally heeded.

Hackers of apparent Russian origin (but actually of Israeli and U.S. origin) established a presence on one or more servers of *JPMorgan Chase* (as well as some smaller banks) and managed to steal nothing more than a list of customers with their physical addresses, e-mail addresses, and phone numbers. Because the hackers appeared to have failed in doing something larger, speculation on their true goals bubbled. Perhaps spending $250 million a year as JPMorgan Chase did on cybersecurity may actually prevent hackers resident in systems for months from actually stealing a penny.

Russia and Ukraine, two comparably advanced countries with first-rate hackers, went to war with each other, and except for some minor DDOS capers, nothing much happened. There were no large DDOS attacks. Neither country went after the other's infrastructure (until late 2015, when a hack apparently led tens of thousands of customers in western Ukraine to lose power for a few hours[18]) or successfully robbed the other's bank accounts. No instances of hacks into the other's military systems have been revealed. Indeed, so absent was cyberwar that the moniker was stretched to cover propaganda (of which there was plenty), jamming, and Russia's takeover of Crimea's phone service.

THE ADVANCED PERSISTENT THREAT

An APT denotes an intruder that can establish a persistent presence in a target network from which data can be constantly extracted and exfiltrated (leveraging a persistent presence also allows a disruptive or corruptive attack to be launched). Most systems are penetrated not to interfere with their workings, but rather to force them to share information with hackers; the number of cyberespionage incidents is far greater than the number of cyberattacks.

The information sought by hackers may not be classified secret. It may not even be particularly sensitive when each hacked piece of information is considered in isolation of others. But the aggregation of each datum into data can be valuable in the same way that a datum about Wal-Mart's inventory is uninteresting, but the way that Wal-Mart manages billions of records can reveal much of how it came to be the world's largest retailer. One defining feature of cyberespionage is that it can deal in quantity—literally terabytes. Exploitation—sorting through all the terabytes to find something of value—is another matter that begins and ends in darkness (unless the nature or volume of exfiltration is noticeable). By contrast, traditional espionage expends a great deal of time and effort to elicit a key fact—for example, where and when is the enemy going to attack—the exploitation of which is more obvious.

The APT moniker has often been used as a euphemism for Chinese espionage into Western (primarily American) systems. Although China may conduct most such espionage, the Russians, especially since 2014, and other countries are not entirely absent.[19] Chinese sources were implicated in *Titan Rain*, a penetration of Department of Energy laboratories from 2003 to 2005.[20] The individual who chased the attacks down marveled at the methodical, efficient, and faultless procedures used. Subsequent attacks targeted the Naval War College, the National Defense University, and the Departments of Commerce and State. One brazen attack, revealed in 2007, compromised the machine personally used by the secretary of defense.

A well-documented case of cyberespionage, *Snooping Dragon*, targeted the Free Tibet movement in general and the Dalai Lama's organization in particular.[21] That the Chinese were responsible is suggested by the exfiltration of stolen data to Chinese servers in Xinjiang and Sichuan, and from the fact that no other country has such an interest in the status of Tibet. The attackers, purportedly posing as members of Tibetan discussion groups, sent e-mail with malware-impregnated attachments to various Tibetan monks. Opening the attachments on the clients' computers released malware into these computers in the form of rootkits: programs operating deep within the operating system, thereby allowing hackers to tell infected computers to do anything a legitimate user could. Such rootkits were designed to evade file searches or attempts to log them as running processes. Infected computers then infected others on the network. Such computers, in turn, ran malware that examined and forwarded e-mails. The investigators concluded that such attacks did not require a sophisticated intelligence organization. A sufficiently diligent individual could have done this by exploiting access to hacker sites: "Best-practice advice that one sees in the corporate sector comes nowhere even close to preventing such an attack. . . . The traditional defense against social malware in government agencies involves expensive and intrusive measures . . . not sustainable in the economy as a whole."[22]

In January 2010, *Google* discovered that it too had been attacked and some of its source code removed via servers in Taiwan. Unprecedentedly, Google executives admitted as much and pressed the U.S. government to raise this intrusion as an international issue.[23] Although the software guarding the repository itself had exploitable errors, it appears that client machines were allowed rather free access into the repository, when more secure practice would have been to require multi-factor authentication (discussed below) for access (although if someone who legitimately wanted to download code had an infected machine, the malware could have gone to work as soon as the connection was made). The route into Google's system was apparently through a vulnerability in Microsoft's Internet Explorer version 6 unpatched by Microsoft (also known as a zero-day vulnerability) but actually known about since the previous September. Once the flaw was exposed in the popular press, a fix was generated within two weeks. Google, on its own, decided to swear off Explorer for its staff (but that may be because they had a rival product, Chrome). The so-called Aurora series of attacks affected thirty-three other systems as well.[24]

In 2011, there were reports that other hackers had attempted to compromise Gmail accounts maintained by U.S. government officials and others. The technique called for sending users a phony e-mail directing them to a fake Google site where they were asked to log in again. The hackers thereby captured the credentials so that they could later log in to user e-mail boxes and steal their correspondence. Note that the security hole that permitted the attack would have been the users', not Google's.

Another series of attacks, *Shady Rat* and *Night Dragon*, showed the industriousness of the Chinese hackers. Shady Rat's researchers at MacAfee found a server through which stolen files from seventy-four hacked firms were cached for later delivery. Most, but not all, of these firms were in the United States; the businesses ranged from industry to commercial real estate. Night Dragon's hackers sought hints on how these companies evaluated certain oil patches and what they were prepared to bid on them—helpful in divining what such drilling rights were worth or how to underbid the oil majors for drilling rights.[25] Similar attacks have been carried out to determine what the target firm's negotiation positions were. Law firms have proven to be soft targets for such penetrations, because they keep highly privileged data but have traditionally not been the most computer-savvy of institutions (or large enough to afford sophisticated information technology staffs).[26]

The 2011 hacks of cybersecurity company *RSA* proved that even companies in the security business can be had. The effect of this attack may not have been limited to RSA, because the hackers stole the seed numbers from which the pseudo-random numbers in RSA's tokens were generated. RSA advised its clients to migrate from a four-digit personal identification number (PIN) to a six-digit one but did not call for a rapid wholesale replacement of digital fobs. A few months after the attack, hackers supposedly used information garnered from the attack to go after Lockheed, but that attack was apparently thwarted.[27]

Lockheed has been a prominent target for the Chinese, who in 2009 managed to break into the systems associated with the *F-35* aircraft under development and purloin several terabytes of data.[28] The impact of what was taken remains debatable. In theory, all the Chinese took was unclassified data, and the amount that they could usefully learn from such data about the F-35 itself should have been limited (China has likely learned far more about making advanced jet aircraft by buying some from Russia and reverse-engineering what they found). Yet rumors persist that the aggregation of these purloined unclassified data might have provided China with information that was equivalent to top-secret data and that substantial cost overruns in building the aircraft may have been exacerbated by the need to redesign it because of what the Chinese learned about the then–current design.[29] There have also been reports that other acts of cyberespionage may explain the rapid increase in the quietness of Chinese submarines; similar stories about Russian submarines also growing quieter very quickly (albeit by purchasing European machine tools) were circulated in the 1980s.

What do all these intrusions say about APTs? First, there is a good reason for the word "persistent." The average time between compromise and discovery is up to a year—and that is only for penetrations that have, in fact, been discovered (including as-yet-undiscovered penetrations would likely raise that average detection time substantially).[30] Oftentimes these penetrations are discovered only because servers that contain information about some penetrated companies are discovered in the course of looking for information on others. Organizations commonly find out from outsiders (such as the FBI) that they have been penetrated when they themselves had no clue.[31]

Second, the Chinese themselves have poor tradecraft.[32] The feeble attempts made to hide the path along which malware came in or data went out seem unimaginative. The fact that the files found on intermediate servers are not encrypted means that those who find such files can read them, guess where they came from, and inform the victims, thereby allowing them to stanch the bleeding. Anyone who uses the same method to penetrate thirty-three companies, à la Aurora, is asking for trouble the first time a penetration is discovered.[33] In 2012, the NSA circulated estimates that a dozen groups in China are responsible for most of the APT intrusions.[34] The Mandiant report presented copious evidence that at least one group, unit 61398, worked for the People's Liberation Army (PLA) and had its own office building.[35] Since then, others have been identified.[36] Nothing is usually done about the hackers—which is why they put so little effort into hiding their tracks.

Third, the United States is not the only victim, contrary to China's line that such accusations are inventions of U.S. media looking to reinvent the Cold War. Accusations have come from Germany (Prime Minister Angela Merkel brought this issue up personally with her Chinese counterparts) and the United Kingdom (which warned companies in public against such threats), as well as Canada, Australia, Taiwan, Japan, and India.[37]

Fourth, cyberespionage is of a piece with many other policies. Chinese or China-associated individuals have been implicated (and convicted) in many physical espionage operations.[38] China has trade restrictions on the import of certain types of content—for example, only a dozen films may be imported in any one year. Meanwhile, commercial intellectual property that finds its way into China is largely stolen; in early 2011, nine in ten copies of Microsoft Windows were bootlegged, which suggests how easily China's infrastructure can be penetrated by hackers.[39] Applications to import products into or start manufacturing in China are frequently held hostage to demands that corporations release a great deal of their intellectual property to native firms before getting permission.

As later chapters relate, the United States has begun pushing back against Chinese APTs, notably by indicting five members of the PLA in May 2014 for carrying out cyberespionage against private corporations and a labor union in the Pittsburgh area. More calls were issued for sterner words with China.[40]

DISTRIBUTED DENIAL-OF-SERVICE ATTACKS

In 1990, major e-commerce sites from Amazon to America Online became inaccessible due to an unexpected volume of web traffic directed their way. This attack, cleaned up after a few hours, was traced to a teenager in Montreal (also known as *Mafia Boy*), who learned how to craft malformed packets that interacted badly with transmission control protocol/Internet protocol (TCP/IP) and then send them out in flows large enough to tie up very large systems. Thus was born the first widely reported manifestation of the DDOS attack.

In April 2007, a DDOS attack was carried out that radically darkened how people viewed them. Earlier that month, *Estonia* had decided to relocate a statue of a Soviet soldier from downtown Tallinn to a military cemetery. Riots ensued (resulting in one death and many injuries), but what caught the world's attention was that Estonia was bombarded by a DDOS attack, which peaked at 4 billion bytes per minute. The attack, directed against Estonian government sites, banks, and other infrastructure, made life difficult in a country that had so enthusiastically embraced the Internet that it called itself "E-stonia." After a few days, Estonia cut its international connections, thereby cutting off most of the traffic. This allowed local access to local sites, but it also prevented overseas Estonians (notably guest workers in other parts of Europe) from accessing sites (such as their banks accounts). After waves of attacks stretching over days and weeks, matters quieted down. Estonia rerouted its Internet traffic with the assistance of router company Cisco and content distribution company Akamai. The option of blocking traffic from just Russia would not have helped much, since the attacks came from all over the world. By one estimate, one packet in six was from the United States.[41] It is unclear whether the attacks were instigated by the Russian state, Russian citizens, ethnic Russians in Estonia, or some mix of them.[42]

Nevertheless, someone in Moscow must have liked the results well enough, because something similar happened in August 2008 against *Georgia*. That attacks started just before Russia's troops moved south into the Georgian lands of South Ossetia suggested some tipoff between the attackers on the ground and those in cyberspace. Because Georgia was not nearly so wired as Estonia, the harm was far less. The primary effect was to complicate efforts by the government of Georgia to communicate its perspective on the Russian invasion to the rest of the world. After a brief interruption, many of Georgia's websites were rehosted on U.S. servers owned by Google and by Tulip, a U.S. firm that employed some Georgian nationals. Unconfirmed rumors allege that the DDOS attacks affected Georgia's ability to command and control its armed forces.

Some DDOS attacks (those on Georgia and many carried out by Anonymous) generate volume by mobilizing like-minded computer owners to bombard a nominated site (also known as a low-orbit ion cannon). But the big attacks find and reprogram other people's computers—thereafter known as bots or zombies—to flood selected websites with traffic.

A common way to recruit bots is to corrupt popular websites (often via their advertisements, which are handled by third parties), wait until they are accessed, and then have the sites download malware onto the machines of the unwary. Bot-herders are indifferent as to who is infected. Theirs is solely a numbers game. For this reason, bot-herders rarely bother with zero-day exploits because they do not need to. Bot-herders might threaten a DDOS attack to shut down a site that expects a high volume of lucrative traffic at a particular time: for example, gambling sites during or just before a major sporting event. Sometimes such sites have to be hit in order to put weight behind such threats. They are also used to knock dissident sites offline or to distribute malware.[43] Botnets also serve other purposes such as spamming or running "pump-and-dump" schemes that manipulate stock prices. Harvesting personal data or distributing banking malware (for example, GameOver Zeus) are other uses. The true attacker need not own a botnet since many are available for rent through one of many black markets.[44]

The September and December 2012 DDOS attacks allegedly carried out by *Iran* against U.S. banks managed to subvert insufficiently protected WordPress blogging software servers rather than individual users to generate large floods.[45] This stands in contrast to most other botnets whose bots were created by subverting thousands or sometimes millions of computers belonging to less savvy users—those who do not patch their machines and may not even notice that their broadband-connected (and sometimes always-on) machines are spewing out a profusion of bytes. Even if they noticed, it is not clear that they would care much as long as their machines did not sputter.

The 2013 DDOS attack on anti-DDOS site *Spamhaus* was large enough to have clogged service to sites that had the bad luck to sit on the routes preferred by the bots.[46] If enough of the wrong type of traffic can be thrown against certain routers, they can crash (and be knocked offline), and then nothing gets through. As of the writing of this book, the largest DDOS attacks were carried out against independent news sites that organized mock elections for Hong Kong's chief executive: one at 500 gigabits per second and an early 2016 attack that reportedly exceeded 600 gigabits per second,[47] both up several-fold from the record 90 billion bits per second of 2007.[48] The attack on *Github* was a very large-scale DDOS attack over a few days in April 2015 that was, in all likelihood, hosted on the backbone of China Unicom, which is not only a major service provider but also a host of parts of the Great Firewall.[49]

By one estimate, as many as 100 million computers were considered to be bots. Some of the larger botnets, such as Mariposa or Conficker, have 5 million to 10 million computers.[50] Up to one in ten packets over the Internet had been considered part of some bot attack.[51] Several years ago, the Internet passed the point where more than half of all e-mail traffic was generated by spam-bots. Fortunately for users, commercial e-mail providers have become quite good at filtering spam. But DDOS traffic still wastes bandwidth. Although bot-herders tend to come out of Russia or eastern Europe, the servers that host the command and control apparatus are commonly American.

Could Internet traffic be kept clean by installing scrubbing devices at key nodes and separating the wheat from the chaff? Unfortunately, nothing obvious distinguishes bot packets from legitimate ones. Examining similarities between the individual pieces of bot traffic within a broader pattern of daily traffic (for example, sources getting too many packets of too similar a nature, especially from previously identified bots) might provide hints of how bot traffic may be differentiated from normal traffic and thereby tossed from the system—but with costs. For instance, dropping traffic from a source that has never communicated with a site may eliminate most traffic but also may keep newcomers out. Filtering DDOS traffic requires accepting all that traffic in the first place and must therefore be done upstream of the targeted site.[52]

Sometimes bot traffic can be squelched by looking at infected computers and seeing where they get their (invariably encrypted) commands from. However, if that technique starts to become a serious problem for bot-herders, they can adopt peer-to-peer command and control networks. Their doing so would greatly complicate the process of figuring out who gave which command.

Nevertheless, botnets *have* been taken down. Cooperation between the FBI and the governments of Spain and Slovenia dismembered the Mariposa botnet.[53] Court action against McColo, an Internet service provider (ISP) that became too chummy with some bot-herders, led to a drastic (but temporary) reduction in spam.[54] Microsoft has taken it upon itself to go after botnets and can claim some success against the Rustock botnet and others.[55] Scott Charney, a Microsoft security official, uses a public health analogy to argue exactly that: users suffer little from being part of botnets, but their victims can suffer a great deal—hence the argument for herd immunity.

Finally, can a DDOS attack take down the Internet by taking down its Domain Name System (DNS), the service that converts names in websites and e-mail addresses to machine locations? The largest such attack, in February 2007, had a limited effect on the DNS thanks to engineering fixes installed since the previous attack in October 2002.[56]

A close cousin to the DDOS attack (in that the victims of the problem are also largely blameless) is an attack that leverages the Border Gateway Protocol (BGP). This protocol picks the route a packet makes to its destination by allowing ISPs to declare to the world that a given site is best reached through its gateways. If an ISP so chooses (or is hacked), it can deliberately misroute traffic by declaring itself part of the shortest route between two points, even if both are on the other side of the world.[57] Mistakes can create the same effect. Indeed, distinguishing attacks from mistakes is not trivial. In 2008, YouTube became unreachable for practically all Internet users after a Pakistani ISP altered a route in a ham-fisted attempt to block the service in just that country.[58] Several years later, an Indonesian ISP took out Google for thirty minutes.[59] In 2010, a large percentage of all U.S. traffic wended its way through China for eighteen minutes.[60] The next year, a large chunk of Facebook's traffic was also diverted to China in an incident that one security expert called an accident and another called an attack ("route hijacking").[61] China was also on the receiving end of such an incident in early 2014: "A large portion of Internet traffic in China on Tuesday was redirected to servers run by a small U.S. company. The company, which publicly opposes China's efforts to control Internet content, says it wasn't at fault."[62] In a more suspicious incident, traffic from a British manufacturer of nuclear components was routed through Ukraine before returning to Britain along the same route.[63]

The weaknesses in BGP arise from the assumption that ISPs are trustworthy and that hijacking is rare enough to justify not having them digitally sign their routing declarations. The more the world's traffic is encrypted, the smaller the loss from route diversion (for example, because it is pointless to divert traffic that cannot be read). So far, these assumptions have more or less held. But this leaves the possibility of an ISP going completely rogue, in large part because its country has as well. A full-scale attack using BGP could seriously bedevil the entire Internet until the offending country is taken off the Internet map—a process that may take hours or longer.

STUXNET AND OTHER DESTRUCTIVE ATTACKS

In 2007, DHS and the Idaho National Laboratories ran an experiment named *Aurora* in which a generator of the sort that powered the Alaskan oil pipeline was fed errant instructions and went into self-destruct mode, eventually shaking itself to death in a cloud of smoke. People learned from this that cyberwar could have kinetic effects (even if the particular flaw was quickly fixed).

Three years later, researchers discovered that first worm, *Stuxnet*, which was designed to break machinery, specifically the uranium centrifuges used by Iran to enrich uranium in Natanz. Even now, Stuxnet still stands out for its sophistication and daring. No one before (or since) has succeeded in so penetrating computers not connected to the Internet or a phone system. The malware crossed from whatever open networks were near the centrifuges (in the sense of being networks of suppliers to Natanz[64]) to the closed network that hosted the computers that could manipulate the programmable logic controllers (PLCs) governing the centrifuges in ways that would ultimately destroy them. The greater the number of infected computers around Natanz, the more the opportunities for such transfer—hence the need for a broad propagation mechanism to infect as many computers and hence as many USB sticks as possible (conversely, some reports suggest the owner of the USB stick was witting).[65] For most computers, the infection would have next to no effect apart from transferring itself to other computers.

How an infected USB stick can infect a computer into which it is inserted is worth noting. Prior to 2008, Windows computers, as a default mechanism, ran programs from the boot sector of USBs upon insertion. Early versions of Stuxnet relied on such mechanisms. When Microsoft awakened to the problematic nature of that mechanism and Windows stopped automatically running programs from the boot sector, the hackers found a flaw in the routine that told the computer what to do when it read the directory of those devices (it had to do with icons of icons). This trick was not widely known; hence, it was a zero-day vulnerability.[66] Stuxnet also had three other zero-day vulnerabilities; they helped escalate the privileges of the program introduced into the computer so that it could spread widely and quickly. Never before had four zero-day vulnerabilities been found on one piece of malware.[67] Finally, Stuxnet also exploited the use of stolen certificates from two reputable companies (that seemed to share a parking lot) so that the computers would recognize rogue code as a legitimately source.[68]

The last step was going from the network infection to a reprogrammed centrifuge. It was initially thought that the centrifuges' PLCs were infected while on the floor. More likely, the PLCs were infected when being programmed on computers running PCS7/WinCC software developed by Siemens, the same company that supplied the PLCs. Thus, the worm did not affect all centrifuges, only those being programmed prior to use (or reprogrammed after being pulled offline).[69] The older centrifuges were not subject to real-time control and thus were not affected by Stuxnet.

More broadly, machinery that cannot be reprogrammed in situ and that does not need programming tends to resist being fed arbitrary instructions (although built-in instructions might be invoked to bad ends by insiders or by hijacking authentication). Those subject to real-time control can have their controls usurped. Normally, such chips require a password to be programmed, but every PLC of that type had the same password, which users could not change. The creators of Stuxnet merely had to go to hacker bulletin boards to find out what the password was.

These centrifuges, having been commanded to execute rapid changes in operating speeds, died over the subsequent weeks and months. Why did the Iranians not suspect that their programming had been corrupted? Perhaps they knew they were dealing with black- and grey-market parts of unpredictable quality. Meanwhile, they were getting no help from Siemens, which never knowingly authorized any such sale to the nuclear facility.

Iranians knew that many problems could make their equipment fail (and some of it had in fact been physically sabotaged prior to arriving at the loading docks). So failure could have had one of a hundred fathers. Thus, the premature death of the centrifuges may have been the unavoidable cost of doing everything under the table. Since the facility was air-gapped, operators may have been confident that the source of failure was not a cyberattack—until they found that it was. Stuxnet also reprogrammed the same chip that controlled how the centrifuges reported on what they were doing. Thus, operators were told nothing untoward was going on.

All this points to a fundamental blunder of process control: never put a controller, which may misbehave, and a monitor, which checks for misbehavior, on the same device, because both may err from the same cause—in this case, a cyberattack. Why were the Iranians insufficiently aware of this axiom? And why were they literally deaf to unexpected changes in rotational speeds that were well within the audible range (normal speeds were 1,000 revolutions per minute [rpm] as opposed to induced speeds, which alternated between 200 and 1,200 rpm)? Perhaps it mattered that Iran is not yet an industrial culture. There was little human oversight on the floor (a centrifuge that breaks while spinning can be a scary thing). Furthermore, Iran was not getting much help from outside vendors.[70]

Stuxnet was discovered when an Iranian whose computer was shutting down sent it to an antivirus company in Belarus, VirusBlokAda, to look for an infection. The company found hitherto unseen malware that, upon analysis, appeared to target industrial control systems—something unusual. Over the next few weeks, as the cybersecurity community analyzed this strange malware and reported it to its peers, the alarming nature of the malware became apparent. By mid-July, Symantec was concerned enough to ping its global sensors to report that over 100,000 computers were infected with the Stuxnet virus, with most of them being in Iran.[71] Its reports on the malware circulated in the trade press and blogs.[72] But exactly what the malware was meant to do and how it was meant to do it remained a mystery. The method by which it spread from thumb drive to machine was rapidly reported to Microsoft and resulted in a quick patch of the relevant vulnerability, also in July (two more zero days were fixed the following October, and the fourth by December).

For the next several months, news of the malware circulated through, but rarely beyond, the cybersecurity community. That so many infections were in Iran led to speculation that whatever Stuxnet was might have been designed to disrupt Iran's nuclear production cycle. By late September, that conclusion had hit the news via the *New York Times*.[73] Initially, it was unclear whether the target was the Natanz centrifuge facility or the Bushehr nuclear plant under construction. A further analysis of the Stuxnet code revealed it was Natanz. Analysts in the United States and Israel publicly estimated that destroying the one thousand centrifuges had set Iranians back several years, an implausible claim on the face of it, given the 2010 inventory of ten thousand, half of which were running (itself far fewer than the 2014 total of twenty thousand, again, half of which were running).

Of perhaps greater importance is that the number of Iranian centrifuges plateaued until mid–2012 before rising sharply again.

So, who was responsible? Based on who stood to benefit, suspicion immediately centered on Israel. Text dropped into the code, such as Myrtus[74] and 19790509 (a possible reference to the date when Iran executed the head of the Tehran Jewish Society), may well have been Israel's attempt to sign the code.[75] In a YouTube video from his retirement party, Israel's chief of staff numbered Stuxnet among his prominent achievements.[76] The second suspect was the United States, a tribute to its interest in stopping the Iranian nuclear program and the assumption that only the United States had the requisite skills to generate such a sophisticated program. The Chinese, who are increasingly looking at the U.S. military as their primary external threat, were quite certain that the United States had done it. But there were other suspects as well. A cyberwar strategist at the Naval War College fingered China, and a prominent cyberwar author indicated Russia, finding some association between the Finnish origin of some equipment in the centrifuge and its next-door neighbor.[77]

If one had to choose a single country, Israel initially had the better claim. With its four zero days (three more than any other malware had ever sported) and two stolen certificates plus a cornucopia of features designed to hide from anti-malware software, Stuxnet seemed to have a lot of style points—a favorite Israeli way of demonstrating overwhelming competence vis-à-vis its hostile neighbors. The U.S. military, by contrast, tends to be far more businesslike.

David Sanger claimed that Stuxnet was essentially a U.S. product that would not have spread if Israel had not tampered with the code.[78] In January 2011, Sanger reported that the Israelis had received a great deal of help from the United States, notably in learning about how to exploit flaws in industrial control systems in general and in Siemens PLCs in particular.[79] He added that the malware was tested in a special mock-up facility located in Israel's closely guarded nuclear plant in Dimona.

Stuxnet was said to begin a new chapter in cyberwar. No prior cyberattack had actually broken things. This one did. Does success now mean that cyberwar is like any other war, with death and destruction the intended consequences? Maybe not. Natanz may well have been the world's most obvious target for a destructive cyberattack (at least in peacetime). Countries normally gain little directly from the woes of others. If hurting another state creates even some risk that the actor itself may be hurt, most countries (like most people) would reason that they would experience net loss from the exchange. But Israel believed, justifiably, that the purpose of Iran's nuclear program was to threaten its very existence. That a nuclear attack would be suicidal (given Israel's nuclear capabilities) may be deemed insufficient assurance given perceptions (however misplaced) that Iran's culture deems martyrdom a holy fate. Its leaders at the time called for Israel's destruction. Even were Iran completely rational, the possession of nuclear weapons would allow it to threaten Israel with destruction should Israel take overly vigorous action against its foes, Hezbollah (which Israel fought in 2006) and Hamas (which Israel fought in 2008, 2012, and 2014). A cyberattack that could delay Iran's nuclear program would increase the odds that Iran would fold or start negotiations to the same effect before generating enough material for nuclear weapons. It would thus improve the security position of Israel and, to a significant if lesser extent, the United States. It would be less a question of making Iran hurt and more a matter of making others breathe more easily.

In contrast to a cyberattack, a military strike carried out by the United States would have come with some obloquy, especially if there were casualties. A strike conducted by Israel carries the same risks and might not even work (Israeli jets lack the air-refueled range of U.S. jets). A cyberattack, however, may go unnoticed forever, as this one almost did, and even if noticed would come without gruesome pictures that could viscerally motivate its victims to seek revenge. And even being noticed would not be incompatible with preserving the veneer of deniability.

When Stuxnet was first reported, Iran initially denied that any of its processes were affected. Two months later, however, a nuclear scientist was assassinated in Tehran, and Iran must have concluded it could no longer hide the fact that someone was making a determined and successful effort to disrupt operations at its "peaceful" nuclear fuel plant. That is when Iran acknowledged having taken damage from worms from the West. Labeling Stuxnet as a vicious and damaging attack on the state of Iran that demanded a response required changing the tenor of its characterization. The conclusion, not necessarily warranted, that insiders may have been involved, notably among the support personnel from Russia, may have caused Iran to retaliate against such workers with expulsions and executions. In early October 2010, Iran arrested an unspecified number of "nuclear spies" in connection with a damaging worm that had infected computers in its nuclear program.[80]

A more lasting effect of Stuxnet may have been psychological. A 2011 report by the Institute for Science and International Security argued, "One official at a Western intelligence agency said that since outsiders knew so much about Natanz as Stuxnet revealed, Iran would tend to hesitate about building a secret centrifuge plant out of fear of getting caught."[81] A former Israeli official speculated that Iran's inability to find Stuxnet until it hit the news meant that even after eradicating Stuxnet, Iran could not be sure that its facilities were free of destructive malware. He hypothesized that such knowledge might inhibit Iran from enriching its uranium from its current concentration of 3 percent U-235 (and, in smaller amounts, 20 percent) to weapons-grade concentration of over 90 percent. After all, Iran would have to kick out inspectors from the International Atomic Energy Agency (IAEA) to do so. Such an act would start the West on a countdown to a military operation to disrupt nuclear facilities or even change the regime before Iran enriched sufficient uranium for a nuclear warhead. Iran might refuse to run that gauntlet if it feared that the corruption of its facilities would jeopardize its ability to complete the bomb before such facilities came under physical attack.

Western observers were sure that Stuxnet "crossed the Rubicon" to put industrial control systems in play all over the world. Worse, now that the object code was publicly available, any competent hacker could use it to target other facilities. But no Stuxnet II has yet emerged, although some code fragments have found their way into malware. Why not? Stuxnet took years of dedicated planning during which certain attacks (creating overpressures) were analyzed and discarded.[82] Today, whoever would write a Stuxnet II would have to generate another set of vulnerabilities to exploit, as the four original zero days of Stuxnet were closed in 2010. Furthermore, the complacency that industrial facility owners might have had in the perfect security of their air-gapped facilities has been broken. Everyone is likely to watch one's industrial facilities a little more closely as a result, making a Stuxnet II that much more difficult to write.

Since Stuxnet hit the news, other pieces of related malware have been discovered. One was Duqu, a keystroke logger. A more interesting follow-up discovery in May 2012 was *Flame*, which was curious from several perspectives. First, at 20 million bytes (fifty times the size of Stuxnet), it was of enormous size. It had a complete toolkit of exploitation techniques—such as turning on a computer's web cam—to be called for at some later date. Second, Flame, as it turned out, was downloaded by target computers that permitted as much in the expectation that they were getting Microsoft updates, which tend to be sizable. Thus, introducing such a large file stirred no alarms. Flame's creators were able to break the MD5 hashing algorithm, relatively weak at the time, used to authenticate the update as being from Microsoft (in the case of Flame, this code may have been lent to others to use under the Microsoft Enforced Licensing Intermediate certificate PCA authority). The computing power required to crack MD5 suggested the help of an intelligence agency (although, these days, a combination of open-source tools and access to cloud computing may suffice). Third, the malware was discovered in Iran's refinery system because the International Telecommunication Union (ITU), a United Nations (UN) agency (a quarter of whose budget came from the United

States), was helping Iran keep its systems free of malware. The ITU, in turn, sent it to Kaspersky for analysis. An analysis of Flame's code carried out by Kaspersky strongly suggested common authorship with Stuxnet's code. Fourth, the infection pattern of Flame, notably in the West Bank, a region the United States has little interest in, is consistent with primary Israeli authorship—which, in turn, suggested Israel's primary authorship of Stuxnet.[83] The day after Kaspersky made that connection, U.S. sources complained to the media that the Israelis had done it to them again.[84]

Several months later, Iran announced that it was putting a billion dollars into developing a cyberwar army. The most notable initial cyberattacks reportedly from Iran took place against certificate authorities to create fake websites dissidents might visit, thereby infecting their machines.[85] More recently, Iran seemed behind the use of the Shamoon malware, which infected and erased files on office computers (but not on industrial control computers) belonging to Saudi Arabian oil production company *Aramco* and to Qatari natural gas company *RasGas*.[86] Iran's efforts may have been prompted by earlier wiper attacks on its own oil infrastructure.[87] Several months later, U.S. intelligence asserted that Iran carried out the aforementioned DDOS attacks on banks via a group referring to itself as Izz ad-Din al-Qassam Cyber Fighters.[88] In May 2013, U.S. intelligence officials claimed that "Iranian hackers were able to gain access to control-system software that could allow them to manipulate oil or gas pipelines."[89] In early 2014, computers at the *Las Vegas Sands Corporation* were trashed, putatively by Iran, in response to statements by the corporation's owner that Iran should be coerced into ending its nuclear program by having a bomb dropped on its soil.[90]

Iran is not the only vandal in cyberspace. North Korea has also started carrying out cyberattacks to render computers unusable. One targeted South Korean banks and media companies (Operation Dark Seoul).[91] Another targeted Sony Corporation for having the effrontery to make a movie (*The Interview*) showing the assassination of its Dear Leader. In late 2014, Germany announced that a cyberattack (of putative Russian origin) had interfered with the proper operation of a blast furnace, thereby damaging it.[92]

Finally, note should be made of *disruptive* cyberattacks, notably on integrated air defense systems (IADS). North Atlantic Treaty Organization (NATO) hackers may have tried to attack Serbian IADS but with unconfirmed results.[93] In 2007, purported cyberattacks (code-named Operation Orchard) on Syria's air defense system prevented the radar from seeing Israeli jets enter or leave Syrian airspace.[94] During the 2011 NATO operations against Libya, defense planners mulled the use of cyberattacks to disable Libyan air defenses. Their request was turned down, in part because of legal concerns and in part because NATO had other tried-and-true ways of countering air defenses. The access required to hack Libyan systems would have taken an indeterminate time to succeed, and prior to the Arab spring cyberwar planners had not identified Libya as a possible target.[95]

CHAPTER 2
Some Basic Principles

Systems are secure to the extent that others cannot make them violate their confidentiality, integrity, and availability. Confidentiality means that a system keeps its secrets (or at least passes them only to those authorized to see them). Integrity means that a system's data and instructions are not tampered with. Availability means that the system is working and accessible. Good systems do what they are supposed to and do not do what they are not supposed to.[1] Some systems are or go bad on their own. But sometimes they have help from others. What follows talks about what happens when systems go bad.

With that in mind, here are a few definitions we will use. A *cyberattack* is an operation that uses digital information (strings of zeros and ones) to interfere with an information system's operations and thereby produce bad information and, in some cases, bad decisions. Specifically excluded from this definition is electronic warfare; despite similarities (for example, both rely on tricks, and in neither case is battle damage assessment easy), one operates on the physical world and the other does not. Similarly, we exclude psychological attack even though cyberattacks often have psychological purposes (for example, e-mail messages that appear to come from commanders but actually came from their compromised computers).

Cyberattacks may cause disruption, corruption, and, sometimes, destruction of the systems themselves or the machines they can command (which means that the machines are built so that some set of instructions can make them destroy themselves). *Disruption* takes place when systems are tricked into performing operations that make them shut down, work at a fraction of their capacity, commit obvious errors, or interfere with the operation of other systems. Erasing information is or should be rare (in large part because backup storage is very inexpensive these days), but sometimes it does happen.[2] *Corruption* takes place when data and algorithms are changed in unauthorized ways, usually to the detriment of their correct functioning. Despite the lack of hard-and-fast distinctions between disruption and corruption, a good rule of thumb is that the effects of disruption tend to be drastic, immediate, and obvious, while the effects of corruption tend to be subtle, hard to detect, possibly lingering, and often difficult to diagnose (for instance, a missile without a good track record whose instructions were corrupted so that it detonated in the wrong place might yield little clue whether the fault was in the original software or in the software being hacked). One can usually tell whether a system is not working, but it is harder to tell that it is functioning but generating the wrong information.

We use *cyberwar* to refer to a systematic campaign of cyberattacks for political or related military ends. Cyberwar comes in two basic types. *Strategic cyberwar*, like strategic war in general, targets a country, notably its critical systems; it is largely undertaken to influence the target or to weaken its ability to resource combat. *Operational cyberwar*, like military operations in general, targets military systems; it is largely undertaken in conjunction with war or a kinetic (that is, force-employing) military operation to enhance the latter's success.[3] An example of operational cyberwar (if true) was Operation Orchard. Those authorized to carry out cyberattacks on a country's behalf (or for a nonstate actor for comparable purposes) are called *cyberwarriors* in this work.

Cyberespionage is the unauthorized extraction of information from a computer system or network and should be distinguished from cyberattacks (not that this rule is always obeyed). Although

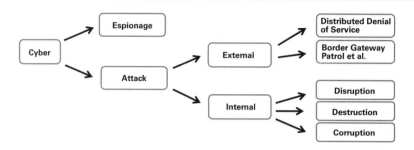

FIGURE 2.1 A HIERARCHICAL DECOMPOSITION OF UNWANTED CYBERSPACE EVENTS

this book is about cyberwar, no treatment of the subject can be complete without due appreciation of cyberespionage. Systems are usually not attacked without being penetrated (DDOS and BGP attacks aside). Once a system is penetrated, it is available for either espionage or attack (which usually entails prior espionage to determine how to attack it). Often, penetration is the most difficult part—and defenses against penetration constitute most of the defenses against both cyberespionage and cyberattack. Those who are penetrated for the purposes of espionage may plausibly believe they have been penetrated for purposes of attack. Finally, cyberespionage and cyberattack sit in the same policy space; respected former officials conflate the two.[4] Those who perpetrate cyberespionage could also perpetrate cyberattack (note that the same individual who heads the NSA also heads CYBERCOM).

Cyberdeterrence is the art of discouraging cyberattacks by others (usually other countries) by threatening reprisals against them, which may or may not take place via a return cyberattack itself.[5] Cyberdeterrence can be explicitly stated or implicit (implied by one side, inferred by the other).

Cybercrime is the criminal use of cyberattack or cyberespionage, but not merely the use of a computer to commit a crime (such as Internet gambling or cyber-bullying). Crimes are defined by governments. A crime in one jurisdiction may not be a crime in another; some contract violations have been deemed crimes.[6] Inasmuch as many of the defenses against cyberwar (and cyberespionage) are also defenses against cybercrime, the three are intimately related, and lessons from one can be used to talk about another, but this book is not about cybercrime.

Cybersecurity entails the state of one's systems being secure; it should be understood as a goal rather than a state, which can only be achieved by making a large number of assumptions. Figure 2.1 shows one way of organizing some of these concepts. The results of operations against computers can be separated into cyberespionage and cyberattack. Cyberattacks, in turn, can be divided into two classes of attack. One class works from the outside, as DDOS attacks and BGP and related attacks do, and do not necessarily arise from faults in the system being attacked. The other class works from the inside and must arise from faults in the target system. The effects of inside attacks can themselves be roughly differentiated into disruption, destruction (rare), and corruption.

This field is hard enough to grasp without metastasizing neologisms; the terms *cyberattack, cyberespionage, cyberwar, cyberwarrior, cyberdeterrence, cybercrime, cybersecurity,* and *cyberspace* (see below) constitute the only words in this book (quotations aside) built from the prefix *cyber*.[7]

CYBERWAR AND CYBERSPACE

One of the confusing ironies about cyberwar is that it is not really about cyberspace, but rather about systems. Although systems are generally accessed *through* cyberspace, there are other paths hackers can use to introduce errors into computer systems without using the (public) Internet. A hacker can be an authorized user (an insider attack). A special forces operator could gain close-in physical access to a system and command it for long enough to make it err. The system may contain rogue logic components inserted prior to its connection to the network; these components could create types of errors based on particular circumstances (for example, if the radar sees a U.S. warplane, a circuit in the radar instructs the screen not to show anything). Short-range, point-to-point radio frequency (RF) connections could be overwritten by a long-range, high-power signal from beyond what would be the understood physical perimeter. Similarly, a hacker could step into Bluetooth range of an unencrypted signal. An infection in one entity can spread to another one connected by private and quasi-private circuits (for example, via asynchronous transfer mode [ATM] communications). A system that reacts to sensory input could be presented with inputs designed to induce specific malfunctions. None of these methods require cyberspace in the sense of a globally connected network to function, but they can create the same effects. Nevertheless, operating through cyberspace is the preferred method of entry for reasons of economy, certainty, and risk.

Careless use of the word *cyberspace* can result in thoughtless policy assumptions. Declaring that it is up to the U.S. government to protect private systems would sound absurd, but declaring that it must defend cyberspace sounds less absurd. Because cyberspace lacks boundaries, so must the government's purview (hence its assumption of responsibility over the attack on Sony, a Japanese company). The United States could plausibly assume the mantle of the world's cop in cyberspace.

Most of what is true about the conduct of cyberwar would be true if the Internet had never been invented; to wit, if communications ran only over phone lines and radio waves (with some exceptions: nontrivial lag times associated with setting up phone calls render impractical attacks that rely on many small exchanges of information from multiple sources). Otherwise, the major themes—notably, attacks by malware—would be themes of circuit-switched telephony much as they are in today's packet-switching world of the Internet. Nevertheless, the myth that the problems of cyberspace arose because the Internet was fecklessly assembled in complete disregard of security concerns persists even through 2015.[8] And so it is on systems, not networks, that we focus.

One way to conceptualize the construction of and hence threat to systems—from whatever conduit it comes—may be to draw an analogy to the layered construction of human speech. All information systems rest on a *physical layer* consisting of devices plus conduits, wired and wireless.[9] Remove the physical layer, and the system disappears as well. It is certainly possible to attack an information system through kinetic means; however, a computer cannot be deceived by destroying its components (although it can be deceived through sly substitution of one component for another). Cyberattacks by definition do not take place *via* the destruction of physical systems, although such systems may (albeit rarely) be destroyed by a cyberattack.

The *syntactic layer* contains the instructions and protocols through which machines interact with one another—for example, device recognition, packet framing, addressing, routing, document formatting, and database manipulation. Some communication infrastructures have more in their syntactic layer than others, but every system more complex than two cans and a string has to have some. This is the level at which hacking tends to take place.

The topmost layer, the *semantic layer*, contains the information that systems have—much of the reason computers exist in the first place. Some of the information, such as address lookup tables or printer control codes, is meant for system manipulation; it is semantic in form but syntactic in purpose. Other information, such as metal-cutting or system-management instructions, is meant for computer-controlled machinery (instructions can be in the syntactic or semantic layer; the difference is whether the device being instructed is a logical or a physical one). Otherwise, the content is made for people's understanding. The distinction between information and instructions is not hard and fast. Indeed, many hacking tricks insert instructions in the guise of information; examples include attachments that contain worms, overly long addresses that create buffer overflows (sending the extra bits into the processing stream to be interpreted as instructions), and web pages with embedded code (or iframe pointers to embedded code). It is possible, but not yet commonplace, to attack computers solely at the semantic level by feeding them false information (for example, harvested from a fake website).

Control over one layer does not necessarily imply control over another layer. A computer connected to the Internet via Verizon's network works pretty much the same as a computer connected via AT&T's network.[10] Likewise, insecurity at one layer may be mitigated by controls at another layer. Protecting the integrity of a database may be done by ensuring that people do not get to write to it—or by ensuring that a valid transaction in one (such as a withdrawal) has to be verified by comparable information in another (such as assets). Social security numbers can be protected from use for identity theft by safeguarding databases that hold such numbers or by rejecting the use of the numbers to authenticate someone's identity.[11] The many weaknesses of supervisory control and data acquisitions (SCADA) systems may be more effectively addressed not by securing SCADA software, but by isolating the SCADA system (the physical layer) or by preventing machines from operating in unsafe modes (the semantic layer).[12] Put another way, systems can be defended by isolating them, by guarding who can instruct them, or by guarding what instructions they can carry out.

At the same time, the importance of physical control over systems should not be underestimated. If the hardware cannot be changed by software, one can build code into it that can use digital signature technology to authenticate not only its own messages but also many of its own internal processes. The hardware, for instance, can determine whether a piece of software has come from a trusted source (notably the hardware's producer) or whether certain process requests can be honored.

Bad system behavior can also be stopped by disconnecting, fixing, and reconnecting it. An approach to errant automatic controls is to override the electronic controls and do things manually. Manual controls have some advantages. For instance, they afford users a way to control a device that can be more intuitive to monitor and harder to hack; compare a sliding tab that can hide a laptop camera to software-based controls that can be overridden or spoofed. But manual override is becoming harder to do. Diagnostics, for instance, are becoming increasingly remote in origin. The old admonition to turn off your work computer when going home is positively discouraged in an organizational environment; updates (ironically, often for the purposes of bolstering security) often take place in the wee hours of the morning.

A broader lesson applies to cleaning out the original infection. One used to be able to clean out machines (after having backed up all the data) by returning them to original factory conditions. But modern machines host not just one logical device, the central processing unit (CPU), but many ancillary logic devices as well. Furthermore, some hardware, such as the basic input-output system (BIOS), has the discouraging property of being hackable but not easily restored by users.[13]

If computers ever build their instructions by learning from their interactions (as humans do), returning them to factory condition would eradicate such learning. Assume that your computer had, over time, learned about something and encoded this knowledge in files. These files were then surreptitiously corrupted. Normally, if a computer is scrambled, one can go to its last known good backup, recover the old information, and pick up from there. But what if instead of being scrambled that information was slowly corrupted, and it was not clear when this corruption started? How would one know the difference between the rules that should have been learned and those that should not have been learned because what they learned from was manipulated to misdirect learning?

HOW HACKERS WORK

Hackers can enter an organization's systems by linking to them and successfully masquerading as legitimate users with the rights and privileges of any other user. In some cases, hackers go further, fooling a network into thinking they have the privileges of a systems administrator (sysadmin). As a sysadmin with appropriate privileges, a hacker can arbitrarily change nearly everything about a network, not least of which is the privileges other users enjoy.[14] Once hackers have wormed their way into a system and appropriated enough privileges, they can do quite a lot. A typical hack may be a three-part process: finding an externally facing computer to compromise, moving malware or escalated access privileges laterally to the most critical parts of the network, and compromising the system as a whole from that point.[15]

Hackers often drop rogue computer code—implants—into systems for later use.[16] Implants are essentially code stubs that call out for additional code when needed. They may lie dormant, only to be activated by commands from the hacker; they can wait for particular events on target machines; or, most commonly, they can *beacon* out to a server looking for new commands. In some cases, implants operate autonomously, searching for computers on the network that lack such implants and making sure they do not lack for long. An implant designed to purloin information on command may be indistinguishable from an implant designed to disrupt systems or corrupt information on command.

The more complex the system, the more places there are for a software or process vulnerability to hide. The software suppliers themselves find a large share of software vulnerabilities and issue periodic patches, which sysadmins and users are then supposed to install. Some let patches pile up, in part because certain patches keep other code from running, and in part because they show up so frequently with no reliable way to discern which ones fix dangerous security vulnerabilities and which do not. Letting vendors know that someone is exploiting a vulnerability usually leads to expeditious patching. Hackers find some vulnerabilities that the software producers do not; these are known as zero-day vulnerabilities until patched. They can plague systems otherwise kept up to date.

Those who seek out zero days are identified with one of many hats. White hats intend to make such vulnerabilities known to those who maintain the code, either directly or via brokers, such as the Zero-Day Initiative or iDefense. Grey and black hats hoard the vulnerability for their own use or sell it to others for them to use. If the vulnerability is converted into an exploit, it is usually for the purpose of penetrating someone else's system—although it is sometimes used by penetration testers to understand how the security features of a system (including its human operators) work or fail. Intelligence agencies have recently revealed themselves to be active customers of gray-hat hackers; brokers that will sell exploits included companies such as Vupen, ReVuln, the Hacking Team, and Endgame (prior to 2013).

A vulnerability that is used and discovered is often brought to the attention of vendors so that they can understand what happened and how to change their code so that it does not happen again. Each found vulnerability means one less vulnerability left for someone else to exploit. Unfortunately, at least for Adobe and Java products, the pool appears to be very large, and the process of draining the pool is going very slowly. Apparently, the ease by which vulnerabilities can be discovered in those two programs is sufficiently great that the rewards for finding them are correspondingly modest.[17]

Fuzzing is a popular method to find vulnerabilities in code.[18] Programs are fed a wide variety of random variables, particularly those that lie at the edge of what normal users would input, in an attempt to figure out which values create unexpected results. These results are in turn a clue to whether a good hacker can persuade the program to do what its creators would otherwise not wish—and hence are a guide to what needs fixing.

Do new vulnerabilities become harder to find as existing vulnerabilities are found? Asked another way: are software vulnerabilities dense or sparse?[19] If there is a finite number of bugs (or at least serious bugs), their ranks are likely to be exhausted faster if both insiders and outsiders looking for the bugs have access to the source code. Andrew Ozment argued, "We find strong statistical evidence of a decrease in the rate at which foundational vulnerabilities are being reported [for BSD Unix's core code]. However, this decrease is anything but brisk: foundational vulnerabilities have a median lifetime of at least 2.6 years."[20] His data indicated that the rate at which vulnerabilities in the core code were discovered did, in fact, decline over time, suggesting that vulnerabilities *are* significantly depleted by discovery. Depleting the inventory of potential cyberattacks means that unless a stockpile of exploits is just waiting in the queue, discovering every successive new vulnerability will require more effort and will take longer.[21] But some bugs persist; a recently discovered bug sat in the code for almost 20 years.[22] Alternatively, if the more serious bugs are found first, those that remain are less serious because they have more subtle and less dangerous effects, because the circumstances under which they can be evoked depend on the user's machine being in a rare configuration, because they create more noticeable anomalies in system performance, or because the effort required to exploit the bug grows greater as the vulnerability becomes more subtle. In other words, the depletion makes those that remain less valuable to hackers.

So, does the world need better bug fixing? Maybe not. Eric Rescorla argued that statistics show that fixing vulnerabilities may make things worse. Issuing a patch leads to more exploitation because hackers can reverse-engineer the patch, discover the vulnerability it fixes, write an exploit, and infect systems at a faster rate than a sufficient number of system owners would patch their systems.[23] If the path between the fix and the attack is short enough, there are bound to be unpatched systems and hence *new* targets for hackers. Yet patch mechanisms that exist today may have reversed the force of the 2004 argument. Microsoft's patch day (formerly "patch Tuesday") is hard to avoid; unless specifically turned off, it comes up automatically whenever the user turns the machine off or after a certain period has elapsed after the patch has been sent out (which means that even continuously connected computers may not be fully patched every minute). Firefox is similar.

Sometimes one vulnerability suffices for an exploit; sometimes it does not.[24] A full compromise may require downloading malware from a website, having the malware escape the browser sandbox, and then defeating an operating system's defenses (for example, address-space layout randomization). Each of the latter three may be considered a vulnerability (sysadmins may consider the susceptibility of users to social engineering an additional vulnerability). However, when we assert that if systems are not supposed to have (and generally therefore do not often have) known unfixed vulnerabilities, *we are referring to the entire vulnerability chain*. It is entirely possible, even logical, to ignore certain vulnerabilities if there are good protections elsewhere in the vulnerability chain. Conversely, a belt-and-suspenders approach means that a single unknown vulnerability cannot be used to compromise a system.

Any attempt to take advantage of a vulnerability to gain access to a system or to get it to accept rogue instructions is called an *exploit*. An exploit, if discovered, should signal to sysadmins that something is not right. Sysadmins may be able to determine where something unusual took place in the interaction between the hacker and the system.[25] Changes in files (data or instructions) or the presence of unexpected files can also be telling. The process is hardly perfect; it is possible to determine a specific vulnerability and miss the broader design flaw of which the specific vulnerability is just a manifestation.

In an important sense, a system's faults, as much as or more than a hacker's skill, determine whether it can be exploited. Insofar as the ability to give instructions to a system that it will accept and act on depends on the system itself, there is no forced entry in cyberspace (good RF signals can be overridden by bad ones, but there are many straightforward ways, such as cryptography, to detect and shut out unauthorized inputs). A hacker can only get into a system from the outside by persuading it to do what its owner/operator did not really want done and what its designers believed they had built the system to prevent. Nevertheless, in any contest between a system's design and use model (for example, a user's intuition that e-mail is information, not instructions) on the one hand and its software code on the other, the code always wins. It is what predicts what the system will do. In the small crack—metaphorically, a bitstream wide—between what design specifications say a system will do and what the code says it will do lie potential *vulnerabilities*. The software may have flaws or may have been misconfigured (administrators established different permissions from what they thought they had established), but a system is what it is, not necessarily what it should be.

Thus, in *theory*, all computer mischief is ultimately the fault of the system's owner—if not because of misuse or misconfiguration, then for using a system with security bugs in the first place. In *practice*, none but the most skilled or well-heeled buyers can avoid purchasing commercial software. Some (but only some) can avoid networking.

Penetration is thus a matter of guile and not force. Certain fundamental properties of guile frustrate its repetition. They are encapsulated in the saying "fool me once, shame on you; fool me twice, shame on me." Furthermore, perfection is theoretically possible. At the risk of doing theology, if one were to ask, "Can the Lord design a computer system that the Lord cannot hack?" the answer would be "Yes." There would be no way to command a system to do other than what it was coded to do. By way of further explanation, consider the notion of being able to broadcast a virus into a system. The only way to do so is if the system was built to run executable code (whether directly or by the internal conversion of data) it received over the air. More primitively, all the broadcasting in the world will not affect a system that lacks an RF receiver. Furthermore, if the system treated such data only as data (a big "if" that depends on what the code really does), then a virus would be treated as data if it is treated at all.

The relationship between a bug, a vulnerability, and an exploit is not straightforward and can be the source of confusion. Statistics on the inevitability of so many flaws per thousand lines of code suggest that vulnerabilities are nearly infinite (because they may arise through an indefinite combination of bugs).[26] Yet only a small fraction of all flaws are those that permit the insertion of malware. Furthermore, not every vulnerability lends itself to an exploit (a standard test of an exploit on a Windows system is to see whether it can cause Microsoft's calculator program to pop up uninvited on the user's screen). The issue of whether the ability to find vulnerabilities or the ability to convert them into exploits marks the most serious threats is difficult to resolve. Finding a vulnerability is a probabilistic endeavor not unlike finding oil: a function of how hard you look, where you are looking, and luck. The price of crude oil is not a function of the cost of finding petroleum (there is no ipso facto reason why the world market price of oil must reflect any one producer's cost to lift oil). Converting a vulnerability into an exploit is closer to the economics of refining, which is a largely deterministic process. Although the cost of refined products is also determined by supply and demand, it invariably reflects the long-run cost of building and operating refineries.

The damage from any given cyberattack will not be the same over all systems and not the same over time. The first is true because systems vary in their vulnerabilities. The second is true because systems change. Sometimes they evolve to have fewer vulnerabilities. Perhaps vulnerabilities are found and then patched. Perhaps as a result of having many discovered vulnerabilities, systems are re-architected in ways that make them more secure (to have fewer vulnerabilities or at least less damaging ones). But systems can also evolve to have more vulnerabilities.[27] Some did so by adding capabilities that create new avenues for mischief. There used to be no way to infect a machine by opening an e-mail. Then, hypertext markup language (HTML) was invented, followed by Java.

When an e-mail was opened, it could try to open itself up as a web page, the result of which was that hidden web code present in the page could infect the machine it ran on. After a few years, the authors of e-mail software decided that the security risks of blithely opening web pages were too great. Those who now click on e-mails have far fewer chances of being infected (opening attachments to such e-mails is another matter). Thus have computers evolved from when e-mail was perfectly safe to when it was potentially unsafe to where it is now fairly safe again.

The exposure to cyberattacks is the price one pays for computer networks and digitization; the two go hand in hand. The challenge, therefore, is to maximize the value one gets from digitization, networking, and related technologies while minimizing the risk that comes from cyberspace. This echoes what was true for industrialization. Before there were the boilers that characterized industrialization, there were no boiler accidents—but also none of the benefits that come from industrialization.

AGORAS AND CASTLES

Claude Shannon is considered the father of information theory for his insight that the enemies of information are not only erasure or destruction but also noise or distortion. This formulation suggests a subtle relationship between noise and deception. Noise can be overcome by retransmission—at a cost of resources, such as time. Noise need not lead to bad decisions, although it may lead to lost opportunities to make decisions in time. It is when the information appears to be correct but is not that real problems arise. From a computer perspective, random bit errors often (but not always) show up as instructions that cannot be executed. Stuxnet did not work by randomly flipping bits in the instruction set of the centrifuge controller but by substituting one plausible (at least to the machine) set of instructions for another.

People have traditionally used three techniques to deal with the risk of misinformation or disinformation. The first is reputation. Trustworthy people can be relied on; the word of others can be relied on only if they lack an obvious motive or inclination to lie (which is why one can take directions from a random stranger). Although computers do distinguish between authorized and unauthorized inputs and could, in theory, distinguish trusted from untrusted sources, they are rarely programmed to make such judgments on their own; it takes considerable artificial intelligence for a computer to discern a user's motive. In the meantime, they have to be told outright.

The second technique is redundancy. This gets easier if human judgment can be applied—that is, if these computers are information gatherers for human decisionmakers. Redundancy also works to guard against noise. If one channel is down or producing garbage, then a second one can be brought in as backup. Multiplying channels is not free, though, and the receiver must anticipate their need in advance.

The third technique is filtration. One filter is to reject information that lies outside certain parameters. If a machine is not supposed to go over 1,000 rpm, then an instruction that indicates that it should go 1,200 rpm would be rejected. Good database design puts in copious boundaries—against not only deception but also error.

Authentication, redundancy, and filtration all have their place in cybersecurity as well. The susceptibility of decision processes to noisy environments varies greatly. A semiconductor plant is a highly noise-intolerant environment because a random piece of dust can interfere with circuitry—hence all the bunny suits that factory workers are dressed in. Similarly, a nuclear power plant is a very sensitive environment where operators trust in their readings and where a badly received or transmitted signal could produce a major disaster (thus necessitating so many fail-safe devices around to stop all processes). Wall Street, however, is a very noisy environment; people make money there by ingesting a gigantic amount of information and rumor and sifting for the few pieces that can tell them more about a stock's movement than the next guy's piece of information. Shoveling in more rumors (rather than falsely documented "facts") would probably not make all that much difference, except that there would be more material to go through.

The distinction between noise-tolerant environments—call them agoras—and noise-intolerant environments—call them castles—is an important but often overlooked element of information security. With castles, the risk from bad information and hence bad instructions is high, but the benefit from having day-to-day access to the world of external information is comparatively low (think nuclear plants). With agoras, the risk from a single piece of bad information is low, but the benefit of having day-to-day access to the world of information is comparatively high (think Wall Street).

A castle protects itself through a series of enclosures: the open field of fire, the moat, the wall, and within the castle, the keep. Each obstacle challenges the intruder, and when one is breached, attention shifts to maintaining the next obstacle and, if possible, throwing the attacker back beyond the earlier breached obstacles. The agora works differently. Recognizing that most individual pieces of information are of little use, possibly false, and usually transient, processes are defended from corruption by putting out more lines to the rest of the world. New information can be used to evaluate the old information, and the sophisticated agglomeration of information is the best path to making good decisions. To use a geometric metaphor, castle processes are defended by circumferential lines that provide rings of protection, while the agora processes are defended by radial lines that provide avenues of correction. If machine decisionmaking entails both sensors and effectors, it is clear that the first is an agora while the second is a castle, because the former can be defended by multiple redundant input channels while the latter can only be defended by clean command channels (and clean internal logic). It should need little further elaboration to note that castles protected as if they were agoras would not remain castles for long, and agoras protected like castles would lose their usefulness quickly.

Distinctions between agoras and castles are echoed in distinctions between clients and servers. The clients belong to the users, not only in the way they are used but, in most environments, also because the user has a great deal of leeway in determining what to put on the client machine. Such machines are numerous, and they travel a lot, often including home with the user. Sysadmins try to make users conscious of security risks, and they may make it difficult for users to install their own software (easier now that everyone uses Microsoft Office than it was in the 1990s, when there was a much greater variety in software), but clients' infections are recurrent. Clients tend to repeatedly be vulnerable largely because cybersecurity is not users' highest priority (compared to getting use out of their machines).

Servers, however, belong to the sysadmins. They are fewer in number and do not travel. Their access is more tightly controlled. They do not surf the web or receive random e-mail. They hold the primary information of the enterprise and can refresh the clients if they get into trouble. Sysadmins tend to control assets such as network monitors, routers, machinery (such as weapons), and databases. Sysadmins are (or should be) trained and sensitive to security issues; they also set the terms by which users (and their systems) interact with the servers.

Yet weaknesses in the client can imperil servers; some clients input directly to servers, and some servers have to extend trust privileges to clients to communicate at all. Infected clients can clog networks, thereby depriving other clients of network services. Assuming that clients are pristine, and hence trustworthy, is asking for trouble. But restricting clients to keep them pristine is also asking for trouble if the enterprise is expected to deal robustly with the outside world. One way to protect the enterprise is to limit what clients can do to servers; the continued wave of cyberespionage from major enterprises suggests, however, that client-server security relationships need better understanding.

Another way that enterprises maintain both castles and agoras is to maintain them as separate zones. For instance, an enterprise's technology and product development systems could be isolated from the rest of the world because others may want badly to steal information in them. Conversely, the office automation systems that support sales, service, and marketing are connected to the rest of the world, because they cannot work any other way these days—and the information in them is of less value to others (unless stolen wholesale). The U.S. military runs a secret Internet (the SIPRnet), which is air-gapped, and an unclassified Internet, the Non-classified Internet Protocol Router Network (NIPRnet), which is not.

But how good is the separation? Infections can sometimes jump from agoras to castles. For instance, the agora might run the heating and air conditioning system that may be considered ancillary to the firm's main business. But bring and keep this system down, and people cannot work in the castle anymore. In other cases, the isolation is not physical but virtual and enforced through cryptography so that messages stay in their own channel: to wit, the castle will not accept (malware-laden) information from the agora, and the agora cannot read information acquired from the castle. Nevertheless, an infection in the agora could crash a router on which the castle depends, and the castle ceases to function. Buckshot Yankee illustrated how an infected NIPRnet (agora) machine can lead to an infected SIPRnet (castle). Someone working with both castle and agora machines may forget which is which and put highly sensitive information on the latter.

Finally, it is possible to attack foes by making them castles themselves. In the age of networking and outsourcing, an increasing percentage of what organizations require in order to function entails them working with others. If such organizations are unaware of what is taking place, the right kind of cyberattacks on such systems can impel them to rely on themselves rather than others. By reducing the trust between the target organization and the rest of the world, an organization that ought to think of itself as an agora starts to think of itself as a castle. In an agora, degrees of affiliation and trust are analog, continuous, and fuzzy. In the castle, one is either in or out. Degrees of affiliation and trust are binary, discrete, and clear. So the organization draws a big circle around itself, thereby cutting what it thinks are its least important lines (or maybe all its lines) to others. It stops learning as quickly, and it finds itself with a limited repertoire of responses to the unexpected. By pruning its twigs and branches, it hopes to save its trunk—but fails to realize that the mark of a dead tree is one without twigs and leaves.

MOST CYBERATTACKS HAVE TRANSITORY EFFECTS

Unlike kinetic attacks, most cyberattacks have only temporary effects. This holds in two senses of the word. First, the direct effects of the attack carry on only until the errant process is stopped; once the affected systems are cleansed, they can return to service. Second, attacks are hard to repeat; defenders themselves often can determine how the attack was carried out and which vulnerability in the system's software was responsible for the attack (and therefore which software has to be fixed). It helps if these companies have a sample of the malware to examine, but merely knowing certain elements of the exploit can help narrow down the search for the relevant vulnerability. Granted, the fix is never instant, although it can be as short as days. In the meantime, the problematic software can be rerouted, or problematic inputs can be prefiltered.

Not all cyberattacks are eradicable, though; DDOS attacks may persist because they are often enabled by the corrupted computers of others, not necessarily because the target is running software whose weaknesses, once exposed, can be fixed. Similarly, the repeatability of other attacks relies on human faults, such as passwords that are too easily guessed. But in the main, the temporary and hard-to-repeat nature of a cyberattack is its salient characteristic.

As a rule, stopping a cyberattack requires detecting it as such. This requires that the induced fault be noticed *and* that it be recognized as something induced rather than an accident, human error, a program artifact (such as an obscure feature of the program understood only by the designers), or a bug (a so-called undocumented feature of the program not understood by the designers).

Cyberespionage is difficult to detect; as noted, the average time between penetration and discovery has been over a year, and that only includes those penetrations that *were* discovered. The so-called Equation intrusion set reportedly went back over ten years prior to discovery.[28] There are techniques to look for penetrations by looking for data exfiltration, but sophisticated penetrations rarely hike the volume of activity in general or even the volume of certain types of activity. Looking at what is leaving the network is frustrated if such data are encoded or are chopped up and buried in common traffic. Encrypted data are hard to distinguish from e-commerce or virtual private network traffic (but not impossible if one can fingerprint data flows by type).

Detection can be helped by a well-grounded baseline of normal behavior that can be compared to behavior under a cyberattack. Yet there is no substitute for understanding how an attacked process works. As a partial corollary, it also helps to have the failed system at hand to analyze. This is generally possible, even for defense systems. But many military systems are unrecoverable if they fail, and some, such as missiles, are unrecoverable even if they succeed (indeed, particularly if they succeed). So if a cyberattack takes out a missile's guidance system, there may be very little to work with unless the missile's operators have good telemetry on the missile itself as it goes wrong. Similarly, a corrupted sensor may stay corrupted for extended periods if there is no way to double-check its readings. Finally, a substantially complete disruption may remove the means for discovering it very quickly. For instance, an attack that takes down Internet connectivity may keep people from using the Internet to collaborate on diagnosing and fixing it.

Attackers have many options to employ if they want to reuse their handiwork. First, malware can be designed to erase itself. Second, malware can erase the memory on which it was stored (erasing the files that log network events is harder). Third, the hackers can use obfuscation tools.[29] Fourth, an attacker's effects may be shaped to suggest an accident or an intermittent flaw; this method requires exquisite knowledge of the target system and a sense of how its sysadmins react when things run awry. Fifth, attackers might create very noticeable effects that can be made to disappear upon diagnosis and repair while the actual, albeit more subtle, damage goes unnoticed. How well this trick works depends on whether sysadmins, who are often under the pressure of time, are content to tinker until the problem disappears and then turn to other matters—or whether they disassemble the software to understand what happened. Sixth, attackers can target systems that sysadmins assume are secure, and thus malfunctions are likely to be viewed as the fault of inherent hardware and software problems (much as those running the Natanz centrifuges did when faced with Stuxnet). If there are still naive system managers left (after Stuxnet), they may be attacked for an extended time. Seventh, limiting attacks to those reluctant to talk to others may permit similar attacks to work against related targets.

A corruption attack may take more work to discover. In any system with sufficient redundancy, errors will be detected. This is why aircraft, for instance, have thrice-redundant avionics; the failure of one device can be detected because the other two are still putting out readings that conform to one another (with just two systems, a discrepancy leaves one guessing which system is working correctly). Even in less technical arenas, storing transaction data in one place and asset data in another can mean that changes to one are not reflected in changes to the other. However, an intelligent corruption attack that works at the outset of a transaction (for example, a clerk pays out $7, but the computer records $70 in both the transactions log and the asset log, with the $63 being shifted to the attackers) could take the redundancy into account. More broadly, a corruption attack has to find the sweet spot between twin faults. On the one hand, if too many variables are too far from where intuition suggests they be, a problem might be suspected. On the other hand, if too few variables are corrupted and none of those are corrupted enough to notice, then the effect may be too weak to be worth the trouble. So the attacker also has to know quite a bit about an organization's crisis response modes to understand how much corruption is too much to stay undiscovered.

The relationship between cyberespionage and cyberattack includes a critical caveat. Typically, a cyberattack involves penetrating a system to understand both how the pieces fit together and what the various parts do. This penetration also provides the opportunity to plant the attack in a system—and this implant, in turn, can be the conduit through which the attack is inserted into the system and/or activated. As long as the penetration remains undiscovered, and if the performance of the target system is essentially unaffected, then the penetration methods remain useful and can be (and typically are) reused, particularly if they use hard-to-generate zero-day exploits. Thus, multiple systems can be penetrated and set up for an attack using the same method; in that sense, cyberattacks are not a single-use technique. However, once a cyberattack is carried out, the half-life of the attack method can drop quickly. Thus, for practical purposes, they have to be detonated all at once (or at least within a very short time span). Furthermore, the strategy of implantation has to be carefully considered; the more often a technique is used, the greater the odds it will be discovered, and its discovery on one system will, in turn, imperil its usefulness when used on other systems. The preparations for multi-system compromise (whether for espionage or attack) are like the dice game of Pig: the more often one throws the dice, the greater the odds of seeing the score drop to zero.[30] Thus, the odds that a very ambitious campaign will succeed may be quite low if the odds that a penetration is discovered in a certain interval are palpably nonzero.

Once an attack is characterized, recovery is not that hard if the system is basically intact. If there are backups of software and files outside of the system, computers can usually be restored to their factory condition, following which the software can be reloaded and the files restored.[31] In today's personal computers, this takes roughly two hours.

Fixing an infected computer on a network, however, requires that all the machines be down at the same time and restored cleanly at the same time, lest one infected machine reinfect those already cleaned. It also requires cleaning all the machines with special privileges to access systems on the network. If the sysadmins do not have access to all such machines (many of which may be owned by business partners), they may have to assume that every external machine is infected when determining which privileges on their own network to grant such machines.

Empirically, the time required to restore service after large attacks has been somewhere between hours and days if the need is sufficiently urgent. Systems that have been down for extended periods were those where system owners wanted to be extra careful that the infection had been eradicated. A full cleanup can take weeks to months.[32] In no case should an attack destroy data that has been properly backed up, although incoming data, as noted, may have been corrupted from entry.

The next step is ensuring that the same attack cannot work again. If the attack comes from malware, there probably is a vulnerability that needs to be, and can be, fixed. Large organizations often have sufficient expertise on call that can determine where the relevant vulnerability is and what mechanisms in the software permitted the attack. But this is under peacetime conditions where any organization can tap into what is now a huge cybersecurity industry. This may not be true if the target (by dint of being small or poor) finds such services unaffordable (or perhaps by dint of having been intentionally isolated finds such services unavailable).

A target's ability to get its purchased software fixed depends on the alacrity with which the vendors respond to reports of the attack. Vendors fix their products' vulnerabilities faster and more assiduously than they did ten years ago; these days, it is the failure to fix that is notable. Generally, once an exploit has occurred in the real world (outside the laboratory), the vulnerability that permitted the exploit is moved to the top of the fix-it stack.

The general rule, therefore, is that attackers who employ cyberattacks should expect either temporary disruption or subtle corruption as a result of their labors. More likely than not, the attack will be discovered and characterized once its effects take place, allowing agile system owners to route around the problem until a patch is generated, days or weeks later. Cyberattacks, at some profound level, are one-time-use weapons.

But again, there are caveats. First, the effects must be detected. Second, they have to be identified correctly as a cyberattack whose mechanisms are understood well enough to be characterized. Third, the system owners have to have ways of disabling a recurrence. Fourth, unless the target can live with a permanent work-around, those who created the software have to be motivated to fix the problem. The first three caveats require good systems administrators. The last requires vendor cooperation (or enough publicity so that vendors cannot ignore the problem) and sufficient circulation of the fix.

Tricks tend to exhaust themselves to the extent that their existence (and thus the need to protect against their recurrence) is obvious and that counters to their recurrence are straightforward to implement. Certain types of attacks will deplete at different rates. The depletion rate for cyberespionage, for example, is relatively slow because it often goes undetected for long periods. The depletion rate for an obvious disruption attack ought to be high, but such an attack tends to be easier to implement than a corruption attack in the first place because it requires only that a process fail, not that it fail in a particular way that meets certain parameters. For corruption, the opposite is true. Depletion is fairly high: *fairly*, because corruption may go unnoticed and hence unaddressed, but *high*, because good corruption attacks are hard. Success requires subtly and consistently altering many parts of a system, lest telltale inconsistencies alert defenders that something is amiss. Rarely will a trick, once discerned, work for very long.

Robert Axelrod and Ruman Iliev have argued that the optimal timing of a cyberattack depends on two variables: the half-life of an exploit before it is discovered during the period before it is used (persistence) and the half-life of an exploit once used (stealth).[33] They reasoned that opportunities to use the attack are not constant (as they would be if the point is ongoing collection against a target); they arise unpredictably. Going after the first good opportunity may prevent using an attack against a later, better opportunity. However, while waiting for a better opportunity, the exploit may disappear (for example, the vulnerability could be patched). Low persistence and high stealth argue for early use; high persistence and low stealth argue for waiting. The authors argued that Stuxnet's use of four zero days meant that the worm's persistence was low; once Stuxnet's creators had made Stuxnet stealthy, they had every reason to use it quickly. Referring to Shamoon, the authors argued that Iran was impelled to strike quickly in order to demonstrate that it could and would respond to Stuxnet. Third, the authors claim that China's APT attacks tend to be used on the early side because the Chinese feel that their exploits have a short shelf life but long stealth. It is unclear whether there was any good reason to wait in any of the three cases, particularly for cyberespionage (where long taps rather than in-and-out are standard). With cyberattack, the opposite is true; one generally waits in peace and deploys in war. Once war starts, it is difficult to know which, if any, attacks should be held back. In practice, between the unpredictable distribution of opportunities and the unobservable adjustments being made in the other side's systems, it is unclear how to collect data that would allow practical use of the authors' insights.

CHAPTER 3
How to Compromise a Computer

T he many ways that systems can be hacked may be grouped into three categories, each of which in turn has multiple attack modes. The first category consists of attacks by authorized or seemingly authorized internal users who abuse their privileges. The second includes attacks in which everyday external users abuse their privileges. The third category consists of supply-chain attacks and malware, both of which directly alter instructions in the target system.

ABUSES BY AUTHORIZED INTERNAL USERS

Insider threat, account hijacking, and machine-in-the-middle attacks are all abuses by what appear to be authorized users. The *insider threat* has been a challenge to computer security for at least a half-century, as bankers can attest.[1] A well-managed system can make it difficult for rogue employees to do a great deal of damage and, in some cases, can limit how much material they can access (even when any individual item is available). Rogue system administrators (for example, Edward Snowden) can create particularly nasty headaches. Organizations used to vetting and trusting insiders must rethink how much damage one can cause; the NSA now requires two system administrators to initiate critical actions.[2]

Insider recruitment by external sources, though, does not easily lend itself to serious cyberwar. Insiders have to be recruited and motivated to carry out mischief, often when and where they work, despite the risk to their person. Tracing an induced flaw to an authorized user can pinpoint the source of the damage and hence suggest its reversal as well as finger the guilty party. Recruiting insiders is hard and failure-prone if it has to achieve scale, because it faces the same constraints of the Pig game: one failure may unmask the recruitment process and force recruitment to begin from scratch, particularly if unmasking the recruitment says something about its target selection and modus operandi. In a heterogeneous American infrastructure with lots of different owners and points of entry and control, it may take a large number of recruits to make a serious difference—except in cases where one insider can create a cascade effect.

A variant on an insider attack may be one carried out by or through wireless devices. This could happen through surreptitiously placing a device sufficiently close to other parts of the network, substituting a tampered device for a legitimate device, or placing a device just beyond what the defense assumed its RF perimeter was based on the equipment it uses itself but within the perimeter that reflects the attacker's use of expectedly powerful transmitters or unexpectedly sensitive antennae.

The problem of user and/or *account hijacking* is prosaic and common. Although some systems allow user access only from physically secured sites, users are increasingly granted remote access, with passwords being the only way to distinguish users from others. Passwords are often broken because users, confronted with a dizzying array of sites requiring their use, become tired and complacent. Even good passwords can be undermined by security questions whose answers are common or easy to look up or can be extracted from examining the user's online footsteps. Passwords have many ways to fail. Users are often conned into revealing them. Passwords can also be intercepted if transmitted in the clear or if they are typed into infected machines that log their keystrokes (hence, key-loggers). Even when users are careful, systems that hold and protect passwords can be broken into, and many passwords are thereby stolen en masse. When asked to change their passwords, users often generate ones that can be predicted from the ones that were compromised. Passwords can be hardened by making them longer, by forcing the use of upper-case, lower-case, and punctuation characters, by generating them randomly, or by requiring pass-phrases rather than passwords. Yet it is unclear that any improvement is sufficiently worthwhile.[3]

Some relief may arise from limiting passwords to trivial operations and requiring harder authentication (or the permission of two individuals) for large ones. Slow-rolling users after several incorrect passwords are entered (as iPhones do) also defeats some attacks. If user actions are monitored remotely and automatically, as they are for credit card purchases, then actions of unusual frequency or nature can be flagged for further inquiry.

Better yet is multi-factor authentication (MFA), the value of which starts from the understanding that every authentication mechanism has its failure mode. Something that identifies you can be faked. Something that you know can be guessed. Something that you have can be taken. Two very different modes, though, rarely fail at the same time.[4] A common MFA process—particularly among U.S. defense contractors—combines a PIN and a hardware token, such as those generated by the aforementioned RSA devices. Typically, the PIN is four or six numbers, and the RSA device regenerates a string of six numbers every minute. The combination of the two can be as difficult as requiring ten billion guesses; a lot depends on how well the PIN was chosen (and how well protected from disclosure the algorithms and the seeds from which these numbers are generated are). Constantly changing the PIN numbers means that an attacker cannot echo a successful session if the authenticating system locks out a second access attempt until the device shows new numbers. Finding the key requires knowing whose it might be and what the PIN is; this also provides a degree of protection.

But will MFA come into common use?[5] Circa 2010, organizations tended to adopt MFA if they thought their customers expected them to. The theft of unclassified material from the F-35 prime contractor sensitized the Department of Defense to the threat from hackers, resulting in great pressure on all contractors to demonstrate security awareness (of which MFA is a major element). Those whose customers did not care or whose other stakeholders (for example, practicing physicians in the case of hospitals) were more sensitive to hassle than security tended otherwise.

The broad philosophy behind MFA can be extended to all ways by which two very different security processes have to fail before the attacker succeeds. The remote diagnosis and maintenance of machinery may be cost-effective, but if all the systems along the chain are not secure, it may be hacked. Conversely, if there is a human in the loop required, for instance, to approve system changes, the hack may fail if the human is trained and alert.

Note that authentication (ascertaining that the person who is asserting privileges is the person to whom the privileges were granted) is not the same as authorization (determining what privileges the person is entitled to). MFA only addresses the authentication problem. A system with optimal authorization can be spoofed either by hijacking credentials or by making a computer do other than what the true user commanded. But a system whose authentication was perfect could be compromised if too many people are entitled to see too much (such as Edward Snowden) or do too much (the downfall of Barings Bank at the hands of a trader, Nick Leeson, who was allowed to risk too much money). Hence, there is wisdom in limiting privileges as much as the business can tolerate (also known as the least-privilege principle).

In machine-in-the-middle attacks, two parties are supposedly communicating only to each other, but a third malevolent party sits in the middle impersonating each user to the other. For instance, a banking customer and a bank are exchanging information. The customer thinks he is telling the bank to pay George $100. The machine in the middle intercepts the request and communicates to the bank: pay Paul $1,000. The bank decrements the account $1,000 and reports the new balance (which, of course, would be $900 less than the customer expects). The machine in the middle intercepts the request and communicates to the customer that the account has been decremented $100 and reports the erroneous new balance, which satisfies the customer—until a new banking session begins. In effect, the machine in the middle is running two conversations: impersonating the bank to the customer, and impersonating the customer to the bank. Machine-in-the-middle attacks require communications to be in the clear (or, if encrypted, to be easily cracked); this is why e-commerce generally requires encryption.[6]

ABUSES BY EVERYDAY EXTERNAL USERS

An everyday external user is someone allowed to interact with the system legitimately but who may then do things that the system is unprepared for. Examples include flooding attacks, semantic attacks, structured query language (SQL) injection and similar attacks, and protocol failures.

Sites can be put out of commission by DDOS attacks called *flooding attacks*. Some rely on millions of bots to clog the lines. Others subvert web servers, which have access to capacious bandwidth. More recent attacks have used the large servers operated by Amazon Web Services to bombard sites.[7] Other attacks leverage Internet services. The reflection attack is one that creates a flood of messages with a forged return address of the victim aimed at an Internet service such as the Network Time Protocol (NTP). Because a small query yields a response that can be two hundred times as large, a few forged messages can drown the target.[8] As a result of recent attacks, NTP servers are being withdrawn from the public Internet.

The DDOS threat is limited primarily to systems that rely on external input to function (such as e-commerce sites) and should not bother other systems unless they connect themselves internally using open external web lines (and maybe not even then if they have dedicated capacity from Internet carriers). One way that organizations can deal with such attacks is by having a very capacious or clever organization handle their connectivity to the outside world. Akamai, a content distribution network, handles that kind of work by hosting sites on sufficiently large companies.

The effect of a DDOS attack also depends on how the servers being targeted process rogue information. If certain inputs cause the servers to initiate complex processes, the unwanted result of being bombarded by such queries may be less one of being clogged and more one of having processing capabilities taken up. One such hypothesized attack could let a single machine tie up a very large server by asking it to search for something within successively overlapping intervals in an indexed database.[9] Other attacks cleverly ping servers with a quantity of requests written to force the server to spend an inordinate amount of time or resources processing them.[10]

Semantic attacks feed false information into a system in order to corrupt the process by which it draws conclusions. One way to do this is to create a phony website that feeds systems information from unauthenticated sites (such as a shopping bot or a Tweet analyzer). Clickstream fraud is of this type. Otherwise, such attacks are rare because systems that draw meaningful conclusions, and particularly those that make consequential decisions without human input, are not yet common.

Some attacks provide inputs to programs to make them misbehave in predictable ways. One prime example is *SQL injection* (SQL is how databases are queried). If hackers can insert carefully crafted queries (for example, by inserting nonalphanumeric characters into the query stream or into the fill-in-the-blank forms that are converted into SQL queries), they can corrupt data files or access records normally off limits to them.[11] In other cases, web servers can be compromised, allowing hackers privileged access to servers on the other end. The gang that broke into the private networks of the NASDAQ stock exchange, Heartland Payment Systems, and others "traded text strings that exploited SQL-injection vulnerabilities in the victim companies' websites to obtain login credentials and other sensitive data, then installed malware that gave them persistent backdoor access to the networks."[12]

Stories about thousands or millions of records (such as prescription accounts or passwords) being stolen are often about SQL injection attacks. One such attacker walked away with 3.6 million tax records from the state of South Carolina.[13] The fundamental weaknesses in SQL that permit SQL injection attacks stem from two sources. First, SQL is a rich programming language, and those who enter queries are being allowed to ask a computer to interpret a potentially unlimited variety of inputs. Second, those who write the programs that use the SQL interpreter often fail to prefilter user-supplied inputs to weed out the use of characters or character combinations that almost never appear in the database to be searched (and so need not be searched on) but do have a special meaning to the SQL interpreter. SQL attacks can be frustrated without great difficulty, but it takes diligence in database design.

Another attack in which legal inputs produce unexpected outputs is nicely exemplified by the exploitation of a flaw in a video poker game and the complicated series of inputs that can be chained to generate an undeserved payout.[14]

Many processes make assumptions about user or system behavior that the attacker need not follow. Ross Anderson, for instance, has written copiously about how successful encryption codes can be undermined by making poor assumptions about authentication and key management.[15] Two other examples of *protocol failures* can be seen by looking at how Chrome works. One involves Google's policy of automatically updating extensions (and not checking whether the extension has been switched from a legitimate provider to an adware provider).[16] Another is a feature in the program that lets users give websites access to a microphone; when users withdraw permission, the red line and camera icons that indicate that the website is listening disappear, but the site can still listen in, thereby allowing a rogue website to monitor subsequent conversation.[17]

Cache poisoning is another type of protocol failure. Normally, a system gets to a particular website by sending a name to a DNS server, getting back an address, and then using the address to route a packet. To save time, a system often looks internally for past contacts with the site and uses the address stored in its own cache. If the information in the cache is changed, a call to a website can take the user to another address entirely.

ALTERED INSTRUCTIONS VIA SUPPLY CHAIN ATTACK

Sophisticated (usually state-employed) hackers can corrupt hardware or software fresh from the factory to make systems fail prematurely or, worse, at will. They also facilitate eavesdropping. One case of successfully compromised components is the British donation of Enigma machines to other nations, which likely did not realize that the British were able to break and thereby read messages from such machines. Another is the installation in the Soviet natural gas network of black-market system controllers altered to malfunction in ways that led to destructive pipeline explosions (although this account is disputed).[18] There are also suspicions that some cryptographic devices a Swiss company sold had an NSA-sponsored back door.[19] Reports in 2013 claimed that the NSA had substituted a computer wired to broadcast to satellites into the Iranian nuclear program in place of an ordinary computer.[20] The Snowden revelations contained a photograph of NSA employees inserting rogue devices into a Cisco router whose path to the customer was temporarily and deliberately interrupted for such ends.[21] Many in the defense community worry that China's growing presence in component manufacturing provides it plenty of opportunities for mischief—which it may not be shy about taking advantage of.

Supply-chain attacks are insidious because users have few alternatives to trusting their hardware, especially if the source code for the hardware's logic is not available for perusal.[22] Even if the flaw is found, if it is not obviously suspicious (as would be an instruction that says: if input equals some random-looking number, then do bad stuff), it is difficult to know whether it arose from a deliberate attempt to subvert a system. It could be just one more flaw to which even uncorrupted systems are heir. Yet there are also limits to what rogue components can do if installed in a truly air-gapped system; for example, they cannot respond to a signal unless the system can receive messages from the outside or a rogue insider.

Corrupting components en masse is a sporty move. If it is caught, the reputation of the guilty party—and even the guilty nation—can be lost, as people will begin to scrutinize everything coming from the now-suspect source. The discovery of lead paint on toys and contamination of baby formula coming from China led to major tremors in that country—and that just was sloppiness.[23] Consider what damage a deliberately queered component would have on China's reputation, much less the reputation of the guilty supplier. A supply chain attack that is feasible, hard to catch, and easy to excuse if carefully targeted may be infeasible, detectable, and hard to excuse if used to corrupt an entire class of components.

MALWARE

We expect our machines to be tools providing us with predictable outputs when we interact with them. The notion of a machine whose instruction set can change without the user being aware of it is quite strange by past standards. But, as with computers, if the instructions they follow can change willy-nilly, their behavior can become unpredictable and unhelpful.

The ease with which a computer's instructions can be changed is the sine qua non of most elements of cyberwar, in large part because systems can be made to misbehave in arbitrary ways rather than in specified ways. Remote code execution—which is what malware allows—permits a hacker to order a computer to do anything a computer *can* do. By way of contrast, a DDOS attack can only flood a system's intakes; an SQL attack only affects a system's databases; and impersonation affects only the privileges granted to an account.

The personal computers the world now depends on were, after all, born as hobbyist toys, oft approached with screwdriver in hand. The whole point was to erect as few barriers as possible between the user and whatever it took for the user to get the most out of the machine.[24] There was no more need to have security guards on personal computers than on Erector sets. Unix was not that much different; in its modularity and experimental nature, it essentially billed itself as the Tinkertoy of software. Neither were serious in the way that an IBM mainframe was.

Personal computers (PCs) were thus meant to have their instruction sets altered easily. Indeed, until 2008, so eager were PCs to absorb new instructions that they "assumed" that whenever someone inserted removable media into them, they *must* have done so to reprogram them. PCs looked at the boot sector of these removable media, be they floppy disks or USB drives, and attempted to run whatever executable file was on that sector. Rarely did they ask the user if that was the user's intention.

The result was predictable. As noted, 1991 saw the Michelangelo virus, which spread from floppy disk to computer and back again. The infected floppy disk put malware into the computer's start-up sequence; with this malware running in the background, the computer made sure to install it onto the boot sector of every floppy disk that was fed to it. Buckshot Yankee arose because someone inadvertently put an infected USB stick into a computer, which assumed that the purpose of the stick was to insert a program rather than present data for transfer. If PCs had remained no more than playthings for geeks, this might have been excusable, but clearly they evolved in importance—as did the Internet.

Another feature of computers that makes them susceptible to malware is their tendency to execute a series of instructions when they boot up. Once hard disks were common, personal computers were designed to execute not only those instructions in their operating system but also those added later (a personal computer could easily run fifty start-up sequences and keep twenty of them running simultaneously). In this way, a computer can be permanently infected if the boot-up sequence is written to execute the hacker's instruction sets.

The threats that people really worry about today would be nearly impossible without the existence of malware. Take the APT. Many techniques can be used to filch files, but without malware's ability to alter such files in multiple ways, it would be very difficult to exfiltrate them past mail guards that flag certain files being accessed from outside the organization (for example, any file containing "submarine"). But clever malware can find such files, bring them back to the infected computer, encrypt and/or chop them up into pieces, and send them out as innocent-looking bytes via normal channels or, more surreptitiously, by packing the information into what looks like DNS calls. Similarly, the Stuxnet worm *had* to be a piece of malware, because what it did was to copy new malign instructions into the computer that rewrote the centrifuge's PLCs. Similarly, not every single mode of attack against the electric grid requires a change in instruction sets, but surreptitious wholesale attacks on them do. It also does not necessarily take malware to make defense equipment that receives signals from its peers (for instance, radar talking to other radar) malfunction in certain ways, such as seeing ghosts when there is nothing there (electronic warfare can also be used). But the only way, in the words of Gen. John Jumper, USAF (Ret.), to "get into the heart and soul of systems like the SA-10 or the SA-12 and tell it that it is a refrigerator and not a radar" is to change its instruction set—a task that essentially requires malware to do.[25] Most DDOS attacks would not work unless there were instructions in the affected computers to convert instructions from the bot-herders into packets sent forth into the Internet. Certain computer crimes also require malware. One example is the sophisticated instructions required for the aforementioned machine-in-the-middle attack (for instance, the Zeus Trojan). Although MFA protects credentials, it is of no help if malware sits on the client's machine and goes to work only when a session with a bank is authorized. This introduces a more general point: if malware gets inside your computer, encrypting its files will not save them from being exfiltrated by malware (only from being extracted after a machine itself has walked).[26]

A variant on malware that codes directly to the machine is the use of Powershell scripts that do likewise but hide in the registry rather than in the part of the file storage where programs reside. Powershell, which was initially shipped by Microsoft in 2006, uses a dynamically typed scripting language to automate low-level administrative functions, typically over a group of machines. In recent years, at least one hacker group has done with Powershell what others do with malware, and to similar effect.[27]

But are mutable instructions necessary for computation (even as cars have had immutable instructions for over a century, during twenty years of which cars were computerized)? To argue the contrary, consider a hypothetical computer, all of whose instructions were permanently burned into the hardware. These instructions could include an operating system, a mail client, networking software, an office automation suite, and a web browser, even with popular extensions such as the Java virtual environment. No instruction would come from anywhere but hardware (to possibly include micro-cards to hold critical patches and updates). Such a machine could, by the estimate of a Microsoft employee who suggested the idea, completely satisfy 90 percent of all users in a typical office. Similar machines, albeit with different program sets, could satisfy many non-office uses, such as factory automation—even if such a machine's usability for the home would be limited (so, no installing video games). Perhaps updating such a machine would be difficult (but updates via micro-SD [secure digital] cards are possible). A machine purchased in 2010 could not run Office 2013. The degree of inconvenience is limited (the two-decade-old Office 97 has most of what one needs for an office, even today).

Now look at the virtues of such a device. Although such a machine *could* host malware (for example, by visiting a corrupted website), once it is turned off, such malware would be gone. The machine's instruction set would be returned to whatever condition it left the factory with (hackers could corrupt necessary configuration files, but to no great end). Malware could not persist on such a machine (corrupt documents capable of corrupting other documents when opened could persist, but document-to-document corruption is not a difficult problem to counter if anticipated). A network composed solely of such machines could not host malware for long if periodically flushed, or turned off simultaneously and then turned back on. Although there may be certain input sequences from websites or documents that can crash immutable machines over and over until such machines are, with difficulty, patched, firewalls can filter out certain patterns, and such input sequences are rare.

But no such machine will be found at the local computer store. Indeed, trends are going the other way. Software that used to come in a box is now being delivered as a service that updates itself. There is a great push to simultaneously network previous stand-alone objects (for example, refrigerators) and make it easier to update their instruction sets remotely. All too soon, it will be difficult to buy a new car that does not update its internal components (for example, braking systems or fuel-air controls) remotely. But in essence, at least one of several things must have happened: too few people feel the cybersecurity pain enough, the cybersecurity industry has convinced people that mischief in their network can be blocked without radical changes in systems, or the possibility of a trade-off has not occurred to enough people. After all, the ease with which a computer's instructions can be changed remains a fundamental feature, despite the many waves of security protections installed over the last thirty years. It gives users greater flexibility—but it also gives hackers more options. It *is* possible to lock down a system and make sure that it is used only in the way that the manufacturer intended or at least anticipated it to be used. This would decrease flexibility, but it would increase security. Indeed, a lot of what enables or disables cyberwar is the trade-off between flexibility and convenience on the one hand and security on the other hand. If we were able to tolerate the elimination of such flexibility and convenience, we would have much safer machines.

A good example of the trade-off between convenience and security is the hack of the Internal Revenue Service (IRS), in which "criminals used taxpayer-specific data acquired from non-IRS sources to gain unauthorized access to information on approximately 100,000 tax accounts through IRS' 'Get Transcript' application."[28] To allow taxpayers to access their tax accounts, the IRS established an electronic portal in which taxpayers verified their identity by answering a number of personal questions—answers to which, unfortunately, were not all that hard to guess by scouring various Internet-accessible databases. The "Get Transcript" service was a convenience to taxpayers, but it came with information security implications. The IRS could conceivably have required MFA of taxpayers (for example, through local post offices), but such a requirement would have been very inconvenient. Less drastically, it could have added questions with more obscure answers—again, purchasing security at the expense of convenience. The IRS' immediate reaction was to close the service and institute back-end tests for fraud (much as banks do with credit cards) in the hopes that it could provide more cybersecurity without compromising convenience.[29]

There is, however, an actual computer that comes close to an unhackable box, suggesting that the world of systems could be a great deal more secure against mischief than it currently is.

Over a billion of these computers have been sold. These are Apple iPhone Operating System (iOS) devices (iPhones and iPads). These devices are theoretically hackable and capable of hosting malware, but with so much difficulty that the instances can be enumerated. In mid-2011, a white-hat hack demonstrated that downloading a particularly convoluted portable document format (PDF) could lead to malware; the flaw was quickly fixed. In mid-2012, a Russian application managed to take undocumented liberties with user contact information (exploiting a bug subsequently fixed). Vupen, a malware firm, claims to have hacked iOS, and others have figured out how to transfer malware onto it. Those who "jailbreak" their own devices to allow unauthorized software to run on them are also susceptible to malware, but putting oneself at risk is the price one pays for tampering with the device. Malicious chargers can hack iPhones, but these require that hackers or their stooges be physically present at some point. In October 2014, malware in the wild was discovered that could insert instructions into intact iOS devices (but it would not reside there, and iOS 8.1.1 quickly arrived to patch the system).[30] There may well be other iOS exploits that have been hidden from view, either because they are being held in reserve or because their use has been completely surreptitious. It is telling that, by one report, the NSA has reportedly hacked the iPhone but by hacking into iTunes, not by putting malware on the iPhone itself.[31] And, as noted, a flaw revealed (and fixed) in early February 2014 made it possible to hijack SSL sessions from iOS devices.

Why has iOS proven to be so malware-resistant? The reason is not because Apple's engineers are so much cleverer than their counterparts at Microsoft or Google.[32] The true answer lies not in the quality of coding, but in the architecture: the major features of a program that indicate which processes can do what.[33] First, nothing is supposed to attach to the operating system. When a device is turned on, there are few applications that start with it (Apple-provided services such as phone, music playing, and location tracking are exceptions). The rest must be invoked specifically. Without such applications running, there is no malware resident when turned on (unless it existed within the operating system, which comes from Apple). Unlike Android, iOS will not allow self-modifying code within its apps. Apple is also a vigorous user of address space layout randomization (ASLR), which keeps hackers from altering programs by poking bits into specific addresses where the programs sit. In order to run malware, a user must acquire it deliberately as an app. Simply going to a bad website will not produce anything that attaches to the operating system, or at least not without a great deal of difficulty. Apple's apps, in turn, have to come from Apple's iStore, where they are vetted and whose providers must supply real identification.[34] Users do not have to go to Google stores to get apps and so they are often unvetted.[35] In addition, Apple does not make its application portability interfaces available to developers.[36]

It is unlikely that Apple did this solely because it is such a security-minded company. Steve Jobs did have strong ideas about what the consumer experience ought to be that made Apple products more closed than their Microsoft or Google counterparts. He also disdained Adobe's products (notably Flash). But the iStore's healthy cut (roughly 30 percent) of all app sales gives Apple sufficient incentive to ensure that software does not land on iOS devices any other way (and thus that the software is trustworthy).[37]

In 2011, Charlie Miller discovered that malware could be snuck past Apple's watchdogs by using an app that was benign but was engineered to pull malicious code from the Internet after it was installed.[38] But compare this to the kind of malware that a PC (or Mac) user could get by going to a perfectly innocent but subverted website and ending up with an infected computer. First, the app's author had to register with Apple (PC apps are not registered). Second, the user had to consciously buy it from the apps store (PC victims rarely know the moment of infection). Third, the app had to be consciously invoked to create mischief (the PC victim generally has no idea that the malware is even running). Fourth, if the app was malign, it is easy to remove; in fact, Apple can do so automatically once the iOS device is connected (removal of PC malware is usually more difficult, although rarely impossible). Last, the app does not spread laterally to other iOS machines (as some malware will). Again, the iOS architecture, *not its coding*, is what makes the difference. (Android machines have more malware than iOS devices, but their rate of overall infection is easily an order of magnitude less than personal computers.[39]) At least two companies whose business is helping government break into networks have revealed their frustration with iOS: Gamma and the Hacking Team (according to analysis by the American Civil Liberties Union's chief scientist, Christopher Soghoian).[40]

iOS machines will not displace all other machines (Apple's market share continues to slide vis-à-vis Android machines, even if Apple's profitability remains strong). It is also too early to predict that tablets will displace PCs. Tablets exist primarily to consume information; office automation relies on producing it. Tablets do not multi-task well, and they do not customize to corporate needs as well as PCs do. Nevertheless, Target's loss of so many credit cards to hackers who figured out how to surreptitiously reprogram the company's point-of-sale devices raises the question of whether the store would have been better off using tablets (iPads) instead of Windows XP boxes for that task.

Essentially, attacks come in two varieties: those that exploit a system's instructions and malware (including supply-chain attacks), or those that insert their own instructions. Both produce unwanted results, but the first set of attacks can only generate particular unwanted effects of the sort a system is capable of generating: an unauthorized user substituting for an authorized one, an unexpected result from processing legal inputs, or information leakage. Their effects are limited to what the software permits. Malware, by contrast, can make systems do anything that their hardware permits. The latter is of far greater concern. It is the difference between a hacker finding an instruction that can be subverted and a hacker finding that all instructions can be subverted.

CHAPTER 4
The Search for Cybersecurity

Unless and until networks rid themselves of easily mutable computers, malware will remain a threat. This chapter looks at many of the approaches that could be used to promote cybersecurity. They include input filtering, operating systems, people, cryptography, firewalls, and air-gapping. This chapter also touches on the broader relationships among machines, systems, and engineering; mixing and matching cybersecurity actions, measures, and countermeasures; and overall lessons from looking at the vast choices available to sysadmins and chief information security officers (CISOs).

APPLICATIONS ARE OFTEN THE WEAK LINKS IN THE SECURITY CHAIN

Many hackers start their attacks by persuading users to visit a specific website that hosts malware either from birth or by subsequent corruption. While users look at what the web page displays, the computer is looking at the embedded code on the web page—be it HTML, Java, or JavaScript—in order to execute its commands. In theory, such commands exist to manipulate what the reader sees, but sometimes such code manipulates the computer as well, typically placing malware in it. This is often an indirect process wherein an "iframe" code redirects users to a bad site. Other hackers start by sending users corrupted documents (for example, PDF files or, somewhat less often, ".doc" files). Such documents infect the client machine as soon as they are opened up.

It is through vulnerabilities in applications rather than in operating systems alone that many, perhaps most, systems are penetrated. Several of them have had recurring problems—notably, Java and Adobe products such as Postscript, Acrobat, and Flash (as well as SQL implementations). Why these? Perhaps their developers failed to use known software quality and security processes (for example, Microsoft touts its software development life-cycle). But a better reason may lie in what these programs are asked to do. Digital computers are state space machines: a system starts an operation in a particular state defined by the variables or parameters it maintains. It gets input (typically, a string of bytes). The computer often enters a different state (at least for non-real-time systems) and sometimes generates output. Most states are safe, but some are problematic, perhaps unsafe. A form of vulnerability analysis entails understanding the extent to which the set of safe states is mathematically closed in the sense that no set of instructions can drive a system from a safe state to an unknown or unsafe state.[1] Ascertaining as much is a combinatorial problem of great complexity—and one nearly impossible to prove for any program of nontrivial size.[2] Hence, there exists the need for approximations in the hope that software developers can be roughly right. But the number of potential input types matters greatly. Toward one end is, for instance, an automated teller machine, where the number of possible entries is quite limited because it has only so many buttons. In the middle is a simple word processor, where the inputs can be grouped as printable characters and a few other things; also in the middle is a browser limited to HTML (or at least its early versions). At the far end sit the aforementioned programs that act as interpreters (in the computer programming sense) for arbitrary user (that is, hacker) input. The more functions these programs treat as valid input, the greater the state space that the code has to process. The problem of ensuring that no set of user inputs can produce an insecure output becomes unsolvable very quickly.

Application vulnerabilities have made hacking simpler than it was fifteen years ago. A poignant illustration of this comes from books such as the 2012 edition of *Hacking Exposed*.[3] Every chapter in the section on exploits deals with the tools of old-fashioned hacking in which hackers successively manipulate the target into revealing more and more about itself, allowing them to give the system commands that will then give the hacker super-user status, albeit from the outside. Toward the end of that section, one learns that hacking need not work that way anymore. Users can be more easily tricked into bringing bad stuff into their computers that converts itself into malware that allows hackers to command them from the inside. Similarly, less phishing is needed if the user is known to frequent certain corrupted websites; this is also known as a "drive-by" cyberattack.

THE ROLE OF INPUT FILTERING

Cybersecurity may be pursued by limiting what applications (acting as program interpreters) consider valid input. Assume a machine accepts only printable characters (A to Z, 0 to 9, punctuation marks, and paragraph markers) and ignores everything else. Such a machine cannot easily get malware from that channel. Thus, programs meant to accept only printable characters for print or display can gather information in sketchy neighborhoods and only pick up semantic garbage (gibberish) rather than syntactic garbage (malware). But as programs get more sophisticated than simply accepting and displaying printable characters, they can pick up instructions (macros are an early version).[4] If so, the possibility for getting malware through that channel is greatly increased.

Take Adobe products. Their primary purpose is to convert a document into something that can be seen on a screen or printer. But they also can let users manipulate the document or secure it against manipulation. As noted, SQL injection depends on the interpreter's tendency to overinterpret non-alphanumeric characters, when few legitimate queries need such characters. As a rule, the more obscure services are what create the most room for problems (not least because well-used services are most thoroughly tested in use).

Are all these services needed? In late 2012, when one particular vulnerability in Java was discovered when it was exploited, Oracle, the organization that maintains Java (and that had known about the vulnerability prior to its exploitation), first indicated it would not create a patch for it until its quarterly update cycle.[5] Many security experts, disgusted with the richness of the Java vulnerability universe, recommended removing the Java client from their web browsers (and did not change their minds even after Oracle relented and posted an out-of-cycle patch).[6] Similar comments have been made about another Adobe product, Flash.[7] Java at least has improved in recent years.[8]

Another approach to reducing complexity would be empowering consumers (or their organizations) to mask unnecessary code easily, but few tools exist to do this. If a filter could be applied to, say, a PDF document so that it only accepts printable characters and converts everything else to a blank, the textual information could flow, but the malware would be avoided—at the cost of omitting the formatting and generally getting a messy document because it is interspersed with all sorts of random characters (roughly three of every eight randomly generated 8-bit bytes are printable).

The question of what criteria should be used to filter input provides a nice illustration of the tension between security and convenience. In theory, a system should only have to filter those inputs that cause known problems. Thus, filtration eliminates unnecessary inputs in the hopes of also eliminating the troublesome ones. But the certainty that all such inputs have been found is elusive—and for good reason. When someone comes up with an otherwise meaningful input deemed invalid because it runs afoul of such rules, either something gets dropped or the rules have to tighten up.

Conversely, although whitelisting (specifying the legal set of inputs) is harder than blacklisting (specifying the illegal sets of inputs), it is easier to audit. Either way, an element of inflexibility is the price paid to ascertain that no bad inputs get through; major program changes on servers could require rewriting the white lists on all the clients.

THE ROLE OF OPERATING SYSTEMS

Fortunately, in recent years, the major software companies have concluded that they cannot rely on the safety of applications. One way to prevent corrupted content taken from websites from infecting everything else a system does is to design a browser that explicitly forbids this: a sandbox. Chrome as well as Internet Explorer 10 and Edge have sandboxes, with Firefox lagging. Researchers comparing Firefox with Chrome (when each had the same market share) found the same number of vulnerabilities in both browsers—but that ten times more Firefox vulnerabilities were "critical" in that they permitted remote code execution.[9] In other words, while coding was important to a safe browsing experience, architecture was even more important.

Another protection, one built into modern operating systems (such as iOS), is ASLR. Because hackers like poking instructions directly into a specific address in the computer's memory, randomizing where the programs sit in memory renders such pokes harmless in terms of injecting malware (the computer might crash, though). There are some countermeasures to ASLR that include such esoteric techniques as return-oriented program and heap spraying, but they work only with difficulty. Thus, if a hacker wishes to embed malware into a system, it has to find an exploitable (and unpatched) vulnerability in a program, but if it is going through the browser, it has to be able to escape the sandbox, and if it is going against a modern operating system, it has to defeat ASLR as well as other protections built into browsers and operating systems (such as Microsoft's Enhanced Mitigation Experience Toolkit).[10] These are not impossible tasks, but the combination of protections complicates what hackers must do and weeds out one-trick hackers.[11]

Only time will tell how well these mitigations work. Microsoft Vista introduced the feature that no program could be installed without the user's permission, but hackers figured out how to install malware by modifying existing programs in ways that did not generate a warning box for the user. More broadly, the field of systems security has seen more than one highly touted security feature prove easier to subvert than initially hoped.

Although these mitigations are not perfect, the code necessary to implement a mitigation tends to be smaller than the code involved in an operating system or the browser—thus having a smaller attack surface and fewer places for bugs to hide. For instance, because the amount of code that governs what happens when a USB stick is inserted into a computer is small and well scrubbed, it may one day become impossible to infect a machine by sticking a USB drive into it (deliberately opening up a corrupted file on a USB stick is another matter).[12] And while small code is not necessarily secure code, secure code may have to be small code (or at least the subset of the code within which a vulnerability matters would have to be small).

Furthermore, it *is* possible to improve the architecture of software in ways that prevent certain systematic faults from recurring, as illustrated by the story of Windows XP Service Pack 2.

THE ROLE OF PEOPLE

Is cybersecurity a technology or a people problem?[13] It is both, but the wiser path to attaining a permanent improvement (or at least cope with an increasingly clever threat) may lie in technology. As Immanuel Kant observed of humans, "Out of the crooked timber of humanity no straight thing was ever made." People can (and should) be trained to be more alert, but the lesson must be repeated and reinforced. Vigilance requires constant attention, and "the only factor becoming scarce in a world of abundance is human attention."[14] Furthermore, as Alfred North Whitehead reminds us, "Civilization advances by extending the number of important operations which we can perform without thinking about them."[15]

The same people who read books read computer screens. Yet reading the wrong book cannot give you an eye infection in the way that bringing up the wrong website can infect a computer. Blaming the victim shifts attention away from the inadequate software and services that let convenience trump security, especially in those circumstances when improving software, systems, and services can be more cost-effective than improving people.[16]

Consider how U.S. highway deaths have fallen dramatically since 1971: from forty-seven to twelve deaths per billion vehicle-miles traveled. It is not because drivers are four times better. Safer cars, limited access highways (versus unprotected rural highways), medical evacuation systems, greatly improved shock-trauma treatment, and the fact that people get their licenses slightly later have collectively made the major difference. Twenty years from now, human nature will be more or less the same as it is now. Technology will be a lot different and could offer a lot more security (granted, it could also offer a lot less security, as it seems to have so far).

Hence, the following tenet: Good personnel practice teaches users to be security conscious, but good engineering practice assumes they will not learn very much. Hence, also a tenet from a notable CISO: If the security of the system depends on the user clicking the right button, it is already poorly designed. Or as one student of cybersecurity argued, "People are not, as is often claimed, the weakest link, or beyond help. The weakest link is almost always a vulnerability in Internet-facing code."[17]

In some cases, people can support cybersecurity in ways that machines cannot. The computer usually has a limited number (mostly one) of ways to sense inputs and other conditions even as humans have several working simultaneously.[18] People are also good at noticing anomalous situations. One potentially good example involves a USB-based attack presented at the 2014 Black Hat conference. This trick leverages the fact that computers trust what any USB device tells the computer about itself. A hacker could embed keyboard-like programs into a USB device that the users, having no ostensible reason to believe it is *not* a memory device, stick into a computer. Unbeknownst to the user, the USB device could be entering malicious commands via simulated keystroke into the computer (which a computer will accept even if not a response to a query). One of these commands could have the computer similarly infect all USB devices consequently linked to the computer, which then infect other computers they are inserted into. This is a tricky but not unstoppable hack. One approach is to have all USB devices signed for what they are and what they are allowed to do; this would require coordination among a great number of vendors (including some who have since left the business and whose devices thus would no longer work once signatures became mandatory). A far simpler approach is for a computer's operating system to announce to the user what device it is (and hence what privileges it has been accorded). A person inserting a USB memory stick, but programmed to act as a keyboard, into a machine would be greeted by a message that a keyboard had been inserted. Many users would then balk and unplug the stick. Not all users would, but any attack that requires spreading the USB throughout the organization without anyone noticing it would have slim chances of success.

THE ROLE OF CRYPTOGRAPHY

Cryptography has two purposes: to hide information (a traditional role) and to authenticate information (a newer role). It comes in two types. Symmetric encryption uses the same key to encrypt plaintext into cipher text and decrypt cipher text into plaintext. Asymmetric encryption uses different keys for the two operations.[19]

Symmetric keys offer two advantages. First, encryption and decryption are relatively quick operations on modern machinery. Second, keys as short as 128 bits—the key length associated with the National Institute for Standards and Technology's (NIST's) Advanced Encryption Standard (AES)—suffice to keep a message secure, even from the best efforts of security services of large countries, albeit using today's computers.[20] The major disadvantage of symmetric keys is that both parties must have the same key, which means that there has to be a separate channel for distributing, exchanging, managing, and revoking keys.

Asymmetric encryption is based on the premise that certain operations (for example, multiplying two prime numbers together) are easy, but reversing such operations (for example, factoring a product into its prime numbers) is hard.[21] Someone who wants to send a message to you (and only you) would ask you for your public key. This public key, which could be transmitted in the clear for all the good it would do eavesdroppers, would typically be the product of two prime numbers. The sender would then encrypt the message with the public key. Only you could decrypt the message because the decryption process requires the two original prime numbers, which only you have and which could not be quickly found out by someone else. Because cracking a prime number is not the same as cracking a random number by brute-force guessing, asymmetric cryptography takes a longer key (to achieve the security of a 128-bit symmetric system). The current standard for such a key is 1024 bits, equivalent to an 80-bit symmetric key; 3072 bits is considered equivalent to a 128-bit symmetric key. Typically, public key cryptography is used not so much to encrypt messages, other than short ones, but to exchange symmetric keys, and these symmetric keys, in turn, are what the longer messages are encrypted with.

Asymmetric encryption is also the basis for digital signatures, a technique that allows someone who receives a message from a specific person to know that it was sent only by that specific person and that the message was not tampered with on the way. A person announces to the world her public key. She creates a message and then creates a hash, typically 128-bit, of that message using, for instance, the secure hashing algorithm. She runs a function that inputs her private key—that is, two prime numbers—and the hash to create a signed hash. The recipient takes the message and signed hash together with the sender's public key to authenticate that only she could have sent the message *and* that the message matches the hash. Had there been a flipped bit in the message (a one converted into a zero or vice versa), the message and the hash would not match. A secure hash algorithm makes it exceedingly difficult to change the right combination of bits in the message and still generate the same hash.[22] Digital signatures have been mooted for several purposes. One is to substitute for passwords on the theory that the private key never has to leave the user's system and thus cannot be stolen in transit or storage like a password can be (in some cases, the authentication message needs a counter or clock bits to prevent echo attacks). Another is to use a digital signature in lieu of a physical signature as a legally enforceable way to tie a message, such as a contract approval, to an individual. A third is to authenticate objects (perhaps a specific sensor) to prevent them from being spoofed by similar adversary-planted objects. Ensuring that every public key is correctly associated with every registered signatory (be it man or machine) is one among many key management problems; public key systems that require multiple layers of trust scale poorly. Suffice it to say that the smaller the ring of those eligible to sign messages, the more secure the total system is.

Historically, cryptography has been a contest between code-makers and codebreakers, and the course of the contest has seesawed back and forth. During World War II, the Germans were pretty confident that messages encrypted by Enigma machines would stay encrypted, but a combination of Polish mathematicians and British computer scientists (such as Alan Turing) managed to crack the code. Nothing in the unclassified world contradicts the notion that the code-makers have won (assuming correct implementation, of course) and will continue to win unless there is a radical change in technology. The reason why is that the difficulty of decrypting messages as keys get longer rises much faster than the difficulty of encrypting messages as keys get longer. Every two years since the 1970s, computers have gotten twice as fast. Thus, key lengths that were impractical to use decades ago have become practical today. The difficulty of using a key of length X rises, as mathematicians would say, in polynomial time (for example, an operation takes four times as long if the key length doubles). So the difficulty of decrypting a message that has been encrypted using a key of length X rises in exponential time. AES' 128-bit key is twice as long as the Digital Encryption Standards' 64-bit key. But the time required to decrypt messages using 128 bits, if you lack the key, is not 4 or 8 times harder but 20 billion times harder. True, cryptanalysis, a set of tricks used by codebreakers, always gets better, but unless there is a trick up someone's sleeve—and these days, many good cryptographers publish their findings rather than keep them secret (as a state intelligence agent might tend to do)—they are not getting better fast enough to break the rule.

Circa 1995, experts mooted the possibility that quantum computers could factor prime numbers in something closer to polynomial time rather than exponential time, thereby restoring the edge to codebreakers. Quantum computers, though, have proven more difficult to build than first hoped, and thus they are still a long way from shifting the balance of power to codebreakers. Even if they did, breaking elliptical curve cryptography does not have a known quantum solution.

Encryption is no panacea. It will not solve all cybersecurity problems. Files that are encrypted may be unreadable to laptop thieves, but the computer has to have the ability to decrypt files in order to use them. Thus, if the machine is infected with malware capable of remote code execution, the malware can use the computer's capabilities to decrypt the file.[23] Similarly, authentication from an insecure machine can yield insecure (yet trusted) sessions.

A ROLE FOR FIREWALLS?

If a cyberattack can be considered a penetration followed by exploitation, then the most obvious first defense is some barrier against such a penetration; hence, firewalls were created.

Firewalls can filter out harmful messages in various ways. For instance, they can scan for a port number on the incoming packets—a two-byte indicator of what the computer is supposed to do with the packets it gets. For instance, 80 is the standard port number for unencrypted web traffic, 25 for e-mail, and 161 for network management. Only a handful of them actually lead to working programs on a particular computer. Those that do not can be rejected. Firewalls can scan for Internet protocol (IP) addresses, either for whitelisting (accepting nothing that does not come from approved addresses) or blacklisting (rejecting what comes from known troublemakers or at least suspected sketchy locations).

Unlike a physical firewall, a computer firewall needs to have a policy that says exactly what to let through and what to block. Even then, if the policy is not well considered, the system is vulnerable to packets that should not be allowed entry (or, in some cases, exit).[24] These days, simple firewalls figure less prominently in the array of defenses because current hacker practice is to pass malware as legitimate-looking traffic such as PDF files or web traffic. Most everything looks legitimate until it does its dirty work.

Complex firewalls in the form of signature-based perimeter defenses scan for content, looking for a pattern of bytes that suggests a known piece of malware, which is then blocked. The Department of Homeland Security is leaning on its version of such a firewall, Einstein III, to protect the U.S. civilian government by detecting and blocking malware (earlier incarnations, Einstein I and II, indicated that something amiss had entered federal networks, but their only response was to warn system administrators that their systems might have been infected). DoD uses something more sophisticated. The defense industrial base enjoys similar protection. DHS had no access to classified signatures, but DoD does, and so do its contractors (in part because they have fewer machines to protect than the civilian federal government does).

Even though DHS has been given responsibility and roughly a billion dollars a year to protect the nation's computers, it has been given scant additional authority except over the federal government's computers. DHS has addressed this dilemma by doing what it is familiar with doing: perimeter defense.[25] Since the only perimeter it actually gets to patrol in cyberspace is that which separates the civilian government from the rest of the world, it stands to figure that this is where it would focus. The construction and operation of Einstein III, therefore, consume over 60 percent of DHS's cybersecurity expenditures. This is *after* the major effort of consolidating the millions of federal government computers in all fifty states so that they touch the Internet only through a delimited set of gateways.

Einstein III's signatures, collected by DHS's United States Computer Emergency Response Team, vary in type. Some are inherent in the malware itself (for example, the packet contains a known exploit). Others are derived from how certain hackers work (for example, the type of e-mail that known hackers use when phishing). Much of what Einstein does is done by antivirus companies such as Norton, MacAfee, and Kaspersky. Such companies acquire malware signatures by reading copious technical notes and polling millions of Internet-facing computers acting as sensors. Microsoft, although not an antivirus vendor, has similar feeds (many of which arise from asking users' permission to look at their computers' contents when a program crashes); much of what it collects would be considered intelligence if done by governments.

Would DHS be better off just relying on antivirus suites?[26] At least military users have additional signatures from classified sources, but it is unclear how much more value such classified signatures provide. A Carnegie Mellon University study concluded that only one of the fifty-odd pieces of malware blocked by the defense industrial base pilot firewall was caught as a result of the classified feed.[27] Admittedly, the larger defense contractors (the subject of the study) are themselves striving to be cybersecurity providers to the federal government and are thus likely to have more powerful defensive capabilities as a result; in other words, the net improvement would be small for them.

The value of perimeter cybersecurity can be illustrated by a series of bars. Many pieces of malware, and almost everything used by, say, bot-herders, cannot clear the bar that exists for computers that are fully patched. A slightly higher bar catches those pieces of malware that exploit vulnerabilities yet to be patched but for which signatures are available—either because antivirus suites code against known but unfixed vulnerabilities or because other information in the malware matches a signature. A still higher bar catches malware whose existence (and hence signatures) is unknown in the commercial world but has been discovered and inserted into the classified feed. Clearing the bar are zero-day exploits (unless accompanied by other incriminating signatures). Such exploits may not be commonly used by those engaged in cybercrime (that primarily prey on the least well protected systems), but they *are* used by state-sponsored hackers.[28]

Unfortunately for the antivirus industry (hence also for Einstein III), the traditional model of antivirus software is becoming obsolete. The number of signatures is proliferating smartly. Malware reflects both the embedded knowledge of the vulnerability that allowed it to infect the computer in the first place and the code that exploits this vulnerability. All that the antivirus software sees is the exploit—but there are almost limitless ways to express an exploit of a vulnerability, and they can be generated automatically. Knowing a vulnerability exists does not necessarily imply being able to block all malware that exploits such a vulnerability. The fact that, for instance, Symantec had 17 million malware signatures on file (in April 2012) hardly meant that commonly used software has collectively 17 million vulnerabilities.[29] Polymorphism means that there may be as many variants as malware writers think they need to have to evade detection. And even that would still leave untouched the next exploit of the vulnerability that did not match prior exploits. The underlying problem is the vulnerability—or in those cases where the vulnerability has been found, the lack of a patch to it, or in cases where the patch exists, its lack of application to the user's machine. If every known vulnerability were patched (and they almost always are, sooner or later) and every patch were distributed and installed, there would be little scope for malware—but also little reason for an antivirus suite. The only malware that antivirus software *could* catch would be zero-day vulnerabilities—the very ones that they are *least* likely to know about. Even classified collection systems will have a hard time seeing zero days exploited by groups that have not exposed themselves to the outside world.

But there are other ways for signature-based firewalls to fail.

- Encrypted material cannot be meaningfully scanned (unless the organization is running an SSL interception proxy on its perimeter). This can be a problem given the increasing share of infected advertising ("malvertising") that is SSL-encrypted. Two individuals can use the Pretty Good Privacy code to exchange files with one another, with the outside colleague unaware of the passage of an infected document to someone inside the firewall. Someone could go shopping on a website whose advertisements have been infected but that are downloaded on encrypted channels using SSL and secure hypertext transfer protocol. Or someone could connect to an infected virtual private network, which stays private by using encryption.
- Firewalls will not see malware brought in by an insider: for example, a troublemaker, a criminal, or an agent of a foreign power, or, more broadly, malware inadvertently borne on USB devices (or that enters the network using transmitters sitting within reception range of network components that accept RF input).
- Firewalls will not see malware already inside the system at the time the perimeter is established.
- Finally, perimeter defenses rarely catch non-malware (for example, SQL injection) attacks.

A broader danger in any perimeter control system, especially when it is provided by third parties, is complacency. Cybersecurity is a multifaceted endeavor. The greater the prominence of a single perimeter approach, the greater the tendency for organizations themselves to avoid the additional effort and the difficult questions already mentioned.

With that in mind, would a national firewall be worthwhile?[30] If the half-billion-dollar annual cost of Einstein III (even without the cost of collecting the intelligence from which signatures are built), which covers the entire civilian federal government (plus associated onsite contractors), constitutes 2 percent of the nation's work-related (in contrast to home) Internet, then a national commercial firewall would probably cost 50 times as much, or $20 billion a year—unless there are positive economies of scale. Unfortunately, so far at least, the economies of scale seem to be negative; many costs arise from trying to manage size.[31] Worse, it is impossible to scan packets for a bad string of bytes without being able to read all such traffic (not just the metadata in the headers). Granted, there may be procedures (for example, put the machines under third-party control) that would prevent the diversion of such traffic to human eyes without something like a search warrant. Yet the post-Snowden era may not be the best of times during which to convince a skeptical public that the NSA could not and would not subvert such a mechanism for its intelligence collection needs or that some future administration would not convert a system for detecting malware into one that detects other objectionable content.

THE ROLE OF AIR-GAPPING

Air-gapping can also help secure networks. Because it deliberately isolates systems from exchanging information (easily) with the rest of the world, it is an option only for operations and assets that organizations can afford to keep off the Internet. Air-gapping can be literal in that there is no electronic connection to the rest of the world. Virtual air-gapping lets a system run over connected networks but accepts or transfers out only those packets that are signed or encrypted within the network itself. If the cryptographic method is secure, the system's resistance to leakage or malware can be relied on, but such a system can be dismembered by a cyberattack against the hardware the virtually air-gapped system rides on.

Air-gapping has to be complete to be totally effective. A system with no real-time Internet connection might nevertheless host a machine with a phone connection, which is nearly the same thing. Air-gapping might fail if computers can pick up over-the-air signals. In specifying a perimeter within which there must be no publicly connected machines, defenders not only must consider the normal range of each RF device on the network (be it a near-field device, Bluetooth, WiFi, and so forth) but also must pay attention to whether a determined adversary might not use antennae tricks to pick up or broadcast signals from much farther away. Other faults to watch for are devices that contain unannounced receiver/transmitters and machines already infected when put into isolation (that may therefore transmit over-the-air signals unexpectedly).[32] Finally, air-gapping also has to be tested to ensure that there really are no leaks.

A network that is intermittently, rather than continuously, connected to the outside world can still be infected by a piece of malware that patiently waits for a connection (or pings for a connection until one is established); Stuxnet proved as much. The intermittent air gap can be crossed by any infected USB device, as well as removable media such as a DVD-ROM used, for instance, to transfer software updates.[33] Alas, modern systems do not run without some sort of intervention from time to time, and so complete and utter air-gapping is harder to do in practice than it is in theory. As noted earlier, however, the portion of the operating system that governs the update of programs from devices that are used solely to transform data (for example, USB sticks) is relatively small; they can more easily be probed for vulnerabilities than the overall operating system itself can be.[34]

The North American Electric Reliability Corporation, which concerns itself with electric grid security, has recommended that there should be a firewall between public infrastructures such as the Internet and the SCADA systems of electric companies. But even when correctly administered (which they not always are), firewalls have proven a relatively ineffective device against good hackers. Even if most critical systems are well protected against sophisticated attackers, because the United States is vast, heterogeneous, and complex, there are lagging sheep in the flock: systems whose owners have not paid adequate attention to cybersecurity, those whose security was undermined by trusted but feckless organizations (for example, a supplier), or those who diverted their attention from the security of their network long enough for vulnerabilities to get in.

Thus, many analysts instead recommend that critical infrastructures be thoroughly air-gapped (that electrical networks preceded information networks proves they can be). Because Internet connectivity saves grid owners money over having to build their own internal networks, abjuring connectivity has costs. Internet connectivity also allows remote maintenance, which may be a necessity for smaller firms that lack the resources to fund their own experts. One alternative would be to have these consultants run dedicated stand-alone machines that can only tunnel through the Internet as part of a virtual private network. Another alternative is to retain remote monitoring (through one-way signaling or even RF broadcasting) but abandon remote control.

Many pieces of critical infrastructure companies are still directly connected in real time. One search engine, Shodan, has proven assiduous at finding, cataloging, and characterizing Internet-connected computers that have the signatures of machine control systems. Over 100,000 so far have been found; in theory, anyone on earth can access them. Fortunately, the major power generation/distribution points are scarce among them.[35]

Yet an intermittently air-gapped system may still frustrate attacks that must execute when and only when called on. The centrifuges that Stuxnet targeted did not have to be destroyed at a specific time; eventual destruction sufficed. But an IADS has to be disabled at a specific time. A cyberattack that takes out an IADS a day after one's aircraft are overhead is useless. A cyberattack that works the day before *and* has effects obvious to the defenders may be nullified if the IADS can be fixed within a day. Unless the malware that crosses the air gap can convert something inside the system into a powerful receiver, there is scant way to issue a command to it. Timing even matters to terrorists who want to pull off simultaneous cyberattacks or time a cyberattack to coincide with a kinetic attack.[36]

There are ways to get the timing right without real-time command and control.[37] One is for the malware to be set to go off at a predetermined time. If this sounds like the tail (the cyber effects) wagging the dog (the kinetic operation), it may be because it is. War is a chancy thing, and asking that the conditions be just right for a kinetic attack at a particular time is no small requirement—although the timing of amphibious military invasions such as at Normandy and Inchon to match predictable tide and moonlight conditions suggests that preset timing is not a complete fantasy. Even then, the attackers have to be confident that the malware is in the right place and can work, indications of which may be reliably pulled from an air-gapped system.

A second way is for the malware to cue itself to external events that make their way into the network (for example, a news item that people would mention in e-mail traffic).[38] A variant on this is an induced crisis or its kinetic operation that creates a pattern of traffic, which then cues the malware. The indicator event has to be unlikely (lest the malware go off prematurely) and not confused with random network events (for example, taking systems down for repair), yet one that circulates reliably.

A third way is to find a system where the mean time between the crossover of information between the Internet and the partially isolated activity is significantly below the time required to detect and repair the infection. Again, if there are such networks, they are worse than intermittently connected; they are near-real-time connected.

Finally, if an infected but air-gapped machine sits close enough to an infected Internet-connected machine, the two may be able to exchange signals over low-power radio or low-frequency sound waves (if the air-gapped machine supports a microphone).[39] Such an arrangement may be infrequent for air-gapped facilities (such as power plants) but common in situations where analysts may have both computers on their desk.

Nevertheless, because there is nothing easy about timing cyberattacks without real-time command and control, even intermittent air-gapping can reduce the attractiveness of a target to cyberattack.

RELATIONSHIPS AMONG MACHINES, SYSTEMS, AND ENGINEERING

Networked systems are made of machines. If machines were secure, systems would be secure. But often that means that the security of a system is no better than the security of its least well secured machines. Worse, many of these machines are considered devices (for example, WiFi routers and printers) that are unexpectedly computer-like; if they are not locked down, attacks on such devices can subvert system security.[40] Networks also have become fuzzy sets with no clear delineation between inside and outside. Organizations commonly extend privileges to external computers to facilitate supply-chain coordination or maintain equipment. Target was hacked because it absorbed infected information from a heating, ventilation, and air conditioning system supplier that was trusted but whose security was not trustworthy.[41] The more machines that face the outside (typically, the Internet), the greater the attack surface of an organization and hence the more opportunities hackers have to subvert the system. Although an individual machine can be resecured by turning it off and on (for infections that never write to disk) or returned to factory conditions (assuming an uncorrupted BIOS), the same is much harder when resecuring systems. One bad machine is enough to reinfect them all. Removing adversaries from a network (which generally means removing all the back doors they installed) would require a general system reboot, which requires understanding every machine that is on the network as well as understanding the extent to which machines not on the network can reinfect the system as a whole.

Failures, in general, are endemic to sufficiently complex systems. Charles Perrow's *Normal Accidents* argues that systems are prone to failure when they are both tightly coupled (errors in one part propagate to cause errors in other parts) and complex (beyond the intuitive understanding of those in charge). To use a non-hardware analogy, the stock market crash in 2008 can be laid at the door of housing valuations coupled with tightly integrated financial markets wired to move at split-second speeds and financial instruments too complex to understand easily. This fed a radical shift in business and personal savings behavior, which mired the economy in a long deep recession. But *Normal Accidents* holds a second lesson: backup systems are down much more often than primary systems are. If primary systems fail, they get repaired because the damage is obvious. If backup systems fail, the damage often passes without notice. Those who think their systems are reliable because both systems are unlikely to fail at the same time must necessarily calculate the odds by looking at failure rates and recovery times in primary systems and remember how failures linger longer on backup systems.[42]

The typical approach to securing systems is to try to secure those machines that face the outside (typically, the Internet) while at the same time assuming that one of these machines will be compromised, thereby forcing system defenders to try to ensure that compromised machines cannot compromise the entire network.[43] One can think of a system's insecurity as a product of the odds of its being breached multiplied by the odds that a breach results in a system compromise.[44]

Another approach is to make almost all of the machines on a system highly secure (for example, use Chromebook, iOS, or immutable instruction sets), and then work aggressively to secure those machines (for example, servers) that cannot run highly secure operating systems. The latter may have to be periodically refreshed to known good states (for example, the condition it was in when received).

A broader approach is to minimize the privileges that all machines have to the network in general, particularly when dealing with subsystems that do not normally need Internet connectivity but that must connect to machines that do (or that need remote maintenance). Limiting communications across such barriers to prespecified messages is an approach whose security can be ascertained, but this will require system reprogramming every time the list of legal messages grows. There should be some set of legal messages that balances the need for security and flexibility.

The last approach is to pay attention to the way in which subsystems are trusted by one another. Ultimately, this may mean flatter networks in which the relationships among machines or between machines and the system as a whole can be specified in advance. It may also call for content-level rather than instruction-level safety and security features within complex systems. One need not pay so much attention to the code in the system as much as one should understand how security faults in one part can lead to security and/or safety faults in another. For machine control systems, this shifts the emphasis from those who know computer code to those who understand how the machines work and, more important, fail. Nancy Leveson's *SafeWare* examines software whose faults had put people in jeopardy (for example, the Therac-25, a radiation-therapy machine that delivered a hundred times more radiation than was safe; two patients died).[45] Software, she writes, should always be written to avoid safety faults; she detailed the features of software creation that would facilitate that process. In many ways, her book is a must-read in understanding cyberwar, although it never mentions deliberate attacks against information systems.

If cybersecurity were simply a matter of fixing poorly engineered systems, the solution to the threat of cyberwar would be better engineering—and nothing further. But cybersecurity sits at the uncomfortable intersection between engineering and conflict. Winning a conflict is not the same as solving an engineering problem, largely because the other side never stops evolving to frustrate the engineering. The fact that attackers cannot get into one's system except through paths already extant in the system, however, suggests that engineering has a stronger role to play in modulating cyber conflict than in modulating physical conflict. In practice, however, attackers surprise defenders all the time—but should they have been surprised?

Another way to understand the distinction is to see system failure arising from two directions: bottomside and topside. A bottomside failure is one in which any hole in the structure leads to taking on water—analogously, any exploitable vulnerability (in a system of interest to a sufficiently serious and hostile military or intelligence agency) is one whose exploitation should be assumed (even, if in practice, adversaries may elect not to use it).[46] A topside failure arises from the conjunction of induced error and unfortunate circumstances: how large the waves are and the wind direction. Bottomside vulnerabilities should be treated as deterministic; topside errors should be treated as probabilistic.

In between these perspectives lies the critical but ill-understood area of threat modeling. Perhaps safety engineering is programming against Murphy (where the error is accidentally or inadvertently induced), while security engineering is programming against Satan (where the error is induced by a hostile intelligent actor).[47] If Murphy dominates, the designer should ask what an attacker *would* do and prioritize security measures accordingly. If Satan dominates, the designer should ask what an attacker *could* do and proceed to ensure that it cannot be done. The vulnerability of a system is only meaningful against the risks it faces.

MIXING AND MATCHING SECURITY ACTIONS

Cyberwar enthusiasts (and cybersecurity pessimists) are wont to cite the Irish Republican Army's warning after failing to assassinate Prime Minister Margaret Thatcher: "Today we were unlucky, but remember we only have to be lucky once. You will have to be lucky always."[48] It is commonly held that the hacker's options are many, while the defender's are few. Hence, the hacker will always win.

In reality, there is a cornucopia of options from which organizations can take in combination to reduce the cost of cyberattacks.[49] To illustrate as much, start with DHS's "Blueprint for a Secure Cyber Future," notably its identification of seventy-five capabilities that it wants to see realized.[50] Read straight through, these capabilities have as much of a theme as a shopping list. But if one works backward from these capabilities to ask what difference achieving them makes (and then what difference the difference makes, and so forth), the effort reveals a huge tree of relationships for which these seventy-five capabilities are leaves and from which twigs, branches, and trunks can be inferred.[51]

Consider figure 4.1. We might label the central goal as minimizing the expected cost of future cyberattacks. The term "expected" allows factoring in attacks that have yet to happen but that would be catastrophic if they did. The term "cost" should be understood broadly to include not only hard-to-measure costs (for instance, the transfer of intellectual property from a U.S. firm to China might not have discernable effects until copycat products hit the market years later) but intangible costs such as lost reputation, reduced personal privacy, and increased risks to national security.

Minimizing this expected cost requires four broad efforts: minimizing assets at risk from system compromise, defeating attempts to compromise systems (repelling them, catching them early, or limiting their damage), increasing resilience in the face of damage, and accelerating recovery afterward. Each of these efforts in turn can be linked to a set of subgoals through a strategy-to-task decomposition.[52] Some subgoals are components (for example, a meal may comprise an appetizer, a main course, and a dessert). Other subgoals are prerequisites (a main course requires buying food, cooking food, and serving food). The goal, for instance, of defeating cyberattacks can be associated with ten different subtasks. Some of these subtasks apply to a particular type of attack: for example, a DDOS attack may be defeated by acquiring more access to network or server capacity, but such a strategy does little against an APT attack. Other subtasks are different approaches to a widely experienced intrusion set.

Each subgoal can be further broken down into constituent actions, sub-actions, tasks, and so on. To illustrate as much, figure 4.2 examines just one of the twenty-five subgoals: repelling

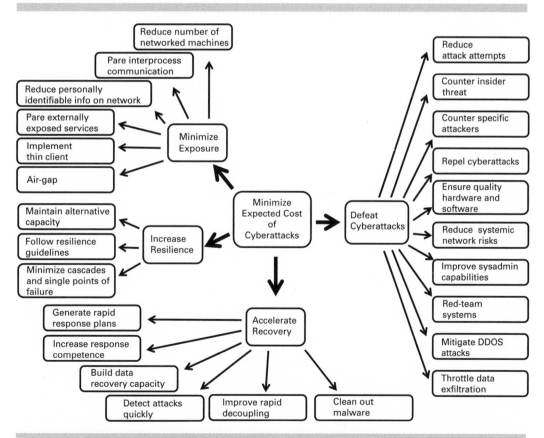

FIGURE 4.1 A HIERARCHICAL DECOMPOSITION OF CYBERSECURITY ACTIONS

cyberattacks (that is, keeping them from getting a foothold within an organization). It has six sub-subgoals, each of which has its own set of prerequisite actions. The overall cybersecurity task can be broken into a vast chart of objectives, goals, subgoals, sub-subgoals, and all the way down into tasks—all before finding a place to situate almost all of the seventy-five capabilities in the DHS "Blueprint." Suffice it to say that the set of all tasks is very large. Conversely, the contribution of most any task to cybersecurity is likely to be small. Granted, many of these actions, if done completely and perfectly, could *individually* address an organization's cybersecurity problems and thereby obviate the need for many of the other actions if they worked perfectly, but rarely are any that reliable. Even so, the contribution that any one action makes is tough to measure or even describe. If an action blocks half of attacks, does that mean that systems are twice as safe? The answer may be yes if it blocks half of *attackers*—or it may be no if its effects are merely to make all attackers mount twice as many attacks to get through. Just because, say, 80 percent of attacks exploited poor computer hygiene does not mean that 80 percent of attacks would be prevented with good hygiene.

Furthermore, the menu of cybersecurity choices is exactly that: a menu. Organizations differ in what they have at stake and what threats they face. No organization is going to carry out every task; each must pick and choose. Before committing itself to any one strategy, an organization might ask itself: what can we afford to lose, and what can we not afford to lose? What are the consequences of losing it (for example, is our reputation at stake, our ability to be first to market with new products, the privacy of our employees)? Who might be interested in our information—or in crippling our operations? Why? How badly? How much risk would they be willing to take to get it? If we carry out operations as part of the business, how time-critical are they? How much flexibility do we have to adjust operations? What is our legal or contractual liability if operations cannot be carried out? Can it get bad enough to make the continuation of current practices unaffordable?[53] Self-knowledge is the sine qua non of cybersecurity.[54] Only after such questions have been asked can organizations determine what needs to be protected, how, and with what tools—at least up to that point, as a prominent CISO observed, where it takes more analysis to distribute security measures optimally than it does to simply distribute these tools everywhere.

A fundamental examination of one's business processes is hard and thus is often avoided. Consider, for instance, the painful dilemma the FBI faced in 2001 when it confronted two pieces of bad news. The first was its discovery that one of its own, Robert Hanssen, had been working for Russia, leading to the death of several agents.[55] Hanssen had access to a great deal of information from the FBI's computers that facilitated his operations. The FBI therefore learned it had to limit access to sensitive information. The second was the discovery that many of the clues associated with the September 11 attacks that *might* have led to the detection and possibly frustration of the plot were already resident in FBI files but never usefully combined.[56] The FBI therefore learned it had to open access to sensitive information. When faced with two contradictory lessons, the FBI beefed up security of its (already air-gapped) network so that intruders could not get access to files they should not see. But the heart of the problem was how to resolve the FBI's business processes: notably, who within the air gap could be trusted with what information. Robert Hanssen did, in fact, get access to the files of others—not because he was a particularly good hacker, but because he knew a social engineering trick or two to use in gaining someone else's access rights and had a fairly good knowledge about what kind of files were where. Cybersecurity would not have stopped him; good policies might have (even if some policies need good cybersecurity to be implemented correctly). What the FBI really needed to do was to systematically analyze which agents ought to have access to which files, so that the proper trade-off could be made between security (which is facilitated by restricting information sharing) and the sort of pattern recognition (which is facilitated by information sharing) that might have forestalled another such terrorist attack. Instead, the FBI swung back

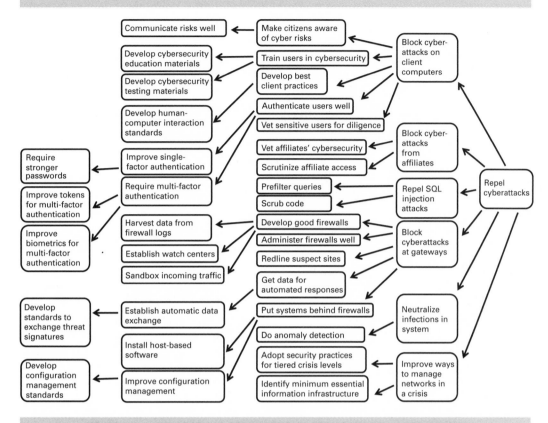

FIGURE 4.2 A HIERARCHICAL DECOMPOSITION FOR REPELLING CYBERATTACKS

and forth between restricting case information to agents (or their field office colleagues) working on a particular case and opening it up to every FBI agent.

It is human nature to address a challenge by making the least profound changes first and hoping that they will fix the problem. An organization beset by cyberattacks may focus on training users better (a high percentage of organizations are initially penetrated because a user clicked on something best left unclicked). If that does not work, it may seek to buy cybersecurity tools. Only later might it decide that it may have to make hard choices about how many devices it allows network access to or how many subnetworks it lets touch the outside Internet. In going step by step from easy to hard, it may suboptimize, for instance, by buying tools to manage the risk from devices and then only afterward deciding to limit such devices, or by training and retaining people on critical networks to be constantly aware of security threats and then isolating networks they work from.

Likewise, it is human nature to attack problems using familiar paradigms. In DoD, cybersecurity can be enhanced by buying secure defense systems, connecting them in a secure manner, and then protecting them against attack once they are established. But it is one bureaucracy (the acquisition community) that buys systems, another bureaucracy (for example, base management, combat operators) that installs them, and a third (CYBERCOM) that defends them. The last is closest to warfighting in its approach to problems. Might not DoD thus end up putting too few resources toward securing systems and too many toward defending them? The same holds for any organization concerned about the state of its cybersecurity: how should it minimize the sum of cybersecurity expenditures and the costs of system compromise that can be expected, given such cybersecurity expenditures? Economics professors Lawrence Gordon and Martin Loeb of the University of Maryland concluded that if one assumes a cybersecurity strategy based on putting a series of multiple barriers in front of attackers, no enterprise should spend more than 37 percent (which equals 1/e) of its expected losses on cybersecurity.[57] Organizations can be exhausted by cyberattacks, but they can also be exhausted by the time, attention, and resources devoted to countering them.

MEASURES AND COUNTERMEASURES

Two instruments may be comparable today, but next year, one might still work well while the other does not (or least not without major updates). One reason is that some are subject to countermeasures and others are not. Although there is no instrument that wily hackers will not try to evade, a countermeasure as used here would meet three criteria: it is specific to the defender's measure (in other words, it would not otherwise be used), it nullifies the measure's usefulness, and it is relatively easy for hackers to deploy. Here are some examples:

- Signature detection is an example of a measure subject to countermeasure. Particular features of packets (for example, the pattern of their bytes, their incoming IP addresses, their destination, their relationship to prior events) examined as they enter a network identify them as part of an individual's or organization's attack patterns. Such packets are discarded or isolated for analysis. A countermeasure would be for an attacker to use a diverse set of indicators so as to make the pattern of its packets look sufficiently different from what defenders are used to that they cannot be distinguished from everyday traffic.
- Anti-phishing training helps sensitize users to certain suspicious message characteristics. Countermeasures, in turn, would be to craft messages that increasingly resemble normal traffic.
- Anomaly detection is also subject to countermeasures. Here, the defender looks for differences between the behavior of its network (for example, traffic patterns) and some behavior set deemed normal. Behavior sufficiently far from normal prompts more intense analysis (what nodes are being controlled by others?)—perhaps isolation and a greater tendency to identify quasi-normal traffic as suspicious. A countermeasure would be to reduce the anomalies caused by penetrating networks.
- Software sandboxing is a technique by which certain classes of inputs (for example, attachments or web pages) are diverted to a special computer designed to detect when such inputs are trying to change its parameters (for example, what programs a computer runs when it starts up). Those inputs are isolated. A countermeasure would be to detect the presence of such machines and go quiet (so as to be deemed innocent and passed to its original destination) or simply hold off for a period that exceeds the time the machine would hold the input and then go back to work.
- Booby-trapped files can infect the hacker's machines when opened and thereby report on what the hackers are doing. They can be defeated through input filtration or by being opened on a machine that the hacker does not mind getting infected.

In fairness, measures subject to countermeasures are not useless. The signals that alert hackers that they need to develop countermeasures may not be received until enough of their targets employ such measures; thus, early adopters of measures can often wring value from their investments. Even in the longer run, they may be useful by dint of diverting the attention of lower grade hackers unable or unwilling to deploy countermeasures. Nor are such measures necessarily one-and-done affairs. Vendors of such measures are constantly innovating: countermeasures may beget counter-countermeasures. But the broader problem remains. The contest may get more expensive for the hackers, but these instruments grow constantly more sophisticated and hence harder to administer correctly, and the contest gets more expensive for the defenders. Unfortunately, next to failure to learn, the second most fundamental mistake in warfare, notably with cyberwar, is failure to anticipate that the other side also learns.[58]

Other classes of measures are not so prone to countermeasures. One example is MFA. Random events that expose one factor (for example, the use of a password for a site that turns out to be insecure, leaving the token where it may be stolen and placed into the black market) do not expose the other. Other such measures might be automated patch management and patch-status detection, subnetwork isolation (of which air-gapping is an extreme form), access control lists (they counter insider threats and can prevent an infection on one user's machine from compromising servers), and thin-client architectures (leaving clients with fewer programs that can be infected).

Other broad distinctions can be drawn between measures that are easy to counter and those that are hard to counter. Measures can be countered if they defend systems against adversaries in order to distinguish their efforts from a more or less benign environment. They have the advantage of not forcing organizations to examine the vulnerabilities in how they use information systems and not forcing them to restrict how their systems are used. They are externally focused. Measures hard to counter are designed to secure systems irrespective of the particularities of the adversaries (many of these measures provide protection against insider threats). They have the disadvantage of restricting how systems are used (or at least how easily they are used) and may require organizations to better understand their own information systems. They are internally focused.

It would be wrong to assume that every measure without easy counters beats every measure that can be countered. These choices can only be made on a case-by-case basis. But it is easy to see how measures that can be countered may appear more attractive than they really are, while those not easily countered may appear less rewarding than they turn out to be.

WHAT COULD WE LEARN?

Several major lessons present themselves from looking at the hundreds of options for minimizing the incidence and impact of cyberattacks. One is the importance of developing a body of knowledge on how to combine these options to generate an optimal level of cybersecurity. Cybersecurity is not simple; there is a great deal to choose from and a paucity of knowledge on the relative effectiveness of any one action standing alone, much less the additional effectiveness of any one action once other actions have been taken. Optimal, incidentally, does not mean best practice.[59] There is no point spending a dollar to save fifty cents of costs from cyberattacks. Furthermore, optimal will be different depending on an organization's mission: for example, protecting the nuclear deterrent versus running a video game chat room.

Second, with so many options, the odds that any one will be a panacea are probably low. The world is full of nostrums. On the commercial side are many vendors of point solutions: for example, sandbox incoming malware, make one's network a moving target, adopt clever biometrics, characterize the top sixty threats, mine all packet flows to look for anomalies.[60] Chances are that if any of these are cost-effective (and some very well might be), they will only address a fraction of the problem. On the policy side are advocates of other point solutions: for example, establish a deterrence posture, collect intelligence to preempt attacks, establish national firewalls, double down on resilience, remove all obstacles to sharing information, and double-check vendors' security.[61] Again, chances are that only some are truly cost-effective, and even those will address just a fraction of the problem. The Australian Ministry of Defence has narrowed the list of mitigations to four, which it claims would prevent 90 percent of all intrusions. However, clues that this is not a panacea can be inferred from the fourth mitigation (Creating a Defence-In-Depth system) and its accompanying publication that lists thirty-five rather than just four such mitigations.[62]

Third is the demonstration that government cannot play a decisive, and maybe not even a major, role in enhancing the cybersecurity of privacy systems. The overwhelming bulk of the actions listed are the responsibility of the organization. Those that the government can do are mostly located at the sub-subtask level of a strategies-to-task laydown. Of the twenty-five primary actions listed, the government has most of the responsibilities for only one: reducing the number of attacks (and that does not take into account that a well-defended system will, over·time, persuade most hackers to go elsewhere). Otherwise, it can cajole. It can mandate. But it cannot do.

CHAPTER 5
Defending Against Attacks of High and of Broad Consequence

Previous chapters discussed how to defend individual systems from individual attacks. But special considerations apply to attacks of high consequence and attacks of broad consequence. Defenses against high-consequence attacks can make use of the mathematics of power-law distributions. Defenses against broad-consequence attacks can make use of the mathematics of the aforementioned dice game of Pig.

ATTACKS OF HIGH CONSEQUENCE

Two basic approaches can be used to prepare for unprecedented but high-consequence events. One is to make a best guess of the event's likelihood and severity and use that to evaluate how much to invest in what. The other is to make a few prudent but low-cost preparations today and wait until events unfold in order to generate a more reliable risk profile against which larger commitments (if necessary) can be evaluated more intelligently.

The justification for the latter approach is that certain types of catastrophes do not suddenly occur out of nowhere. Instead, they may well be foreshadowed by smaller catastrophes, the nature and frequency of which can be used to calibrate the odds of something larger. Thus, worry about someone creating a major catastrophe only after someone succeeds at creating a near-catastrophe. The near-catastrophe signals that an attacker might come closer than earlier believed to creating a major one—and at the very least permits defenders to recalibrate the odds of a major catastrophe. But the element of time is also important. Once the attacker gets that close, chances are that some attacker is likely to use what happened as a template for more focused attempts to overcome those obstacles that prevented complete success. Simultaneously, alert defenders could use what happened to generate more focused defenses. Whoever learns best and first determines whether a catastrophe ensues.

The September 11 hijackings would seem to be the kind of hard-to-forecast event that lacked precedent. But a day before Christmas 1994, an Air France flight was hijacked from Algiers by a militant Islamist group to be used against the Eiffel Tower (the airplane was seized by authorities in Marseille).[1] In retrospect, such an incident should have raised the a priori probability that the next hijacker would be interested, perhaps to the point of suicide, in using aircraft as bombs, when hitherto there was only evidence-free speculation of such a motive.[2]

Similarly, the Stuxnet worm appeared to be an event without precedent, but even so, it was foreshadowed by the Aurora experiment and Buckshot Yankee. The first should have shown that bad instructions could break machinery, and the second, that an air gap does not guarantee cybersecurity if it is crossed from time to time.

Many catastrophes obey a power-law distribution, wherein the top values (major catastrophes) are rare and the lower values (minor incidents) are common: more precisely, the size of the nth ranked event (or item) is inversely proportional to logarithm of n. Power-law distributions can be generated from processes that resemble a series of coin flips with double-or-out rules.[3] If the first flip is heads, the score is one, and another flip is allowed; if tails, the score is zero, and no more flips are allowed. With every successive flip, heads doubles the score and tails freezes it and ends the flipping. A commonly cited power-law distribution describes the population of U.S. metropolitan areas. There is one New York City, two Chicago-sized metropolitan areas (the other being Los Angeles), four Philadelphia-sized metropolitan areas, and so on. Power-law distributions describe quite a number of phenomena, not least relevant of which are the "sizes of power outages."[4] Thus, before one sees a full-fledged catastrophe, one should expect to see a few near-catastrophes and multiple could-be-near-catastrophes. Conversely, if there are no near-catastrophes to point to, the odds of a full-fledged catastrophe may be low. The emergence of a near-catastrophe, in turn, could be a random event or it may signal that the odds of a full-fledged catastrophe have risen from notional to possible.

One reason that a power-law distribution is plausible is that systems have multiple layers of defenses, each one of which has to be breached in order to have the maximum desired effect. Typically, failure at one level alerts system administrators to the heightened possibility of intrusions, and post-mortem analysis suggests which approaches worked and perhaps also what the attacker's signatures were—hence, which avenues of attack to block. Earlier traces of the hacker's work can be cleaned out. *If* that particular path is then forever blocked, either because the lock is changed or the key can be detected as soon as it slips into the lock, then hackers must start again from square one (rather than as far as they got before being stopped) and try another approach.

For a cyberattack, a critical step might, for instance, include gathering enough people with the right distribution of skills (perhaps some computer types, some electric power types), any one of which may defect and end the enterprise or even put the conspiracy at risk. If money has to be raised (for example, to pay people to search for vulnerabilities), more potential failure points arise. If the team is assembled and financed, team members need to scope the system unnoticed. If they need to recruit an insider (from the system being targeted), this, too, can be risky and a possible source of failure. Breaking through to office automation systems of power companies is of moderate difficulty, but staying resident long enough to understand the system from the inside could be harder. Then comes the difficult task of penetrating what is normally an air-gapped system from a vantage point perhaps gained on the office automation network. Next comes figuring out which changes in machine controls will cause power lines to trip, and then determining (perhaps by guessing) which power lines are single points of failure that can create cascading effects across regions. If the point is to break machinery, that too involves a risk of incomplete success. The first few attempts to take down a major complex may fail or, at best, succeed incompletely. Thus, before people succeed at bringing down the North American electric power grid for a substantial length of time, it is likely that they will try and meet with incomplete success (if not fail entirely), which may include taking down something small and being able to go no further.

None of this says what the *odds* are that any of these transitions will lead to failure, particularly a failure that terminates the effort (rather than a temporary setback). Nor does this formulation predict the number of hackers that will march up to the starting line. Therein lies an analytical problem. We might think the probability curve looks like a power-law distribution without knowing the number of attempts that will be made (data points for the curve) or the transition percentages from one level of success to another (the higher the transition probability, the more likely it is that lesser events will be harbingers of larger ones—and the more likely that intermediate catastrophes may not take place to serve as warnings). Finally, it is unclear what kind of states represent lower transition points. From the perspective of understanding what it takes for a hacker to succeed, what constitutes one failure or two failures or three failures away from success?

IDENTIFYING NEAR-CATASTROPHES TO GET AHEAD OF CATASTROPHES

So, what *does* constitute a near-catastrophe? This is a problem, for instance, that the U.S. Federal Aviation Administration has wrestled with.[5] Its interest in near-accidents arises from the perception that a near-accident is the result of faulty human/system behavior that produced a range of out-comes, some percentage of which could have resulted in an actual accident—but fortunately did not.[6] Figuring out the distribution of possible outcomes relative to actual outcomes is not trivial. For instance, trains routinely pass each other at high relative speeds without being considered near-accidents, but when two trucks do so, people are right to be worried, and when two airplanes do so, they are right to get excited. The difference is that the statistical range of train locations relative to their location controls is tightly bounded by the layout of train tracks, whereas the predictable range of trucks (given that some come quite close to each other) is not so constrained, and that range for aircraft is even less constrained. So the inference from a near-collision involving trains to knowing the odds of an actual collision looks a lot different depending on whether trains, trucks, or aircraft are at issue. More broadly, the qualifying characteristics require a fine understanding of the (soft-ware and protocol) failure modes of the systems at issue.

A catastrophic cyberattack on a system requires that defenders be ignorant of or indifferent to the risks associated with its vulnerabilities. Knowing that hackers were one step from success in creating catastrophe requires a sense of what that one step is. Since obvious flaws rarely remain flaws for long, that step may be hard to describe in anything but the most general terms. A costless inci-dent (for example, the hackers got to the point where they could input instructions to the machinery but the instructions they inserted did not have the effect that they hoped for) may be closer to a catastrophe than a costly incident (the hackers caused a power outage by interfering with communi-cations among machines). Systems analysis would likely uncover multiple paths by which to create a catastrophe and, therefore, many different potential near-catastrophes, the latter attacks that could have created a catastrophe but for failure or incomplete success at the last step.

Most analyses undertaken to prevent system failure rightly concentrate on how the *attacked* system ought to work in order to detect changes from that baseline that may indicate its being close to failure. But the approach of this chapter concentrates on how the *attacker* succeeds. Ori-enting defensive efforts to how the attacker might fail (and/or be induced to fail) is reflected in Lockheed's "kill chain" for defending networks.[7] The kill-chain approach assumes that attackers must complete six tasks to get what they want: reconnaissance, weaponization, delivery, exploita-tion, installation, and command and control. Failure at any one means failure for the attack. That noted, Lockheed's method was not designed to detect near-catastrophes, although it might be adapted to do so.

Forcing a hacker to surmount a succession of difficult barriers rather than one super-difficult barrier drastically minimizes the odds of a lucky hacker breaching a system quickly. Take two sys-tems. One can be broken by finding a single vulnerability that takes, on average, a year to discover. The other requires that six vulnerabilities be discovered in succession, but each takes two months, on average, to discover (assume there is no ipso facto correlation between breaking one early and breaking another early). The hacker in either case will take, on average, a year to break into each system. The odds that the first system can be broken in half a year are one-quarter.[8] But the odds that the second system could be broken in a half year are far less: 1/128. Against an impatient foe, one who will quit if a compromise takes too long, the second system is far more secure.

HEDGING TO DEAL WITH EXCEPTIONS TO THE POWER-LAW RULE

The power-law rule can be broken. If attackers can build and attack test systems, they can fail in silence as they build up their competence; they do not have to start afresh every time. The best (and, so far as known, only) example of a hacker test lab was the reported construction of an Ira-nian centrifuge cascade by Israel in its Dimona nuclear plant.[9] By contrast, outside the laboratory, their failures may well be detected by defenders, leading to the whole scheme being unraveled and tougher defenses subsequently put in place.

But there are other exceptions. The attackers may get lucky, and their first attempts may succeed. Alternatively, the failures may take place so early in the process that they do not register as near-disasters and hence are not subsequently blocked. Or the transition probabilities between successive steps are low only early in the process; by the time one gets deeply into the process, transition rates are high. Thus, most attacks that get deep go all the way. Finally, a power-law distribution may fail to apply in a particular case.

The possibility of exception calls for a hedging strategy, one that first determines a worst-case scenario and then works backward to generate policies that convert the worst to something that is merely awful. This then requires some thought about what a worst case really is.

Consider, again, the power grid. If the worst case is that a cyberattack destroys hard-to-replace generating equipment, then worst-case policies might provide, say, stand-by generating equipment, nationwide (or at least regional) bootstrap recovery mechanisms, and perhaps an autonomous sense-and-communications network to detect when generators are entering a self-destruct mode. If, on the other hand, the worst case is something closer to the August 2003 blackout, then the emphasis should be on preventing power-loss cascades coupled with stand-by mechanisms to permit power to restore itself quickly (otherwise, bringing every system back on at once creates grid instabilities). In the wake of that blackout, power companies emphasized understanding their single points of failure so that no one outage—whether caused by hackers, weather, or error—could precipitate a cascade.[10] Other systemic catastrophes require their own approach. A natural gas distribution failure can be ameliorated by a combination of local inventory and allocation mechanisms. A financial market failure may be mitigated by roll-back mechanisms and Federal Reserve policies. A transportation failure may call for stand-by capacity and offline backup of shipping and passenger manifests. From a general cybersecurity perspective, comparable steps include figuring out in advance which users (and their machines) should be given access to which processes (or at least not without further permissions)—with the understanding that the trade-off between ease of access and security may need to shift toward security as hacker-induced catastrophes loom larger in planning. Overall, it is prudent to have a menu of options prepared in advance against the possibility that shifts in the threat environment make their implementation worthwhile, even urgent. Understandably, these steps only turn full catastrophes into somewhat less catastrophic events. The latter may be costly. But a modicum of planning and foresight may help ensure that the worst case is not as bad as it could be.

SCALABILITY INFLUENCES HOW WELL A NEAR-CATASTROPHE PREDICTS A CATASTROPHE

Whether an attack scales well can indicate whether it can evolve from a demonstration to a serious incident and then to a near-catastrophe and a catastrophe. For instance, an attack on a gas pipeline that exploited a vulnerability common to multiple gas pipelines might scale; a similar attack that exploited a singular vulnerability or that used an insider might not scale.

Scalability has several dimensions. One is breadth: multiple systems can be attacked. Another is depth: a scalable attack may only need to hit one electric power company, but if the attack leads to a cascading failure, the effects may be regional or nearly national in scale (the North American grid has three quasi-autonomous subnetworks: east, west, and Texas). The last is duration, which may characterize attacks that can infiltrate multiple systems and remain undetectable until activated.

Attacks that require physical access, particularly in peacetime, scale poorly. This is why many of the clever attacks demonstrated at the Defcon or Black Hat conferences, while relevant when the target is an individual, are irrelevant for cyberwar purposes. Apple's iPhone, for instance, can be compromised by someone who convinces its owner to charge the phone using a specially corrupted charger.[11] One can imagine a few iPhones being compromised that way, but it is difficult to see how to get many of them so corrupted without eventual discovery and reversal. More broadly, any attack that puts the attacker at physical risk, however notional such risk might seem, is one that is hard to replicate too often. Granted, an attack that breaches physical security (for example, to access an untended machine[12]) may yield outsized effects because many security protocols assume that hackers enjoy only remote access and fail when that assumption is untrue. Yet any catastrophe that requires multiple examples of physical access faces long odds (except perhaps when physical risk is expected, such as in war zones, and new intruders can be sent forward when their predecessors fall).

Understanding why attacks may fail to scale may help. As a general rule, attacks will not scale well if they must succeed multiple times to acquire their strategic effect, the odds of any one attack being detected in an interval are nonzero, and detection leads to the discovery and hence winding back of earlier attacks (for example, because the latter can be characterized by now-obvious patterns). Or an attack may have to lie undetected for long periods of time before a critical mass of infected machines is achieved. The scalability of such an attack depends on several factors. Does using the infection or the malware it leaves behind create anomalies on the system or network whose detection would alert defenders to look for similar instances? Will infections be overwritten by the next software patch? Does the infection require constant (and telltale) communications with its owner? Finally, if such an attack requires that multiple infections *all* be activated at the same time—lest the activation of one cause defenders to scramble to find others—can simultaneous activation be achieved (particularly when doing so requires reliable communications to the infection)? If an attack requires the use of witting collaborators, then the larger the number of people, the greater the cumulative odds that one squeals, possibly initiating investigations that may unearth silent coconspirators. An attack against a singular vulnerability may not scale (absent cascading effects) unless such an attack has broader features that permit analogous vulnerabilities to be detected and exploited (for example, tools that accelerate the time required to detect certain classes of vulnerability or vulnerabilities in certain classes of systems). Or an attack may require the affected system to be in a state that rarely occurs naturally or is very difficult to induce.[13] Such an attack might succeed once in a blue moon, but it may take nearly forever for multiple such attacks to succeed at the same time.

ATTACKS OF BROAD CONSEQUENCE

One unique aspect of operations in cyberspace is the role played by the reusability of tools, such as exploits, obfuscation tricks, social engineering tactics, and suborned servers. It takes a great deal of time, energy, and even luck (in finding vulnerabilities) to generate a set of usable tools; once they work, hackers tend to reuse them (albeit with variations). Although nothing prevents hackers from approaching each individual target with a unique set of tools and techniques, they rarely do so (even Stuxnet may have been recycled against North Korea). This holds whether the hackers are Chinese (the signatures of APT1, for instance, or the repeated attacks under the Aurora label), Russians (see Snake[14] or BlackEnergy[15]), or otherwise (Regin,[16] the Equation Group[17]).

Therein lies a potential defense against certain classes of *broad* systems compromise. Typically, the identifying characteristics of these tools are not apparent until after a particular intrusion set is discovered and analyzed. Once that happens, one can begin to understand what signatures such tools leave behind (multiple discoveries help with clarifying these characteristics). Once these identifying characteristics—signatures—are generated, they can be distributed to defenders so that any sufficiently well-instrumented organization can discover whether it has been attacked or is under attack by the group that used the tools. Finally, once the signatures of the hackers' tools are understood, they can be searched for within the patterns of network traffic and the log files kept by networks to look for indicators of *past* compromise, thereby helping reverse the effects of prior infections. Such knowledge can be used to frustrate intrusions either at the border (between trusted and untrusted machines) or, failing that, once inside but before they have done any serious harm. The APT1 report from Mandiant provided enough signature information to force APT1 to step back for several months to a year before it could build and deploy new tools.[18]

The faster that system compromises by a group can be detected and characterized, the harder it would be for the group to mount a broad strategic campaign of national or global compromise. Although a major cyberattack itself *could* be a one-time sally against a network, in practice it takes a great deal of repeated espionage to understand the target system well enough to attack it with (quasi-)predictable effect. For a broad strategic campaign, many systems must be compromised in turn (but not necessarily starting at the same time). Finally, if a campaign is to work coherently, all the disruptive/destructive cyberattacks have to be triggered simultaneously. A sequence of attacks going off at different times gives the defense an opportunity to diagnose the problem, infer which tools were used, and search for evidence of such tools in other systems with fair odds that the discovery of such tools permits the affected systems to be restored to an uninfected state. What then should have been a mass attack becomes a singlet, or at worst a set of them.

The attack dynamics resemble the game of Pig, in which slightly raising the odds of zeroing out a turn or the total score can drastically increase the number of attempts required to reach even one hundred. Likewise, the greater the odds of discovering a set of tools quickly, the more attempts hackers must make to compromise a certain predetermined number of systems, and the longer the odds of getting all of them before their tools are discovered and all their previous compromises reversed.

That now raises the question of how to accelerate the discovery of compromises, extract the tools associated with them, and distribute the signatures of these tools in such a way that future compromise attempts using them would be quickly defeated by dint of being detected.

The toughest of the three questions is how to detect an infection and *quickly*. Gadi Evron, founder of cybersecurity start-up Cymmetria, has raised the concept of placing throughout an organization sensors that are not otherwise seen by normal traffic. Thus, what touches these sensors would be interpreted as malicious contact, likely by an attacker trying to move laterally throughout a system after having penetrated its borders. Once the sensor is touched, it can start extracting information from the contact—notably, what it was trying to do and where it came from. By tracing the contact's route backward through the system, the system can acquire more defining characteristics of the tool set (the process is similar if the wake-up call is an induced system malfunction, but in that case, the damage is already done and the purpose of analysis is to prevent a repeat in the system).

If hackers are aware of the danger of touching otherwise quiet nodes, their malware might limit the nodes touched to those also touched by the overall network; this might be a countermeasure. A counter-countermeasure may be to establish stereotypical communications among all nodes, the nature of which will be obvious to the sensor (and hence factored out) but not to hackers. Another countermeasure may be for the hacker to create evidence of tools that are actually manifestations of legitimate traffic; using such indicators to block suspect traffic also blocks legitimate traffic. White-listing IP addresses and normal behavior might be a partial counter-countermeasure.

Normally, sensors sit on Internet-facing nodes, but such sensors will likely harvest bushels of inconsequential pings and lame penetration attempts (for example, those that exploit long-patched vulnerabilities). Furthermore, unless such a node can simulate a human operator, it would not really see attacks that start when attachments are opened or corrupted websites visited. By facing outward, these sensors will also capture a great deal of extraneous traffic; such noise interferes with the processing needed to distinguish changes in computer memory arising from normal interactions from those changes arising from interacting with malware. Furthermore, such sensors have to be placed at *all* outward-facing nodes—thereby adding even more noise. By contrast, the inability of a subsurface sensor to see attacks so weak that they cannot successfully penetrate the system's borders (which is a useful feature if such attacks merit no further concern) is actually a virtue. That they do not observe the initial penetration directly, however, is not a virtue. Robust logging (that goes back long enough to detect attacks that linger in the stricken computer before venturing forth in search of internal computers to infect) will be necessary to capture IP addresses used as well as the social engineering tricks or the exploit meant for initial penetration. Analysts would have to count on being able to work backward from intrusion detection to find the patient zero of the network and thereby the vector of penetration.[19] To the extent that the purpose of a sensor is to generate indications that can be given to intrusion detection systems to filter out attacks at the border *and* that many intrusion detections sit at the border, the difference between what subsurface sensors see and what intrusion detection sensors see has to be reconciled. But that is not as critical as one might think—if the purpose of a sensor system is to characterize and *broadcast information on* the tools as a form of deterrence rather than defense.

Tool components will vary in how difficult they are for defenders to capture and how difficult they are for hackers to change in response. For instance, an exploit built around a vulnerability that then gets fixed is difficult to change, because it means finding a new one to build an exploit around—but if the tool (exploit) is used only to penetrate a system's border, it will take work to detect and characterize. The signature of a piece of malware is relatively easy to capture, but it is easy for the hacker to alter (for example, via polymorphism). The characteristic IP addresses used in an attack are easy to capture; altering them may be of middling difficulty (it may require compromising another intermediate server) or even less difficulty if the hackers have figured out whether and how to use techniques such as fast-flux DNS. Social engineering tricks are of moderate difficulty to both capture and alter (and after-the-fact detection may require a well-trained workforce with a good memory). Various obfuscation and counterdetection techniques (which allow the software to evade detection by cybersecurity tools) are relatively hard to distinguish but also relatively hard to alter. Both the tricks and the tricks by which tricks are detected are subject to the same measure-countermeasure contests that characterize cybersecurity in general, particularly if such a sensor system is widely implemented around the world.

The most reliable measure (and counter-countermeasure) is a smart analyst who can use human experience and intuition to detect when malware rather than legitimate traffic is touching the sensors and infer tools from instances of sensor disturbance. But while software scales well (in that it can be used anywhere), humans do not; furthermore, the ones that can do these jobs are expensive. Not surprisingly, the optimal man-machine ratios will shift over time. If serious infections are rare (for example, if the average organization goes years between attacks), scalability is less important, and throwing smart people at the infection in order to extract tool signatures can be justified.

The fate of these tool signatures depends on the value of impeding further cyberattacks by the fingered hacker group vis-à-vis deterring that group (by forcing them to build new tools) and discouraging all other groups (newly aware that being caught will also force tools to be rebuilt). If the goal is impeding further cyberattacks, then sharing is not necessarily recommended; the less widely the discovery of the tools is broadcast, the lower the odds the hacker group will discover that its tools will fail against the few who know. Without that news, the hacker group will have to deduce as much from a declining payoff rate. If the goal is deterrence, then broadcasting the news is preferred; distribution need not be 100 percent.[20] Furthermore, deterrence (forcing the hacker group to retool and putting others on notice that they might have to later) benefits organizations without intrusion detection systems, just as everyone benefits from the reverse-engineering that lead to exploits of vulnerability discoveries and thence to patches. Yet broadcasting the discovery has the disadvantage of making it obvious to the group why its efforts are not working so well; if the group has a second set of tricks, it can start using them immediately or at least develop new tools sooner.

How can organizations be persuaded to accept such sensors, particularly if they come with the expectation that analyses (or at least pings) from such sensors will be shared? If the organizations themselves own the sensors, their motivation for sharing may be negative; not only is the gain going to others, but if these sensors are effective, their possession also can signal to hackers to go elsewhere because an attack may well cause them to lose their tools, and then they cannot attack others. Once these sensors are widespread, there may be nowhere else to go, and hackers will end up redoubling their efforts to evade the impacts of touching sensors—so the additional layer of dissuasion possessed by owning a sensor is likely to be vitiated.

There is also a public interest in defeating large-scale attacks by widening the distribution of sensors—hence, a rationale for encouraging the hosting of such sensors (and analyzing their results). The benefits of hosting such sensors can be sweetened if a third party pays for the analysis that would follow such a sensor being pinged. A further sweetener may be a promise that only those who host sensors will get threat signatures, although that promise will come at the expense of maximizing dissuasion. Technical measures to protect personally identifiable information that comes from the sensors (which should not be a problem on otherwise quiet sensors, but "should not" does not equal "will not") as well as organizationally sensitive data (for example, proprietary information) will have to be worked out. The latter considerations are arguments for otherwise quiet internal sensors over Internet-facing sensors. Economies of scale favor the widest distribution of sensors, especially overseas among countries that are friendly (or at least unlikely to use such data to strengthen their hackers' efforts against U.S. targets).

Finally, the design of a large-scale tool-detecting sensor system should be compatible with the business interests of cybersecurity companies whose talents will be needed to ensure that such a sensor-analysis-distribution system keeps current with technology and the threat. The business of diagnose-and-tell was, after all, their invention.

All this assumes the sensor system works (for example, by avoiding false positives and negatives), and this still leaves nontrivial issues of standardization (in terms of minimum reportable quality and how signature information is rendered in some common format) and organization. Confidence in such an approach will likely require more research and development.

IMPLICATIONS FOR LEARNING

As may already be clear, cybersecurity and system compromise are games of competitive learning. If those who are hacked realize that and understand how, they can take steps to make sure the same attack cannot happen again. If hackers understand how defenders detected them by differentiating their activities from those of normal network traffic, they can take steps to make their activities (and the network's reaction to their activities) look like everyday ebbs and flows and evade detection. Just watching how defenders react teaches hackers what to do next, and just watching how hackers work teaches defenders what to do next. Everything else being equal, faster learners beat slower learners. Small cyberattacks may have an immunizing effect if they promote learning, absent which organizations are heir to large cyberattacks. Unfortunately, as Dorothy Denning and others have noted, the attacks also provide learning opportunities for hackers as well. Also, attackers will have more experience from which to learn than defenders for two reasons. First, individual attackers usually deal with more hacks (their own) than most individual defenders do. Second, many sallies into target network attacks fail, thereby yielding lessons for attackers but leaving defenders none the wiser.

One of the reasons that cyberattacks, particularly the more clever ones, do not repeat themselves very well is that people have learned from the more well-reported attacks what the tricks are to avoid becoming a victim. One ramification is that some very clever ideas have a shelf life of between zero and one successful attempt. Consider the vulnerabilities of hitherto mechanical systems that are now electronic systems with network connectivity (wireless and/or wired). One intriguing example entails a prison door.[21] Imagine, therefore, a clever hack that exploits this trick to free your soldiers kept as enemy prisoners. The results would be spectacular—and very difficult to repeat. The other side would likely learn at the level of code (the faults that allowed this hack) and at the level of architecture (the perils of entrusting guard systems to electronic systems without using backup).

Exactly what hackers have to learn has changed—and in some ways to their benefit. Twenty years ago, when legacy systems such as mainframes and minicomputers had a larger role in the office, and when specialized computing equipment was more common in factories and militaries, attackers would have to study specific target systems in great detail. What was learned with one did not necessarily translate into another system; furthermore, the experience base for any one system was sufficiently low that it was similarly difficult to predict how a given system would react. These days, far more servers are built on the Microsoft/Intel architecture, with most of the rest being some variant of Unix/Linux. General-purpose personal computers have also replaced the specialized systems that controlled industrial and military processes. Thus, someone today who finds or learns about a vulnerability in a general-purpose machine has a greater chance of getting into a random system than was true when there was a greater heterogeneity of machines.

Conversely, the variety of cybersecurity products that have become available to trap the hacker has proliferated, and each one seems to use a slightly different trick to detect an infection. Thus, if and when such defenses are deployed in sufficient numbers (which is contingent on their doing what they advertise they can do), the hacker has to determine what they are and figure out how to elude their many grasps.

What defenders learn about their own vulnerabilities plus what they learn about attackers should together be more valuable than what the attackers learn about the defenders. If so, then constant cyberattacks should ultimately favor defense. But attackers can shape their attacks to avoid revealing all of their tricks—notably zero-day exploits—particularly if they are going after targets that can be hacked without needing them. More generally, the side with less at stake can test its cyberattacks against the other side, knowing that it cannot afford to pull punches (in the interest of hiding its capabilities) and that the side with the lesser stake can. Indeed, victories at preventing compromise often go undetected, almost by definition.

The more useful goal of information sharing may well be the construction of a systematic knowledge base on cybersecurity. With rare exceptions, one can view every successful cyberattack in terms of one or more failures of systems administration, just as one can view aircraft crashes as a result of failures in the art of building, maintaining, and piloting an aircraft.[22] Indeed, the more defensive components a system has—each of which has a shot at catching an attack in action—the more failures are required to result in system compromise.[23] As Ross Anderson has observed, one of the reasons for the enormous progress in airline safety vis-à-vis computer security is that airlines crash outdoors and computers "crash" indoors.[24] Once an aircraft goes down, the National Transportation Safety Board (NTSB) is figuratively and literally all over it. Their efforts, building on decades of knowledge on understanding accidents, have resulted in a dense body of knowledge of what not to do.[25] In a related fashion, medical knowledge has advanced as people have learned about human system failures. A similar knowledge of all the ways that systems have failed could improve cybersecurity. Exactly how to get such information is unclear, but, as a general rule, having professionals talk to each other in a professional (and non-fault-finding) setting can go a long way. It should be considered unprofessional for cybersecurity professionals not to share information about how mistakes (or should-have-done-betters) in cybersecurity lead to problems, and it should be illegal for cybersecurity contracts to muzzle discussion of found faults. Such norms apply to medical workers, aircraft designers, and safety professionals. That noted, the plural of anecdote is not data. Systematic learning requires systematic, well-funded analytic work to correlate cybersecurity practices to cybersecurity outcomes.

IS INFORMATION SHARING A PANACEA?

Information sharing can be useful in defeating deep cyberattacks and broad campaigns of system intrusion. It can also promote learning. But these effects require that information be not only shared but also analyzed and molded to fit particular ends: for example, adjusting the odds of a catastrophe, detecting the use of certain tools, or creating a systematic knowledge base of practices. It requires, in other words, the systematic use of such information.

Unfortunately, information sharing has become, at least in the United States, yet another panacea to where it is common wisdom that information legislation represents the difference between having and not having cybersecurity. To be sure, there are benefits to unfocused information sharing. Researchers, for instance, have argued that if banks shared their lists of suspect IP addresses with one another, each would be more secure and $300 million a year less of financial cybercrime would take place.[26] Companies believe that they do not get enough threat information and that they could prevent cyberattacks if they did.[27]

As it stands, neither the federal government nor private organizations are particularly happy with the current level of information exchange. Government officials say they simply do not get enough information and suspect that companies do not want to reveal what may be embarrassing or detrimental to maintaining their stock price. Industry, in turn, has complained the government does not let them in on the good stuff, or at least not fast enough.

Part of the problem may be misunderstanding what needs to be shared. With terrorism, we want to know who is going to carry out an attack, where, and how (by what means): Colonel Plum, in the ballroom, will detonate a satchel bomb. In this case, "who" is important, and "where" is important, but "how" is of somewhat lesser interest—satchel bombs are figuratively a dime a dozen. Knowing that one weapon rather than another is being used contributes modestly to whatever measures are being taken for self-protection. More important is targeting "who" and guarding "where." Information sharing in cyberspace has to meet different needs. The question of "where"—which is to say, "to whom"—is interesting but, again, what does one do with the information? Systems administration entails more than raising firewalls when someone heralds an approaching attack. But the "how" is vitally important, because it indicates the weaknesses to check for (and fix).

It also matters who gets the information being shared. Consider the poor sysadmins who hear that among the PDFs that their organizations get daily is one that exploits a particular flaw. They could write scripts that would sideline the PDF if it has a particular signature (that is how antivirus software works), only to find that such script would have to be kept continually updated and would have to be rewritten if numerous signatures are (typically) associated with any one vulnerability. By contrast, informing a software maker about a vulnerability can lead to a fix that, when sufficiently well proliferated, ends that particular problem forever and for everyone, whether or not they are sharing information.

The question of "who" may be less important, even though it is the focus of congressional action on cybersecurity. It is not clear what to do with the knowledge that it is the Elderwood Project rather than the Comment Group (also known as APT1) that is after your information—unless this knowledge comes with information about their particular techniques.

Threat-centric information therefore tries to correlate "who" with "how." It calls for organizations to report instances of being attacked together with relevant details of the attacks such as malware samples, attacker modus operandi, IP addresses, social engineering methods, and so forth. These instances, in turn, are used to create a profile of specific threat actors and signatures of their activity, which, in turn, would be circulated to organizations so that they can better prepare themselves, notably by putting such signatures into their intrusion prevention/detection systems.

The usefulness of threat-centric information may be specific to certain classes of cyberattack that come from groups that carry out multiple attacks using the same or similar signatures *and* are spread out over enough time so that signatures from early attacks are still relevant. It helps that not all hackers are conscientious about altering their tools, and some features of their tools may not be obvious to them (and would thus not necessarily be changed over time). Forcing hacker groups to use multiple signatures, evolve their signatures, or group their attacks means more work for them. Some hackers will drop out; others may not be able to attack as many organizations. Furthermore, even if threat-centric information sharing does not work, the efforts that organizations would have to make to understand what is going on in their networks in order to share information effectively would, as a side benefit, also help them protect themselves absent any information sharing whatsoever.

A better approach may be providing incentives not to the targets of cyberattacks but to the cybersecurity firms they work with. Such firms have a much better idea than their clients (who are rarely in the cybersecurity business themselves) do of what is going on in the clients' networks. Second, because they can do this analysis, their presence obviates the need for private organizations to hand raw packets to the U.S. government for the latter's analysis. Third, because these organizations have multiple clients, their reporting creates less risk of embarrassing any particular one of their clients (who would then be more amenable to the distribution of such reports). Fourth, such companies have a keener need for U.S. government information than their clients do. Not only do they understand such data better but they also can make money from getting it and distributing it to their clients, while network owners can use it only to protect themselves. Such cybersecurity companies are more apt to drive the bargains that can persuade the intelligence community to swap its information for the information they, the companies, hold (which is likely to be one or two orders of magnitude more than any one individual organization sees).

CHAPTER 6

What the Government Can and Cannot Do

Much of what the government already does to protect systems is written in the language of budgets and administered in the language of bureaucracy. Bureaucracies tend to grasp problems largely by reference to the tools they can bring to bear; possessing only hammers, they see every problem as a nail. Within the intelligence community, cyberspace insecurity is seen as a counterintelligence problem (or as a wonderful intelligence opportunity).[1] Within the rest of DoD, it is a military problem of warfare's fifth domain. Within the State Department, it is a diplomatic problem. Within DHS, most of whose manpower works for Immigration and Customs Enforcement, Customs and Border Patrol, Transportation Security Administration (TSA), and the Coast Guard, it is understood as a perimeter security problem—hence, its focus on Einstein III. The various regulatory agencies—for example, the Securities and Exchange Commission, Federal Energy Regulatory Commission, Federal Communications Commission, and Federal Deposit Insurance Corporation—see it as a regulatory problem; they are inserting cybersecurity into their regimes but as consistent with their allowed toolkits. Within the Justice Department and Secret Service, it is a crime problem. Hacking violates laws such as the 1986 Computer Fraud and Abuse Act (which criminalizes the unauthorized penetration of systems). The 2000 Digital Millennium Copyright Act criminalizes the production and dissemination of technology, devices, or services intended to subvert digital rights management schemes in order to gain unlawful access to copyrighted works; sometimes the law has been used to go after those who expose security holes, but, thankfully, with no great success.[2]

Apart from letting bureaucracies extend their missions into cyberspace, what *else* can and should the United States do *further* to combat insecurity in cyberspace?

FIRST, WHY SHOULD THE GOVERNMENT DO ANYTHING?

A basic tenet of economics is that when people are left to their own devices, they will optimize their spending, leaving no scope for government policy intervention into their decisions. This should be as true for spending on cybersecurity as for any other spending. So why should the government help with cyber security?

It matters whether organizations bear all the gains and all the losses from their decisions and whether their decisions are fully informed. Take an organization where the only cost of system insecurity is the risk that its network might fail at day's end and that it has to pay people to work overtime to restore it. Because the organization bears all of the costs of insecurity, economic theory suggests that whatever it chooses to spend is the right amount. But how often *are* organizations hacked with no external consequences? Personal records such as credit card numbers and transaction records that are stolen from an organization by hackers can be used to run up charges on customer credit cards—or to learn incriminating details about some customers. Such impacts are clearly external; even if the organization compensates the banks to make good its clients' accounts (most of the losses from the Target cyberattack fell to banks[3]), customers may have work to do to restore their credit. If the circulation of credit card data in black markets cannot be associated with a particular retailer, that retailer has no incentive to stop such crimes and therefore lacks reason to spend sufficiently on cybersecurity. This is one reason why California requires that corporations inform customers whenever their social security numbers are revealed to hackers.

Similar forces affect the decision to protect personal computers from becoming part of a botnet. The infected computer itself may work as it always did, but it can be controlled by others to spam third-party sites. The computer user will likely not care and will therefore be disinclined to spend money on, say, antivirus software, even if doing so would make these third parties better off. Therein lies the case for compelling the home user to keep his or her computer secure (whether the cost of doing so exceeds the benefits is a different matter).

When cybersecurity requires collective effort, the incentives to invest vary with the relationship between each member's contribution and outcomes. If the quality of defense came from average effort, then the trade-off between effort and security would represent the community consensus. But if the quality of defense is a result of the weakest link (for example, the feckless user mentioned above), the quality of defense will suffer accordingly. Ironically, this is also true if the quality of defense reflects the strongest component (for example, the rare individual who can find and patch the organization's firewall). In both cases, the results are socialized, but the costs are privatized.[4] Ross Anderson has further observed that the incentives that persuade a system owner to protect itself against a limited attack that takes out a single, say, refinery may be insufficient against an attack that takes out a nation's entire refinery system.[5] If one refinery goes down, consumers can turn to others—but if all of them go down, a great deal of economic activity grinds to a halt. "Cybersecurity and the North American Electric Grid" explains that power companies underinvest in cybersecurity because, "first, given the interconnected nature of the grid, the benefits of these investments are likely to extend beyond the footprint of an individual company. . . . Second . . . individual companies may have a difficult time determining which investments to make beyond the minimum required for compliance with mandatory standards [particularly because] current compliance and enforcement programs . . . fail to reward—instead they potentially penalize—entities that go beyond minimal compliance."[6] From a national security point of view, it is a bad idea for foes to think that they can manipulate a country's sovereignty and freedom of action by threatening or attacking its critical systems, but this is a minor consideration to power company stockholders. And crippling some civilian systems affects a country's ability to fight wars.

Be wary, though, of the argument that private corporations cannot compete against countries that attack them wanting their information. Were that always decisive, no private U.S. corporation could compete against foreign state–owned enterprises (for example, in selling software or aircraft). Yet they do so all the time.

Martin Feldstein argues that "the infrastructure companies should be required to meet a high standard of protection and to cooperate with government agencies in preventing incoming malware. But the cost of doing that [in his case, a national firewall]—should be borne by the country as a whole, just as we pay for the military or other public goods like the weather service."[7] But should it? Normally, such costs would be paid for one way (taxes) or the other (increases in the cost of newly protected goods and services). But any scheme that has the government fund such costs either directly or indirectly via tax breaks would tilt the decisions of owners from costs that are hard to write a bill for (for example, a secure architecture that leads to less convenience for users) to costs that are easier to write a bill for (for example, hiring a cybersecurity contractor).

Software suppliers, for their part, have found ways to indemnify themselves against the costs borne by customers when their products are insecure by requiring they accept the software's "as-is" contracts.[8] Presumably, they would invest correctly in securing their products if they could charge a premium for more secure software—which would require customers to be able to tell which features were better at lowering their expected costs from hacking. But when markets are young, time-to-market is critical so that the winner can benefit from network effects—and security is an afterthought.[9]After all, the costs of security arise not only in additional labor costs for programmers and testers. Adding security to a base product, such as word processing software, can complicate writing applications that run on top of the base product. Given two base products—one secure but hard to write applications for, and the other insecure but offering fewer barriers—application writers will first write to the easy rather than the secure base product. This gives the former that much more momentum in the time-to-market race. Unfortunately, many of the security problems are not discovered until after users and supporting vendors commit to a product—whereupon switching away becomes costly.

Optimization also assumes that consumers *can* judge the security of products—but is that really so for software? If not, they will assume that software is insecure and, in their skepticism, drive quality products from the market.[10] Many of the methods used to convey quality do not work very well. Some products acquire a reputation reinforced by groupthink—as per the phrase, "No one was ever fired for buying IBM." Formal evaluations can often be corrupted, in part because those who carry out the ratings are paid by those whose products are being rated, creating incentives to pass products whose flaws are not obvious or likely to be obvious any time soon. As with mortgage-backed securities, everything would be fine until the day of reckoning.

In some cases, the world cannot afford products to be deemed failures. One cannot flunk certificate authorities (they verify that software came from a particular source) without major disruption.[11] For instance, if GoDaddy were deemed compromised, the 26 percent of all websites that relied on hypertext transfer protocol–secure (HTTPS) circa March 2013 would need to be immediately issued new certificates. Overall, the credibility of the certificate authority *system* depends on the credibility of the least well secured authority. The current system of certifying software has six hundred authorities; the Iranians needed only to subvert two weak ones to spoof dissidents into clicking on Iran-run websites when they thought they were going to safe locations such as Google.[12] So what buyers are paying for (such as the perception of security, a liability shield, and trust signals to third parties) does not really correlate with security.

Another distortion of the marketplace might arise from the exercise of monopoly power. In 2003 Dan Geer and his coauthors argued that Microsoft's monopoly was bad for cybersecurity in two ways.[13] It led to complacency when securing cyberspace's most important pieces of software: the operating system and major office applications. Also, exploiting a single unpatched vulnerability could put most of the Internet at risk—especially if it could be exploited by a self-replicating worm. Yet heterogeneity is not free. It multiplies what sysadmins must learn and must do; a different patch for each of ten groups of one hundred computers is harder to administer than one patch on one thousand computers. It complicates configuration management because each application must talk to many other clients, often in different languages or protocols. Fortunately, Microsoft has cleaned up its act since the article was written in 2003. Unfortunately, the two most vulnerable commonly distributed products—corrupted PDFs and Flash files on the one hand, and Java on the other hand—are not directly purchased by customers, but rather they show up in browsers. This further dulls the incentive to keep them vulnerability-free.

Open-source software, whose source code is available for public inspection and improvement, has also been touted as a panacea. Eric Raymond, a fierce early advocate of open systems, contrasted Linux to Windows NT (1998) and argued that with open systems, "all bugs are shallow."[14] Because the code was public, all users—not just the original programmers—could look at what the code said, not just what the machine did. He further cited F. P. Brooks' aphorism, "More users find more bugs." Unfortunately, recent years have not been kind to the argument that open source leads to better code. A survey of open-source Java components showed 7.5 percent had known vulnerabilities.[15] Heartbleed showed that SSL code had flaws in it that arose, in large part, because no one was paid to maintain it, and very few people actually took a hard look at it.[16] The Shellshock crisis arose because another piece of open-source software, the Bash shell, was found to have critical flaws; as Robert Graham, the chief executive officer (CEO) of Errata Security, observed, "If many eyes had been looking at Bash over the past 25 years, these bugs would've been found a long time ago."[17] This was by no means the last such embarrassment of 2014.[18]

In other words, there is more than ample justification for the government to intervene on behalf of cybersecurity—if it can do so wisely.

WHAT THE WISE MEN RECOMMENDED

The problem of cybersecurity and its intimate link to cyberwar, and hence national security, makes it hard for governments to do nothing, both here and overseas.[19] Unfortunately, this circumstance does not prevent governments from making fatuous statements. Four reviews in the last twenty years stand out in terms of importance: the 1997 Presidential Commission on Critical Infrastructure Protection (PCCIP),[20] the February 2003 "National Strategy to Secure Cyberspace,"[21] the 2008 "Comprehensive National Cyberspace Initiative" (CNCI),[22] and the 2009 "Cyberspace Policy Review."[23]

The PCCIP recommended establishing information analysis and sharing centers (now called information analysis and sharing organizations), which until recently were informal discussion groups (the one run by banks was uniquely useful). The report also called for shared responsibility (that means it is always the other guy who should have done something differently), federal coordination, adaptation, best practices, well-tuned laws and regulations, and more research and development (R&D). Who could possibly object?

The 2003 National Strategy emphasized the risk from home users, lamenting that if only they would immunize their machines, innocent others would not be infected quite so easily. Suggested remedies for the home user were the usual ones (for example, passwords, virus protection, staying current on patches), but these were only suggestions that told few what they did not already know. Other core principles were public-private partnerships, an *avoidance* of further regulation, a respect for civil liberties, coordination with Congress as well as state/local governments, plus hortatory injunctions.[24]

The 2008 CNCI focused on what the government could do for itself. Its recommendations included the aforementioned Einstein program to protect the *federal* civilian government, the coordination of *federal* R&D emphasizing leap-ahead technologies, the integration of *federal* network operation centers, stronger counterintelligence, expanded cybersecurity education, and the recommendation that thought be given to deterrence strategies, the management of supply-chain risks, and securing the critical infrastructure. At least it allocated real money.

The 2009 "Cyberspace Policy Review" started with fine words: that the nation is at a crossroads, that the status quo is no longer acceptable, that the national dialogue must begin today, that the United States cannot succeed in isolation, that the United States cannot abrogate its role, that the country needs objectives for its next-generation infrastructure, and that the White House must lead the way forward. Recommendations included a "cyberczar" (whose appointment was a painful process entailing over a dozen rejected offers before someone accepted), an updated national strategy, the designation of cybersecurity as one of the president's key management priorities, a privacy and civil liberties official within the National Security Council, the convening of "appropriate interagency mechanisms to conduct interagency-cleared legal analyses of priority cybersecurity-related issues," a public awareness campaign, an official international cybersecurity policy framework, a cybersecurity incident response plan (which effectively said: in case of an incident, please let DHS know what you are doing and DHS will tell you what others are doing), an R&D framework focused on game-changing technologies, and a call for what would become the 2011 "National Strategy for Trusted Identities in Cyberspace."[25] All in all, this business of developing cyberspace strategies appears to have been dreary work, recycling clichés for over a dozen years— the consequence of not being able to decide that cybersecurity is not a government problem but not being willing to do much about it either.

In many cases, if commercial firms are positioned to end cyberspace threats, they work faster than the government can. Consider a thought experiment. Assume the president issued the *draft* version of the 2003 national cybersecurity strategy that placed such great emphasis on bulwarking the defenses of the home user in order to quash worms. Assume further that the policy resulted in laws to regulate ISPs (so that they could ensure the security of the home and small business user).[26] Getting legislation might have taken years (not until the end of 2015 did Congress pass *any* serious cybersecurity legislation). Regulations might have taken a few years more (the bulk of the Affordable Care Act program was designed for implementation in 2014, four years after it passed). If any ISP balked, court decisions would have been needed to force the point, adding even more years. By contrast, as noted, Microsoft put the problem of fast-replicating worms to bed in August 2004.

The point is not to never regulate, but to appreciate how much of what happens in cyberspace occurs because of decisions made by private actors for their own reasons—and who, with the right awareness and incentives, can make them in ways that favor security.

GOOD POLICIES

We now look at potential government policies. Some are good. Some are panaceas. Some are bad. We conclude by examining two difficult policy choices. The first examines ways to address the current shortage in cybersecurity professionals. The second moots whether the government is even capable of keeping up with the unexpected problems that cybersecurity throws up.

Authenticating Identities in Cyberspace

The government could authenticate identities in cyberspace (much as it authenticates physical identities via passports) by maintaining infrastructures that associate public keys with individuals. This would let people present themselves in cyberspace in an auditable way so that they could, for instance, sign documents electronically. Similar technologies would allow institutions to authenticate themselves as well; for instance, a digitally signed college transcript could be generated for students and would not have to be repeatedly requested from the college. The current credentials system as argued above is broken.

Sharing Classified Information on Vulnerabilities and Threats

In 2009, the chief of cybersecurity for the National Electric Reliability Council could legitimately lament:

> Threats like those suggested by the April 8th *Wall Street Journal* article discussing the existence of "cyber spies" in the electric grid, for example, have been challenging for the industry to fully evaluate and address. Without more specific information being appropriately made available to asset owners, they are unable to determine whether these concerns exist on their systems or develop appropriate mitigation strategies. A mechanism therefore is needed to validate the existence of

such threats and ensure information is appropriately conveyed to and understood by asset owners and operators in order to mitigate or avert cyber vulnerabilities.[27]

Since roughly that time, the government has begun granting short-term security clearances to selected individuals within the critical infrastructure so that they can get classified material on threats. Far more could be done. Selective revelation does not meet the needs of less concentrated industries such as truck driving and small and medium enterprises or of foreign-owned institutions (the risk that they may leak information to their own governments is a problem that DoD has addressed for decades with foreign-owned defense firms).

Understandably, the intelligence community may be leery about revealing how it learned about threats, but since 2009 there has arisen a fairly large cottage industry that specializes in threat collection based on its own resources—and behind which threat intelligence could be masked without much suspicion (for instance, by telling them and letting them tell the world). As for vulnerabilities, they can be found in many ways, ranging from white-hat investigations to the revelations of cybersecurity firms working with targets of network intrusion to whatever the hackers themselves reveal either directly (for instance, in plea bargaining) or because their malware has been reverse engineered. Again, there is plenty of cover to mask sources and methods. The wealth of alternatives means that an adversary that learns that one of its favorite tricks has been revealed may not necessarily conclude that it was stolen by spies, much less know *how* it was stolen. Indeed, if the adversary believes as much but is wrong, then revealing the vulnerability may prompt the adversary to tear itself up looking for what it cannot find for its not being there in the first place.

The fear of supply-chain attacks provides another good lesson in revelation. Suppose that the intelligence community finds a deliberately corrupted device; should it reveal as much?[28] Here, the case for revelation is easy. First, the United States should not want to hide the finding to use the information for offensive operations.[29] Second, revealing the compromised code in the product can embarrass the perpetrator, discouraging further such attempts by the perpetrator or third parties.

The case for revelation may rest on how *and how well* the intelligence community knows about the specific supply-chain vulnerability. Was it from examining the product or through intelligence? If the latter—for example, indications that some company intended to compromise the code, did so, and was happy with the results—can the specific flaw be found? If not, then the case for disclosure is weak, not only because of the intelligence gain/loss calculation but also because the credibility of the accusation—which is inevitably an accusation against someone—may be doubted. If the flaw *can* be found, then credibility is unlikely to be such an issue, and the flaw could plausibly have been found without collected intelligence at all. The product's manufacturer and the spymasters it worked for may, nevertheless, suspect that there was a leak, but revelation itself may not say much about where the clue came from. Finally, some revelations are worth risking sources and methods for. They may include the first credible evidence that a major foreign company has deliberately corrupted electronic components for the purposes of cyberattack. If corrupted components were behind a cyberattack that merits retaliation, then some explanation will be required.

Creating Bug Bounties

Many propose that the government accelerate the search for software vulnerabilities so that they may be fixed.[30] Until a few years ago, the primary bug-bounty programs applied to software in general and were not richly rewarded: iDefense and the Zero-Day Initiative (founded by TippingPoint) were the main players, with HackerOne a more recent addition. In the last few years, Google (with its Project Zero), Facebook, Microsoft, and even United Airlines have gotten into the act—some to fix their own software, others to fix Internet software.[31] Yet the total sums involved are still small.

Total annual payout can be expressed in double-digit millions—several orders of magnitude lower than the estimated $80 billion spent annually for cybersecurity. Adding modest amounts of money could make a difference.[32]

Exactly how the government would convert resources into discovered vulnerabilities is a nontrivial question. It could use civil servants (or civil servants augmented by federally financed research and development corporations), but even the NSA uses contractors for such work. Contractors, in turn, could be paid per annum or per discovery. Alternatively, government might reward contributions from all comers.[33] In doing so, there should be methods to distinguish critical from noncritical vulnerabilities (a well-understood distinction) and (more controversially) to favor the discovery of vulnerabilities found in the more popular or critical software.[34] Ten years ago, the link between the discovery of a vulnerability by outside researchers and a patch of the relevant software was an iffy process. Many white-hat researchers went outside the system to create pressure to fix the problem; their motives ranged from altruism to careerism (resume-building) and spite (for example, they found the vendor cocky). These days, patching is more responsive; Microsoft and Firefox's Mozilla, for instance, make it hard for individual users *not* to install patches. No longer need the government publicize the fact that it is handing a vulnerability over to the software producer—or at least not until after a patch has emerged. Patching enough vulnerabilities in a given product, incidentally, can alert producers of fundamental architectural flaws within it, thereby resulting in new versions.

If bug-bounty programs seem unfair because they use tax dollars to do what software companies ought to do on their own, would it help if software producers bore the costs imposed on third parties created by their vulnerabilities? The conversion between a software flaw and an exploited vulnerability is not straightforward. The target may not be faultless. Were the parameters set correctly by the organizations that deployed them? Did the victim keep current with their updates? Did individual users (for example, employees) blow past warnings or automatically click on what was presented to them? Were data backed up? Were networks monitored correctly—or at all? What provisions were made for resiliency and recovery? The list of actions that could be taken to reduce the costs of insecure software could go on and on. The important point is that creating a liability regime for software, if not written into software licensing agreements, would embroil judges in the determination of fault in the case of a hack when all sides were responsible.[35] Software companies, faced with liabilities the consequences of which were very hard to predict, may simply declare they could no longer serve the market. Even if they did, they may set such stringent conditions under which the software may be safely used that they indemnify themselves from any practical application of liability (because no one would restrict their use to these abstruse conditions).

In all fairness, even a robust zero-day program would not solve the problem of zero-day attacks, since there is no guarantee that a white hat will find a flaw faster than the black hat. As a practical matter, if one has information on a vulnerability, it is often faster to block an incoming attack by checking signatures in a national firewall to which information on the vulnerability has been added than to fix the vulnerability. The latter requires reverse-engineering the vulnerability, generating a patch and testing it to determine that it will not break systems in other places, distributing it, and ensuring that all who should patch their systems do, in fact, do so. In the long run, however, fixing the flaw is both more reliable and more efficient.

Mandating Air Gaps

Mandating systems isolation may be a cost-effective hedge against a catastrophic attack on infrastructures that move physical goods: electric power, natural gas, water, chemicals, and transportation. These are sectors for which Internet accessibility is helpful for convenience and optimization purposes but not essential for basic operations. Such infrastructures used to work quite adequately before there was Internet (and even earlier, phone) connectivity. Such a standard would mandate that no one starting from the Internet and the phone system should be able to enjoy write (that is, command) access to such systems. This standard can be subject to external testing by having authorized and well-monitored red teams attempt to do just that. If they get in, the company they penetrated has work to do.

Variations on the test depend on which threat merits attention. If one fears rogue insiders, then such a standard is inadequate, but eliminating all vulnerabilities from SCADA and other machine control systems will be a long, painful, and likely incomplete process. If one fears hackers who do not care *when* the target is disrupted, then, as argued, complete air-gapping may be necessary (alternatively, data can be allowed to leave the system as long as nothing is allowed to enter it). If one fears only hackers who themselves need to exercise real-time command and control over their target (so as to disrupt it when they want to), then the air gap can be penetrated intermittently (for example, for software updates) without great compromise.

Although such mandates require enabling legislation, the congressional fate of less strict mandate proposals leaves few grounds for optimism. However, there is within existing legislation a mechanism that could be used to test the notion: Chemical Facility Anti-Terrorism Standards. Broadening the terrorist threat to include cyberattacks (such as the feeding of damaging instructions to potentially dangerous machinery as happened in Bhopal) may provide a useful test bed for this approach.

PANACEAS

The following are not bad ideas, but they are ideas that are too easy to see as solutions for the cybersecurity problem, when far more modest expectations are called for.

Standards

Executive Order 13636 calls for cybersecurity standards and suggests that companies who manage the nation's critical infrastructure adhere to them (many Democrats would do more than suggest). This has problems.

First, critical infrastructure tends to be defined too broadly. If the goal is to prevent a September 11 in cyberspace, then it is disruption (rather than espionage or corruption) that matters. That being so, one must figure out which processes are critical and cannot be disrupted for a period measured in days (or however long it takes to restore most services), and, conversely, what can withstand such a disruption without much effect. The civilian federal government is routinely considered critical, but well over 90 percent of it hardly functions in the 110 hours starting the Wednesday afternoon before Thanksgiving. By contrast, a four-day closure of convenience and grocery stores (rarely considered on anyone's list of critical facilities) would have far more serious consequences. A similarly long power outage (or gas outage in the winter) would be very disruptive, perhaps even fatal. Disruptions of some obscure back-office functions that are nowhere near that list could bring important computer services to a halt. DHS had originally defined eighteen sectors as critical, but they are sectors that are important vis-à-vis terrorists with exploding bombs, not hackers with logic bombs. One of the eighteen, for instance, consisted of iconic national monuments. A more recent list of sixteen sectors had no national monuments, but it is still not oriented toward cyberattacks.[36] Most recently, in response to a 2013 executive order, DHS identified "61 entities in five critical infrastructure sectors where a cybersecurity incident could reasonably result in catastrophic regional or national effects on public health or safety, economic security, or national security."[37]

Second, standards may be overrated. There is a broad consensus on which processes are correlated with good computer hygiene: for example, hard user authentication, rapid patch management, diligent network monitoring, and complete and accessible backups. Unfortunately, the list of good practices is long, and the effort required to audit that these processes are in place can be very intensive.[38] Some firms may bitterly oppose external auditing; companies are very tight-lipped about their own security measures for obvious reasons. If the point is to grade organizations, then the need-to-have and the nice-to-have measures have to be differentiated, and these measures are meaningful only after one understands the nature of the particular businesses and the types of risks they face—which vary widely from one to another. Specifying good hygiene sounds simple, but defining and auditing for good hygiene are anything but. That noted, funding (or subsidizing) the rating of security products or even testing such products themselves may be a sound use of taxpayer dollars; in mid-2015, Underwriters Laboratory and Peiter Zatko (also known as Mudge) took up the challenge.[39]

Third, the correlation between a good security process and a good security outcome is rough, at best. It is a bit like asking whether a bridge will bear traffic by looking at the education and training credentials of the bridge-builders; more education cannot hurt, but how much does it really help? Measurable criteria for cybersecurity would be more telling but have proven elusive. Furthermore, even if following standards was correlated with better cybersecurity, so is just spending more money on cybersecurity. Finally, the knowledge of standards in and of itself may be helpful. Consider A, B, and C, all of whom spend equally on cybersecurity: A is ignorant of the rationale for International Organization for Standardization (ISO) 27001's controls; B is knowledgeable about them but decides for itself whether to pick and choose; and C is knowledgeable about them and consciously conforms to them. Even if C enjoys more cybersecurity than A, does it necessarily enjoy more cybersecurity than B? If not, then the value of standards lies in what they teach, not what they compel. The current search for cybersecurity is messy but vibrant. The last thing that public policy should do is abandon it for an emphasis on the degree of conformance to an ever-lengthening set of requirements. A large percentage of the federal government's efforts to promote cybersecurity have been diverted to checking off Federal Information Security Management Act requirements. More research is badly needed in how to write useful standards.

Insurance

Will insurance markets persuade organizations to take cybersecurity seriously? Insurance transfers both the obligations and costs of cybersecurity from infrastructure owners to insurers; the latter acquire the onus of determining whether the insured have adopted, if not secure systems, at least systems that have been secured using good processes for doing so. The cyber-insurance market is growing, but it is still small.[40] It features hefty premiums, high deductibles, and low maximum payouts. Insurers may not be entirely to blame. Assessing the risk from cyberattacks is very difficult; because insurers are not in the business to lose money, they hedge their bets very carefully. Third-party damage claims from cyberattacks have few precedents to make estimates from. The courts have yet to provide much guidance on which expenses can and cannot legitimately be recovered from hacked organizations. Furthermore, even if the cost of a really serious cyberattack can be catastrophic, none has yet occurred, and thus assigning odds to such an event is a total guess. Insurers are much more comfortable dealing with weather events, whose occurrence might be estimated based the more common less-than-catastrophic events.

Alas, the government may be moving in the wrong direction by promising to indemnify infrastructure providers for their failures if they follow rules and fill out their paperwork. There may already be some indemnification for major cyberattacks to the extent they are likened to acts of war. It would encourage cybersecurity more if the laws provided that any third party that suffered damage because a systems owner failed to secure its infrastructure would be made whole by such owners.

Preempting Attacking Computers

The urge to strike back at an attacking server is powerful and hard to resist (it gives CYBER-COM a role to play in protecting the U.S. infrastructure).[41] Although abjuring all active defense options may be a poor idea, exercising such an option would be nearly useless against a subtle and determined adversary (even as the less subtle and determined ones can be thwarted using good defenses).[42] Putting major resources against it may be both wasteful and problematic (particularly if mistakes were made in an innocent party's network).

It is hard to deny the satisfaction of stopping an attack by stopping the attacking machine. Active defenses appear attractive when they can quickly put the attacking computer (temporarily) out of business over the course of the attack. One ploy used was to throw a rapid series of windows onto the attacking machine, thereby rendering it useless, but that particular incident entailed technology of the late 1990s. It is also relatively easy for attackers to build mechanisms that filter out everything except what they expect to see coming back—which would filter out the commands that tie computers into knots.

Indeed, many of the things that one might do following the discovery of a particular attack method make more sense when applied to the defense than when applied to the offense. For instance, if one discovers that a particular website has been corrupted in ways that infect everyone who visits it (also known as a "watering hole"), one can wipe out the server that has been corrupted, but if the server's owner is just feckless rather than complicit, a certain difficult explanation may be in order. However, there are other responses. One is to ask the server's owner to remove the malign code. Another is to block access to that particular website while its content is cleaned up. A third is to determine what vulnerability the malware is designed to exploit and patch it (or install preexisting patches). If certain computers have already been infected, then knocking out the server does nothing about them; the proper defensive measure starts with finding out who has been infected and then isolating them (or limiting their access) until they are cleaned.

It is possible to get some relief from an annoying DDOS attack through a counterattack, but it takes weeks and months rather than minutes. But some types of attacks, notably those involving bots, do not necessarily have a single point of origin—or even a single point of command and control.[43] Botnets cannot be quickly destroyed by a cyberattack without taking the risk of disrupting a lot of innocent computers in the process (for instance, if the botnet is using normal traffic in abnormal amounts, any normal user that goes to the attacked site may be seen as part of a botnet attack). Given enough time, the ranks of the botnet can be thinned by intensive discovery and reporting. If the botnet server can be penetrated and the commands reverse-engineered, someone could essentially tell the bots to turn themselves off and destroy the modules that allowed them to be commanded.[44] But a clever botnet commander could prevent them from listening to anyone else pretending to be the master controller (for example, by digitally signing commands).

If the attack is coming from a big server with a lot of bandwidth—rare but not impossible these days—then disabling the server should stop the attack, but so would blocking any communications from that server—something that, with traditional Internet protocol addressing, can be easily determined.

Cleaning Up the Ecology (to Eliminate Botnets)

Are botnets a problem the government should try to solve? Under current circumstances, cleaning up the perhaps hundreds of millions of infected clients is hard to justify when the cost of botnets to the U.S. economy is limited (DDOS attacks have been used to suppress free speech, but such a problem can be inexpensively addressed by rehosting beleaguered sites on capacious networks).

Countries, acting alone, may be similarly uninterested in reducing the bot problem because no one country, not even the United States, accounts for the majority of all bots. Anything done at the consumer level (for example, mandating that antivirus software be run) multiplied by billions of computers gets expensive fast.

Should ISPs accept the responsibility to block bots? Should their governments indemnify them against angry customers if they do so? The larger ISPs often have a fair idea of which customers own bots based on the pattern of their outgoing traffic. They could demand that such clients be isolated from the Internet (or at least have their outgoing bandwidth throttled) until they clean themselves up (with or without ISP help). But should an ISP be able to cut a user off if the user has merely failed to keep his machine up to date with patches and anti-malware; should the ISP provide the necessary software to do this? Would the U.S. government indemnify ISPs from being sued by angry users (or, more prosaically, be forced to spend the millions to field thousands or millions of angry phone calls)? Australia has asked the ISPs to filter out bots, but, as an island, Australia is used to exercising strong border controls.[45] More troubling, if customers can be denied service for being infected, would doing so put ISPs under pressure to go further and threaten the service of customers who, say, have bootleg MP3s on their system, spread controversial material, or even fail to host software that prevents certain sites from being accessed?

If there is no cost-effective way to suppress bots and DDOS attacks, then imposing such a requirement on other countries is hardly the counsel of wisdom. Yet because there are no guarantees that bots might not become far costlier in years hence, what makes no sense today may make sense tomorrow.

Dot-Secure

Circa 2010, some security experts started pondering the notion of a "dot-secure" network, one that would serve only those organizations whose cyber security was important. This idea was discarded as a false hope largely because the odds of preventing all breaches in it were close to zero, and once a machine within the dot-secure network was compromised, other networks would be no more protected from subsequent infection than they would be from an infection from outside the dot-secure network.[46] Worse would occur if membership in the dot-secure network bred complacency about cybersecurity.

However, a dot-secure network, membership in which was prudently restricted, could form a defense against DDOS attacks that interfered with communications between members. Although a DDOS attack could originate from within or cross over into the dot-secure network, quelling the effects of such an attack on communications internal to the dot-secure network would be far simpler than it is today. It would, though, do little to prevent DDOS attacks from blocking access by, say, customers from outside the dot-secure network (for example, of the sort that connected banks to end-customers).

Whether establishing a dot-secure network (and many organization-to-organization communications links are already separate from the Internet) is worth the cost is another issue. Not surprisingly, it depends on the likelihood of future DDOS attacks that might affect interorganizational communications.

BAD IDEAS

Many of the bad ideas are those that tend to focus on cybersecurity as something bad guys do to the United States against which a national defense of some sort is recommended.

Converting Cybersecurity into a National Security Problem

On September 11, 2001, terrorists attacked the United States. Three thousand people died, and the physical damage was upward of $200 billion. On September 12, the country responded. The United States strengthened its homeland security—and went to war twice. The United States lost nearly seven thousand people in combat. Between ten thousand and twenty thousand were seriously injured. Total additional expenditures may well reach $2 trillion by the time both wars are wrapped up. Even though a future attack on the United States may be damaging, the cycle of response and counter-response may be far more consequential. This was so in the physical world. Why would cyberspace be immune to similar overreaction?

The presumption that a widespread cyberattack is a national security matter has consequences. It puts the weight of the policy machinery on identifying and punishing attackers. It takes the pressure off those whose failure to secure their own systems created the problem in the first place. Both the Deepwater Horizon oil leak of 2010 and the Fukushima nuclear power plant disaster of 2011 demonstrated that governments have a very limited ability to fix problems in someone else's system. Unfortunately, it also demonstrated the existence of unreasonable expectations that the government do something (even Malia Obama expected as much when she reportedly asked her father, the president, "Did you plug the hole yet, Daddy?" in response to news items about the BP spill[47]).

If making strategy requires maximizing options, there is something to be said for not owning a crisis that you do not have to. If, in fact, U.S. interests lie in quelling an international crisis precipitated by a domestic event, then perhaps the last thing the leadership needs is to be pressed to greater crisis by hungry media and expedient politicians. To be sure, there will be circumstances under which such sentiment allows leaders to plead that they must have concessions from the attacker lest they be overwhelmed (a good-cop, bad-cop logic). But there is risk in generating such sentiment only to find others exploiting that sentiment to prevent reaching a later modus vivendi.

So, just as cyberwar is really not about cyberspace, the metaphors of war may not be the best approach to cyberwar. Granted, the techniques of cyberattack can be used in conflict. Granted, too: no hackers, no hacks. If everyone who thought to spy on, disrupt, or corrupt an information system was absolutely inhibited by the fear of punishment, the many insecurities of our systems would not matter nearly as much as they do.

But these tenets do not prove that such insecurities are best seen through the lens of war, because with war comes baggage. Thinking in terms of combat perforce focuses on the adversaries: who they are, what they want, what they are trying to do, how they can be detected, how their efforts can be stopped, how they can be deterred from starting, and how they can be put away if they go ahead anyway. One could, instead, think of the rain of cyberattacks like rain itself, something that cannot be stopped by any conceivable means but the damage from which can be reduced. Coming inside when it rains, covering what may be damaged if it gets wet, fixing holes, as well as building soundly and away from floodplains all can convert what could be a disaster into something merely annoying.

Wars have to be won. The test of a war is who is left standing when it ends. It is not properly subject to tests of cost and benefit. There is, we are taught, no substitute for victory.

Rain has to be endured. It is foolish not to spend a dollar to prevent ten dollars' worth of damage (over the lifetime of such an investment); it is equally foolish to spend ten dollars to save a dollar's worth of damage. The trick, therefore, is to find the lowest-cost approach to dealing with what cannot be entirely avoided.

Somewhere on the spectrum between war and rain lies the best approach to cybersecurity. No one who advocates cybersecurity would have hackers act with impunity. No one who would go after hackers would recommend against greater cybersecurity.

This has a key caveat. To the extent that hackers penetrate systems for the information they contain (rather than cyberwar), the value of cybersecurity (one's reputation, importantly, aside) has everything to do with how they would use the information—which means getting inside their head. Such an orientation is clearly not rain, but it is not war either (since their interests may not necessarily be to your disadvantage).

In theory, the U.S. government's approach puts DHS in charge, tagging it with all the responsibility, few of the resources, and none of the power to do very much. DHS can educate, cajole, and coordinate, but little more. In practice, far more resources go toward DoD, the intelligence community, and law enforcement. They have deep wells of technical expertise, in part because the NSA (and hence, it hopes, CYBERCOM), CIA, and FBI are considered elite institutions. Their work is respected. They *do* things. But they only do certain things because they are organizations built to do certain things, which creates their perspective on the world, which guides them to view problems in terms of the strengths they bring. U.S. defense officials also argue that should some digital September 11 occur, they will have to answer why DoD stood aside and did nothing to protect the country in this domain.[48] But that logic is not good enough to assign them the responsibility to protect the civilian economy.

Convert Cybersecurity into a Counterterrorism Problem

To date, cyberterrorism has been a nearly empty set, proof that just because something has a name does not mean that it exists (see "unicorn"). It is difficult for anything confined to cyberspace to cause terror to humans because it is hard to cause visceral fear without threatening someone's viscera. Today's terrorists also have little interest in or capability for causing mischief in cyberspace.[49] However, two attacks in 2014 had some resemblance to cyberterrorism in that they sought to use pain to squelch the expression of ideas: the Las Vegas Sands attack and the Sony attack. These attacks also smell like terrorism in other ways. The two were considered soft targets since neither was part of the U.S. critical infrastructure; thus they were considered of little interest to hackers, particularly malicious hackers, and thus were only indifferently protected. In neither case did the hackers gain anything tangible.

The U.S. reaction to the Sony attack echoed its response to terrorism. The matter was treated as a law enforcement issue, albeit at the strategic level. Shortly thereafter, the U.S. government formed the Cyber Threat Intelligence Integration Center, which was directly modeled after the National Counterterrorism Center and announced by the assistant to the president for homeland security and *counterterrorism* (emphasis added).[50] It was established, ostensibly, to coordinate and reconcile the varied threat assessments made by different U.S. government agencies. Several months later, DHS started certifying companies "under the SAFETY [Support Antiterrorism by Fostering Effective Technologies] Act, providing their customers protection from lawsuits or claims alleging that the products failed to prevent an act of cyberterrorism."[51] Dan Blumenthal of the American Enterprise Institute has suggested that Congress create a cyberattack exception to the Foreign Sovereign Immunities Act as was done with terrorism so that foreign countries can face lawsuits in civil court from the victims of cyberattack or cyberespionage.[52]

The logic that converts the cyberattack problem into a terrorism problem can be insidious. First, cyberspace is deemed ungoverned territory—just as certain failed states are ungoverned. Second, direct action against hackers is required. Third, protecting sources and methods forbids the display of proof before going after bad guys. Indeed, the use of unmanned aerial vehicles (UAVs) to go after terrorists raises questions that could just as easily be used in thinking about going after hackers guilty of cyberterrorism.[53] Of course, a major difference is that regardless of how ungoverned one thinks cyberspace is, once the problem of defending ourselves from the depredations of cyberspace is converted into operations against hackers, one is back to the real world where many hackers have serious governments to protect them.

Yet cyberattacks are just not terrorist attacks. Countering them requires very different forms of intelligence, not least because cyberattacks, unlike terrorist attacks, are enabled by the architecture and implementation of the attacked systems. A great deal of counterterrorism consists of identifying terrorists and killing them. Is the U.S. government prepared to do this to hackers, particularly those working for and in other countries? Fortunately, the current tendency is to pursue hackers with lawyers rather than UAVs—so far.

An Internet Kill Switch

Should the president be allowed to isolate all or much of the U.S. Internet from the rest of the world—or even from large parts of itself (as a clause in the original Collins-Lieberman cybersecurity legislation might have permitted)? In theory, this would protect parts of the Internet from contagions arising in other parts of the Internet (particularly overseas). In practice, the problem of rapidly proliferating malware has been muted since Windows XP Service Pack 2 was released in August 2004.

A kill switch may become pernicious, particularly if decisions to sever the "healthy" bits are automated so as to outrun malware spreading at (as popularly labeled) the speed of light. An automated process would create a very tempting target for hackers who want to shut down the U.S. portion of the Internet and cannot do so by their own methods (because the Internet is large and highly variegated) but hope to trigger the government's automated mechanism (which would override the Internet's size and heterogeneity) to do so. Even if the process is not automated, its existence and the ease by which it can be summoned may tempt some future president to squelch the distribution of troublesome content (for example, classified material, incitements to terrorism) by invoking a mechanism originally designed solely to protect the health of the Internet. The lesson that such a maneuver backfired in Egypt may not necessarily remain learned forever.[54]

Hard Authentication for Internet Users

Stewart Baker, the NSA's former chief counsel, used to argue (circa 2010) that because the Internet cannot afford the luxury of anonymity, all online activity must be associated with a real person. The architecture of the Internet, which allows, even encourages, anonymity, was born flawed because it trusted users (including the untrustworthy). If people had to register themselves to use the Internet, the odds of detection, and hence punishment, would supposedly be sufficiently inhibitory to make the Internet safe once again.

But would it? Like many such ideas, it is expensive to implement and easy to evade. It also makes censorship and surveillance that much easier. To begin with, a hard requirement would be something at least as intrusive and expensive as a national identification (ID) card. Not only is this idea considered undesirable by a majority of Americans, but even weaker requirements to standardize state driver's licenses (the Real ID Act of 2005) were bitterly attacked as an unfunded mandate (not to mention a threat to liberty); their implementation was constantly delayed. Worse, any ID that has to be checked by a machine is easier to spoof than one checked by a human. Credentials can always be stolen; it happens constantly in the physical world. Furthermore, such a requirement would have to be enforced *in every country* to guarantee that every attack could be traced (and every country would have to cooperate with the United States and eliminate corruption in the process) and on every Internet-accessing device (notably cell phones, but in the future, intelligent devices).

Finally, such a proposal assumes that anything coming from a user's machine (or a user's account on a machine) can be legally ascribed to the user beyond a reasonable shadow of doubt—even as there are a hundred million computers that have already been converted into bots, obeying commands some hacker sent them regardless of what the user wants or even knows.[55] *If* the means were available to prevent computers from being zombies, such a scheme would work—but if cybersecurity *were* that good, hard authentication would no longer be needed because the cybersecurity problem would have shrunk beyond recognition. Finally, eliminating user anonymity can chill free speech on the Internet, as well as facilitate surveillance (not only from the U.S. government but also from hackers who can more easily associate purloined Internet traffic with real users).

Encouraging Hack-Backs

Should the law allow victims to hack attackers' systems back? There are constant rumors that organizations have done as much, but no one organization has outright confessed to doing so.[56]

The term "hack-back," like its cousin "active defense," is subject to several interpretations. It may connote letting criminals steal a file crafted so that, when opened, it creates a beacon in the thief's network that allows the owner of the information to trace where it went.[57] It may also include erasing files on intermediate servers before they have been transferred to the thief (although exactly how one determines that such files have moved no further is unclear).

Alternatively, an active defense may be a destructive attack that promotes the message that targeting a particular organization is unwise; in effect, the hacker-back wants to make a reputation as someone not to be trifled with. Such activity could be motivated by spite; think also of the many drivers who vow to teach road jerks a lesson even though their profiting from such education is unlikely. Otherwise, such a message has to spread to the universe of potential hackers to do much good. The hacker-back therefore must be able to surmount the defenses that hackers themselves put up, must assume that tales of their retaliation reach a wider population, and must hope that the hackers do not ape Anonymous when it retaliated against H. B. Gary for going after it.[58] All this is a tall order.

Of late, hack-backs have been mulled against public or quasi-public servers whose users have been compromised so that hackers may exploit the copious bandwidth provided to such users via the server itself. Perhaps needless to add, hacking back against such servers would disrupt the access (perhaps livelihoods) of users whose systems have not been compromised. In the absence of norms and regulations that would have server owners cut off infected accounts, the motive of those suffering DDOS attacks is understandable but may not rise to the level of permissible.

In general, a hack-back recommendation can only be the counsel of desperation, as it shows the world that the United States (which essentially invented cyberspace) has abandoned establishing and enforcing any rule of law in that medium. It also gives hackers yet one more excuse if they get caught: he hit me first. A country that condones hacking back may also get into trouble if the hackers-back are caught and the target assumes that their country was just using private hackers as proxies.

Many of the supposedly innocent (and putatively legal) tricks for hacking back are brittle; they cease being effective once they fall into common use. Consider scattering within one's network interesting-looking but corrupted PDF documents. When a hacker steals one, takes it home, and opens it up to read its contents, the document creates an opening in the hacker's computer that allows the original owner of the document to compromise the hacker's computer.[59] Hackers who anticipate as much can easily avoid this trap either by reading such documents offline or filtering out troublesome meta-content in PDFs before reading them.

Automating hack-backs would mean more trouble. Attackers who anticipate as much can make their attacks appear to come from somewhere else, such as orphanages, mosques, opposition media, or trusted allies.

ON USING EXTRAORDINARY INCENTIVES
TO JUICE THE CYBERSECURITY WORKFORCE

Organizations constantly complain that good cybersecurity professionals are hard to find and expensive to employ. The real supply crunch is for great cybersecurity professionals, variously estimated as the most talented 2 to 5 percent of the total cybersecurity professional workforce.[60] The latter are good at finding vulnerabilities in software for both fixing and exploiting them. Others excel at finding out whether and how a system has been attacked (notably by advanced persistent threats). If great hackers are born rather than made (some of the most ingenious exploits have been developed by those "naturals" well under eighteen years old), then policies to increase training may be secondary.[61] What matters is discovering promising individuals, encouraging them to make cybersecurity a life's work, providing them with educational opportunities, and inculcating them with requisite ethical norms. That noted, the lone anti-social genius pursuing his wizardry may not describe how elite hacker *teams* function.[62]

Although many started their careers with the NSA (or, for example, Israel's Unit 8200), by the time their skills mature they can command salaries well in excess of what the government can pay. Correspondingly, there have been increasing calls for the U.S. government to accelerate their production (even the number of computer science degrees still lag its late 1990s peak).[63] Several approaches for increasing supply may be offered, but there are reasons for tempering enthusiasm about each of them.

Early Recruitment

If the requirement for upper-tier cybersecurity professionals were important enough, policymakers might think about channeling people with a talent for cybersecurity into that profession irrespective of their other talents. Israel, with its heightened awareness of national security and its universal draft, does that—and has created a substantial cybersecurity export industry as a byproduct.[64]

An early start is essential. Nearly four in five (78 percent) U.S. science, technology, engineering, and mathematics (STEM) college students said they decided to study STEM by the time they graduated high school. One in five (21 percent) decided in middle school or earlier.[65] The growing importance of hacker competitions (hack-a-thons) coupled with the media emphasis on cybersecurity suggests that early encouragement is taking place.[66] Opinion is mixed on hack-a-thons. Some find them useful; others think that performance under artificial conditions is a poor proxy for what employers really need.[67]

A full-court press throughout the country to find upper-tier cybersecurity specialists could increase the eligible labor force by a full order of magnitude—a proposition underlined by the ability of local cybersecurity establishments to meet many of their requirements locally. In one Center of Academic Excellence (which specializes in protecting machine controls from hostile manipulation), a third of the students came from a catchment area that held only 1 percent of the nation's population. NSA talent searches focus on high schools in the Baltimore and Washington, D.C., metropolitan areas, and recruiters are reasonably satisfied with what they get.

Should an accelerated junior college curriculum be established to graduate specialized cybersecurity professionals?[68] The new Cyber Student Initiative, which is part of the DHS Secretary Honors Program, announced in late 2012 that it would engage community college students, including veterans, to work in DHS on cybersecurity.[69] However, it is not clear that people brainy enough to become good cybersecurity professionals would be satisfied tracking themselves into an educational path that ends short of a bachelor's degree. Emphasizing cybersecurity training vis-à-vis education would make sense if the requirement were urgent and temporary (as would be in wartime if there is no tomorrow if the war is lost), or if the cybersecurity field is likely to present the exact same problems tomorrow as it does today. Neither seems to be true. The transition between lone-wolf hacker circa 1999 to today's hacker as tool-maker suggests that the needed skill set is still evolving.

Importing Foreigners

What about letting foreign students convert into immigrants via the H-1B program, through the L-1 visa for intracompany transfers, TN visas for Canadian or Mexican citizens, or by extension of the Optional Practical Training program? Cautions abound for those who think this is the fix.

First, a great deal of cybersecurity work, particularly at the high end, is already internationalized. Examples include writing computer code or finding bugs in it (companies such as Microsoft and Google have branch offices around the globe). Indeed, any problem that does not require hands-on interaction can already be shipped overseas.

Second, security clearances are almost always required for government and related contractor employment. Foreigners are not citizens and cannot, therefore, get security clearances before six years have elapsed—and this assumes the individual applies for citizenship as soon as possible, gets it immediately, and can turn immediately to getting a security clearance. Before that point, a surge of foreign-born cybersecurity professionals into this country would depress the supply of native-born cybersecurity professionals—but not directly address the government's problem. In the short run, suppressing the non-cleared compensation levels will shift demand from uncleared to cleared positions (thereby helping employers of cleared professionals). Yet it is unclear what the cross-elasticity between these two submarkets is (gaining security clearance takes at least a year for citizens, and cybersecurity positions may be considered particularly sensitive and hence take longer to clear someone for, particularly in today's post-Snowden environment). In the longer run, the short-term expedient of using immigrants will suppress the market's tendency to equilibrate supply and demand by drawing more U.S. citizens into the profession.

Outsourcing

This will not solve all problems, either. First, many military tasks and some civilian tasks cannot be performed by private contractors. Some of the reasons have to do with being deployed in war zones or on warfare platforms such as ships; other constraints are associated with the chain of military command. Second, it takes federal employees to oversee the contracting process: for example, establishing requirements, evaluating proposals, selecting contractors and overseeing them. If federal employees lack the skills to write such specifications (and particularly if the contractors understand as much), they are likely to be spending federal money inefficiently. Third, outsourcing creates a vicious circle. If the "cool jobs" are given to contractors, then extant and even prospective federal employees will have that much less motivation to stay or join the federal government to work on cybersecurity or cyberwar problems.[70] This then reduces the quality of the federal labor pool, which then reinforces the initial tendency to assign the "cool jobs" to contractors.

Differentiate Job Categories More Precisely

Many believe that if cybersecurity fields were more narrowly defined—DHS's National Initiative for Cybersecurity Excellence program divides the field into thirty subcategories—they could concentrate their attentions (salary offerings, training, and so forth) on the harder-to-fill specialties. Such subdivisions assume that job categories are not fungible: someone trained in one cybersecurity field such as information assurance cannot be useful in another such as forensics. But how much more precision is needed? There really is no set of unique predispositions among the career-choosers (or career-switchers) that suggests that placing people precisely into subcategories beats letting people sort themselves out. There is little evidence to suggest that all the best hackers major in computer science, either. Deep curiosity and a drive to understand how things work have been found to be better predictors of top-notch cybersecurity capabilities.

Using National Guard and Reserve Units

Joining the National Guard or Reserve allows people to serve the national defense in emergencies while keeping their civilian jobs. Cybersecurity professionals in such units would be current both with military perspectives on cybersecurity (thanks to their reserve training) and with trends within the broader commercial sector. Proponents speak highly of the National Guard's 262nd Network Warfare Squadron, whose ranks include employees from Microsoft and nearby high-technology companies.[71] But might this address the military's need for cybersecurity at the expense of the rest of the economy's needs in a crisis?[72] Also, to the extent that defending a system requires knowledge of the systems being defended, such units still have to climb an onsite learning curve once deployed in order to offer useful contributions. The infiltration that allows a cyberattack to take place in a crisis perforce occurs before any such crisis begins; by the time the Guard and Reserve show up, it may be too late to secure networks from such malware.

CAN GOVERNMENTS COPE WITH SURPRISE?

The September 11 hijackers all had to go through airport security, and every last one of them passed. The prevailing airline security model was designed to look for guns and unattended luggage (or third-party luggage) because it was based on how the system failed against prior attackers, not suicidal hijackers. After September 11, the amount of resources going into airline security rose severalfold. Yet in a world where the Twin Towers had fallen to a more successful version of the truck bomb attack that took place on February 26, 1993, today's homeland security dollars would likely have been spent very differently. When Richard Reid tried to destroy an airplane with shoe-borne explosives, TSA started to require that shoes be removed so that they could go through X-rays. After the underwear bomber failed, TSA ramped up its use of body-scanning.

The tendency of governments to focus more on ensuring that past disasters do not recur than ensuring that novel disasters do not take place can be ascribed to many reasons. Some are good. Among the many types of disasters that *could* take place, there is at least an existence proof for those that *have* taken place. Some are self-centered. Government officials are much more likely to be blamed if they permitted something they should have foreseen than if they permitted something unforeseen to take place. In the latter case, they could plead: who could have known? In the former case, there is no easy out. This is human nature: it applies to military acquisition (military specifications reflect everything that has gone wrong in the past with similar programs) and economic management (consider how few in the Bush administration took responsibility for the financial collapse of 2008).

It is not clear that this logic works the same way in the private sector, not because the business people are wiser, but because people in business are more likely to be judged by outcomes (notably profit and loss) while politicians are judged by inexpert opinion (for example, voters) on the basis of discrete choices (few of which are publicly acknowledged). The who-could-have-known argument thus carries less weight. Conversely, the premium on being able to anticipate the unknown so as to thereby profit or avoid loss is higher.

Not all cyberattacks are surprises; many victims simply were not paying attention to either past events or consequent fixes (notably, software patches). But those that go after the more sophisticated targets—and by extension, those that have the greatest shock if they succeed—have to have a large element of surprise. The history of cyberspace is littered with examples of "I did not know they could do that."

Anticipating surprises is difficult by its nature. But the difficulty of that task has to be harder if nonpublic enterprises are being constantly monitored, much less regulated, by public officials who would more fear being shocked by something that should have been anticipated (perhaps because it happened before) than fear being shocked by surprise. In cybersecurity, there is a premium for getting ahead of the attacker. It would be a shame to see that premium washed away by perverse incentives arising from public oversight.

PART II   POLICIES

CHAPTER 7

What Should Be Secret

In a book about cyberwar, there are several reasons for discussing what should be secret—that is, classified if the secrets belong to the government, or private if the secrets are personal. First, because a purpose of cyberespionage is to steal secrets and the purpose of cybersecurity is to keep secrets from being stolen, some consideration of what ought to be secret helps in understanding the value of computer security. Second, operational security (OPSEC), a component of which is keeping secrets, is part of the broader rubric of command and control warfare (as it was known circa 1992) of which cyberwar is also a subject; so is military deception, a fact whose significance will be explained. Third, the institutions of cyberespionage and cyberwar are often the same.

So, what *should* be secret?[1] To set the table for this question, we observe that although the loss from information going into the wrong hands constitutes the core reason for secrecy, it is not the only reason. Some information may merit protection because the originator (or distributor) of such information was so promised; because people may not be forthcoming in policy deliberations if they think their words will leak; and because how we know this information is sensitive and thus its being leaked can allow others to infer sources and methods and thereby frustrate their continued employment (and put lives at risk in some cases). With privacy, the psychological discomfort arising from having one's secrets leaked (being naked, as it were) cannot be totally ignored; neither can the fact that people find it "creepy" when their privacy is invaded.

That noted, we now focus on the value of secrets: first of government secrets (classification), then of personal secrets (privacy). The cost of maintaining classification or privacy regimes, though important, is not covered.

THE CALCULUS

The value of making a datum secret arises from the harm that its possession by others can do to your interests. For example, say someone knows something about you and then makes a decision that harms you (such as calling in a loan) that would otherwise have been made in your favor. Alternatively, someone may fail to make a decision that helps you (such as giving you an award) that would have been made without the information. Such unhelpful decisions in turn are made more likely because the adversary knows something that it did not know—or, again, speaking in probabilities, knows something with greater or lesser certainty than it knew before. The possession of (or confidence in) such knowledge must have been influenced by the information that has come into its possession from you. Finally, the information must have become available because of a failure to secure information sufficiently—and not classifying it or not classifying it enough is a major factor.

Rendering the formula forward, rather than working backward, leads to this: to be classified, material should meet four criteria. First, the failure to classify has to result in more information going to potential rivals or adversaries. Second, this information must affect the knowledge that such adversaries have. This change in knowledge ought to be nontrivial and helpful (in the sense that the additional information moves them closer to rather than further from the truth). Third, this change in knowledge must be of the sort that plausibly affects decisions that the adversary makes or might make. This effect, again, ought to be nontrivial and helpful (to the adversary). Fourth, the decisions that the adversary would make should harm national security (it could also harm other national interests, but the national security rationale is the only one that can justify classification as per U.S. law).

If the failure to classify a piece of information means that an adversary is more likely to have it, *and* if having it changes what the adversary knows, *and* if the change in knowledge alters what it does (or the odds of doing so), *and* if what it does harms the United States, then there is a rationale for classifying it. Whether the benefit exceeds the costs of a classification regime also has to be answered (but not here).[2]

Conversely, if the classification does not change what the adversary learns, *or* what the adversary learns does not change what it knows, *or* what the adversary knows does not affect what it does, *or* if what it does is not detrimental to U.S. interests, then there is *no plausible case* for classifying such information.

It is not enough that each of these criteria can be passed by some adversary; there must be at least one adversary for which all four criteria matter. To illustrate this distinction, consider the following hypothetical. A datum shows a vulnerability in a U.S. base that will permit it to be successfully attacked by mortars. We assert that classification would reduce the likelihood of the datum's distribution outside DoD; the datum reveals enough to permit a particular type of attack; the revelation of such a vulnerability would make such an attack more likely; and being attacked would harm the United States. So, should the datum be classified? Not necessarily. Posit two (and only two) adversaries: a terrorist group and a large state. Each has different capabilities and motives. First, classification makes it very difficult for even the large state to access such information—but it would make little difference to the terrorist group, because the latter lacks the ability to access *unclassified* information held by DoD in its protected but unclassified systems. Second, the large state has no interest in mortaring U.S. bases (for example, because it raises the risk of general warfare). Finally, the large state does not share information with the terrorist. Thus, the fourfold test for classification is not met when each of the adversaries is viewed individually. The terrorist cannot get the data even in their unclassified state. The large state would not use the data because it lacks any desire to exploit the vulnerability. And there is no leakage between the two information/decision chains. Neither path—via terrorist attack or via large state attack—passes all four criteria. Classification is thus unwarranted. Now, take each of these principles in turn.

DENYING AN ADVERSARY SOMETHING

The first principle is that classifying the data must actually result in adversaries having less information. Classifying information is similarly not justified if an adversary cannot get it in its protected but unclassified state (most small states and all known terrorist groups with the possible exception of Iran's proxy, Hezbollah). For DoD, the question is whether the data should be on the protected NIPRnet or only on the air-gapped classified SIPRnet. In either case, the information is less accessible than if on public websites. Moving the information from the NIPRnet to the SIPRnet would protect it better.

AFFECTING ADVERSARY KNOWLEDGE

Next, the leaked data would have to affect what the other side *knows*. There is little point in classifying data that an adversary already knows from other sources. Although exactly what they *do* know is hard for others to ascertain, they presumably have access to data that is freely available in soft or hard copy. To this, one can add broad assumptions about the information collection abilities of specified states or nonstate groups of concerns: for example, what their satellites or their tourists could see. The easier, the cheaper, and more risk-free it is to get such data, the weaker the argument for restricting their circulation.[3]

Might data be useful to the other side by increasing its confidence in what it already thinks it knows? Before the Navy SEAL team went into Abbottabad, Pakistan, in May 2011, President Barack Obama's team estimated, a priori, that there was a 60 percent certainty that Osama bin Laden was there. Perhaps no one among the president's advisers would have gone in if the certainty had been, say, 20 percent, and no one of them would have counseled against going in if the certainty had been 80 percent (in that bin Laden *was* there, the probability was, in retrospect, 100 percent). A piece of information that strengthens the confidence and moves the needle from too-much-doubt-to-proceed to confident-enough-to-proceed is therefore meaningful by this criterion. But not every piece of information will move people to the correct choice (for them). It may confirm a perception of a fact that is false: for example, a mostly honest person lies, but someone only sees the lie and so deems the person dishonest.

The chain between a datum and the information that goes into decisionmaking can often be long, with several interdependent steps. Consider a hypothetical Israeli intelligence agent in October 1973 who comes into knowledge that Russian sailors have been told to stay out of Cairo markets (a datum). An inference from that might be: Russian forces are leaving suddenly (information). If that war would put Russians at risk, their departure may mean that Egyptians are about to launch an offensive against Israel, and that Israel might have to react (knowledge to support a decision). Even if the intelligence is accurately read, it may not be credible and hence does *not* enter decisionmaking. The longer the chain of inference from datum to decision, the lower the odds that the new datum would affect much.

Finally, human nature almost always tends to reduce the correlation between data and knowledge. Decisionmakers may use new data to confirm their existing understandings and biases even when they should not. New data may be overvalued relative to old data or not otherwise interpreted objectively (a datum may be viewed as more credible than it should be because it is secret or because it was obtained from an official source). Or adding data may produce information overload that hurts all decisionmaking. Although whether or not such things *will* happen as a result of the release of a specific data source will likely be difficult to anticipate before the fact, that they *could* do so cannot be ignored when considering information security or classification decisions.[4] People have strong a priori notions of what is and is not plausible.[5]

AFFECTING ADVERSARY DECISIONMAKING

For the classification of information to be justified, it must be of the sort that could plausibly affect a decision to act. If getting such information has no serious effect on what the adversary *does,* how can stealing such data hurt its victim? If someone is already intent on doing something, then acquiring new—even clearly relevant—information may have no influence at all on what is done.

True, sometimes purloined information results in making no decision rather than trying to make a less well-informed one. Information may alter the terms of a decision by removing options:

for example, a choice between *A*, *B*, and *C* now becomes a simpler and less hazardous choice between *A* and *B*. Or the decision is the same but is made faster (and can be implemented faster) or cheaper (expenses to gather new data can be foregone). Information may also call an adversary's attention to a decision that needs to be made—for example, data on a new weapons system convince the other side to make decisions about countermeasures.

For new information to alter the choice, it must be significant enough to outweigh or at least influence other elements that are part of the consideration. Where new information serves to reduce uncertainty, how much that reduction will affect decisionmakers is an open question. Put another way, will being 90 percent confident of a particular fact about U.S. forces lead an opposing nation's military planners or operators to a different decision than if they are 80 percent confident of that fact?

Measuring the enthusiasm or desperation of foes for more knowledge about the United States may be quite misleading in evaluating the harm from their satisfaction. They might want the information for reassurance. The well-observed phenomenon of "confirmation bias" suggests that people seek and value information that confirms their view of the world and devalue information that does not. Uncertainty, doubt, and ambiguity are conditions that many find uncomfortable, and in their discomfort people seek evidence that will erase their doubts and thereby relieve anxiety. This urge is particularly intense *after* having committed to a decision. Again, the theory of cognitive dissonance suggests that commitments drive perception. So, intelligence may not necessarily be introduced into decisionmaking in a particularly rational way—thereby diminishing its value as well as the case for its restriction. That said, a particularly vivid piece of information sometimes does change minds. Pictures of Soviet missiles being erected in Cuba in late 1962 sufficed to convince skeptics—even those who were inclined to believe that Moscow would not do something quite so provocative and stupid—that a very dangerous development had taken place. But how often is intelligence so clear-cut?

These three factors—the relationship between restrictions and leak of a datum, the relationship between the leak of a datum and the change in a decision's considerations, and the likelihood that changing a consideration changes a decision—can now be combined. To resume the Russo-Egyptian scenario, assume that the Egyptians face a decision between keeping their warning to the Russians close hold (only a hundred know) or very close hold (only ten know). They face the following parameters. The odds the information will leak are 40 percent if close hold but 20 percent if very close hold. Given the datum, the odds that Israel will infer that Soviet forces are leaving for a very long time would rise from 30 to 50 percent. Given that inference, the odds that Israel will conclude that Egypt is thinking of invading over the next month would rise from 5 to 20 percent. Finally, if Israel concludes that Egypt is thinking of invading, there is a 60 percent likelihood that it will reinforce the front against attack (the 40 percent odds that it does nothing may reflect the need to balance defenses against other foes, or the fear that its own mobilizing may induce Egypt to invade). Assume Israel's reinforcing the front costs Egypt the equivalent of $1 billion (the cost of obtaining just enough added equipment to offset Israel's greater readiness). Thus, the *value* of keeping the datum very close hold is 20 percent (the shift in the odds of leakage) times 20 percent (the shift in the inference that Soviet troops are leaving for a very long time) times 15 percent (the shift in the likelihood that Israel will conclude that Egypt is thinking of invading next month) times 60 percent (the odds that the imminence of an invasion leads Israel to reinforce the front) times $1 billion (the cost to Egypt if it does). This equals $3.6 million (a number that should then be compared against the cost of enforcing the very close hold and the inefficiencies that occur when one's own people operate with insufficient knowledge).

Lastly, foreign governments are not unitary actors. A datum may be sought not to improve a country's decisionmaking but to bolster the argument of one faction vis-à-vis its rivals. There is no a priori reason that the faction that wins the argument operates to the greater detriment of the United States.

ADVERSE TO US

The fourth principle is that the action made more likely by the leak of information harms U.S. national security. For example, foes might glean information of ongoing military actions, future military actions, current capabilities, and future capabilities and, with that information, decide to counter U.S. plans—and do so more effectively based on what they have newly learned.

Not every adversary decision harms U.S. interests. It typically does when two adversaries commit to fighting to the death. But some decisions made by adversaries, even if made on the basis of better information taken from us, may benefit them and cost us little. For example, confirmed adversaries may seek information from us to inform their diplomatic or military choices with respect to third countries. Even though gaining such information might make it easier for them to advance their interests, their resulting decisions may have a neutral or even positive effect on U.S. interests. Even the current conflict with the Islamic State of Iraq and the Levant (ISIL) does not have this character as decisionmakers on both sides have multiple goals and are devoting resources to multiple ends simultaneously (for example, neither they nor the United States want to extend Bashir Assad's reign in Syria).

In some cases, the decisions others make help some Americans and hurt others. To use a commercial example: if Chinese hackers, for instance, steal the secrets of a technology that improves their industrial firms' ability to cut their costs and reduces their emissions of greenhouse gasses, this would most likely be bad news for U.S. companies that compete with them or might otherwise have sold them such equipment. But it would advance global environmental goals that the United States favors.

The ability to steal information may allow foes to cut expenditures in other areas (for example, they would have less need to send out spies, allowing increases elsewhere in their intelligence budget). But savings are not always used to harm the United States, either; they may be used to increase civilian expenditures.

SOME IMPLICATIONS OF LOGICAL CLASSIFICATION RULES

The implications of this four-part rule can be illustrated by working out some examples.

Consider the logic of classifying news reports of leaks. Because the classified State Department cables in WikiLeaks remain classified even after exposure, the Air Force almost ruled that airmen who read such cables on the *New York Times* website would be reading classified information on unclassified computers—a security violation.[6] But would that have made sense? The whole purpose of not putting classified data on unclassified computers was to deny foes access to information they lacked, which was hardly the case with a newspaper article. The secondary reasoning was that finding such information on an *airman's* computer would make it seem more credible; this is why knowledgeable sources are enjoined from confirming rumors of sensitive information. But that assumes that the presence of such information on that computer provides any confirmation of its truth value at all. Incidentally, if adversaries believe that a piece of information is true precisely because it is classified, then one of the purposes of classification is to make such information believable so as to improve the credibility of any deception campaign that relies on the disclosure of classified information. Of course, try explaining that "we classify in order to make our leaks disproportionately credible" to your security manager.

To pose another question, assume someone with a security clearance has already communicated information to the world based on open sources. The speaker is then told that such information is classified. Should she stop talking? Remember that her saying that something was true does not necessarily mean that others listening to her believe that it *is* true. They may respect her, but remember that her words lack the government's imprimatur; therefore, they may deem the information probable but not proven. If people then notice that she stopped talking about the topic, they may infer that what she said was false and she preferred not speaking falsely, or, conversely, that what she said was true but classified and she preferred not revealing classified information. The more that adversaries lean toward the second view, the more likely they are to (correctly) raise their confidence in the truth of that information. But what if she stopped talking about one thing because she found other things more worthy of her attention? Conversely, unless adversaries had other ways of knowing she was read in to matters that she only speculated about, continuing to talk about the matter gives adversaries no new information. Ironically, *less* information is conveyed by her continuing to talk; the only saving grace from ceasing conversation is the possibility that adversaries may be deceived.

However, matters are not so simple if classification is understood as a tool of information warfare whose point is not just to refrain from helping adversary decisionmaking but to worsen its quality in one's favor. Consider a hypothetical al Qaeda intent to attack an installation. Knowing that the guard post behind the gates is not manned between, say, three o'clock and four o'clock in the morning on Thursday might be a usable fact, the knowledge of which can influence the timing of its attack. The fact that the installation has a hotline to a second military base equipped with special forces on call is also quite sensitive. But would leaking *that* latter information to al Qaeda be harmful? It *might* induce them to attack the link between the installation and summoning of forces from that installation, thus perhaps spawning a strategy that might not have occurred to them. Or it *might* dissuade them from attacking at all. On net, the defenders may be better off if the decision to search for a way to attack the leak is less consequential and/or less likely than the decision to call off the attack (deterrence is why countries often show their hand when it comes to military power). Now reconsider whether it is a good idea to "leak" information about the special forces backup when no such nearby forces, in fact, exist—and that therefore cannot be classified, as such. If a "leak" about the backup were convincing, then it is just as effective as the fact of the backup. As a general rule, several orders of magnitude more information are classified than leaked for the purposes of deception. True, this strategy can backfire: misinformation can be hard to keep straight, and the odds of its being contradicted are often nontrivial. If such information is revealed as bluster, then others may interpret similar information ("we can do this and that") as bluster; it thereby loses credibility as a deterrent. Leaking is not free—but sometimes it does help security.

And this is where we get back to why information warfare includes *both* OPSEC and deception. OPSEC is easy to demand and hence routinely demanded. It may be a weak cousin to deception. Deception, though, requires that information warriors actually have a handle on what decisions the adversary is trying to make, what the basis for these decisions is likely to be, and how the basis for these decisions can be corrupted in one's favor. If we really think that we are guarding information of such importance, we should be surrounding it, in Winston Churchill's words, with a bodyguard of lies. Alas, doing so requires taking adversary decision processes seriously—while bureaucracies are more comfortable just making rules for others to follow.

Strategic deception is hard to get right. Michael Howard's analysis of strategic deception in World War II concluded that it was difficult to conclude that *any* of Britain's operations benefited the war effort, with the vital exception of Operation Fortitude (the attempt to misdirect the Germans as to where the Allies would enter France).[7] And this despite Britain's unique advantages: it had turned every German spy, and Germany had no aerial reconnaissance. Between the fact that

British operational plans constituted only one input into Germany's knowledge and the fact that German decisionmaking operated under many constraints of which its knowledge about the Allies was only one element, not much useful deception took place.

THE IMPORTANCE OF AGGREGATE PRIVACY

Although broadly understood in terms of one's ability to keep information from others, privacy combines four related but distinct needs.[8] First is somatic privacy, the deeply felt desire not to have people see you naked (hence the term "private parts"). Another is domicile privacy: the right to keep hidden what takes place in the house. This one enjoys some constitutional protection and may be extended to other spaces not readily accessible to observation (as in a "private conversation").[9] There is a political privacy associated with political and religious expression; it also enjoys some constitutional protection in terms of secret ballots and judicial protection for anonymous opinion on political topics. Note the progression: from privacy to protect something that almost no one sees, to privacy to protect something witnessed by few other than friends and select professionals, to privacy to protect something the results of which many people, even strangers, can witness.

The fourth, aggregate privacy, is the topic that merits discussion here. It can be understood as the right to control information about oneself *even if* such information was generated in public, before complete strangers that lacked a professional obligation to keep secrets (as doctors and lawyers do). Such a right would not require that any information was per se embarrassing individually, and, in some cases, even if it were not per se embarrassing collectively. The broader the collection of information on you that is accessible to any one person or institution, the greater is the violation of such privacy rights. This privacy right has generally *not* been legally recognized as a right in the United States, although other countries, notably European ones, do recognize such a right and therefore limit what data can be collected from individuals. Nevertheless, its validity is widely held. Decades ago, few worried about such privacy.[10] But with more digitization and networking came the increased collection of information and the greater ease with which such information can be aggregated. Hitherto, your grocer, druggist, or bookseller could, at most, remember only the odd fact or two about you and your habits. But once your transactions with them are digitized (if not already born digital, as it is with e-commerce), they can be amalgamated, distributed, and stored indefinitely. Unless you insist on surfing privately, your every movement in cyberspace is probably tracked. Express an interest by searching for or viewing some product or service and expect to see it advertised in subsequent unrelated websites. Smart phones are constantly leaking data.[11] From these small bits, revealing stories about each of us can be written. But is aggregate privacy about what others know about you or what others *presume* to know about you?

To explore as much, start with a story about tuna fish. Circa 2000, I did most of my food shopping at a mini-supermarket too small to issue affinity cards (tokens that help associate specific grocery store purchases with particular individuals). One day, in pursuit of last-minute cooking supplies, I found myself in another grocery store that *did* take affinity cards. After having checked off the shopping list, I noticed that canned tuna fish was on sale cheap—but only to those with affinity cards. Because canned tuna keeps forever, the price break provided a nice opportunity for stocking up. But would I give up my privacy to save a few dollars?[12] Well, that store was unlikely to see much of me over the course of a year. All they would know is that I once bought many cans of tuna fish. That, I concluded, was less revealing than misleading. They would not know the real me. My true identity (insofar as it was reflected in my shopping habits) would be safe. And thus having rationalized my purchase, I refilled my larder with canned tuna fish and thereby satisfied my hunger, wallet, and privacy simultaneously.

Or did I? It is a paradox of privacy that data on someone need not be true to be of concern; it need only be plausible enough to be *accepted* as true. Verity is not as important as verisimilitude. Imagine someone stumbling upon a person's dossier held by a large data consolidator. At first glance, the details are accurate and therefore disturbing: the dossier holds his name, address, phone number, where he lives and how much he paid for the house, arrest records, divorce records, and the like (all of which, incidentally, are somewhere in the public domain). The next page has his travel history with detailed flight records—again, seemingly accurate. He *did* fly to San Francisco several times and took the train to Manhattan on many occasions. But upon closer scrutiny, some of the dates seem awry. As he reviewed the record, he found flights he knew did not take. A glance at his credit card history revealed stores he did not patronize. When it came to his medical history, nearly everything was wrong. He concludes that the report, once it departed from the public record, was largely concocted. So, should he be relieved that his privacy is intact, or distressed wondering what kind of decisions have been made about his life?

For some circumstances, such as in negotiations, he should feel better. One side to negotiations that holds a dossier on the other side can strike a harder bargain by knowing his go-no-further point or what arguments he finds particularly appealing. False data in the dossier negate such advantages. Conversely, however, such a person may not necessarily be better off if the negotiations fail or the persuasion is ineffective because he was being sold something very different from what he wanted. Here, two forces are at play: the *knowledge* of who someone is, and the *presumption* that the possession of such knowledge is a legitimate basis upon which to base negotiations.

In other contexts, the ills that befall the object of a true dossier would also befall the object of a false dossier. On the basis of the latter, a person could still be tailed by federal agents, be hassled at airports, face tax audits, encounter unusual difficulties getting permits much less government contracts, and be denied house loans or life insurance. The person's only saving grace in all this is the possibility of proving such information false—a nontrivial process. But if the existence of the dossier and its use in making decisions were not obvious, how could one know that there *was* anything to challenge? Some of the logic that might be used to discern the existence of an incriminating dossier verges on the paranoid: am I being subject to more than random surveillance, audits, or commercial difficulties? Proving that one has not done something is hard. How does one produce nonexistent tickets, credit card slips, and the like? So, yes, you can have your privacy violated even if you do not know that it has been.[13]

But is primary abuse the collection and amalgamation of information (indeed, if it was entirely fictive, no information had actually been collected) and abuse of discretion in public and commercial life? Had private transactions data not been collected on individuals as a matter of course, people would not have been able to base decisions on them. Yet that may be putting the cart before the horse. Would we be better off if local gossip rather than transactions data was the source of such arbitrariness? To echo David Brin, the problem in this vignette may not be that someone's life is transparent so much as it is that *the decisionmaking processes* that affect someone are not transparent.[14]

To what extent is the right of privacy the right to be free from the consequences of having others know who you really are? Is privacy violated if key details of one's life are known by someone who takes in everything and lets out nothing? What if, to go to extremes, the details of one's life are known by space aliens who promise never to set foot inside the solar system? If the NSA intercepts every phone call made from the Bahamas and never takes actions against individuals (maybe the target was thought to be here but was elsewhere), then who suffers—particularly if no one is aware that this took place?[15]

Must the knower be sentient? Defenders of mass surveillance programs such as the Defense Advanced Research Projects Agency's Terrorism (or Total) Information Awareness research or the

NSA's Section 215 metadata program for telephone calls argue that only the computers know what has transpired; no humans were told. Is one violated if the details of one's life are known by a computer that has no output device—or, perhaps to be more realistic, can only be unlocked by free and open permission of the person whose life has been so recorded? If the answer to any of these questions is "yes," then the next logical question is, "Why *do* you care what is known by those who will not tell?" A response that indicates the fear that such information will inevitably leak is making the case for better cybersecurity, not more privacy.

Judge Richard Posner, also an author on economic topics, has gone so far as to stipulate that the right to privacy is really the right to deceive.[16] Absent data, we would be free to present ourselves as we would like to be presented. Yet to the person who has to make a decision about us, our ability to present ourselves as we would like may well involve deception if it is at variance with reality. Here, privacy is deception, which in military garb is a component of information warfare. Another perspective is commercial. Companies that provide free services in cyberspace—for example, Gmail—make their money by creating user profiles that they then provide to advertisers who target their wares more accurately as a result. To Google, such information has value. Does your right not to have that profile created always exceed the value that Google and its advertisers realize from being able to create profiles?

Some would argue that it is bad for the government to "know" all the details of one's life because there is no conceivable way for the government to take all this information in and *not* be in a position to do something about it. Even though personal information circulates much more vigorously outside of government than inside of government, many are far more wary about what the government knows than, say, what Google knows. The latter can annoy you, but it cannot arrest you. Needless to add, however, if the government learns what Google (or Amazon, or Microsoft) knows, then such a distinction is moot.

THE BENEFITS OF DISCRETION

The horror of George Orwell's dystopia, the all-seeing state, for instance, rested in large part on the premise that it was also the all-powerful state. Defenders of surveillance in America, however, may point out that such institutions as rule of law and an independent judiciary mean that someone blameless can be subject to round-the-clock surveillance without fear of consequence; only the guilty need fear the government's gaze. Arguing that once the requisite databases are assembled, the transition to a totalitarian state will be a mere detail is a stretch, to put it mildly. The reverse is more likely to be true: once a state has abandoned due process, then gathering the data needed to persecute people is secondary. Again, if the government is going to arbitrarily arrest, say, a thousand people, is it better if the thousand were selected in a completely random fashion or on the basis of some personal detail that the government should not have known about? That depends; arrests on the basis of political speech or religious practice seem to be more deleterious than random arrests (qua the third definition of privacy offered above), but, with special cases excluded, where is the difference between the two? The evil from collecting invidious information is clearly secondary. It is the loss of due process that is primary.

Nevertheless, rule of law does not obviate the discomfort that round-the-clock surveillance imposes. Very few of us have not, at one time or another, driven in excess of the posted speed limit, failed to come to a complete stop at intersections, or appeared to be other than in full control of our vehicles. Who does not feel relief when state troopers turn away from following you to pursue other quarry? This holds true outside the car. Modern life is so complicated (and the urge to cheat here and there so omnipresent) that few of us could withstand full scrutiny of our everyday lives.

Furthermore, anyone can feel the brunt of the law's occasional errors. Indictment, even without conviction, can bring with it incarceration (lasting months in some cases), costly legal fees, the alienation of friends, the removal of one's children, and a lasting blot on one's reputation. Arrest and, to a large extent, indictment, at least, are a matter largely of government discretion. So are other elements of government discretion: for example, from the privilege of holding a passport to flying on airplanes and the frequency of tax audits. Nevertheless, the U.S. government's scope for discrimination is limited precisely because due process is so widely applied.

The private scope for discrimination based on access to private acquisition is wider, not least because victims can only get recompense—for discrimination—if their membership in specifically enumerated groups was the problem. Mere arbitrariness or decisions taken on the basis of secret knowledge (and who can prove that?) are much less likely to violate the law: people can be and are fired without explanation. Outside the workplace, the freedom of arbitrary decision applies to, for instance, life insurance, credit ratings, and the ability to join certain organizations. Companies commonly use customer profiles to determine who should get better or worse service.

In other words, it is not the collection of otherwise innocent information that is necessarily bad so much as it is presumption that such information may be used to make decisions that affect people's lives. This presumption retains its bad taste whether the information is true or false. If it is true, then the details of one's lives *have* been used in judgment; if it is false, then the privacy invasion may be less, but the arbitrariness is greater. The way to nullify the effects of violating privacy lies in transparency (ironically or seemingly so).

These criteria can be used to think about the harm to those (22 million Americans) whose records were compromised in the OPM hack. Whoever took the data—and Chinese are the prime suspects—walked off with not only millions of social security numbers but also particularly sensitive data about the lifestyles of U.S. citizens being evaluated for security clearances. Analysts believe that such data can help in recruiting spies (and identifying those with U.S. contacts); hence, the United States was putatively harmed. But were individuals themselves harmed? If it was the Chinese *and* they protected their own files from being transferred to third parties, then the only individuals harmed were those affected by the decisions that the Chinese might want to make: for example, to recruit or pressure individuals or their friends, family, and contacts—a very small fraction of the 22 million. Were the Chinese to sell such information into black markets, then the risks of identity theft would be substantial. If the FBI were to retrieve such files (for example, by dint of their own hacking into, say, Chinese servers) *and there were no legal restrictions on what they could use*, many people would have far more to worry about.

CONCLUSIONS AND IMPLICATIONS

Espionage, classification, and privacy protection all rest on the presumption that something one person knows about another can help the former and harm the latter. Setting aside the (quite valid) personal preference for privacy, the truth of that statement has everything to do with the use that can be made of this information because, ultimately, information is about decisions (or else it is mere entertainment). Thus, if information is to have value—or if losing sole control over information is to have costs—there has to be some relationship between the acquisition of hard-won data, the conversion of data into information, the subsequent application of information to a decision, and the decision itself. It is too easy to get caught up in the excitement (or depression) of knowing something previously denied. Correspondingly, it is too easy to get caught up in the effort to acquire knowledge (to justify the tens of billions being spent on it) or the effort made to keep it from being acquired.

Understandably, it is difficult for one side to know what use its information is to another. The hacks on OPM (and related hacks) initially looked much like a criminal operation to acquire personally identifiable information such as social security numbers; thus, OPM expensively offered credit monitoring to those affected by the hack. Later, when the theft was traced to China, speculation arose that building a huge database on U.S. federal workers would permit the identification of useful recruits for China's human intelligence collection. More recent speculation is that China wanted to find U.S. spies in China, a third reason altogether.[17] Knowing the certainty with which another country holds the knowledge it gets is even more difficult; few calculate such things with sufficient self-awareness, much less precision. Nevertheless, if a case is going to be made that collecting or protecting information from cyberespionage is important, it is incumbent upon those who collect or protect information to tell a plausible story of how it might matter.

CHAPTER 8

What Does China's Economically Motivated Cyberespionage Cost the United States?

In response to all these incidents of Chinese cyberespionage, U.S. officials have voiced stern displeasure in face-to-face meetings with their Chinese counterparts; they may well levy costs on China until these attacks stop or at least are opposed by the government.[1] It is not entirely inconceivable that the Chinese would pledge to refrain from stealing intellectual property (as President Xi Jinping did in September 2015) and live by what they pledged. Conversely, the United States, not entirely convinced that China is conducting itself accordingly, may apply threatened trade sanctions. The Chinese could counter, and trade relations could deteriorate.[2]

Before such a confrontation goes much further, it might be worthwhile to determine what the U.S. economy would gain from persuading China to cease all economically motivated cyberespionage (EMCE). The term "economically motivated" distinguishes such espionage from the more traditional use of espionage to protect national security. The United States and its allies can argue that they do not do EMCE (not even Snowden's revelations suggest as much) and that EMCE violates international norms, particularly as embodied in international trade agreements (the General Agreement on Tariffs and Trade) to which China is a signatory and organizations (for example, the World Trade Organization [WTO]) of which it is a member. Conversely, because the United States and its allies are unlikely to foreswear traditional national security espionage, compelling China to do so would be viewed as hypocritical and thus less likely to be effective than concentrating on EMCE. Note that if national security were considered a valid motivation, many acts of cyberespionage of the sort traced to China would still be considered something that nations can be expected to do. They include cyberattacks on DoD and other U.S. government systems, on defense contractors (for example, Lockheed), on security vendors to defense contractors (for example, RSA), on opposition groups (for example, the Free Tibet movement), U.S. politicians, U.S. media, and, to some extent, even Google.[3] But an agreement to foreswear EMCE would put cyberattacks on, say, Coca-Cola, Exxon, or Telvent off limits.[4]

It matters whether EMCE is closer to a $1 billion a year problem for the United States or a $1 trillion a year problem. If it is a $1 billion problem, then trying to solve it through confrontation risks far more costs than it saves. Confrontation also makes it difficult to work on problems (for example, North Korea) that carry greater risks for U.S. interests. Conversely, if EMCE is a $1 trillion problem, then the gain from solving it may top all other Sino-U.S. issues and may well be worth risking a trade war. Calculating the benefit from making China stop its EMCE is tantamount to calculating the cost that these cyberattacks have on the economy.[5]

So how much *is* EMCE hurting the U.S. economy? Figures of $1 trillion a year have been bandied about—and by none other than the president of the United States.[6] General Keith Alexander, who headed the NSA and CYBERCOM, repeatedly called EMCE, at $300 billion a year,[7] the "greatest transfer of wealth in world history." A 2013 MacAfee–Center for Strategic and International Studies report estimated the cost at $25 billion to $120 billion a year.[8] Even in 2008, one could find estimates of over $100 billion worth of annual damage in the United States alone.[9] Others talked about EMCE being a "death of a thousand cuts" from inexorably hollowing out the U.S. economic (mostly manufacturing) base. Backing for such claims is thin.[10]

No reliable damage estimate is likely to be precise. First, no one knows exactly how much EMCE is actually going on, what has been taken, and what the take has been used for. Second, the relative efficacy of EMCE as a means of technology transfer is unclear. Third, much of the damage may be unobservable today because the conversion of stolen information into altered economic activity (for example, greater Chinese exports) is not instantaneous. Most known EMCE has taken place since roughly 2007, but most of the effects may have yet to occur.

Nevertheless, we will argue that a set of heroic assumptions would be required to generate an estimate that China's theft of intellectual property (for example, know-how, product designs, and formulae) costs the U.S. economy much more than $10 billion to $20 billion a year (a number that excludes what is often labeled intellectual property theft such as bootlegged DVDs).

We approach this question in pieces. First, we examine what might happen to U.S. trade flows when China improves the price performance of its own products and services as a result of having copied U.S. information. Second, we estimate how much U.S. trade, notably export trade (for reasons explained below), might be at risk from such intellectual property. Third, we assess the relative role of EMCE among all factors that could contribute to China's ability to displace U.S. exports. Fourth, we lay out the formula that estimates the loss to the U.S. economy as a function of several factors.

WHAT'S AT STAKE?

The most straightforward measure of an adverse action on an economy is its effect on its gross domestic product (GDP).[11] But intellectual property theft is unlike classical theft in that its original possessor is not deprived of anything directly. Those who had the information before have the information afterward.

If neither the productivity of the United States nor its stock of capital or labor is affected by cyberattacks, then the first-order effect of EMCE on current GDP would be zero. China's copying U.S. intellectual property may raise its own productivity, but there is no ipso facto reason to believe that it lowers U.S. productivity. This formulation, however, no longer applies if, as a result of EMCE, U.S. productivity is deflected from its year-to-year upward rise. This might happen if resources devoted to product and service development were to be curtailed—for instance, as it might be if the ability to hold onto the exclusive use of such R&D long enough to pay back the effort is jeopardized because EMCE allows the Chinese to come out with a competing product sooner (reducing the duration of patent protection could produce a similar effect). Yet if such reduction is taking place, there has been no mention of it within the trade press. U.S. R&D ($465 billion in 2013 and $495 billion in 2014) accounts for over 2.8 percent of U.S. GDP, still a high measure by historical standards.[12] Furthermore, the choice between generating R&D only to see it copied and abandoning R&D does not take into account the many ways that corporations, which hitherto may have underestimated the threat to their intellectual property, can adapt to the newfound realization that their intellectual property is at risk. For instance, they could keep doing R&D but confine its circulation to isolated intranets (a practice of the semiconductor industry). Granted, these alternatives raise the cost of and thereby must reduce the incentive to carry out R&D—but the disincentive should be measured not in ex ante terms of how much organizations already lost from having the Chinese copy their files, but in ex posteriori terms of how much more organizations have to pay to protect their R&D from future loss now that they understand the threat against it. Because the latter is almost certainly smaller, the impact on the incentive to undertake R&D is correspondingly smaller—but not necessarily zero.

The lack of a primary impact, however, does not mean that there is no secondary impact. The Chinese could use copied technology to take over markets held by U.S. firms. Assume that Chinese copying allows a completely Chinese product to replace a completely American product overseas; the U.S. balance of trade falls $1 billion, and the Chinese balance of trade rises correspondingly. One train of logic holds that some U.S. factory lost $1 billion worth of sales; workers were laid off, thereby reducing their spending on goods and services, which, in turn, reduces ancillary employment, and so on—so that the overall cost is some multiplier of the initial loss of sales. Macroeconomists, though, would argue that there is no ipso facto relationship between trade flows and national employment levels (especially for very large and heterogeneous countries); the latter are almost entirely determined by macroeconomic factors (for example, the money supply, the fiscal balance). Nevertheless, a $1 billion shift in the trade balance matters because, ultimately, accounts must be balanced. The primary adjustment mechanism for a shift downward in the trade balance (vis-à-vis China) would be a devaluation of the U.S. dollar versus China's yuan. U.S. goods are cheaper overseas to sell in higher quantity; imports are more expensive so that they sell in lower quantity. U.S. consumers lose by having to pay more than they would have for imports, notably but not exclusively for Chinese goods.

But calculating the gains and the losses (particularly to the U.S. economy) arising from the copying of intellectual property is not straightforward. Consider a few vignettes.

In the first vignette, a U.S. company invests in R&D that produces a marketable process, which the United States wants to sell to others. The Chinese copy the secrets of this process and decide that they, too, want to sell the process (the effects are similar but smaller if the only effect of having copied the information is that the Chinese no longer have to buy the information). The only markets for this process are outside the United States. The competition between the United States and the Chinese copycat makes it unprofitable for the U.S. company to market the process. The U.S. company loses the stream of revenue that selling such intellectual property would have provided. The Chinese company gains a stream of revenue, but probably not near what the U.S. company lost (since the Chinese company would have had to underprice what the U.S. company was asking for in order to win customers). The other gainers are foreign customers overseas, who get the technology at a lower price than they would otherwise have gotten, albeit from Chinese rather than U.S. sources. Note that the size of the loss is not necessarily related to the amount of R&D the U.S. company spent (it could have spent little but gotten lucky) or how much R&D the Chinese company would have had to spend to invent the process themselves (perhaps they could not have generated this process even had they spent ten times the money). Here, the logic is straightforward.

In the second vignette, this American company has valuable intellectual property that is used to create a product for the marketplace. This intellectual property finds its way into the hands of a Chinese company, which puts out a competing product and thereby displaces sales *in the United States*. Assume for the nonce (but unrealistically, as argued below) that the Chinese company's product is identical in price and performance to the U.S. product so that no gain accrues to U.S. customers. One billion dollars a year's worth of U.S. sales vanish. However, this does not represent a $1 billion loss for U.S. GDP, because some, say, 30 percent of the value added of the U.S. product originated overseas. The Chinese company, for its part, serves the U.S. market from its U.S. manufacturing plants; but in the latter case, 50 percent of the value added of the Chinese-made product comes from overseas (defined to include profit remitted to the Chinese company). Thus, the net impact on the U.S. trade balance is not $1 billion but 20 percent as much ($200 million). The distinction between the interest of the United States (as reflected in its trade balance) and U.S. companies (as reflected in their sales and profits) is a feature of globalization, especially as foreign investment in U.S. manufacturing rises. Although China does not supply U.S. markets from its U.S.

plants to the extent Europeans or even Japanese do, it *is* starting to invest heavily in U.S. manufacturing facilities.[13]

As one variant of the second vignette, assume that this product had also been exported, but what previously were U.S. exports were displaced by Chinese production. In such a case, the U.S. company may well be generating most of its value added in the United States (if the product came from a U.S.-owned overseas plant, it would not have been considered an export), and, typically, very little of the value added of the Chinese product would have originated in the United States. This situation is the one where the damage to the U.S. economy is likely to be significant.

As another variant of the second vignette, assume the U.S. company had competition from Europe. The illegal transfer of U.S. intellectual property to the Chinese company might not necessarily come at the expense of U.S. sales, but rather of European sales. Take cars. U.S.-based companies tend to dominate the North American market for full-sized automobiles and utility vehicles (for example, pick-up trucks). Foreign companies are much more competitive in selling mid-sized and compact vehicles. U.S. car manufacturers have likely been hit by cyberespionage, but that hardly portends China's starting to make cars that look and feel like Buicks any time soon (although General Motors sells almost half a million Buicks a year in China). It is more likely that they will use bits and pieces of what they find to improve the price-performance ratio of the cars they are already making—and those cars are more likely to compete with automobile imports than with U.S. models. In such a case, the net cost of Chinese cyberespionage is likely to be small or might even provide a positive boost to the U.S. economy (albeit at the expense of U.S. friends).

In the third vignette, a U.S. firm has done a great deal of research on a product but has decided that it could not make money introducing it (and finding a licensee is not worth the license fees). The Chinese copy the technology and conclude they *can* make money on it (for example, because their wage rates are lower) and introduce a corresponding product for which there is no directly comparable U.S. product. The U.S. company loses little if any sales. U.S. consumers are better off having greater choice.

In the fourth vignette, a U.S. company, aghast at the erosion of a core product at the expense of Chinese competition, concludes that it must shift its R&D from pursuing incremental improvements to its erstwhile core products to pursuing a product that will make the original core products obsolete. In this case, its efforts succeed. Its new product consigns the original product—and the Chinese copies thereof—to a stagnant low-profit commodity-like submarket while the U.S. company makes large profits from the new product. Consumers, both here (which counts in calculating costs to the United States) and overseas (which does not count in such calculations), are better off, not only because of increased competition for the old product but because of the unique performance features of the new one. The story, of course, could be told in reverse. That is, the Chinese company, having acquired the technological secrets of the old product, is also in a better position to develop a new one. The Japanese (circa 1980) pursued a successful strategy of first copying (albeit almost entirely legally) and then later innovating. But if the best way of learning to innovate is to innovate rather than copy, then the U.S. firm still has a decisive advantage in this vignette.

In vignette five, China copies U.S. expertise of shale gas extraction, a field in which U.S. companies are dominant. The Chinese may otherwise have to pay for U.S. expertise; by copying U.S. technology, they may avoid having to pay for U.S. expertise—a clear loss to the United States were it so. But would China really want to depend on U.S. expertise, when many countries less avowedly socialist than China (for example, Mexico) take pains to run their own energy sector (for example, Pemex)? Suppose that China can extract far more shale gas after having copied U.S. fracking technology. As a result, China uses more gas and hence less oil, thereby reducing the pressure that its currently burgeoning economy puts on oil markets. The trajectory of oil prices stays depressed.

Until the United States becomes a net hydrocarbon exporter, the U.S. economy is unambiguously better off as a result.

The point of these vignettes is not only to illustrate the worst-case scenario (at least from a near- and mid-term perspective), but also to show the many circumstances under which the loss to the U.S. economy would be less than the worst case, and, in some circumstances, may even be a net positive.

As noted, lost sales can be translated into harm to the U.S. economy by their weakening the dollar. Exactly how much the dollar has to devalue vis-à-vis the yuan to make up for a $1 billion shortfall is unclear; much depends on how quickly the market will force a devaluation to rebalance accounts (as a rule, the influence of price changes—and devaluation is a price change—grows stronger over time as short-run adjustments such as driving less when oil prices rise are joined by long-term adjustments such as buying more fuel-efficient cars). The elasticity of the trade balance with respect to currency values equals the sum of the elasticity of imports plus the elasticity of exports minus one (a more expensive foreign currency means the total spent on imports in dollar terms can rise even if volumes fall). Estimating these elasticities is tricky because it is hard to disentangle the effects of currency devaluation from the effects of the forces that created the trade imbalance that forced devaluation. Research by Jaime Marquez suggested a general figure for export and import elasticities of roughly one.[14] A 2000 paper he coauthored suggested that short-run elasticities were perhaps half as high (but this was limited to trade vis-à-vis the affluent Group of 7 countries); for the United States, the long-run export price elasticity was 1.5, and long-run import price elasticity was 0.3.[15] A policy paper by Josh Bivens calculated that the 9 percent decline in the dollar's value (between February 2002 and July 2003) could be associated with a $100 billion to $160 billion shift in the U.S. trade deficit, but only by raising the cost of imports by $60 billion.[16] Given this wide divergence of estimates, a nice round number that posits that the cost of a dollar shift in the U.S. trade balance requires raising the total cost of imports by one dollar is not provably wrong. But this adjustment is hardly instantaneous; in the short term, differences in trade flows can be washed out by equal and opposite differences in capital accounts.

Economists would also note that a rise in China's income, in and of itself (that is, net of the composition of its export sectors), is a net gain for the U.S. economy. A richer China means more consumer (and investor) demand for goods and services of all sorts, not least of which would be U.S. goods and services. Currently, China has a large direct trade surplus with the United States; if China were to look more like Europe in terms of its income and economic composition—a likely consequence of its becoming more technologically sophisticated—trade flows between China and the United States would be closer to a net balance, just as they are between Europe and the United States. Or to reverse the question: would the U.S. economy be better off, in the long run, if Europe's economy tomorrow came to look like China's today? If the answer is no, why would China's achieving Europe's economy make the average U.S. citizen worse off?

HOW MUCH TRADE IS AT ISSUE?

We now try to put some numbers on how much foreign trade could be displaced because of EMCE. Foreign trade will be divided into three parts: trade losses as Chinese exports to the United States displace U.S. domestic production, trade losses as U.S. exports to other countries are displaced by exports from Chinese firms, and value added losses as production from U.S. majority–owned facilities is displaced by production from Chinese-owned facilities.

We start with the assumption that the Chinese copied files from nearly every sector that has information accessible to the Internet—rather than starting with reported cyberespionage incidents and working up from there. Doing so deliberately avoids the standard argument that counting known penetrations understates the cost (because much more EMCE takes place than is known but that victims are either ignorant of what they have lost or are reluctant to discuss it).

The illicit acquisition of U.S. technology by Chinese firms could also displace U.S. home production and thereby exacerbate the balance of payments in the same way that displacing U.S. exports can. But, as noted in several of the vignettes, there are offsetting benefits to U.S. consumers arising from improved price-performance ratio of Chinese exports to the United States.[17] Furthermore, in cases (albeit less common ones) where the elasticity of Chinese exports (relative to price) vis-à-vis U.S. production is less than 1.0, such price improvements would *reduce* the dollar cost of U.S. imports. In light of how many Chinese exports to the United States compete with imports from other countries rather than U.S. production (so that lower prices from China result in lower imports and/or lower import prices from third parties), lower Chinese prices may often result in less money spent on imports. Finally, if the price elasticity were under roughly 2.2, the gains to U.S. consumers from the lower prices from China would exceed the loss to consumers arising from the compensating rising in the yuan required to re-equilibrate accounts (assuming a response adjustment and the elasticity of 1.0 as noted above). Such price elasticities for intercountry trade are considered rather high. Thus, while the potential for Chinese companies to displace U.S. goods in U.S. markets (roughly $5 trillion worth) is likely higher than the potential to displace U.S. production in foreign markets, there may be gains to the U.S. market (because consumers get greater choice and lower prices) that offset the losses to the U.S. trade position. Furthermore, the great bulk of Chinese exports to the United States (roughly $39 billion a month in 2014) are competitive solely by virtue of China's lower wage rates—and there are many other countries that can offer low wages (albeit without some of the advantages that China offers, such as a deep supply chain and a well-disciplined and literate labor force).[18] For most items, therefore, the cost to the U.S. public if the yuan gained a great deal of value would be the difference between what we paid China for its exports and what the next-cheapest exporting country would sell at. For all these reasons, if there are costs to the U.S. economy from EMCE, they are much more likely to arise from the displacement of U.S. exports by Chinese production than from the displacement of domestic production by imports from China.

DISPLACED U.S. EXPORTS

To assess the costs of EMCE to the U.S. trade balance, we start with exports. We ignore the trade in services as being largely unaffected by intellectual property issues (for example, of the kind that can be captured by copying blueprints).

In 2012, the United States exported $1.55 trillion in goods. The exports are divided into six groups in government statistics.[19] Of these, $130 billion were in foodstuffs, a sector in which China's ability to displace U.S. exports by dint of (illicit) technology transfer is quite limited. These are materials where the U.S. advantage lies in natural endowments, including its relatively low energy costs (notably, natural gas).

Roughly $500 billion was in "industrial supplies and materials." Of this total, however, roughly $300 billion came in the form of raw or semi-processed raw materials—subsectors in which China's ability to displace U.S. exports by dint of illicit technology transfer is also quite limited for similar reasons.[20] Figure that $200 billion of exports are potentially vulnerable to Chinese exporters using technology transfer as their wedge in.

Roughly $530 billion was in "capital goods, except automotive." This is the sector that would be most vulnerable to Chinese exports that gained market share through technology transfer. But even in that category, there are U.S. strongholds that the Chinese will have a hard time displacing, in large part because of the depth of knowledge and experience required to do well there: for example, civilian aircraft and aircraft engines and parts ($100 billion), measuring, testing, and control equipment ($25 billion), and semiconductors ($45 billion). Figure, therefore, that the remainder, $300 billion worth, is vulnerable to Chinese exporters.

Automotive parts constitute $150 billion. Most of that consists of intracompany transfers within North America and thus is hard for the Chinese to displace. Figure $50 billion worth is vulnerable.

Consumer goods plus other goods constitute $240 billion, but $50 billion are pharmaceuticals (which have patent protection, which is worth something if not everything, in foreign markets), and another $40 billion are made up of jewelry, gems, and antiques. Figure $150 billion is vulnerable.

This leaves roughly $700 billion worth of U.S. exports, all told, that the Chinese could possibly displace through the transfer of technology (including, notably, the illicit transfer of technology through cyberespionage). In truth, however, this $700 billion overstates the vulnerability. Many of these products have patent protection, which may not necessarily mean much in the Chinese market, but it would in other countries. Other U.S. products are globally unique. The United States (as well as other developed economies and many developing economies) has many specialized products that are the province of a particular company based on closely held processes, a well-managed brand identity, an active product upgrade and R&D effort, and strong ties to ultimate customers (who, in turn, contribute cues that help guide further product upgrades and innovations). All of this makes it very hard (and expensive) to compete with, even by someone who has managed to purloin all the written material associated with a product's production.

Thus, the total volume of U.S. export trade at risk from Chinese production made uncompetitive by its increasing technological sophistication—from all sources—may put most but not all of this $700 billion at risk with the rest being essentially unassailable, at least by means of illicit technology transfer. Figure $400 billion as exports that really could be displaced. One of the reasons that this number is not higher is that Chinese production has already displaced production from the United States (and other countries) for low-technology goods and the assembly and light manufacturing component of medium- and high-technology goods. Those markets are already lost and cannot be lost again through technology transfer.

Finally, as per the second vignette, one should take account of globalization when extracting from trade statistics. A large percentage of what counts as foreign trade is actually the transfer of goods between different branches of the same company (for example, between U.S.-based manufacturing and China-based assembly). Conceivably, a U.S. company might shift sourcing from its own U.S.-based manufacturing facility to one owned by a Chinese competitor who copied its technology, but it is also understandable that the U.S. company would resist shifting production that way (vis-à-vis shifting component sourcing from an *unaffiliated* U.S. manufacturer to a Chinese manufacturer who had copied technology from the erstwhile U.S. source). If so, the $400 billion may be a bit overstated.

Technology transfer is only one way that countries move up the technology ladder in foreign trade; illicit technology transfer is not the only form of technology transfer, and EMCE itself is not the only form of illicit technology transfer. It would be convenient to be able to estimate the role that EMCE plays in the possibility that the Chinese could displace $400 billion in U.S. exports by improving their technological capabilities. Yet such an exercise, as will be clear, is hard enough even without accounting for possible substitutions (for example, the Chinese would buy U.S. companies if they could not copy files from them) or complements (for example, it takes Chinese educated at U.S. universities to understand the files they copy from U.S. companies). So, what follows will be approximate.

We start by looking at China's broad efforts to acquire technology as a context for understanding the role that EMCE may play. As a rule, countries can acquire technological capabilities by developing them on their own or by getting them from others (or some combination thereof). With R&D accounting for 1.5 percent of China's gross domestic product in 2008 and closer to 1.95 in 2014—a very high ratio for a country at China's stage of economic development—it is hard to argue that the theft of foreign technology has allowed China to forego developing its own.[21] Similarly, education levels in China are rising rapidly as well, as is its cumulative work experience. Both public and commercial investment levels are a very high percentage of total national income. Combined, this means that a China without any technology transfer whatsoever is still likely to substitute higher-technology production for low-technology production as the latter migrates to lesser-developed countries such as Vietnam or Bangladesh. In the process, Chinese goods would compete more successfully to displace U.S. exports absent any technology transfer.

The modes of technology transfer vary. To begin with, the entire purpose of the world's scientific and engineering publication establishment is to transfer knowledge as well as create it, and much of this knowledge (particularly for engineering) is tantamount to technology. The Internet is facilitating this transfer of knowledge, and the Chinese are learning English by the millions, in part to access all this technological knowledge. The West generally deems this a good thing—even if the Chinese were to generate no new knowledge of their own, which, of course, they will, and their patent activity suggests they already do.

At a more direct level, almost a half-million Chinese students educate themselves overseas (200,000 of them in the United States). In so doing, they inevitably learn about Western technologies; most Chinese overseas students are studying science, technology, engineering, or mathematics. Again, the West deems this a good thing (as it is, many Chinese students stay in the West, and among those who eventually go home, many spend their most intellectually productive period of their lives in the West).[22]

Moving from general technology transfer to the transfer of specific technologies, the latter can take place in many perfectly legal ways thanks to globalization. One obvious (and easily overlooked) way by which technology is transferred takes place when Western firms export products to China. The product itself may not say how to make it, but, at a minimum, it says that a particular item is technologically feasible.[23] Disassembling the product can generate broad knowledge about what it was made from, thus, to some extent, how it was made, and thus how to make something like it. The fact that many Chinese weapons systems, for instance, look like their U.S. counterparts is not necessarily testimony to their having copied the technological details by stealing files. Instead, it may reflect Chinese appropriation of the visible aspects of such weapons coupled with the perception that such designs can work, and that U.S. engineers—who must know what they are doing—have chosen such designs over all possible alternatives. Recent versions of Chinese military equipment more resemble the Russian equipment that they previously purchased from Russia rather than the U.S. equipment whose designs they have been supposedly acquiring from EMCE.[24] Technology transfer from exported products goes beyond mere examination. There are printed design specifications, repair manuals, service calls explaining the fit between a product and its usage, visits to the factories where these products are made, and various trade fairs that help transfer knowledge.

Technology is also transferred when Western firms put factories and, of late, R&D facilities in China. This educates Chinese workers, engineers, and researchers; when such firms establish their supply chains, they educate the latter's workers. Learning how to make components to Western standards is learning how to make components that can be sold globally. Western buyers often work directly with potential suppliers to share design and production know-how with them. Those educated by working for or with Western corporations, in turn, are available to work for (or establish) Chinese corporations. From time to time, the Chinese government requires Western firms to transfer more technology than such firms intended, if they are allowed to sell into China. The

propriety of such Chinese behavior is iffy, because it contravenes the spirit of the WTO, and Western countries have complained—but it must yield something, because the Chinese keep insisting.

Chinese companies can also acquire technology through acquisition. They can hire Americans with experience of technologies of U.S. origin; although such employees sign contracts with
their former employers forbidding the transfer of specific designs and product information, there
are no barriers to transferring the tacit knowledge that comes from working with such products
and designs. Or the Chinese can and do purchase entire companies. Although the Committee on
Foreign Investment in the United States sometimes limits which companies the United States lets
fall into foreign hands, there are non-U.S. companies available for purchase from countries with less
national security sensitivity.

Finally, the Chinese can license technology from Western companies—but at this point, they
have shown less enthusiasm for forking out hard cash for such technologies than the Japanese do
now, or even did when Japan was at a comparable level of development.

So, the Chinese can and do employ many ways of acquiring Western technology apart from
simply reinventing it from scratch. These methods are entirely or largely legal. Western governments have allowed such methods to be used and, in many cases, have encouraged them.

That then leaves illegal methods, notably espionage—both human and cyber. Of human espionage, there is no shortage of examples. When the administration wanted to demonstrate its opposition to EMCE shortly after the Mandiant report was released, its report had twenty examples of
spies caught in the United States trying to hustle files out the door; eighteen of them were Chinese.
Overall, Chinese connections have been found in 44 percent of all Economic Espionage Act pros-
ecutions since 2008.[25] Human spies are often people who worked at the facility they are stealing
from; they thus have an insider's knowledge of what information to copy and what its context is.[26]
But humans get caught; such risks put an upper limit on how much information China can receive
this way. From a policy perspective, the question is whether pressure on the Chinese to cease EMCE
would also reduce the amount of physical spying that took place. Perhaps China may pull back on all
activity that would irritate the United States. Alternatively, cracking down on hackers might have
the reverse effect if a shortfall in one leads to greater effort in the other. The Chinese could also
argue that they have enforced the law over their own hackers while insisting that it was up to the
United States to enforce its own laws over spies that were physically present in the United States at
the time of their espionage.

That leaves EMCE as a source of technology transfer. Even assuming that it takes place in huge
quantities, how efficient a mechanism is it? Technology is often compared to a set of recipes—ways
of combining ingredients in a certain sequence and manner to achieve a particular result. The recipes that most people are familiar with as such are stored in cookbooks. Julia Child's cookbooks,
for instance, have sold in the millions. Yet possession of a Julia Child cookbook does not a Julia
Child make, even with lots of practice. Cooking—and technology in general—is a mix of explicit
knowledge, such as a cookbook has, and tacit knowledge, which only comes with work, talent, and
at-the-elbow assistance. It is the last that, in large part, distinguishes the efficiency of illicit technology transfer from the efficiency of legal technology transfer. Those who copy intellectual property
in the form of files (much of which shows what but not how and is thus less informative than a cookbook) lack such at-the-elbow assistance.[27] The master, so to speak, is not there to evaluate the work
of apprentices or answer their questions. Individual files, for their part, do not always come with the
kind of context that would indicate the relationship of the part to the whole. All this reduces the use
that can be made of these files.

Furthermore, a great deal of technology simply does not transfer well. Only a certain percentage of all R&D carried out by a company is actually worthwhile to another company; the rest

solves problems unique to a company's product line. Consider the rewards of stealing information about how to produce a Chevy Corvette. Perhaps one major problem is protecting the lifespan of a car from the consequences of withstanding the vibrations of a 400-cubic-inch engine. This is an interesting topic, and some elements of what is learned may be broadly useful. But if the Chinese have no interest in building such a powerful car, they would have a correspondingly modest interest in solving the problems associated with building such a powerful car. Process R&D is another type of intellectual property that is hard to transfer inasmuch as it is about tweaking a production line (broadly understood); such lines vary from one company to another. To use another example, every steelmaking country has had to develop its own processes based on the ores that were available to it—and each ore body had its unique set of impurities to be dealt with.

If time-to-market is an important consideration, as it tends to be in many industries with a high R&D content, then thieves are always going to be behind the curve. The stolen research has already been completed and documented by the time it is transferred to someone that can use it. The receiving country has to be able to acquire, understand, and exploit the research during the interval between the completion and the owner's exploitation of the R&D. The corporation from which the information was stolen may well have gone on to the next versions of the product.

There is a paucity of public data on how such copied files are actually being used. If these files were distributed so widely throughout the Chinese economy that China could make a serious play for the hundreds of billions of dollars' worth of exports, where is the someone who has admitted seeing and/or utilizing such files? Could it be that such files requested by Chinese ministries do not circulate outside the Chinese government?[28] After all, the U.S. intelligence community itself shares next to nothing outside government circles. What makes it obvious that China's ministries (which operate in a much more closed society) are far more generous with their take? At first glance, this logic seems off. Why take all this information if those best placed to use it never get to see it? At second glance, while unlikely, it is not completely inconceivable that a large share of these files are used not to transfer U.S. technology but rather to assess it for purposes of, say, reducing technological surprise.

Alternatively, the circulation of this information could take place but be controlled to China's many—and stodgy—state-owned enterprises. Or, alternatively, the circulation of such information is restricted (to a few trusted corporations) to minimize the leakage to the public that would expose the sources and methods used to carry out EMCE (although it is hard to believe that most of it has not already been exposed to the Mandiants of this world). The more tightly the disbursement of such information, the less use can be made of what has been copied; this may be a trade-off that Chinese cyberspies are willing to live with for operational security reasons. But it also does reduce the damage that EMCE can wreak on the U.S. economy. If the take goes to state-owned enterprises rather than the more dynamic privately owned enterprises, then boosting the former at the expense of the latter retards China's ability to move upmarket.

DISPLACED VALUE ADDED BY U.S. CORPORATIONS

Chinese EMCE could lead to the displacement of sales by U.S. affiliates manufacturing overseas. Although most of the loss in value added from such displacement would occur in the country whose production was being displaced (to be offset by the possible gain in value added if displaced by a Chinese-owned affiliate in that country), a fraction of this value added would be lost to the United States. Some of this loss would occur in the form of lost profits. The rest would occur in the form of lost value added that typically would take place in a headquarters country when a foreign affiliate loses sales: for example, management services, marketing services, and product R&D.

In 2009 (admittedly a recession year), majority-owned foreign affiliates of U.S. corporations generated $1.1 trillion of value added, of which manufacturing accounted for 60 percent ($668 billion).[29] If we make the generous assumption that all of it is subject to displacement by Chinese-owned affiliates, this compares to the $700 billion worth of U.S. exports that are subject to displacement. Thus, *if* the U.S. share of value added is estimated as high as one-third, then by using a logic similar to that carried out for U.S. exports, one could argue adding the loss to the U.S. economy from the displacement of U.S. value added from majority-owned affiliates adds one-third to the calculations for the loss of U.S. exports.[30]

But even that may be quite an overestimate. This total, for instance, includes the roughly $100 billion worth of sales by China-based U.S. subsidiaries that could conceivably be displaced as a result of EMCE.[31] Although it is easy to see how low-cost labor can allow a Chinese company to convert U.S. intellectual property into products that undercut similar products made in the United States, the case that such products can undercut products made in U.S.-owned Chinese factories (using similarly low-cost labor) is harder to make. Furthermore, the strong position of U.S. multinationals overseas is strongly related to their superior brand management ($180 billion of this $668 billion is food and chemicals, such as those from Proctor and Gamble). China's firms have very weak brands relative to the size of China's manufacturing base.[32]

SUMMARY CALCULATIONS

The Chinese must be benefitting from EMCE. Otherwise, why would they do it—particularly in the face of growing Western irritation? That the Chinese get more from it than the United States loses is also likely—this is generally true of all technology transfer (unless and until the provider reduces its investment in technology because it cannot hold onto it, of which there is scant evidence yet). We start by assuming that EMCE is ubiquitous: that the Chinese are copying everything they can from as many sectors as they can reach. But how much does the United States lose from all this?

We start, as noted above, with U.S. exports (to China and other countries) subject to serious competition as China moves upmarket in technology: roughly $400 billion worth.

First, the value added that would have gone to U.S. sources but is instead going to Chinese sources as a result of the shift in exports is less than the value of sales.[33] The Chinese may compete by exporting from their U.S. factories. Alternatively, they may source components in the United States even as U.S. products sourced inputs from other countries. Call the ratio between shifted value added and shifted exports A.

Second, China is unlikely to displace all exports in the face of ferocious competition from incumbent providers, new U.S. entrants, and manufacturers from every other country in the world. Call the percentage of eligible exports the Chinese actually manage to displace (over, say, a ten-year period) B.

Third, where the Chinese have succeeded in displacing U.S. exports, some part will have been because of their indigenous development of capabilities and some part because of technology transfer. Call this latter percentage C.

Fourth, of those exports where the necessary edge (to displace U.S. exports) arises from technology transfer, only a certain fraction of this technology transfer arises from illicit technology transfer. Call this percentage D.

Fifth, cyberespionage is only one form of illicit technology transfer, albeit probably the major share. Call its share E.

Sixth, although our initial assumption is that all U.S. exporters have had all their files copied by the Chinese, the reality is a fraction less than 100 percent. Call that fraction F.

Thus, the amount of exports transferred to the Chinese as a result of EMCE can be calculated as $400 billion multiplied by A x B x C x D x E x F—where B, C, and D are all likely to be less than half (and A, E, and F are certainly less than 1.0).

As noted, the loss to the U.S. economy (as expressed in terms of higher import costs) is roughly the same figure as the shift in the trade balance as calculated above. Unfortunately, these calculations cannot deliver a definitive number. But it would take a heroic set of assumptions about the various factors cited above to conclude that the U.S. economy is losing much more than $10 billion to the Chinese to EMCE. To demonstrate as much, start with the $400 billion, assign a figure of 0.8 for A (the shift of value added per dollar of shift in export sourcing from the United States to China), 0.4 for B (the share of U.S. exports that the Chinese themselves can, in fact, displace), 0.4 for C (the percentage of price-performance accounted for by technology transfer), 0.4 for D (the percentage of technology transfer accounted for by espionage), 0.8 for E (the percentage of benefit from espionage that is a benefit from EMCE), and 0.8 for F (the percentage of companies that account for the $400 billion whose files have been copied by either human or cyberespionage). The conclusion from these multiplications is that the illicit transfer of technology from EMCE accounts for $12 billion worth of value added shifted from U.S. to Chinese sources *if these parameters are right*—and they may well be overstated.[34]

To be fair, EMCE has another cost, and that arises from the theft of proprietary business information. Examples include data from U.S. energy companies on the value of certain oil properties, the illicit learning of negotiating positions from Hollywood, and the cyberespionage carried out against Coca-Cola when the latter was trying to purchase a Chinese company, Huiyuan Juice Group. The effect of stealing business proprietary information is similar to the effect of stealing intellectual property in that they both come down to how they change trade flows (and international flows of revenue, such as from oil leases). Nevertheless, estimating such costs requires understanding the relationship between the recipient of the information and the victim of the EMCE, not just examining trade statistics. Several other differences merit note:

- A large share of business proprietary information is stolen through more traditional methods associated with intelligence such as bugging telephones, subverting laptops, or wiring local hotel rooms.
- Business proprietary information tends to be much more volatile; taking it can, at best, cause a onetime gain, while copying intellectual property can move its recipients up the knowledge ladder, thereby altering advantage for a longer time.
- Business proprietary information can largely be used only to gain an advantage against the specific company that the recipient is competing against, while intellectual property can be used to gain an advantage over all competitors.

Finally, finding out the negotiating strategy of others can backfire. Normally, one purpose of finding out someone else's negotiating strategy is to determine the maximum that it would pay for something and hold out for that price. But the hackers' discovery of Coca-Cola's negotiating strategy (to buy China's Huiyuan Juice Group) led to a canceled deal. If China had really wanted to crush the deal, it hardly needed cyberespionage to do so.

This analysis assumes that the Chinese have stolen data from most U.S. corporations, support for which would seem to come from a report that in 2013 the FBI informed 3,000 corporations that they had been hacked.[35] We had further assumed that what they stole was intellectual property, which supposedly gave their recipients a permanent leg up in the market, rather than business proprietary information, which tend to be more short-lived data (for example, to find and seize an advantage in business negotiations or legal actions). The indictments of the five Chinese hackers in May 2014, however, suggest that the search for business proprietary information currently dominates.

According to press releases associated with the indictment, six organizations were hacked and the following was taken:[36]

- Westinghouse: technical and design specifications for piping and e-mails associated with the construction of a Chinese facility for a state-owned enterprise
- Solar World: information about cash flow, manufacturing methods, production line information, costs, and privileged client-attorney communications related to ongoing trade litigation
- U.S. Steel: information on servers, probably associated with a trade case against Chinese steel companies
- Allegheny Technologies Incorporated: information on network credentials, probably associated with a joint venture and with a trade dispute with a state-owned enterprise
- United Steelworkers: e-mails associated with strategies related to pending trade disputes
- Alcoa: e-mails including internal discussions about a partnership with a Chinese state-owned enterprise.

Note that every single organization that was hacked was dealing with the Chinese, either as a business partner or as a commercial disputant.[37] There are few indications of intellectual property theft. There is a reference to the "manufacturing methods" of Solar World. The information on "piping" associated with Westinghouse piping might indicate intellectual property but might also be useful in understanding the cost basis for Westinghouse's bid in an effort by the Chinese to find a more advantageous price to buy Westinghouse's services.

Can the paucity of intellectual property within the mix of the take be otherwise explained? Perhaps it matters that the sample is small (six) and geographically concentrated (western Pennsylvania, which has less high technology than, say, Silicon Valley); thus, the take is not necessarily indicative. Or the U.S. government believes that revealing intellectual property theft would be more harmful to those organizations cooperating in its prosecution than revealing that business proprietary information was taken (although how that choice would survive the discovery process if the indictments went to trial is unclear).

If, however, the Chinese are predominantly stealing business proprietary information rather than IP, several implications follow. First, it helps explain the conundrum of figuring out where this information goes (the answer would be: to very specific recipients, predominantly government owned). Second, it would confirm the argument in this chapter that converting stolen data files into the kind of know-how that permits a permanent shift in market position is considerably more difficult than made out to be. Third, therefore, the impact of Chinese EMCE on the U.S. economy is, while still substantial, even lower than the calculations below would indicate. Fourth, the distinction that the U.S. government is trying to make between Chinese EMCE and what the United States does (for example, acquire data to assist international trade negotiators) is finer than imagined.

As a sanity check (and an order-of-magnitude comparison) on the *total* cost to the U.S. economy from the theft of intellectual property and business proprietary information, consider the amount of money spent by U.S. corporations to limit the damage from EMCE. After all, U.S. corporations have no less reason to spend money to reduce the costs that accrue from EMCE than they do to eliminate all other costs that affect their bottom line. Globally, around $80 billion was spent on cybersecurity worldwide.[38] The U.S. government spends about $10 billion of that; perhaps other governments combined also spend $10 billion (militaries are particularly heavy spenders on cybersecurity, and the U.S. military is roughly as large as everyone else's military combined). Figure end-consumers spend another $15 billion, leaving $45 billion to be spent by organizations, of which the United States likely accounts for a third (just as it accounts for a third of all corporate activity). This yields a $15 billion estimate of organizational spending on cybersecurity—but this money covers organizations with little intellectual property at stake (for example, banks, retail) but that have threats from cybercrime as a reason to improve their cybersecurity. Furthermore, within worried organizations, spending is motivated by risks apart from Chinese EMCE; they include insider threats, other cybercrime, and database confidentiality (for example, the SQL injection attack). This leaves a few billion dollars at most directed against EMCE. Granted, this number is rising largely because many companies that felt themselves immune from EMCE have rethought their position. Yet unless one can argue that U.S. corporations are systematically stupid about risk management, the billions that they are willing to spend to reduce EMCE throws into question estimates far in excess of $10 billion a year that EMCE is costing them.[39]

As a final sanity check, note what a large percentage of complaints about Chinese cyberespionage come from the intelligence community, DoD, and the FBI (none of which have economic growth as their primary responsibility). By contrast, note how few have come from the President's Council of Economic Advisors, the Special Trade Representative, or the Departments of Commerce and Treasury. It was not until the Xi-Obama Sunnylands Summit, whose U.S. top agenda item was Chinese cyberespionage, that a secretary of the treasury complained to Chinese officials.

CONCLUSIONS

Even were all fair in love and war, the same cannot be said for international trade. There are rules and regulations governing trade. China has accepted such norms by dint of being a WTO member with its trade-related aspects of intellectual property rights clauses.[40] Insofar as China's EMCE results in the theft of intellectual property, it likely violates these rules (whether these rules are violated by stealing business proprietary data is less clear). The United States has a right to forbid the import of goods and services that have benefited from such theft (notwithstanding the difficulty of proving as much) and the right to persuade like-minded nations (many of whom are also victims) to react similarly. And although there is little to no evidence that U.S. firms are currently contemplating pulling back on developing intellectual property as a result, this could change, making the United States worse off.

Yet notwithstanding what the United States has the *right* to demand, the *wisdom* of confronting China with deeds (not just words) does not automatically follow. Everything depends on what the United States can gain by persuading China to abjure such behavior compared to the risk of irritating China.[41] This chapter has raised arguments for believing that the net cost to the U.S. economy from EMCE is limited.[42] For this reason, the wisdom of a confrontational strategy that risks such costs should be compared against the benefits to be gained by such a confrontation. And such considerations should also factor in those issues between the United States and China in which China's cooperation may be useful (for example, managing North Korea or reducing carbon dioxide emissions).

CHAPTER 9
Return to Vendor

The NSA not only employs a hacking crew far more talented at finding ways to compromise systems than their civilian counterparts (as well as contractors on call), but it also purportedly spends an additional $25 million paying others to find vulnerabilities for it to use.[1] Zero days are an important, perhaps the most important, tool in the hacker's kit bag, particularly when going after hard targets. Knowing about a zero-day vulnerability permits exploits for which few *specific* defenses exist. This makes them valuable for U.S. government agencies that need to penetrate foreign computer systems. Unfortunately, this also makes them valuable for foreign agents and criminals who want to grab the contents of U.S. information systems.

WHAT SHOULD THE NSA DO ABOUT ZERO DAYS?

Does the NSA's buying or even developing zero-day vulnerabilities put it in the business of making cyberspace less secure? In addressing this question, recommendation number thirty of the "Report and Recommendations of the President's Review Group on Intelligence and Communications Technologies" argued, "U.S. policy should generally move to ensure that Zero Days are quickly blocked, so that the underlying vulnerabilities are patched on U.S. Government and other networks. In rare instances, U.S. policy may briefly authorize using a Zero Day for high priority intelligence collection, following senior, interagency review involving all appropriate departments."[2] The deputy assistant secretary of defense for cyber "has said that the government discloses vulnerabilities it finds to software companies."[3] Michael Daniel, President Obama's cybersecurity coordinator, has offered similar assessments of the trade-off.[4]

What considerations should go into *whether* to return vulnerabilities back to their vendors rather than retain them for intelligence work?[5] *When* should such vulnerabilities be returned? In asking these questions, we posit an informed decisionmaker that can weigh the damage from leaving vulnerabilities unfixed against the benefit to the United States (or collectively the intelligence-sharing Five Eyes: the United States, Canada, Australia, the United Kingdom, and New Zealand) from using such vulnerabilities to acquire intelligence. Granted, actual costs and benefits are nearly incalculable. Government rarely makes or at least publicly reveals such calculations, in part because, as noted, a long train of judgments links any particular piece of intelligence to any improvement in decisionmaking.[6] Furthermore, judging the value of retaining a zero-day attack for intelligence purposes requires some sense of how successful its use is likely to be, and—what is less knowable almost by definition—what will be found by successful hackers.

True, hacking does not require zero days.[7] Organizations in which even a few machines exposed to the outside are not fully patched may be penetrated without them. Very little cybercrime uses zero-day attacks because there are enough poorly patched systems to steal from. Most bots would probably be bots in a world without zero days as well. Thus, a world without zero days is not necessarily a world without hacking—but it is a world in which the harder, and often more critical, systems would be hacked far less often.

RETAIN OR RETURN: SOME CRITERIA

Two factors that could tilt the NSA's return-or-retain decision are who else might know about the vulnerability and whether the vulnerability more likely characterizes the systems of friends than the system of foes.

The disposition of a discovered vulnerability should weigh on the odds that the NSA can use it for U.S. interests against the odds that others can use it against U.S. interests. The latter will often depend on how many vulnerabilities a product has (or, what is similar, how quickly vulnerabilities are depleted by discovery) and how long a vulnerability lasts between its discovery by someone who intends to use it for exploitation and its eradication.[8]

The NSA's discovery of a vulnerability ought not to affect the odds that someone else has discovered it—but only if the NSA does not *use* the vulnerability. If it uses the vulnerability on a sophisticated target with ties to intelligence agencies, such a target might determine that and then figure out how it was hacked, unearth the vulnerability that permitted the hack, and determine that it is a zero day. The target or its friends can then use it to carry out its own zero-day attacks (but probably not against organizations given privileged access to the NSA's vulnerabilities). Much depends on how often the victims of the NSA's intrusions discover they had been hacked. In practice, examples are rare.

Research suggests that a given product's vulnerabilities do deplete.[9] Roughly one hundred zero days are discovered by bounty-paid researchers over the course of a year; a comparable number are unearthed a year by the Zero-Day Initiative over a multiyear period.[10] This suggests that the number of undiscovered *and practically exploitable* vulnerabilities *in any one product* is in the hundreds, and, in some cases, lower.[11]

Another way of understanding vulnerability discovery and depletion is to look at the number of zero-day vulnerabilities that have been found twice. Roughly 3 to 5 percent of all vulnerabilities reported to vulnerability reward programs have been discovered by others.[12] One paper disclosed, "Our Firefox dataset does not indicate independent rediscovery, but we have limited data from personal communication with a Firefox security engineer. . . . He indicated that there had been at least 4–7 vulnerabilities reported through the VRP [vulnerability rewards program] for which there had been two independent discoveries, a rate of 2.7% to 4.7%, which is consistent with what we see in our Chrome dataset."[13] A reported vulnerability, at the time of the article, was patched after an average of 120 days.[14] Putting these data together suggests that a vulnerability that is found by someone has roughly a 10 percent likelihood of being found by someone else in the course of a year. In other words, if every vulnerability were equally obscure, its typical half-life would be ten years.

In practice, there may be clumping. Scientific discoveries, for instance, are correlated in that when the time is right, multiple people make the same discovery.[15] If, similarly, when the time is right, a certain class of vulnerabilities will be discovered by disparate researchers (who may not tell one another), then the odds that something discovered by the government is *also* discovered by someone else would be that much higher (as noted, the Heartbleed vulnerability was a near-simultaneous discovery). That noted, it is unclear what mechanism would lead to simultaneity.[16]

Sharp differentiations between U.S.-used software and foreign-used software are unlikely. Most of the world runs the same packaged software, and almost all of the packaged software that people use is supplied by American companies. It is fair to say that the percentage of all critical software vulnerabilities that are found in non-U.S. software is in the low single digits; only 1 percent of all vulnerabilities reported to the Zero-Day Initiative came from non-U.S. software (defined to exclude international foundations with heavy U.S. participation such as Mozilla, Linux, and Apache).[17] Thus, few are the vulnerabilities that affect the targets of U.S. espionage but not U.S. (or, more broadly, Western) users themselves. Otherwise, the case against returning the vulnerabilities to the vendors would be a lot easier to make.[18]

This universality of software, by contrast, does not characterize defense equipment, notably electronic warfare equipment. During the Cold War, neither side made each other's equipment. Even today, U.S. foes rarely get their kit from U.S. sources (although ISIL has armed itself with *stolen* U.S. equipment). Insofar as, say, electronic warfare systems used by the other side have vulnerabilities, our government has an easy choice of what not to do when it finds them (why secure equipment that only adversaries use?).

Might there be subtle differences between the ways various countries use software that could tilt the return-or-retain decision? One is that the percentage of personal computers that run modern operating systems (notably Windows Vista forward) is currently lower in China (and many other developing countries) than it is in the United States.[19] Everything else being equal, therefore, vulnerabilities discovered in Windows XP but not in later versions of Windows are better candidates for keeping (particularly given the reluctance of Microsoft to keep patching Windows XP after April 2014). Also, while few in the United States (and to a lesser extent, the West) run Huawei and ZTE equipment, many in developing countries (notably China) do. So, vulnerabilities in *those* products may be worth hoarding. The UC browser is a very popular app in China and India but is practically unknown in the United States—hence, its value as a locus of injected malware.[20]

AFTER HOW LONG SHOULD A ZERO DAY BE RETURNED TO VENDOR?

The argument for the *initial* use of an exploitable vulnerability can be strong. Since the best way to determine that a vulnerability is exploitable is to write an exploit for it, researchers can have something to use once they confirm a vulnerability. On the first day the exploit is available, it could be tried against high-priority but not-yet-penetrated targets. Afterward, the exploit could be used on successively lower-priority targets. At some point, the value of keeping a vulnerability dips below the value of fixing the software.

But that logic may depend on certain assumptions. *First,* can the not-yet-penetrated targets actually be penetrated that quickly? That depends. If the exploit, for instance, can be quickly mounted on a site that the target uses (also known as a "drive-by attack"), then *yes.* If the penetration requires, say, social engineering whose likelihood of working on any given day is small, then *maybe not.* If it requires someone inadvertently walking a USB device from a penetrated system to an air-gapped system (à la Stuxnet), or if it tends to spread slowly from one device to another, then the answer is *definitely not. Second,* once a patch comes out, will the organization whose systems have been penetrated be willing or even able to go back to its logs, determine that it has been hacked, and remove the source of its troubles? A *yes* answer argues against returning the vulnerability, particularly if its purpose is to provide a continuous tap on day-to-day information. Conversely, if the purpose of penetrating a system can be satisfied quickly (as it might be if the purpose was to pinch particular files, collect particular criminal evidence, or set up a cyberattack), then perhaps not. *Third,* is there a list of not-yet-penetrated high-priority targets that such an exploit can be applied to, or do high-priority targets surface unpredictably on a day-to-day basis? If the latter, then the value of the exploit on the day it is ready may not necessary decline so quickly over time.

By contrast, there is no ipso facto reason that compels *others* that know about the vulnerability to use it any more on the day the *government* finds it than they did the day before or the day after. The value of the exploit to these hackers (and correspondingly, the cost to organizations whose cybersecurity matters to the United States) declines much more slowly over time (largely as the likelihood of its being patched ratchets upward).

Assume, conversely, that the value of the vulnerability declines only slowly over time. What considerations should go into *subsequent* decisions on when to return the vulnerability?

Start with what should be an easy one. If the vendor patches or writes over the vulnerability, there is nothing to return, and thus the decision is moot. Whether or not the vulnerability works may depend on how the patch is distributed (for example, faster in the case of Microsoft operating system updates, slower if the cleaner version of the product needs to be separately purchased: for example, a new version of Office). If the vulnerability is not discovered but overwritten in the course of producing a new version of the software, older versions of the software may be unpatched, and the decision to return the vulnerability to the vendor still involves trade-offs. Even if the software update is universally applied, the vendor may still get an insight into its own software process and design features from having the vulnerability revealed.

What if the vulnerability is known to have been discovered by others? The government might have learned as much through its intelligence collection or by unpacking something fishy in the networks or firewalls it monitors. If so, others are probably exploiting it, and the decision should tilt toward returning the vulnerability—unless those using the vulnerability (for example, U.S. allies) are actively avoiding friendly targets and have no interest in selling such a vulnerability.

What if the government concludes that the exploit is working less and less frequently? This may be true if, say, the module the vulnerability was in was increasingly being routed around or the exploit was part of a broader class of blocked traffic. If so, then the benefits of continued exploitation go down, and the decision would tilt toward returning the vulnerability to the vendor.

What if none of the three discoveries (by the vendor, by other hackers, or by potential targets) is known to take place? At what point does the likelihood that the vulnerability has been discovered tilt the decision toward returning the vulnerability? After all, the likelihood that a vulnerability has been discovered (even if not disclosed) always rises over time; it never falls. However, if analyzed à la Bayes, the opposite case may be made: the longer a vulnerability stays undiscovered, the harder it must have been to discover it, and thus, in retrospect, the less likely it is that someone else *has already* discovered it.

If the government has a surfeit of similar vulnerabilities, the odds that it gets to use the nth vulnerability on its list becomes small (and zero when the vulnerable software is rewritten). If so, the loss to the government of returning vulnerabilities to the vendor is small; other hackers may not be so well endowed with zero days and would find even mediocre ones worth using. Given the risk that returning the vulnerability may lead to unearthing prior penetrations, the government's strategy would be not to release the already-used vulnerability but those it needs least, which may well be the newest one discovered (this then becomes an argument for redirecting resources otherwise used for finding vulnerabilities in a particular piece of software).

All this assumes that vendors will fix the vulnerabilities that the NSA points out to them. But vendors inevitably prioritize patching the many vulnerabilities they face; those actively exploited are usually first in line. Thinking thus, a vendor may push NSA-discovered-but-not-yet-exploited vulnerabilities lower on the to-do list, unless prodded. It may well figure that even if the NSA discovered a vulnerability, no one else has, and given the NSA's reputation, the odds that someone else could do so is lower than if the discovery came from elsewhere, because the NSA can find vulnerabilities better than anyone else can.[21]

The impact of there being an active civilian bug bounty program on the exploit-or-return decision depends on particular modalities of such a program. If the intelligence community can itself be paid for bugs, it may decide to return more of them (even though, from a national perspective, the costs and benefits have not changed). If individuals are rewarded, incentives are created that may persuade intelligence community employees to sell to vendors what they find in their day job (but perhaps surreptitiously, given conflict of interest rules).

Some further effects of a white-hat program on the black-hat world may be surmised. For instance, the mere existence of such a program may convince some on the intelligence side that the government overall is doing enough to help the software firms do what they should have been doing for themselves all along. Government hackers therefore have less obligation to help improve software, especially if it comes at the expense of intelligence collection (the argument may be felt even if white hats and the intelligence community are each finding very different vulnerabilities).

A white-hat bug bounty program may also increase the demand for bugs and thereby raise the cost to the intelligence community of buying vulnerabilities. Inasmuch as the U.S. government does not like competing against itself, the establishment of a white-hat bug bounty program may be accompanied by having just one entity buy such vulnerabilities. For each acquisition, an exploit-or-return decision would follow, promising to disappoint at least one side of the keep-or-return divide.

Finally, if the bug bounty program is run by a civilian government agency (for example, DHS), might the intelligence community try to override that agency's decision to return the bug in order to keep it for exploitation purposes—or at least get some inside information on the vulnerability so that it can be exploited in the window between when it is handed off to the vendor and when a patch is distributed?

IRRELEVANT CONSIDERATIONS

Several proffered arguments made against revealing vulnerabilities hold little water. One, revealing the vulnerabilities also reveals how they were found in the networks of adversaries. This can apply only to a small fraction of discoveries, in light of the many other ways the bug could have been found. More so, if adversaries really do know such vulnerabilities, the argument for returning them to the vendor is all the stronger.

Two, U.S. competitors (for example, Russia, China) are not sharing.[22] This is likely true, unquestionably unfortunate, difficult to imagine otherwise in the real world (where the recipients of such information would almost certainly be U.S.-based companies), but largely irrelevant to the keep-or-return dilemma. When both the United States and its geopolitical competitors are trying to crack a third party's system and the one who gets there first "wins" (in the sense that it then locks the other side out), then oversharing with vendors might be considered unilateral disarmament. But such situations are quite the exception. If there is a competition, it is more likely to be waged over how well competing countries can penetrate U.S. systems—in which case better cybersecurity that results from using less-vulnerable software helps the United States. More broadly, neither the cost nor the benefits of returning particular vulnerabilities to vendors is terribly much affected by whether U.S. geostrategic competitors do or do not share vulnerabilities they themselves find.

Three, being forced to turn over such vulnerabilities might discourage such efforts within the NSA and tempt analysts to withhold information on them in the hopes that they could use them without being caught. The Review Group's twenty-fifth recommendation states that the "Information Assurance Directorate—a large component of the National Security Agency that is not engaged in activities related to foreign intelligence—should become a separate agency within the Department of Defense." The unlikely event of its implementation, though, might *remove* some incentives for the NSA to consider information security equities in such decisions.

CONCLUSIONS

When the government finds a vulnerability in software, it faces the choice between returning it to the vendor and exploiting it to penetrate systems (for intelligence or attack purposes). In late 2014, Michael Daniel argued that the government does not "stockpile *large* [emphasis added] numbers of zero days for use," suggesting that the number nevertheless is nonzero.[23]

Several factors should influence its decision: whether the vulnerable product is used more often in target countries than in the United States or the West, whether the U.S. government has alternative ways of protecting systems critical to the country, and how fast the value of the exploit falls over time. Overall, the choice of whether and when to return a vulnerability to its vendor depends on whether the United States (and those it wishes to consider in its calculus) gains more from having the security that comes from using software with fewer security bugs or from gaining information from hardened systems (that is, those that require zero-day attacks). This is almost incalculable. Nevertheless, note that those who head or headed the FBI, the Joint Chiefs of Staff, the Department of Defense, and the nation's top intelligence position have all labeled cyberattacks either as an existential threat or as the country's most serious near-term threat.[24] No such case has been made for the possible consequence of leaving the "golden age of surveillance" and "going dark."[25]

Let us conclude with a question. Assume that it becomes known that the NSA has had (legal and acknowledged) access to the source code of a U.S. product. Should others, notably foreigners, feel worse or better about purchasing the product? In Snowden's wake, "worse" would seem more likely and difficult to argue against. In a world in which the NSA red-teams such products intelligently and with a view to improving them by returning their vulnerabilities to vendors to be fixed, "better" would be the correct answer—and, perhaps in time, the more likely answer. Which world is better for U.S. interests?

CHAPTER 10
Cybersecurity Futures

W̶ill systems become easier or harder to compromise over time? Three factors seem to dominate this question: the quality of offense, the quality of defense, and, oft overlooked but perhaps most important, what systems allow users to do. Better offense and more applications favor the intensification of cyberwar. Better defenses would diminish the risk. If each factor were of equal importance, the power of cyberwar—the threat from insecurity—is likely to increase. But each factor needs to be independently assessed.

BETTER OFFENSE

Clearly, attackers are getting better. Perhaps twenty, maybe even ten years ago, clever (and morally challenged) underemployed youths may have been unaware what a lucrative career move it was to get into the hacking business. These days, it is difficult to envision any corner of the world where such opportunities are unknown. Also growing is the understanding by countries of what can be gained through cyberattacks on their foes (in the case of cyberwar) or anyone with information of value (in the case of cyberespionage). That said, when people say the sophistication of cyberattacks is increasing, they might mean that the hackers' ability to sidestep measures designed to distinguish their efforts from the noise level may be increasing, not necessarily that the hackers' ability to overcome defenses may be increasing.

In recent years, networks of criminals have improved their ability to specialize their services so that no one hacker needs a complete set of talents—penetration, asset removal, fencing credit cards, converting them into cash—when such talents can be purchased on hacker markets.[1] Hackers also have access to better and easier-to-use tools—although script kiddies are so last decade and were overrated at the time anyway. If practice makes perfect, hackers are certainly getting practice.

But have such trends plateaued? In 2009, one could hear predictions that nonstate actors would, in two to three years, have the sophistication of national intelligence services because they would be able to buy the requisite tools. Although similar claims are still being made, the old ones have not been borne out, and the new ones should be regarded with a grain of salt.

Another factor that may add to the talents or at least options available to the offense is the popular legitimization of certain cyberattacks. Anonymous and Lulzsec may have crossed the authorities, but they have added a sprinkle of panache to the business by going after the arrogant (such as H. B. Gary) or the obnoxious (such as the Westboro Baptist Church). Stuxnet, for its part, amounted to state legitimization of cyberwar as a national tool—something the victim of Stuxnet may think covers its own mischief, such as DDOS attacks on banks.

Might hackers simply be the beneficiaries of expanding attack surfaces? If so, can they still make progress against targets whose attack surface is not increasing? Gregory D. Koblentz's "Strategic Stability in the Second Nuclear Age" presumes that cyberattacks represent a "longer-term" threat to strategic nuclear capability.[2] But if the information architectures of strategic nuclear systems do not change (and such systems are managed extremely conservatively), then the pattern of vulnerabilities—and hence the opportunity for their exploitation—will not change either. Given the relentlessness with which such vulnerabilities have been tested for established strategic nuclear systems over the last few decades, the basis for the "longer-term" assessment is not obvious.[3]

A LARGER ATTACK SURFACE

The opening of formerly closed corporate networks to customer penetration also bears watching. One example is the Smart Grid, which allows electric distribution decisions to reflect customer-generated inputs such as usage patterns and adds home-generated electricity into local power generation options. Fortunately, there has been so much concern that the Smart Grid is not so smart from a cybersecurity perspective that by the time it is fielded, hackers may be blocked from being able to work backward from consumer meters into grid management; unfortunately, as Ross Anderson has shown, it provides opportunities for every customer's power supply to be individually hacked (and perhaps all of them at once).[4]

A similar trend, somewhat later down the road, is the increasing population of things that think, also known as the Internet of Things.[5] The digitization of cars is an old story; the average car has twenty to fifty computational units in it. But the networking of cars (for example, General Motors' OnStar system) is a new story. Hackers have already demonstrated that they can force networked cars into very unsafe acts.[6] Although regulators are already mindful of this risk, their concerns can be overrun if one such yet-to-be-fully-security-tested application becomes a must-have item (if not by consumers, then by those who make cars and want to monitor and/or maintain them after they are sold). Perhaps automobiles will start generating conversations with intelligent transportation systems and vehicles that they share the road with, creating interaction that produces problems not inherent in either vehicle or road.

The cybersecurity impact of making devices Internet-addressable, especially if by default, also bears watching.[7] True, most devices tend to be special-purpose, and thus many of the vectors by which they can be attacked (for example, via web-surfing or social engineering) do not apply. Furthermore, although cell phones and consumer tablets introduce another vector into organizational networks, they can substitute for many non-work-related uses of personal computers. Knowing this, adroit organizations can now remove those features of personal computers hitherto retained for office morale and return the computers to machines of limited functionality (to wit: e-shopping on cell phones produces fewer problems for organizations than e-shopping on networked computers). Nevertheless, the secure use of non-computer devices does require some discipline in limiting which messages and which senders they can respond to. Even if corrupted devices are not given privileged access to an organization's network *and* their own failures can be tolerated (clearly not true for medical devices), their insecurity has to merit concern. A hacker who can read others' devices may learn too much about someone's personal habits or an organization's work routines. A device's memory may also yield passwords to networks or network services.[8]

Allowing manufacturers to update their devices over the Internet by sending out digitally signed software updates poses only a small risk to security (compared with having no updates at all). Opening up such devices to third-party software creates more risks, but ones that can be managed if they go through trusted portals. Allowing such devices to communicate freely with all ports open is asking for trouble.

If such an Internet of Things comes to pass, it is important for the security, and hence often the safety, of their users that vendors should avoid mistakes made several decades earlier in building personal computers (and related networked devices). Even if deficient cybersecurity was a reasonable price to pay for starting an information revolution, most of what the Internet of Things would improve already works today (albeit perhaps with less customization, efficiency, and adaptability than vendors of smart devices might promise). Manufacturers of smart cars may want to understand the problematic architectural issues they may have to face:

- *Software installation.* The earliest personal computers were designed to have their instruction set altered easily. Now malware can do so via multiple channels without the user noticing, much less approving, let alone initiating, such changes. How might, say, automobile instruction sets be validated as authorized *and* benign before being installed?

- *Software maintenance.* It has taken a long time and decades of maturity for software makers to understand their responsibility to keep their already-purchased software free of vulnerabilities, once they are pointed out (often, by figuring out how hacks succeeded). Many observers of the Internet of Things worry that suppliers do not understand lifetime support and the proprietary nature of their code that may prevent others from providing it.[9]

- *Trusting inputs.* Rarely do computers demand sufficient proof of good intentions when executing or receiving instructions (especially from websites). There may well be similar demands for third parties to offer services associated with intelligent cars and roads. It is unclear whether methods will be developed to ensure that such services are undertaken for honest reasons.

- *Configuration management.* The Internet has so reduced the cost of interacting with machinery (for example, electric power generators) that people have connected things that should have been more isolated. As important as decisions of what to connect are decisions of what not to connect (or connect only with one-way links).

- *Time-to-market.* Just as competitors for ruling the information economy believe the market will reward time-to-market over security (which can be fixed later), so will those competing to supply the Internet of Things. Can the trade-off be better this time—especially in businesses where security means personal safety?

The problem of hackable cars was said to be one that would persist for decades, not only because automakers lacked familiarity with writing secure software but also because it would take that long to retire every insecure vehicle. But will it? Read the two leading articles on the Jeep hack and you will not see the word "recall."[10] On the Friday after the articles appeared, this omission was rectified when Fiat/Chrysler, under pressure from the U.S. National Highway Traffic Safety Administration (NHTSA), recalled 1.4 million cars to fix the defect (vulnerability) that allowed hackers to imperil drivers.[11] In essence, what was a huge unsolved problem was converted into a solved or at least solvable problem. The NHTSA possessed two essential tools generally missing in the whole cybersecurity debate: a regulatory paradigm within which the problem of insecure vehicle control software could be easily fit, and the legal authority to solve problems according to that paradigm. To wit, a cybersecurity problem could be understood as a discrete safety problem and NHTSA had the tool—mandatory recall—to address it (and even if some drivers chose not to install the USB-based fix, the cost of such a recall may persuade carmakers to take cybersecurity more seriously next time). The Consumer Product Safety Commission also has recall powers. The Food and Drug Administration regulates medical devices. Building codes can be applied to forestall the installation of problematic home fixtures. The Occupational Safety and Health Administration has the power to make the workplace less hazardous (for example, by making industrial machinery safer). Indeed, safety is something the United States has been dealing with for over a hundred years, with increasing success over time. Any cybersecurity problem that can be conceptualized as a safety problem can be worked as well.

Yet some aspects of the cybersecurity problem are not easily framed as safety problems. One is that hacking into many of the devices can provide surveillance on individuals (for example, where your car goes, when you are home, what your medical condition is). Whereas harming safety is always a bad thing, politically, we are not as ready to declare that surveillance (for example, by law enforcement) is always a bad thing or at least not all that important. So the authority to force recalls because devices can be tricked into leaking information is far less well established. Another aspect is that whereas we have the legal structure to enforce safe software if it is embedded in a device, no such legal structure exists to enforce the safety of software downloaded from third parties or resident in the cloud.

There is a comparable impetus for a military Internet of Things. Consider a battlefield swarm composed of devices that used to take orders only from warfighters that now take them from one another as well. One major difference between intelligent transportation systems, for instance, and battlefield swarms is that while the motivation for an outsider attacking the former is speculative (what does success gain the attacker?), the latter is obvious. The problem with machines taking their cues from one another is that doing so makes it difficult to determine the source of unwanted behavior. The failure of a device to carry out a human command may be laid to its being compromised, but devices made so that they do run only official instruction sets cannot go too far wrong. A device, however, that makes a decision based on input from another device, whose input is, in turn, colored by the input from a third device, and so on, is one in which an indefinite set of interactions can lead to unwanted activity. The broader the state space of a machine, the greater the potential sources of error. Natural systems can afford self-referenced (such as flocking) behavior because there are no intelligent malign actors and because persistent maladaptive behavior is gradually eliminated through evolutionary forces. But manmade systems used in war and programmed to react to a range of external inputs such as observable elements may encounter inputs carefully engineered by the enemy to induce behavior that the enemy wants. The military that wants useful outcomes from its swarms lacks the millions of years or, more to the point, may not be able to generate the number and breadth of equivalent test cycles required to engineer maladaptive behavior out of the system once the enemy figures out how to induce it.

As argued, it is architecture (as a reflection of architectural choices) as much or more than coding that explains why systems are subject to malware in the form of arbitrary remote code execution. But complexity is still the leading source of unwanted responses of programs to carefully manipulated input (for example, SQL-I, or the recent rash of SSL flaws). Even though the unwanted responses are limited to responses that exist within the software's repertoire (rather than responses that exist within a processor's instruction set), these can still be costly errors to fight against, and they are never going to stop as long as software is so soft.

BETTER DEFENSE

An organization's defense can often be understood in terms of two components: the quality of software on each processor (also known as attack surface) and systemic defenses established to protect the system as a whole by detecting attacks as such and eradicating their presence.[12]

There is considerable money devoted, hence considerable activity under way, to improve systemic defenses. Overall spending is near $80 billion a year; venture capital is pouring in,[13] in large part to find a replacement for the antivirus model, which even its vendors[14] now admit is close to complete failure.

The advent of cloud computing—or more generally, the outsourcing of computation—may help cybersecurity.[15] True, with cloud outsourcing, the number of places an attacker can grab information has risen from at least one (your computer) to at least two (your computer and its servers). Public cloud providers, as a late 2012 *Wired* article revealed, have not always been particularly fastidious about not letting hackers reset one's account.[16] However, the general trend toward outsourcing security in general (also known as managed security services or "security-as-a-service") could put server security in the hands of a relatively small number of providers—for example, IBM, Oracle, Google, Amazon, Microsoft, Rackspace—that are more likely to have specialized professional cybersecurity services than their customers do because of the size of cloud providers and because cybersecurity is a big selling point in their gaining business. These days, few Americans rely on their own farming skills to eat—why, in the long run, should everyone have to rely on their own computing skills to manage their information and services? Nevertheless, these systemic defenses must still surmount the challenge of separating false alarms from real ones (while not missing the latter) against the wits of hackers endeavoring to make their effects look as much like noise as they can. Furthermore, although clouds can contribute to server-side security, client-side insecurity remains a major source of network compromises and is unlikely to be helped so much—unless organizations put so much processing into the cloud that they replace PCs with much thinner or at least more locked-down clients.

This then leads to the question: can software become so good that few if any hackers will be able to place malware into a system (without taking advantage of onsite presence or by suborning legitimate users) and even then only with great effort? A great deal depends on how exploitable vulnerabilities in software are distributed.

The most optimistic software vulnerability model is that any one piece of software has a finite number of vulnerabilities. Once such vulnerabilities are found (and fixed and patched), hackers will have no way in (taking any human element out of the picture). Unfortunately, this model fails to account for the tendency of new software to replace old software well before all the vulnerabilities of the old software are discovered—as well as the possibility that new software introduces its own vulnerabilities. A perfectly bug-free piece of software is only an update away from having new vulnerabilities: both recent SSL vulnerabilities, Heartbleed and Apple's, occurred in the newer versions dating from January 2012 and November 2013, respectively. A former Microsoft vulnerability researcher has observed that the succession of subsequent releases coupled with the lead time associated with fixing vulnerabilities meant that any one version would only see a limited number of patches before being superseded by its successor. Serious analysts believe that a more realistic model of vulnerabilities is that their numbers are essentially unlimited, but the difficulty of finding successive vulnerabilities rises as the easier-to-find vulnerabilities are discovered (and eradicated).[17] As noted, a rough guess is that the half-life of a given vulnerability is ten years. If, however, the industry improves sufficiently that vulnerabilities are truly scarce, the half-life is likely to rise; the fewer the bugs, the less often one is found twice.

One recently used metric of how difficult it is to find a vulnerability is the number of fuzzing test cases that have to be run to find a flaw. In a March 2014 Pwn2Own competition, Chaouki Bekrar, president of Vupen, observed, "The Firefox zero-day we used today we found it through fuzzing, but it required 60 million test cases. That's a big number . . . that proves Firefox has done a great job fixing flaws; the same for Chrome."[18] To some—but only some—extent, the race between software companies and hackers (of whatever colored hat) to find vulnerabilities has a lot to do with how much fuzzing capacity each has (plus the efficiency of their fuzzers, which can vary greatly). In that regard, Google claimed in 2014 to have as many as three thousand fuzzers running their code full-time, with Microsoft having a tenth as many. Thus, to the extent that finding vulnerabilities in software takes an increasingly large number of fuzzing cycles, one could trace its increasing hardness over time and, correspondingly, predict the declining number of hackers capable of finding zero days. That noted, fuzzing is not the only way to find vulnerabilities.[19]

Successive versions of Microsoft operating systems tend to be better than what came before: "Scans of real-world systems show that XP systems get infected six times more often than computers running later editions, including Windows 8."[20] The aforementioned president of Vupen observed, "It's definitely getting harder to exploit browsers, especially on Windows 8.1. . . . exploitation is harder and finding zero-days in browsers is harder."[21] Indeed, "Left unscathed [at the 2014 Pwn-2Own contest] was the highest single prize of the contest, $150,000 for the 'Exploit Unicorn.' This rare beast demanded a specific hack: system-level code execution on a Windows 8.1 x64, in IE 11 x64, with an Enhanced Mitigation Experience Toolkit bypass."[22] More recently, however, hacker groups who used to rely on vulnerabilities in Adobe and Java to ease their way into networks either may have concluded that such vulnerabilities have been firewalled from the operating system or are returning to look for vulnerabilities in Microsoft's own product line.[23]

Improvements are available even at basic levels of architecture. Windows computers, for instance, no longer automatically run code from boot sectors of removable devices—the "design feature" that enabled Buckshot Yankee and the early versions of Stuxnet. Google's Chrome is notable for its sandboxing, which has proven very difficult, albeit not completely impossible, to break. The Chromebook's OS is similarly malware-resistant. An alternative route to defect-free software is to switch from those open to the insertion of new third-party code to those that are more locked down. The iOS operating system, noted earlier, is one candidate for such an approach, particularly if Apple can successfully get iOS features into MacOS (and vice versa) and thus ease its path into the corporation without losing its current security attributes.[24] And although it may seem like a minor point now, spam is not the problem (for end-users) that it was five to ten years ago (it still clogs networks, though).

Granted, eliminating malware in new programs would not eliminate malware in old programs. In a world in which a third of all users relied (circa mid-2014) on an operating system that has not been sold since 2007 (to wit, Windows XP), the victory of the new requires the retirement of the old. The longer the history of computers (which grows one year every year), the longer the tails of obsolescent equipment.[25] Their security vulnerabilities could be ignored when they were stand-alone machines but cannot be now when they are connected to the entire world.

NEW TOOLS FOR DEFENSE

Will tomorrow's more secure software suffice? Many investors doubt it; they are bankrolling companies that assume that the attack surface of organizations will never be good enough to keep an intruder from establishing a presence on at least some box, and leveraging that presence to scurry around their networks.

Prominent among these products have been those that seek to distinguish normal traffic (itself growing increasingly complex) from traffic made abnormal as a result of attack. Vendors of these tools (CrowdStrike is a good example) rely on a combination of big data analytic techniques and focused intelligence on specific hackers. Some of them (FireEye's tool is a good example) work by sandboxing incoming traffic to instrumented test hosts to see if the latter become infected. Even the former director of the NSA has started up a company.[26] Their emergence—even if beneficial—is not itself a positive sign. First, people would not be selling such tools unless they expected buyers to have foregone defending their organizations by using better software and different information architectures. Second, these tools are more like treating than curing the disease.[27] Such measures beget countermeasures more readily than do other measures such as those that improve an organization's ability to manage its own systems (such as what the patch level is or what is connected to what). Countermeasures to cybersecurity measures that work by distinguishing signal (of attack) from noise (of everyday networks) would entail making the attack signal look more like noise.[28] Just as malware writers are eager buyers of antivirus software to determine what will or will not get detected, the better-heeled hackers could easily get their hands on such measures and continually refine their techniques until their efforts no longer garner attention from them. True, part of the secret sauce may be retained by the vendors who could vet their customers and not sell to hackers. Or vendors may anticipate some of the countermeasures and withhold counter-countermeasures until subsequent versions of the product. Nevertheless, the cost of riding a measure-countermeasure treadmill is real.

A THREE MILE ISLAND IN CYBERSPACE

Technology almost always marches toward sophistication, power, and complexity; it rarely advances, halts, and backs up. But sometimes it does. In the aftermath of the 1979 Three Mile Island (TMI) accident, no ground was broken on a nuclear plant until 2013.

Could something like TMI take place in cyberspace? At what point or after what precipitating incident would a consensus emerge (howsoever justified on technical grounds) that insecurity in cyberspace had become intolerable? Furthermore, would it be recognized that conditions have become intolerable largely because today's networks had become too complex and promiscuous to defend affordably? If so, would organizations (and end-consumers) turn away from today's computer and network architectures and toward more secure, albeit less flexible and adaptable, alternatives?

Several assumptions are packed into these questions. *One* is that we have not, in fact, yet passed that point. Despite the crescendo of alarm coupled with rumblings (notably from the technical community) that completely new architectures are needed, most organizations have yet to experience their *Network* moment (as in "I'm as mad as hell, and I'm not going to take this anymore!"). Most CISOs are not ready to abandon the hope that increasing user education and buying defensive tools will permit managing the risk from cyberspace at acceptable cost. *Two* is that the world is no more ready to abandon networking today than it was to abandon electricity after TMI—but it may accept a different set of trade-offs to get the networking it wants. *Three* is that stepping back is preferable to walking forward faster. The leading edge of the security industry deprecates "patch and pray," and it prefers to pursue greater sophistication, not less. But rethinking architectures is not the same as rethinking technologies. Stepping back may, in fact, require a higher level of technology. Does Apple's iOS necessarily represent less technology, because it supports a locked-down machine redolent of the mainframes and mini-computers that were popular before personal computers came along? *Four* is that we get to TMI through a crystallizing incident rather than the constant accretion of bad news.

So, what would a TMI moment look like? If a precipitating incident would have the requisite effect, it probably could not be psychologically dismissed by blaming the perpetrator or a victim. What if Chinese hackers took down the U.S. electric power grid? Would organizations fundamentally reexamine their cybersecurity? Or would they hope that a more aggressive U.S. stance vis-à-vis Chinese hacking would suffice to protect their own networks? Or would they focus on features particular to the electric grid industry (for example, the insecurity of hardware-based SCADA systems)? The latter two reactions do not lend themselves to a TMI moment. Similarly, if there were a highly destructive worm that affected only Windows XP machines, would this be read as a lesson about networking per se or a lesson about the urgency of replacing XP machines? A great deal depends on which narratives resonate (and among whom). Events are mute; it is what people make of them that matters.

Nevertheless, that still leaves many potential events that could be disturbing, widespread, and indicative of internal architectural issues. Consider the following as potential TMI events.

Super-Shamoon

Every computer capable of hosting malware can host malware that trashes computers; modern trash attacks have all used the Shamoon virus or variants thereof.[29] A TMI event could be the rapid erasure of tens of millions of machines as a result of a worm that had spread widely before being detected or its malign nature understood. Almost every home router has vulnerabilities that could result in its trashing (fortunately, the vulnerabilities of each model class tend to be different, making an all-fall-down event harder to pull off).

Super-Zeus

E-banking rests on the premise and promise of safety, but malware, notably the Zeus Trojan, can void this promise by worming its way into sessions between customers and banks and siphoning off money while neither is aware of its presence. A wave of attacks frequent enough to make e-banking hazardous may echo into e-commerce as well.

A DDOS Attack that Crashes the Internet

A botnet might successfully attack the Internet's routing or DNS structure over an extended period. As recent attacks have shown, a combination of capacious home networks of clueless users, poorly guarded cloud servers, and packet reflection services could have the requisite effect.

JPMorgan Chase, Only Much Worse

The JPMorgan Chase hack was 86 million customers wide but not deep: the bank kept operating, no money was lost, and no critical personally identifiable information was compromised. Had worse happened, other organizations (for example, multinational corporations) might reasonably conclude that even spending the quarter-billion dollars a year that JPMorgan Chase spent was not enough to protect a network against hackers. They might then wonder whether any amount of money spent on defending networks as currently architected could protect them.

An Industry Lost

A precipitating event may be one in which a U.S. industry had to close shop and the leak of intellectual property via cyberespionage was perceived to be why. This may persuade organizations to keep closer tabs on whether and how they expose their intellectual property (and corporate e-mails) to the Internet.

Military Defeat

Should deficiencies in cybersecurity be associated with military defeat (and one lost battle may suffice), a TMI reaction may be expected. Admittedly, military command and control systems are hard to penetrate in real time, while more open networks are less essential to warfighting outcomes. But unexpected dependencies between open and closed networks may permit attacks on the former to compromise the latter. In the face of such a reversal, nonmilitary organizations may tell themselves that at least they lack enemies dedicated to their destruction, but that would be thin comfort.

Unrestricted Cyberwar

Most systems are compromised for reasons of crime and espionage rather than disruption, corruption, or destruction. A shift in attitude within a country with capable cyberwarriors may raise the damage from cyberattacks to where they are much harder to ignore. Neither China nor even Russia is likely to do so absent overarching circumstances (for example, actual kinetic combat); Iran,

North Korea, or the Russian *mafiya* (perhaps operating under nod-nod-wink-wink imperatives) just might. Exactly how much damage even they could do is another question.

None of the above events have transpired; none is individually likely over the next ten years. But if one did occur *and* if the subsequent narrative stressed the difficulty of protecting systems as is done now, then current network architecture could come under severe scrutiny.

Or would it? Radical change tends to be infrequent because it is difficult. For cybersecurity, the necessary changes may easily cost hundreds of billions of dollars—and no one incident of the sort limned above may necessarily reach that cost threshold. Incumbent technologies are supported by powerful organizations that make a living selling such technologies and that are both motivated and resourced to promise that the next version will cure the ills of current versions. Behind them lie cybersecurity products whose vendors promise to solve today's cybersecurity ills without customers having to rethink the fundamentals of their networking. Finally, the argument that a radical change is needed is poorly articulated today and has few natural advocates.[30] As desperate as people might be after a TMI event, it is hard to beat something with nothing. Nevertheless, what are the more fundamental, perhaps radical, solutions that may arise?

- *Trusted distribution.* Ensuring that system software cannot be changed except by going through a trusted source could prevent malware from establishing a permanent presence on such machines. Apple's "walled garden" approach with iOS is an example where it plays the role of trusted source. A similar architecture for military (and perhaps also defense industrial base) equipment could require a digital signature from, say, the NSA's Information Assurance Directorate prior to installation.
- *Intensified air-gapping.* Isolation helps keep systems from being communicated to, and hence commanded, by hackers. This isolation could be physical or it could be virtual in that the public Internet is used only as a transport device for shuttling encrypted traffic between protected nodes. A softer version is to allow traffic (such as performance indicators) to move out of a system but not into it (data diodes are one such mechanism). Softer versions of isolation may be available from intense filtration in which allowable messages are whitelisted in advance.
- *Conformance monitoring.* Tools that ascertain that all machines in a network are fully patched are ones that, by definition, cannot be infected except by zero-day attacks. The complete use of MFA would add security.
- *One-touch system restoration.* The costs of seeing computers bricked might be alleviated if they could be readily restored to factory specifications—and then from there to where programs, configuration data, and working data are easily, perhaps automatically, restored as well. The latter would come from servers (or the cloud). Although clouds are not fault-free, it would take two faults—in the bricked client and in the corrupted server—to cause serious problems.

This list is hardly meant to be complete; technological development and human ingenuity may provide other ways to ensure that architectural choices are reflected properly in the performance of systems. But the ability to compile a list suggests that desperation—or giving up entirely on networking—is not the only response. Again, there is no reason to believe that a TMI in cyberspace is inevitable. The harm from cyberspace (and the costs of keeping such harm under control) may be containable. The current suite of cybersecurity products may prove workable even in the hands of customers who, today, are not too certain how to set and operate such tools correctly. The industry may evolve from current dilemmas as software and hardware vendors face increasing pressure from customers. But it never hurts to ask: what if?

CHAPTER 11
Operational Cyberwar

Cyberattacks against military targets and military-related civilian targets carried out during or just prior to war can be a decisive force multiplier if employed carefully, discriminately, at just the right time—and the opponent uses networks in the first place.[1]

POSSIBLE EFFECTS

The effects of cyberattacks on warfighting systems can be inferred from what cyberattacks do in general. We focus on disruption, corruption, and eruption (which has little role outside a military context)—as well as real-time cyberespionage carried out to support military operations.

Disruption

Disruption takes military systems down or cripples their workings. By doing so, it can create a short-lived window of opportunity—one that generally must be exploited vigorously before defenders can return their systems to full service. Disruption comes in many varieties: communications not sent or sent but not received; command and control systems that neither provide useful information nor transmit commands; sensors that go dark; or weapons whose electronics go haywire (which can prevent them from functioning, even in a debased or manual mode).

As with other forms of combat support, cyberattacks help more if warfighters know how well they worked—even if warfighters could just go ahead and conduct operations, pocketing any enemy paralysis as a bonus. In terms of effects, dark lights and missing signals are a good clue; reduced electronic traffic is a fair clue. Good in-the-net intelligence or echoes elsewhere (internal complaints, for instance) may also provide indications. Determining how much slower the other side made decisions requires a sense of how well their command and control would have worked if not attacked. Measuring degradation in the *quality* of the adversary's decisionmaking is harder. Foes that expect their command systems to be attacked (even if unsure of how or where) might generate spurious indications of woe: ostensibly paralyzed units are operable, or inoperable units appear to make decisions, albeit not well-informed ones. Military strategies that would exploit enemy paralysis may require operators to be confident that paralyzed units are, in fact, paralyzed—and such information may not be forthcoming. Intermittent disruption may be hard to verify if the target cannot distinguish a system with induced error rates from one that errs often on its own. Disruption may be particularly useful against a foe whose strategies are so precisely synchronized that small perturbations can upset large battle plans. Ironically, therefore, although cyberwar may depend on the close synchronization of virtual effects (the radar is knocked out) and physical effects (the jets fly unimpeded overhead), it can, itself, kill plans that rely on tight synchronization.[2]

Exactly how services provided to the other side would be disrupted by a cyberattack would depend on the details of the system. This requires deep intelligence not only on the system itself (such as how an SA-400 surface-to-air missile system works) but also on how the system's parameters are set and how the system fits into the broader network. Before personal computer architectures were standardized and ubiquitous, doing something to an opposing command and control system would have required painstakingly acquired insight. These days, the task is somewhat easier because exploitable faults in one personal computer (or server, router, and so forth) are often exploitable faults in others. But the defenses—including the quality of human defenses—that keep exploitable faults from harming the system are often unique to the system itself.

If, for a cyberattack, longer downtime is better, then trashing computer systems would seem to be the ultimate goal. It may not take many computers to make a network inoperable, and such flooding can be turned both off and on as needs dictate. Yet if foes realize that their systems have been trashed, as long as their data were backed up, they can swap out to new systems and continue as before; if flooded from the inside, it is not hard to detect the source of the byte flood. A more worthwhile goal may be to induce faults that are hard to detect (or at least hard to characterize as deliberately induced rather than an accident or some software flaw) or, if detected, hardest to diagnose, and, if diagnosed, hardest to fix. A brief outage may be militarily valuable if well timed, but the scheduling of follow-up operations to take advantage of disruption need not be so precise if the outage persists. Even in an age of standardization, intelligence on the other side's information systems—not only how networks are wired together but also how information is used—can be helpful. Alternatively, a network can be flooded by infecting its computers and commanding them to conduct a DDOS attack on their local neighbors.

Disrupting civilian systems communications or transportation systems may help cripple military command and control and hence operations (and if military systems are separate, then at least hinder military mobilization). Nevertheless, many civilian targets that may be plausible targets for air raids (for example, manufacturing plants) are not necessarily fruitful targets for cyberattacks. Cyberattacks mostly offer only temporary disruption. Thus, little may be gained by delaying for, say, a few days a process that is weeks behind military operations in the supply chain when schedule fluctuations can often be absorbed by reducing slack elsewhere in the supply chain. Furthermore, using certain exploits against civilian targets reduces their efficacy against military targets. A cyberattack on a civilian target may also be perceived as escalatory (although not as escalatory as a physical attack).

Corruption

Corruption is what makes systems function badly: for example, a missile that fails to point in the right direction; a sensor that fails to pick up on certain types of signals, is less sensitive than it should be, or misinterprets what it sees; a communications system that misroutes packets or leaves some nodes mysteriously quiet; a logistics system that fails to update itself when stocks change. Corruption is not always easily detectible. The attacker has the advantage of knowing what kind of corruption to look for. The victim should be more familiar with the system's normal parameters, is almost always better placed to measure its performance (for example, by feeding it test inputs), and can more easily probe the system's software. Multiple systems producing similar errors or anomalies may point to deliberate corruption (even if the source is a mystery). The target can also fool the attacker by creating spurious indications of corruption. Corruption has the virtue of persisting longer the more subtle its effect—but the less information or the fewer the instructions corrupted, the more modest the impact.

Eruption

Eruption is the temporary but intense virtual illumination that operational cyberwar can bring to the battlefield. Among other things, it can highlight the presence and location of military targets for immediate destruction. Making adversary systems light up may also help in discovering "hiding places" (apart from those too deep to emit detectable signals) that thereafter cannot be used again, or at least not so easily. The attacker may even be able to estimate adversary strength by counting what lights up (either because everything lights up or if there are ways to determine what percentage lights up). Knowing how enemy forces are physically arrayed may also yield a sense of the enemy's immediate strategy. Exploiting eruption requires that target systems emit on command—and that the attacker can acquire these emissions, identify their sources, localize them, and strike them before they disappear (which defenders will be in a hurry to do if and when they realize that their emissions are giving them away). Getting the timing right matters. If multiple targets emit at the same time, they will create a sudden wave of electronic noise; telling one target from another may then be difficult. There may also be limits on how many targets can be struck in the hours that constitute a window of opportunity. Prosecuting such signals would require detailed coordination with operational units: to acquire many signals, determine which are spurious, correlate them with targets, evaluate the targets, and sequence them for prosecution. Pulling the same trick twice will be challenging—somewhat harder if the target cannot detect that it is being forced to emit energy but suspects that its assets are being targeted with unexpected accuracy, and much harder if the target *does* detect that it is emitting and thereby being detected.

Interception

Interception is the collection of real-time intelligence on enemy targets and dispositions; it may not be, strictly speaking, operational cyberwar, but it can often be more powerful than whacking their systems. Anyone who can get the right kind of malware into a laptop equipped with a blue force tracker (or something comparable) can grab any information that the user can—such as the precise location of the many assets that blue force trackers are meant to show. If, as typical, usurped computers run no worse than clean ones, penetration may go unnoticed, and an implant may linger unnoticed far longer than a system stays down following a cyberattack. Granted, the ability to filch this information in real time requires a real-time conduit from the system that has or gets the information—which means that a truly air-gapped system (for example, one without an RF signal that can be acquired) cannot be usefully attacked for such purposes (although even non-real-time information has intelligence value). This conduit also has to be able to transmit (or at least slip its information through extant networks) undetected.

In some circumstances, active hacking and passive listening can complement one another. As noted, a hack can make a system leak more information that can be captured inside as well as outside cyberespionage channels. To the extent that surveillance is used as deterrence ("we know when you move here or do this—so don't"), a clever hack or even the demonstrated ability to hack can increase the target's doubt that it can act unobserved.

TIMING CYBERATTACKS

Because most cyberattacks have temporary effects, their use in warfare presupposes that one can schedule kinetic operations to take advantage of a window of opportunity (measured in hours, days, and occasionally weeks) during which the other side is disabled or confused. Although cyberattacks on adversary military forces at peace may force them to spend money in clean-up, they become harder targets next time. Thus, unless war is imminent, the cyberattack is wasted in terms of its *direct* ability to support kinetic attack. But there are exceptions: for instance, a continuous surveillance platform could be blinded long enough to hide forces or an activity (India's nuclear program eluded U.S. oversight because work that had to take place in the open was scheduled for hours when surveillance satellites were known not to be overhead). Surveillance systems, usually air-gapped, are very hard targets, though.

Detonating cyberattacks in clusters has its benefits. Confusion may be created when many things go wrong unexpectedly at once. A foe bent on executing its own plan suddenly has to confront the difficult problems of discovery, diagnosis, and triage among multiple systems that fail for no apparent good reason. If the specialized forensics, recovery, and mitigation resources available to address simultaneous problems are limited, the affected systems may be disabled longer than if problems had occurred sequentially. If systems are cross-linked (for example, system diagnostic machinery is down waiting on parts from logistics systems being taken offline for lack of diagnostic machinery to bring them back up), then restoration may lag further. Parallel attacks may leave few healthy systems to cover for their stricken colleagues. Although a well-prepared or at least mentally agile commander may cope, not all commanders are so cool when facing disasters in systems they barely understand; confusion breeds paralysis, and paralysis breeds defeat.

But taking advantage of multiple failures may tax the physical resources of kinetic attackers. Worse, using a novel attack method to penetrate second-order targets may render them unavailable for first-order targets that may emerge later. The advantages of parallel attacks are less pronounced if the attacks are designed to corrupt rather than disrupt. Indeed, if effects are sought through anomalies too subtle to be recognized as being unusual, simultaneity may defeat the purpose—a correlated set of otherwise unremarkable disappointments may actually strike someone as out of the ordinary, be assessed as the result of cyberattack, and be reversed after investigation.

Cyberattacks tend to be easier to set up in peacetime than in wartime. Even if the attack is novel—and successful cyberattacks against hard targets have to have some novel elements—the techniques required to prepare the environment or maneuver the attack vector (for example, the implant) into place will resemble those used for cyberespionage. In fact, they may be the same techniques, used one day for espionage and the next day for attack. Such techniques work more easily before the target's security posture is tightened. Putting the attack in place entails attention to a few precautions. First is to avoid creating a large spike in suspicious activity within the target network—or any other network being monitored. Second is to carefully coordinate cyberattack and cyberespionage activities, not least when using the same penetration techniques that intelligence agencies employ to gain access for collection. The risk is that discovery and elucidation of the attack preparations may hint at intelligence collection penetration methods that, when found in other systems, may permit unraveling other attacks and permit struck systems to be cleaned.

Timing, as noted, matters in a cyberattack; for example, the IADS has to be down when the jets are overhead, not after—and given repair or substitution times, not much before. For some attacks, such as Stuxnet, while success is likely, the timing of success is not. Randomly timed success can nevertheless be exploited if one can tell from outside whether and when a cyberattack has succeeded *and* has the forces that can exploit the chaos and confusion (that is, effects) that a cyberattack can produce *while* these effects last *and* the victim reaps no great countervailing advantage from knowing that a cyberattack presages an imminent military attack. Those are three big ifs, not least of which is some confidence that critical capabilities of the victim will, in fact, be down for as long as it takes to start and carry out the kinetic attack. There are opportunities aplenty for the intended target to discover the cyberattack and then spoof a response so that those carrying out a follow-on kinetic attack meet a prepared response. In practice, doing so is quite hard.

THE ROLE OF SURPRISE

The essential nature of cyberattack is that it entails deception, and the essence of deception is surprise. A surprise cyberattack might remove capabilities that the adversary relied on to complete its military missions. Such capabilities can be defensive—perhaps a surface-to-air missile failed to engage its target correctly or at all. They can also be offensive—perhaps the command and control required to synchronize an invasion fleet is suddenly crippled by a consequent loss of efficiency, hampering synchronization and coordination. Surprise works best at the outset of conflict when the other side is unprepared. Afterward, it is difficult to surprise the same system twice in the same way—and if the defender takes broader precautions, it may be difficult to surprise the second system twice at all.

Although the effects of any one attack may be enhanced if the *possibility* of an attack is unimagined, true surprise is rare. As Richard Betts has concluded, "[t]here are no significant cases of bolts from the blue in the 20th century. All major sudden attacks occurred in situations of prolonged tension during which the victim state's leaders recognized that war might be on the horizon."[3] Correspondingly, a cyberattack bolt from the blue originating from a country on fair to good terms with the target would be historically novel.

Several strategic-*level* surprises are nevertheless possible. First, an attacker could attack civilian infrastructure during a period of tension when the expected course is to attack military targets. Many military surprises appear in retrospect to have succeeded because attackers found unexpected ways to neutralize defenses or other advantages that the victim thought should have precluded such actions.[4] But the efficacy, hence plausibility, of such a surprise rises by the extent to which a cyberattack on *civilian* infrastructure would reduce the victim's *military* effectiveness. Perhaps the target was unaware of how important its own civilian assets were to its ability to employ military force. Starting cyberattacks at the strategic level also threatens strategic retaliation from the outset (possibly trumping on-the-ground gains). Although such surprise would be irrational, as Richard Betts has observed, "apparently irrational behavior is one of the most important elements in several past surprise attacks."[5]

A bolt-from-the-blue cyberattack on military systems could be launched just prior to a surprise military attack. But in what sense would a cyberattack *be* a surprise? Why would a military be unprepared for cyberwar even though it faces constant penetration attempts? Perhaps it is because in peacetime, it may accept the risks of more open access to gain its benefits (for example, faster learning). It may relax its constant testing for security vulnerabilities or corrupted files lest fixing them as each arises proves expensive. Furthermore, a military at peace may have many potential challengers, each with a different mode of potential attack. Similarly, militaries may spread their own collection efforts against each of them. War brings focus and concentration on the one actual foe among many potential ones. If hostilities proceed without a preceding crisis, some level of surprise, even in cyberspace, can be expected.

Operational surprise is still possible after war starts and presumably after the target has hardened its system to wartime modes. The target may have yet to see exploits that the attacker has in waiting or has implanted but not yet activated. For this, the attacker needs a good bag of tricks that it has yet to use (or at least has not used widely enough for them to be recognized) against vulnerabilities the target did not realize it had (or at least has not fixed). Thus, a cyberattack can still be a bolt from the blue, even if hostilities are imminent or under way. Because operational cyberwar can still work if there is *operational* surprise, it can still be used by countries, such as the United States, whose war policies do not include *strategic* surprise—but it is even more useful for states that find strategic surprise appealing.

Once initial phases of conflict end, cyberattacks are likely to transition from a general purpose to an opportunistic weapon. True, just because the best cyberattacks can only be used once does not mean they have to be used immediately; there may be targets that are better hit later in the conflict. However, the odds of success are greater against an unprepared adversary because a prepared adversary is likely to have adopted greater operational security as a result of having been made aware of what cyberattacks can do—offset somewhat by the tendency for speed to trump security in carrying out particular warfare operations. Later in the conflict, attackers may choose to press their foes so as to reveal mistakes that can be exploited for cyberattack. Otherwise, cyberattacks would be prudently husbanded for special occasions and special targets. Such targets would be thoroughly researched to discover uncommon vulnerabilities whose exploitation depended on crucial timing or that could be set up via social engineering or the cultivation of insiders. Potential attackers would have to know the target and its defenders, perhaps better than its intended users would. Because the scope of subsequent operations would be limited (largely to forestall depletion), they would have to be thoroughly prepared, precise, and closely monitored, since effects can rarely be assumed in advance. If operational cyberwar works, kinetic consequences almost always have to follow on its heels.

Many of these considerations disappear if the purpose of a cyberattack is not so much to cause direct effects such as disruptions as it is to cause indirect effects such as a loss of confidence. War-fighters who cannot count on their systems being available, their data retaining their integrity, or their communications being safe from enemy ears are likely to make adjustments to restore their confidence in their ability to fight—and an initial and perhaps lingering component of restoring such confidence is to be wary of their devices. Done right, the cost of these adjustments should be less than the costs of suffering cyberattacks—but overreaction in the face of fear is not unknown (as noted, Iran probably lost more centrifuges to post-Stuxnet caution in installing more centrifuges than from the attack itself). A military made skittish about its systems will remain skittish for far longer than the days required to restore its systems to functionality. The correlation of forces will be shifted in the attacker's favor for an extended period, relieving pressure to exploit the window of opportunity a cyberattack yields. Not surprisingly, culture and military professionalism matter in shaping long-term responses to an attack. Furthermore, if the military is already wary because it fears cyberattack, an unimpressive cyberattack may have the opposite effect. Ironically, whether the point of a cyberattack is to startle naive foes or to engender long-term doubt among them, the efficacy of cyberattack is still front-loaded.

HIDING THE ATTACK TO FACILITATE ITS REPETITION

In some types of carefully formed attacks, the target may not see the faults that hackers induced. Transient failures, for instance, can be hard to diagnose. Even if seen, they may be ascribed not to cyberattack but to bad design, human error, accidents, or natural causes. Until Stuxnet was discovered and revealed, the Iranians knew that their centrifuges did not last very long but were uncertain why. The longer targets are in the dark about what caused systems to work poorly or not at all, the longer it takes them to diagnose and reverse the real problem for having reinforced their contrary assumptions.

A variant on making attacks look like, say, accidents, is to shape attacks so that no systematic lessons can be learned from them, the better to frustrate the erection of defenses against their repetition. Attackers could find ways to jostle the targeted system to persuade the target that secondary problems have been detected and fixed. They could exploit vulnerabilities that only a painstaking search could uncover. They could try to generate attacks that are relatively insensitive to simple countermeasures (disconnecting systems that really should not have been connected in the first place would, by contrast, be simple). Or attacks could be shaped and targets chosen so that *others* do not learn to defeat such attacks. So thinking, attackers might want to go after system-specific vulnerabilities rather than generic vulnerabilities (the latter, when patched, make many systems harder to attack again), or concentrate their attacks on those unlikely to share their experiences with others.

Last, if the choice exists, attackers can use exploits likely to become obsolete soonest and save those with later use-by dates for later contingencies. All this is easier said than done.

AN OPERATIONAL CYBERWAR SCENARIO

To illustrate how a cyberattack may implicate larger warfighting issues, consider a scenario that starts by Taiwan moving toward independence. China decides it is time to take the island but concedes that the United States will intervene on Taiwan's side—so it tries to complicate and hence delay the transit of U.S. forces over the Pacific. It hopes that by the time the United States does arrive, the war will be over, or at least the Chinese will have a secure lodgment on the island. To do this, the Chinese carry out a full-fledged operational cyberattack on U.S. military information systems with the hopes of turning the data they contain into gibberish. Even before 2000, James Mulvenon, an authority on Chinese cyberwar, argued that the Chinese might corrupt the time-phased force deployment data accessible through DoD's unclassified Internet.[6]

To the extent that the United States *might* use force—which the Chinese, in this scenario, already assume is inevitable—a cyberattack on such a force (before it has started to fight) is an understandable use of military power. Because it is entirely possible that such a cyberattack never hits the news (at least not until after the lessons-learned analyses take place), it would not automatically evoke a narrative of attack and defense (as an opening Chinese attack on U.S. critical infrastructure might). The workings of U.S. military logistics may not be secret, but they are often esoteric. If such a cyberattack were to take place after Chinese forces had begun irrevocable moves toward Taiwan, and if the fact of U.S. intervention was already determined, then the U.S. military would have little choice but to work around the disruption or corruption of its databases.

To make matters more complex, imagine further that the Chinese are holding back on using kinetic force while waiting to see how badly U.S. forces have been delayed by the cyberattack. The Chinese may be looking for indications that are visible, but they may also be collecting from listening posts already emplaced within unclassified DoD networks. If these indicators reveal that the hoped-for effect has taken place, then the PLA may conclude that it has achieved a favorable correlation of forces and start fighting. If, however, the hoped-for effects fail to materialize, then perhaps the correlation of forces is not so good, and they may stand down and deal with the fallout from the cyberattack later, perhaps by denying everything.

Would a cyberattack on U.S. forces actually degrade mission effectiveness? If the military knew the specific vulnerabilities that such an attack would exploit, then presumably these would have been fixed already. But determining whether such a cyberattack would work may be secondary to whether the Chinese *think* that they can alter the correlation of forces by so doing. If the answer is yes *and* they find themselves debating whether to go to war, their confidence may impel them toward going ahead with both a cyberattack and a kinetic attack (incidentally, a similar argument can be made for outer space). In such a case, if they carry out a cyberattack and it turns out that the United States can fight its way through it with little effect, then although U.S. forces will be in a better position to fight, war will have begun anyhow.

Therein lies a challenge for the U.S. military: first, to determine to what extent its ability to carry out its missions is at risk from any cyberattack; second, to ensure that it has the resiliency to fight through cyberattacks; and third, to make everyone else aware of how well it can withstand attack—in reverse order. In January 2011, the secretary of defense said that "Chinese technological advances in cyber- and anti-satellite warfare posed a potential challenge to the ability of our forces to operate and communicate in this part of the Pacific."[7] That suggests that the third task had not yet been accomplished. Perhaps this is because the second task remains unfinished as well. It is unclear that DoD believes it understands the risk from cyberattack is to its mission effectiveness in requisite detail. These are not impossible tasks; DoD can make its networks into what it will—and do so in ways that nullify temptations to mischief that our weaknesses would otherwise engender.

WOULD CHINA USE OPERATIONAL CYBERWAR THE SAME WAY?

All weapons of war are apt to be used if their use is efficacious and cost-effective; if they are not heinous; if their use does not put one's own forces at great risk; and (at least for the United States) if their use comports to the law of armed conflict (LOAC). But that does not answer everything one can ask about how countries would use cyberattacks. It may also help to understand how a country's strategic culture—revealed and reflected in how it uses other forms of warfare—may predispose its use of cyberattack.

For instance, how will cyberattacks be allocated against military targets over the course of a campaign? As noted, attacks early in a conflict could succeed spectacularly if the other side is surprised (and if they have not thought about their defenses against cyberattack seriously enough). But husbanded attacks can be saved for targets that do not exist or are not vulnerable early in the conflict, and those who wield them will benefit from experience (on how to exploit such attacks) that they lacked at the outset of conflict.

So other factors may come into play. One is whether front-loaded attacks solve a problem that a particular country has—such as China's aforementioned desire to delay the entry to U.S. forces off its shores. If the goal is important enough, such a country may be willing to utilize exploits that it might otherwise have husbanded for later in the conflict in order to gain a decisive early edge. Another is whether national leaders bet on quick wins or hedge and hold reserves to prosecute what may turn into long wars. The tendency for countries to mount surprise attacks is also a factor; those that believe in surprise attack are likely to count on initial victories to shape the outcome and thus front-load operational cyberattacks. Cyberattacks, in and of themselves, may be attractive by dint of not requiring obvious buildup of the sort that creates indications and warning for surprise kinetic attack. But leaders who count on a surprise attack working *because* their cyberattacks are effective also have to believe that cyberattacks *can* be militarily effective and they have to have requisite confidence in their cyberwar forces in the first place. This confidence would cover not only the efficacy of such forces but also their ability to report diligently and accurately on the effects of cyberattacks. Not all leaders have such confidence.

Which countries might withhold attacks on networks and systems from which they are or could be collecting (notably, command and control systems in contrast to weapons systems) valuable intelligence? Military leaders could reason that they may be able to attack such systems because their efforts would be particularly hard to discern (for example, selective corruption attacks or disruptive attacks on systems that are prone to failure anyway). Alternatively, they may reserve their cyberattacks for systems with little information to harvest (such as an IADS) or whose destruction is imperative. A military orientation is associated with early use; an intelligence one, with later (if any) use. Countries whose cyberwarriors are aligned with their intelligence agencies would, it seems, adopt or at least understand the latter's orientation and favor using penetrations for intelligence rather than attack. Those whose cyberwarriors are aligned with their electronic warriors should favor using cyberwar in conjunction with electronic warfare (and perhaps space warfare as well)—and strike at the outset of conflict.

Cultural factors matter. The American way of war highlights the merciless application of overwhelming force.[8] China's military thinkers pay homage to Sun Tzu, who famously emphasized winning without fighting (in fairness, there are multiple Chinese military texts, and others have a more conventional orientation). One recurring trope in Chinese strategic thinking is the stratagem, an attack or maneuver that is relatively small in scale but, if correctly timed and aimed, is capable of catching the adversary unprepared, thereby having an effect disproportionate to its size. The instrument is often known as an "assassin's mace."[9] From a strategic perspective, though, the use of an assassin's mace by *inferior* forces necessarily contains high risks because the fact, much less the effect, of surprise is by its nature difficult to test. Cyberwar's use of an adversary's computers against them fits with the Chinese strategic inclination to "attack with a borrowed sword." All this suggests that the Chinese may opt to put disproportionate resources into looking for breakthroughs in the hope that such investments can give them a niche capability that can hold overall U.S. superiority at bay.

After cyberwar has been used to try to delay the entry of U.S. forces into Asia, its steady-state role would be part of China's integrated network electronic warfare (INEW), whose aim is "controlling the flow of information in the adversary's system and maintaining the PLA's information superiority on a traditional, physical battlefield." The PLA's goal, according to two Chinese generals, is being "proficient at electronic feints, electronic camouflage, electronic jamming, virus attacks, and space satellite jamming and deceptions, leading the enemy to draw the wrong conclusion and attaining the goal of strategic deception." Proponents of the INEW strategy apparently believe that the goal is to attack only the key nodes of the adversary's command and control and logistics information flow; if true, this suggests that China's information warriors (or at least their planners and doctrine writers) see information as something to throttle, not corrupt. It is a very physical approach to the virtual world. Deterrence constitutes a third role for cyberwar as per General Dai Qingmin's *The Science of Military Campaigns*: we must send a message to the enemy through cyberattack, forcing the enemy to give up without fighting. A fourth role is cyberwar as a subset of a broader information operations campaign designed to "attack the enemy's perceptions."

Four similar but distinct roles for cyberwar may not necessarily get along. For instance, using cyberwar as an assassin's mace calls for something like a bolt out of the blue; using it as part of an INEW campaign also works better if the target is not given enough time to raise its defenses. The 2001 book *Science of Strategy* states that in a war of annihilation, nodes must be attacked to break up the network before attacking weapons systems. Other Chinese military academics argue that those who do not preempt will lose the initiative in what may be a very short-lived information operations war. Conversely, using cyberwar for deterrence or as part of a broader psychological operations campaign requires that China's willingness and capability to use cyberwar be evident before conflict begins. The two are contradictory.

WHY SUPREMACY IS MEANINGLESS AND SUPERIORITY UNNECESSARY

Because cyberattackers really cannot be disarmed by cyberattacks, cyberwar lacks a counterforce rationale familiar to other forms of warfare. Offense cannot defend because the prerequisites for a cyberattack are few and hard to damage from cyberspace: talented hackers, intelligence on the target, exploits to match the vulnerabilities found through such intelligence, a computing device, and a network connection. Cyberattacks against an unprepared computer sitting on the network at the time may be reversed if it can be rebooted, recovered to factory conditions, or, at worst, swapped out for a new computer (that costs less than a thousand dollars). The threat to end network connections to the target country, although very difficult to carry out in practice, is at least a theoretical possibility. However, any serious cyberwar-capable state has probably figured out how to carry out cyberattacks starting from someone else's territory; the most subtle ones can start from within the territory of the country it is targeting.[10] Powerful hardware may also be needed for breaking codes (see Flame[11]) or decompiling software, but they need not be online; if not online, they are very difficult to reach, much less break with a cyberattack. Indeed, if hackers phone in their work, physical attacks, with the possible exception of targeted assassinations, may not dent a state's cyberattack capabilities much. Even if defenders can detect that a particular server is about to launch a particular attack or command slave computers to do so and disable it, hackers who are just mediocre can find another server, and those more competent will already have had another server in place to begin with. Although there may also be value in attacking the attacker in order to capture the tools it may have stored awaiting use, those who anticipate as much may keep a copy offline. Because cyberwar is not a like-on-like affair, superiority is not inherently necessary.

Operational cyberwar simply cannot win an overall war on its own; it is a support function. It cannot occupy territory, put people's lives at risk on its own, or, except in specialized cases, break things. Otherwise, most effects are reversible in hours or, at most, weeks. A support function is hardly a euphemism for a worthless endeavor, though. The current U.S. space constellation is a support function but is also indispensable to conventional war. The Middle East has provided many examples of how airpower can convert the prospects of slow heavy combat into a rout (the 1967 Six-Day War, the 1991 Gulf War). But this does mean that operational cyberwar can be analyzed only in the context of the military functions it *does*, in fact, support.

Is supremacy in cyberspace useful in the same sense that it is useful, perhaps vital, for one's air force to prevent another from flying (very long), or one's navy from keeping the other side's navy in port?[12] It might be if cyberspace were a unitary domain, which it is anything but. Two (military) organizations can simultaneously keep the other off its own networks at the same time. Granted, hackers *do* get into other people's networks—but hackers cannot claim physical control, and physical control can be made to dominate all other forms of control. Owners can physically add or remove machines from a network and can install software directly. If worse comes to worst, owners can discard and replace systems. Owners with the wit to have backed up their data (including configuration files) and applications can resynthesize their networks regardless of who has messed with them. Furthermore, there is no ipso facto relationship between keeping the bad guys out and getting into where the bad guys live—even if such underlying factors as the relative quantity and quality of each other's hackers predispose success or failure at both. In short, there is no such thing as a single cyberspace, but at least two: yours and theirs. Without a *common* space, there is no such thing as supremacy.[13]

The importance of having superior cyberwar forces vis-à-vis adversaries is also easy to exaggerate. Everything else being equal, militaries would rather have better than worse cyberattack capabilities. However, improvements are not free and may not always be more worthwhile than alternative investments. Specific investments need to be evaluated for what they can bring to the fight. The question of military superiority is really a second-order question: must one invest in cyberattack capabilities if the other side does so?[14] Put another way: does the cost-effectiveness of investing in one's own cyberattack capabilities rise if the other side's cyberwar capabilities increase? Merely ascertaining the value of investing in cyberattack capabilities is fraught with uncertainties enough; there is no obvious reason why such a number would shift if the other side had, itself, invested in cyberattack capabilities. Cyberattack is not a force-on-force affair; one's offense goes against their defense of their systems, and their offense goes against your defense of your systems.

CODA: A NOTE OF SKEPTICISM ON THE POTENTIAL OF OPERATIONAL CYBERWAR

It is hardly obvious that operational cyberwar will prove to be particularly effective in wartime. True, further digitization and networking will add complexity to warfighting systems of systems fielded by advanced militaries. With complexity, the attack surface of any system rises faster than its size, in part because complexity and interactivity create vulnerabilities in the connections among systems that do not appear, or at least are not evident, within the individual systems themselves. So militaries are likely to become *more* susceptible to operational cyberwar, thereby increasing the latter's scope and influence.

Nevertheless, penetrating the warfighting (machine control) part of a military network is harder than penetrating the administrative end. Weapons networks are not built to surf the web or exchange PDF files (although they are often built atop commercial processors and operating systems built to permit as much). Warfighting systems tend to be mobile, hence linked by antennae rather than wires, and parsimonious in their communications (compared to the prolixity of communications over fiber optics). Because they communicate over the air, they are, or should be, built for encrypted communications from the onset.

The attacker therefore has three barriers to overcome in usurping the command and control of opposing systems. First, attackers must surmount electronic barriers. For many reasons, primarily to counter jamming and interception, military communications use techniques such as frequency-hopping or spread-spectrum (for example, via code-division multiple access [CDMA]). Exactly how systems hop among frequencies or spread their spectrum is a closely guarded secret. Although such tricks can be overcome through patient analysis (perhaps aided by a little eavesdropping), they still constitute barriers to infiltrating instructions or exfiltrating data (or feedback on how the instructions are working). All that assumes that the attacker can get transmitters and receivers with requisite power and sensitivity in the right place to acquire the signals.

Second, attackers must surmount the cryptographic barrier—the encoding of information required to cope with the vulnerabilities created by having to communicate out in the open. In theory, the mathematics of encryption is daunting, and standard algorithms with very long keys are almost provably impossible to break fast enough to make a military difference. In practice, protocols are often misconfigured, cryptographic keys can prove difficult to manage, random number generators are not so random and sometimes their seeds can be guessed (hardware that can sample the nth digit of an analog process would produce truly random numbers). Steps taken to ensure that the electronics have not been tampered with are not completely foolproof. So cryptographic barriers are not absolutely forbidding—but they are quite daunting.

Third, the attackers, if they can carve a channel into the target systems, must be able to get the various weapons systems to ingest and run the attackers' instructions, or else react to the attackers' inputs in ways that compromise their functionality. Having discussed the matter at length above, suffice it to say that it, too, is possible but hardly easy and results are not guaranteed.

To be fair, foes may have inordinate confidence in one of the three barriers and therefore may neglect one or two others. If they think their communications are unbreakably encoded (for example, using CDMA), they may get complacent and ignore cryptography. Or, if they think their cryptography is guaranteed unbreakable and always on, they may ignore cybersecurity. Thus, attackers need not surmount all three barriers. Conversely, perhaps foes are justifiably confident and the barriers they maintain cannot be overcome.

Compounding these technical barriers are grave questions about what kind of authority and resources will be given to operational cyberwarriors. It is unclear what kind of seat cyberwarriors can get at the command table when it comes down to figuring out how to combat enemy forces. Their techniques have to compete against those proposed by kinetic warriors; the latter can bring hundreds of years of history, physics, and the ability to prove battle damage to the argument. Cyberwarriors also must compete against electronic warriors who have proven their ability to affect combat since 1940 and also have physics to rely on even if battle damage is hard to prove.

Cyberwarriors that rely on intelligence agencies for their penetrations into systems face other obstacles.[15] The conversion of a penetration into an attack puts the penetration at risk, either directly, because the system is destroyed, or indirectly, because knowledge of the attack may be converted into an understanding of how the targeted system was penetrated. Worse, if many systems were penetrated in the same way or if indications of penetration in the attacked system can be found in other systems that have been penetrated (but not attacked), penetrations into the latter systems may be discovered and reversed. Thus, the conversion of a penetration into an attack could jeopardize not just one but many sources of information. It is unclear whether the intelligence community will be so eager to turn its access methods over for cyberattackers to use.

CHAPTER 12

Organizing a Cyberwar Campaign

The trope of the cyberwarrior has changed radically. Circa 1999, cyberwarriors at the Joint Task Force Computer Network Defense worked under the U.S. Space Command. It seemed like a poor fit. Space operations require the careful orchestration of many different parts, huge checklists, and a zero-defect culture in the face of literally thousands of possible errors. Every move is choreographed. Cyberwarriors, at least then, did not work that way. They entered systems silently. When there, they braced themselves for surprise regardless of how thoroughly they were briefed. They learned to orient themselves quickly, looking for handholds that let them manipulate the system before the system found and expelled them. They innovated when they had to. They left as quickly as possible. It sounded as though the Special Forces community would have been a better fit.

But the hacker as cyberspace commando no longer fits today's practice. Most successful hacks these days do not involve an intruder as such, but a piece of malware created to sneak past a system's defenses and put itself in a position to take control over a system to execute a series of instructions and then call out for further instructions. Hacking, like many human endeavors, has been automated. Hackers are like toolmakers—closer in spirit to the space community than in 1999. Although hackers no longer work for U.S. Space Command, they work for CYBERCOM, which, together with the U.S. space community, operates under U.S. Strategic Command.[1]

Understanding as much, we examine several issues associated with the command and control of cyberwarriors: the role of operational cyberwar to combat operations, the logic of cyberwarfare campaigns, the chain of command, delegation, and the rogue cyberwarrior challenge.

WHY A CAMPAIGN?

How should offensive cyberwar capabilities be commanded and controlled over the course of a conflict? Consider three alternatives.

- Cyber operations are "fires." Commanders identify targets, and then cyberwar units determine how to generate effects for such targets.
- Cyber operations are organized as a campaign to generate an overall effect, one planned and executed by CYBERCOM.
- The cyber operations campaign is planned and executed by the regional combatant commander.

A call-for-fires model can be likened to a World War II–type scenario in which Marines are taking a South Pacific island but need gunfire support from a battleship. The targets are well specified. The likelihood that the fires actually take place is fairly high. The immediate effects are fairly predictable (for example, a blast of a particular force radiating from a blast point of a particular location) and, to a somewhat lesser extent, so is the ultimate effect (for example, a pillbox is destroyed).

The effects produced on Thursday are only modestly affected by whether there was fire support on Wednesday. Immediate ammunition stores in battleships permitting, there is no good reason to husband fires for later use. Finally, the lag time between choosing a target and seeing it destroyed can be as short as minutes.

In cyberspace, calls for fire may not find a ready response. Those who do call likely have less idea what the art of the possible is; although CYBERCOM will have a better idea, cyberwarriors know that the answer does not lie in the physics. The timing and sequencing of cyberattacks matter because combat in cyberspace can be a rapid measure-countermeasure game. The certainty about the effects of a cyberattack is substantially less than for a physical attack because such effects depend critically on the details of the target system and the ability of the target's system administrators to restore functionality and integrity quickly. Last, the better-defended targets cannot be detected and affected on short notice; to determine their vulnerabilities, targets have to be investigated for periods of months or years.

Managers of systems suffering under unexpectedly damaging effects can respond by reducing the access to such a system even at the expense of its agility and usefulness. If they do, cyberattackers face diminishing returns, perhaps sharply diminished returns, unless the use of such attacks is paced to the rate at which new vulnerabilities in target systems are found. Thus, calling for fires on Wednesday will likely erode what Thursday's call for fires produces. By Thursday, the target's managers may well have altered their system—either by fixing a specific vulnerability or by reassessing the vulnerability of its overall architecture (such as which systems are accessing which services) and adapting accordingly. Conversely, to provide extended support, cyberwarriors have to take into account how fast foes learn, how well the lessons stick, the extent to which attacks can induce architectural rather than simply software changes, the rate at which lessons learned circulates, and how the speed of learning depends on the nature of the attack.

Targets cannot necessarily be hit at a moment's notice. Everything else being equal, the more critical a target to the other side, the more diligently it is protected, and the longer it takes to penetrate such targets and cause them to misbehave. During the first few months of a conflict, particularly one against an unexpected adversary, there may be few targets that can be struck because none were thoroughly scoped beforehand. Under a call-for-fires model, warfighters may find some overlap between the targets they want serviced and those that have been investigated, but hoping for a coincidence is hardly a planning method. The development of a cyberwar campaign would provide a forum for mutual dialogue between those who have to scope targets and those who may have an a priori sense of which targets may be more important to the war effort. In some cases, the kinetic campaign may inform the cyber preparation of the battlefield; in other, likely fewer, cases the art of the possible in cyberspace may color the choices made in kinetic campaign planning.

A third and related reason for planning is to capture the relationship between strike planning and battle damage assessment (BDA). For all military operations, BDA is part of the observe-orient-decide-act loop, a process by which feedback on the last operation informs the next one. With cyberattacks, BDA is nontrivial. Understanding how an attack has harmed a system (and how fast and how well it recovers) takes penetrating a system and keeping the monitoring implants communicating with the attacker even after the initial effects are noticed. It takes forethought to determine what needs to be monitored, what indicators need to be collected, where the monitors need to sit, and how they can collect and exfiltrate data undetected. This cannot be easily started and brought to completion *after* the fires have been called for. If one is looking to change the target system's behavior, one needs to know its baseline performance; thus, monitors have to be emplaced well before the attack. Even as the attacker is using BDA to fine-tune the next attack, the defender is simultaneously using its own BDA to understand and thus minimize the effects of the next attack.

Campaign planning is also necessary if one is to carefully weigh the intelligence gain-loss factor in carrying out cyberattacks, notably those against command and control or network targets in general (rather than against weapons systems that rarely merit eavesdropping upon). Knocking out a command and control center, whether by kinetic attack or cyberattack, for instance, also knocks out a source of intelligence. If the attack is physical and the source returns to service, the opportunity to eavesdrop on it usually returns as well—but after a cyberattack, the source that returns to service may well have cleaned itself up, especially if the penetration or penetration technique that enables the cyberattack is also used to enable cyberespionage. A temporary loss of enemy warfare capabilities may lead to a much longer loss in collection capability. Thus, the trade-off parameters are different. Calls for fire, unless integrated into a campaign plan in which equities are carefully considered against one another, are likely to fall subject to snap judgments one way or another.

A last argument for campaign planning rather than calls for fire is, as noted, that a cyberwar campaign can erode the confidence foes have in their information systems. If the cyberattacks also affect weapons operations, warfighters may lack confidence that their digitized weapons will work when called upon. Such doubts may inhibit them from taking digital weapons to battle in favor of more primitive analogs. Perhaps, in the absence of their information systems, they will not be able to count on their military to retain effectiveness when performance is most urgently needed.

Ironically, if the primary purpose of a cyberwar operations campaign is to affect the adversary's thinking, then perhaps this should be undertaken in coordination with (or in direct support of) a broader deception operation—which, in turn, is likely to be run by psychological operators rather than digital mavens. This returns us full circle to an older notion of information warfare as an overarching discipline—or it simply reminds us that everything really is connected to everything else and that our organizational principles are not meant to be (even literally) carved in stone (on headquarters buildings) but are just notions that seem to make sense at the time.

To the extent that eroding the adversary's confidence is the main point of a cyberattack, the character and sequencing of cyberattacks might make a great difference. The United States wants to create a narrative that convinced the adversary not to trust its machines. To the extent that narrative formation—that is, story-telling—is more than a set of random words, the decision to carry out a cyberattack on Thursday, having done so on Wednesday is more than incidental. It requires a campaign.

True, planning of some sort is required for the call-for-fires model as well as the campaign model. The difference, a big one, is that planning for a call-for-fires model is largely a matter of capabilities planning where the nature of the adversary enters as something to be overcome (by analogy, knowing whether one has the capability to strike the adversary's capital requires knowing how well an adversary's surface-to-air missile systems work). Planning for a campaign, however, requires understanding much more: for example, one's own goals and constraints, the foe's goals and constraints, how they envision combat, the capabilities of specific systems that one would penetrate, how fast they learn, or how they would react to the unexpected. Operating a campaign requires attention to how the adversary reacts as events unfold. Operating a call-for-fires model settles in at the tactical level: what was done, what worked, and how much did it help the kinetic effort.

These considerations then raise the question of how to integrate cyber operations acting in support of the main event, kinetic operations.

THE INSERTION OF OPERATIONAL CYBERWAR INTO KINETIC OPERATIONS

Perhaps the greatest obstacle to planning an offensive cyberwar campaign is convincing commanders raised in the world of physical force that cyberwar has something to contribute. Apart from temporarily shutting down jihadist websites, it has been nearly impossible to see the impact of operational cyberwar (outside highly classified channels) even as the potential to have major effects has been mooted in the early 1990s. Predicting effects, as argued, is iffy. Yet the cyberwarrior may argue that it *could* work and do so without eating into the resources (such as, for example, gasoline) otherwise used to prosecute combat.

One approach is for cyberwarriors to prove their bona fides on their own and then leverage success to get a better seat at the planning table. But how? Perhaps they could show off their strategic warfare campaigns—which do not need integration with operational combat commanders to be carried out. Yet even if cyberwarriors succeed visibly, kinetic operators may deem civilian targets softer than defense systems (even if effects on civilian office networks suggest how military networks may be affected)—and hence less impressive. The effects of operational cyberwar against targets that the kinetic operators are not focused on (and thus not monitoring) may be hard to prove; kinetic operators will have to take the word of cyberwarriors.

Cyberwarriors could also demonstrate their power against military targets if given permission to act. But at what point in the campaign? Early strikes, as argued, are most likely to be telling because as combat proceeds, defenders tend to tighten up. But once attacks start, both sides will be reacting, and the question will be who reacts best and first. The slower the defenders' adjustments, the larger the window of opportunity. Defenders may well be quicker on the mark: they would have immediate battle damage reports (at least for disruption attacks) if not necessarily certainty about what caused the damage. But if the capability to conduct cyberwar depletes as a result of use, by the time enough effects are created to impress their cohorts in warfare, the efficacy of cyberwarriors will have been correspondingly weaker.

If cyberwarriors aim to make foes doubt their own information system, the results of their confidence-eroding or will-eroding cyber campaign may be ambiguous, slow to register, and a tough sell to a skeptical audience—even if historians later deem their efforts decisive.

Cyberwarriors might also bide their time, watching for opportunities to complement kinetic operations. For instance, planners of a kinetic attack may worry about prevailing against a counterattack. If hacking the adversary's command and control can create confusion or delay orders and thereby retard the counterattack, the original mission may have a better chance of succeeding with lower casualties. Command and control, cyberwarriors may well argue, is often difficult to target directly by other means: for example, specific targets may be buried or hidden within adversary command and control centers. The airspace required for a bombing run may be too well defended, a particularly daunting proposition if significant on-station time is required to find the target. Anti-jamming capabilities may be present to frustrate electronic warfare. Perhaps needless to add, if the objective is to confuse the minds of the adversaries rather than paralyze them with fear, kinetic approaches may not offer very much. A low chance of success with cyber operations may trump a zero chance of success with kinetic ones.

Cyberwarriors can then argue the prime attraction of cyberattacks: they are cheap to do once the requisite capacity exists and the intelligence has been collected on the target (which may have been already collected for other purposes ahead of time). The major operational cost driver—which applies to only some cyberattacks—is mounting an air sortie (which could be unmanned) to inject an RF signal into an adversary receiver. Otherwise, such an attack is riskless (to its operators) and primarily requires the time and attention of cyberwarriors with little else to do. By contrast, kinetic operations can be costly in both men and matériel.

Many of the costs of a cyberattack, and hence the basis for objections to mounting one, are other than in men and matériel. One is collateral damage, discussed further below. The not-always-well-founded fear of violating LOAC may be another (lawyers love to chew over cyberattacks but perhaps because the targets of cyberattacks are seen as civilian, such as banks). Maybe preparations for cyberattack can reveal more than comparable preparations for kinetic attack, allowing defenders to infer the importance that an attacker places on a target and perhaps its strategies as well—but this logic applies more so to nonobvious targets. By contrast, cyberattacks against the adversary's central command and control system are so obviously inviting that discovering preparations against them would not say much. Even if troubling, such inferences can be confounded by cyberattack attempts on both critical and noncritical sites—if cyberwarriors are willing to waste a good exploit just to divert the adversary's attention.

Finally, if cyberattacks are given the time to work while other attacks are withheld, planners may have to be convinced that waiting is either tolerable or unavoidable. A problem for cyberwarriors is managing the trade-off between the time required for preparation (often months) and the time during which the target is held off-limits for other attacks. As it is, cyberwarriors can and perhaps should prepare many targets in case one gets chosen for a cyberattack, but the resources of cyberwarriors are not infinite. In some cases, cyberwarriors may recognize that the need for destruction outweighs the hope of causing confusion.

WHOSE CAMPAIGN?

Originally all cyberattack operations came under the command and control of CYBERCOM, whose units were originally *not* chopped to combatant commanders but exercised directly. As General Alexander emphasized in a written statement provided for his confirmation hearings: "The Commander of USCYBERCOM will have freedom of action to conduct military operations in cyberspace based upon the authorities provided by the President, the SECDEF [secretary of defense], and the Commander USSTRATCOM. Because cyberspace is not generally bounded by geography, the Commander of USCYBERCOM will have to *coordinate* with U.S. agencies and COCOMs [combatant commands] that would be affected by actions taken in cyberspace."[2]

Since then, command shifted to the regional commanders. Was that the right decision? On the one hand, only CYBERCOM will really know whether worthwhile strategic targets have vulnerabilities that can be exploited and to what effect. By contrast, the existence of kinetic targets is easier to demonstrate (for example, by imagery). Esoteric knowledge on cyberattack targets may influence the options that the U.S. cyber commander presents to the regional combatant commands for the latter's coordination. But the regional combatant commanders will have a much better understanding of their own goals and strategies, the adversary's goals and strategies, the course of the kinetic campaign, how the adversary might react to shifting fortunes on the battlefield, and what its red lines are.[3]

To be sure, regional combatant commanders do not command space and strategic nuclear assets, either. As with cyber assets, they reside under STRATCOM. But space and strategic nuclear assets are global in the sense that cyber assets are not. Satellites do not hover above regions; furthermore, they are used to support U.S. missions rather than affect the enemy directly—and work similarly regardless of who they are being used against. Thus, a model in which the regional combatant commander requests certain functionality from them (such as take this picture, give me bandwidth) works. Strategic nuclear weapons, by definition, also do not sit in theater. They, too, function more or less the same regardless of who the adversary is. Finally, if one of them is actually used in combat, the regional outcome will fade in importance relative to the strategic one—at that level, decisions are made by the president, not combatant commanders, anyway. The global properties of almost all cyber weapons are more limited.

Because zero-day vulnerabilities in commercial software can be used against systems around the world (if the software is military, it can still be used as widely as the targeted equipment is deployed), CYBERCOM has a legitimate interest in ensuring that such vulnerabilities are not burned by being used against low-value targets. CYBERCOM also has an interest in promulgating rules of engagement that apply nationwide in ways that protect the integrity of the cyberwar force. But these interests, at most, allow CYBERCOM to exercise a veto over a regional combatant commander's campaign (such as by not releasing certain assets); they hardly enable the commander to plan or conduct such a campaign. Conversely, if the only cyber weapons that the combatant commander may use are those that do not compromise the secrets buried at Fort Meade, then they may well buy exploits, find their own, or, failing that, use exploits that worked against patched vulnerabilities in the hope that their own hackers can find accessible systems whose maintenance leaves something to be desired. A successful exploit will not be without consequences (it will teach foes and even friends to make sure to install certain patches), but those consequences are limited.

Escalation concerns also argue for putting campaign planning into the hands of the regional combatant commander. The use of cyber weapons may cause the adversary to react in unforeseen and unhelpful ways. Although cyber weapons, by dint of being largely nonlethal and nondestructive, seem less escalatory than kinetic weapons, their newness, overall spookiness, and the unclear nature of their collateral effects suggest they might, in fact, be more unpredictably escalatory. After all, it is always what the *other* side thinks is escalatory that determines whether they themselves escalate after a cyberattack. In using cyberattacks, one must gauge where their red lines lie. The regional combatant commander may have a different risk assessment and tolerance than CYBERCOM. Chances are that his assessment will be better because understanding specific regional adversaries and their decisionmaking is part of a regional combatant commander's job. Furthermore, whereas CYBERCOM may have an institutional interest in proving the operational or strategic effectiveness of cyberwar, a regional commander is far less likely to. On balance, therefore, CYBERCOM's tolerance for risk may be higher for the wrong reasons.[4]

Last, under what circumstances should lower-echelon units carry out cyberattacks? If a cyberattack is not directed against civilian, dual-use, nuclear, or otherwise sensitive targets, then it is a combat weapon like any other combat weapon (and nonlethal to boot). In theory, therefore, its use should be delegated down to the lowest possible echelon, but this assumes sufficient understanding about collateral effects and acceptable ways to allocate scarce exploits.[5] Even then there are limits to how small a unit can get and still support a sufficiently talented team of cyberwarriors. The U.S. Army's organization, for instance, reflects the requirement that units be at a certain echelon (essentially, be of a certain size) before they get specified units of their own, such as helicopter squadrons. A great deal of who gets which cyberwarriors depends on how much talent is needed for operations. If cyberwarriors have to analyze opposing systems, understand their unique features, and devise a cyberattack that exploits such features, then they need to be so good as to be quite rare (and thus cannot be assigned to any unit but the largest ones). Those capable of using generic tools developed elsewhere are easier to find.[6]

THE ROGUE CYBERWARRIOR CHALLENGE

Controlling the effects of cyberattack entails controlling cyberwarriors. In the physical world, both command and control are getting better thanks to increasingly ubiquitous surveillance and the proliferation of communications networks. The effects of war can be meticulously documented and attributed (much as police now operate under more effective scrutiny because of cameras). In cyberspace, keystrokes can come from anywhere. Standard operating procedures are a poor guide when one cannot state a priori exactly what the means of attack should be for a class of target, much less what the likely effects of attacks are. Any policy designed to attack up to some boundary but no further is subject to the two aforementioned differences: between intent and effect and between effect and perception.

So, will cyberwar commanders act appropriate to the crises, follow standard operating procedures, or be allowed to think beyond them? As Barry Posen, for instance, observed, "During the Cuban Missile Crisis, the U.S. Navy ran its blockade according to its traditional methods, disregarding President Kennedy's instructions," adding that for the Air Force, "orders to cease U-2 flights near the Soviet border were either not received, or were ignored; Soviet detection of these flights hindered the negotiations to end this crisis." Richard Smoke argued that one of the reasons that Britain found itself mired in the Crimean War was that it perceived that Russia's devastating defeat of the Turkish fleet at Sinope was interpreted as an insult to the British themselves using the following logic.[7] Britain implied that it would not respond if the Russians fought at sea as long as they did not attack a Turkish port. The tsar concluded from this that naval action was acceptable as long as it took place at sea. But Russian admirals interpreted matters consistent with their desires and carried out their actions within the port of Sinope (without actually attacking the port facilities themselves). The only source of comfort from these examples is that standard operating procedures for cyberwarriors are still nascent enough to forestall arguments that they have always done things and will do things that way—but how long will that be true?

Rogue cyberwarriors will not necessarily respond to constraints when freelancing except as warnings as to what to avoid being seen doing. Because they do not have to work in military formations or with unique military hardware, their operations are harder to detect and, hence, control than their equivalents in physical combat: for example, the militias of developing nations.[8] Effective militaries have ways of filtering out most such rogue warriors and engineering social controls that keep potential rogue warriors in the force from straying. Having done what they can, states then have to determine whether the risks of violating self-imposed constraints merit reducing every cyberwarrior's access to the intelligence and tools necessary to mount the more sophisticated attacks. Or it may suffice to parcel out the intelligence and tools to each attack squad in ways that if a rogue employee does attack, one can determine where such an employee worked because no other squad would have had the means to mount that kind of attack. Broadcasting confidence that rogue activities will be inevitably detected may dampen unwanted mischievous enthusiasm—as long as the confidence is warranted. Furthermore, the more sophisticated the attack, the larger the source code of the malware required to carry it out, and the less that any one individual would have the ability to develop it on his or her own. Time will tell whether the problem is the rogue warrior, or the rogue organization, or neither of the above.

CHAPTER 13
Professionalizing Cyberwar

D eveloping a capability is only the first step in its integration into the toolkit of the professional warrior. Weaponization is the process by which a device or technique is made ready for military use. It is the difference between the lab and the battlefield and, in many ways, between a militia and a military. Consider many of the wickets that a device or technique needs to go through before it can be successfully considered weaponized:

- the ability to forecast battle damage beforehand and measure it afterward
- conformance with recognizable norms of conduct
- deployability in time and space
- integration into combined arms
- rules of engagement
- safety in storage and use
- integrated logistics support
- training

Nuclear forces had to make such an evolution. Alamogordo proved the physics was valid; the ability to measure effects in terms of TNT showed an understanding of potential effects; BDA was obvious; and the precedent of World War II's mass air attacks on civilian infrastructures gave them a basis in warfighting norms. But to turn nuclear devices into nuclear weapons required, at a minimum, that the device be designed and built so as to be put on an aircraft, the B-29, with the characteristics necessary to go from U.S. bases to its target. After Nagasaki, the United States turned to building a nuclear establishment in order to increase warfighters' understanding of their effects, promote safety in their storage and transportation, create a logistics infrastructure, write doctrine for integrating them into overall operations (admittedly, a controversial task), and train people in their use and management.[1] Issues of command and control pervaded the entire nuclear era.

BATTLE DAMAGE ASSESSMENT

Understanding which weapons to bring to bear on the fight and whether the results of using them are worth their cost is a big challenge. Warfighters need to know what a cyberattack can do to a target. With kinetic weapons, DoD has developed Joint Munition Effectiveness Manuals (JMEMs) that indicate the characteristics and size of a weapon's detonation. By contrast, the effects of a cyberattack—or, more specifically, a piece of malware—on a target have everything to do with the target itself (DDOS and BGP attacks, again, aside). In some cases, when the target is simple, the list of potential vulnerabilities is large, and the resulting change in behavior is limited to what a piece of malware can induce, some predictability is possible because some attack will get the malware in. For more complex targets, uncertainty is the rule. An attack that has a devastating effect one month may have no effect a month later. If one knows the target thoroughly in advance and can confidently assert that it has not changed appreciably since it was observed or has no hidden protection mechanisms, then one might forecast the *immediate* effect of a cyberattack. But inasmuch as most effects are temporary, it is difficult to determine when the other side will recover its capability or know how it will respond to having been attacked. Simply put, no reliable JMEM is possible for cyberspace, despite some fervent wishes that it were otherwise.

Warfighters also need to know what a cyberattack *did* to the target (for instance, can the attacked radar still imperil my air strike forces?), in part to know whether further attacks are needed. Good BDA for cyberattacks requires answering many questions correctly: Was the target penetrated? Did the attack affect the functioning of the target? If the system supports human decision-making, were decisions made badly or late? If the intent was to coerce, did it do so persuasively? Normally, the target of a cyberattack is a system that is not (or at least was not supposed to be) easy to get into. If the attack had any code that had to replicate itself to other systems before the full measure of damage was wreaked, access to the target system may be yanked (even literally if a network wire is pulled) well before the full propagation has taken place. Without a resident monitor within the target system or being fed by it, the only way an attacker might know what happened is if the attack was designed to disrupt a service visible to the outside: for example, the lights go out. But these are not necessarily the most sought-after effects. Note that the attackers in the Stuxnet case had to use the equivalent of a fire-and-forget weapon and thus had no direct access to the Natanz plant via the worm itself (there may have been other sources for intelligence).[2] That the IAEA was counting centrifuges was a fortuitous circumstance that allowed the world to hazard a guess as to what happened after the fact.

In contrast to kinetic attacks, cyberattacks may leave even the victim scratching his head about what the damage was. With disruption, the fact of damage (if not initially its cause) may be felt. But the point of corruption is to ruin processes in ways that defy detection so that errors are not immediately detected as such (ruining processes in *obvious* ways can only be a second-best outcome from the attacker's perspective). Indeed, the attacker may have a better fix on what happened in a corruption attack since it knows which systems or processes were being targeted, while the target can only guess. But the attacker may have no good idea which downstream systems relied on the systems being attacked; perhaps only the target will know that. So, neither side may know entirely, unless they collaborated—an unlikely possibility.

Pulling the infected system off the network and thus, in most cases, from observation is easier than withdrawing a damaged target from overhead scrutiny, especially if the scrutiny takes place as or just after the target is hit. That said, sudden disconnection is itself some evidence of effect. Finally, as noted, defenders may try to fool the attacker as to how much damage occurred. In fairness, BDA has always been a problem in war when the target cannot be inspected directly. From World War II through Vietnam to the Kosovo campaign and beyond, attackers have generously estimated the immediate effects of their actions as well as the time it would take to restore functionality of what was struck.

The existence of other systems, invisible to cyberespionage (for example, because they are not networked), may also serve to limit the damage from an attack (as well as from accident, human error, bad software, and so forth). Imagine a networked temperature sensor that can be disrupted by a cyberattack. Surveillance indicates that such a cyberattack would succeed—were it not for a standalone mechanical device, installed just in case but invisible to hackers, that cuts off the heat when the room gets too hot. Fortunately for the authors of Stuxnet, there was no mechanical governor in the centrifuges that kicked in when the revolutions per minute went too high—but in a well-engineered system sensitive to such failures, there could have been.

The imminence of conflict may also affect the reliability of BDA. Posit that one country's attacker, in pursuit of a deterrence policy, has painstakingly surveyed the systems it wishes to hold at risk at another country. The survey, repeated as late as Monday, shows such systems are ready to be hacked. The other country decides to carry out an attack on Wednesday but wants to avoid the full force of retaliation. On Tuesday, it therefore alerts owners of critical systems to reduce their connectivity and otherwise make penetration difficult for an unspecified (but clearly temporary) period. On Wednesday, that country launches a cyberattack. On Thursday, the target country retaliates, only to find that the systems it hoped to disrupt were far harder to access than previously thought, precisely because the first opportunity for retaliation came *after* the original attacker ordered its systems to enter a defensive crouch to accompany the original attack.

Because software changes with every add-on, tweak, and patch, the vulnerabilities that can be exploited today may be gone tomorrow. True, if the attack is already implanted and beaconing, then preserving the ability to initiate an attack is simpler (unless the defender knows about the beaconing but is playing along). In general, though, maintaining entrée into an evolving network requires constant efforts—and these efforts must succeed often enough if one is to hold a system at risk. If the access architecture of a system—which people and processes can get access to which levels of privilege—changes, then mere maintenance may not be enough. Today's accessibility may not faultlessly predict tomorrow's.

Several other factors bedevil BDA. The same complexity of systems that makes it hard to know they are secure also makes it hard to know what damage introducing an errant process or terminating an active process can do. Sometimes the process that has been shut down is one path of many to generate or affirm an answer. Consider a weather prediction that relies on a great deal of usually correlated data; the one data feed that has been corrupted will likely be treated as an outlier, and useful predictions can be made based on every other intact data element, albeit with modest loss of certainty, accuracy, or speed. At other times, the process being targeted feeds multiple downstream processes—much as when power in the northeastern United States went down in August 2003, telephone service and water supply followed. As argued above, attackers will not always know which functions call on which services (the server may know where the call came from but not how the information was used). Similarly, an obscure service (for example, name reconciliation for when lots of people have identical or even similar names) may be a prerequisite for more well-known services such as credit checks.

Some cyberattacks are undertaken to cause a cascade of events: one failure leads to another. An attack on an electric power system epitomizes the phenomenon; again, note the August 2003 blackout wherein a power line that shorted when it touched a tree deprived 50 million of power. But the differences among an event, a limited cascade, and a general cascade are often unpredictable. The only barriers to that outage spreading southward were relays in PJM Interconnection (a regional transmission organization) that cut off when upstream traffic became sufficiently anomalous. How confidently can such a reaction be predicted?[3]

As a rule, the degree of damage that can be wreaked with any cyberattack can be related to a system's recovery time. If the attack crashes a network, for instance, the extent of the damage is roughly proportional to the time that the network is down. Similarly, if a process or database is corrupted, the length of time that the process or database stays corrupted provides a guess for the amount of damage the attacker caused. Forecasting how long an attacked system will stay down may depend on understanding how long the other side takes to recognize and repair the damage. The Iranians probably did not know that their centrifuge controllers had been corrupted for months—perhaps not until they read about it in the trade press, or even later, in the *New York Times*. But that may not be typical. So, return to the question: how can one predict the behavior of unobservable individuals asked to carry out a task (system recovery in the face of infection) that they may never have had to carry out before (particularly under the pressure of time)? Perhaps one's own sysadmins have been run through the same exercise and their reaction time used as a proxy to the reaction time of the targets, but a great deal of variance between your side and their side has to be assumed away to have any confidence in the results. This is not a test range issue but a people issue and, worse for prediction, a people-doing-novel-things issue.

Can forecasts be improved by building and operating test ranges where attacks are run? Test ranges for cyberattacks do exist.[4] But the same attack on instrumented test ranges (where all parameters can be prespecified) can yield widely varying results. In today's computers, internal processes of one or another sort (for instance, self-examination, polling software threads to see what needs attention, context switching between tasks) are always going on; computers do not go to sleep between user-initiated commands. It is not unusual for an attack to elicit a weak response if the computer happens to be in a state that is subtly different from the state it had when the attack worked. The ability to know all a system's parameters beforehand is hardly guaranteed—and this is for a relatively short "beforehand" that may apply over the planning of an attack.

Attacks *could* be tested in vivo. Probes can check whether altered codes or files are still there (whether they are still being referred to by running code is another issue). The brave might run an attack just before the point where they create effects of the sort that would be noticed by the target's defenders (the sought-after effects have to be loud enough to be detected by witting attackers but not unwitting defenders). Implants can be pinged to see if they respond to test signals correctly. Too much testing, though, will alert defenders and may prompt them to find and patch the vulnerabilities that permitted such attacks (and the in vivo tests) in the first place. Even successful in vivo testing that pulls up short of creating an obvious effect still leaves open the question of how dynamic the target system administrators' detection and repair practices are.

COLLATERAL DAMAGE

Any attempt to create wanted effects (for example, on the battlefield) risks creating unwanted effects. Some of them can be termed collateral damage (even if a strict definition of collateral effects refers only to unlawful military targets), but there are many reasons why certain effects are unwanted. Inadvertently bringing new classes of targets into the conflict (for example, from outside the zone where war is taking place) can put one's own counterpart's targets into play for a retaliatory cyberattack or even kinetic attack. Effects that reveal their own cause may also be unwanted: consider how the unexpected spread of Stuxnet led to its discovery when Iranians might otherwise have been clueless as to why their centrifuges died so soon. Although many of the unwanted effects from cyberattack are similar to those of kinetic attack, there are important differences arising from choices about how cyberattacks are carried out, the larger role played by secondary effects, and the responsibility of the victim.

Any cyberattack that uses a replicating attack vector—a virus or worm—is problematic in that it has the potential to spread uncontrollably. The Stuxnet worm did exactly that; although its target was a handful of computers (those that programmed specific Siemens PLC chips), it ultimately infected more than 100,000 machines, many of them outside Iran. Had the Stuxnet worm been written to turn itself off if it appeared outside Iran's IP address space (after initial delivery), or if its time-to-live were not so long, such problems might have been avoided (albeit, perhaps, at a somewhat lower likelihood of mission success). Although unintentionally infected machines were not damaged, cleaning out the infection imposed nontrivial costs on their owners.[5] If any such worm-based infection mechanism is still viable (most of the vulnerabilities that permitted USB sticks to spread malware were fixed years ago), then those who use them must trade off mission success with intended consequences—even if these consequences are exaggerated (none of the hundreds of thousands of machines that did not host PLC software ran particularly worse for having been infected).

Another problematic attack modality is the drive-by attack, wherein a website is corrupted and those who surf there are infected by downloading its content (loaded with bad iframes). Drive-by attacks are typically used to recruit bots, in which case the effects are wanted (albeit not necessary licit). They are also used in the hopes that a *particular* target might frequent the site and thereby become infected. The latter leaves open the question of what to do with the other infected machines, which thereafter may be repeatedly beaconing out for instructions (generating collateral damage similar to that associated with Stuxnet).

A third attack modality that risks creating collateral damage is to infect a few computers in a network, which then carry out a DDOS attack to disable all the machines that they connect to. Predicting what services are lost if one system goes down is easier than doing so if a network goes down—particularly if the network is defined by which computers talk to which other computers rather than which ones are connected to the same router. The same lesson holds: those who use such attack modalities have serious trade-offs to consider.

A fourth related attack modality is associated with the use of DDOS attacks (or flooding attacks in general). They may be precise in the sense that the *primary* target is the intended one, but all too often those nodes that can be reached only through the deliberately congested artery also find their communications throttled (as was the case in the Spamhaus attack).

Otherwise, most sophisticated cyberattacks are used against targets that have been so well studied that both their weaknesses and their contribution to adversary warfighting are understood. With so much knowledge about the target system, those that are affected are likely to be what hackers think they are, and they can be found where attackers think they can be found.

Unfortunately, there is a large gap between knowing what a system does (something required to justify interfering with it) and knowing it does nothing else. In system terms, dependence is asymmetric. Examining a system's code will indicate what information and/or services it feeds on, but not what information, decisions, and/or services it feeds. The latter would require looking at all code of every system that links to it (both permanently and intermittently).

Determining the *other* functions that a potential target supports is a problem not necessarily limited to computers. Consider a satellite that looks for the characteristic infrared signatures of missile launches: Scuds but also nuclear missiles. Any attack—whether virtual or physical—on an asset that supports conventional warfighting could also take out a nuclear-related capability. Indeed, if the wiring diagram between systems is sufficiently complicated, the target may not know that its strategic systems have been crippled until afterward. Similarly, the dual-use nature of some command, control, communications, computers, intelligence, surveillance, and reconnaissance (C4ISR) systems means that the virtual connections between systems are less visible. Attacking, say, global positioning systems not only degrades the performance of U.S. weapons systems but also adds hazard to civilian aircraft operations.

Networks such as those that support logistics, health care, environmental monitoring (mostly weather forecasting, so far), command and control (including mission planning), and intelligence often serve multiple purposes. But most military targets tend to be self-contained. A cyberattack on an IADS is unlikely to have an effect outside air defense; ditto for an attack on a ship or any military platform in general. But weapons platforms tend to be the hardest targets to attack, as noted, because doing so requires surmounting radio frequency and cryptologic defenses before getting to cyberwar defenses.

There may also be obscure links between military and commercial services. Consider an air freight system shuttling boxes both to end-consumers and naval customers in, say, San Diego. An attacker might want to confuse shipments to the latter and may, in fact, be able to rewrite information about contents or a package's dimensions at the box-by-box level, but if it lacks access to such information and its only intelligence is the knowledge that *some* boxes on a flight are going to military customers, it may feel it has little choice but to try something like scrambling information about what is on that flight. Even if it attacks DoD's logistics systems directly by corrupting information about the characteristics of military packages, the confusion generated when loading the aircraft with packages whose dimensions have been falsified may delay the arrival of commercial packages. Worse, if the air freight company suspects that *some* of its data were corrupted, it might end up delaying all shipments in an effort to ascertain that *all* of its data were reasonably correct.[6] Similar stories could be told about interfaces between military and civilian hospitals, or the reliance of weather forecasts on military databases that have been corrupted.

Analogs in the physical world can highlight some critical differences in cyberspace. An attack on a power plant that cuts power to a military facility could also cut power to a civilian facility, but charting the power lines can suggest what connects to what. In cyberspace, neither physics nor economics yields particularly good clues as to which servers satisfy which clients (although hacking into the server may reveal some information). With cloud computing, a single server farm may support very different customers, many perhaps in neutral or even friendly countries.[7]

Does this argue for close inspection of the targeted system? That might allow the services that a system or network supports to be traced, grasped, and evaluated for sensitivity. But this choice is not only technically difficult but also potentially counterproductive. Understanding *all* the services that a system supports takes far more cyberespionage than required to understand its basic function. Worse, the more cyberespionage, the greater the likelihood of discovery—which, by way of repetition, often reveals how such spying worked, hence what vulnerabilities it exploited, and thus what vulnerabilities need to be closed, thereby making repeat attempts harder. In fairness, the NSA has had a good record in doing a great deal of cyberespionage without its methods being revealed (pre-Snowden). But will such risk-free cyberespionage characterize future activity? China's alarm at having been penetrated, for instance, has spurred President Xi Jinping to personally supervise the country's improvement in cybersecurity.[8]

Worst, consider an attacker being caught scoping systems that are *not* targets in order to ascertain that their processes do not depend on systems to be targeted (for example, corrupting military logistics does not result in corrupting civilian logistics). Will the other side tell itself that the attacker is exploring such systems to ensure they are not collateral damage—or conclude that the attacker is poking into such systems precisely because it *does* consider them legitimate targets? Such suspicions were raised in the United States when Chinese intrusion was discovered into the office networks of natural gas pipelines; what could have been the theft of intellectual property was seen by some as intelligence preparation of the battlefield.[9] Although there is no virtue in being ignorant of what a system does for whom, one cannot ignore the risks of getting caught when vigorously trying to fill in the gaps.

The situation is not hopeless. Understanding what a comparable domestic system does may yield a good guess on what an adversary's system does. Understanding how information is used in an adversary's society may yield a good guess on the difference between adversary use of information and one's own use of information—a potentially useful refinement of the estimate. Furthermore, because it is well understood that certain systems are politically sensitive (for example, health care, personnel pay, police files), they could be put at the bottom of any cyberattack targeting list. Finally, if an attacker is careful to signal that it will not target certain systems, avoids targeting them directly, and establishes a corresponding track record, then the adversary is more likely to deem its being harmed in the course of going after military systems to be inadvertent rather than deliberate. Thus, a mistake should be likely to engender a tit-for-tat response from them.

But should collateral damage always be avoided? Maybe not. Part of any deterrence strategy is the implicit threat that the response to aggression may be uncontrolled and perhaps disproportional.

If a war breaks out, both sides may find it in their interest to prevent escalation. Yet until a war breaks out, or if the other side persists in fighting when it could choose to settle, is it always a good idea to assure others that escalation will never take place? Thomas Schelling wrote of the threat that left something to chance. Similarly, the threat that cyber operations will put at risk more systems and services than the other side believes it can afford to lose may help preserve or encourage restraint. Recall that John Lehman's 1980s-era maritime strategy explicitly called for the U.S. Navy to sink Soviet ballistic missile submarines in the Barents Sea—even if the conflict began as non-nuclear and the United States had no plans to go nuclear first. The United States may not want to declare outright that no targets are off limits lest it give the other side a green light to act as if cyberspace were entirely safe—but it may hint that its vaunted ability to wage cyberwar with exquisite precision is easy to overestimate.

The victim's responsibility for the damage done, conversely, may be larger in cyberspace than in physical space. In theory, well-written software should not operate in ways that break hardware (even, one can argue, if hijacked). Yet flawed software and promiscuous connections among systems may allow faults in one to infect the other. A cyberattack meant to disrupt electricity for just a few days may cause power-generating hardware to fail unexpectedly, disrupting electricity for months. Would such damage lead others to judge acts disproportionate? If the (ill-advised) practice of security through obscurity makes it hard for attackers to know whether disrupting or corrupting an operation has serious downstream attacks, who is at fault when an attack yields excessively broad effects? Is it fair to hold the target state—which, after all, may otherwise be a completely innocent victim of aggression—responsible for dangerously commingling systems (or at least no more than business logic would otherwise dictate)? If the knowledge were deficient and damage resulted, would opacity on the part of the adversary mitigate the attacker's responsibility? What constitutes a reasonable presumption of connectedness?

The responsibility for secondary impacts is always contentious. Assume that as a result of a physical attack on a military target (for example, a military base), citizens of the target country panic and as a result of their panic cause great havoc with greater costs (for example, by not coming to work in their civilian jobs) that could have been avoided if they had remained calm. Or suppose a military attack that is predominantly focused on units staffed by one ethnic group gives rise to ethnic conflict that yields far more damage than the original attack did (a loose analogy of the terrorist attack on the Shia al-Askari shrine in 2006, which was clearly not a legitimate military target). Conventionally, these second-order effects are not counted among the tally of collateral damage. The key distinction is that giving in to panic or vengeance is a matter of human choice. The attacker's responsibility ends before that point.

Now consider an analog. The adversary changes the information going to a human operator, which causes the human operator to make a mistake that hurts civilians (as well as harming military targets). Does the latter count as collateral damage? Or consider the Stuxnet-infected PC that reprogrammed the PLC whose corrupted instructions led to the premature death of the various centrifuges. Now replace the PC with a human and replace the malware with a corrupted set of instructions (for example, the real manual was surreptitiously replaced by a phony but authentic-looking manual). Does the harm to machines signify that force was used? What makes the two examples different?

At what point do law and custom then hold that computers, which are growing steadily more intelligent and potentially discriminating, should have acted wisely? If a computer is programmed to make choices with as much sophistication and sensitivity as humans, does that mean that nothing a computer does is the responsibility of the attacker? Must the defender argue that the computer cannot pass a Turing test and hence cannot accept responsibility for its mistakes? What about all the computers whose operations are affected by the attack on the original computer (for example, the computer holding the instructions may be dumb, but the computers calling on the instructions may be smart); must defenders argue that none of *those* computers could have passed a Turing test? If a computer's having intelligence lets the attacker off the hook and thus puts the target on the hook, what prevents the target from ensuring that its machines have no such intelligence and just do as they are told so that the target can avoid blame? Or do we simply declare that in an interconnected world of increasingly intelligent and semi-opaque machines, the burden of proof is *always* on the attacker to ensure that *no* corruption of a machine's logic can hurt anyone?

In 1996, then–CIA director John Deutsch testified before the Senate, "The electron is the ultimate precision-guided weapon." As the argument above suggests, this may have been a case where precision is not the same as accuracy. Collateral damage is possible with cyberattack, just as it is with kinetic weapons. The difference, though, may be that whereas the error range of cyber weapons is contained, it is not understood as well as it is with kinetic weapons. Put another way, while the known unknowns may be smaller, the unknown unknowns may well be greater.

OTHER PARAMETERS

Deployability in time and space ought not to be much of a problem. Hackers can operate day and night with effects carried around the globe. In practice, the susceptibility of an information system to attack depends critically on its details. Not only are months and, sometimes, years required to scope adversary systems, but the result must also be constantly inspected and occasionally renewed to validate its ability to work at the time and place of attack. And even then, the descent into crisis and war (when systems are locked down) is often the moment that access to a system is likely to change. But the advantages of hackers being on the spot should not be completely dismissed. Some cyberattacks need propinquity (for example, insertion via RF means or by using Special Forces) in order to penetrate target systems or to collect intelligence (for example, via dumpster-diving). Gauging the effect of a cyberattack has everything to do with the relationship between the affected information system and a human decisionmaking system. Gaining such knowledge sometimes requires being there. Last, if commanders are to give cyberattack options the weight they deserve, it may help for cyberwarriors to be literally in the same room with proponents of competing options. Similar considerations govern integrated logistics support even if physical movement is not an issue.

At least safety in storage and use is relatively straightforward (once the blowback risks from a cyberattack are taken into account). Ironically, certain aspects of network defense bear more watching, if for no other reason than that some of them are constantly running. Among these are active defenses, intrusion detection systems, anomaly characterization, counter-virus measures, and techniques to deceive hackers. All of them could, in theory, flag or even attack user processes as well as attacker-inserted processes. The risk is not necessarily in their design, but in the possibility of error or oversight in their implementation that lends them undesirable behaviors.

Training cyberwarriors is not problematic as such, but it is time-consuming and difficult. Training serves to simultaneously inculcate a set of skills and evaluate which of the many students are among the few who are really good at hacking. It provides a winnowing function whose dropout ratio may be similar to that characterizing Special Forces. From the military perspective, evaluation is helped by the fact that the defense of military systems has much in common with the defense of civilian systems and the ranks of defenders are large enough to ensure that their performance vis-à-vis one another can be measured well.

The importance of readiness and sustainability to cyberwar operations may be exaggerated in that they are not meaningfully achievable. Readiness is largely a matter of having enough of the right people and a modicum of equipment. Cyberwarriors need less tailoring for their destination than their physical counterparts—but they have to be acutely aware of the details of systems that vary from one country to the next. Sustainability, as repeatedly noted, is also not a useful expectation for operational cyberwar. Attacks exploit vulnerabilities. Exploited vulnerabilities, for that reason, are more likely to be fixed (if elucidated) or at least routed around (if not). That attackers need new tricks that are slow in coming (if they come at all) helps explain why operational cyberwar may be mostly used as a bolt from the blue and only later in special cases.

Standard rules of engagement in cyberspace remain elusive.[10] For instance, a standard rule of engagement in kinetic combat allows return fire because of the heightened risk to warfighters if they cannot return fire. Few question its purpose. The hostile shooters have little moral basis to objecting to a return shot. Also, expecting warfighters to ignore threats to their lives is awful for morale. Yet the human that is the target of a cyberattack will live another day—and the target of a cyberattack is rarely a system that can carry out its own cyberattacks.[11] True, a cyberattack may indirectly allow kinetic weapons to be far more effective, but such a formulation applies to only some cyberattacks, and return fire may more wisely be directed toward those wielding the *kinetic* weapon. Furthermore, for many cyberattacks (DDOS attacks aside), the damage has already taken place by the time the attack is felt—again, in contrast to kinetic attacks, which often require repeat application for a kill. Thus, returning fire is usually unrelated to the target's ability to avoid damage. Finally, as noted, cyberattacks cannot disarm cyberattackers.

As for conformance with recognizable norms of conduct, tools and techniques to defend networks are certainly on safe ground, even if active defenses—preemptive counterattacks—are still matters of controversy and caution. Cyberespionage is hardly more offensive than eavesdropping on RF signals. But the legitimacy of cyberattack has yet to be fully accepted, particularly if directed against civilian infrastructures.

PROGRAMMING AND BUDGETING FOR CYBERWAR

Part of the professionalization of cyberwar is finding a way to program and pay for it—hence some way to analyze program and budget requests. This is something that admittedly was, for kinetic weapons, an art hovering between embryonic and nascent even *after* Robert McNamara introduced systems analysis to the Pentagon circa 1961.

In popular and media imagination, the big budget question is the balance between offense and defense in cyberspace. Tilting toward offense is taken for aggression; tilting toward defense is taken for prudence or, to some, pusillanimity. Thus are proposed ratios between defensive and offensive teams within CYBERCOM evaluated.[12] But the either-or notion is misleading, in large part because most of the work of defense takes place within the various services, defense agencies, and combat commands because those who build and run networks must defend them. Taken alone, CYBERCOM might look offense-oriented; when cyberspace activities are examined across the entire U.S. Department of Defense, the reverse is true. The competition between offense and defense is rarely relevant anyway; they are mostly financed separately by separate outfits and rarely compete directly.

One of the more difficult challenges in programming and budgeting for *offensive* cyberwar activities is working through the measure-countermeasure exchange. Once an offensive measure is used and discovered, countermeasures are likely to emerge, some of which can be up to 100 percent effective. Contrary to the popular notion that offense dominates in cyberspace, countermeasures are often cheaper to develop than measures. Oftentimes it is a matter of "oops, I shouldn't have done that." What can make countermeasures expensive is testing and distributing them, but the second of these costs can be brought down by tight network management. Granted, almost all military measures are subject to countermeasures (while some are just copied by the other side). But the linkage was tighter and the cycle times lower for electronic warfare (EW) than they were for traditional weapons—and even tighter and faster for cyberwar, whose cycle times can be measured in days or even hours.[13] Thus, the development of every offensive measure has to be coupled with the question: how long will this measure be viable once used? In fairness, not every measure creates countermeasures so quickly. A useful tool may create repeatable (albeit low-level) effects as long as the degree of time and attention (and hassle) required by the other side to ward off such effects is relatively high. The latter is affected by whether the other side realizes it has been attacked; its access to resources required to fix the problem, where resources may be internal ("can I afford it?") and external ("can someone sell it to me?"); and the costs that can be imposed on the other side by having to fix it.

More telling are the divisions *within* defense and offense. In defense, a key question is the relative emphasis between defending unclassified networks and defending classified (hence air-gapped) networks. Unclassified systems are easier to penetrate—it pays to monitor them constantly for anomalies—but they play a lesser role in warfighting. Classified systems are harder to penetrate—monitoring them for anomalies is likely to yield far fewer true positives of hostile activity—but they play a greater role in warfighting. An emphasis on unclassified networks reveals a focus on frequency over criticality and, correspondingly, of peacetime protection over wartime protection, even though militaries exist for wars. In offense, a question is the emphasis of operational cyberwar vis-à-vis strategic cyberwar. Operational cyberwar is useful only in wartime; a war against a foe sophisticated enough to merit electronic warfare attacks will likely entail operational cyberattacks. Strategic cyberwar speaks to the U.S. deterrence posture. At the risk of being a little unfair, this raises the question: Are we serious about cyberattacks as a warfighting tool (hence classified and operational) rather than as a posturing tool (hence unclassified and strategic)?

Last, how many people are needed for cyberattacks? Start with a general proposition: the number of successful attacks, notably on the harder targets, depends on how many exploits there are in hand. As it is, good general exploits are rare, while specific exploits can be used only against certain systems. The belief that more is always better runs into shortages of first-tier hackers. Because exploits tend to depreciate rapidly after exposure—and thus often after being used in a cyberattack—these should be reserved for first-tier hackers. Using too many second-tier hackers spoils the stew, and their activity might alert the adversary and provide it hints about the attacker's target sets and operational methods and, worst, high-level exploits and implanted code. Even giving second-tier hackers low-level exploits to play with may be more likely to immunize rather than infect the target. Better tasks for these individuals would be mapping networks, maintaining implants, and dredging through exfiltrated data.

CHAPTER 14
Is Cyberspace a Warfighting Domain?

Like everyone else who is or has been in a U.S. military uniform, I think of cyber as a domain. It is now enshrined in doctrine: land, sea, air, space, cyber. It trips off the tongue, and frankly I have found the concept liberating when I think about operationalizing this domain. But the other domains are natural, created by God, and this one is the creation of man. Man can actually change this geography, and anything that happens there actually creates a change in someone's physical space. Are these differences important enough for us to rethink our doctrine?

—Gen. Michael V. Hayden, USAF (Ret.)

Take two warfighting "domains." Operators in one domain have been achieving significant military effects for seventy years; many airmen (among others) owe their lives to their efforts. Losing control in this domain could shut down many operations beyond line of sight. Within their ranks are tens of thousands of highly trained individuals backed by billions of dollars' worth of highly specialized equipment. However, no single commander represents this domain. Within the four services, the highest rank of any individual whose primary responsibility is to operate in this domain is a one-star flag officer (in two services) or a colonel.

Operators in the other domain have yet to achieve more than modest effects (as far as published reports go), and if worthwhile effects have been achieved (accounts vary), they were only within the last dozen years against third-rate opponents, such as Serbia (as some reports claim), or fourth-rate opponents, such as jihadists. No one really knows whether significant effects in this domain, in fact, *can* be achieved against first-rate opponents or achieved by such opponents against us. The development of a military career path in this domain, or even the definition of military occupation specialties, has just started. Little specialized equipment exists. This domain is overseen by a four-star flag officer.

No prizes will be awarded to readers who guessed that the first domain is the RF spectrum (for electronic warfare) and the second domain is cyberspace. The former is not considered its own warfighting domain. Yet somehow it is considered obvious that the latter should be. Cyberspace, we are told, pervades the other domains in that warfighters in prior domains would be severely handicapped if their access to cyberspace were successfully challenged (this is no less true for the RF spectrum). Thus understood, cyberspace has become the new high ground of warfare, the one domain to rule them all and in the ether bind them. But is this the right way to think about cyberspace and what militaries can do by operating "within" it?

Whether cyberspace does or does not have the essence of a warfighting domain as per some platonic ideal is not at issue. Connotation rather than denotation is the problem: does understanding cyberspace as a warfighting domain promote or hinder understanding what can and should be done to defend and attack networked systems? To the extent that such a characterization leads strategists and operators to presumptions or conclusions that are not derived from observation and experience, it may mislead.[1] The argument that cyberspace is simply a very different kind of warfighting domain begets the question of what end is served by calling it a domain in the first place. Our purpose is, therefore, akin to what our ancient Chinese friends would have called the rectification of terms: making the name of the thing match the nature of the thing.

CYBERWAR OPERATIONS ARE ABOUT USURPING COMMAND AND CONTROL

Cyberwar is about usurping the command and control of an adversary's systems; as argued, it is rarely about cyberspace as such. Even if sending bits through cyberspace—the Internet and like lines—remains the most common way of accessing other people's information systems, there *are* other ways. Concentrating on the medium through which attacks move rather than the systems (more precisely, logic processors) in which instructions vie for control is what gives rise to the illusions of cyberspace as a combat medium. It is like describing World War I as a contest in rail-space because both side's trench-dwellers got to the battlefield on trains.

Everyone concedes that cyberspace is manmade and, as such, different from its physical predecessors. Most then proceed as if the difference between a natural and a manmade combat medium is of no greater importance than the difference between cotton and polyester. But it is not the manmade nature of cyberspace that makes it different.[2] Cities are manmade, but city combat shares many of the rules of country combat. Cities, though, are not particularly mutable (at least not by those defending them). Cyberspace *is* highly mutable by its owners, hence defenders, in ways other media are not. If systems were not mutable, they could not host malware, the most prominent way in which the behavior of systems is wrenched away from what was intended for them.

How mutable is cyberspace? In the commercial world, there are many givens: the majority of all machines run some version of Microsoft Windows. Most software product lines are dominated by a handful of firms, often just one. Communications with the outside world use various protocols of the Internet suite (for example, TCP/IP, the Border Gateway Protocol). Most communications travel over fixed hardware infrastructures. Nevertheless, all this still leaves users considerable scope for adjusting the terrain, even doing so quickly: for instance, which systems are connected to the outside, which services and data stores are accessible through systems so connected, what provisions are made for back-up or process validation, how networks are managed and secured (including which products and services are used to do so), where encryption and digital signatures are used, how user and administrator identities are authenticated, how such individuals are vetted for their privileges, what version of software is used and how diligently its security is maintained, what security settings are applied to such software (and who gets to change them), and so on. As the prior discussion on iOS or the system-in-hardware example suggests, vulnerability is not an ineluctable attribute of cyberspace.

The U.S. military has both a real need and a serious capability to shape its information systems. Unlike most of the civilian world, DoD's foes have a clear interest in preventing its operations from working, particularly while fighting a war (that is, when warfighting capabilities matter most). Thus, DoD should be and is willing to make trade-offs that ensure its systems do as they are told, even if doing so makes systems somewhat costlier and less convenient. Many DoD systems *are* air-gapped. Encryption is widespread, particularly on RF links that connect warfighting platforms. DoD vets users tightly and imposes many restrictions on what they can do; access to the NIPRnet, for instance, requires a Common Access Card. It has its own Internet domain and runs its own domain name server. It has acquired most of the source code for Microsoft Windows so that it can understand, and in some cases alter, the latter's security features. It operates a complex system of document security (that is, security classification). DoD (notably the NSA) has hired some of the world's smartest cybersecurity folks. In sum, it has even more scope than most organizations do to shape its share of cyberspace, and it uses this discretion vigorously. *Its* cyberspace is definitely mutable. Thus, it is not a given that it maneuvers there on equal basis with its foes.

CYBERSPACE AS MULTIPLE MEDIA

The use of "*its* cyberspace" when discussing DoD indicates another feature of cyberspace—it is not a single medium as, say, outer space is. Cyberspace consists of multiple media: yours, theirs, and everyone else's. Each of these media often contains sub-media. *Your* cyberwarriors are trying to get into *their* cyberspace as a way of getting their systems to misbehave, and theirs are trying to get into yours for similar reasons.

As a rule, the more sophisticated and well financed the adversary, the more of a separate network it runs, particularly for maintaining connectivity among mobile units (for example, warfighting platforms). Conversely, the less sophisticated and well financed the adversary, the less likely it is to be able to afford any of the kind of networking upon which the United States and comparable militaries have grown so dependent. That may not be a pliable middle ground for hackers if countries are either too technically sophisticated to allow their critical systems to depend on the Internet or too unsophisticated to afford (and hence depend on) networked systems. The ability to command or at least confound the *civilian* Internet of foreign countries is likely to be of modest direct *military* value. This is far from saying that such countries are impervious to operations against their systems. It does mean, however, that carrying out such operations requires playing in their corner of cyberspace, and they too have considerable scope to shape what they become dependent upon—cyberspace is not a given for them either.

What about this broad cyberspace in the middle; is it worth trying to dominate or preventing others from dominating? To some extent, it is. Cyberspace operations can keep a state's leaders from communicating with their population easily, as Russia's operations did against Georgia in 2008. It can make life uncomfortable for citizens of another state, as the operations of Russians against Estonia did in 2007. The ability to interpose messages into media can have psychological effects. The ability to take down (for example, jihadist) websites can complicate recruitment efforts. Interfering with services from, for example, electric and transportation utilities or maintenance organizations can reduce the support that militaries receive from them. But these operations are carried out not so much against cyberspace, which is to say the Internet per se, as against systems connected by cyberspace to the rest of the world. Such systems, and to some extent their connections, are themselves mutable. Thus, Estonia reduced its vulnerability to DDOS attacks by having Akamai redo its network architecture, and Georgia did likewise by having U.S. companies, such as Google and Tulip, rehost their websites. Electric power companies do not have to be vulnerable to hackers; they can air-gap their generation, transmission, and distribution systems. If they feel the consequences of their failures to do so beforehand, they can correct matters afterward, albeit not instantly. Maintenance companies can adopt back-up methods (for example, phones and modems, very small aperture terminals) so that they can continue to serve their customers should they isolate their subnetworks.

Compromising large chunks of the world's communications infrastructure allows unencrypted (or weakly encrypted) messages to be intercepted—and metadata (from, to, when, where) of even encrypted communications to be collected. This capability is powerful but can be enjoyed by both sides at once (even without each being aware of the other's activities). In the latter case, there is no media dominance.

DEFEND THE DOMAIN OR ENSURE MISSIONS?

Thinking of cyberspace as a warfighting domain tends to convert the problems associated with operating in cyberspace—creating useful effects in their systems and preventing the same from being done to you—into a warfighting mold shaped by the four older domains. This shifts the focus of thought from the creation and prevention of specific effects to broader warfighting metaphors, such as control, maneuver, and superiority. It emphasizes the search for analogs to standard attributes of kinetic military operations, such as mass, speed, synchronization, fires, command and control, and hierarchy—but it does so at the expense of other ways of creating or managing effects: for example, through engineering.

To talk of defending networks, for instance, is to think in terms of defense even though securing them through engineering may be more cost-effective. Accordingly, the problem of preventing effects arising from enemy-created instructions should have a strong engineering component. Other disciplines that can be used to secure networks include design/architecture (how the various parts fit together influences how faults echo throughout a larger system), administration, and policymaking (how to make intelligent trade-offs between values such as security on the one hand and cost and convenience on the other). Warding off bad effects that may afflict systems too complex to grasp readily may also call on the talents possessed by scientists of complexity theory.

Granted, some elements of network management *are* like warfare. Even well-designed systems have to be tended to constantly (and good design facilitates such management). Systems managers may even be lucky enough to see incoming or circulating malware and intervene to limit its malign effects by isolating and neutralizing it. There is a point to having warriors "live in the network." But is such a reactive ability important compared to systems engineering, or is it simply something to be emphasized in order to make network defense look like warfighting?

The same question may be asked of "active defense." Cyberwarriors want to take the fight to the enemy by finding, targeting, and disabling the servers from which the intrusions came. This is probably not a bad idea if foes lack the care or sophistication to launch an attack in other ways (such as by using fire-and-forget weapons à la Stuxnet) or lack the wit to operate from multiple servers up to and including peer-to-peer networks (for example, of bots). Against better foes, search-and-disable missions are likely to be much less productive. Here, also, the conventional imagery of cyberspace as a warfighting domain creates distortions in understanding.

More broadly, the emphasis on defending the domain puts the information assurance cart before the mission assurance horse. Militaries adopt networked systems in order to facilitate kinetic operations. Adversaries target these networks in order to neutralize the help that networked systems provide to operations (or worse, to exploit the dependence on such systems to render militaries less effective than if they had never adopted networked systems at all). Information assurance is about how militaries minimize such a threat, but it works in service of the more important goal: mission assurance. A large facet of mission assurance is being able to carry out operations in an environment in which the enemy has penetrated the militaries' networks. This requires understanding the relationship of operations to information flows and managing risk accordingly. It also includes training to ensure that warfighters can function when networks are not always available and information is not necessarily trustworthy. But if cyberspace is viewed as a domain that needs to be mastered by warfighting, the subsidiary nature of this domain to kinetic operations fades and the emphasis shifts to achieving control in this domain for its own sake rather than understanding exactly why such control was needed in the first place.

AS FOR OFFENSIVE OPERATIONS

Could understanding cyberspace as a warfighting domain help in understanding at least *offensive* cyberspace operations? At first glance, yes. It is easy to envision teams of cyberwarriors metaphorically entering the networked systems of adversaries, controlling, disrupting, and corrupting as they go.

At second glance, not quite. Much of what offensive cyberwarriors do is reconnaissance or exploration; in no other military endeavor is intelligence quite so integral to warfighting. But the nature of the reconnaissance is not simply to observe and report. The real work has a more scientific bent: to examine a logical structure and determine its flaws, either by observation or by experimentation. The center of gravity of such an operation is the act of determining the target system's vulnerabilities and creating a tool, often embodied in malware, to exploit them.

As often noted, cyberspace operations can be hard to repeat because they work by surprise. A target attacked once is a target harder to attack again—hence, the logic of front-loading them in a campaign.[3] By contrast, fights in other domains retain importance throughout a campaign. Indeed, one can fairly characterize offensive cyberattacks as a set of carefully prepared one-offs that have a well-defined role to play as niche operations in certain phases of a conflict. Such a characterization ill fits the notion of cyberspace as a continuous warfighting domain in the same way as land, sea, air, and space.

As a practical matter, cyberattacks have a niche quality to them: they can only be used against certain systems whose vulnerabilities can be exploited in certain ways in certain circumstances. At a bare minimum, they require foes to have *and depend on* their information systems. As a practical matter, these systems have to be accessible in real time to the rest of the world in order to be struck at a militarily useful time and place: neither too soon nor too late. The circumstances may not be known a priori.

IT RAISES THE ATTENTION TO DDOS ATTACKS

Thinking of cyberspace as a military domain seems to lead people to focus on that form of cyberwar most like conventional warfare: DDOS attacks. They are about cyberspace; they would be unimaginable without it. Such attacks do bear many of the characteristics of military attacks: for example, there is forcible denial of entry to others, the faults being exploited are generally not those of the target, the intervening (network) terrain matters, these bytes take a particular route to the target, the effects take place at the same time as the attacks, and the attacks can be shut off. A DDOS attack starts in a particular location under the active command and control of a particular source (ultimately, for the most part, a particular computer). Defenses against DDOS attacks are possible without changing the affected systems; thus, such defenses can be employed even if the target is private and resists opening itself up to government eyes. By severing sites from the Internet, DDOS attacks can be said to restrict the "freedom of maneuver" in cyberspace, a familiar leitmotif of the maritime and outer space domains. Inasmuch as the effects of a DDOS attack—to sever links in a communications chain—are similar to what jamming might produce, it looks like electronic warfare, a well-recognized facet of modern war. The fact that DDOS attacks take place in real time creates the beguiling possibility that such attacks can be preempted by going after the command and control computers of the attackers, shutting them down in progress.[4] This metaphor is even more pronounced if the DDOS packets are generated from thousands of large sources rather than millions of small ones. They can be stifled with the cooperation of those who really own cyberspace (for example, the major ISPs).

The policy responses also look like those of war. Generally, the target of a DDOS attack is usually not at fault from having been victimized. The only "flaw" in the case of most DDOS attacks is not having bought bandwidth well in excess of its day-to-day needs (so as to withstand the volumes involved in a DDOS attack).[5] Addressing DDOS attacks has to take place at the national or international level rather than by assigning the blame to the victimized organization. This is a fight the government can run; it can pressure intermediate countries to tamp down the flows. One can even envision a patriotic campaign—for example, is *your* computer taking down the network?—to reduce its impact.

By contrast, the more typical—and serious—cyberattacks require the victim's complicity. There is no forced entry. Volume is usually beside the point. The ability to mimic legitimate traffic is more important. An attack cannot necessarily be shut off by shutting off the source (a lot depends on how much command and control is needed for its success, but there is also a great potential for fire-and-forget malware). Governments cannot defeat such attacks directly and cannot easily shut themselves off from most such attacks (particularly if the attack vector lacks a recognizable signature) without shutting themselves off from global communications entirely. It is easy to see why militaries are less comfortable making such attacks the basis for understanding all cyberattacks when DDOS attacks fit the kinetic model much better.

One danger from conflating DDOS attacks with all cyberattacks arises if military and/or intelligence entities are authorized to carry out such preemptive attacks because *some* threats fit the DDOS case and then use such authorization to counter cyberspace threats that look nothing like the ones that lent themselves to war metaphors. Many of the proposed "solutions" to the problem of insecurity in cyberspace dwell on those that specifically address DDOS attacks. For instance, much of the draft-for-comment 2002 National Strategy to Secure Cyberspace dwelt on how to get home users to practice safe computing so that their infected computers would not be used to attack others; this metaphor had DDOS attacks as well as self-replicating worms in mind—but not APT attacks.[6] Finally, the notion that nations have a responsibility for the bad packets that exit their borders tends to reflect DDOS attacks (where the unexpected volume of traffic is a sign that some channel should be suppressed) rather than cyberattacks that rely on deception (whose packets are initially hard to distinguish from innocent ones but that can be filtered at the target's border once they are distinguished). Similarly, a DDOS attack may cross a neutral country and thus raise the question of its responsibilities to prevent its territory from being used as a conduit of war.

But DDOS attacks are just not all that powerful; their military uses are modest. They can neither steal nor corrupt data. They can rarely interfere with the internal operations of networks.[7] Malware attacks on machines that cause them to flood internal networks are a different matter, but one readily dealt with by finding and shutting off such machines until they are cleaned up. The only harm DDOS attacks do is to make networks that depend on public access temporarily unavailable to the public—or panic people into doing the bot-herder's work for them. According to someone close to such deliberations, a DDOS attack coming out of North Korea in 2009 almost persuaded U.S. officials to disconnect South Korea from the U.S. portion of the Internet.

Despite this, there have been arguments that DDOS attacks can be a weapon of actual interstate combat. The author of "Carpet-Bombing in Cyberspace" argues that a DDOS attack against a network-centric military could stop or delay any operation it intended.[8] The U.S. Air Force, he argued, should equip itself for such combat by returning machines it would otherwise discard back into service, booting them up on a flash drive filled with bot software, and letting them flood our enemies' networks—ignoring the fact that most target military systems are air-gapped and those that are not can still function without much public access. Furthermore, any set of attacks bearing ".mil" addresses are easy to detect and delete at national (or at national defense system) gateways. It would also be a dead giveaway to who was doing what. At least the author admits, "Our enemies would know it was America that attacked them. Precisely." Even if such an attack worked, which is highly unlikely, the fundamental effect would be to create short-term disruption, not the kind of corruption that would make militaries doubt the information in front of their eyes and keep doing so in the long term.

DDOS attacks are the duck-billed platypus of cyberwar. Although they are unquestionably attacks and unquestionably of cyberspace, the many differences between DDOS attacks and other attacks suggest treating them as a separate category. Otherwise, anyone making valid generalizations about cyberattacks will constantly have to remember to add, "with the exception of DDOS attacks." Yet envisioning cyberspace as a domain makes DDOS attacks seem like the epitome of cyberwar.

OTHER ERRORS FROM CALLING CYBERSPACE A WARFIGHTING DOMAIN

Calling cyberspace a warfighting domain also drags in misleading warfighting concepts from the earlier domains of land, sea, and air. Consider "domain superiority," the idea that power in a domain can prevent adversaries from doing anything useful in it. In the air or on the seas, whoever's fleet can keep the other from taking off or leaving port has achieved superiority. But how can this be so in a medium that is really composed of independently defined sub-media? The metaphor that air control means "I can hit you and you cannot hit me" is not even close to an accurate précis of what competent cyberwarriors permit. The best hackers in the world can do little to interfere with a truly air-gapped network of their adversaries.

Ground warfare is another source of misleading metaphors. Take "key terrain." True, in any network, some physical nodes and services are more important than others. But offensive cyberspace operations generally cannot break physical nodes, and the services provided by networks can be, and are, increasingly virtualized. The very plasticity and mutability of software make gaining the "possession" of key terrain an empty victory. The same analogy may be drawn with naval choke-points even though networks are almost limitlessly replicable given time (and not even all that much time). Notions of cyberspace as a high ground whose dominance presages the dominance of all other domains are similarly meaningless, not least because every modern military owns its own high ground (its core routers).

Or take "maneuver." Again, no self-respecting cyberwarrior wants to stay in one place waiting for the enemies to arrive, but by the time this metaphor of place is translated into cyberspace, it may be drained of all effective meaning. Should malware be polymorphic? Should it be hopping from client to client? Should systems dynamically reconfigure their address space? Should server capacity be distributed across the cloud? These are all good questions, but it is unclear how translating all of them into some aspect of maneuver helps answer them. What works does so because it solves a problem.

If cyberspace is like other domains, then under current rules of engagement for kinetic combat, U.S. forces, for instance, are allowed to fire back when under fire—but, as also noted, this assumes that your returning fire can suppress their fire (not least by eliminating those firing on you). This hardly works against an even halfway-sophisticated adversary (DDOS attacks aside). And as noted, hackers cannot be destroyed or even disarmed by a cyberattack.

In recent years, the U.S. military has begun to see that cyberspace is best seen as a layered construct, with software sitting upon hardware (as described above). But instead of putting information as the top layer as a way of conveying the purpose of cyberspace (that is, a device for collecting, manipulating, and presenting information), its top layer is the "cyber persona" as if cyberspace were just another medium in which people did things.[9] Even today, most of the IP address space belongs to unattended things, not persons—and all this is before the Internet of Things arrives in force to the civilian world or autonomous sensors or systems arrive in force to the military world.

Finally, warriors in given domains tend to see their counterparts as the true adversary. To wit, the best weapon against a tank (or aircraft, or submarine) is another tank (or aircraft, or submarine). Likewise, cyberwarriors may be tempted to focus on their counterparts when these should be, in fact, their hardest targets, owing to the high classifications at which cyberwarriors work, and the fact that they should take security most seriously (although *pace* H. B. Gary and RSA and the Hacking Team,[10] sometimes the cobbler's kids do go barefoot).

Fortunately, although these issues make writing concepts and doctrine an error-prone exercise, the influence of concepts and doctrine on what people actually do on a day-to-day basis is limited. Cyberwar in the trenches is intensively practical. But why burden cyberspace warriors with having to master, only to later jettison, such concepts in the first place?

NO DOMAIN, NO CYBER EQUIVALENT OF BILLY MITCHELL

Elevating cyberspace into a military domain feeds the quest of proponents for another Billy Mitchell—a visionary strategist who will declare to the world what great power lies therein. But should it? Such visionaries are often more trouble than they are worth. Consider three examples. The primary U.S. sea power strategist, Alfred Thayer Mahan, wrote *The Influence of Sea Power upon History, 1660–1783* to argue for battle fleets large enough to dissuade other states from asserting sea control. The book was a deliberate counterpoint to the Jeune Ècole preference for commerce raiding. Mahan's work inspired Theodore Roosevelt's Great White Fleet and enchanted both Kaiser Wilhelm and the United Kingdom's Sea Lord Jackie Fisher (the Dreadnought's proponent). It helped spur the battleship competition that exacerbated the Anglo-German naval rivalry just prior to World War I. But did Mahan's work do its adherents any favors? The Kaiser's love for his fleet kept it in port for the two and a half years after the Battle of Jutland, preventing it from trying to break the blockade on the Central powers, the maintenance of which caused them to collapse before the Allies did. Meanwhile, the naval action that nearly broke Britain was the success of German U-boat attacks—to wit, commerce raiding—on Britain's supply lines to North America. Airpower strategists (Billy Mitchell, Hugh Trenchard, and Giulio Douhet) emphasized the role of strategic bombardment in not only winning future wars but also shortening them. Yet World War II was longer than World War I. Furthermore, the emphasis on the strategic air campaigns wasted the Luftwaffe's strength during the Battle of Britain and cost the 8th Air Force alone more than 26,000 dead. Richard Overy's defense of strategic bombing maintains that it was worthwhile, less for the harm it inflicted on Germany than for impelling Germany to spend too much money countering it (but compare "air power will demoralize foes" to "air power will cause foes to overreact in self-defense").[11] Admittedly, a B-29 loaded with nuclear weapons could defeat (or at least destroy) adversaries on its own, but that said less about air power than nuclear weapons. Among the writers of nuclear strategy, Bernard Brodie ("Thus far the chief purpose of our military establishment has been to win wars. From now on its chief purpose must be to avert them. It can have almost no other useful purpose"[12]), Albert Wohlstetter (second-strike capability is essential), Tom Schelling (strategies that "left something to chance"), and Herman Kahn (escalation dominance) stand out. Their nuclear confrontation featured ultra-cool decisionmakers rationally facing the prospect of numerous deaths and maneuvering deftly to avoid surrender and holocaust. But when a real nuclear crisis took place over Cuba, world leaders stared at the abyss, realized they had come far too close to a nuclear holocaust, and vowed never to get that close again (hence the hotline and Nuclear Test Ban Treaty a year later). Rather than each side making noises as if it would throw the steering wheel out the window (*pace* Schelling's work), each instituted measures to ensure and assure others that it had a much better grip. The opening of the Soviet archives in 1989 indicated that the delineations that occupied such U.S. strategists (for example, nuclear/conventional firebreaks or counterforce versus countervalue) mattered nearly not at all to their Soviet counterparts.

Finally, two other domains—space and the electromagnetic spectrum—have no comparably memorable strategic doctrines associated with them; neither suffered as a result. More to the point, does cyberwar merit being called a battlefield revolution? Can operational cyberwar capabilities force warfare to be reinvented? Such questions cannot be addressed without remembering that operational cyberwar attacks only digital systems and networks. Prior to the 1960s, militaries had no digital networks to attack. A cyberattack carried out against a military today can, at worst, return to its prenetworked condition (assuming it has something to revert to). Thus, to argue that operational cyberwar is revolutionary requires arguing that digital networking is revolutionary. Even then, the former must be less revolutionary than the latter, because it cannot entirely nullify the latter. So, is digitization revolutionary? RF communications predated digitization (and remain quite analog). As helpful as network-centric warfare may have been for the United States, every other military in the world is less digitized and therefore less susceptible to cyberwar than the U.S. military.

That said, militaries cannot revert to their predigitized network state easily—and the longer digitization proceeds, the harder such reversion will become. Yet if true, it says either that such militaries have abjured that option because they *correctly* recognize that the impact of cyberwar is something they can manage, or the revolutionary impact of cyberwar is *incorrectly* underappreciated by militaries who therefore digitized without giving sufficient thought to what would happen if cyberwar *were* efficacious. If the former is true, the issue is settled. If the latter is true, then the only way cyberwar could be revolutionary is if those victimized by it fail to see it was going to be revolutionary.

Maybe in years hence, cyberwar will have changed everything we know about warfare—or maybe not. True, just as aircraft grew ever more capable from their invention forward, so societies are growing increasingly digitized, with little prospect that they will move backward (unless, as noted, to counter the risk from cyberattacks). But the correlation ends there. Aircraft improvement was a contest against a fixed target (the laws of aeronautics, physics, and chemistry); cyberwar is a contest against a moving target wherein offense contends with defense. It is not obvious that offense will get continually better, particularly when defense (the target's software and network configuration) defines what the offense can do.

Perhaps we should be thankful that cyberwar may evade the "classic" treatment. If a cyberwar classic looked like its predecessors, it would likely say that cyberwar is all-important and that those who wield its power should fight wars on their own rather than helping warriors in other domains.

To say that war in the virtual world can match the horrors of war undergone or contemplated might seem a stretch, but anyone who ventured such an opinion would not stand alone. Joining them would be the U.S. Defense Science Board (which imagined a cyberattack so severe as to merit a nuclear response),[13] some Chinese generals (one of whom casually opined that a cyberattack could be as damaging as a nuclear attack),[14] and even Russian president Vladimir Putin (who said that a cyberwar could be worse than conventional warfare—this from the head of a country that lost twenty-five million in World War II).[15] There is nothing quite like a good nuclear analogy. Yet the mere argument that cyberwar is going to be very important hardly says what to do with cyberwar capabilities, apart from keeping them well fed.

As the U.S. Army Air Forces did in the 1940s, cyberwarriors may wish to be seen as part of a military organization capable of creating strategic effects rather than just supporting other warfighters. If talented cyberwarriors convince themselves that strategic warfare offers a better shot at top command slots, they will migrate accordingly. Perhaps if cyberwar *is* that important, there will be enough resources and manpower to go around—although the current difficulties in finding enough cybersecurity professionals suggest that their supply is not infinite and only time will tell how elastic. Serious choices must also be made when allocating knowledge of those vulnerabilities in software that allow cyberwarriors into many of their targets. To the extent military and civilian systems rely on the same software and hardware—as they increasingly do, although there are still major differences—then a vulnerability exploited for disruptive/destructive purposes (rather than espionage) is likely to be a vulnerability that can be used only during a small time window. Its availability for strategic purposes limits its availability to support combat. Because systems have to be penetrated well before they are attacked, such choices may have to be made well before the character of the upcoming conflict is clear.

CONCLUSIONS

The desire to see cyberspace as a warfighting domain is deeply ingrained in doctrine and the minds of those who carry out such doctrine. This chapter argues that this concept is misleading, perhaps pernicious. Faced with the question: if cyberspace is not a "domain," what is it? one answer may be that "it" is a set of tools that have a related set of objectives in common. Such a stance suggests that the term be totally avoided, but since the author himself has no intention of following such advice, the second-best alternative is to use the term carefully. Take a sentence with "cyberspace" in it phrased to suggest that cyberspace is a domain (for example, the United States must achieve superiority in cyberspace) and restate it in terms of usurping systems control. The resulting sentence will likely be wordier, but if it is also nonsensical or excessively convoluted, perhaps so is the underlying thought. As for the argument that the military's calling cyberspace a domain is necessary if it is to organize, train, and equip forces for combat in that medium, what is wrong with focusing on the problems that such forces must solve—defending networked systems, interfering with those of the adversary—and then organizing, training, and equipping to solve such problems?[16] Militaries do this for electronic warfare without its having been elevated into a separate domain.

CHAPTER 15
Strategic Implications of Operational Cyberwar

Even relegating operational cyberwar to a niche capability within conventional warfare does not mean that its existence lacks strategic implications. This chapter examines three of them: its influence on the digitization strategies of others, military strategies that presume that operational cyberwar can shift the correlation of forces, and the challenges of alliance defense.

INFLUENCING OTHERS AGAINST DIGITIZATION

Can the specter of cyberwar inhibit other countries from arming their forces with networked and digitized equipment? It might—setting up the next question of whether it is in the U.S. interest to manipulate such fears.

As a rule, although a weapon in the hands of a capable warfighter can do more than the same weapon in the hands of a less capable warfighter, the difference may be particularly sharp if the weapon is networked and digitized. Poorly defended systems may, under pressure, leak information, buckle unexpectedly, or provide bad data to warfighters and other decisionmakers. Errors or omissions in defending or recovering defense systems can convert what should be a capable weapon into a liability. This is less true for other deficiencies: for instance, even though an F-16 is likely to be flown more effectively (and maintained better) in U.S. Air Force hands than in the hands of a developing country's air force, it is still a lethal war machine in anyone's hands.

Developing countries lag behind developed ones in handling stress from cyberspace. The difference between a great and a merely good hacker can be orders of magnitude (and much more than the difference between a great and a merely good hardware repairman), and factors such as education and career opportunity matter more in finding and growing the great ones. Similarly, a country's limited access to others' source code or a limited ability to write its own renders its military systems all the more vulnerable to cyberattack. The militaries of less developed countries with turnkey systems are likely to be less confident about using nonstandard configurations; thus, the effect of attacking them would likely be more predictable than it would be against those who understand their systems well enough to tune them to their unique circumstances. Unless such countries are under U.S. sanction, their systems could be maintained by U.S. firms (in the event of hostilities, such firms may well retain enough detailed knowledge of target weapons systems to assist U.S. cyberwarriors). If the prevalence of cloud computing comes to match the current enthusiasm of its vendors, critical components of their systems may be stored in other countries and operated by other entities, of which U.S. firms now appear the most likely hosts. If such assistance is withdrawn and countries have to defend such systems themselves, they may not even know where to start, particularly if their being on the outs with the United States inhibits global firms from offering their services. Although restoring software to original factory conditions may permit countries to recover their capabilities in the wake of a cyberattack (albeit at the loss of more recent configuration files), cyberattacks against firmware may not be so easily repaired without specialized tools.

If states fear their networked systems being penetrated and their defense systems suddenly disabled, they may foreswear network-centric warfare altogether despite the increasing difficulty of finding nondigital systems. Conversely, for the United States, if it really *can* defeat the other side's network-centric military capabilities through cyberattack, what would be the point of dissuading opponents from slipping into committing themselves to networking? Some answers may be mooted. One reason might be that the United States cannot be certain it can defeat such capabilities but might be able to look as if it can. It may want to dissuade any military buildup because it would lead others to adopt a more aggressive security policy, and U.S. security is better served by its not blustering in the first place even if lacking the capacity to follow through. However, if the United States believed that the other side would go ahead anyhow, then it may be better off keeping quiet about its confidence in being able to defeat such capabilities.

If hostile others have already stepped into digitization and internal networking, playing on the fears of cyberattack might conceivably make them wary of networking the equipment they already have to the *outside* world, the better to reassure themselves of the inherent capabilities of their own weapons. War promotes self-reliance, paranoia (someone really *is* out to get you), and the realization that security mistakes may have deadly consequences. Organizations have a natural tendency to close in on themselves when under threat. Emphasizing a capability for operational cyberwar can play on such tendencies. The adversary could be made continually aware of the possibility—and consequences—of a successful cyberattack.

Might carrying out actual cyberattacks, or at least compromising actual systems, help matters along? The point would be to emphasize not U.S. power but rather the vulnerability of *their* systems to puzzling cyberattacks. Proving a system was, is, and will stay hacked may be impossible, but a hinted attack (as compared to a real attack) may leave little evidence (especially if it did not take place), hence no specific trace and no specific fix—while a one-time penetration that erases its tracks but captures data may be comparably hard to trace. Even if system owners react to rumors by making general fixes, such as selective disconnection or the installation of anti-malware guards, until another attack comes, there will be nothing that suggests which of these general fixes worked. Hints *can* speak louder than facts sometimes. After all, it takes twice as long to find nothing in a room as to find something there. Worse, if finding is conclusive but sweeping and finding nothing is inconclusive and thus has to be repeated, then it takes far longer than twice as long. System owners may be unable to rest completely assured after having found supposedly rogue code because there is no proof that what was found was the rogue code that rumors referred to; such code could be a glitch unrelated to any malevolent actor or could have been placed there by a third party, while stolen credentials leave few traces apart from the denials of those accused of carrying out a rogue operation. It cannot be overemphasized that the target of such an attack is not the system itself but confidence in that system and any other system an adversary depends on.

What really helps is convincing others that their systems cannot be protected even after painstaking attention to their security. They may have checked everything three times. Yet the cyberwarriors find their way in. The effect is necessarily prospective rather than retrospective; it is rare these days that people are attacked, the attack makes the news, and yet there is no good idea how the attack was carried out or at least what vulnerability was exploited to enable the attack.[1] Many of the indicators of the attack remain with the target system nestled in its log files or even in the malware itself. Even if the targets of the attack (for example, the Iranians) cannot figure out what was done or how (for example, Stuxnet), there may be others (for example, the Belarus firm VirusBlokAda) who can. The number of prominent attacks whose workings, notably penetration and propagation methods, remain a mystery is small.

Incidentally, to the extent that brandishing U.S. proficiency at the dark arts of cyberspace is important, Edward Snowden has unwittingly done the U.S. cyberwar community a large favor. His many revelations—all the more credible for his hostility to the NSA—made it appear that there is no system that the United States cannot get into.

If foes cannot be persuaded to abjure networking, perhaps they can be persuaded to go too far in protecting their networks. This ploy may be likened to competitive strategies: an approach to defense planning elaborated upon by DoD's Office of Net Assessment. One example (circa 1982) was the U.S. focus on long-range penetrating bombers, hoping that the Soviet Union would bankrupt itself purchasing air defenses.

A foe may thus also react to a threat by radically restricting access to its beleaguered network. In a network lockdown, more activity would be isolated within compartments, and access to them would tighten.[2] Users would find it more difficult to get on machines and stay logged in; dealing with information systems would become generally more onerous. They would have less discretion to adapt systems to their needs or even to use the available tools in unprescribed ways. Organizations that wall themselves up, even if they have carefully fit their command and control to the possibility of a lockdown, would be unable to react with agility to the unexpected or to reintegrate their operations in response to emerging opportunities and threats. Poor ideas will fester longer for their adherents having less opportunity to compare them with alternatives. Lockdowns can also erode coalitions between militaries, especially those cemented by exchanges in cyberspace. Such exchanges are becoming more important even to war. The more easily information flows among coalition members, the more easily they can coordinate action. The strengths of one partner can cover the gaps of another. The longer a conflict continues, the more important it is that warfighters learn—something helped by unconstrained access to information. Lockdowns can also make it harder to deal with partner organizations in the civilian world.

But supporters of coalitions—for all their value—must necessarily acknowledge that seams between the networks of allies may be relatively soft targets, hence loci of infection. Rarely does a common security administration cover the target military and adjunct institutions (including other militaries). This makes unifying security architectures on the fly complex and error-prone if attacks can slip through the seams between very different systems. Imagine that one system makes it very difficult for unauthorized users to gain access but gives its users a considerable amount of freedom within its boundaries; a second system erects fewer barriers to unauthorized users but restricts what authorized users can do more tightly than the first system. Now, glue the two systems together. At this point, a hacker may be able to gain access to the second system and acquire the privileges of a user. By being an authorized user of the second system, there may be privileges it can assert on the first system. This, in turn, allows it to access or corrupt that first system because it gave trusted users freer rein than the second system. Hence, a vulnerability is present in the combined systems that existed in neither individual system. Cyberattacks can be crafted accordingly; an attack that crosses, strikes close to, or exploits the seam between institutions may result in finger-pointing and erode trust. Allies and allied organizations would face higher barriers to interacting with each other's networks. From the inside looking out, external information sources could be cut back, and access to them from the inside would be restricted. True, data can be conveyed through hard copy or freshly unwrapped thumb drives. But any added difficulties would reduce the flow of information and reduce the ease of working with allies and allied organizations compared to working entirely in house. Furthermore, the next generation of computer users may well find working with anything other than a Web interface difficult. Future exchanges that may involve real-time interaction (for example, let me show you how this operation would work by putting you in a simulation) may be nearly impossible to transfer without network-to-network interaction.

Can a locked-down military work? Today, probably yes. Deadly militaries have traditionally been closed organizations. No one expects nuclear establishments to be particularly accessible. Even the U.S. military, with its vaunted degree of networking, cannot operate seamlessly in cyberspace with allies—and it does not even come close to sharing all its operational information with those it works with daily. Yet it is hard to create organizations without networks that are at least partially open to the outside; logistics provides a good example, particularly if supply corps must work with outside suppliers.

Could Russia be frightened away from digitization? Unlikely. First, Russian capabilities at cyberwarfare are very advanced, as befits a state so devoted to *maskirovka* and blessed with a surfeit of good but underemployed mathematicians. Russians may fear our military capabilities, particularly in digital electronics, but are unlikely to regard them as puzzling (especially if physical or supply-chain attacks on electronics are not part of the U.S. cyberwar package). Second, Russia's military long suit is not the systems integration of complex electronics and networks. It is precisely because the Russians lack confidence in most of their conventional military that they lean so heavily on their nuclear arsenal and, as Crimean operations suggest, their special forces. Russia, so far, has lacked an investment strategy that could have been diverted by the U.S. development of cyberattack weapons.

What about China? The Chinese have certainly shown enthusiasm for penetrating systems, but their talents lean more toward quantity, as befits a focus on cyberespionage (and deep pools of well-trained but cheap labor), than on the quality required to get into hardened military systems. Furthermore, China's military investment strategy is quite different from Russia's. The Chinese have less interest in achieving nuclear parity and more interest in pursuing anti-access strategies that rely on sensors, surveillance, and missiles, which normally require high levels of systems integration, hence networking.[3] These factors leave some—but only some—scope for a U.S. dissuasion posture based on using cyberwar capabilities against China.

So, would success in dissuading a potential adversary from a high-technology challenge to U.S. superiority be in the best U.S. interest? Much depends on what kind of wars the United States worries about. If the goal is to make it very difficult for others to use conventional forces for purposes of invasion or coercion (rather than fighting an insurgency), then there is sense in the dissuasion; large low-technology forces are no match for the United States. With low-technology wars, the question may just not come up.

The target of such a dissuasion strategy has many ways of reacting. It may observe that the effects of cyberattacks are temporary and hard to repeat. Thus, even if its weapons falter when first used, they can be recovered for later use *if they survive*. But recent trends make high-tech wars short ones, leaving little time for recovery. Furthermore, once a system has become flaky, warfighters may not want to bet their lives on it until it has been provably cured, a lengthier process than simply having its symptoms relieved.

Another counterstrategy may be to digitize but not connect weapons (or at least not let individuals and their devices into the network that connects weapons). This permits air-gapping as a defense strategy and avoids some of the vulnerabilities arising from human error (notably those associated with authentication, such as passwords and tokens). Perhaps a self-denial-of-service policy reduces a military's ability to learn from others and, to some extent, itself, but such militaries may believe they have nothing to learn from others.

This question can also be turned around: should the United States itself abjure digitization and networking in the face of threats from cyberspace? A Defense Science Board report called for reversing some of the digitization associated with nuclear systems to ensure that no digitally savvy adversary could convince itself the U.S. nuclear deterrence capability was nullified by such tricks.[4] The need for such a trade-off assumes that vulnerabilities to cyberattack are inherent in digitization and networking per se. In reality, they adhere to specific digitization and networking choices. Defense systems do not have to be built atop software architectures optimized to accept third-party software; if instructions must be changed, there are trusted distribution mechanisms for doing so that can limit the risk of malware. As argued, systems can be built to white-list allowable and known safe commands. Unguarded (or, in war, captured) servers need not permit access to everything. Digital systems and MFA could be adopted.

Might a well-placed cyberattack remind countries that they face the prospect of losing control over their defense systems when they need them and dampen their urge to start a fight? The answer depends on how such countries react to having their military systems penetrated—particularly if implants were left behind. Opting against war requires such a country to believe that it has been so hacked, it has no choice but to go with the systems and equipment it has, and its estimate of a war's outcomes is decidedly worse as a result. And even that may not suffice. First, nearly all defenders and a surprising percentage of attackers believe that they had no serious choice but to wage war because the alternative, such as fighting later at greater disadvantage, is worse. So the Germans believed in 1914 and the Japanese believed in 1941. Fear had already failed to deter them. Second, how badly would their twenty-first-century equivalents need high-technology systems to succeed? Many high-technology systems (for example, electronic warfare) are only needed against similarly sophisticated opponents—not, say, guerrillas. A cybersecurity threat that looks big in peacetime (when systems are vulnerable by dint of being connected) may look smaller in wartime (when systems are configured for survival, in part, by being disconnected from the outside world). Finally, the target may simply not believe that U.S. cyberattack capabilities are good enough to stymie military forces completely—not during peacetime and certainly not when the war drums sound. Going to war requires surmounting a great many fears; the fear of systems penetration may simply be another one.

Other cautionary notes bear mention. If the United States really can scramble adversary systems to great effect, then persuading the adversaries of as much is counterproductive if it only forces them to pay intelligent attention to cybersecurity. Conversely, if the winds of alliance shift and the United States has to interoperate with such countries, hints of earlier penetration may complicate matters. Previously benign liaisons with a target country may become more difficult if the "partner" suspects that interacting with U.S. forces will reveal how its systems are operated and networked and thus where and how the United States could implant malware in them to the best effect.

Once other states think the United States is behind their fears, reality may be secondary. Countries that are certain that their militaries have been attacked may be less inclined to blame their unsophisticated neighbors in favor of blaming a technologically advanced country, such as the United States (or Israel). Indeed, the spread of cyberattack capabilities makes it easy for such countries to hold the United States responsible for *any* failure in military equipment (unless failure was clearly not in the U.S. interest), even if it was caused by an accident or human error. The instinct to blame others predates cyberspace. Egypt convinced itself for a few days that its air forces could not have possibly been destroyed in June 1967 by Israelis; Americans must have done it. Militaries that can give themselves a pass from their public by using such an excuse may be insulated from the effects of their own mistakes and might maintain their influence and power longer than they should (but if they come to believe their lies, they may fail to learn from their own mistakes). If you convince people you are a magician, there is a great deal of magic one can be blamed for by people with insufficient motive to figure out, much less admit, what the real problem is.

Militaries may also conclude that depending on foreign sources for logic-processing devices is dangerous. This could spur them to build more indigenous production capability or, alternatively, pressure their suppliers—disproportionately U.S.-based companies—to hand over source code with the systems they buy. The same suspicions may extend to civilian gear, such as routers. If foreign governments convince themselves that adherence to the, say, Windows/Intel standard is the root of the U.S. ability to hack their systems, they may lean toward more open operating systems or make common cause with other countries, such as China, that are striving to build a network foundation from components and code believed to be not controlled by U.S. companies.[5]

THE IMPORTANCE OF CONVENTIONAL DISSUASION

Assume a country discovers that its logistics system has been corrupted in ways that would complicate moving forces. Yet no one is shooting. The normal instinct in such matters is to ask, "Who did it?" followed by, "How can I get back at them?" But if one understands network systems as instrumental to war rather than simply as venues of war, many other questions need answering first. By answering them, one can understand another strategic implication of cyberwar and cybersecurity: as temptation for or protection against starting wars.

Thus, the first question after such an attack should be, "Is there a war coming soon?" The word "soon" matters because the effects of most such cyberattacks are temporary (if no hardware has been broken and information can be recovered from somewhere else). The window of disruption, hence disability, is likely to be measured in days as system administrators scramble to find out why the logistics databases are not working or at least not working reliably and have to move to backup to support operations. If the attackers mean to use such an attack to facilitate a kinetic conflict (rather than, as above, to discourage networking or belligerence), such a conflict is likely to take place within that window. If attackers tarry, not only will much of the damage to systems have been repaired, but also the logistics system may well be stronger the next time (albeit perhaps less efficient for having additional built-in safeguards). To the extent that a cyberattack telegraphs a kinetic attack, delays will leave the target that much more time to prepare.

Exactly how long systems will be down is a question for which there are little good data. The more subtle the damage, or the harder it is to identify the source of the damage, the lower the odds that the victim will guess that the problem was an induced fault in a computer system. As noted, the centrifuges in Natanz were repeatedly allowed to break because their managers did not envision a cyberattack on their air-gapped facility; they may have convinced themselves that problems were caused by faulty gray-market parts or inexperience at running centrifuges. Militaries that give defenders free rein to diagnose system failures will lead to faster response times than those told to follow procedures. Those with access to cybersecurity experts (especially those in a position to poll their peers worldwide) will react faster than those without (the difficulty of finding cleared forensics experts may make the time needed to diagnose classified systems longer and hence overcome). Some militaries are surprisingly adept at reacting to surprise (Israel's creative reaction to Egypt's TOW missiles during the October 1973 war comes to mind); others, not so much. Militaries that may react well to known unknowns (expected glitches) may not react well to unknown unknowns (problems never before seen). Disabling the troubled functions may speed short-term recovery but can hinder functionality in the long term until addressed.

Other explanations for such cyberattacks merit note. They could be carried out to distract the target—raising the question of exactly what the attackers want to distract victims *from*. They may be used to exhaust defenders sent to the ramparts repeatedly, but attackers with a limited bag of tricks pay a price for doing so.[6] The cyberattacks may be tests to see how well defenders react, in preparation for some later, larger attack. Attackers would be asking many questions. Can enemy sysadmins determine what happened and why? What workarounds do they use? Might corruption be detected? If the target knows it has been so tested, would it retaliate? But these may be expensive tests if they *also* reveal a great deal about the attacker and what it knows about the target's vulnerabilities. The target, if it understands the purpose of the attack in time, may want to react in ways that deliberately leave a particular impression in the attacker's mind. The attacker may also want to know whether the victim will fold or fight in cyberspace as a clue as to whether they would do so in the physical world—but inferences may be tricky. A defender may reduce some capabilities in its systems as a way of wisely correcting the functionality/security balance in light of new information on the threat from cyberspace—but this may be seen as a lack of desire to defend a challenged resource.

If some preparations for war have been discovered but no war has started, the second question for the defender is, "How can the attacker be persuaded that its ability to operate in the physical world remains intact?" Presumably, an enemy that understands that its cyberattacks have done little may therefore stay put. Ideally, the goal is to be able to make this claim: "Yes, perhaps you have broken into our systems, but notice that it has not slowed us down, increased our casualties, or decreased our ability to wreak damage on you." Recoverability is a key aspect of robustness—it may include the ability to get some systems to cover for those that have been damaged while the compromised portions are being isolated, diagnosed, fixed, checked out, and returned to service. Exactly how confidence is supposed to be projected may depend on what has been affected and what kind of listening posts the attacker has in place to monitor reactions. Such reactions need not necessarily take place within the logistics infrastructure. Indications may be reflected in other military traffic (or even social media). The victim may be able to fake confidence by carrying on with its logistics, even if what is moved is not exactly the right gear. Perhaps the fact that the wrong gear is what is moving is hard to detect until after the fact.

The third question is, "How fast can we recover?" Nothing helps looking healthy than getting better. And if the war comes anyway, then getting better faster yields better outcomes. In any case, expect a great deal of activity by and sleepless nights for sysadmins. Triage may be necessary in order for the more critical systems, such as those that schedule shipments, to take precedence over, say, financial systems that reconcile the books at a later date.

Only later should the target ask, "How should this cyberattack be responded to?" If a war does start, then responding to the *cyberattack* would be quite low on the priority list since it would be overshadowed by the response to the kinetic attack. If the war does not start, the response may be influenced by what the target wants the attacker to believe. A cyberattack on the logistics infrastructure—unless it disabled civilian operations (for example, FedEx)—is unlikely to be public knowledge (at least not immediately). Whatever lessons may be taught may be those learned only by the attacker.

Perhaps retaliation could discourage what exactly took place: a cyberattack *without* follow-up into a kinetic attack. But would it convince the attacker not to carry out cyberattacks? Or would it convince the attacker that a cyberattack that is not followed up by a kinetic attack still would be punished? Hence, having committed to a cyberattack, it might as well commit fully to a kinetic attack as long as punishment is inevitable. Conversely, the prospect of retaliation would at least reduce the attractiveness of a cyberattack. Otherwise, it might be deemed risk-free because the worst *expected* outcome is that nothing happens (the *actual* worst outcome is that the attacker continues with a kinetic attack based on the likelihood of success but then loses). If the attacker believes that preparations for a follow-on kinetic attack raise the odds of retaliation for a cyberattack, then it may elect to suppress such preparations and thereby limit its ability to follow up a successful cyberattack. Or retaliation might persuade the attacker to prepare for a physical attack using less detectable cyberattacks the next time. Retaliation is somewhat more attractive if the cyberattacker is not the physical attacker but is acting on the latter's behalf—because it is likely to stand out more clearly (and not be confused with the subsequent kinetic conflict). The credible threat of retaliation might therefore persuade potential cyberwarriors to think twice before putting their hackers at the service of another state's military goals.

Can one rest assured that good defenses will ultimately bring a foe's efforts to naught and thus that the foe will not follow up with a kinetic attack? Not necessarily. First, those carrying out such cyberattacks may commit to kinetic war before finding out whether the cyberattack worked. Or they may be psychologically primed to see victory irrespective of actual results. Proponents of cyberwar may want others to believe that their efforts worked and thus may proclaim success to combatant commanders without fear of contradiction (from those not allowed to see the details). Commanders may reason that taking advantage of a successful cyberattack requires their kinetic forces be mobilized before the cyberattack begins—and once they mobilize, they will be observed doing so and could be counterattacked if they do not attack first. Or commanders may figure that a successful cyberattack will lead to a reciprocated kinetic attack and conclude that if any cyberattack leads to kinetic war, outcomes would be more favorable if they started on the kinetic attack.

Thus, if the defender wants to guarantee peace, it needs to impress upon potential attackers that a cyberattack will not yield ultimate military victory. This requires demonstrating that hacking will not work on its own terms (that is, the targeted systems do not fail) and/or that even if it does (that is, systems fail), the target's ability to defend itself militarily, even with systems crippled, remains unaffected.[7]

If John Mearsheimer is right that countries are deterred from starting a fight not by the rising prospect of losing but by the dim prospect of winning cheaply, then a country that seeks to deter aggression is better off investing in the sort of deep, nested, robust defenses that make it difficult for the invader to win quickly than those defenses that minimize the odds of an eventual victory.[8] Investments that may offer just the possibility of an eventual turnaround or offensive maneuvers in general would, everything else being equal, have less deterrent value. The same may hold for cyberspace: invest in robustness, protect core information system capabilities, train to fight with degraded and suspect information systems, and emphasize the ability to reconstitute smartly following an attack. The last thing a state wants is an enemy that thinks it is only a successful cyberattack away from paralyzing the state's ability to respond militarily. Thus, as important as it is to ensure that information systems are robust in and of themselves, it is more important to ensure that the military can offer a respectable defense in the face of a wide range of plausible cyberattacks. Whether that means an ultrahigh assurance of retaining 10 percent or 90 percent of its information capabilities depends on the relationship between military power and that least important 90 percent or, alternatively, 10 percent of the network.

How, indeed, does a military convince others it is not vulnerable to cyberattack? A successful cyberattack (DDOS attacks aside) require passing two wickets. One is getting into a system. The other, once inside, is making the system misbehave. If the defenders are successful in keeping attackers out of their system, they start with the presumption of invulnerability. But attackers could easily have a much better idea than the defenders do of how deeply they penetrated. If the attackers cannot penetrate enough systems, they will likely judge that their hacking cannot succeed well enough to change the correlation of forces appreciably; if they are informed and rational, they will not attack. Nothing the target does (apart from repelling such penetration) will make much difference to the attacker's logic.

The second tack would be to convince attackers that even if they got into the system, they could not do much damage. What details should be revealed in order to bolster the claim that missions have been hardened against cyberwar? It is not like measuring the armor of a battleship. Detailing defenses against enumerated vulnerabilities and their exploits would show hardening only against a known threat—not against unknown threats (for example, zero days) that, by their nature, cannot be easily tested against. As a general rule, the cyberwar community takes as given that the ability to penetrate a system is the ability to bring it down. What is less obvious and has rarely been demonstrated is that the ability to take a system down implies the ability to keep a system down long enough to generate significant battlefield consequences.

The difficulty of demonstrating hardness against cyberattacks suggests stepping back in the logic chain and arguing in favor of the defender's broader resilience. A military that can demonstrate that its people are sufficiently agile and its capabilities sufficiently robust against all manner of disasters may, by doing so, demonstrate similar immunities to disasters from cyberspace. The defender that cannot demonstrate its ability to blunt an attack nevertheless could show that its missions can succeed *even though the cyberattack worked*. Thus, what would be demonstrated are features such as the technical resiliency of its warfighting system, the adaptability of its warfighters, the diversity and redundancy of its communications paths, the error tolerance of its control and decision systems, the multiple layers of its error detection and error correction protocols, the safety and failsafe features of weapons systems, and the ability to revert to earlier, less sophisticated (perhaps analog) systems if digital ones stop working well. What needs to be demonstrated is the quintessentially *military* nature of battlefield resiliency. At issue is not how well one side can defeat cyberattacks—for who can prove that the attacks were strong enough to count? It is how well it can operate if cyberattacks get in the way. The ability to completely repel a series of created attacks may be laudable but misses the point.

Many techniques of resilience are well understood. One element is redundancy, the provisioning of standby capacity that is unused or little used normally but is available for emergencies. Another, correspondingly, is the ability to identify and suppress low-priority applications whose use of resources gets in the way of high-priority applications (some customers, for instance, pay less money for electric power because they allow the power company to impose intermittent outages on them). Diversity is another element in redundancy that comes in handy against attacks that target particular types of systems: for example, satellites are used as standby for landline telephony. A rapid response capability—such as the ability to deploy medical teams or evacuation teams—also helps, particularly if the disaster threatens people's lives. Loose coupling (à la Charles Perrow's *Normal Accidents*) helps insulate complex systems against cascading failure through a combination of slack and circuit breakers. The latter would sit between downstream systems and upstream shocks (for example, battery backup that permits an orderly shutdown of systems, such as aluminum smelters, when main power goes). Attitudes are an important component of resiliency. If power goes out, are people prepared and willing to move to tasks that do not require power? Do they own flashlights? Can they read maps? Can they use sextants? Testing is an oft-overlooked component of resiliency as well. Many disasters take place because the backup capability died or at least lost its ability to compensate for the magnitude of the disaster it was designed for—and no one noticed. Analysis and engineering matter; they provide an educated guess as to how much of what kind of resiliency to put into a complex system.

The best dissuasion of adversaries enamored of operational cyberwar as a way to shift the correlation of forces is not demonstrating that operational cyberwar can be defeated on its own terms, but that its consequences can be managed.

THE CHALLENGE OF ALLIANCE DEFENSE IN CYBERSPACE

Defending allied systems from cyberattack is not straightforward. NATO provides its own computer-emergency response team, the NATO Computer Incident Response Capability, to assist states that think they have been attacked. But as a general rule, organizations—that is, national militaries—have to do most of what it takes to defend themselves in cyberspace, notably in vetting their employees, assigning them privileges, selecting software and setting its security parameters, developing routing architectures, and deciding on what information to isolate. There are exceptions—for example, perimeter defenses (there are economies of scale in acquiring signatures) and indications and warning (similar economies of scale) as well as post-attack detection and forensics (which are both specialties)—in which collective action is called for. But the efficacy of collective services remains to be seen.

If external help is needed beyond what NATO can provide, it need not come from the United States directly (a requirement that normally drives alliance formation). Private companies have emerged specifically to bolster their clients' defensive capabilities (a major problem, however, is ensuring that private companies assess such capabilities objectively when their ability to sell products and services depends on scaring customers). That being so, cybersecurity does not necessarily require the help of NATO member countries—even if Fort Meade does have experts it can and does lend to the owners of victimized systems. As noted, Estonia called on Akamai and Georgia rehosted its websites on Google to defend itself from Russian DDOS attacks.[9]

Although all alliances face the free rider problem, it is muted because the failure of an entity to protect its own systems cannot easily be overcome by efforts made by others. Should an ally's cybersecurity fall short, such failings might be treated much as other shortfalls are. For instance, the inability of a country to defend its helicopter support systems is like its inability to keep enough spare parts to keep its helicopters flying. In both cases, its ability to contribute helicopters will have fallen short.

The problem shifts if collective defense implies a collective network. Military effectiveness often requires the networks of member states be connected to those of other states—but how deeply connected? Each nation could run its own military units and networks, and interfaces between high-level commanders could take place on a separate NATO system run by NATO rules.[10] But warfare is trending toward greater interoperability. Aircraft and ships from member states must talk to one another to carry out combined operations. Weapons may have to talk to platforms and vice versa. Ground units, with their ever-larger radii of operations, must coordinate closely in tactical operations. Blue force trackers of member nations must exchange information to avoid friendly fire incidents. As the U.S. Navy's Cooperative Engagement Capability has demonstrated for shipborne or airborne radar, the ability to illuminate the battlefield to detect, track, and target enemy assets works much better if the various sensors of each platform from each member state can coordinate their readings. Finding the right unit to best prosecute the discovery of the adversary's assets also requires coordination. Although in some cases such unity can be achieved through NATO-specific systems, efficiency and efficacy in combat may favor combining systems of member states.

Combining member networks, however, raises problems. A weakly defended system can erode the defenses of a strongly defended system if the latter extends privileges to the former. Making things worse is that many of these privileges are undocumented; they have to be inferred from the code that runs the network. A member state's contribution could therefore be negative in cyberspace in ways that are harder to imagine in the physical world.

There are several ways to address this dilemma. Several are nonstarters: for example, ignoring the problem in the belief that the impacts of network penetration are overstated, abjuring networking or at least treating every other state's networks as suspect, or having one state establish a network for all (expensive, and possibly resented even by its beneficiaries).

Two other possibilities merit thought. One is to have a single guardian over the enclave within which sit the collective networks of NATO's member states. A common enclave approach allows for a common perimeter defense, with all the benefits (and limitations) of that approach. Yet herding the communications of NATO's member states through a set of gateways could mean adopting a circuitous and possibly expensive network architecture. Furthermore, the country whose computer inspects the contents of each packet looking for suspect material is, in effect, reading the traffic of other member states, something sure to raise eyebrows, perhaps even hackles. Yet providing each member state with its own monitoring equipment inherently means providing each with what is today considered highly classified information on threat signatures—which providers may not want to do (but perhaps should, anyway).

The other approach, vetting NATO members' systems against standards, avoids these problems but introduces others, as discussed in the section above on standards. To recap: standards are hard to write, technology change makes doing so harder, and they often default not to defining correct system behavior but to management processes that are supposed to lead to correct system behavior. Furthermore, countries have to be judged against such standards. A serious test is one that alliance members can sometimes fail—but calling out failures can be detrimental to alliance cohesion. Incidentally, the assumption that the United States would be the one judging others is not obvious. True, the United States has the resources that allow a very sophisticated approach to systems defense. Yet the U.S. perspective in favor of network-centric warfare—more information for more warfighters is almost always better—is not necessarily the most conducive to information security.

Fortunately, NATO has taken the challenge of information system security to heart. U.S. deputy secretaries of defense and their staffs have made many visits to Europe to ensure it does. Nevertheless, this problem will not be solved easily. Note that the notion of collective defense (NATO Article V) seamlessly includes both attack and defense.[11] That is, all can defend much better than one, because a collective effort can disarm an enemy much more effectively than a single effort. But, as noted, because defenders cannot disarm their cyberattackers, collective defense is just that: defense.

CHAPTER 16
Stability Implications of Operational Cyberwar

By disrupting systems or inserting hesitation into human command networks, cyberwarriors could conceivably stymie or cripple the other side long enough to win a short, intensive kinetic conflict. If such conflicts thereby become more attractive, might operational cyberwar change the dynamics of crisis and stability?

With the expected caveats—contexts vary widely, nuclear weapons trump everything else, and operational cyberwar must be presumed militarily effective to matter—this chapter sketches some general factors that would make crises more or less stable. For each such factor, it addresses whether the proliferation of cyberwar capabilities would help or hinder stability (for example, if offense dominance is bad for stability, would cyberwar add to or subtract from offense dominance?).

Stability, we argue, obtains when neither party in a crisis has a desire to attack the other. It fails when one or both sides believe there is much to gain by attacking or at least much to lose by not attacking. Because stability involves the decisions of two or more parties, any one change in the balance can sometimes have indeterminate effects. If, for instance, one side becomes stronger, it can simultaneously increase the other's fear and thus *increase* its motive to attack—or reduce the other side's confidence of victory and thus *decrease* the latter's motive to attack.

Generally, instability is more likely when:

- those who attack are more likely to win (also known as offense dominance)
- getting the jump on the other side makes victory more likely
- the risks of acting are reduced
- the risks of not acting are increased.[1]

Consider each in turn.

ATTACK WINS

Aggressors are more likely to go to war, not because they smell ultimate victory, but because they taste quick (hence, low-cost) victory. When such prospects seem bright, wars are more likely, and stability suffers. Offense-defense theory argues that when the attacking side is expected to beat the defender, the rewards for attacking go up, and states are therefore more likely to attack.[2] Although World War I turned out to be defense-dominated (immobile artillery, machine guns, and barbed wire meant that those who charged prepared positions bled more than defenders did), its onset was hastened by leaders who looked at the quick wars of German unification and convinced themselves that offense was superior and that a quick offense outperformed a slow offense. Come World War II, however, and a combination of tanks, radios, and aircraft (coupled with German storm trooper tactics) really did allow a clever offense to run roughshod over naïve defenses. Since success at conventional warfare generally requires movement, offense dominance suggests that those who maneuver (in the physical world) do relatively well.

Cyberwar has been oft described as an offense-dominant activity.[3] In some ways, it is. Much less money is spent on getting into systems than on keeping people from getting in. As long as the attackers can operate undetected, they can try again and again if there is at least one route in; defenders must succeed all the time, everywhere.

But it is one thing to concede the difficulty of keeping Internet-connected systems free of all penetration and so conclude that cyberespionage is offense dominant; it is quite another to conclude that today's *kinetic* systems are *therefore* offense dominant because offensive cyberwar exists. There is no ipso facto reason to believe, for instance, that cyberattacks favor maneuvering units over dug-in defenders; indeed, the converse is more likely.[4] Cyberattacks can be understood as a countermeasure to the advent of C⁴ISRTA (command, control, communications, computers, intelligence, surveillance, reconnaissance, and target acquisition) systems. C⁴ISRTA is what makes maneuvering units easier to target than static ones (between two equally matched adversaries). Movement itself disturbs or stands out from the environment and hence can be spotted. If C⁴ISRTA systems, therefore, favor the defense (that is, non-maneuvering units), the degree of digitization inherent in such systems makes them susceptible to operational cyberwar. That being so, operational cyberwar *restores* the offense to the extent that it can complicate the use of C⁴ISRTA systems. This is offset to the extent that maneuver requires fast, responsive command and control, which is similarly susceptible to operational cyberwar.

Conversely, the threat from operational cyberwar may favor the slow introduction of systems onto the battlefield and thereby aid the defense. Why? Digital systems all have potential vulnerabilities, most of which are unknown by their owners. Systems in storage can be made nearly impenetrable if not connected to a network (or at least not to a network that extends beyond some RF perimeter). Once fielded, they tend to communicate to do their jobs. To function, they often have to get within weapons range of their adversaries. This makes their electronic signals more accessible and therefore potentially vulnerable—"potentially" because getting inside systems that are connected only by RF links, as noted, means having to first break signal encoding *and* cryptographic encoding. The owner of such systems, knowing the other side is working to make them fail, would want to avoid the catastrophe of having all its systems all fail at once. If it introduces its equipment one by one, and those introduced are attacked, their owners may well determine which vulnerabilities allowed such an attack, fix them, and return the systems to service (and do so faster than were its weaknesses in hardware design). Preserving the option for midcourse adjustments suggests caution to any attacker—which favors defense. The defenders, for their part, may be able to limit the exposure of systems to cyberwar to those actually engaged in combat at the time.

The converse question is whether one side thinks it can take down the other side's critical digital systems at the outset using cyberattacks. The side that believes it can do this before the war starts may think it can win a first battle. The defender, unaware of its vulnerabilities, may not acknowledge as much beforehand and thus may not make the sort of concessions (to the potential attacker) that the weak might otherwise offer to the strong in order to avoid war. What the attacker cannot win in advance through intimidation, it may be tempted to achieve through force (and hope no third party intervenes to spoil things). A great deal depends on how confident the attacker is. It may attack in hopes it would win outright, or it may test the proposition by carrying out cyberattacks unaccompanied by violence in the hopes of seeing encouraging results without alerting the other side (lest the tested vulnerability is discovered and fixed). Otherwise, the ability to bring down the other side's systems would be another case of hoping for the best but not counting on it too much.

The opening act of World War I, however, suggests that leaders do not have to first *prove* that offense wins if their faith is strong. Why leaders in the conflict so completely misunderstood the nature of modern warfare is a question less of technology than of politics, sociology, and psychology.[5] Today's psychology is mostly different. Yet leaders who are transfixed by the power of cyberwar and who lack a firm understanding of how and why it works may be convinced by their cyberwarriors that it is more powerful, and hence decisive, than it really is. As did their predecessors with earlier weapons, cyberwarriors will have an obvious motive for exaggerating the effectiveness of their tools. In their case, the secrecy of their craft will keep others from vigorously challenging their claims in ways that skeptics of more traditional weapons could. Thus, leaders may be susceptible to systematic misunderstanding, with its various malign effects.

The nature of cyberspace also permits attackers to misjudge defenders in ways that may yield false confidence. For instance, the attacker corrupts the defender's computer systems expecting a reaction, but receives none. Perhaps the defender did not notice. Perhaps the defender is sufficiently resilient that it really makes no difference. Or the attacker determines that the implants it put into the defender's networks have been found and removed; the attacker knows they were prefatory to attack but does not know the defender sees them as part of an espionage campaign and thus elects not to make a big deal of its discovery. The attacker infers that the defender failed to react because it is weak and afraid. It calibrates its aggression level accordingly—and erroneously when the defender reacts vigorously to the heightened aggression level.

GETTING THE JUMP WINS

A strong first-mover advantage may tempt one or both sides to move first and disarm the adversary. For instance, because the nuclear confrontation was thought to favor the first mover, strategists urged building a survivable second-strike capability in the interests of stability; to some extent, mutual assured destruction was considered a *good* thing. No such fear should attend pure cyberwar because one country's offensive cyberwar capabilities cannot, in and of themselves, do much to reduce the ability of another state to carry out cyberwar. Analogously, introducing a military system that is both influential and fragile may spur the other side to knock it out first.[6]

As per the Taiwan scenario outlined in chapter 11, a bolt from the blue (against, for instance, a soft target such as logistics) may well be *the* key cyberspace risk: An attacker convinces itself that an otherwise infeasible military attack can be made feasible by leading off with a wave of cyberattacks. Even if the attacker is wrong, everyone suffers.

The temptation to jump first could be magnified if it takes a large commitment to get the jump. The inability to start small and test the way forward leaves two choices: going big or staying home. Eliminating an aggressor's incremental options may not necessarily reduce stability, though, if the risks of going big and failing are substantial. A lot depends on the risk tolerance of leadership and its military. A variant of that occurs when leaders really do not know how deeply they have committed themselves to conflict; again, the impact on stability is mixed. Cautious leaders may therefore be very conservative, but leaders with incautious cyberwar subordinates may find themselves committed to war before they know it. Technical circumstances (such as the railroad schedules of 1914) may make it harder for leaders to pull back from the edge. Adding uncertainty to calculations may dissuade the cautious—but aggression is rarely started by cautious people.

If a crisis involves another country that was not earlier deemed a risk, the first country may not have done the cyberespionage necessary to understand which targets in cyberspace are worth hitting and which vulnerabilities can be exploited. It may choose to hold off military action until such information is at hand. Holding off allows time for nonviolent resolution of crises. Conversely, if the cyberespionage has been done (because the two countries already see each other as potential adversaries), cyberattacks can be launched immediately, and the pace of crisis would depend on whether follow-up kinetic forces are ready to exploit openings created by cyberattacks.

The dynamics of operational cyberwar may also create subtle spurs to aggression. To the extent that cyberattacks work, they are likely to catch the defenders by surprise, in terms not only of how they work, but also in their potential to work at all. Surprised defenders are apt to both attend with alacrity to revealed vulnerabilities and reexamine the broad trade-offs they had earlier made between system security and convenience and consequently start to favor system security. A post-Stuxnet Iran, for instance, is far more careful about which devices attach to the network that controls its centrifuges and much more alert to variations between how centrifuges are supposed to work and how they are actually working. Even though the target may be taken down by other tricks, they would have to be *other* tricks, and the latter would likely have to be even more subtle and complex than those that initially surprised the defender.

Knowing this, the attacker may opt to go big all at once even if it has a deep reservoir of potential attacks almost as sneaky and effective as the first ones. The reason to start big is because a gradual course allows defenders to fix their vulnerabilities as they are revealed. Otherwise, attackers might husband attacks as a way of figuring out how and where such attacks are best employed (likewise, a cat's paw attack on Pearl Harbor was out of the question). In many ways, operational cyberwar is not only an untested weapon but also an untestable weapon. Whatever can be learned by interfering with the other side's systems while leaving them unaware they have been tested is a poor guide to what happens when such systems have to be taken down and kept down in ways that cannot be hidden from defenders. Cyberwar is a tool that the plunger rather than the doubter would be more comfortable with using. Stability would seem to suffer correspondingly.

Several other aspects of operational cyberwar militate against using it confidently in a program of calibrated escalation of kinetic operations (as distinct from calibrated escalation of cyberwar-only operations). Taking down systems requires penetrating them in advance. There is a risk that if such penetrations are discovered and the correct inferences are drawn from such discoveries, then the defender may guess its adversary's strategic plans and may react not to what the adversary is doing but to what it infers the adversary will do. Crisis escalation may be unexpected inasmuch as discovering a penetration is an iffy event.

Another source of instability is the disjunction between what the attackers intend and what the targets infer from a discovery. There is no ipso facto reason that those who discover the preparations will therefore correctly know what the attacker is trying to do—or how the attacker's goal in cyberspace relates to its goal in the physical world. Although such fog is present for many types of attack, in cyberspace, while the target knows about its own systems and how they work together, the attacker can only guess about connections that are expressed solely at the systems level and thus have no externally visible relationship. Granted, the target, recognizing that the attacker can only guess at what the target knows, may hold back from drawing too many inferences. Perhaps it was just probing when it finds its systems penetrated; it could choose not to react as if attack was imminent. It may recognize that cyberwarriors, particularly if they work with signals intelligence folks, may see nothing particularly wrong with penetrating adversary systems in peacetime to understand how they are built and used. However, targets that will not make that assumption (perhaps their own cyberwarriors are aligned with their electronic warriors who reserve their craft for war, as they do in China) may jump to unwarranted and destabilizing conclusions. Thus, a strategy in which countries respond to crisis by intensifying their cyberespionage may inadvertently turn toward war.

Use-it-or-lose-it considerations may also prompt action. A leader who is otherwise inclined not to push matters may be told that the correlation of forces is as good as it is ever going to be now that adversaries have bad code (or stubs that can quickly grab and attack bad code) implanted into their systems; thereafter, the target may discover it has been compromised and would react in ways that make further system penetrations very difficult. The use-it-or-lose-it argument is more intense if undertaken against an air-gapped system vulnerable to malware transferred by removable media (à la Stuxnet). Activating such malware at a particular time is difficult if such transfers are occasional—and so the only way such an attack might work is if it is preset to go off at a given time. If the time comes and the cyberattack takes place and there is no corresponding kinetic attack to take advantage of the resulting confusion, the vulnerabilities and techniques that permitted such an attack would be revealed and defenses against it erected. A second try would be correspondingly far more difficult. Thus, starting the kinetic attack, irrespective of all other circumstances, may be deemed by cyberwarriors the only sound course of action once implants go off.

The prospect that cyberattacks will be far more fruitful early in the conflict rather than later may tempt a country that feels its cyberattack capabilities exceed those of its foes to press for a short war. Initially, it may figure, attackers may enjoy a positive correlation of forces; later, such advantages will be vitiated. To be sure, every aggressor hopes the wars it starts are short and costless and often ignores contrary advice (the best known example being Admiral Yamamoto's warning to Japan's war council planning Pearl Harbor: "I can run wild for six months . . . after that, I have no expectation of success"). When aggressors are wrong (World Wars I and II provide classic examples), everyone pays the price for their optimism. The glittering prospect of cyberwar can only exacerbate this unfortunate human tendency.

THE RISKS OF ACTING ARE REDUCED

When attacking presents risks, anything that reduces such risks (which may include public embarrassment) emboldens attackers. If getting the jump on the other side could succeed gloriously or fail silently, the odds shift toward jumping. A similar logic may hold if the attack planners stood to gain if the move worked but would lose little if the move did not. If the decision to attack can be made independently by any of several commanders, the odds of an attack tend to rise because the most aggressive will be the one calling the shots by initiating its own attacks—hence the importance of understanding if and how cyberwar institutions can take a country to war or which aspects of cyberwar allow subordinates to start a war unsupervised.

Failure, for instance, may be deemed costless. Imagine attackers laying the groundwork for a kinetic attack by penetrating defense systems prior to conflict. Perhaps they target logistics systems. They can succeed (in which case they may well attack), or they can fail. Not all forms of failure are evident to the other side, though. For instance, the system cannot be penetrated, but failed attempts may be indistinguishable from the unlucky attempts of random hackers. Alternatively, perhaps the attackers have penetrated the system and wreaked some mischief but not enough to make it very clear what they wanted to do; for instance, some instructions were changed, but whether to facilitate spying or attack is hard for defenders to determine. Or it may be clear what the purpose of the attack was but not who did it—particularly if the crisis has yet to arise or if the target is facing more than one foe. In the first case, the target does not know that anything happened; in the second case, the target may know that something happened but not what; in the third case, the target may know what happened but not who did it. The target cannot justify a reaction without confidence in what and who. If the attacker believes that it can fail and yet remain hidden, obscure, or at least anonymous, it may calculate that failure is costless while success can be exploited. So thinking, it could try to bring down its adversaries' systems ahead of conflict—something it might not try if failing would lead to disaster.

Alternatively, cyberwarriors may be able to act without their superiors knowing about it immediately. Cyberattacks neither use visible weapons nor generate immediately visible effects—and cyberwarriors work at or with intelligence agencies that are expert at covert operations and professionally paranoid when it comes to exposing what they do to others. Indeed, although intelligence agencies could have made war (for example, through covert action or financing others) before cyberwar was invented, now they have one more way, which scales nicely from covert action to what may be full-fledged conflict. But if cyberwarriors cannot command kinetic force, can they really increase the odds that their country goes to war? Perhaps if operational cyberwar efforts lead the target to believe that war is coming, then a war may start even if the aggressor in cyberspace is not the one starting the (literal) shooting. If cyberwarriors actually manage to break something, a response from their victims is more likely since it may be motivated by arguments of reprisal and self-defense rather than just preemption.

Kinetic warriors who are (or think they are) unexpectedly presented with opportunities to prevail over their counterparts may add their voices to those of the cyberwarriors in pressing political leadership to go forward, when hitherto they may have been more cautious. Bear in mind that kinetic warriors may have little independent way of validating or refuting what cyberwarriors claimed to have done (although, in fairness, their lack of comfort may also keep them from recognizing true advantages because they had no confidence in how such advantages were produced). Strong confirmation biases may induce leaders to capitalize on what they hope was success, even when they might have held back given more time to consider what a rush to war might produce.[7]

As noted, the window of enhanced opportunity following a cyberattack is brief. If success in the physical world is contingent on success in the virtual world, and the onset of operations has to start before anyone knows that the foe's kinetic capability was significantly reduced by a cyberattack, then armed forces may have to start rolling before the cyberattack starts.[8] If the cyberattack fails invisibly, then the target's prewar intelligence on the potential attacker may be ambiguous; it is unclear why the attacker moved forces to the border or carried out a "training" exercise. However, if the attack fails visibly, the hitherto ambiguous prewar intelligence takes on a new and more sinister coloration—even without forensic confirmation of attribution.

THE RISKS OF NOT ACTING ARE INCREASED

Countries may be inclined to attack if they are afraid that the failure to attack will jeopardize them more than attacking will. Either way, they reason, war is coming; there is grave risk in holding back and hoping otherwise.[9] One side may want to go first because it has a critical use-it-or-lose-it capability (by contrast, in the brittle-system case, it is the other side that is tempted to go first).[10] Another such risk arises from the fog of war when one side fears that the other side may be attacking but is unsure whether an attack is under way and therefore interprets (rightly or wrongly) many extraneous pieces of evidence as indicators of attack and concludes it has no choice but to preempt. A third case, but in reverse, arises if a new capability (such as cyberwar) becomes a prerequisite to using an existing capability but the attacks on the newer capability are more easily recognized than attacks on the older one was; if so, sneak attacks become harder to pull off. After all, World War I could have been narrated as a quandary in which all protagonists were defense-minded but each feared that it had no choice but to act lest it find itself at great disadvantage. Fear can motivate war, and the threat of cyberwar can give rise to a great many fears.

Commanders, for instance, may find some equipment mysteriously inoperable, blame a cyberattack, and convince themselves that more of their equipment could become inoperable soon. So thinking, they resolve to use it while they can—thereby motivating attack if already within a political crisis. True, in this case, the other side may have carried out a cyberattack first (albeit not one damaging enough to warrant overreaction). But an actual cyberattack may not be necessary—if the fear of cyberattack is so pervasive that it is the first thing to be blamed when things fail inexplicably (and there is pressure to react before forensics can establish otherwise).[11]

Active defense—in the sense of prompt action against machines on the attack—also presents opportunities for light-speed reaction that could lead to escalation that, with a little contemplation, could be foreseen and forestalled. The potential for one side's cyberwarriors to catalyze a war is multiplied if the other side has delegated the authority to *respond* to its own cyberwarriors (perhaps in the belief that others higher in the command chain cannot respond fast enough).[12] Because the parameters of cyberwar are poorly understood by the laity, cyberwarriors may also be trusted to determine when an incoming cyberattack is under way. In other words, specialists (mindful of their own community's status) may be entrusted to interpret both signs of early warning and the right opportunity for hitting back. Perhaps one should not bewail the tendency for lawyers to want to vet cyberattacks at least in countries that enjoy rule of law (not for nothing does the number of law review articles on cyberspace exceed the number on, say, electronic warfare).

Or, as noted, a crisis may be exacerbated if evidence of successful cyberespionage is perceived as prefatory to a successful cyberattack of greater scale—because no one will assume that all penetrations have been discovered, and thus one sighting may be extrapolated to many intrusions. Although this variant requires making both a logical leap from espionage to attack *and* projecting from a cyberattack to an existential defeat, successful cyberespionage in peacetime is commonplace. Over time, this path to instability should decline as commanders begin to understand that weapons are not that much more vulnerable when used than when not used (where they are connected is a different issue), and that because the damage from cyberattacks is usually temporary, the wiser path may be to start nothing, withdraw the system, clean it out, and return it to service, and return to the status quo absent physical evidence of impending aggression.

Conversely, the advent of cyberwar could, in some contexts, give defenders *more* confidence that they can see an attack coming from farther away, thus reducing their need for preemption. By way of analogy, assume that the United States fears a North Korean nuclear missile launch. It then gets a reliable ship-based anti-missile system (for example, the Standard Missile 3), which convinces North Korea that if it wishes to attack the U.S. homeland, it first must disable the anti-missile ships offshore. Thus, what was a small interval between detecting a missile launch and the missile's impact turns into a long interval that starts with detecting an anti-ship attack whose success must be ascertained before the North Koreans are confident enough to launch nuclear missiles.

Consider now three analogies in cyberspace. First, the defender may believe that the attacker has to carry out a *successful* cyberattack before it starts a kinetic conflict (which means the defender believes the attacker would rather benefit from a well-prepared battlefield than from total surprise). Any success at detecting the attack would therefore warn of a kinetic attack—and any confidence the defender feels in being able to detect the attack will decrease its twitchiness and therefore serve stability, even if the defender is wrong. Unfortunately, cyberattacks *are* difficult to detect, and the defender's ability to detect one *correctly* is important lest it detect a false positive and react as if a kinetic attack were coming (as argued above).[13] A lot depends on how the defender balances false negatives and false positives; there is a big difference between assuming a nuclear attack is coming if the aforementioned ship carrying standard missiles is painted by radar and assuming as much if the ship is sunk. The saving grace (so far) is that such a model is speculative and may be ignored by leaders.

Second, the ability to penetrate information systems promotes stability in the same way that traditional surveillance did. The more deeply one can see into the other side, the greater the difficulty that either side would have generating a bolt from the blue. There is an important distinction, however, between, say, space-based reconnaissance and cyberspace-based reconnaissance. Most U.S. adversaries have a fairly good idea what the United States can see—and even when (for example, as certain satellites are overhead). But they have far less direct indication of what the United States (or any other hacker-endowed country) can see in cyberspace. It is in the interest of stability that the power of surveillance be overestimated.

Third, if those worried about a kinetic attack believe the attacker must remove the potential target's surveillance implants from its own (the attacker's) system before starting a war, then the target can rest assured that it is safe as long as its implants are functioning. This could *increase* stability—if the defender really believes it can detect tampering with its implants *and* that such implants do provide useful indications and warning. Neither assumption is obviously true. A clever (kinetic) attacker may be able to remove or spoof the implants without the kinetic defender noticing. Conversely, if the (kinetic) defender panics when the (kinetic) attacker does remove the defender's implants in the attacker's network systems (when it could be an attempt to clean out the infected systems or a side effect of a software update), it may do something rash.

A MISSING ELEMENT OF CAUTION

Although those who wield conventional military power must think of the troops (and machines) that they put at risk by engaging in combat, cyberwarrior commanders know that neither their people nor their machines are at risk. The primary downside is that expending zero-day vulnerabilities (or tricks in general) may reduce the inventory of the better weapons in their kit bag (leaving the exploits that can do useful work against the many systems with incompletely patched or otherwise poorly defended machines). Yet exploits tend to deplete over time anyway, and an exploit not used for combat may be siphoned away to be used for espionage. Granted, cyberwar is not the only weapon whose use in combat does not risk human lives; UAVs or, more broadly, robots have this quality. But while the command and control of robots may be exercised by commanders of units with people at risk, the command and control of hackers is exercised more independently.

Finally, although cyberespionage is not cyberwar, the dangers to international relations associated with current levels of cyberespionage should not be ignored. The U.S. umbrage at China's APT and China's at what it thinks the NSA is doing carry their own dangers. The problem is that implicit norms that deem spying tolerable reflect the expectations of an era in which espionage was limited to human spies, overhead photography, and esoteric signals interception. The information revolution that has so drastically lowered the cost of amassing and processing information has also lowered the cost of collecting information from others. Economics reminds us that the more you have of something, the less valuable an addition to the pile is. But human nature suggests that the irritation of the millionth person to have his or her privacy violated is not less than the irritation of the first, tenth, or hundredth person to have suffered so. Bureaucracies tend toward what has been termed functional autonomy—the continuation of behavior that works regardless of whether its rationale has survived. The more esoteric and secret the activity, the more it resists oversight from those outside the bureaucracy. Might cyberespionage have reached the point at which changes in its quantity may lead to changes in the quality of its tolerance?

CONCLUSIONS

Operational cyberwar counters stability in two-and-a-half of the four ways by which stability is threatened. Granted, it does not automatically help moving forces vis-à-vis defending forces. But it does provide a way to get the jump on an enemy. It can often be used as a first strike with reduced risk: certain types of failure go unremarked and hence risk little reprisal, even as significant success can be exploited. Finally (and where the "half" comes in), although successful implants may hasten conflict lest an irreplaceable advantage be lost, a defender that discovers its own equipment is infected is not necessarily in a use-or-lose situation. That noted, leaders overly sensitive to the potential of cyberwar may convince themselves that any probes, implants, and so forth that they have discovered signal imminent attack and hence demand an imminent countermove. In this respect, it is not operational cyberwar that is destabilizing so much as it is thinking so that makes it so.

CHAPTER 17
Strategic Cyberwar

S trategic cyberwar is the systematic use of cyberattacks on the society of another country (or de facto country). In discussing its potential, we assume either that no kinetic war is going on or, if it is, that it is clearly secondary to an attack on the homeland. This assumption, in turn, raises the question: is a cyberwar-only or cyberwar-mostly scenario plausible enough to merit attention? As it is, there has been precious little cyberwar, with or without kinetic war to accompany it. Nevertheless, a country could carry out a cyberattack without intending a broader war; it could be trying to signal (for instance, we do not like your sponsorship of your friend's hostile activities) or achieve an effect (for instance, to cripple a defense program). Or both countries could be attacking each other, but each regards the use of violent force as crossing a firebreak (much as going from conventional to nuclear war crosses a firebreak). Strategic cyberwar can accompany more general economic sanctions in situations where the attacker is very casualty averse and the target clearly has the lesser kinetic military force. A small kinetic war can escalate into a major exchange in cyberspace if operational cyberwar attacks escalate (whether deliberately or accidentally) into attacks on dual-use infrastructures and then to more general attacks.

Strategic cyberwar could have external and internal objectives. The external objective would be primary: to bend the other side to one's will. The internal objective would relate to war's conduct: modulating its scope (for example, by not putting life-protecting systems in play), avoiding unwanted escalation (for example, into violence), or compelling a cease-fire. The two objectives may conflict. Teaching some a lesson that cyberwar does not pay by hitting them back harder calls for more aggression; inducing them to reduce their aggression by showing forbearance calls for less aggression.

Some aims are simply outside the scope of strategic cyberwar itself. One is disarming the enemy, despite occasional opportunities for destruction. Another is occupying territory. Regime change is a very unlikely outcome as well. Absent such aims, a pure strategic cyberwar contest becomes, in the words of the Duke of Wellington, a matter of "who can pound the longest" and take it better.[1]

STRATEGIC CYBERWAR MAY FOCUS ON POWER GRIDS AND BANKS

If strategic cyberwar is meant to inflict pain or at least high levels of annoyance, a key question is: how? Because the effects of cyberattack are generally temporary and difficult to repeat, countries are unlikely to use strategic cyberattacks as they would use strategic (conventional) air attacks, much less nuclear attacks.

Power grids are an obvious target for disruption. In 2013, the director of national intelligence deemed a large-scale cyberattack on the nation's critical infrastructure (of which the electric grid is the most prominent part) the greatest short-term threat to the nation's security.[2] One analyst has calculated that even a temporary shutdown of the power grid could cost the United States $700 billion (that is, more than the defense budget).[3] Destroying power systems, were that possible, could yield power outages lasting months or even years (it hardly speeds recovery that replacement U.S. electrical equipment would have to be imported), but many experts believe that wide-scale damage would require an exceptional set of circumstances.

It might seem odd that a power grid that worked well before the Internet arrived could be so vulnerable, but over the last several decades, power companies have concluded that it is far cheaper to have each of thousands of power stations, transmission lines, and distribution centers answer to a central information service than to send people on trucks to check on equipment every time something does or might happen. Therein lies a problem if hackers can work their way into the electric grid system and send it the kind of commands that tamper with, say, voltage levels. Overloaded circuits, for instance, can create a cascading failure that takes down entire systems.

But how likely are such cyberattacks? The August 2003 outage in the Northeast threw 50 million into the dark and was said to cost $7 billion to $10 billion.[4] It still serves as a template for such disasters—but did it result from a cyberattack? No, said the final report produced by the U.S.-Canada commission.[5] Power outages are among the most thoroughly researched incidents in the United States, and if the 2003 power outage had been caused or even substantially exacerbated by deliberate systems failure, it would not have gone unnoticed. One story published in the *National Journal* quoted unnamed intelligence sources as suggesting that the Chinese may have been behind the 2003 outage. The same report averred that hackers who fiddled with the wrong controls caused a 2008 power outage in central Florida—which later engineering reports pinned on human error.[6]

Perhaps such an attack is being prepared for later contingency use. A widely quoted article in the *Wall Street Journal* claimed that foreign hackers—presumably Chinese but also Russian—had worked their way into the nation's power control system; it was based not on an examination of code in the power grid but on "intelligence" gathered from overseas.[7] More recent reportage suggested Iranian efforts to find power grid vulnerabilities.[8] There was also a kerfuffle over the discovery that a Chinese researcher had published a paper trying to work out how to cause a cascading failure in the power grid.[9] This suggested to some that the Chinese planned to do precisely that to the North American grid (but if such plans were under way, why would the Chinese see fit to tip their hand?). In late 2014, CYBERCOM's chief testified (without releasing supporting details) that China, and perhaps other countries, could take down the U.S. electric power grid.[10] Several months earlier, DHS analyzed the BlackEnergy malware that infected human-machine interface products in power grids but could not identify any attempts to damage, modify, or otherwise disrupt the victim systems' control processes.[11] Evidence suggests that BlackEnergy malware was created not for destructive attacks but for cybercrime and cyberespionage purposes and that the infections are incidental.[12]

Indeed, the sensitivity of the homeland security community to the very possibility of such an attack led to a report of an overseas computer intrusion of a water system in central Illinois from Russia, which in turn led to a pump's being burned out. Later investigation indicated that the so-called hacker was actually an employee of the firm that had accessed the system when on a trip to Russia.[13] But a contemporaneous hacker did show, by way of demonstration, that it was possible to access a water system from the outside by hacking into that of south Houston.[14]

Such forebodings have also characterized the reports of the otherwise even-tempered Government Accountability Office (GAO). One report in 2008 led off with a description of how calamitous an attack on the power grid would be and proceeded to score points off the Tennessee Valley Authority's cybersecurity.[15] The utility confessed to its sins and agreed to reform, but at the end of its response reminded the GAO that its systems were, in fact, isolated from the Internet.

Experts believe that security may also be imperiled by the switch to the Smart Grid (to accommodate services such as time-of-day pricing, discrete load management, and the measurement of user-generated power sent back into the grid). Although such functions can be separated from bulk power generation, transmission, and distribution, smart grids may allow hackers to simultaneously affect every individual's access to power by infecting power meters with malware.[16]

Actual incidents, however, have been rare; the Ukrainian hack was the first true one. As it was, Idaho Falls Laboratory reported a sharp increase in attacks on machine control systems since Stuxnet.[17] Furthermore, in 2012, Gen. Keith Alexander, then head of CYBERCOM, on several occasions noted that the number of attacks on infrastructures as reported to the U.S. Computer Emergency Response Team rose by a factor of seventeen since 2009 (forgetting to add that in 2009 such a reporting service had just gotten started and thus was not on the radar of most of those who might have had news to report).[18] An examination of the many incidents revealed that none of them (at the time he reported as much) breached machine control systems; all of them affected office automation systems, including the aforementioned breach affecting the domestic natural gas industry in the spring of 2012.[19]

Another infrastructure that has begun to attract considerable attention as a cyberattack target is the banking sector. In 2007, the director of national intelligence told the president that "if the 9/11 perpetrators had focused on a single U.S. bank through cyberattack and it had been successful, it would have an order-of-magnitude greater impact on the U.S. economy."[20] But no sector is as aware of the threat as the banking sector is. The Federal Reserve System itself has a large, well-paid staff precisely to counter it.[21] Finally, anyone who wants to make that argument has to dream up an attack that has the level of access sufficient to crash the global banking system but not good enough to actually remove any serious money from it. Otherwise, if such an attack did put hackers in a position to siphon off great sums of money, why has such a crime not already taken place? Who would be a cybercriminal at civil service salaries when riches await those who strike out on their own?

Last is the possibility that a major cyberattack would strike consumers en masse, not producers. A hacker who can infect a computer at the rootkit level can generally also render its hard drive useless, thereby crippling it; recovery can permit the hardware to return to service, but all files that have not been backed up would be irretrievably lost. Thus, if every infected computer were infected by an enemy country (rather than cybercriminals), and if all these computers could be infected without a pattern being detected,[22] and all these computers were bricked at once, and if there were no backup (for example, from the cloud) that would make restoration easy,[23] then the disruption would be substantial—but that is a plenitude of *ifs*.

HOW COERCIVE CAN A STRATEGIC CYBERWAR CAMPAIGN BE?

Casualties are the chief source of the kind of war-weariness that causes nations to sue for peace while still capable of defending themselves—but since no cyberattack has caused direct human casualties, the next such casualty will be its first. Otherwise, the coercive strength of a cyberattack would depend on the stakes at issue, how much economic cost it could impose, what the defender could bear, and how badly the defender wanted to protect a reputation for resisting coercion.

If the stakes are high enough, a society, even a quasi-affluent Western one, can and will take a great deal of punishment and still not yield. Historically, a siege (particularly if coupled with starvation) was one such campaign. In the Franco-Prussian war, the Prussians surrounded Paris for several months, attempting to starve the city into surrender before administering several days of artillery shelling as a coup de grace. But one can hardly compare what even a vigorous cyberwar might do to what the inhabitants of Sarajevo had to endure from 1992 through 1995 or what those of Jerusalem endured in 1947 and 1948. In both cases, solidarity held. If Russia has suffered from the West's embargoes (following Russian actions in Ukraine), it had yet to show any political give as of spring 2016. Few nations have yielded to trade embargoes alone, even to universal trade embargoes. Examples include Southern Rhodesia (now Zimbabwe), Cuba, and Iraq between the two gulf wars, and, to some extent, Iran (prior to the 2015 agreements). North Korea suffers from a largely self-imposed strategic economic warfare (its *juche* self-reliance policy). It still stands. Myanmar withstood years of Western investment boycotts (it only yielded when it realized that the alternative to getting along with the West was to become dependent on China's investment strategies). It is unclear that a cyberwar campaign would have any more effect than even a universal trade embargo, which can affect all areas of the economy and whose effects can last decades.

Even a complete shutdown of all computer networks would not prevent the emergence of an economy as modern as the U.S. economy was circa 1960—and such a reversion could only be temporary, since cyberattacks rarely break things. Modify "computer networks" in the prior sentence with "publicly accessible" (if matters get so bad that only isolation provides sufficient protection), and "circa 1960" becomes something closer to "circa 1995." Life in 1995 provided a fair measure of comfort to citizens of developed nations (even if today's kids swear that life would be meaningless without cell phones and social media). Finally, low-tech countries are inherently more immune than high-tech states are to being deprived of network services and are therefore less susceptible to damage. True, the effort of going from now to back then may not be easy—people have become dependent on the Internet. Many techniques that were used to make life work in a nonnetworked era will have to be relearned. But if the price of a country's having stable networks is the loss of its sovereignty, how many would make that choice?

Perhaps the most important reason that a strategic cyberwar campaign would not have the effect of a strategic bombing campaign is because, as argued above, the effects of almost all cyberattacks are temporary and the impact of such cyberattacks depletes over time. Depletion is both specific (attackers have to find new vulnerabilities) and general (systems tighten up and reduce their exposures). All this suggests that the damage from cyberattacks may be self-limiting in ways that do not apply to other attacks. There may well be an effective upper limit to the cumulative damage that can be induced through the disruption of critical systems. In contrast, recurrence is more likely for attacks on low-priority systems because the ability to take advantage of bad user habits (for example, allowing a bot to take over your computer or yielding a password to a phishing attack) appears endless.

Further weakening strategic cyberwar as a coercion strategy is that the object of coercion, the government, is not the one responsible for protecting most networks (even overseas). Most infrastructures and banks are privately owned and operated. In the face of cyberattack, governments could well try to redirect popular ire to infrastructure owners whose poor defenses allowed the public to feel the inconveniences of cyberwar. If voters look persuadable, this would permit the government to resist coercion. Although infrastructure owners might try to refute such arguments, their refutations would likely be seen as self-serving and overly technical and hence weak.[24] Government computer systems, for their part, do not present so tempting a target for coercion-minded cyberwarriors. Granted, some U.S. government computer systems cannot take interruptions: for example, Fedwire (because of follow-on effects on financial markets), the Global Positioning System (heavily protected for military reasons), and the Federal Aviation Administration's air traffic control system (whose primitive nature makes it more invulnerable to attack than its rickety structure would otherwise suggest). Others, such as Social Security and similar benefit programs, cannot go down for too long without consequences. The rest can go down for several weeks with only minor inconvenience to the average citizen.

STRATEGIC CYBERWAR AS INFORMATION WAR

The Russian campaign for the Crimean peninsula and eastern Ukraine has involved the heavy use of propaganda carried out so effectively that according to some, it is not information warfare anymore: "The second component of Putin's 21st-century warfare is cyber. Calling it propaganda diminishes the insidious and poisonous nature of this information battle."[25]

The relationship between propaganda and cyberwar is a curious one. The first tries to influence human thinking; the second tries to exercise some control over computer "thinking." Fifteen years ago, both were considered part of information warfare; a few years earlier, information warfare was a subset of "command and control warfare."[26] Psychological warfare operates at the semantic level; cyberwar operates at the syntactic level. They differ substantially.

Yet the two may not be so different after all. At one level, the most common reaction to cyberwar has been fear—a function, in part, of the fact that no one has yet seen full-blown cyberwar against a society. Cyberwar must therefore have strong psychological elements that some may be tempted to manipulate.

The more important reason not to dismiss the connection is the possibility that a strategic cyberwar operation against an authoritarian state may consist of actions that try not to break the morale of its citizens but rather to erode the bonds between the citizens and the state. Authoritarian governments know this all too well. The four countries most often mentioned as problems for the United States in cyberspace—Russia, China, Iran, and North Korea—all fear citizen unrest, and all hobble their citizens' access to the Internet. All of them are therefore vulnerable to information reaching their citizens about the less-than-perfect behavior of the state and its rulers (many of whom have amassed fortunes well in excess of what civil service salaries can explain). China went so far as to penetrate the networks of the *New York Times* looking for sources behind reporting that "the relatives of Wen Jiabao, China's prime minister, had accumulated a fortune worth several billion dollars through business dealings."[27] Russia's classification of information about casualties as secret indicates a sensitivity that can be exploited in an information campaign.[28]

From this one can see the glimmerings of a strategic cyberwar campaign operating largely at the psychological level. It would have two components. One would be to unearth documents indicating state or leadership malfeasance. The other would be to inject such documents into the public media of these countries.[29] The Russians themselves are not above such tactics.[30] Witness their doxing of Assistant Secretary of State for European and Eurasian Affairs Victoria Nuland, whose barnyard deprecations of the European Union in a private conversation were captured and leaked to the media to her embarrassment.[31] Witness also what looks like an Iranian hack to expose the diplomatic cables of Saudi Arabia.[32]

THE CONDUCT OF CYBERWAR

No one really knows what a productive coercive cyberwar campaign would look like. Both sides would likely be making it up as they go along. Students of crisis management suggest that most world leaders are likely to proceed incrementally into crisis, making carefully calibrated and implemented moves and observing and evaluating their effects.[33] Caution arises when leaders fear losing control of a crisis, either by engaging in behavior that may provoke an unpredictable reaction or by empowering third parties to pursue their own not-necessarily-perfectly-aligned aims. Analyses of U.S. decisionmaking during the Vietnam War suggest that leaders feared the loss of control more than they feared the loss of war.[34]

At first glance, cyberwar lends itself to an incremental approach because it presents such a broad range of options for contemplation. Attacks may range from introducing modest but inexplicable changes into the enemy's information systems to making wholesale attempts to collapse all the adversary's infrastructures at once. At second glance, maybe not. The relationship between effort and effect may be nonlinear—perhaps nothing, followed by ratcheting up, then again nothing, followed by ratcheting up, then almost imperceptible annoyance, more ratcheting up, and nothing again, yet more ratcheting—and suddenly the players have crossed into strategic-level conflict. Incremental efforts may thus not always produce incremental effects.

The course of cyberwar also depends on the systems being targeted, which in turn will depend on which ones have which vulnerabilities and to what extent exploiting them can sway countries. Cascading or ripple effects are often a bonus. Good attack methods work in nonobvious ways, have few good countermeasures, do not reveal and hence do not exhaust vulnerabilities (that may come in handy for operational cyberwar), and can thus be used again.

The classic case for starting a conflict with a series of probes is to learn how to employ one's own weapons systems, test the opponent's defenses, and discover its weak spots—feeling your way forward (or, as Deng Xiaoping has said, crossing the river by feeling the stones). Presumably, practice makes if not perfect, then at least predictable. In cyberwar, however, weapons effects cannot be considered independently of the adversary's vulnerabilities, its ability to recover, and, most important, what it has learned from being attacked. For this reason, early probes, feints, and jabs may be informative to answer high-order questions such as: Is the adversary an easy or tough opponent? At the operational level, opponents may know less after these early moves than before if the terrain has changed radically in response to these attacks. With all this, there may be no good operational reason not to throw everything at once—surprise has a great operational advantage here—but every good strategic reason not to. If cyberattacks are a sideshow to a shooting war or if cyberwar is deemed inevitable, strategic cyberwar considerations may be secondary, and the logic of getting cyberattacks to succeed technically may suffice. This will not be so if conflict is limited to cyberspace.

INDICATIONS AND WARNING

Because successful surprise—Pearl Harbor, the Chinese crossing the Yalu—usually works against defenders, indications and warning of attack are considered very helpful. But are indications and warning of a surprise attack possible? Perhaps. Spies may have penetrated the attackers' networks, but it is hard to believe that military units charged with developing offensive cyberwar capabilities do not live in closed compartments where the only way in or out is through human intelligence. Human spies planted among cyberwarriors are not impossible. The exploit may be observed being tested in the real world; criminals sometimes try out malware in small quantities a day ahead of its full deployment. If so, intercepting a test may indicate an imminent attack of some prespecified nature, if not necessarily who the attacker or what the target is likely to be.

Similarly, a major DDOS attack may be preceded by minor or singular DDOS attacks—something the attacker can get away with because for a victim, knowing that a particular type of DDOS attack might be coming is not enough to blunt it. By contrast, knowing about an attack that depends on particular vulnerabilities may suffice to blunt them.

Otherwise, the problem, as noted earlier, is that there is no ipso facto relationship between discovering the means of an attack and when such an attack is to take place; cyberattacks take place in ordinal time, not cardinal time. There is no engineering sequence that is associated with an attack as there might be for launching a liquid-fueled intercontinental ballistic missile, where tasks must be completed in a particular order with particular lead times (and cannot be undone)—or as there might be for placing kinetic forces on alert when this cannot be sustained indefinitely without becoming costly. Hence, such movements are indicators.

Empirically, there have not been enough cyberattacks to know what kind of events proceeded them, except to note that real-world events (for example, the moving of a statue in Tallinn or the build-up of agitation between Russia and Georgia over South Ossetia) tend to precede events in cyberspace—as well as many kinetic events (a riot and invasion, respectively). It used to be thought that finding a collection of unrelated smaller attacks indicated that either a big one was coming or that at least a big one composed of multiple small components was in process. But that notion has yet to be backed by example. It also has a weak theoretical base—smaller cyberattacks put the target on notice in ways that lead to its reacting in ways that frustrate the larger cyberattack that the smaller attacks were supposed to lead to.

Implants—insertions into the target network that prepare it to execute arbitrary instructions sent later—may be a precursor to some attack someday. Whoever discovers an implant knows that someone is interested in doing something nefarious with the specific system and perhaps the network on which it sits, and maybe even the systems connected to that network. But one cannot necessarily tell what instructions the implant is going to get; it could be an order to spy on a machine, or it could be an order to disrupt or corrupt something. If the defender is lucky in that the implant or the manner of its entry into the infected system clearly characterized some particular foe, it may know who is planning the mischief. But there is likely to be little clue as to when the mischief is going to take place. So what kind of warning is this if "what" is unclear, "who" is only occasionally known, and "when" is just a guess? What can one do with it—other than clean out the implant (which should be done regardless) so that the particular infection does not lead to any attack? The likelihood that finding an implant sparks a crisis depends on what inferences the target draws from its discovery: for example, does the implant indicate an attack is coming soon? The answer may depend on how long the implant was there. A recent implant may raise more panic. An old one may be interpreted either as espionage or as evidence that the attacker plans to use cyber threats in a crisis. If no crisis exists, the target may be slightly more relaxed.

A related issue concerns the role of information operations conditions (INFOCONs, the cyberwar community's answer to defense conditions, or DEFCONs): what should cause them to rise? Clearly a real-world crisis, as noted, might qualify—but if this is the only rationale for raising INFOCONs, why bother with a distinct set of them; why not just button systems up as a response to DEFCONs? The only justification for a separate INFOCON is a situation where the risks of a cyberattack rise without a corresponding rise in the kinetic threat. But not only are such situations hard to define, a successful cyberattack that is not followed up by a kinetic attack also is not particularly useful for the attacker since the system can be restored in short order.

A more strategic version of indications and warning is to determine when the broader cybersecurity climate has changed in ways that justify shifting the balance between security and convenience-cum-cost to security. With rare exceptions (several attacks by Iran and North Korea come to mind), today's mischief in cyberspace is carried out in the service of either crime or intelligence collection. Discovering preparations for more disruptive or destructive attacks would indicate a disjunction between current cybersecurity practices meant to counter ordinary threats (and hence plausibly optimal for the defender who faces many other like threats) and the much higher level of cybersecurity required to counter extraordinary state-sponsored threats (and hence plausibly rarely achieved in today's more benign environment). Can such an inflection point be spotted correctly? The aforementioned attacks on natural gas companies (and Telvent) have been cited as preparation for a strategic cyberattack, but were they?

MANAGING THE EFFECTS OF CYBERWAR

Nuclear warfighting (in theory) paid attention to keeping some targets in reserve lest the other side, having nothing left to lose, had no reason to yield or quit. Even countries that see no reason to spare their opponents might leave targets untouched in the hope that restraint might persuade the other side to do likewise, thereby limiting mutual destruction. Mutually respected safe zones may even provide an exemplar for mutual de-escalation.

There is no easy analogy in cyberspace. One can whack every conceivable target one week, and all could be back in service the next week, available to be whacked again (albeit with more difficulty unless the implants and back doors remain in place). Even never-struck targets are likely to be better defended—the flare-up of cyberwar would be expected to persuade all system owners to pay more attention to security.

Furthermore, it is harder to show that some targets have deliberately been spared from cyber-attacks than from kinetic attack, where what is hit is more or less obvious. A target unstruck may communicate reserve on the attacker's part—or that the target was too hard to hit. Conversely, failed attempts, even if detected, do not prove that the adversary was attempting to violate such a zone; it may be some form of collateral damage unanticipated because the relationships among systems were indiscernible.

Third parties may complicate achieving finesse. Even with the optimistic belief that countries alone can take down certain targets, the list of those who can make failed attempts to strike certain targets may include third parties. To the extent that third parties can complicate signaling during strategic cyberwar, both parties may benefit if each one endeavors to distinguish the other's handi-work from that of hackers. Such differentiation would help gauge the strategy and relative efficiency of adversary attacks, assign blame (or credit) correctly when something is hit, sense possible adver-sary de-escalation, or discount what may otherwise seem to be adversary escalation. Even if some attackers would make their attacks appear to come from somewhere else, others may want to inflate their strength and thereby get credit for attacks others pulled off.

Shaping cyberwar to permit the other side to recover quickly—as an inducement to settle, for instance—can be easier than shaping kinetic conflict thusly. This is because the art of a cyberattack lies not in destroying but rather in confusing target systems. Systems can be set straight by revealing the sleeper code that was placed, which algorithms were corrupted and how they can be restored, or what key was used to encrypt and make inaccessible which data files. But would promising such "repairs" be advised if hostilities might recur before systems turn over, rendering then-current vul-nerabilities obsolete anyway?

TERMINATING CYBERWAR

War strategies have to be ultimately about war termination.[35] Strategic cyberwar, as noted, is highly unlikely to be terminated by dint of the adversary having been disarmed (much less overturned) by force unless by kinetic force. Such wars are more likely to end by exhaustion or by concession. Indeed, how can one be sure that the other side has, in fact, stopped its attacks?

Consider three war termination paths: negotiation leading to termination, tacit de-escalation, or petering out. Monitoring peace pacts in cyberspace poses challenges not found in physical space. If either side still believes it can, if unpunished, reap unilateral advantages from an attack, then attri-bution and BDA will likely remain as difficult afterward as they were beforehand (the same applies with even more force to espionage). Each could cheat by shifting from visible disruption attacks to subtler corruption attacks. Both sides also must contend with the possibility of potential mischief from third-party (including state) hackers masquerading as the other side.

In physical wars, peace pacts are often followed by unilateral disarmament (after World War I, for instance, Germany's army was limited to 100,000 soldiers) and multilateral disarmament (for example, the Washington Naval Treaty). But disarmament in cyberspace means little inasmuch as cyberwar is less about arms (exploits) than vulnerabilities.

Mutual transparency may help keep the peace (in much the same way that formerly warring sides exchanged hostages), but no state (not even a friendly one) exposes the secrets of its security architecture to another. If it did, the transparency would have to be bilateral rather than public, lest mischievous third parties profit from the newfound knowledge. Even then, each side could attack the other from third parties outside the transparency agreement.

Mutual tacit de-escalation, compared with explicit war termination, has the advantage of not requiring formal adjudication of the original issues. Prospects for peace rest on both sides believing that neither would make much headway against the other through further cyberwar. Unfortunately, tacit de-escalation presents many of the same validation problems as negotiations—made worse by the lack of much consensus over what (for example, an attack on which target) was and was not considered a violation. How could one tell that the other side is even cooperating, absent clarity on what constituted cooperation?

The third path to a return to former conditions (a complete cessation of cyberspace activity being unrealistic) would be for attacks on one or both sides to peter out. Each side could unilaterally conclude that cyberattacks were growing more difficult to conduct, showing decreasing returns for the effort, and thus pointlessly irritating, when caught, as some invariably would be. The part of the equation in which one side decides that the effort no longer pays is not strategically problematic because it does not require the other side to recognize that the first side has changed its behavior. But the party that quits being irritating might hope to see some reward for its restraint. As long as the one side had not negotiated or declared restraint, the other side would not be able to hold up some future cyberattack as evidence that it had been lied to or cheated (although it could still be evidence of hostility). Furthermore, if the other side still found advantage in cyberattack—or any other attacks—it may have no motive to acknowledge such restraint. But if the other side also finds that the advantages of hacking have waned or that they are trumped by the rewards of friendly engagement, it too might work itself into a modus vivendi.

If cyberwar turns into real war, how the real war ends will dominate how cyberattacks alone end.

CONCLUSIONS

The coercive effects of cyberattacks are speculative. There are targets, but there are grounds to believe that the better targets are the hardest to penetrate. Furthermore, damage usually is temporary and not necessarily repeatable. As a threat, strategic cyberwar may not be believed; as a reality, it may not cause enough cumulative damage to make the target cry uncle—but could create enough annoyance to exacerbate a bad relationship. Attacks, once both sides start engaging in them, may be hard to terminate through mutual agreement. Although these may not be proofs against the wisdom of strategic cyberwar, they do suggest that cyberwar is neither a good adjunct to nor an adequate substitute for more conventional forms of strategic coercion.

PART IV STRATEGIES

CHAPTER 18
Cyberwar Threats as Coercion

Never attempt to do with war what can be achieved by merely threatening war. Wars are costly, chancy, and hard to disengage from. In many circumstances, it is easier to wring concessions from a country one has yet to harm than from a country that one has harmed and that has consequently committed itself to enmity and resistance in the belief that the stakes have become existential.[1] As with conventional war, so too with cyberwar. So let us see what the coercive potential for cyberwar might be.

A LIMITED CYBERWAR CAMPAIGN

First, can limited strategic cyberattacks influence other countries to make specific decisions in the interests of the attacker? To explore this question, posit a scenario in which Taiwan shuffles toward independence and China concludes that it will have to take the island. China hopes that the United States can be pressured not to intervene and uses a cyberattack to take out, say, the U.S. power grid. Its message is: "Do not delude yourself that the costs of intervention will occur only in our neighborhood. Your citizens will suffer directly. Stay on your side of the Pacific." It does not attempt to hide its hand. Following the cyberattack, China then invades Taiwan.

Will the United States be inhibited from intervention? Based on its reaction to Pearl Harbor and September 11, probably not. The United States has a long history of reacting nonlinearly to being attacked. Moreover, the Chinese, who do take history seriously, would likely understand this. Indeed, once the United States is struck, the nature of the Taiwan Straits struggle would likely shift from being a regional affair in which the United States has some sort of (not-so-hard-to-fudge) legal obligations under the Defense of Taiwan Act to a strategic affair where the outcome matters directly to the United States. The conflict would have been transformed into a matter of credibility in facing what would consequently have become the primary threat to the nation's existence (or so it would be argued). That being so, the *failure* to intervene would appear to most people, both at home and abroad, as evidence that the United States was too scared of having its networks disrupted to intervene—that is, to counter this newly existential threat. Just as the outcome in South Vietnam or Afghanistan, otherwise backwaters in a vast globe, became a vital interest of the United States once the country had committed its credibility, the outcome over the Taiwan Straits would become a vital interest once the Chinese had carried out a digital 9/11.

Such an attack would change the narrative of the conflict to China's disadvantage. Prior to the cyberattack, the Chinese could argue something like: Taiwan is part of China. Its separate status is an artifact of history. China is only rectifying the past to restore the nation's historic sovereignty. Taking Taiwan does not mean that China has designs on Japan, South Korea, the Philippines, or Vietnam—which are clearly different countries.

But once the lights go out here, the United States will hear a different narrative about China: China is rising and the United States is falling. The United States dare not intervene in China's part of the Pacific because it fears being hurt. If the Chinese understand what narratives they are communicating by their attack—and they very well might—they will conclude that a strategic cyberattack is a very poor coercive tool and its application may well backfire.

The depletability of cyberwar also limits its coercive effectiveness. Generally, the reaction of someone who has been hit will be some mixture of anger and fear. Anger is the emotion that says, "You can't do this to me." It is based not only on emotion but also on the fine calculation that if you are perceived as someone that can be hit with impunity, others will be more likely to try. If the law of the jungle prevails, your survival time is drastically reduced. Compliance is contraindicated. Indeed, doing things that you know the aggressor will not like *just because you were hit* is an element of deterrence. Counterattacks are one such reaction, but the perception of being hard to coerce may be expressed through less drastic steps such as reducing cooperation or making common cause with the aggressor's foes. Estonia, having been struck by Russia, reinforced its anti-Russian posture and snuggled that much closer to NATO.

Fear, however, both emotional and rational, represents the feeling that *not* responding as the attacker wants will leave one open to more punishment. Anger has a large retrospective component; it reflects what has happened (consider the urge to get back at a driver who cuts you off even though your benefit from having one more chastened driver on the road is miniscule). Fear, by contrast, is more a function of what will or may happen. If fear dominates anger, then coercion works. If anger dominates fear, then coercion backfires.

Compare, therefore, two situations in which an attack produces both anger and fear. In one, the prospects for greater punishment grow over time. This was the case with the confrontation between NATO and Serbia over Kosovo, where the continued failure of Serbia to bend to NATO's will foretold indiscriminate air attacks and maybe even the introduction of ground forces. When the fear component rises while the anger component is a given, fear—which would lead to concessions—would seem to have the upper hand.

In the other situation, the prospects for greater punishment fall over time. Anger—which leads to no concessions or counterconcessions—would have the upper hand. In cyberwar, the first demonstration that networks are too open for the defendant's good is likely to yield a drastic reduction in the openness of vulnerable networks; the odds of comparable damage drop. Under such circumstances, the anger component remains but the fear component may drop—and since fear tends to be prospective rather than retrospective, the balance between anger and fear is likely to tilt toward anger. In other words, coercion through cyberattack would likely be more self-defeating than coercion through kinetic attack.

Lastly, would one attack suffice to coerce? Most attacks exploit vulnerabilities. If, following the coercive attack, the specific vulnerability (or class of vulnerabilities) can be identified and fixed in every system that mattered, the party to be coerced might feel that it has regained its invulnerability and hence its resistance to coercion. It would thus take a second attack—but then, the same cycle of discovery, patch, and resistance might require a third, and so on. Psychological factors, though, may allow one attack to suffice. The first three of the four September 11 airline hijackings succeeded because of a security vulnerability: passengers presumed (as they have been taught) that they would survive the hijackings if they did not resist. Passenger resistance to the fourth hijacking demonstrated that such a vulnerability had closed by noon. Nevertheless, the attention paid to airline security then rose sharply, even though the susceptibility to hijacking was lower after 9/11 than before.

A COERCIVE CAMPAIGN

What about wielding the threat of cyberwar for coercive ends with a cyberattack at levels high enough to hint at what is possible but lower than would spark revenge?[2] A cyberattack against a military that is not at war may be worrisome and annoying, but ultimately disruptions are temporary and, when reversed, leave the physical hardware largely intact (even if software may be shown too insecure to be left in place). Thus, the threat of a cyberattack on military forces is unlikely to be very persuasive unless the country is in one of two states. The first is being at war with a third party—raising the prospect that it could suffer battlefield reverses because and while its military systems are being disrupted. The second is if a cyberattack threat is coupled with a latent kinetic attack threat (for example, from the same country) and the prospect of disruption of military defenses makes the other side's leaders feel nervous about being even temporarily unprotected. Otherwise, because system recovery is straightforward, suffering the attack only means longer hours for the military's sysadmins; it is like threatening to close a fine dining kitchen during the wee hours of the morning.

For these reasons, threatening a cyberattack against a military is unlikely to produce the requisite coercive effect. By contrast, the civilian sector needs and produces services every day around the clock, in peace and in war. If electric power is out for a week, that would be a week in which economic activity would fall sharply (not to mention a very uncomfortable week, unless the weather cooperates). If bank records are scrambled, people lose access to their money until and only if the true records can be recovered. If government payments are delayed, people living on the edge may go sick or hungry.

Several factors, however, suggest that a *denial* strategy on the part of the coerced party (the defender) is more tenable for a cyberspace threat than a kinetic threat. First and foremost is that the difficulties of brandishing cyberwar capabilities by the would-be attacker make it easier for the would-be victim to deny they exist (at least in sufficient strength to require concession); this ploy is not so easy with kinetic threats. If a bully rolls thousands of tanks up to your border and asks you to accommodate its interests, you may well consent without forcing him to demonstrate that the tanks are as capable as they look. The same credibility calculus does not work in cyberspace. You may be entirely unsure of what a cyberattack may do to your economy and society because you are unsure of how capable the bully is and how vulnerable you are. Indeed, because its threats presume your vulnerabilities, you may not believe that the bully knows more about the vulnerabilities in your state's systems than your people do (for if they knew about them, they would fix them). The fact of the threat may similarly suggest that the bully knows something that you should know; this threat may then be a wake-up call to install all the current patches, make another scrub for vulnerabilities and aberrant system behavior, and reexamine the system's architecture. With all that uncertainty, the weak persuasive power of such a threat that leaves so much to the imagination is not hard to grasp.

As it is, *no* country (yet) openly boasts about its cyberwar capabilities. The best, partial, exception is that the United States (and Israel) have been deliberately coy about Stuxnet and that DoD's latest cyberspace strategy openly speaks about using such weapons.[3] The United States also benefits from Snowden-revealed documents, which (if true) revealed how deeply the NSA can burrow into the systems of others. Otherwise, everyone else's capabilities can only be inferred from what third parties claim about the extent and authorship of this or that intrusion set. Recent observations that today's hackers are not taking great pains to cover up their national origin may be part of their strategy to gain implicit credit for clever hacks they may still explicitly deny carrying out. Or it may reflect the fact that national (in contrast to personal) attribution is of little consequence and thus is not worth making much effort to avoid.

The less obvious a country's capabilities in cyberspace, the more easily the leaders of a target state can argue that they do not merit great concern. True, leaders may risk embarrassment if they call the attacker's bluff and cyberattacks follow with consequential effects. In some cases, ignoring rather than denying threats may be wiser. Either way, the target can buy time, pushing back against political demands to accede and thereby forcing the onus back onto the would-be attacker in ways that are more difficult to do if the coercer's capability to punish were easier to display to the world. The vaguer the threat, the easier to ignore as a threat that never was made. Threats that can only be conveyed by the victim's intelligence community have the property that leaders can deny ever having received the memo.

If threats are used to compel (rather than deter) *and* the target takes them seriously, they may respond not through deprecation but by working to bolster the necessary defenses. This is a more plausible strategy when the threat is a cyberattack rather than a kinetic attack. Systems, after all, are vulnerable to the extent that their defenses were previously not taken seriously because they were set for peacetime (non-threat) conditions. Take banks. In peacetime, they protect their systems against theft; the odds of a malicious disruption or corruption attack that does not profit the attacker directly are small. In times of war or threatened war, such threats must be taken more seriously. Pains that are not worth taking in peacetime may have to be taken when war looms. Corrective actions are not instant, but the time required to carry them out can be measured in days, weeks, and months, rather than the months and years required to bulwark against a physical threat (for example, by upgrading a weapon). The longer the potential victim can ward off an attack, the less damage it can expect if attacks come, and the sooner leaders can switch from (insincerely) talking eventual accession to outright denial.

Potential attackers, for their part, may anticipate as much and therefore not give their targets much time to respond. But attackers (even if more knowledgeable about what systems are being targeted) are less likely than the other side to know how much time it would take to bring systems up to snuff. And they will certainly know less about how much confidence the other side needs before switching from accommodation to defiance. Furthermore, a coercion strategy that hustles a compliance date forward to short-circuit the stall-until-hardened ploy is not free either. It cannot easily be used to coerce the other side into a form of compliance that takes time to monitor (for example, dismantle a particular facility) or accompany any campaign in which some minimum time must transpire between the making of the threat and the mobilization of all the forces that the coercer needs to have ready in order to make good on the threat. For instance, a do-this-now threat of cyberattack also cannot easily be made against a country not already on the target list (*pace* the non-operation against Libya). Here, too, is where threats of a cyberattack differ from threats of a kinetic attack to the latter's disadvantage. The United States can, for instance, bomb pretty much anything pretty much anywhere it wants to within 24 hours. But cyberattacks take time to plan because penetration can be unpredictably long—sometimes easy, sometimes hard. Those who would coerce can pretend that they scoped out the target system well before there was a crisis or that they started recently but succeeded quickly, but the other side may recognize the bluff for what it is.

A similar logic may attend the use of cyberattack as deterrent, particularly if the country making the deterrence threat uses it to discourage actions that the target state feels it has a right to do. If the target wanted to do so and was met with a deterrence threat, it may postpone its actions long enough to bulwark its systems against a retaliatory cyberattack. The difference is that the target state has to move more stealthily in doing so, lest it signal its intent to do what it was forbidden to do (so that the intention to act draws the very cyberattack that was reserved for the act itself). Again, defenses against cyberattack threats may be easier to mobilize in stealth than similar defenses against kinetic attacks.

The dynamics of coercion reflect the mutual asymmetry of information associated with any cyberattack. The attacker may know what systems it penetrated and what first-order effects could be generated from such a penetration, although its information on whether access to the penetrated system is still usable may be iffy (particularly if the system under attack has no real-time connection with the attacker). The potential victim may not know exactly what was penetrated (in some cases, it may have a good statistical guess), but it should have a better idea than the attacker about what the failure modes of the likely targets are. The potential victim should also have a better idea than the attacker about how resilient its systems are, what the recovery path and lead-times may be, and, most important, how well it can get along without the system under attack (the latter may also characterize a kinetic attack). The notion of "should" rather than "will," however, covers the possibility that neither side has much clue about resilience and recovery because cyberattacks of the sort that call for resilience and recovery have so far been quite rare.

A denial strategy works better if the potential attacker is actually reluctant to carry the attack out and so prefers winning without fighting. Any cyberattack, after all, carries risks. It may attract world condemnation; if the threat is made public or looks implicit in its context, people may attribute any subsequent cyberattack accordingly. An attack risks angering target state populations in ways that render concessions politically impossible. Similarly, an attack would more likely lead to retaliation than a threat would. The response may be limited to cyberspace, but not necessarily—particularly if the victim's strength lies elsewhere.

The attacker, itself uncertain about how well its proposed attack would work, may regard the victim's unwillingness to yield as a clue that the proposed attack would not impress. The logic is Bayesian: the more confident the target is that it can brush off the attack, the more likely it is to ignore the threat. Therefore, ignoring the threat is evidence that the anticipated effects of the attack are nugatory. Of course, since that is exactly what the victim wants the attacker to believe, such logic may be discounted by the attacker.

Two other factors may predispose the victim to ignore the threat. One arises when the threat is to private systems. Leaders can point out that no failure of these private players to secure their own systems should cripple the latitude of leaders to act in their country's best interest. No similar argument can be made if the threat is kinetic because countries are expected to defend their people and property against kinetic attack; that is what militaries, after all, are for. By contrast, governments lack the tools to defend otherwise poorly defended systems from hackers and hence cannot be expected to be responsible if such systems go down. Indeed, because private parties can undermine a denial strategy by wringing their hands in public about how vulnerable they are, a strategy to blame them in advance (preferably in advance of the threat) for any disruption may keep them quiet and allow leaders to put up a good front.

The other factor is harder to justify but cannot be totally discounted. To wit, it would be a *good* idea for the country to experience a major cyberattack, the better to take cybersecurity seriously (and thereby nullify future such threats). One need not hang out with cyberwarriors terribly long before hearing exactly that from someone followed by a round of knowing nods. Admittedly, this is a tough argument for leaders to make out loud (unless citizens were culturally predisposed to see themselves as sinners deserving of punishment). Indeed, the notion that suffering such an attack yields more benefits than costs presupposes organizations that are excessively short-sighted about cybersecurity investments, a very nonlinear relationship between cyberattack and cybersecurity response (weak for small attacks but great for large ones), and a belief that as bad as a major cyber-attack might be, far worse could be in the pipeline. But one need not buy the calculus to conclude that there *would* be some offsetting advantages from calling serious attention to cybersecurity. The relatively modest impacts arising from the Iranian DDOS attacks on banks nevertheless served as a wake-up call for major banks, which now spend hundreds of millions of dollars annually on cyber-security. If leaders convey an attitude that their people need a wake-up call, a coercive strategy to do just that will have less coercive effect.

One advantage of a partial attack is that it might give pause to a country that feels itself constrained to act abroad until its home front is secured. Thus, in the Taiwan scenario, a partial attack on the power grid may give the United States pause while utility officials scramble to safeguard themselves (either by scrubbing or by disconnecting their control systems). Only then would the United States intervene—but in waiting, the opportunity for the United States to beat invading forces before they have dug in goes away. Here, a strategic attack has operational implications.

Cyberattack threats are not without a few advantages vis-à-vis threats of force. It is precisely because such threats are untested that the fearful can exaggerate their impact as well as the less fearful can downplay it. Perhaps the best guess is that those inclined to resist can find reasons to do so, and those inclined to accede can also find their own reasons.

Nevertheless, if one assumes that people will react to threats in rough proportion to their ultimate seriousness, it appears that a coercive strategy that uses the threat of cyberattacks as its primary thrust is likely to be weaker than a comparable strategy that uses *equally damaging* kinetic (or even financial) threats. Simply put, the unknowns are larger, and therefore the victim may profit from calling the coercer's bluff or at least pursuing a stalling strategy to play for time that it can use to boost defenses.

CONCLUSIONS AND IMPLICATIONS FOR MUTUALLY ASSUMED DISRUPTION

That, in turn, is why mutual assured destruction (MAD)—more like mutually assumed disruption—in cyberspace lacks the necessity that MAD carried when the subject was nuclear war and why the discovery that one's foe has developed a coercive cyberwar capacity pointed at you need not force you to run out and do the same in return.

It pays to remember that nuclear MAD is a weird creature. Normally, one side sees nothing good in the acquisition of an assured strike capability by the other side. In the nuclear case, however, it was felt that an insecure foe would not trust that it could ride out an attack and still have some deterrence capability left. Insecurity would breed twitchiness because leaders could see great danger in not responding to ambiguous threats; hence, they would exhibit a stronger tendency to launch on warning (rather than impact). The combination was unstable, hence dangerous. Therefore, the "assurance" component of MAD could help both sides sleep better.

In cyberspace, however, the inability to disarm is coupled with the greater likelihood that the target of coercion could, thus would, bluff its way out of a coercive threat, thereby forcing the potential attacker to either back down or carry out an attack and thereby risk being on the wrong side of the anger-fear balance. The weaker the coercive threat, the lower the need to spend the resources and run the risks of building up a countering coercive capability. MAD is not necessary for peace in cyberspace, if threats are unable to impress and thereby coerce.

CHAPTER 19
The Unexpected Asymmetry of Cyberwar

I t is considered nearly self-evident that because the United States is the world's most wired power, it therefore has the most to lose in a cyberwar; the other side will come out better if significantly less developed. Correspondingly, the emergence of cyberwar gives small countries an unprecedented ability to reach out and touch large ones.[1]

But is that so? In early 2011, Amos Yadlin, a former director of Israeli military intelligence, expressed a very different perspective on asymmetry: although developed countries had more vulnerabilities than underdeveloped countries, the superior ability of developed countries to master cyberwar more than made up the difference. Stuxnet underlay this argument. Perhaps one can go further: not only do developed countries have an edge over underdeveloped countries, but also the United States has a greater edge than most other developed countries do. Put another way, vulnerability does not equal dependence; a country's ability to repel attack, its resilience in the face of attack, and its ability to recover all have to be taken into account.

But that fact does not necessarily complete a net assessment: because people can help in cyberspace without showing up, a contest between two countries (or coalitions thereof) is not completely determined by what each side brings to the table.

THE THIRD WORLD DISADVANTAGE

Twenty years ago, cell phones were a luxury. Now they are everywhere, including nearly everywhere in the third world—and almost all cell phones these days are essentially computers. All the switches and routers without which cell phones would not work are also computers—and very complex computers produced by a limited number of suppliers in a few countries. Looking at communications alone shows how all countries could be affected by cyberwar (even isolated North Korea has cell phones and more than one hundred externally accessible websites as of late 2014). It is not as if underdeveloped countries only have underdeveloped, that is, analog, technology; such devices were long ago withdrawn from the market (even as used equipment, for the most part). It simply does not pay for an advanced manufacturer with a global customer base to maintain, much less build, analog machines when finding support engineers and components becomes increasingly difficult (and digital components are both cheaper and programmable). Thus, a developing country buying process control machinery, unless it finds and buys something used, must buy something similar to what developed countries purchase. Iran's Natanz centrifuge facility had to use digital components (even as its predecessors from, say, the 1960s did not) whether its operators wanted to or not. Furthermore, if digital systems need to be maintained, it is often more cost-effective to connect them to the Internet even if, years ago, they used to be maintained using house calls or even phone calls.[2] If the management of such systems is computerized, then when computers fail, so do the systems they manage.[3]

Granted, the digital technology is not spread equally thick everywhere. Much of the developing world, for instance, is underbanked, and hence attacks on banking systems would not directly affect the unbanked billions in currency in developing countries (at least not directly; problems with banks may affect enough businesses to impede overall economic activity). The large digital data-bases (public records, affinity programs) where our vital identifying information is stored may be smaller in developing countries—until people in developing countries start to transact a large share of their business on the web. Indeed, more e-commerce takes place on the web in China than in the United States.[4]

Conversely, there are large differences between the ability of developing countries and developed countries to defend their systems that greatly favor the latter. Cybersecurity firms are dispro-portionately American (albeit with a growing Israeli presence). Developing countries that must tend to security often do so through local subsidiaries of large corporations headquartered in the West.

To understand asymmetry simply in terms of rich versus poor or big versus small may also be too simplistic. Consider a stand-off, for instance, between China and Taiwan. China is the larger country, but Taiwan, on average, is the more highly developed one. China's networks are also large, but the security management of its large networks has not quite caught up to their scale. A determined Taiwan could easily put China's networks at risk, creating at least temporary chaos; demonstrating as much (without enraging China at the same time) may give China one more rea-son to reassess the costs of what might otherwise be a relatively affordable military takeover (absent U.S. involvement). That cyberwar favors the small, highly advanced, and disciplined should benefit countries such as Israel and Singapore as well. Cyberwar also has a dead-hand quality to it that may offer a modicum of deterrence against an attack that seeks to absorb or change the governance of a determined country. Because all of the inputs for a cyberattack—computers, network connections, hackers, and intelligence—should be mobile, they can be carried out from anywhere, particularly if the identity of the hackers is not known to countries. Thus, the hackers' capital may fall and fresh attacks may continue in ways that are much harder to do with any other form of warfare. A coun-try under threat may remind others that its disappearance will not eliminate its ability to wreak future havoc. That noted, the stock of intelligence will need to be renewed, and that will not come cheaply—so that, barring outside funding, the dead-hand capabilities of the exiled hackers are likely to dwindle over time.

Perhaps less developed countries or nonstate actors can bootstrap their offensive cyberwar capabilities by exploiting markets for malware in general and zero days in particular. They thereby become as fearsome as big ones.[5] This threat has been voiced since at least the mid-1990s and repeatedly since then, but there is little evidence that it has come to pass.[6] Several reasons why may be adduced. First, the notion of malware as a weapon of cyberspace (analogous to terrorist groups with nuclear weapons) downplays the work required to adapt it for exploitation purposes *and* use it against a specific target. Understanding the target and its fault modes well enough to create serious effects requires an intelligence and analytic capability that cannot easily be purchased off the shelf. Second, the various malware markets bifurcate into two types, neither of which is particularly help-ful for small and nonstate actors. One type deals in malware for criminal purposes: for example, stealing money or information convertible into money. Criminals mostly go after the least well protected individuals and indifferently protected businesses. The population of such victims is large enough that criminals rarely need zero days—which is why zero days are rarely found in black mar-kets.[7] The other type entails grey markets that traffic in zero days (for example, Vupen, ReVuln) but the latter (say they) deal only with NATO or NATO-friendly governments (with exceptions: Team Hacking *had* zero days and dealt with illiberal governments). Third, the playing field is constantly rising; to look at nonstate or small state actors and play up their rising competence does not tell the entire story if the defenders (or at least their tools) are becoming increasingly sophisticated. None of these are insurmountable challenges and certain nonstate actors (for example, Hezbollah) may be lent the capabilities of state actors (for example, Iran).[8] But panic is somewhat premature.

THE PARTICULAR U.S. ADVANTAGE

The great majority (perhaps as much as 98 percent) of all vulnerabilities that permit cyberattacks come from U.S. software: U.S.-headquartered corporations or nonprofit organizations. It is hard to think of any other product so dominated by one country even if, as explained below, this dominance is neither permanent nor inevitable. While it lasts, however, U.S. cyberwarriors can *potentially* take great advantage of circumstances. For instance, the software corporations are more likely to share the same broad cultural values of the U.S. population, and by extension the U.S. government, than they will with the population (and hence governments) of other countries, notably those less democratic and advanced. Indeed, in many ways (the many cybersecurity startups being formed by ex-NSA employees), they are literally the same people. The U.S. intelligence community and U.S. software firms occasionally even swap employees (under the Intergovernmental Placement Act). This fosters a dialogue that allows U.S. cyberwarriors on the one hand and software developers on the other hand to understand each other's mindset. This facilitates not only mutual accommodation but also predicting each other's next moves. Furthermore, this also makes it easier for cyberwarriors and software writers to talk to each other as technical peers.

Nevertheless, there are limits. Only occasionally do U.S. companies consciously adapt their products to U.S. or, more broadly, Western values (for example, favoring privacy over surveillance)— even assuming there was a single set of Western values in the first place. Commercial entities optimize their products to meet the expectations of their customers and related stakeholders[9] and their own business objectives.[10] Many U.S. companies, for instance, supply equipment and software to foreign governments for use in suppressing Internet use, although their use within the United States would likely raise howls even from their own employees. Furthermore, although it might seem that U.S. officials may have better luck in getting access to the source code, in practice, companies either share with all the major players (for example, Microsoft shares with the United States, but also with Russia and China) or none of them. With open source, everyone gets to see everything anyhow.

Yet imagine a conflict in cyberspace so consequential that corporations and other organizations headquartered in the United States feel pressure (externally, but also perhaps from their employees, suppliers, and counterparts) to work with U.S. cyberwarriors even as these corporations protect the cybersecurity of their customers worldwide (except perhaps in countries at cyberwar with the United States). If the other side was clearly a pariah state, the tilt of U.S. companies would be fairly clear; they already avoid business in certain states (largely under pressure of U.S. law, with its many extraterritorial features); today's rogue states would constitute a very small percentage of their market anyway. In contrast to what large U.S. (and German) companies could and did do in World War II, it would be difficult to split off local affiliates of software companies to do their own thing in foreign lands. So, despite what software companies might maintain, they would have to choose sides.[11] If they did, they would almost certainly side with the United States (and with likeminded countries such as those in Europe). That being so, might there be several advantages to be reaped from their cooperation?

First, they can be expected to prioritize patches that are necessary to defend U.S. (and Western) systems at the expense of patches that implicate no such interests; they may even be tempted to overlook vulnerabilities (assuming these were even brought to their attention) that U.S. cyberwarriors are using but, as far as anyone can tell, are not being used on U.S. systems. Will any company exert itself to fix a vulnerability that only terrorists or rogue nations suffer from; indeed, would there even be robust channels for vendors to find out about it? To the extent that patches engender attacks as soon as they are announced (see Heartbleed), U.S. software companies would likely tell high-priority customers (including those so deemed by the U.S. government) before they tell anyone else.[12] Once they release their patch, however, prospects for keeping it out of an adversary's hands are doubtful. If hackers can reverse-engineer patches to discover which vulnerability just got fixed, then such fixes would find their way everywhere. As a rule, adversaries would likely get their patches later than those in countries not at cyberwar with the United States; the many Chinese who run bootleg copies of Windows have to get their security updates from their ISPs. With open source software, the difference in update lag times between friend and foe could be smaller. Finally, it is unclear whether it is possible to make sneaky patches, ones in which it is less obvious what is being patched or which break systems that use software components common only in adversary systems.

Second, such companies in theory may be able to engineer their products for national security customers in ways that make them somewhat more secure than the normal products in circulation. But can they do so in practice? Many sufficiently complex software components already have various security settings, but selecting these settings almost always comes at the expense of convenience and adaptability. If software companies can engineer a better security/convenience trade-off, why are they not doing so already? What would change? Two answers might be offered. One is that in a full-fledged cyberwar, the necessary tilt toward security may allow restrictions to be implemented in software at the expense of convenience. Similarly, the second answer is that extant security weaknesses might be a result of deliberate architectural choices. One example may be an application that provides consumer information to those who supplied it.[13] Another has paths in it that permit easier maintenance (for example, via back doors). Both create structural weaknesses that may permit hackers to enter the same door.[14] During a serious cyberwar, such trade-offs might be made differently. Again, these extra-security versions can be made available to designated customers while being denied to the adversary—but this is no guarantee that the adversary cannot reverse-engineer something for itself, albeit later.

Third, compliant software companies could, in such circumstances, brief cyberwarriors about the more problematic or brittle elements (understood only by those with access to the source code) in the software so that the community can find vulnerabilities and build workarounds more efficiently. It is less likely, but not provably impossible, that some could put weaknesses into their software that only they and the cyberwarrior community know about. Indeed, there are (weakly denied[15]) accusations that the NSA permitted—or, worse, may have inserted—a faulty random-number generator to be embedded in RSA software.[16] Deliberate insertion, though, is a particularly dicey step, and it would take a great deal to persuade companies to weaken their own products, even in the interest of national security. Asking for deliberately weakened products may strike corporate employees as unprofessional, dangerous (who can guarantee that the bad guys will not discover the flaw and use it against other systems?), and damaging to a company's reputation outside (and even inside) the United States (today's allies may be tomorrow's targets for cyberespionage, if not cyberattack). For proof, reflect on Apple's refusal to help the FBI break into a dead terrorist's iPhone.

Fourth, U.S. cloud providers may retrieve customer information from overseas (as well as domestic servers) when so asked.[17] That noted, discovery that data are already being requested has motivated many countries to mandate that data that is provided by local customers not leave the country, and they are willing to favor local providers (not subject to U.S. laws) to ensure that this is so.[18] U.S. corporations are eager to get out from under that obligation,[19] and Google announced a service in June 2014 that will prevent it from determining the contents of its cloud (and hence passing such information to others) for concerned customers.[20] With the rollout of iOS8, Apple announced that it would no longer hold the decryption keys to customer phones, thus preventing it from readily yielding them to government officials.

Although the major sources of open source software (for example, Linux, Mozilla, Apache) are U.S.-dominated, the influence of U.S. cyberwarriors over their products is apt to be limited.

Their distribution is global, hence easy to replicate. Furthermore, it is impossible to put hidden content into open source software (although content of obscure purpose is possible). That said, some influence may be wielded to prioritize some patches before others, build more secure versions, and convey its weaknesses preferentially.[21] On the flip side, adversaries can also repair their own versions of open source software, but it is more likely that adversaries, in doing so, would have to use a forked version, which, as explained below, is likely to be less secure than the mainline version. To demonstrate as much, it may help to ask: how would the patch sequence of Heartbleed have gone if the United States were in a real cyberwar?

All this noted, these features constitute an edge in the game, not guaranteed victory. This level of cooperation would require sufficient crisis *and* enough time for this edge to be translated into an operational advantage. If a serious cyberwar were to erupt tomorrow, the playing field would start at today's far more level ground.

Will the United States come to lose its overwhelming superiority in software? No empire lasts forever, as Percy Bysshe Shelley's "Ozymandias" reminds us (and the fate of General Motors over the last half-century confirms). Twenty years ago, critics of the U.S. software industry such as Edward Yourdon were convinced that the U.S. dominance of software would yield before the more systematic approaches of others (stories pictured rows of uniformed Japanese programmers sitting in front of terminals).[22] But the United States has many built-in advantages ranging from global network effects that make it difficult to dethrone those who dominated existing lines of business to an exceptional startup infrastructure (reflecting education, capital-raising mechanisms, immigration, attitude). Although many traits foster continuous improvement in software security, one is the desire of and freedom for hackers to show up powerful software providers by demonstrating weaknesses in their products. How compatible are such conditions with authoritarian governments?

The most important challenger to the United States has to be China, whose writers bemoan U.S. hegemony (however odd the word "hegemon" sounds to U.S. ears). It can point to the aforementioned popularity of U.S. software and content (for example, Hollywood) and the fact that so much Internet traffic routes through the United States. Chinese authorities argue that U.S. dominance is an artifact of a time when the United States was advanced and China was not. China's attempt to internationalize the governance of the Internet (for example, Internet Corporation for Assigned Names and Numbers [ICANN]) by empowering the ITU reflects such attitudes; so does its determined efforts to keep major U.S. Internet services such as Google, Twitter, Facebook, or Amazon down in favor of local firms such as Baidu, Sina Weibo, Tencent, or Alibaba. China, though, has fewer champions in operating systems and applications. As noted, China is rapidly developing engineers and raising the money to fund research. Yet it is unclear whether, in the long run, educating so many engineers, spending so much on R&D, and tilting the domestic playing field in favor of local companies will translate into the kind of edge that U.S. companies have outside the United States.[23] Will international customers who are now nervous about using clouds inside the United States be sanguine about using clouds inside China? Will those nervous about whether major U.S. software companies have put back doors in for the NSA's use trust that their Chinese equivalents have not done as much or more for China's use?

WAS THIS ALL AN EXERCISE IN NOSTALGIA?

Readers may be forgiven for wondering if the last few pages were an exercise in nostalgia for a pre-Snowden world. Many foreigners have convinced themselves that U.S. companies have been (at best) easy for the NSA to manipulate or (at worst) active connivers in corrupting their products or services to make the NSA's job easier. This has, as noted, affected cloud-related sales of U.S.

companies. In some cases, this has redoubled the interest that many countries, most notably China, have already evidenced in trying to transition from U.S. software and services to native and, they imagine, more secure brands. Granted, the Chinese suspected as much before Snowden's revelations, long practiced techno-nationalism (that predisposes them to favor local products even in contravention of free trade norms), and were driven to express their suspicions even more strongly after the May 2014 indictment of their citizens. But the Snowden revelations hardly helped the U.S. market position in China.

Therein lies an important lesson. If the United States (or any other country) would use the dominance of its software producers as a thumb on the scales of some potential conflict in cyberspace, it needs to avoid leveraging such dominance unless and until it really needs to (which, arguably, has not happened yet). Once leveraged, such dominance erodes and will not be available next time. Other countries may well weigh the economic benefits of allowing U.S. dominance (for example, because U.S. goods are better or at least better supported than their home-grown equivalents, and everyone profits from free trade) against the risk to their national security from doing so. Otherwise, while they suspect such dominance can be used against them, they have only suspicions to go on whilst the managers of U.S. companies swear to their neutrality and act the part. The hint of evidence gives wind to the suspicious and deflates the trusting.

This consideration leads to the question of why the NSA risked the ability to conduct cyberwar by taking actions that may erode the dominance of U.S. software manufacturers and service providers.[24] The publicly delivered (and most likely) rationale for its actions was to combat terrorism.[25] This then leads to the next question of whether enhancing the capability to go after technologically unsophisticated terrorists (whose capability to harm the United States was considerably reduced after post-9/11 fixes to airline and domestic security) justified eroding what could have been a considerable advantage in a conflict in cyberspace against large sophisticated foes.

A SILVER LINING ARISING FROM KERCKHOFF'S PRINCIPLE

Fortunately, even this (Snowden) cloud has a silver lining, but to explain why requires a small detour into one of the primary tenets of practical cryptography. Kerckhoffs's principle states that the strength of a cryptosystem should rest in the difficulty of finding the key, not the difficulty of figuring out the algorithm that uses the key to decrypt cypher text. Put another way, one ought to design systems under the assumption that the enemy will immediately gain full familiarity with them. Both are warnings against security through obscurity. A well-tested yet unbroken cryptosystem is more secure than one designed to repel investigation by being hard to figure out. In the former case, there are communities that want to see it work but, more important, want to ensure that it can—and the only way to do so is to try to break it themselves. The more their efforts fail, the greater the trust it merits. In the latter case, the only people who are testing the cryptosystem are those who would profit from seeing it broken, to wit, its enemies, who are motivated to devote the time to decipher the algorithm and then look for flaws in it—which are then more likely to persist if the products they are in lack the validation that a public algorithm would have given. This principle works in favor of the United States, whose products are global standards and hence the target of people who want such assurance about these products.

Reported efforts of the NSA to subvert some cryptographic protocols coupled with deep suspicions that the NSA tampers with all U.S. products (reality notwithstanding) have convinced China to build and use its own operating systems and routers (even with Huawei's market clout, Cisco still sells well in China, albeit not as well as before). Despite China's size, any operating system the Chinese use for their own purposes (perhaps a large chunk of the government subset of China's market) is likely to be far less well tested than Microsoft's (a universal standard).[26] Thus, barring the unlikely event that Microsoft Windows has deliberately opened back doors to the NSA (and as noted, China has been given most of the Windows source code, leaving that much less room for the back doors to hide), whatever China produces is bound to have more vulnerabilities by virtue of being less poked at (and perhaps because individual Chinese may be inhibited from bragging about the holes they found in an operating system favored by its authoritarian government). A similar logic suggests that the forced transition from Cisco to Huawei routers comes at the expense of China's cybersecurity. This is a victory for those who favor less cybersecurity in Chinese networks.

A more telling example is al Qaeda's attempt to roll its own cryptographic system. Bruce Schneier argues that this is an even bigger victory for the NSA, inasmuch as very few cryptographers are going to share their bug reports with al Qaeda.[27] Ditto for North Korea.[28]

THE INFLUENCE OF THIRD PARTIES ON THE BALANCE OF POWER IN CYBERSPACE

No net assessment in cyberspace can be complete without taking account of third parties. Earlier sections mooted the potential contribution of third parties in complicating the results of a strategic combat in cyberspace—but they remain "potential" because, apart from minor acts of web deface-ment and DDOS attacks, third parties have not played much of an offensive role in contests between two countries or in attacks on noted targets.

However, third parties have played a noticeable *defensive* role in cyberspace. The Belarussian firm VirusBlokAda was the one who found the Stuxnet worm. Kaspersky, operating on behalf of the ITU, found the Flame worm inside Iran's oil refining system.[29] These incidents raise the ques-tion of whether the outcome of a full-fledged conflict in cyberspace might not hinge on the efforts of talented third parties (not necessarily always from the former Soviet Union) who volunteer to help (ostensibly) in the interest of improving cybersecurity for everyone. This tendency may be all the greater if the attacks are anonymous or at least not formally acknowledged. That way, organiza-tions could help the victim (that everyone will assume fell to U.S. attacks, anyway) without facing accusations that they are working against U.S. interests (because the United States has not admitted to intruding into the target's systems).

During the Cold War (or even in a world where the Cold War had survived the Internet), such a development would be hard to imagine. Everyone in the developed world took sides, and the Soviet Union would have been very nervous about letting Western companies explore its systems. But today and for the foreseeable future, such a division does not exist. Not everything the United States does is applauded by others—the global (and even domestic) reactions to reports of the NSA's goings-on provide proof enough. Furthermore, it would not be hard to generate enough interna-tional sympathy for the victims of strategic cyberattacks to motivate a few outfits to lend a hand in forensic analysis, eradication, and bulwarking of attacked systems.

Perhaps needless to add, the hurdles to providing help in cyberspace are a great deal easier to surmount than would be the case for physical combat. No one has to show up in dangerous places or be blocked trying to get there. If the helping outfit has halfway decent operational security, it can keep its own name out of the news (indeed, analysts may not even know whose system has the malware they are looking at if even half-hearted efforts are made to mask that fact).

Granted, issues of trust may be more difficult to surmount in the vast anonymity of cyber-space: how would the besieged country assure itself that its "friend" is not secretly working with the United States? But there *are* ways. The party may be vouched for. The target country need not give the helper a live connection to a system if it can provide a sufficiently reliable image of the system. Even if the cost of accepting help is that the United States acquires a deeper insight into the target system, if the United States has already successfully attacked it, the target may assume that it has already lost control over that secret anyhow.

Thus, while the United States, on paper, can prevail in a cyberspace conflict with a developing country (despite the greater dependence of the United States on cyberspace), these odds should reflect the possibility that the country works with clever third parties.

CHAPTER 20
Responding to Cyberattack

Future administrations will have to consider new declaratory policies about what level of cyberattack might be considered an act of war, and what type of military response is appropriate.

—SECRETARY OF DEFENSE ROBERT GATES, 2008

If a country would respond intelligently to a cyberattack, it helps to understand the attacker's motives, factors that affect what should be revealed, the set of response options, and issues of timing a response.

FIRST-STRIKE CYBERATTACKS MAY HAVE A VARIETY OF MOTIVES

Understanding what the attacker wanted to achieve with the attack suggests what the target of a cyberattack might want to frustrate in order to dissuade further mischief. It may also provide clues about how the attacker will receive any retaliation. Sometimes the breadth, scale, sophistication, persistence, or use of a consistent set of methods can provide good hints. Small attacks, for instance, are unlikely to be carried out for coercion. Large attacks are unlikely to be accidental. Certain classes of attacks affect only the military and thus are meant to influence kinetic capabilities. Attacks that are hard to discover are usually not meant to elicit retaliation or to impress third parties. Context, such as the state of world tensions at the time, may provide a clue. In some cases, the attacker may make it fairly clear who is attacking and why. But in the end, whatever response ensues may well have to proceed under a thick fog of doubt about why it was done and by whom. So, here are some possible motives for an opening cyberattack.

Gain a Military Advantage

Cyberattacks can facilitate kinetic attacks; if so, the motive would be obvious fairly soon and the proper response would be informed by whatever kinetic attack ensues—unless the goal of the cyberattack is to *preempt* an attack by the target. The more intriguing cyberattacks are those not immediately followed up by the use of force. Some may be feints or distractions to divert attention. Some may be used to reduce the target's confidence in its own forces so as to perhaps gain a psychological edge in a crisis. In other cases, a follow-on attack was contemplated but abandoned at the last moment. The cyberattack may have failed to change the balance enough to make a kinetic attack worthwhile. Or warriors may have gotten cold feet (although, given the haste with which cyberattacks must be followed up, they only have a few days for their feet to cool). Again, in all such cases, the proper *immediate* response will be determined by political context and the military balance.

State Coercion

Earlier chapters analyzed this motive, and little more need be added—except that "shock and awe" may work more effectively against a military forced by physical circumstances to respond than against a society that faces no such forcing function. The potential to create "shock and awe" gets harder with every shock. Cyberattacks may, however, be used to put others on well-deserved notice that their civilian systems are too unreliable to allow the targets to confidently start a fight in cyberspace without suffering much in return. Again, the success of such a strategy will depend on what the target initially believed before the attack. If the attackers were already deemed capable, then further demonstration will say more about an attacker's intentions than its capability—and as noted, the more confidently defenders say, "We're all right," the greater the letdown if they are wrong. A variant on coercing the target is coercing big foes by going after their unsophisticated friends. It helps if the effects of such attacks are visible (for example, turning off the lights) even if other less visible attacks would have a greater impact on decisionmakers in the target state. Such a trade-off is less urgent with physical attacks.

Nonstate Coercion

This motive was exemplified by the attacks on Sony by North Korea. The effectiveness of such coercion depends, not surprisingly, on who is being coerced. Although states often stand on principle and refuse to yield to coercion, businesses may feel that they have little recourse if such stands harm their bottom line. A country's response has to weigh the message it sends to the attacker (for example, do not coerce private firms) against the message it sends to the victim (for example, do not come crying to us if you have not made sufficient efforts to protect yourself).

Civilian Preemption

One aim may be to silence certain communications (Georgia suffered that fate during the initial period of the 2008 Russian attack[1]) or divert an attack that would arise from bots. In most cases the attackers are just buying time; if the attackers are under threat, their efforts may be deemed by others to be understandable. Unless this is a case of mistaken identity or purpose, the target state's highest priority may be to reconstitute the preempted capability.

Test Attacks

Because the weapons of cyberwar do not lend themselves to Joint Munitions Effectiveness Manuals, countries serious about acquiring an arsenal, so to speak, may want to test how such attacks work and what reactions they engender in their targets. The Russians may have carried out such attacks on the electric power grid (via the Havex malware engineered to cross firewalls by being packaged as part of a software update), the French television station TV5, and perhaps even NASDAQ.

Malice

The attacker may wish to create problems for the sake of doing so (consider Iraq's spiteful attack on Kuwaiti oil fields in 1991 upon its troops departing the country). It may even have a rough redistributive justice in mind: as you did unto me, so shall I do unto you.

Discredit the Target

The attacker may want to erode the target's reputation and perhaps thereby convince third parties that the target cannot be a trustworthy partner in cyberspace (in which case the consequences of the attack must be visible). It may want to impose costs on the target or make the target's citizens lose faith in their own government. Many of North Korea's attacks on South Korea (for example, Dark Seoul) seem to have this character. It is unclear how well-considered such motives are. Not only can societies function even when most people have lost faith in the competence of governance institutions, but also in times of crisis, people fall back on governments for lack of any other protector.

Notwithstanding the U.S. government's competence or lack thereof after the September 11 attacks, citizens rallied behind their leaders.

Distract the Target

Similarly, attacks to hinder a government's ability to see or respond to a looming challenge have to assume that such a government is easily distracted. It must perforce assume that such a government lacks internal organizations (bureaucracies) able to function without day-to-day direction and the victim will not refocus on the attacker when the proximate crisis passes. Because warfare tends to concentrate the mind once hostilities begin or even appear imminent, the effects of a pure cyberattack are likely to recede rapidly in importance. Conversely, a major cyberattack, if traced back, is certain to focus the victim's attention on the attacker, thereby obviating any advantage of surprise that the attacker may have hoped to profit from.

Retaliation

The original attacker may have been retaliating against a very small attack that should have been ignored for its imperceptibility or against an act that is not traditionally held to be a casus belli. For instance, the target country may be supporting an economic embargo against the attacker. Or (qua the Sony attack) the attacker may be taking umbrage that a private corporation was planning to release a movie that showed the assassination of the attacker's supreme leader.

Elicit Retaliation

Perhaps Osama bin Laden, who saw the Soviet Union being mired in Afghanistan and collapsing thereafter, hoped for similar luck as the United States reacted to the September 11 attacks. Conflict between the United States and elements of the Islamic world might polarize the Islamic world and rally fundamentalists around ISIL.[2] The next such terrorist may embrace a similar logic but via cyberattack.

Crime

Completeness suggests that criminality and "hacktivism" should not be completely ignored as motives, but the motives of individuals do not transfer readily to states. A country could, for instance, attack the computers of a foreign bank to transfer funds to itself.[3] However, states have a great deal to lose if they are caught—and far better ways to raise revenue. Less implausibly, attacks could come from criminal elements protected by government officials for one of many reasons (for example, solidarity, blackmail, kickbacks), but if such crimes are discovered and attributed, the target could ask for prosecution first—and retaliation only after the cover-up has been established.

Protest

Finally, the attack could be a protest, but again, countries have other ways of garnering attention—that do not garner attention for the wrong reason.

SOME SUPPOSED ATTACKS ARE NOT

What looks like a cyberattack carried out ab initio could be otherwise.

Mistaken Characterization

Some system compromises result from the inadvertent spread of malware generated for another purpose entirely. As noted, it is unclear whether Buckshot Yankee was a deliberate attack in its opening stages or the inadvertent spread of some malware.[4] More recently, the virus found in the networks of South Korea's nuclear plant may not have been deliberately planted but just got in; if so, it was just the background pollution of cyberspace.[5]

Mistaken Retaliation

The attacker could have suffered its own cyberattack and retaliated incorrectly. Apologies and compensation may put the matter to bed, but how often is error confessed? Although not a case of retaliation, after the United States shot down an Iranian Airbus in 1988, then–vice president George H. W. Bush proclaimed, in effect, that superpowers do not apologize (but they do pay compensation).

Accident

The attack could have been the inadvertent effect of something not expected to cause so large an effect. The attacker may have attempted to steal information or test the target system's reaction to a partial cyberattack but its efforts ended up erasing or corrupting important process-control files (as reported, albeit baselessly, of the alleged cyberattack on Florida power). Or there might have been an unexpected interaction between the breaking-and-entering activities and the defense mechanisms of the target system.

SHOULD THE TARGET REVEAL THE CYBERATTACK—AND WHEN?

The likelihood that what is an attack will, in fact, be revealed as one should reflect the visibility of the effects multiplied by the likelihood that they will be publicly ascribed to a cyberattack (rather than to human error, physical accident, or buggy software). Both halves of the equation are far from certain. Cyberespionage is rarely apparent until an investigation reveals it (for instance, by finding someone's information where it ought not to be). Corruption may go unnoticed until a discrepancy appears between what a system does and what it should do. Sometimes even disruption may go unnoticed; for example, if a sensor is silent, it may be unclear whether such silence means it had nothing to report or it has been tampered with.

When an attack is correctly characterized, full disclosure, one might think, ought to be the best policy. Governments too often believe they can control information much better than they do.[6] Very post hoc revelation eats at government credibility—not to mention competence if playing catch-up with events makes the government look bad. Revelation is even more necessary if the target state is going to respond visibly, either with retaliation or with legal, diplomatic, or economic measures. Going public provides an opportunity to be clear about the aims of the response. Incidentally, revelation may also be necessary for sub rosa retaliation (see below). Just because the retaliator is silent about the attack does not mean the attacker (as the target of retaliation) will be silent about the counter-retaliation.

Yet silence has its virtues. Revelation may expose the fecklessness of the target's system security, reducing the public confidence in it and making it a target for repeat (or third-party) attacks.[7] Evidence to support the attack claim may reveal sensitive information about system security. Silence, after all, is not the same as doing nothing—just not doing something publicly (sub rosa responses are still available for undeclared attacks).

If the target does not follow up its claim of an attack with attribution, its inaction could raise the difficult "why now" question and encourage others to conclude as they will about the target's willingness to finger attackers. Announcing a poorly supported attribution allows the (alleged) attacker to scream, "Slander!" as North Korea did.

Once it has revealed the attribution, the potential retaliator may have to resist pressure from its public to retaliate and from others (often foreigners) not to. When the United States announced it would retaliate for the Sony attack, it stated that it would do so when and in a manner that it thought best—with the caveat that "some [responses] would be seen, some may not be seen."[8] That the American people did not rise up and demand reprisals then and there helped give the president working room. It is not clear that such a formulation would suffice if the pressure to retaliate were strong. Israel has repeatedly proved that it does respond to physical attack and provocation. No one, not even Israel, has much of a record in cyberspace. Thus, in the absence of such credibility, some sort of decision on retaliation may have to follow quickly once attribution is announced (and as of spring 2016, nothing impressive had followed the Sony attack). The longer the gap between attribution and retaliation, the more time the forewarned attacker has to prepare for a return blow, especially if by cyberattack.[9] If retaliation is delayed, third parties (for example, super-patriot hackers) may take matters into their own hands—but policymakers should recognize that they may do so in any case, even after retaliation has taken place (and it is unclear how effectively they could harm the attacker). Indeed, within hours after the United States officially declared that it was North Korea that attacked Sony, North Korea's access to the Internet was cut off for much of a day. Most indications were that the United States did not carry it out even though it initially appeared as though it had. Because the bandwidth going into North Korea is so small, any number of parties could have done it.[10] With third-party retaliation, the target loses some control over events, but the attacker cannot use the threat of counter-retaliation to avoid paying some price for the original attack.

In some cases, attribution may take a few weeks (as it did in the Sony case), or it may require months and years of work. Even in the physical world, a dozen years separated the Lockerbie crash and a court conviction. In the United States, successful prosecution of a crime requires the marshalling of evidence of judicial quality (for example, "beyond a reasonable shadow of doubt"). The decision to retaliate, however, can be informed by intelligence information and does not require utter certainty. If investigators are unsure who did it, however, they may also not know whether the case is a criminal matter or a military or intelligence matter. Jurisdictional conflicts between the criminal, military, and intelligence authorities (also known as United States Code Title 18, Title 10, and Title 50 authorities) could further delay attribution of a cyberattack.

Is retaliation delayed retaliation denied? Eventual punishment for crimes is considered justified; it is less clear whether the prospect of eventual punishment would deter a state-sponsored cyberattack. Because criminal justice systems have hundreds of years of history, no one doubts the will of states to detect and punish long-past crimes. In cyberspace, which has (as of spring 2016) yet to see its first open retaliation, the principle is not so well burnished and thus may be doubted.[11] Until retaliation actually occurs, deterrence qua judicial punishment may lack credibility. If the attack has coercive elements, the coercion may linger. Attackers, for their part, may see no reason to stop attacking. They cannot distinguish between the target's lacking a deterrence policy and its taking time to retaliate. A lack of will, a lack of capability, and a lack of justification all explain inactivity.

By the time the knowledge arrives that provides clarity for retaliation, it may be overtaken by events. The attacking state may be on better terms with the target (as was Libya vis-à-vis the West by 2001 when Lockerbie was in the courts). Late retaliation may sour a relationship that the target may come to value. The attacker's regime may have left, and successor regimes may have in effect disavowed earlier actions. Irrespective of regime, if too much time goes by, the attacker may consider that the rationale for retaliation was just an excuse—especially if there were no new attacks.[12]

NON-RETALIATORY RESPONSES

Many responses to cyberattacks are within the rights of sovereign states and ought not to raise questions about the use of (virtual) force. In some cases, the hackers can be prosecuted, especially (in the unlikely case) if the attacking country cooperates (for example, because it was unaffiliated with the government or, if affiliated, then a rogue attacker).[13] Individuals, even those in official positions asked to carry out implied instructions, may be deterred the next time; ditto for higher-ups. Attack methods may be legitimately laid out in the course of prosecution. If the attacking state balks, perhaps for such reasons, its lack of cooperation provides an opportunity for the target state to press the matter to convince others that the attacker has something to hide.[14] But if the attacker lives under the protection of a not-altogether-friendly country (and avoids foreign travel[15]), the question is less criminal than political.

If prosecution is unlikely, the United States can bar the entry of named individuals or prevent them from doing business here. It can forbid organizations under U.S. regulation (notably banks) from doing business in such countries or with certain organizations and individuals. By defining a cyberattack as terror, it could brand accused countries of sponsoring terrorism.

If public attribution is the primary response, the risks and complications—as well as the benefits—of retaliation are avoided. A few motives for cyberattack would shrivel in the sunlight of disclosure. If the attacker thought the target attacked first, disclosure could help clear up misunderstandings. Disclosure alone might persuade the attacker to tighten control over its rogue operatives. Attacks meant to boost the attacker's prestige (relative to the target) could backfire if the existence and purpose of such attacks were revealed. The same holds with more force if the attacks were designed to get a third party in trouble. If the motive was weak but the fear of disclosure was great, the attacker could see the downside of starting trouble.

If the U.S. accusations against Chinese cyberespionage (admittedly, not an attack) are any indication, the attacker may deny and keep on denying its involvement in the face of what a neutral party would consider conclusive evidence. The accused may demand evidence; if it asks for specific evidence, it may force the accuser into a difficult choice: refuse to hand it over and thereby cast doubt on the case, or hand it over and reveal forensic sources and methods, the knowledge of which suggests what to avoid to evade attribution. If serious purposes, such as strategic coercion or operational cyberwar, are involved, disclosure alone may not do much more than cause temporary embarrassment, if even that.

How hard to push is an open question. What would be gained by continuing to show the attacker in a bad light on this issue? Can the rest of the world be convinced to pay attention and align against the attacker, or will the target state get the reputation of being a hapless whiner, seeking to make something out of virtual nothings? Need the target be completely innocent of any similar mischief itself to be a credible accuser? The ability to garner allies directly affects the efficacy of a diplomatic or economic response. The imposition of unilateral restrictions, even by the United States, may hurt the imposer more than the imposed upon. This is why *who* the attacker is makes a great difference. Limiting the attacker's use of cyberspace may be poetic justice of sorts, but pressing the world community to cut the attacker off completely would probably be impossible and might backfire (an isolated attacker may behave worse).[16]

Whether and how one country presses another should depend on what else is on its agenda. Take the U.S.-Chinese relationship. The United States simultaneously wants the Chinese to help it keep North Korea under control (and not test nuclear weapons), not press its maritime claims in the South China Sea, buy U.S. Treasury bills, and reduce carbon emissions. If the United States were to add "behave nicely in cyberspace" to that list and could get past the expected denials ("we *do* behave nicely" or "*you* don't behave nicely"), it might have to decide what it was willing to give up to reach a mutual accommodation.[17] Would it put more on the table (that is, do more of what China wants the United States to do) or cut back on U.S. demands? If the United States wants it all, can it expect its allies to join in pressuring China, when their agendas might be completely different (they themselves might want to see less U.S. cyberespionage)? The ability of the United States to persuade China (during the Xi-Obama 2015 summit) to agree not to carry out economically motivated cyberespionage may belie such cautions, but what issues did the United States avoid pressing China on in order to win such agreement?

With a country whose cooperation in other matters is less critical (say, Russia, for argument's sake; it buys fewer U.S. Treasury bills), enforcing good conduct in cyberspace may come higher on the U.S. agenda. The bargaining leverage may come from being more willing to apply pressure.

ECONOMIC RESPONSES

A nation with which the United States trades (notably China) may be pressured against cyberattacks by threatening a trade war—unless a trade war would rise spontaneously as a result of cyberattack.

To illustrate as much, consider the conflict scenario described in Richard Clarke's *Cyberwar*. China claims the entire South China Sea. The United States says no and by way of warning, it conducts military exercises with concerned Southeast Asian friends. The United States also leads an attack in cyberspace, first by sending China a warning in the form of an image of a sinking ship e-mailed from within China's supposedly closed military network, and then by turning off the power around the ports at which a potential Chinese amphibious invasion of disputed islands is being assembled. This cyberattack unfortunately blacks out the province of Guangdong. China retaliates in kind against San Diego—and also blacks out more of the West Coast than intended. Things go from bad to worse. Key financial databases are scrambled, and the control computers for the major U.S. railroads and airlines go down. So the United States ups the ante only to discover that China has disconnected itself from the Internet, thus blocking the most obvious route into its cyberspace, and has phased down power interconnections among its regional power grids, thus limiting the possibility of cascading failures. Finally, China placed its railroads under manual control. In the end, the United States decides it has less stomach for conflict in cyberspace than the Chinese appear to and throws in the towel.

This weekend-long scenario ended before each side's susceptibility to a trade war was introduced. But in the real world, matters might have lasted long enough to bring trade policy into play. China's willingness to cut itself off from the Internet is likely to affect its ability to export. China's export sector, much of which consists of products made to order for large customers (as long as few Chinese companies have a strong brand presence), depends on large data flows. Some are associated with product specifications from and production coordination with U.S. manufacturers; some exchange sales data from U.S. marketers. If the disruption lasts more than a few weeks, Western investors in China could lose money. China's attraction as a manufacturing base would sink relative to other low-cost producers. Meanwhile, U.S. store shelves would start looking threadbare, and large U.S. exporters would see order books shrink.

Were China's efforts to include supply-chain attacks, the damage to the United States may be much sharper, depending on how many zombie components exist in U.S. systems and whether they can be accessed and activated by hackers when needed. A scenario of a supply-chain attack outside the context of war is implausible largely because the effects they would produce are temporary while the blowback would persist. Zombie components can be replaced over time—admittedly, months and perhaps years, compared with the hours and days associated with restoring penetrated systems.

But discovery of such supply-chain attacks would put China's export base—particularly its electronics export base—at great risk. The echoes may well last a generation; indeed, China's decision, in the wake of some dispute over islands, to stop exporting rare earths (notably to Japan) came back to haunt it as other customers have proven willing to pay a premium for resources (and not just rare earths) coming from a secure source.

In deciding whether to escalate from cyberwar to a trade war, other factors enter the equation. Is the cost of a trade war low compared to whatever concessions are entailed in losing a cyberwar? Can a credible threat to start a trade war convince the other side not to take advantage of its superior cyberwar capability? Will the other side back down first? Would the ever-tightening chain of global sourcing also make noncombatant states much worse off? How much damage would a trade war wreak on the world trade system?

Popular reaction to a cyberattack by China would also have to be taken into account. The prospect of a boycott may be scarier than the prospect of retaliation from a country that could suffer counter-retaliation. Individuals might ponder the prospect that their country may suffer as a result of their collective actions, but unless they are worried about getting caught for doing something illegal, they themselves are not at risk.

SUB ROSA CYBERWAR

War tends to be obvious. A Pole waking up in September 1939 facing a German tank would probably be under no illusions about what is being done by whom. Few leaders have the effrontery to deny as much.[18] All this is not necessarily so in cyberspace.

Accordingly, one can define sub rosa attack and retaliation as those operations not obvious to the public. They are distinguished in large part by their targets more than just by their techniques. Eligible targets might be those that belong to parts of the government or to internal systems of institutions likely to keep matters private (so that, by contrast, power grids might be off-limits) and whose difficulties either do not create obvious effects outside the gates or can credibly be explained as accidents if they do. The best targets of sub rosa cyberattacks are those whose very existence target states are reluctant to admit (that noted, many such systems are isolated and thus very hard to penetrate). Open societies such as the United States do not offer as good a set of targets for a sub rosa attack because of the difficulty of keeping such attacks secret. Similarly, because secrecy is emphasized in war, states at war offer more sub rosa targets than those at peace.

Normally, coercion—especially against democratic states—requires that the pain be publicly visible and hard to explain away. Yet adversary actions may coerce leaders without the public being the wiser. Often, the less the public knows, the more easily leaders can offer hidden concessions.[19] As long as the policies that result from making concessions do not appear too foolish or too inexplicable, leaders need to hide only the fact that their policy choices were driven by fear. Keeping mum has other advantages for the target. Reducing the public itch for revenge (or its desire to demonstrate resolve) may facilitate negotiations or mutual de-escalation. Obscuring the fact of or at least the damage from the attack may also mask the state's vulnerabilities from the eyes of third parties (even if the attacker will know which vulnerabilities it had exploited). Done right, therefore, sub rosa responses are likely to be less destabilizing than overt attacks and responses; done wrong, they are likely to be perhaps worse for their having been sneaky. For sub rosa attacks to work, though, the attacker's leaders must also keep silent (contrast this with someone who "accidentally" let self-congratulating PowerPoint slides appear on YouTube after Stuxnet).

One way to understand basic sub rosa responses is to see them within the context of a broader attack-response matrix. The attacker has three options: an overt attack (which is noticeable and acknowledged or of otherwise unmistakable origin), a public attack (noticeable by the public but not acknowledged by the attacker), and a covert attack (whose effects are hard to see and thus whose origins are not at issue). If the target chooses to retaliate, it can retaliate openly, retaliate in a public manner, or retaliate covertly.

If the attack is overt, the target is almost being dared to respond. It could take the dare openly. Even if it would avoid credit for responding, it could be assigned credit anyway because it alone has an obvious motive. It could respond covertly, leaving the original attacker with a choice: reveal the retaliation and perhaps the justification of its original attack, or let retaliation pass without comment and refrain from openly boasting that it attacked with impunity. If the target state retaliates quietly and the original attacker keeps at it, the target state may have to answer to its public (and others) about why it did nothing. Its motive for keeping matters covert may be the hope that it can persuade the attacker to stop because it will not be obvious to others *why* the attacker stopped; the attacker saves face by not being seen as backing down under the target's counterpressure.

If the attack is public, the target's choices depend on its confidence in knowing who did it. Overt or public responses present similar considerations. Even with public responses, the target may be blamed for the retaliatory cyberattack because it alone had a clear motive (even if other countries that were also attacked or that even just carry a grudge against the attacker might also have done it). The only reason to deny what is otherwise clear is to indicate a desire to keep things from getting out of hand in ways that let both sides save face while they come to a modus vivendi. The target could concede that it had been attacked but claim that it knew too little to warrant a counterattack and hope that the original attacker also keeps quiet. A covert response will not deter third parties, though.

If the attack is covert, the responder has a deeper dilemma. It can respond overtly in order to make an example of the attacker; the attacker may then deny its culpability and may even demand proof that the initial attack took place. An overt response may help mobilize public opinion against the attacker, particularly if the initial (covert) cyberattack presages overt hostilities or probes the other side's will. A public response may be chosen because it permits a wider target list; one need not avoid striking systems whose induced failure would be clear. If the original attacker later reveals the retaliation, its doing so will suggest to others who started things. The risk to the retaliator is if it is fingered, it cannot argue that it was attacked first covertly without its case appearing contrived.

The purest case is one in which each side attacks the other covertly. The attacker may wish to pressure the target state's leadership without causing a public reaction that may constrain that leadership's ability to respond by cutting back or stopping. The retaliator may wish to discourage further attacks without riling the attacker's public. In other words, each side believes that the other side wants to keep the public out of the dialogue. In the event that both sides' leadership consists of hawks afraid that their publics are dovish, they can carry on at each other without undue interference. And so the game goes on until someone concedes (either explicitly or implicitly) or until one or the other side's attacks are made public. One side could do this itself. Or some action in cyberspace may end up not being as covert as the actor originally thought.[20] Alternatively, the exchange may continue indefinitely until enough target systems have so hardened themselves that attacks are no longer worthwhile.

The retaliator may also wish to limit itself to covert responses because of attribution problems. If it is confident that it knows who the attacker is but cannot or will not provide a convincing rationale to others, then a covert response puts the onus on the target to explain that it is being attacked and why. But a covert response has a sneaky way of indemnifying the retaliator against the consequences of its own attribution errors. If the retaliator is correct, the attacker will probably have a good idea who hit back: the target of the initial attack (unless the attacker hit many countries at once). If the retaliator is incorrect, however, the unfortunate victim of retaliation may be left hurt but confused; it does not know about the original attack and therefore has no reason to suspect the retaliator—barring, of course, other evidence.

Sub rosa cyberattacks can be quite tempting, particularly within the covert community. No one has to produce evidence of attribution if the attack is a reprisal. There is also less pressure to reveal the particulars (methodologies and targets) of the original attacks that sparked reprisal cyberattacks. No one has to justify the reprisal to a potentially skeptical public (note the comparison to UAV strikes on individuals where a country is judge, jury, and executioner). Because there are fewer people likely to know about the planning for the attack, there is less need to gain permission to carry it out (as President Obama had to seek in order to respond to Syria's use of chemical weapons). Thus, the victims of reprisals can pretend that nothing happened if they believe that they have no good counter-escalation options or wish to contain the level of overall damage. The lack of prisoners also explains why covert operations in cyberspace carry less risk than those in the physical world.

Yet what tempts can also trap. Those who work in the highly classified arena can avoid the *public* oversight under which the more overt parts of the national security community operate (private oversight exists, but it is carried out by members of the same community that inevitably share similar assumptions and perspectives). If the cyberattackers wish to justify their actions, they have more control over what evidence is collected and presented—and less to fear from contradictory material provided by neutral or hostile parties. They can evade the question: if the evidence of who carried out the original attack will be unconvincing to others, how good can it really be? Members of the covert community, despite their personal probity and honesty, tend to operate in a sealed world. Mistakes (such as would be judged so by the greater public) can go uncorrected for longer than those made by public figures.

Sub rosa strategies are also hostage to the discretion exercised by the other side, not to mention accident and error. Once revelations start and what was sub rosa is exposed to sunlight, many parties will be embarrassed—not only the attackers on both sides but also the targets for being vulnerable and hiding the fact that these vulnerabilities were exploited. Although a rationale for keeping matters covert is to ease coming to terms later, covert communities are not always motivated by the desire to reach accommodation with the other side. Indeed, by virtue of their occupation, they tend to distrust everyone else. So each side has to weigh whether it is better off pulling back the shades on these sub rosa exchanges or letting matters continue on their shadowy course. The result may be a game of chicken. Each knows that revelation will make its side look bad not only to the public but perhaps also to its own masters, but each may hope that the *threat* of revelation may make the other side accede. Each side may therefore be in a position to concede things to hide its mutual activities in ways that might be impossible were its "negotiations" subject to public scrutiny. The retaliator may threaten to go public during the implicit or explicit negotiations in the sub rosa exchange, but it is unclear whether such a threat would be taken seriously. Once the crisis starts, however, the national security elite would be acting against type to relinquish that sort of control to its enraged population.[21]

The assumption that no one third-party state knows about the original attack may also be wrong; two states with little in common but their dislike of the United States often swap intelligence.[22] The original attack might not have been so secret prior to the attack, or its existence might have been revealed after the fact. Such a revelation may be deliberate (perhaps someone in the know is bothered by any major mischief in cyberspace) or may simply reflect the universal difficulty of hiding secrets. Finally, the retaliator may have overstated its ability to keep itself anonymous. A country that suffered undeserved retaliation may not be certain who did it, but its suspicions may sour its relationship with the retaliator—and if it did not know why the retaliator acted as it did, it may be angrier than if it understood that retaliator's motivation.

DOING NOTHING IS ALSO AN OPTION

The do-nothing option is not entirely crazy. The failure to respond may indicate one of two things: that the resulting annoyance is beneath its notice, or that the fault is with those whose cybersecurity was too weak. Either way, the target is unmoved. If the attacker's rationale for carrying out a cyberattack required a reaction—whether from anger or fear—its strategy will have been defeated.

An attacker that hears a yelp of pain may figure that it is close to achieving its goals—giving wind to its cyberattack strategy. For a country's chief intelligence officer to testify that cyberattacks constitute its most pressing short-term national security concern hardly promotes insouciance. Conversely, a country that can foster the impression that it can bear the pain of cyberattacks, keep calm, and carry on reduces such temptation. How the *attacker* responds to the target's insouciance may depend on whether the cyberattack was its best punch. If so, it may give up (at least in cyberspace). Otherwise, it could try to land a bigger punch and see if that would have any effect. In the latter case, the target's insouciance strategy might have backfired, and retaliation may be in order. But it need not be. Because cyberattacks rarely hurt anyone or break anything, calls for action are unlikely to have the emotional resonance that would arise from a bloody terrorist attack.

Broadcasting a disinclination to respond may convey a country's refusal to own a crisis arising from the inability of private infrastructure owners to protect their own systems. After all, the government has little privileged insight into specific vulnerabilities of private systems, and that is exactly as most private system owners want. Conversely, any promise to raise an attack on a private company to a federal case could well weaken its incentive to protect its own systems for the sake of third parties (for example, those that would lower power if electric facilities were hacked). The threat that angry customers could sue the company ought to be uppermost in the minds of its chief information security officers (and their bosses and boards). Any policy that stipulates or even hints that a cyberattack is an act of war (or even terrorism) tends to immunize private system owners against such risk. A cyberattack would be considered on a par with other events (for example, bad weather, being bombed from above) that lie beyond the organization's power to abate—even though this is demonstrably not true.[23] Private organizations—notably infrastructure providers—could declare force majeure and thereby evade their obligation to provide continuous service. Similarly, persuading the public that such attacks are beyond what infrastructure owners can protect themselves against would reduce political pressure on them to keep their systems clean and could induce owners to postpone the vigorous search for vulnerabilities in their own systems.[24]

CONCLUSIONS

In the end, a country may retaliate immediately in response to a cyberattack. But it should at least consider the attacker's motives in or before doing so in order to assure itself that it is defeating the attacker's strategy as well as altering the attacker's calculus. Even if it retaliates, it need not do so immediately. And, there are responses other than state-on-state retaliation.

CHAPTER 21
Deterrence Fundamentals

History teaches us that a purely defensive posture poses significant risks. . . . When we apply the principle of warfare to the cyber domain, as we do to sea, air, and land, we realize the defense of the nation is better served by capabilities enabling us to take the fight to our adversaries, when necessary, to deter actions detrimental to our interests.
—GEN. JAMES CARTWRIGHT, USMC, COMMANDER, U.S. STRATEGIC COMMAND, 2007

When atomic bombs were first used, most strategists thought of them as powerful and efficient means for doing what the United States already demonstrated it had the capacity to do—devastate cities and kill tens of thousands of people in the process. But it quickly dawned on some that changes in quantity—one aircraft could substitute for thousands—were changes in quality. Normally, for instance, if you could encounter an attack fleet of one hundred aircraft and shoot down ninety, you had a spectacular victory and the damage to your city would be correspondingly reduced. But if the ten survivors were carrying atomic weapons, millions of your citizens would die anyway. Bernard Brodie publicly intuited in 1946 that the point of having atomic weapons was not to use them, but to keep the other side from using them—by threatening to use yours on them if they did (and hoping never to have to make good on that threat).[1]

Thus was born deterrence theory, and RAND in the 1950s was where the theory was refined.[2] There, analysts explored trade-offs between the countervalue use of nuclear weapons (to hit cities) and the counterforce use of nuclear weapons (to attrite the other side's forces, notably nuclear forces), the need for a second-strike capability (it was not enough to have nuclear forces if the other guy could wipe all or most of them out before you had much chance of using them), and extended deterrence (how to assure European allies the United States would treat a nuclear attack on one of them as if it had hit U.S. soil).

Now fast forward. Cyberattacks are a large and seemingly growing problem where offense appears stronger than defense. Even with $80 billion spent worldwide on defense every year, breaches are reported all the time. Many have therefore suggested that the United States pursue a deterrence policy in the (warranted) belief that it kept the Cold War cold and the (questionable) belief that the lessons of one form of combat can be transferred to another.

From a policy perspective, the decision to embrace deterrence[3] as a policy has several possible components that can be phrased as questions:

- Should the United States rely on deterrence in the hope that it can substitute for defense (or at least significantly reduce the level of expenditures on defense)?[4]
- Should the United States make its deterrence policy explicit and deterministic?
- Should the United States invest in the ability to carry out retaliation in cyberspace (*pace* General Cartwright's quote)?
- Should the United States retaliate for attacks of the sort and level that it has endured from other countries (notably Iran and North Korea)?
- Should the United States *ever* retaliate for a cyberattack?

Deterrence, to begin with, is *not* the same as retaliation. It is a state of mind one hopes to induce in foes that persuades them not to attack; it depends on the *threat* of retaliation.[5] Retaliation comprises the punishment that takes place after the attack. Retaliation is what happens when deterrence, as such, fails. Somewhat paradoxically, retaliation may be part of the strategy of restoring deterrence after it has failed. To wit: "We said we were going to punish you if you attacked; you did; we did; now, don't do it next time." Although deterrence (by punishment) requires the ability and willingness to retaliate after an attack, retaliation is measured in terms of post-attack effect while deterrence is measured in terms of pre-attack dissuasion. It entails a capability in cyberspace to do unto others in response to others doing unto us.[6] Nuclear retaliation could disarm *and* reinforce subsequent deterrence. Retaliation in cyberspace, as argued above, cannot disarm. Thus, retaliation has no other rationale but deterrence to fall back on.

CYBERDETERRENCE DIFFERS FROM NUCLEAR AND CRIMINAL DETERRENCE

Cyberdeterrence is symmetric (it takes place among peers within the international system) and has to be repeatable. In that respect, it differs from criminal deterrence (which is asymmetric) and nuclear deterrence (which may not be repeatable).

Symmetry means that the target country (the potential retaliator) does not, a priori, occupy a higher moral ground than the attacking country—as it does with criminal deterrence where the law has an authority that criminals lack. There is also no reason to believe that the target, by dint of being a target, can automatically win any confrontation with the attacker if things go too far. Thus, the retaliator for a cyberattack always has to worry about counter-retaliation (as it does in nuclear conflict) and cannot help but shape its deterrence policy with that in mind. Cyberdeterrence is not unique in being repeatable and symmetric. Such deterrence typically characterizes interactions among quarreling states (or quarreling tribes and gangs, for that matter), each on guard against depredations from the other side and each willing to defend itself against small slights. Deterrence in such situations does not necessarily keep the peace; in an anarchic system, violence is endemic. Fights, in retrospect, often look like they have no larger issues than themselves.

Criminal deterrence, the threat that crime will be punished, is repeatable and asymmetric. It has to be repeatable because many first-time offenders could become second-time offenders. The prospect of counter-retaliation from criminals, meanwhile, is rarely a serious problem in the United States and other developed countries. Police and other officials of the justice system are rarely at personal risk from those they prosecute, thanks in large part to the legitimacy the law is accorded and the latent ability of law enforcement to mass force against criminals. Countries or regions where this is not the case (for example, drug-infested regions in the Americas) are clearly troubled, and their criminal justice has been rendered far less effective. Cyberdeterrence has to be repeatable because no feasible retaliatory cyberattack is likely to eliminate the offending state, lead to its government's overthrow, or even disarm the state.[7] Thus, a country could attack, suffer retaliation, and live to attack another day.

Nuclear deterrence, for its part, is singular and symmetric. It is singular in that the point is to make the prospect so frightening that no one dares invoke it. If nuclear retaliation ensues, by the time retaliation and counter-retaliation have run their course, the landscape and hence the strategic circumstances underlying the deterrence are likely to have become quite different. One or both parties may have been eliminated or rendered powerless. The nature of deterrence the second time will also be different. The same largely holds true for heavy conventional deterrence: if retaliation is invoked, it too could run its course and lead to a major war, which one or another regime also may not survive.[8]

THE RATIONALE FOR DETERRENCE

One major purpose of a deterrence posture is to reduce both the likelihood of future attacks and the money that would otherwise have to be spent on defenses (in absence of deterrence); it would therefore be part of a cost-minimization strategy. Correspondingly, the case for cyberdeterrence—the threat or retaliation following a cyberattack—rests on two premises: that the level of damage from a cyberattack could be intolerable and that relying on defense is not cost-effective. The latter often rests on the premise that offense-defense curves *at levels that characterize today's conflicts in cyberspace* favor the offense: another dollar's worth of offense requires far more than another dollar's worth of defense to restore prior levels of security. Thus, defense alone may be a losing game. This is illustrated in the lower left-hand side of figure 21.1. Part of the reason offense is rather inexpensive at today's levels is that neither individual hackers nor their state sponsors are at risk—which means there is no cost in their trying repeatedly until they succeed (except, as noted, if they have hard-to-replace tools exposed by their efforts). The offense-defense curves at levels beyond today's (the rest of figure 21.1) are unknown. They might still favor the offense. If true, countries might adopt a competitive strategy in which they threaten adversaries and force them to go bankrupt paying for cybersecurity—were not gearing ratios between raising offensive expenditures, the resulting additional threat to adversaries' networked systems, their perception of the additional threat, and their spending more on defense as a result so speculative. Alternatively, there may be an upper limit to the damage that hackers can do, regardless of how hard they try; for instance, it may take heroic efforts to compromise air-gapped systems to the point at which they can be commanded in near real time.

What we do know is that the failure to have an explicit deterrence policy has yet to cost the United States anything—*if nothing done to the United States to date has merited retaliation.*[9] In other words, the reason that the United States had yet to retaliate for any cyberattack as of spring 2016 was not for lack of a policy but for lack of an event that would warrant it. No country has yet been attacked at a sufficiently serious level by another country in cyberspace. Thus, it may already be profiting from an implicit deterrence stance that warns other states against any seriously hostile act. This is not to say that state hackers have given U.S. systems a pass; witness the attacks on Las Vegas Sands Corporation and Sony. State-sponsored hackers have undoubtedly penetrated U.S. systems, if

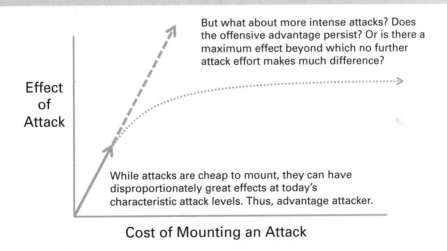

But what about more intense attacks? Does the offensive advantage persist? Or is there a maximum effect beyond which no further attack effort makes much difference?

Effect of Attack

While attacks are cheap to mount, they can have disproportionately great effects at today's characteristic attack levels. Thus, advantage attacker.

Cost of Mounting an Attack

FIGURE 21.1 COST-EFFECTIVE CURVES FOR CYBERATTACKS

only to steal information. But in the absence of serious attacks, adding a threat to retaliate in cyberspace offers little upside in terms of reducing *today's* run of attacks.

The attraction of cyberdeterrence is that, if it works, it can reduce the cost of defending systems against *potential* attacks. Instead of having to put more money into making systems more secure, the defender inhibits the attacker's efforts by threatening retaliation against successful attacks (or, if the defender is sufficiently confident in its forensics even when the attack fails, then against serious attempts to attack).[10] If the attacker can be persuaded to reduce its efforts in the face of punishment, the defender can save some of what it would have spent on defense and still achieve the same level of cybersecurity. A variant on this argument is that without deterrence, the United States would have to spend money it could not afford to protect its critical infrastructure against an unlikely but not-provably-impossible full-press attack by an extraordinarily skilled state actor.[11]

How much money a successful cyberdeterrence policy can save should not be overstated. Even in a world in which no country penetrated the computers of other countries or offered to protect those who did, the bulk of cybersecurity spending would still be necessary to deal with insiders, rogue individuals, criminals, and other nonstate threats. Furthermore, unless such retaliation was extended to cover cyberespionage (which is far more common than cyberattack), money would have to be spent on cybersecurity to protect organizational secrets and personally identifiable information. The United States has not disavowed cyberespionage nor has it offered to do so if others pledged to; no other country has, either. Thus, the amount of money saved by even a completely credible cyberdeterrence policy would be quite modest.

A case for deterrence has to presume potential foes have preparations for cyberattacks that go much further than anything seen to date. Rather than let matters get to that pass, the argument goes, the United States should make clear to potential attackers that reprisals will follow. This could affect their calculations today over what to invest in such a capability. If they are dissuaded today, the odds of a full-fledged conflagration tomorrow go down. But would it?

Last is the argument that the failure of the United States to respond to a cyberattack may persuade others that it will not respond to physical attacks either—*unless* the United States made it obvious that it treats the two differently (which it does not). More broadly, if one believes that *foes* will see cyberwar as a real contest (but with nonviolent effects), then to some, there can be no acceptable outcome except victory. If the North Koreans attack the United States and the United States does *not* respond, then they have won, and therefore we have lost—and losing is unacceptable. If, presumably, the other side will attack until victory is achieved, then deterrence—and its instantiation, retaliation—may in fact be a cost-effective way to minimize future costs; but that is a lot of *ifs*.

WHAT MAKES DETERRENCE WORK?

Civilization is said to advance when societies make the transition from arbitrary rule to explicit rules. People can govern their conduct with the expectation that if they stay within the lines, their lives and property are safe. The same logic applied to international relations would state: rules moderate the behavior of states that otherwise exist in an inherently anarchic environment. Rules, of course, are only hortatory unless there are ways to monitor compliance and punish noncompliance. Deterrence policies constitute a set of rules in the sense that a state declares that a particular behavior is unacceptable and, if such behavior is observed, will be countered with punishment.

The point of imposing rules is to change the calculus of the attacker to where the expected value of unwanted actions is negative.[12] The benefits of a cyberattack as far as the attacker is concerned are related to the odds of success and the useful consequences of success. If the threat of retaliation is absent, the attacker's costs are just the cost of mounting the operation. Deterrence then puts its thumb on the cost side by persuading the attacker that an attack *might* lead to retribution, which hurts the attacker (or the interests on behalf of which the attacker is acting). If victims of a cyber-attack lose more than attackers gain (as is ostensibly the case with vandalism), even a weak threat ought to tilt the logic against acting. This would leave a rational adversary no choice but to desist.

The calculus of deterrence takes place entirely in the attacker's head. Just because, by your estimates, the odds of your retaliation and the consequences to the attacker thereof *should* be sufficiently dissuasive does not mean that the odds as perceived by the attacker *are* dissuasive. Foes may believe that you lack the will to strike back or that they are invulnerable (no small consideration in cyber-war where vulnerability or even dependence is so hard to know). Or attackers may figure that there is value to standing firm before such deterrence threats, the better to communicate resolve and other manly virtues. Some aggressors are thus *more* likely to act if they are threatened by consequences.

Conversely, even a lame credibility posture may nevertheless look credible enough to the attacker to inhibit cyberattacks—which was the point. The attacker always has to factor in some likelihood that an attack will engender a response. The questions are: how likely and how bad?

A lot depends on the likelihood *in the mind of the attacker* that the target of the contemplated attack detects the cyberattack (something that is not obvious in a corruption attack), identifies the attacker correctly with an actionable level of confidence, judges that these attacks crossed some threshold, decides to strike back even in the face of counter-threats that the attacker can make to ward off retaliation, can strike back, and thereby cause the attacker real pain.

Bear in mind that with or without a deterrence policy, a thinking attacker will always go into the decision calculus with some notion about the possibility and pain of retaliation. An explicit deterrence policy may remind people of what they may have forgotten, but a declaration only succeeds as policy if it *shifts the odds* against the attack. The attacker may well reason that having to make such a retaliation threat explicit signals the retaliator's belief that the threat has not registered, thereby making the purported attacker wonder why something that should have been regarded as obvious had to be spelled out.

Attackers may not necessarily want such considerations to look as if they mattered. Doing so concedes that those who would deter can legitimately make the rules—a presumption that may not be shared by those who would be deterred. The latter may have to accede to the lower power position by accepting as much, or conceding to something inherently unfair.

Deterrence is also tethered to questions of legitimacy. To the defender, the cyberattack is illegitimate. If the attacker believes that earlier events legitimized the cyberattack, its concession to deterrence would indicate otherwise; hence it would want to delegitimize the application of the deterrence rule. It might do so in advance, arguing that, for instance, respectable states do make international threats for something as arcane as, say, the violation of intellectual property laws (if cyberespionage is at issue). It may offer counter-threats to change the retaliator's own calculus.

Where attribution is less than obvious, the attacker may want to react perversely. If it can make the target wonder whether attribution is correct, its leadership might reconsider its decision to keep hitting back (and question whether it really occupied the moral high ground). Assume a nonzero a priori doubt in the target's mind. If attribution is correct, the attacker may respond to retaliation (that exceeds what it had already conceded would happen) by rethinking the logic of cyberattack and backing off. If the target is incorrect and punishment is misdirected, the real attacker (which escaped punishment) has been given no reason to back off, and the presumed attacker cannot back off because it was not doing anything in the first place. Thus, if attacks continue after retaliation commences, the a posteriori odds that attribution is correct decline (because having little to no effect is only one of two possibilities), while the a posteriori odds that attribution is incorrect are unaffected (because having little discernable effect on future attacks is by far the most likely possibility if the true attacker was not affected). The probability needle swings toward the likelihood that attribution was in error. Thus, the failure of retaliation to make much difference may shake the target's confidence in its own powers of attribution. Accordingly, the attacker's strategy is to act as though it had nothing to do with the original attack. Since the attacker knows where the real evidence lies, it can feign a limited degree of openness to investigation. Meanwhile, attacks could continue, or they may stop because the attacker's strategy changed, the target's defenses are so good that nothing registers, or the attacker wants to reinforce the target's false belief of who attacked it.

Another consideration is that retaliation has to preserve some daylight both above and below the level of cyberattacks. If the retaliation promised or delivered against a cyberattack is comparable to, say, that delivered against a kinetic attack, then an attacker contemplating a cyberattack has no reason not to contemplate both if the combination gets it closer to its objectives. Conversely, if the target is already punishing the attacker severely for lesser or earlier infractions, the potential attacker may figure that nothing worse will happen if it goes ahead. As noted, the United States, for instance, cannot threaten to (re-)embargo Iran or embargo North Korea for cyberattacks after it has embargoed them for their nuclear programs.

THE CORE MESSAGE OF DETERRENCE

One way of understanding the many dilemmas of cyberdeterrence is through the core message of deterrence: *if you do this then that will be done.* The key words are "you," "do," "this," "that," and "(will be) done": to wit, attribution, detection, thresholds, capability (to punish), and determination. Such a statement fits the model of behavior modification that rule of law was invented to do (remember that deterrence is but one form of behavior modification).

An alternative formulation, "If you do this, then *I* will do that," would have put the emphasis on "I." Although clarity about *who* is retaliating helps the credibility of the threat, it suffices if the attacker believes that retaliation will come from somewhere. Indeed, declaring who "I" is gives attackers someone to counter-retaliate against: if you hit me back, I'll hit you back twice as strong. This can alter the calculus of the potential retaliator much as deterrence might alter the calculus of the potential attacker. If there is no "I," then counter-deterrence requires the attacker to threaten who it thinks "I" is or threaten someone else and hope the "I" cares.

Normally for attribution, "you" is a country. Individuals or even small groups do not carry out invasions or drop nuclear weapons, but small groups, even individuals, *can* carry out cyberattacks, perhaps quite devastating ones. This creates a disjunction between the attacker and the target of retaliation and thus raises questions of when and why a state can be held responsible for an individual's attack. This is more than a quibble; many current techniques of tracing attacks, if successful, terminate in a box and maybe a person but not a government. Finally, in common with most deterrence policies, those who would deter have to decide whether "you" refers to anyone or is tailored to a particular set of countries.

"Do" provides a reminder that the cyberattack has to be detected. For the larger, more obvious attacks, this is not a problem. For the smaller, more subtle attacks (particularly those that selectively corrupt records or instructions), it might be. If the proscribed act is cyberespionage or laying in an implant, discovery is not at all ensured.

The "this" has to be well communicated, specific (enough), and measurable, or at least to the point where there is some clarity on what was done. If the threshold for retaliation (rather than criminal prosecution) has any specificity, then some effort must be made to indicate where the threshold lies and how to measure it. But the "this" need not be confined to cyberattacks on U.S. soil. A nasty cyberattack on an international institution may hurt the global, hence U.S., economy either directly or indirectly by reducing confidence in international records systems (for example, bank records). Cyberwar erodes trust in people as well as systems. Getting away with cyberattacks because they hit a weak unallied state erodes the rule of law across the board.

The retaliator needs a credible "will"—the likelihood, in the mind of the potential attacker, that an attack will result in retaliation. An attacker may doubt the will to retaliate for many reasons, not least being that the retaliation will make life even worse for the target. Fortunately, the target need not prove the certainty of retaliation to gain the benefits of deterrence. A rational attacker may be dissuaded if the possibility of retaliation multiplied the extent to which the pain of retaliation exceeds the gain of attack. Yet the perceived odds of retaliation have to be high enough so that when it does come, it does not look entirely arbitrary (much as a one-in-a-million death-penalty response to jaywalking might). Nor should it look opportunistic to the point where the attacker, having been hit back, may reason: this was not retaliation, it was an attack under cover of retaliation that was carried out because circumstances were particularly propitious for the retaliator.

The "that" has to be sufficiently distasteful to the original attacker to, in fact, alter the calculus; that is, something must be held at risk. Whether the reaction is going to be in the physical world or in cyberspace matters. The attacker may reason that a physical attack is unlikely because it puts the two countries into a very different conflict than a tit-for-tat in cyberspace would. If the attacker then concludes that it has nothing vital at risk from a cyberattack that the retaliator can affect, the deterrence threat may be unconvincing. If, as suggested, successive rounds of retaliation yield less and less pain, then attackers may continue their mischief (albeit with reduced efficiency as the target also grows harder). Proving to a stubborn attacker that diminishing returns are not setting in may require multiple attacks—if possible.[13] Conversely, all this may be an academic quibble: despite professional optimism that the original vulnerability has been laid to rest, the public may believe otherwise, and it is the public's reaction that may shape the attacking state's behavior.

But need "this" and "that" be the same for every country? A state with a tailored deterrence policy sets different thresholds or imposes different classes of punishments on different states. It can pursue a tougher strategy against a potential attacker whose capability for counter-retaliation is weak or whose sensitivity to damage is high compared to a more cautious strategy against an attacker whose counter-retaliation can sting or whose sensitivity to damage is low. Some tailored threats are necessarily context-sensitive. In American eyes, it makes sense to draw a red line against Iran's acquisition of anti-ship missiles because Iran's leaders have made threats against Persian Gulf shipping and sponsored terror. But drawing the same red line against, say, Syria's acquisition of such weapons is different: the country threatens no one's shipping and has not sponsored much external terrorism. There is no easy equivalent to context specificity with cyberwar. Thus, tailoring—or, not to put too fine a point on it, inconsistency—comes at the expense of legitimacy. A cyberattack is essentially a crime, perhaps a high crime if damaging enough. Crime is crime. The punishment for crime should not depend on the power of the criminal. Hence, a tailored cyberdeterrence approach is not blind justice. Adopting such a policy can easily convince others that the goal of deterrence is not to reduce the likelihood of cyberattacks but to justify wielding yet another stick to beat up the usual suspects. For potential attackers to balk at carrying out a universally acknowledged crime is to concede to norms; to balk when the threat is against you is to concede weakness. What reduces legitimacy raises the cost of retaliating and thereby lowers its likelihood when the retaliator cares about the good opinions of others (as the United States does).

The statement "If you do this, that will be done" need not be explicit. The point is to get the prospect of retaliation inside the head of the potential attacker. It can be privately communicated. It can be implicit in a state's history or behavior. It can be inferred from the statements of those who can be said to speak for or at least predict the country's actions. Although stating it outright makes it more credible, this credibility is not free, as discussed below. An explicit statement makes it difficult for a state to back away from its commitment to retaliate—but, in the end, what matters is not what a state says, but what other countries believe. Conversely, it *cannot* be secret, either. Fans of the movie *Dr. Strangelove* may recall the good doctor plaintively asking the Soviet ambassador: "What's the point of having a doomsday machine if you don't tell anyone about it?" Similarly, any tailored thresholds or punishments also must be communicated to potential attackers—which implies some willingness to tolerate public disclosure that different attackers are treated differently (bear in mind that privately conveyed distinctions are only as private as those being threatened want them to be). A deterrence capability based solely on the ability to retaliate in cyberspace is subject to the same conundrum. How, in fact, do you tell anyone about it if the presence—and hence the efficacy—of such a capability is a secret and is, anyway, only as good as the target is vulnerable?

We will now argue that cyberdeterrence is problematic. The most commonly bruited problem is that "you" may not be easy to determine—a question of attribution. But other problems are that making "this" explicit requires establishing thresholds. Furthermore, making "that" fearsome (without overreacting) requires being able to convince the attacker of the effects of cyberattacks (if retaliation is to be in kind), which is not so easy. Even if the "will" component is less fraught than for nuclear retaliation, it is not a given.

Finally, every deterrence policy needs an assurance component: not only "we will do X if you do Y" but "we will do X *only if* you do Y" (although Y may stand for a range of unwanted behavior that includes cyberattack).

One alternative to an explicit policy is to wait for easy-to-attribute attacks, retaliate in kind, and if these retaliatory attacks succeed, retroactively justify them. Others could infer a deterrence policy (and a threshold) from such action. The advantage of waiting for a good opportunity is that it tamps down whining about insufficient attribution. But will a one-time response mean that a deterrence policy *will* be inferred? Other potential attackers may focus on the weakness of the country that suffered retaliation. Retaliation, itself, may lead to counter-retaliation or escalation that suggests that the retaliator learned its lesson and would not retaliate further. If the goal is to establish a policy of deterrence by action, there is no requirement that retaliation actually force the other side to stop. But if it does not, the inescapable conclusion is that the deterrence policy, when called for, did not, in fact, deter.

By way of recapitulation, therefore, the key prerequisites of a deterrence policy are credibility (the will to retaliate), attribution (the ability to determine who to retaliate against), thresholds (the distinction between acts that merit retaliation and acts that do not), and capability to retaliate. The next chapters discuss each in turn.

CHAPTER 22
The Will to Retaliate

D eterrence is fine if it never has to be called upon. But when an attack does come, the victim has to weigh the gains from having one's threats taken seriously against the pain from the attacker's counter-retaliation. Thus, the decision to retaliate—at least in the nuclear domain—has to be at least somewhat irrational particularly if there was valid cause to believe the original aggression had aims short of annihilation. Yet if the aggressor believed that the victim would *never* act irrationally and retaliate, deterrence could easily fail.[1]

Several strategic scholars tried to deal with the nuclear deterrence problem in different ways. Thomas Schelling argued for a deterrence that "left something to chance" in that the original nuclear strike might set off a cascade of uncontrollable events that would culminate in some retaliation irrespective of what decisionmakers in the target country might have calmly chosen. Patrick Morgan argued that "rationality" may be the wrong standard and that thinking in terms of a "sensible," rather than a rational, deterrence policy might avoid some of the conundrum.[2] Henry Kissinger called for the United States to have a capability to fight a limited nuclear war (with mutual agreement on its limits); retaliation therefore need not mean suicide. Nevertheless, the question of "will" was central to strategic thought, and there was also considerable debate on how a state would express its will to retaliate before actually having to do so.

At least in that respect, retaliation for cyberattacks has fewer problems than retaliation for nuclear attacks.[3] But the will to retaliate is still problematic—in a field of contention where the opportunities to demonstrate will are far more likely than with nuclear weapons.

THE RISKS OF REPRISALS

The decision to retaliate is necessarily buffeted by a plethora of uncertainties. One is that the pain induced by retaliation is hard to predict. An attacker that fears a return blow may take short-term steps to insulate its systems from the rest of the world; in such circumstances, it may find advantage in trading the certainty of losing some of the benefits of connectivity for the hopes of weakening the reprisal. As noted, recovery time is also just a guess.

Attackers may well deliver a counter-retaliatory blow. They may not believe retaliation is merited or at least appropriate. They may face internal pressures to respond in an obviously painful way.

Concerns over escalation add uncertainties. The attacker may believe it will lose in a tit-for-tat contest in cyberspace but can prevail in kinetic domains where it enjoys superiority. Those who would deter a cyberattack by threatening retaliation in kind may lose to an attacker who counters by threatening escalation out of kind; this threat is known as cross-domain deterrence.

Attackers may also escalate if the target's retaliation crosses a threshold of theirs—even if the retaliation is in kind and appears proportionate to the retaliator. Where the ultimate effects of the attack are so uncertain and the ground rules nonexistent, the risks are incalculable. Indeed, any state that carries out a seriously damaging cyberattack on a nuclear-armed state necessarily runs the risk—small, but not zero—that nuclear war may ultimately ensue. In the 1990s, it was Russia's declared policy to react to (what it deemed) a strategic cyberattack with the choice of any strategic weapon in its arsenal.[4] If an attacker believes that the benefits of a cyberattack merit running a slight risk of nuclear war, how much would it be daunted by the additional (albeit more plausible) risks of a retaliatory cyberattack? By contrast, nuclear strategists did not worry about escalation beyond the nuclear level (although they worried about deterrence *within* the nuclear level) because there was no "beyond."

THIRD-PARTY CYBERATTACKS

Third-party intervention cannot be ruled out (assuming the tit-for-tat in cyberspace is public knowledge). Hacking *is* one of the activities in which some third parties (for example, Russian organized crime) can play in the same league as most states. A serious interstate exchange could legitimize hacking to a community that is otherwise constantly lectured by governments on how immoral and immature such activities are. After all, if states that adhere to "rule of law" do it, the only difference between legitimate and illegitimate hacking is official imprimatur. Hackers are not particularly impressed by imprimatur. A general dogpile cannot be ruled out, particularly if the exchange appears to put certain assets "in play" (much as a takeover bid for a corporation makes it a feasible target for others).

The emergence of third-party hackers could further complicate attribution and confuse the relationships among attack, retaliation, and counter-retaliation by making it very hard to cease hostilities.[5] All this weakens an implied promise of deterrence: If you stop, we stop. The potential for third-party hacking drains strength from the "we" promise. What attackers want to hear—if you stop, it stops—may not be something the retaliator can promise. Conversely, third-party attackers may strengthen an implied threat of deterrence: Do not even start, because who knows where it will lead.

That noted, third-party pile-on has been rare.[6] Attacks against hard targets take time to plan; if a confrontation arises, third parties may simply not be ready to weigh in immediately for lack of their having scoped targets on either or both sides. In a sense, the activities of Anonymous, Lulzsec, and the Lizard Squad are good examples of *potential* third-party pile-on, but they may illustrate the limits of nonstate actors who lack a professional criminal interest in attacking systems. Their attacks are annoying, perhaps embarrassing, but hardly consequential.

THERE MAY BE BIGGER ISSUES ON THE TABLE

Consider the conventional top four threats to the United States in cyberspace: China, Russia, Iran, and North Korea. For each country, whatever has happened in cyberspace so far has hardly been the biggest issue that the United States has had with these countries. As noted, for instance, the United States asks much of China (for example, helping control North Korea) and maintains a trade (and increasingly an investment) relationship worth close to $1 trillion a year. If it chose to retaliate against China's EMCE (putting aside the DDOS attack on Github, which is more like a cyberattack) by, say, banning the importation of a Chinese product that may have benefited from such EMCE, China may well retaliate through its own import ban. Although the United States would have to ask itself whether whatever reduction in harm it achieved by discouraging Chinese EMCE was worth the risk to a very large trade relationship, the United States did succeed in gaining the Xi-Obama agreement, and no risk materialized.

With Russia, there are many complicating factors to consider if the United States were to retaliate against a (noncatastrophic) Russian cyberattack. One is nuclear weapons, which Russia's president likes to remind others of (far more casually than he should).[7] Another is Ukraine, Russian activity in which has already brought sanctions on its head (as a result of which the Russian economy is deliberately becoming more autarkic)—thereby limiting further sanctions as a form of response. This raises the question: Is the value of reducing Russia's mischief in cyberspace worth jeopardizing the West's ability to influence Russia's behavior in Ukraine?

With Iran, the big issue is adherence to the July 2015 nuclear agreement. If the value of stopping Iran's nuclear program is comparable to the value of stopping Iraq's weapons of mass destruction (and doing so without leaving chaos behind), then, based on what the United States spent in Iraq, it is in the trillion-dollar class. By contrast, neither the DDOS attacks on the bank nor the attacks on Saudi Aramco and Las Vegas Sands were in the hundred-million-dollar class. Again, the question: Is limiting Iran's mischief in cyberspace worth possibly jeopardizing a nuclear deal with Iran?

With North Korea, nuclear negotiations are currently moribund, but because of North Korea's hostile attitude, the U.S. military currently maintains 29,000 troops in South Korea—something that adds at least $10 billion to the U.S. military budget. The added cost to the United States associated with North Korea extending its attitude into cyberspace was well under 1 percent of that amount. Again, one is the dog and one is the tail.

Conversely, those who would attack in cyberspace have issues with the United States that outweigh whatever gains they can reap through contemplated cyberattacks. Indeed, the cessation of DDOS attacks on banks and the putative diminution of cyberspace activity since nuclear talks started suggest that Iranians may think this way.[8] The important point, however, is that larger considerations may reduce the credibility of a U.S. retaliatory threat unless that threat is specifically linked to these larger issues.

Overall, the relatively small costs associated with cyberattacks (none of which has crossed $100 million in costs or hurt anyone) make it difficult to retaliate for future attacks of that magnitude without worrying that more important issues that the United States has with other countries may be jeopardized. The counterpoint is that the run of past attacks may not indicate the value of deterring future—and potentially much larger—cyberattacks. Prior to September 11, U.S. casualties from terrorism were in the single digits. Hence, the question for gauging the value of cyberdeterrence is: Has great damage been avoided because the intentions of cyberattackers were restrained (in which case something like deterrence is necessary) or because the potential for damage from cyberattacks is limited (in which case, far less so)?

The problem is complicated by the fact that many of the responses that any sovereign state can make without going to war (or even war-like measures such as blockades) are off the table for these countries. The United States does not allow commercial and financial trade from North Korea. A similar embargo covers Iran (although the nuclear agreement suggests that will start to lift). Sanctions, possibly tightening ones, cover Russia. When softer forms of response are unavailable, what is left risks counter-retaliation.

CREDIBILITY MAY NOT BE EASY TO ESTABLISH

As noted, the United States has a history of reacting violently when attacked, whether at Pearl Harbor or lower Manhattan. This history raises the question of why any rational country would carry out such an attack—even in cyberspace—*of similar consequence* and not expect to see the United States react disproportionately (or, colloquially, go nonlinear). A country blind to the prospects of such a reaction must perforce be blind to a great many things and probably would not respect, say, a formal declaration of intent. So, there is no advantage at the high level to crafting a deterrence policy on the high end.

The United States might try to indicate that its temper can be motivated at lower levels of pain. By analogy, we would react as fiercely to a 3/11 (the 2004 Madrid train bombs that killed over two hundred) or even a 7/7 (the 2005 London bombings that killed over fifty) as to a 9/11—but saying so would not necessarily make it so if attackers do not believe these smaller attacks would be large enough to trigger the kind of sustained popular commitment that 9/11 did (although, in practice, terrorists probably sought a U.S. response).

Many low levels of cyberattack are treated as crimes, and the willingness of the United States to prosecute crimes (vice prosecute countries) is longstanding and suffices to establish at least some level of criminal deterrence in cyberspace. The United States pursued the Russians who hacked Citibank in the mid-1990s, extradited a Russian hacker from the Maldives in 2014, and has a substantial award out for the arrest and conviction of the progenitor of the GameOverZeus malware. But in no case was the United States willing to punish Russia itself for protecting these hackers.

That leaves the middle between crime and 9/11 as a place where the U.S. will to respond to a cyberattack can be made manifest in such a way as to move the needle in the calculations of would-be attackers—lest any declaration to get tough on cyberattacks be seen as mere wind. The basic problem is that unless potential attackers impute to the United States both the will to respond and the (approximate) threshold at which the United States would respond, they have no reason to factor a U.S. response into their planning.

Furthermore, until the United States actually *does* retaliate and with consequence, the *will* to take the kind of risks that retaliation entails can be questioned. Nothing the United States has done to North Korea (as of the end of 2015) or Iran (fingered by the director of national intelligence as the perpetrator of the Las Vegas Sands hack) impresses. A response that is not obvious to the public, to be sure, may create deterrence in the minds of North Koreans, but unless the latter announce their pain to other countries, these others will have no reason to be sure that the United States will respond. And what if potential attackers with the capacity to inflict painful counter-retaliation deem that North Korea was retaliated against because it was weak rather than because it did wrong?

THE SIGNALS ASSOCIATED WITH CARRYING OUT REPRISALS MAY GET LOST IN THE NOISE

Deterrence is also a form of signaling, and such signals are apt to lose fidelity in cyberspace for the same reasons that other signals do.[9] The Israeli-Palestinian dynamic is an object lesson in how easily deterrence signals get lost. In theory, Israeli policy is to retaliate following acts of terrorism. This would signal to Palestinians in general, and Hamas in particular, that perpetrating or even condoning terrorism would cost them. In contrast to cyberattacks, terrorism in Israel was straightforward. Attribution was easy: It was almost always a Palestinian, and even if not, Palestinians cheered anyway. The threshold—loss of life—was obvious and all too frequently crossed. Retaliation consisted of killing leaders or key members of Hamas (or Fatah, Islamic Jihad, and so forth). But the retaliation cycle was not particularly clean. One problem, ironically, was that the Israelis believed that retaliation could, in fact, disarm (or decapitate) the group. If Israel saw a good opportunity to strike at its enemies, it was likely to do so, whether or not such a strike could be tagged to a prior Palestinian attack—so its foes probably figured that they were going to be targeted if they were vulnerable, whether or not they had just done something specific (the assurance component of Israel's deterrence policy left something to be desired). Hamas, for its turn, discovered what a bloody nuisance could be created by firing rockets across the Gaza-Israel border. This created a threshold problem for Israel. Since it has not responded to every attack (the vast majority hurt no one and break nothing), Israel could not begin to do so without its reaction being widely viewed as highly disproportionate.[10] No number (for example, retaliate after ten attacks in a day) would be seen as anything but an arbitrary threshold. Retaliating after Hamas got "lucky" and caused horrific damages (for example, by hitting a kindergarten) would convert deterrence policy into a game of Russian roulette. Eventually, Israel, having been fed up, struck back in January 2009 (Operation Cast Lead) as well as in August 2014 (Protective Edge), but the lack of a temporal relationship between the rockets and the reaction fed suspicions of ulterior motives—and all this for a case with fewer ambiguities than present in cyberspace.[11] Because cyberspace is noisy, both the easily understood and subtle signals (thought to be) present in the nuclear realm may be nearly indecipherable in the new medium. Noise destroys communication, hence signaling. Without clear signaling, it is difficult to distinguish deterrence from aggression.

THE IMPACT OF GOOD DEFENSES ON CREDIBILITY IS MIXED

A good defense against cyberattack would add credibility to a cyberdeterrence posture in several ways (but detract from it in one). First, good defenses reduce the odds that an attack would succeed and thus that a cyberdeterrence policy would be tested—and the longer such a policy goes untested, the more credibility it acquires, if only through longevity. Second, a good defense adds credibility to the threat to retaliate by reducing the attacker's power to threaten counter-retaliation; the costs of sparking a full-fledged cyberwar would fall disproportionately on the other side. In a similar vein, Herman Kahn argued that having bomb shelters made nuclear deterrence more credible.[12] Third, good defenses have a way of filtering out third-party attacks, or at least those that lack the sophistication of state-sponsored attacks. This takes the wind out of one argument against retaliation: that it puts a country's assets in play vis-à-vis third-party hackers. Reducing the incidence of serious third-party attacks in turn facilitates attribution by elimination ("since our defenses are good, X could not have done it—and therefore we are down to Y and Z as suspects"). This should not be overstated, since the differences between state and nonstate attackers may be subtle, and there remains the problem of distinguishing between attacks from even two countries with good cyberwar skills (for example, was it Russia or China?).

Conversely, a good defense may indicate that punishment is less likely. Israel's nonstate foes, notably Hamas, have argued that Israel's Iron Dome anti-missile defense *detracts* from deterrence because the substitution of machinery for boots on the ground means that Israel will *not* risk pain to punish intercepted rocket attacks (whether Hamas believes its own arguments is another matter). Such arguments, however, do not look as solid in light of Israel's violent incursion into Gaza in August 2014 carried out to erode the ability of Hamas to launch rockets at will—even though the Iron Dome had worked quite well.

Finally, a country that is all too aware of the rickety state of its networks—as China is[13]—might logically be easier to deter because it knows the consequences of being caught and suffering retaliation. But such a country may also be very sensitive to probes and unexplained anomalies in its network and therefore less likely to give potential attackers the benefit of the doubt when assessing the latter's intentions. Thus, it may be quick to take offense at attacks real or imagined and may want to establish its own deterrence capability by not letting any slight go unanswered.

CAN EXTENDED DETERRENCE WORK IN CYBERSPACE?

During the Cold War, the United States promised Europe that a nuclear attack on it by the Soviet Union would be met with U.S. nuclear retaliation. One reason for giving this assurance was to keep NATO together in the face of threat and blandishments from the East. Another was to inhibit Europeans (notably Germans) from developing their own nuclear weapons.

Correspondingly, should a cyberwar power offer to retaliate (not to be confused with the ability to help defend) against attacks on its alliance partners? After suffering DDOS attacks from Russia in 2007, Estonia wanted NATO to decide that such attacks could trigger the alliance's collective defense clause; NATO said no.[14] The Russian attack on Ukraine may have changed NATO's mind.[15]

Arguments in favor of extended deterrence draw on familiar lines of thought. A big retaliator may have the capacity to retaliate that the little target may lack. The little target may be more vulnerable because of insufficient infrastructure redundancy or the inability to afford forensic and mitigation services. Cyberdeterrence could remove one avenue for the attacker to pressure another state's allies.

Technical issues, though, cast doubts on extended deterrence. Start, not surprisingly, with deterrence. How does the big retaliator trust the little target's read of the cyberattack? Perhaps the little target gives the big retaliator deep access to its systems (despite the fact that no state trusts another's intelligence operatives). Perhaps the damage is obvious (as it was with Estonia). Otherwise, when it comes to knowing what the attack did and who did it, the big retaliator may have to take the little target's word for it ("Why dig into our systems? Don't you trust us?"). It would not be unprecedented in the annals of diplomacy for a state to fabricate or exaggerate evidence that implicated a traditional enemy for carrying out an attack that may or may not have happened and, even if so, caused damage that may or may not have crossed a threshold. Even if the big retaliator exercises due diligence and demands to see the evidence, who knows whether it has been denied access to exculpatory evidence? How would NATO react if the member state refused outsiders access to the more sensitive parts of the affected system, arguing that it has secrets to keep and that its accounts of what happened should be trusted? One can understand the potential for a crisis that would rend NATO if one of the less trustworthy members asked the rest of the alliance to risk war by responding to an attack whose nature had to be surmised because the request for a thorough investigation beforehand would reveal that NATO did not, in fact, trust that member. Also, would NATO really want to be dragged into a war because one of its member states had failed to secure its information systems diligently and, as a result, had opened itself up for an opportunistic attack that might otherwise have been avoided?

Analogies that use mutual defenses in the physical world to create a template for mutual defenses in cyberspace have to overlook the very different nature of where an attack takes place. An attack *into* France is an attack *on* France. Now, imagine an attack on the information system of a credit card company that disables all of its global transactions for an extended period; should it matter that the (hypothetical) critical server was located not in Germany (a NATO country) but in Switzerland (not a NATO country)? Should the fact that Sony is mostly owned by and headquartered in Japan (even if its movie-making division is headquartered in the United States) have made a difference? If not, can whoever retaliates (and it would be mostly the United States) assume such a right regardless of where the attack took place? Indeed, who, other than their owners, actually knows where the relevant servers sit (a question of more than theoretical relevance as more organizations put their computing in the cloud)?

Or does the potentially anonymous nature of extended deterrence work in its favor? Cyberdeterrence still can work if attackers believe that an attack on *anyone*, rather than a specific someone, will have deleterious consequences (recall the discussion about third parties above). Thus, if *some* states were willing to retaliate for attacks on other states, this could simultaneously create a broader deterrence without necessarily implicating the true retaliator—unless only one state could possibly step up to the role (while the target conspicuously does not). Indeed, how far is assuming the responsibility for retaliation for any cyberattack anywhere in the world from taking the position that the United States is responsible for law and order in this domain and should be accepted as the global policeman? One caveat: If the nature and effects of the original attack were not of the sort that would be universally visible, the attacker may feel, in the wake of retaliation, that the target state was culpable even if it did not carry out the retaliation itself. The target's revealing enough information to a third party to enable retaliation may suffice to justify counter-retaliation. If the target can be made to believe as much, it may keep quiet even to its friends.

Although the primary purpose of extended deterrence is to deter attacks on its members through collective action, achieving the secondary goal of reassuring allies that they will not be attacked *because* of this mutual defense treaty may be unattainable. The United States cannot even assure itself that its systems are secure from the wiles of others, and given the large number of non-state attackers coupled with the problems of attribution and actionable thresholds (discussed below), optimism on that score is premature. At best, some reduction of cyberattacks may be promised for alliance members—but knowing how much, if any, is hard. It scarcely helps that others must take on trust the U.S. ability to defend their systems using offensive means (whether via deterrence or the gauzy promise of preemption). There is no equivalent of their being able to determine the U.S. capability and commitment by counting tanks (much less tanks on their side of the ocean). And there is no equivalent of their knowing that U.S. capability is not directed against them (via cyberespionage).

WHY CREDIBILITY MAKES ATTRIBUTION AN ISSUE

A friend of mine, hawkish on cyberdeterrence, posed me the following: Consider a suitcase nuclear bomb detonated on U.S. soil. Technical attribution, he argues, can be quite difficult, not least because such a bomb could wipe out all the hardware associated with its composition (hence origin) and placement. Yet there is no doubt in anyone's mind that the United States would retaliate, and harshly, if it found the perpetrators. Conversely, no one would quibble if the United States announced that it would do so in advance of such attacks in order to deter them (they might quibble with a declaration that promises a nuclear response). Why should a comparable cyberattack not be subject to the same rules?

Some answers can be offered, the first three of which rest on the premise that attribution for the suitcase nuclear weapon is likely to be better than attribution for a comparable cyberattack.

First, the process by which the accretion of evidence over time leads to more confidence in attribution is likely to work better for a suitcase nuclear attack than for a comparable cyberattack. The attacker in cyberspace would be motivated to look like someone else, and evidence on the modus operandi of that someone else can be inferred from deconstructing the many intrusions that countries around the world have done. No such knowledge exists with suitcase nuclear bombs because the next one would be the first one; hence, there would be no one to masquerade as. The best technical forensics rely on the post-detonation pattern of radiation and fallout debris, but duplicating the patterns that characterize another country's devices may be impossible without having gotten hold of the fallout from a recent test of theirs. Further evidence may as likely confirm the false attacker as the real one.

Second, technical forensics constitute only one part of how terrorists are identified (figuring out where the box cutters for the September 11 attacks were bought did not play a major role in the investigation). The full range of police methods is used; terrorists who used a suitcase nuclear weapon are likely to number among known terrorists who reveal themselves by interacting with the physical world; by contrast, the real identities of many individual hackers are unknown (even if they do reuse their hacker handles).

Third, acquiring and detonating a suitcase nuclear bomb requires a larger infrastructure than even a big cyberattack does. Such people have to interact with the rest of the world by traveling, moving objects, casing the detonation site, and making purchases. By interacting with the physical world, the chances that investigators will get a break are far higher than they would be in a cyberattack, where the only thing that moves is code and little, if anything, need be bought.

If these arguments hold water, the odds of finding the perpetrator of a suitcase nuclear weapon would be higher than the odds of finding the perpetrator of a comparably broad cyberattack—even if initial technical factors are equally unrevealing. But are the odds different enough to justify certainty that a deterrence posture makes perfect sense in the case of the former, but dubious sense in the case of the latter? Perhaps not. So, dig further.

Fourth, because the seriousness of detonating a suitcase nuclear weapon is likely to far exceed the seriousness of carrying out a cyberattack, it is much more plausible to hunt down anyone who had *any* culpable role in the former. By contrast, whereas many people could have a comparable role in a cyberattack (for example, by exchanging information on hacking techniques with the attackers), its moral taint may not necessarily be large enough to merit moving heaven and earth to find them and bring them to justice. A cyberattack large enough to cause as much *economic* damage as a suitcase nuclear weapon is likely to kill few if any people and hence is unlikely to cause nearly as much moral outrage; cyberwar is far less heinous than kinetic war. This argument, however, is less about deterrence than about the relationship of cyberattacks to other attacks. It also speaks to why the *credibility* of ultimate punishment is higher for a nuclear attack than a cyberattack.

Or one can shrug and argue that countries can no more rely on strategic (versus criminal) deterrence to ward off a nuclear threat than we can in the case of cyberattack. In practice, the threat of a suitcase nuclear device is dealt with proactively: for example, by investigating and disrupting the many precursor steps to detonation (for example, rounding up loose nuclear material), concentrating fire on terrorist groups with an interest in such devices, and closely monitoring states (North Korea?) with some interest in fostering the use of such a device. Against cyberattacks, the best methods are defensive ones (whereas defenses against a nuclear detonation are nonexistent).

Or perhaps the attribution is not central to either case. In the case of both a suitcase nuclear detonation and a comparably destructive cyberattack, the United States would pursue individuals who did it without much regard for any statute of limitations, just as it pursued the bombers of Pan Am Flight 103 (Lockerbie). In both cases, if a state was deemed ultimately responsible, then the act would be considered quite hostile and would justify corresponding treatment by the United States of such a country. But if a country were found responsible for detonating a nuclear weapon inside the United States, it would be hard *not* to consider such a detonation an act of nuclear war that would merit even nuclear retaliation. If U.S. nuclear weapons cannot be contemplated as retaliation for such actions, for what actions *can* they be contemplated? And if the answer is none, what was the point in having them? Indeed, what is the point of having *any* retaliation policy? Furthermore, what would then keep any nuclear power from attacking the United States with impunity?

With a cyberattack, different considerations come into play, not least of which is whether it is worthwhile making this a casus belli in the first place. Retaliation meant to convey great ire at having been attacked may lead to counter-retaliation, which may set off a cycle of tit-for-tat that might stay in cyberspace or might result in violence. This consideration is not an argument against establishing a deterrence policy, but it is a caution. That then introduces the question: Is retaliation, if only to bolster deterrence, the most cost- (and risk-) effective way to reduce the future threat? In nuclear deterrence it appeared to be the only way, and a suitcase nuclear weapon is essentially the same problem albeit with a different delivery mechanism. But with a cyberattack, there are many other options to consider. Some of them, as noted, are within a state's sovereign rights. Some of them focus not on the attacker but on improving the defenses of U.S. systems so that a similar attack next time either fails or is not so devastating.

And so we return to the core dilemma of any deterrence policy—worthwhile if it deters, problematic if the bluff is called. With a suitcase nuclear bomb, the prospect of retaliation ought to be so painful that deterrence should hold—as it has in the nuclear arena since 1949. With a cyberattack, the many ambiguities associated with it—determination, thresholds, and, yes, attribution—argue against assuming that deterrence will never be tested. The consequences of carrying out retaliation have to be considered. Because cyberattacks sit toward the bottom rather than the top of the escalation ladder, such consideration may argue against putting too many chips on a deterrence policy for a cyberattack while not necessarily affecting the wisdom of a deterrence policy for a suitcase nuclear weapon attack.

CONCLUSIONS

Although the case for a robust deterrence policy—declared and frequently resorted to—against cyberattacks is weaker than it is for policies to ward off being attacked in the physical world, two points in favor of such a policy should be adduced.

As explained in greater detail below, one reason to be careful about promising deterrence is the difficulty of figuring out who did it coupled with the difficulty of determining whether such an attack was or was not beneath notice. However, if the other side boasts of having carried out such an attack without retribution, then retaliation may be in order. An important purpose of a deterrence policy is not only to ward off further cyberattacks but also to maintain a reputation for not being openly trifled with.

Maintaining a reputation may also help ward off a physical attack, particularly an attack on an interest that the attacker is not sure the United States would defend (by comparison, everyone thinks the United States would respond to an attack on its homeland). The attacker, presumably, would be looking at the U.S. response to a cyberattack as a way of determining how strongly the United States would defend what might otherwise be a peripheral interest. A strong response to a cyberattack should indicate a feisty United States, thereby raising the odds that the United States would mount a response to a physical as well as a cyberattack on what might have seemed an interest not worth fighting over. But this logic should be handled carefully. No cyberattack prefatory to a kinetic campaign has ever taken place.[16] Furthermore, the clues that might associate a particular cyberattack with an imminent kinetic attack (especially if against a different target) are subject to ambiguous interpretation. Similarly, the other side's interpreting a vigorous U.S. response to a cyberattack (for example, on the U.S. banking system) as evidence that the United States would militarily defend, say, some miniscule Asian island is not particularly obvious—but not entirely vacuous either.

CHAPTER 23
Attribution

The ability to attribute with confidence is the difference between a deterrence policy that says, "Don't do this" and one that says, "Don't get caught doing this." Both false positives and false negatives are bad for such a policy. False negatives—failure to punish the guilty— weaken deterrence directly by reducing the odds of getting caught. False positives—fingering the innocent—erode legitimacy; if retaliation visits the innocent, the retaliator may have made a new enemy. Even if the presumed attacker deserved punishment for other bad behavior, its incentive to behave well may be attenuated: If punishment follows both innocence and crime, why avoid crime?

To retaliate wisely, a country must convince itself that it is probably right, but if retaliation is public, it should also be able to convince third parties that the attribution is correct. Because today's threats are less existential than those of the Cold War, considerations of morality and conformance with international norms carry greater weight than they did when survival was primarily what mattered. Even leaders of U.S. allies may be skeptical. They themselves have constituencies to bring along and may fear being collateral damage in a cyberwar prompted by ill-considered retaliation. Last, if the United States retaliates on the basis of evidence that does not convince others, these others may be given an excuse to retaliate for other cyberattacks on the basis of evidence that does not convince the United States.

It also helps to make a credible case to the attacker. Granted, the attacker should know who did it (although if carried out by, say, a rogue intelligence faction, leaders may not know immediately). However, a good case helps convince the attacker that it faces retaliation not just because it is unloved but because of the attack alone. This is needed even more if the target has failed to respond to earlier attacks, either because it chose not to or because it was unsure who did it.

All this speaks to how good attribution should be. First, it must be good enough to convince authorities that the consequences multiplied by the odds of not responding when response is justified (the false negative) exceed the consequences multiplied by the odds of responding against the wrong party (the false positive). Second, it should be persuasive enough to get a pass from the rest of the world when judging the response; active support would be even better. Third, it should convince the attacker that retaliation is what it purports to be—a serving of just deserts. Note that unless attribution has to be proven before a court of law, certainty beyond a reasonable shadow of a doubt is not required. In a sense, the standards are closer to the preponderance-of-evidence standard of a civil case.

WHAT WILL CONVINCE?

In the Cold War, the United States faced an existential threat from the one foe that had as many nuclear weapons as it did. These days, more than one hundred countries are supposedly developing what are described as cyberattack capabilities (many may just be cyberespionage, though).[1] But there is no *single* dominant threat; the most putatively capable threats (for example, Russia, China) are not necessarily the most hostile to the United States (although Russia's hostility rose sharply in 2014). Third parties may not even be immediately convinced that the attack occurred—much less who did it. If the attack's purpose was to corrupt a target system, effects will be apparent only to the attacker and the target (if even then). Even if the effects are public, the cause of the malfunction may be apparent only to the target (if correct) and the attacker (who should be able to assign the failure of the target system to its having been attacked).

As hard as it is to make a good confidence estimate for oneself based on evidence, it is harder to determine how others will judge your assessment. One must factor out information that you know but you believe that they do not know, guess what they know that you do not know, and then try to factor in how much weight they give your assurance (or lack thereof). After all that, the normal human tendency is to mirror-image others: if I'm convinced, then the case is convincing, and thus they should be convinced. But it is not always so.

What *will* convince skeptics? Al Qaeda's responsibility for the September 11 attacks is accepted in the United States ("truthers" aside) but for a long time was the minority view in Islamic countries.[2] Syria's deadly use of chemical agents was difficult to attribute convincingly, particularly to those who oppose U.S. retaliation against Syria. At least those who accused Syria had considerable evidence on their side (vis-à-vis claims that Syrian rebels carried out the attack); the area of attack was, grudgingly, opened to UN inspection. By comparison, it is harder to imagine knowledgeable neutral inspectors being allowed to examine, let alone in sufficient detail, the systems that hackers had struck. Hampering the efforts to attribute the Syrian attack was the U.S. government's insistence on classifying the incriminating details that congressmen were shown—and even they were not shown everything.[3] Given the great secrecy associated with cyberwar coupled with the understandable desire not to reveal proprietary features of the systems that have been attacked, it is highly unlikely that attribution of a cyberattack would be more transparent—or convincing—than in the Syrian case. With the Sony attack, the FBI, in the face of skepticism over who did it,[4] released a case against North Korea that rested entirely on three pieces of evidence contained in 140 words in a document.[5] Bruce Schneier's continued ambivalence about attribution at that point was nicely expressed:

> Many of us in the computer-security field are skeptical of the U.S. government's claim that it has positively identified North Korea as the perpetrator of the massive Sony hack in November 2014. The FBI's evidence is circumstantial and not very convincing. The attackers never mentioned the movie that became the centerpiece of the hack until the press did. More likely, the culprits are random hackers who have loved to hate Sony for over a decade, or possibly a disgruntled insider. On the other hand, most people believe that the FBI would not sound so sure unless it was convinced. And President Obama would not have imposed sanctions against North Korea if he weren't convinced.[6]

It was only several weeks later that the head of the FBI added that some of the IP addresses used by the group claiming responsibility for the attack (Guardians of Peace), through a slip-up, used the same IP addresses known to be used by North Koreans in other attacks.[7] And it had to be added that "we are still looking to identify the vector—so how did they get into Sony."

Because information on attribution accumulates over time, a strategy that advises for immediate retaliation on the theory that others will trust your word on things may look good in the short run but takes risks. Indeed, it is unclear why the FBI chose to make attribution as soon as it did. Is there any evidence that North Korea had stockpiled further cyberattacks and would have released them but for the unexpectedly strong U.S. response? Did the administration conclude that its certainty was 100 percent and thus was never going to get better? Informal evidence suggests, conversely, that even pro-American foreigners who take cybersecurity seriously were not satisfied by the FBI's explanations.

It is in the attacker's interest to feign innocence, the better to persuade the target to give out the methods by which attribution was made—so that it might evade attribution next time. The attacker may know that it carried out an attack but also knows that it had been carrying attacks out for years *and* that other countries had carried out attacks as well. The attacker might then ask two questions after retaliation: Why me? Why now? What the attacker concludes may have little to do with the fact, much less the particulars, of the cited attack. (The notion that the target reexamined its deterrence policy and *then* found out who attacked may be plausible to others but not necessarily to those who knew that the attack in question preceded the change in policy.) Instead, it may reflect other events—a bureaucratic tussle within the retaliating state, a nasty trade dispute, an attempt to win a third state's favor. So thinking, the attacker may decide to halt attacks anyway and give the retaliator no further excuse. Or it may figure that further attacks are unlikely to raise the odds that it will be subject to retaliation, especially if whatever evidence the retaliator offered was unconvincing. The attacker may feel attribution and retaliation were arbitrary and resulted not from what it did but from being unloved by the target. Last, bias may arise from a push to retaliate quickly where one potential attacker is hard to retaliate against (because, for instance, its systems have not be analyzed for a vulnerability) even as another can be struck quickly.

Politically speaking, it helps if the burden of proof can be shifted to the accused. The target might show that the traffic came from the latter's servers and force that country to prove that the attack was just hopping through these servers en route from somewhere else. Realistically, however, governments that do not feel themselves accountable to a discerning public can resist attempts to place the onus on them far longer than might seem reasonable to U.S. citizens. A case in point is Russia's denial (and then later its unembarrassed concession) that its forces were not involved in the Crimean takeover of March 2014, or China's assertion[8] that the United States faked the evidence in its May 2014 indictments.

HOW GOOD WOULD ATTRIBUTION BE?

Former defense secretary Leon Panetta observed in mid-October 2012, "In addition to defending the department's networks, we also help deter attacks. Our cyber adversaries will be far less likely to hit us if they know that we will be able to link to the attack or that their effort will fail against our strong defenses. The department has made significant advances in solving a problem that makes deterring cyber adversaries more complex: the difficulty of identifying the origins of that attack. Over the last two years, DoD has made significant investments in forensics to address this problem of attribution and we're seeing the returns on that investment."[9]

In early 2012, information leaked from the NSA suggesting that it could trace most of China's APTs to a dozen groups. Former assistant secretary of homeland security Stewart Baker argues that there has been an "attribution revolution" that puts paid to the notion that cyberattacks can be carried out with impunity.[10] These days, it is difficult to read about a major act of cyberespionage or cyberattack without some confident assertion that it came from a particular country, and often a particular group within a country. The same, however, cannot be said for many cybercrimes apart from a vague attribution to eastern European (mostly Russian) organized crime elements.

That noted, it *is* in the U.S. interest that bad guys believe they will be caught irrespective of the odds they can actually be caught. To meet its deterrence mission, CYBERCOM has been "establishing 13 teams of programmers and computer experts who could carry out offensive cyber-attacks on foreign nations if the United States were hit with a major attack on its own networks, the first time the Obama administration has publicly admitted to developing such weapons for use in wartime."[11] Alan Friedman has argued that from a diplomatic perspective, it is a smart strategy for the United States to be overconfident in assigning blame for the cyberattacks.[12] In many ways, a country's assurance that it was struck by X and its willingness to take action may reassure others who reason that the United States would not take the risks if it lacked confidence in its attribution.[13]

But what exactly can the United States attribute—and to whose satisfaction? The United States has yet to convict a state-sponsored hacker (even though foreign criminal hackers have been convicted). Claims of North Korean culpability for the Sony attack have not entirely cleared the court of public opinion—even with strong hints that more evidence exists but is classified and hence cannot be revealed. This is not to say that agencies cannot make attribution *claims*. For instance, the United States has come out and blamed China for stealing information from U.S. organizations, and the accusation was repeated by President Obama at the 2013 Sunshine summit; a year later, five PLA officers were indicted.[14]

WHEN ATTRIBUTION SEEMS TO WORK

When attribution is reliable, one reason that attackers (such as Chinese APT groups) nevertheless keep carrying out similar attacks, persist for a long time within target systems, exfiltrate a large quantity of data back, and seem to exercise very poor operational security is that they feel themselves immune from punishment.[15] Indeed, hackers should, individually, fear no consequences are as long as their activities are condoned or, as argued in the Mandiant report, ordered by their government—U.S. indictments notwithstanding.[16]

Four characteristics—repetition, persistence, exfiltration, and impunity—make attribution easier. Repetition means that characteristics of attacks can be matched against earlier ones attributed to a source; the more attacks, the more likely that they will leave incriminating clues (not least of which is attacking a target, such as the Free Tibet movement, believed to be of interest to only one country[17]). Persistence means that communications between the attacker and the target recurs frequently even though potential changes in the attacker's modus operandi are undertaken to masquerade cyberattack activities.[18] Exfiltration, particularly in large quantities, means that there is a route from target to the attacker that is traversed by large volumes of data; if individual transfers are kept small to avoid triggering suspicion (and that step is often skipped), then the frequency must be correspondingly greater. Because high volume lends itself to a standardized modus operandi, once that is established, it may be possible to find something similar when analyzing subsequent cyberattacks. Operating at high volume leads to repeated patterns, the use of automation (such as bots), or enlistment of an army of less sophisticated (albeit trained and well-disciplined) hackers using similar methods.[19] Conversely, an attacker that believes it is important to preserve anonymity for cyberattacks may isolate its cyberwarriors from those who carry out cyberespionage.

In the case of North Korea, things were simpler. The Guardians of Peace lacked the discipline to avoid identifying themselves in communications apart from the attack. The Sony attacks themselves employed the same tricks used in the 2013 Dark Seoul attacks. Because of the presumption that most attacks on South Korea come from North Korea, putting one and one together yielded a plausible two.

With Stuxnet, by contrast, there were only a handful of actual attacks, little if any communication flowed between the malware and the controller (there appears to have been some updating activity), few large files were exfiltrated, and the authors took pains not to be discovered (a lot depends on whether the aforementioned clues in the code were deliberately put there). At the time of discovery, there were no forensic clues that definitively linked Stuxnet to any country. The accusation that the United States and Israel were behind Stuxnet was based on the sophistication of the code and the presumption that no other two countries were so motivated to hobble Iran's nuclear program.[20]

The notion that one can narrow down the list of potential attackers and thereby increase confidence in attribution because only sophisticated countries carry out sophisticated attacks is tricky, especially if a stronger claim is made that only *one* country knew how to carry out a particular type of attack. In the first case, narrowing the accused down to two is far different from narrowing it down to one. In the second case, proving that no one country can do *X*—when offensive cyberwar capabilities are so highly classified—is proving a negative.

A one-time fire-and-forget attack (even if preceded by some surveillance) carried out by a country that actively wanted to avoid blame offers different and far less promising material for technical attribution than a set of similar APTs designed to exfiltrate large amounts of data. Therefore, advances in attribution associated with persistent system penetrations may not necessarily mean that attribution of fire-and-forget cyberattacks that would merit retaliation has gotten significantly easier—*unless* a destructive cyberattack requires a great deal of cyberespionage to work. In that case, the characteristics of cyberespionage that facilitate the attribution or prefatory cyberespionage also facilitate the attribution of a consequent attack, even if the latter is a one-time fire-and-forget attack. Such logic, however, can mislead if *two* attackers have an interest in a target for *either* espionage or attack purposes.

Nevertheless, recent advances in attribution have not gone to waste. They have forced potential attackers whose countries wish to escape attribution to pay attention to operational security (which at least increases the cost of mounting attacks and weeds out hackers who cannot). They could limit the amount of information that stealthy attackers can exfiltrate in planning attacks. Finally, as noted, catastrophic attacks that require setting up many small attacks (to go off at once) run risks of exposure similar to those that carry out repeated intrusions for espionage purposes.

WHAT COULD MAKE ATTRIBUTION SO HARD?

In a medium where, it was once observed, "nobody knows you're a dog,"[21] it may not be so easy to know whether anyone is *the* hacker everyone is looking for. Computer attacks do not leave distinct physical evidence behind—neither gunpowder residue nor fingerprints.[22] The world contains billions of nearly identical machines capable of sending nearly identical packets.

Attacks can come from anywhere.[23] Granted, the act of bouncing packets from one machine to another in near–real time is not as risk-free as it was once thought to be. Nevertheless, such attacks can be routed through zombies that only need to erase the packet's originating address and substitute their own to mask the true origin; it helps further if the packets are reencrypted at every node and if delays in retransmission exceed the interval during which network log files are kept. Attacks can be implanted beforehand in a compromised machine. Hackers could operate from a cybercafé, a public library with WiFi access, many airports, or most U.S. motel lobbies, or through a cutout (someone who operates on behalf of another). Finding incriminating packets that can be traced back to the IP address of a government ministry is unlikely unless the ministry is stupid or arrogant, runs so many hackers that it cannot be anything less than obvious, or operates a network that has been hijacked by the actual attackers.[24] That noted, data mining, cloud computing, and access to cooperating ISPs could facilitate correlations that point to traffic patterns that may serve as clues.

A state's failure to cooperate with the investigation of a particular incident may be telling and may thus be construed as an indication of guilt—or nothing more than evidence that it places a great value on its sovereignty or has some *other* state secrets to protect.[25] Even friendly countries whose cooperation may be needed to trace packets back to their source may hesitate if they think successful attribution will increase the likelihood of reprisals that culminate in some war (even if they themselves are not involved). Furthermore, rejection may be entirely innocent; U.S. (or European) courts, for instance, could reject some investigative techniques that other countries employ because such techniques violate their conception of privacy rights.[26]

Last is the false flag complication. Consider a crisis between the United States and China over the fate of Taiwan. Taiwan believes, not without reason, that a cyberattack by China on the United States will raise the odds of intervening on Taiwan's side (even if, for instance, Taiwan is flirting with declaring independence contrary to U.S. desires). When the United States fears a cyberattack by China, Taiwan has an incentive to carry one out on the hope that the United States fingers the "usual suspect," China. A U.S. policy that brushed off such cyberattacks or at least took a pains-takingly deliberate approach to determining attribution would tempt Taiwan less. During a 1990s RAND game on cyberattacks in the context of a Taiwan Straits crisis, three of the seven teams thought that Taiwan carried out cyberattacks that looked as if they came from China.[27] False flag attacks are rare, but a late 2014 attack on France's TV5 may have been by Russian hackers pretend-ing to be from Daesh.[28]

Ironically, the more that a country knows about the modus operandi of one group, the more confidently it can emulate it in carrying out its own cyberattacks; thus, better attribution by one may lead to worse attribution by another. If the source of the attribution shares its indicators of a suspect group with the rest of the world, everyone would have an easier time in emulating that group; again, better attribution today may lead to worse attribution tomorrow.

Finally, as hard as attribution is today, when being fingered as the source of cyberespionage or even cyberattacks carries few penalties, it would likely be much harder if attackers faced serious retribution if caught. Deterrence may inhibit states from attacking in the first place, but it could persuade them to cover their tracks more carefully and continue attacking. After all, they have many ways to do so, including working from overseas and avoiding tools, techniques, and hackers with which they have already been associated.[29] In that sense, attribution is good only until it is useful, at which point it will gradually stop being good. Stated another way, if cyberattacks are measures, and attribution is a countermeasure, it may look as if attribution has won until attackers are motivated to develop counter-countermeasures.

Incidentally, recovery may suffer if the threat of retaliation persuades attackers to hide better. Attribution improves diagnostic forensics (specific attack groups have signature operational meth-ods), which, in turn, helps reveal the source of the damage and thus may hint at how to reverse it. Anything that persuades the attacker to erase evidence that may lead to attribution also tends to reduce the amount of information that defenders can use in system repair.

WHEN CAN COUNTRIES BE BLAMED FOR WHAT STARTED WITHIN THEIR BORDERS?

Even if attribution can be localized to a country, or even to within a government network, that fact does not in itself prove that the attack came from someone operating under national command. It could also be a rogue element in the government, perhaps operating on behalf of what it perceives to be state interests but without specific or at least not clear authorization (for example, it may have permission to spy but not to tamper). Or the attacker could believe its activities were winked at by a government that wanted to preserve its deniability. Or the attacker could be a proactive bureaucratic faction that acted when it deemed command authority wimpy. Or an attacker could be an entrepre-neurial group of hackers who were looking to create effects, confident that they would be appre-ciated and perhaps even rewarded—in outright cash, by future contracts, or by having their other illicit activities overlooked.[30] Hackers may be working off the government payroll but be linked to a particular political faction or to individual politicians (more likely in non-Western states). They may want to advance state interests as their friends perceive them or may want to get the current regime in trouble—the better for their friends to assume more power or to exacerbate tensions between the target and the attacker, perhaps fearing that its own country would otherwise buckle under to external pressure. The hackers may be organized criminals (for example, the Russian *mafiya*) who have co-opted large parts of the state apparatus.[31] The hackers could be "superpatriots" without connection to the government (for example, the sort that defaced websites in China and the United States in spring 2001), perhaps motivated by striking foes in lieu of or in advance of where they want the government to go.[32] The cyberattacks could have been carried out by a group that considered the attack a favor to the country most likely to be accused: a role that could be played, for instance, by Hezbollah on what it believes is Iran's behalf. The greater the government's authority, the less likely rogue attackers are because most governments intensely dislike their functions being assumed by others; thus, many of these threats are notional. However, trends toward less government authority in some regions coupled with the proliferation of cyberattack knowledge suggest that rogue attacks may become more common.

Even knowing that intelligence for the attack was collected under official auspices does not conclusively prove the attack was authorized. Intelligence preparation of the battlefield may have taken place as a contingency for cyberwar or for combat using entirely different means—and then been passed to or taken by others. Good oversight in cyberspace can be trickier than its equivalent in real space. One keystroke looks much like another on casual inspection (even as serious inspection can easily distinguish one set of keystrokes from another). The effects of such actions on target systems are even harder to monitor in real time. Because cyberspace remains arcane to conventional warfighters, much less to their political leaders, much of what operators may report can get lost in translation. All this multiplies the scope available to rogue operators. Leaders may not know with any confidence what mischief has been perpetuated in their name against other people's systems. The cyberwarriors may not know themselves what effects they wreaked. Even if they did, leaders may not understand them. And even if the leaders do understand, they may not necessarily understand the cyberwarriors when they say "oops."

A country that deliberately shielded attackers from criminal enforcement should expect little sympathy after suffering retaliation. From a strategic perspective, however, if the actual attackers are working on behalf, but not under the direct command, of the "attacking" state, is retaliation wise? Would it forestall future attacks? Foregoing retaliation means that the target has no deterrence policy against countries that choose to carry out cyberattacks using freelancers. The only compensation is that freelancers are unlikely to be called on to carry out certain types of attacks: for example, serious attacks on the target's military and those meant to coerce or goad the target.

Yet if the target state wishes to create or enforce a set of global norms by retaliating or threatening to do so, it must forge some link between the attackers and their government. Convincing the attacking state to call off such attacks or prevent their taking place is harder when the offenders are freelancers. The logic (see above) that acting innocent may strengthen the target state's doubts about who did it is stronger when retaliation depends on both finding the hackers and linking them to the government. Retaliation presumes that pressuring the attacker-government link can end the activities of the freelance attackers themselves.[33] This may hold if the attackers were directed and paid by the government, but the looser the connection, the looser the gearing between punishment and cessation. There is a big difference between cutting off funding to or otherwise discouraging freelancers and ending their activities by prosecuting them. It is hard to justify retaliation against a government that apparently would like to but cannot prosecute, or even find, mischief makers that other states believe are in the country; the justification is stronger if the government knows who and where they are but prevents others from taking action against them. Governments, notably in the third world, that can legally prosecute individuals may find it politically difficult to do so if the accused are politically influential. The distinction between will not and cannot can be very difficult for an outsider to make, much less prove. Perhaps no retaliation can effectively stop or even slow freelancers with multiple customers, hence defenders.

If retaliation nevertheless takes place, how could the attacker's government convince the retaliator that it has done all it can to rein in its hackers? Must it turn over all records that the injured state claims are relevant? If the accused state lacks the technical capability to find hackers, is it obliged to give personnel from the injured state carte blanche to conduct investigations within its borders? If rogue employees, especially those connected to intelligence services, are under investigation, what aspect of their "work" for others can legitimately be kept from such investigators? These are questions of law, right, and wrong (and hardly exclusive to cyberspace), but they speak to the usefulness of deterrence.

Even *if* a deterrence posture can reduce the odds of being attacked, would emphasizing the serious consequences of unrestrained hacking by government-associated elements prompt other countries to take the pains required to control such elements? Or would retaliation prompt the other side to ask: Can you justify attacking us because we could not do everything possible to prevent an attack by others who may be in our country? Would such a country then dig in its heels? If retaliation followed, would such countries be inclined to accept it as their just deserts, or strike back? What if the attacker's government convinces itself that the only way to relieve the pressure is to counter-retaliate? Perhaps it hopes that the retaliator finds that the long-term costs of going after the attacker's government exceed the benefits from the small likelihood that the pursuit might limit freelance activities. Worse, after retaliation, the original hackers may attain the mantle of heroes— they struck a state whose subsequent harmful actions gave retrospective justification to the original attack. Hezbollah emerged from its 2006 confrontation with Israel much more deeply embedded in Lebanon, even though its kidnapping of Israeli soldiers brought war down on the citizenry's heads.[34] Note that if the retaliator is going after states that could have stopped the attack but did not, the rationale for retaliation shifts from juridical (punishment is the legitimate consequence of crime) to the harder-to-explain pragmatic (punishment is a useful way to get the other party to take corrective actions). That is a much higher standard than "not doing what you could have."

The best case that linkage can be legitimate comes from the widespread acceptance of NATO's action against the Taliban for al Qaeda's September 11 attack on the United States. There is little evidence that the Taliban government knew that such an attack was planned, much less that it was conducted by or even on behalf of the Taliban. However, the Taliban's refusal to help bring al Qaeda to justice afterward provided sufficient casus belli, rendering irrelevant the question of original culpability. Still, states balk at giving outsiders too much influence over how they enforce their laws. In 1914, Serbia had accepted all but one part of the ultimatum that the Austro-Hungarian Empire imposed after one of Serbia's citizens shot Archduke Franz Ferdinand in Sarajevo; it resisted making Austrian officials part of Serbia's state justice mechanism. Austria then declared war.

Can freelance hackers be distinguished from government hackers? The degree of organization might be inferred from their actions. Freelance hackers are more likely to use techniques that have been circulating throughout the hacker community; they likely have fewer novel exploits. Government hackers can tap a larger and more secretive research effort that can consolidate discoveries, tools, and techniques across their own organization; thus, their bag of novel tricks is likely larger— not least because governments are much more likely to buy malware kits and tools on the black market than to sell them into the black market. Government hackers are apt to be more methodical and uniform (as befits a uniformed military, for instance) and less likely to be experimental or whimsical.[35] They should be more disciplined in attacking certain targets for certain reasons and avoiding others that may look equally interesting but are not part of the plan. They are likely to provide more consistent and even coverage through a 24-hour day, patiently waiting until people are least likely to be standing guard over their systems. Style points matter little to most states (Israel perhaps aside), but they matter greatly to those freelance hackers eager to impress their friends.

The boundary line between government hackers and organized criminals, however, is less easy to distinguish (particularly in Russia). As one cybersecurity company argues, "The lines are blurring between run-of-the-mill cyber criminals and advanced state-sponsored attackers; the former grew more sophisticated and the latter used off-the-shelf tools to camouflage their moves . . . [with the result that] attribution is becoming more complicated as different kinds of threat actors increasingly share the same tools."[36]

Perhaps most tellingly, only government hackers are likely to start with substantial knowledge of the target's military operational systems (for example, how surface-to-air missiles fail) rather than simply its military information systems (for example, how surface-to-air missile *computers* fail). To cause the desired effects, they must understand the machinery they are trying to interfere with. If such knowledge is classified, few on the outside will know. Although the use of heavyweight code-breaking tools would normally point to a government attacker (because few private hackers can afford to maintain the requisite supercomputers), with cloud computing (or botnets), this is decreasingly so. In 1999, RSA Data Security announced that a longstanding encryption standard had been broken using the brute force of networked computers.[37]

WILL THE ATTACKER ALWAYS AVOID ATTRIBUTION?

Attribution is not always a lost cause. Attackers may be stupid (for example, in operating from an address linked to the state). They may be arrogant and thus sloppy. Open chatter may prove a state's unmaking, especially if it uses hackers who also freelance or have previously freelanced and then talked about what they did. Finally, states may be penetrated by intelligence assets belonging to or working on behalf of the target.

Under what conditions might an attacking country reveal itself? A lot might depend on why it attacked. Consider the several reasons, adduced above, for carrying out unprovoked cyberattacks. Of those, *crime* hardly needs self-attribution; neither do *test* attacks. Because *protest*, *discrediting the target*, *preemption*, and *malice* are about the target much more so than about the attacker, self-attribution can get in the way of the messaging. In other cases, such as *military* motives, *conducting retaliation*, or *eliciting retaliation*, attribution would seem to be obvious—unless the country is carrying out the attack on behalf of another country or faction.

That leaves coercion (against state and nonstate actors). Telling another "do what I want" without identifying "I" is hard, not impossible. Suppose a country (for example, an Islamic state) has allied its interests with those of a larger community (for example, the *umma*), particularly one with powerful nonstate actors. If so, then some correlation can be made between the timing and nature of the attack (for example, following action against Islamic individuals) and the behavior required from the target (stop attacking Islam) without necessarily indicting the attacking state. Others may be willing to help if there are multiple states with a particular interest, such as Vietnam, Indonesia, or the Philippines, all of which fear Chinese bumptiousness in the South China Sea. A state accused of a cyberattack could plead that it has friends that it cannot control but whose righteous ire should be acknowledged.[38] So-called patriotic hackers may be citizens of an accused state without that state appearing hypocritical as long as it makes a credible attempt to bring them under an ostensible control. Alternatively, the state can express satisfaction in cyberattacks that punish behavior that contravenes the community's interests. At the same time, it need not admit to the support, much less protection or even sponsorship, of such attacks. The attack's coercive potential may be limited to promoting those interests held by the community—normally just one among its overall interests (for example, good for taking action against a common enemy but not so good at asserting particular interests such as water rights). But that may be enough in some cases. If the attacker wants to be clear about what the target is supposed to do or not to do, then announcing itself may be in order. Absent explicitness, the target may have implicitly blamed someone else and thereby take away the wrong message.

Or the attacker may want to get the attention of third parties and believes that either the target will not publicly identify the source or that third parties will not credit the target's evidence and thereby not believe the identification. Revelation can be private (to the target) or public. Private revelation can be carried out through diplomatic or intelligence channels or by leaving "calling cards" in cyberspace (for example, information that only the attacking state would have). The attacker may also go public because it believes that private "calling cards" may not get passed up to the target state's command authorities. Public revelation would probably have to come up with evidence that gave such announcement credibility. Indeed, confessing to carrying out an attack can be a form of brandishing a capability to attack (of which more below).[39] Confession, at least, should end the problem of attribution—unless the confessor is lying, which it might do to take credit for something someone else did (if so, it helps to be sure that the real hacker will not contradict such claims) or is protecting another, perhaps weaker, state more likely to be subject to retaliation than the confessor state would. Many examples of misattribution can be drawn from the world of crime and terrorism; Khalid Sheik Mohammad confessed to far more terrorist incidents than he was entitled to take credit for.

One final consideration. If you cannot tell who did it or even communicate what the damage was, you also cannot tell who did *not* do it or what the damage could have been. As long as the burden of proof is not heavy or, better yet, if it can be shifted to the accused, who has to prove the negative, a target can claim an attack (that may not have happened) from someone who probably did not do it. But anyone who goes down that road is probably not interested in the calculus of deterrence and is more interested in justifying aggression and sowing mischief and just needs some rhetorical cover.[40] Such purposes may be incompatible with U.S. behavior, but establishing or at least supporting norms that legitimize cyberdeterrence may give less fastidious governments yet one more excuse to wreak international mischief.

WHY AN ATTACKER MAY FAVOR AMBIGUOUS ATTRIBUTION OVER NONE AT ALL

Attackers that want to coerce their targets but worry about retaliation may find that the calculus of attribution can be made to work in their favor. Assume that whoever openly attacks loses more from retaliation than it gains in coercion. Assume, too, that the attacker cannot coerce if its identity remains a complete mystery. It would seem that all intermediate levels of assurance would also yield net negative benefits. For instance, if the target thinks that the odds that the attacker was State Z are 50/50, then the coercive benefits are half of what they would have been if the target were certain and so are the odds of retaliation. From State Z's perspective, both the benefits of coercion and the expected cost of retaliation are reduced by half. This still leaves a net negative. So, it appears that the attacker cannot win.

But are the odds of retaliation really the same as the perceived likelihood that Z was the attacker? Are the odds of retaliation a 50/50 proposition if the target thinks the odds are only 50/50 that Z was the attacker? A great deal depends on how risk averse the target is. If the target fears the consequences of retaliating against an innocent country more than it fears the consequences of *not* retaliating against the actual attacker, then it needs considerable confidence in its attribution before it hits back. In that case, the odds that the state will retaliate when it is only half-sure that Z did it would be less, perhaps far less, than 50/50.[41] Z therefore gets half of the coercive benefit but suffers far less than a 50/50 chance of retaliation. It may be a net gainer.

Thus, an attack that might not be attributable may be worthwhile for the attacker even when a more obvious attack is not. The target state, for its part, may do its best to exaggerate its likelihood of retaliating, the better to throw off the attacker's calculations. Yet given the nature of crises coupled with the natural ambiguities of cyberspace, the attacker is likely already dealing with a great quantity of ambiguous information.

Perhaps the fact that since 2014 the Russians are becoming easier to see is because they want to be seen by those prepared to see. Intimidation may be part of their broader information operations strategy. But the virtue of keeping them guessing is not unique to cyberspace. The extent of Russian involvement in eastern Ukraine was not always crystal clear to everyone. Russia denied that its troops were in Ukraine, going so far as to claim that captured Russian troops had gotten lost. To any impartial observer with access to global news coverage (that is, outside Russia, for such purposes), Russian coercion was obvious. But Russia's denial, and the difficulty of proving its participation beyond a penumbra of a doubt, served three purposes. It let Russia convince its own citizens that it had no troops in Ukraine. It let Russia avoid a commitment that could have prevented it from withdrawing forces if it had to. And last, the wisp of deniability allowed countries reluctant to take action against Russia to argue that they were not convinced that Russia really carried out an invasion; a clear admission might have demanded a response.[42]

What Russia did on Eurasian soil could easily work in cyberspace where a soupçon of doubt could convince citizens unwilling to believe their government could do bad things or dissuade governments unready to face the consequences of admitting that something bad had taken place. The failure to admit complicity in cyberspace could also allow others to think that the attacker was not completely committed to carrying out a vigorous campaign in cyberspace.

WHAT SHOULD BE REVEALED ABOUT ATTRIBUTION?

What evidence for attribution should be laid out? Much depends on what the purpose of attribution is:

- If used to prosecute an individual, then the answer is a function of the legal process.
- If used solely to characterize a potential adversary's intentions, motives, capabilities, and modus operandi, then it is intelligence and the requirements would be set by the intelligence process.
- If used to affect the policies of the U.S. government toward the attacker, then it matters whether these policies are executed where people can see them (for example, via diplomatic measures) or whether they are executed sub rosa. A lot also depends on whether the responses are within a sovereign state's rights (for example, denying visas to hackers) or whether it goes beyond them (for example, an embargo).
- If used to justify overt force, then the need for public attribution is that much stronger, especially if UN concurrence is sought.

The nature of the attribution evidence should also color how public to make it. If the *primary* source of attribution evidence is intelligence collection, revelation could be costly (in terms of sources and methods and ramifications therefrom). But if intelligence is just one reason to be confident about an attribution call, then presenting the *other* evidence can be a workable compromise (more protection of sources and methods but a weaker case). Last, if intelligence provides a clue that permits forensic evidence to be marshaled, then the case for the latter's revelation is stronger. What if disclosing the forensic technique lets hackers know what signature to avoid leaving? If so, the case for revelation may stand on the hope that by the next time revelation is required, the technology will have moved so far that the hider-finder game in cyberspace works far differently. Or it may rest on the trade-off in which credibility rises because of punishment confidently delivered, even if the difficulty of attribution also rises. Or the accusing country may hold off burning an attribution method until a new one is in place (lest burning it prematurely lowers the odds of using this alternative method). Finally, the more complicated the case for attribution, the fewer people will understand it directly.

Revelation may not be a once-and-for-all process. Can the intelligence community reveal some sources and methods without being pressured to reveal more—and will it believe that it can resist the pressure to go further? If the community believes that revelation will happen anyway, can it modulate the risk to sources and methods by going out and changing its mix of techniques among, for instance, open-source fact-gathering, forensics, human intelligence, or signals intelligence? What role would deliberate indirection—for example, putting out the "news" that the information came from one place when it came from another—play in that mix? Or will it just have to throw up its hands and back away from public attribution?[43]

There will be times when the clues to attribution are classified and explaining how they were generated could blow the source. In some cases—such as when credibility on attribution is needed to justify major retaliation—blowing a source is justified. In other cases, when attribution is hortatory, or the planned response is well within a state's sovereign rights, there is less need. Clearly, sources cannot be blown often. Attribution for the less critical incidents in cyberspace is, for that reason, likely to be worse than attribution for those critical enough to blow a source for.

After the Snowden revelations, the omniscience of the NSA has become a matter of belief to many. How, believers ask, could the NSA *fail* to attribute cyberattacks? But these newly credited powers raise new questions.

First, assume the NSA is that good. Is it reasonable to conclude that it is also good enough to be able to characterize attacks and prevent them before they take place? If so, is the NSA actually doing all this? Even though *some* secret sauce was provided to the intrusion prevention systems that protect the dot-mil domain and the defense industrial base, Iranians did manage to penetrate the Navy–Marine Corps Internet for months.[44] Nor is it obvious that the NSA is transferring *all* the knowledge about the vulnerabilities that overseas hackers may exploit to those who run intrusion detection systems. But seeing everything that might implicate hackers may not shed enough light on the actual work of crafting, testing, and distributing malware. Thus, the ability to indict may not imply the ability to prevent.

Second, can this information do any good if the revelation of how it was collected jeopardizes future collection? The May 2014 indictment of the five Chinese hackers cannot help but raise the question of what evidence the U.S. government can present in open court (on the off chance that the suspects show up). If the NSA (is the source of the information and) is not prepared to open itself up to the legal discovery process, then would it reveal its information in a public forum where the case can be made but need not be defended (for example, something like former secretary of state Colin Powell's unfortunately erroneous indictment of the Iraqi regime before the UN General Assembly in February 2003)? Or would an administration consider the NSA's job done if it merely gives the president confidence to retaliate irrespective of public opinion (or if it chose to respond sub rosa)?

Third, the U.S. government may have to release far more than what is narrowly needed to makes its case (if for no other reason than the legal discovery process).[45] Much of what makes a convincing attribution case is that the evidence from an attack in question resembles evidence from past attacks attributed to the same source and does *not* resemble evidence from attacks attributed to other sources. Making *that* case requires displaying evidence on multiple attacks, and not just for the accused party but for others; this only multiplies the sources and methods problem. The FBI's assertion that the hackers had used an IP address that was used by North Korean hackers cannot prove the hackers were North Korean—until it is established that the *only* users of that IP address were North Korean. The intelligence community's reluctance to use its own data may be assuaged by the existence of private corporations with similar data.[46] Since the Mandiant report, other cyber-security firms have established a reputation for assigning a series of attacks to one or another group whose national origin they can establish. They include Symantec (the aforementioned Elderwood Project), CrowdStrike (which tracks over sixty groups, including Energetic Bear and Hurricane Panda), Cylance (which tracks Iranian groups), iSight, and Kaspersky (which revealed the Regin and Equation series of intrusions).[47] Several private companies, such as Symantec and Kaspersky, maintain vast surveillance networks to discover malware and, secondarily, to aid attribution.[48] The advent of private attribution has, some argued, made it easier for the U.S. government to go public with its own attribution claims. But to what extent would a private corporation be willing to share its own sources and methods in an open forum? And are private sources always right?

Fourth, how might a belief in the NSA's omniscience (howsoever correct) affect the other side? One might hope that others would be deterred from a cyberattack to the extent that they would concede both attribution and U.S. confidence in such attribution sufficient for retaliation (assuming sufficient will to retaliate). A lesser hope is that the other side will take greater pains, thus pay greater costs, to carry out operations, which ought to reduce the volume of activity. Conversely, unless they think that what the NSA does is magic, those who really want to get the NSA off their networks can make considerable progress in doing so, largely by employing air gapping and tightly filtering bytes that must cross the gap between the dark and the light side. This may create a basic dilemma of attribution: you can convince others that they are being watched, or you can watch them—but not both.

CHAPTER 24
What Threshold and Confidence for Response?

H ow bad must an attack be to justify retaliation? We examine the use of a zero-tolerance policy, the establishment of specific tests as part of a threshold, the risks of trying to deter cyberespionage with retaliation, and a comparison of explicit and implicit deterrance policies.

A ZERO-TOLERANCE POLICY?

Certain classes of attacks such as DDOS or defacing websites are so common that strict adherence to the broken-windows-in-cyberspace theory would entangle a country in a constant state of
retaliation (and maybe counter-retaliation) to the point where distinguishing initial attacks from
responses would be a lost cause.[1] If implants that might be prefatory to attack are deemed worthy of
retaliation, the crossover point will likewise be breached continually because it is very difficult to
distinguish an implant that precedes espionage from one that precedes attack. Minor attacks often
leave less damage than what would merit the attention of a U.S. small claims court. Merely cranking
up the machinery of retaliation or even the machinery of investigation for something so small would
entail costs that would greatly exceed the actual damage. If retaliation for a cyberattack follows a
first discovery of a recurrent activity, the accused cannot help but ask, "Why me, why now?" and
perhaps draw the wrong lessons.

Furthermore, invoking retaliation for small matters may complicate its effectiveness for large
measures. After facing retaliation, space-sponsored or state-condoned attackers will improve their
operational security. They could also develop countermeasures against forensic methods, much as
they can create countermeasures to defensive measures. Because compromising a system is usually a
painstaking rather than a spontaneous effort, such adjustments can be readily built into how hackers
work.

A zero-threshold posture, nevertheless, may inhibit the attacker's employing of a cat's-paw
gambit: the target did not retaliate against this, so I will try that next. If an adversary believes that
it can carefully calibrate increasing levels of attack (notwithstanding the necessity of predicting the
effects of an attack in the face of variegated and shifting defenses), it may hope to replicate what is
(misleadingly) said to be frogs put into slowly boiling water. Conversely, the first retaliation against
such a strategy may appear disproportionate (especially if it is meant to respond to the accumulation
of crimes past) and thus illegitimate, hence inviting counter-retaliation.

Another advantage of a zero-threshold policy is that the target country could demonstrate its
will to retaliate for large attacks (yet to occur) by retaliating, even if in lesser measure, for small
ones. A low threshold for responses also allows the target country to establish a set of norms against
which the behavior of others can be held. These norms, in turn, constitute a basis for deterrence.
Israel's tit-for-tat policy against terrorist attacks (whether by ground or air) is understood to be part
of a constant strategy of deterrence that "connects a series of acts of force to create and maintain
general norms of behavior for many military actors of an extended period of time"[2] (also known as
"cutting the grass"). Correspondingly, one can ask whether the failure to respond to date put the
United States at greater risk of cyberattack.

Conversely, small attacks often leave small signatures. Even if very large attacks can come only from a handful of large countries, no such relationship covers small attacks; there could be a limitless list of possible perpetrators. Small responses may also be problematic; if *not announced* as such, the fact that they were intended as punishment may go unnoticed in the noise of cyberspace. Even if the attacker received some specific indication that the attack was an act of retaliation, such signals may not necessarily reach the attacker's public (or the third parties the retaliator wishes to impress).

Because the smallness of the attack suggests that it be created as a crime rather than an attack, national-scale retaliation could seem provocative, and using cyberattacks to retaliate against low-level cyberattacks legitimizes cyberattacks as an everyday use of state power (Stuxnet, by contrast, was an extraordinary objective). Would that be in the U.S. interest in a world in which other countries might see this as license to do as much to weaker neighbors?

NON-ZERO THRESHOLDS

Skipping across the scale, one obvious threshold for a hostile state-level response is the loss of life. Death has the advantage of being unambiguous. The U.S. strike against Libya in 1986 was justified as retaliation against a Libyan-sponsored bombing in Berlin that killed two Americans; similarly, for the (supposed) incident that started the Mexican-American war (the death of eleven U.S. soldiers at the hands of Mexican infantry in territory that both nations claimed). Few in the United States thought that either constituted an arbitrary flash point.[3] That said, the source of death may sometimes be ambiguous, especially if indirect (for example, someone who dies because 911 service was hacked), or, worse, statistical (for example, increased suicides caused by unemployment when companies shut down in the wake of a cyberattack).

The problem with looking for casualties is that devastatingly expensive cyberattacks may simply not produce any but cannot pass without notice. Basing thresholds on economic criteria—for example, retaliation will follow if the attack cost more than $1 million—allows costly cyberattacks to qualify for retaliation. Yet thresholds can be hard to define. How does one price secrets, lost privacy, or lost trust (admittedly, consequences of cyberespionage, not cyberattack)? If cyberattacks are followed by systemic improvements in security to prevent a repeat, does the cost of buying the latter count (such expenses are determined afterward by the target and aimed at future, not past, attackers)? What about attacks or even system compromises that convince the target to expensively rebuild the system (doing which, to add further confusion, has ancillary benefits)? What about the cost of poorly considered responses (such as the credit checks offered by OPM following an attack almost surely carried out for intelligence purposes)? How does one count services that the hacked organization withdraws from customers using the hack as an excuse ("sorry, we cannot process your loan")? An attacker could unintentionally cross the threshold through inadvertence or cascading effects (even if this is not legally exculpatory).[4] The potential retaliator would have a double burden: not only establishing causality between an attack and the subsequent damage but also making a convincing case that the damage exceeded the threshold.

The wisdom of placing a specific threshold can be subject to cost-effectiveness tests. Assume an earlier billion-dollar threshold. After several attacks in the $40 million class (for example, Saudi Aramco, Sony), the threshold is lowered to $20 million. Assuming that lowering the threshold actually deters (rather than goads) attacks—say, down to nothing—helps form an estimate of how many attacks in the $20 million to $40 million class were avoided. In that sense, the defender comes out ahead—or more, if doing so establishes the credibility of the deterrence policy for larger attacks. Conversely, the cycle of retaliation and counter-retaliation may leave the United States with the cyberspace equivalent of the Vietnam (now Iraq) syndrome.

In some cases, damages from systems compromise can be substantial. South Korea has concluded that it had to redo its national identity system after attacks by North Korea; the cost is said to be $1 billion (if business as well as government costs are included).[5] This is equivalent to sinking an empty warship.

Some of the economic threshold problem can be mitigated by requiring that, in practice, the damage be much larger than the announced threshold. This only works if the number of attacks whose damage exceeds the nominal threshold but not the actionable threshold is small. Otherwise, retaliation against an attack that crosses the unannounced real threshold may seem arbitrary because no such response followed attacks that also crossed the announced threshold (but, unbeknownst to others, did not cross the real threshold).

The threshold question remains even if states respond to cyberattacks with actions that are within a state's prerogatives (for example, name-and-shame, visa controls). A norms-based threshold would require defining, or helping the community of nations define, what constitutes bad behavior (for example, that hacking is not simply "boys will be boys" or "spies will be spies"). But with retaliation against cyberattack, the stakes in getting it right are higher, and the arguments about proportionality may surface only after it is too late to take things back.

To illustrate other difficulties of setting thresholds, note that U.S. retaliation against North Korea for its attack on Sony was justified by the chilling impact that the attack had on Sony's freedom of speech *and* because computers were wiped and not just read from. This was a problematic threshold for several reasons. First, any justification that has two legs creates questions about what behavior it is trying to warn others away from: the first, the second, or only something that combines both? Second, the right of Sony to make whatever movies it wants to is an element in commercial, not personal, speech; the perfectly legal threat of a private lawsuit is perhaps even more chilling.[6] Third, Sony is a Japanese company (even if its moviemaking subsidiary is headquartered in the United States). Fourth, the movie's distribution to theaters was cancelled only after major movie chains pulled out in the face of a *physical* threat to moviegoers.[7] Fifth, the United States did not respond thusly to the Las Vegas Sands hack, which both was destructive and affected its owner's right to free speech. Sixth, it is not entirely impossible that when the final accounting is done, Sony may have made money from the hack; early estimates of $100 million in damage now look exaggerated, and before the film was consigned to Netflix, Sony had realized $40 million in sales.[8] Although the company may have hoped for more ticket sales (say, $100 million), the movie reviews were very mediocre. All in all, the U.S. decision to respond to the Sony hack did not lead to the cleanest of red lines.[9]

One DoD official has made a quasi-specific statement about thresholds: "About 2 percent of attacks on American systems, officials say, may rise to the level of prompting a national response led by the Pentagon and through the military's CYBERCOM."[10] This raises the question, though: 2 percent of what (since there is no lower bound on what constitutes a cyberattack)?

Earlier, the same official would moot the notion that a single threshold could not capture a long series of cyberattacks akin to "death by a thousand cuts." As Director of National Intelligence James Clapper testified in reference to his 2015 threat assessment, "Rather than a 'cyber-Armageddon' scenario that debilitates the entire U.S. infrastructure, we envision something different . . . an ongoing series of low-to-moderate level cyberattacks from a variety of sources over time, which will impose cumulative costs on U.S. economic competitiveness and national security."[11] So maybe cyberattacks are collectively costly, but so are cybersecurity investments.

One *could* define such a death-by-a-thousand-cuts threshold by adding up a series of related cyberattacks. But would spacing a series of small cyberattacks over time in lieu of one big attack be a likely or an effective strategy by hackers or other states? The tendency for cyberattacks to induce victims and onlookers to invest in cybersecurity argues otherwise. What if what is billed as death by a thousand cuts is really death by a thousand infections: potentially fatal if they arrive simultaneously or in quick succession—but less worrisome if they are spaced out well enough for later attacks to meet an immune system primed by earlier ones?

SHOULD PULLED OR FAILED PUNCHES MERIT RETALIATION?

Should a country respond to a pulled punch—for example, a cyberattack that goes only far enough to demonstrate that it could damage a system but does not, in fact, damage it—as it would respond to a delivered punch? A "yes" answer would inhibit demonstration attacks and hence inhibit coercive strategies that depend on such attacks; all punches in cyberspace, pulled or not, would have to factor in possible reprisals. Because a demonstration attack is, essentially, an act of communication, the attacker is going to be very interested in a response, and retaliation may be part of the dialogue from which the attacker (and others watching) draws inferences. Unfortunately, a failure to respond could be interpreted either as the target not seeing the attack, not wanting to bother itself over something ambiguous, or lacking the courage to get into a fight.

Yet the argument that only attacks that follow through should count cannot be brushed off. First, if some proportionality matters, then retaliating requires determining what a delivered punch would have done based on what a pulled punch did. Estimates could be quite wrong (unless the attacker indicates what it had tried to do). Second, unless the retaliation is sub rosa, the retaliator has to make the case that such an attack could have been disastrous had the aggressor not consciously withheld a critical step *and* that it is legitimate to retaliate on the basis of intention and not just effects. This is something the law of armed conflict does not support unless the intention implies an imminent attack. Third, it may not be in the target's interest to deter a demonstration attack in the first place. It may actually want to know what the other side can do (especially if its own fears subsequently prove exaggerated), and it may want others such as private network owners to know as well, the better to spur them into raising defenses. The target of a demonstration attack may wish to establish the aggressor's intent and gain insights as to what the aggressor thinks might scare the target. Finally, any concrete demonstration will reveal vulnerabilities to which attention may be focused, thereby likely reducing them.

The argument is similar for failed attacks with only subtle differences.[12] Failure is not an act of communication. Also, attribution for a failed attack will likely be harder than for a demonstration attack where the attacker is trying to make a point.[13] Thus, the target can afford not to respond without fearing that it has lost face.

WHAT ABOUT RETALIATING AGAINST CYBERESPIONAGE?

Does the failure of the United States to establish a deterrence policy against cyberespionage explain why it suffers so much of it, especially from China? Clearly, the United States is upset, but perhaps it is not just the espionage but also the volume of the intrusions (in terms of both number and bytes exfiltrated), their apparent brazenness (for example, going after the computer used by the secretary of defense[14]), and the mess made in the course of doing so. The problem is not limited to the United States: German chancellor Angela Merkel felt confident enough in this attribution to complain to China's premier in person.[15] China has steadfastly denied all responsibility.

But would a retaliation *policy* be wise? Cyberespionage can go years without detection; a policy that reacts harshly not to all acts but to those few that are discovered may seem arbitrary, much as harsh punishments for rarely detected crimes do.[16] The law of armed conflict does not recognize espionage as a casus belli, and a good case for changing this has yet to be made, even though the means of espionage have changed (so that changes in the quantity of espionage from cyberespionage might be deemed a change in quality). Finally, every country that can do so carries out cyberespionage.[17] Those who try to establish deterrence policies to prevent others from doing what they do themselves perforce reveal themselves to be fools or hypocrites—unless they are so powerful that they can get away with it. It is doubtful whether even the United States qualifies as being that powerful.

There are also practical hurdles to such a policy. One problem is communicating exactly what was objectionable about the behavior—was it the fact of espionage, its volume, the mess it left behind, or its purpose? The United States used to argue that it did no commercial espionage; after the Snowden revelations, it had to refine its distinction to include commercial espionage—but not for competitive gain.

A second problem gets back to the threshold question, in an area where the no-threshold rule is likely to lead to great inconsistency. But what threshold? Many estimates of the cost of purloined information tend to measure loss by the cost. Yet, as argued, estimating the cost of EMCE can, at best, be done only years later when the information is converted into competitive products (if, indeed, one can determine that such a product required that such espionage had to take place). Proportionality requires that punishment reflect how much was *actually* taken, not just how much was *discovered* as having been taken. In a realm in which very little is detected, it is unclear how to infer unseen, hence unmeasured, activities.

Also, how could one tell that an act of retaliation had any effect on the behavior of the offending country? Facing pressure, those who carry out cyberespionage might do nothing different (while claiming they are doing nothing, doing something, or leaving the matter in doubt), swear to carry on but stop anyway, swear to back down and not do so, or swear to back down and actually do it. If the retaliation (both effects and retaliator) is public, the accused has little to lose by asking for proof; the accuser, however, puts its sources and methods at risk by providing that proof. Even if one assumes away the attribution question, the measurement question is nontrivial; in mid-2015, the FBI reported "that economic espionage cases surged 53 percent in the past year, and that China accounted for most of that."[18] But such a number is a product of the number of intrusions, the percentage that are discovered, and the percentage of those discovered that are reported to the FBI and become cases (which in turn reflects how organizations feel about the FBI and what threshold is used to designate a case). Because the last two variables can go up or down on their own (the trend these days is up), the correlation between compromises and cases can be quite inexact.

A similar argument bedevils any attempt to punish the implantation of code into sensitive sites (for example, a country's energy infrastructure). If the United States were to confront another country about having done so, its response could well be threefold. *One*, prove it was us—the typical attribution problem. *Two*, unique to this threshold: prove that what you found was prefatory to an attack. Finding a weaponized code on the far side of an air gap may be incriminating; finding an implant that could easily receive espionage as attack code is anything but. *Three*, prove that you have not done the same to us. Inasmuch as careful espionage that communicates sparingly is very difficult to detect, the accuser would have more than the usual difficulties proving a negative. Nothing prevents the United States from giving private warnings to other countries that it will apply its own standards in evaluating such matters and react accordingly—but if it does something nasty or risky in response, the public justification will be that much more difficult than it would be for a response to an overt cyberattack.

A country that steals personal information and then also uses it for criminal purposes (for example, bank fraud, identity theft) or transfers it to someone who uses it this way has crossed a line from permissible to impermissible behavior according to most norms. The United States could warn

China that while stealing personnel records is what countries do, selling them is *not* what countries do (that said, there is no evidence as of spring 2016 that the Chinese have any intention of selling the twenty-two million personnel records from OPM).

A DETERMINISTIC POSTURE

Should a deterrence policy be explicit and deterministic—if you do this, we will do that—or implicit and hence probabilistic: if you anger us enough by your behavior, we might strike back? The latter policy may be understood as the default for all sufficiently powerful countries. U.S. history—see Pearl Harbor or September 11—provides sufficient basis for believing that once past some of the insult and injury, it becomes bent on destroying their source. Even in World War I, the United States, "too proud to fight," tolerated submarine attacks (for example, on the *Lusitania*) until the Zimmerman telegram and Germany's announcement of unrestricted submarine warfare; then it was off to war. And before that was popular reaction to the sinking of the USS *Maine*. Indeed, in a democratic society like the United States, responses are often driven or at least strongly supported by popular sentiment, which dilutes a counter-coercive strategy by the attacker and is hence a strength from the viewpoint of deterrence. All this should suggest to potential adversaries that the United States would respond harshly to sufficient provocation even if the exact nature of the provocation was not prespecified.

Characteristic of a deterministic policy is that there is no response until a red line is crossed; after that, response is certain (a set of multiple red lines is possible but, mathematically, they are simply the addition of binary responses). With a probabilistic policy (for example, certain punishment if red lines are crossed, but possible if not—or possible punishment if red lines are crossed but certainly not otherwise), no threshold is declared but the probability of a response as a function of provocation starts off very low (but not necessarily zero) and ends up very high (but not necessarily 100 percent). From the potential attacker's perspective, incidentally, it matters little if the United States had a probabilistic red line (that is, it declared fixed probabilities of response and then tossed the dice after each provocation), or if the United States did have a red line but the attacker was uncertain of where it lay. Either way, the perceived likelihood of a response rises as the seriousness of the contemplated attack does, but in neither case are these probabilities very clear. A nonlinear dose-response curve may be either deterministic or probabilistic; it is not the difference between apathy and overreaction that matters, but the obviousness of the line separating the two.

Unless a country thinks it can get away with unilateral declarations of what constitutes a red line, it may want to negotiate appropriate norms in advance. To wit: if you are going to draw a red line, you have to offer negotiations over what rules should not be broken, your intention (and maybe plan) to adhere to such rules, and (perhaps) the means by which rule-breaking would be detected. For the United States, it really helps if allies are on board (because the United States is pledged to protect such allies from, increasingly, cyberattack). Last, a credible case has to be made that such rules could be plausibly acceptable to those being deterred. But behind the offer can be a threat to go unilateral in the face of foot-dragging.

A policy of determinism has its advantages. It creates a serious penalty for stepping over the threshold. Thus, it should induce self-restraint by the adversary as this or that act threatens to breach the threshold. It also colors the response to crossing the threshold as foretold rather than arbitrary. But when is determinism deterministic? The nuclear weapons use that Cold War deterrence was designed to prevent would have been unmistakable (not only was radiation a tell-tale sign, but also the smallest nuclear weapon was more powerful than the biggest conventional weapon). However, the likelihood that the United States would respond in kind to a nuclear attack, particularly one that was meant to be singular and not followed up, was never 100 percent. Schelling's advocacy of a deterrence that "left something to chance" was a way of creating a deterrence policy that suggested to the Soviet Union that there was always *some* likelihood that the United States would respond to something that crossed a line, even if the United States faced a devastating counter-retaliation by doing so.

Determinism for cyberattacks can be problematic. The relationship between effort and outcomes in cyberspace, for instance, is chancy. A full-throated cyberattack may be stopped or substantially weakened by unexpected defenses (the headlines say which attacks succeeded; they rarely report those that have failed completely and only occasionally report those that worked their way into systems but to little ultimate effect). Conversely, a cyberattack may overachieve in the sense that a precision attack meant to disable a capability (such as providing electric power to a radar) may create cascading effects, as explained above. In cyberspace, perceived effects may be alternatively greater or less than actual effects. Attacks could corrupt systems so that they produce incorrect results rather than rendering them obviously useless, thereby driving their knowing owners to seek correct results elsewhere. From a military perspective, there is considerable value in breaking a system in ways that are not obvious until someone tries to use it. Conversely, if such corruption is obvious to users, they may suspect that many other systems have been corrupted even if the adversary knows it did not strike them. So the target's damage estimate may be much higher than facts warrant.

Thus, a major advantage of a deterministic policy—a bulwark against inadvertent escalation—is not a guarantee. Because of the disjunction between cause and effect and between reality and perception, an attacker can think it has not crossed into the danger zone because its intent stayed left of some red line. Yet the target may think otherwise if the perceived effect wandered to the right of the red line. Hence, retaliation lands on the table and, with it, the risks of a greater confrontation.

Clearly marking red lines can inhibit others from crossing them, but that inhibition also can be eroded—in this case by difficulties in attribution. Granted, attribution should be a neutral factor in comparing a deterministic versus a probabilistic deterrence policy. They both reduce the odds of retaliation by the same amount. Similarly, difficulties in attribution ruin the credibility of both policies—but not the same way. Credibility matters more for a deterministic policy than it does for a probabilistic one. One country declares a red line and avers that punishment would follow its crossing. Another crosses it but attempts to conceal itself. Punishment never comes. The attacker would be justified in asking: Did I hide well enough, or did the target, knowing who did it, nevertheless refuse to respond, perhaps for fear of starting a nasty fight? If the target shrank back, how credible is its threat of cyberdeterrence? Worse, the attacker may be asking: If a cyberattack did not draw a response when a response was solemnly promised, then how credible are all the threats in other domains such as where the issue was one of death and destruction? The same scenario, played out against an ambiguous deterrence policy, may cause the attacker to wonder whether it did hide well or it was found out but the provocation-response curve lies to the right (greater provocation needed) of where it was previously thought to be; the possibility that the declaration was a sham would get less emphasis.

The corrosive effects of doubt are exacerbated, so if others assume that the intelligence community of the United States is so good (particularly after the Snowden revelations), the United States must know who did what. After all, the entire Cold War was fought without any country calling any other country's bluff—even though there were serious questions about whether any sane country would retaliate in full against a nuclear attack that destroyed a few things if the cycle of retaliation could end up destroying everything.[19] No one really wanted to call anyone's bluff in the nuclear arena, because the price of being wrong was catastrophic. Catastrophe is nowhere near such a threat in a cyberwar; hence, a U.S. deterrence policy might be considered a testable proposition if the attacking country did not fear that a U.S. response could ultimately escalate, perhaps even to the nuclear level (a prospect not to be casually dismissed[20]). Bluffs may well be called. The major difference is that the probabilistic deterrence strategy is less brittle and loses less credibility if difficulties in attribution prevent a response. Even if the target state had deterministic deterrence policies for other types of attacks (for example, nuclear), the credibility of the latter would not be damaged by the ambiguities of its policy in cyberspace.

Lastly, one country's decision to announce a deterministic policy may influence another country's decision to do likewise. The United States has been edging toward a more deterministic policy over the last few years. China, by contrast, lacks one altogether. Not only has it refrained from drawing red lines, but it also is not clear when talking to its academics and officials whether it has thought through how it would react to this or that cyberattack. But, as in a game of chicken, the side that declares a deterministic deterrence posture eliminates options (to back down) by doing so. It gives itself an edge in a confrontation—but may also prompt the other side to seek a similar edge in a confrontation. Thus, advocates of a deterministic posture may want to ask: Would the United States be better off if its own declaration prompted China to do likewise, thereby creating the potential for a showdown in which neither side could back off?

OTHER ADVANTAGES OF A PROBABILISTIC DETERRENCE POSTURE

A probabilistic deterrence posture has many other advantages in an uncertain world.

It establishes no safe zone. If there is no red line, there is no area left of the red line where attackers can play without consequences. Everything that rises above some noise level risks retaliation in the same way that walking in a mine field is not safe even if the first footfall is unremarkable. Indeed, if Americans determine that the accumulation of injuries—for example, the continual theft of intellectual property by one actor—had excited the population enough to demand a response, the fact that such behavior had passed muster before would be beside the point.

It thus does not make the world safe for cyberwar. A stated red line may also raise the question of what an appropriate punishment would be. The declaring state has a choice. If it says it will react with violence to a cyberattack, it may enhance deterrence, but, if tested, such a policy may drag the state into a very costly war when perhaps a less costly response in kind might have sufficed to give teeth to deterrence. If it says it will react *only* in kind, then it sets a top limit on the amount of damage the attacker can expect. And if the attacker, say, by dint of having less infrastructure at stake, determines it can outlast the target in an all-out tit-for-tat, it may not be deterred at all. The optimal solution, *if the means of retaliation are specified*, is to make the punishment fit not only the crime but also the criminal. Discriminate deterrence, however, sends a very mixed message and may evoke the Melian dialogue (the strong do as they will and the weak suffer what they must), which is anathema in a rules-based world. Ambiguity in specifying the means of retaliation has its virtues.

It does not reassure unpredictable allies. The United States is no stranger to ambiguous deterrence policies (for example, would it launch nuclear weapons in response to a Soviet invasion of Europe?). The United States wishes to have the Chinese believe that attacking Taiwan after the latter declares independence will lead to retaliation—but also wishes to leave some question in Taiwan's calculus, lest it pocket the U.S. guarantee and then do something that sets China off and culminates in a U.S.-China confrontation. There may be a cyberspace equivalent.

It weakens counter-deterrence. Many a deterrence policy fails or leads states to danger when the potential recipients of such warnings threaten counter-retaliation. However, if the impetus for retaliation is not calculation but the outrage of the population, the recipient of the warning may want to think twice if it believes that it can ward off punishment by the counter-threats. The population is unlikely to understand the requisite nuances. If it is driven by anger, it may not be in a mood for doing its sums, anyway. The leaders of the target country can plead to the attacker: I'd like to hold my fire, but I fear more from my own people than I do from anything you can do to me. Incidentally, the basis for retaliation need not be public ire, if calculation coupled with public acquiescence suffices. But the fact that it *could* be public ire suffices to neutralize what the attacker *thinks* will be the effect of the counter-deterrence strategy.

It permits tailored deterrence.[21] There are practical reasons for the target to tailor the reprisals for an attack based on who carried it out. The situation's context may matter (one country but not another may be involved in a real-world crisis). The attacker's history may matter. The attacker's ability to counter-retaliate may matter (having nuclear weapons or a large volume of bilateral trade may actually make a difference). The lessons that others may take away may matter (reprisals against a neutral may play differently than reprisals against a foe of long standing). In some cases, avoiding retaliation may be wise; in others, one might as well go ahead. No explicit deterrence policy that seeks to make a country's response to a cyberattack look as if it were the blind application of law (that is, the natural response to crossing a red line) can state (or at least not with a straight face) that the rules apply to some but not others. Since an implicit deterrence policy declares nothing, it need not speak to the issue of tailored deterrence, making the tailored application of reprisals easier to contemplate.

It creates less need to explain. Any explicit deterrence policy creates the risk that its intended recipients will not take it at face value. Instead, they will try to infer the state's underlying posture by asking, perhaps out loud, why the policy was declared at a particular point in time, and why the red line was set as it was ("Why here? Why now?"). Such questions could undermine not only the legitimacy of a policy but also its credibility. If potential attackers infer that an explicit deterrence policy is needed because implicit postures are inadequate, they may conclude that the declaring state has discovered that it could not achieve cybersecurity or that it has more to lose in a cyberattack than was previously assumed. If the retaliation promised for cyberattack is limited to a cyberattack, the attacker may begin to wonder whether kinetic means have been taken off the table. By contrast, if retaliation follows the expression of popular anger—as it could in probabilistic policy—it need not be declared in advance, and thus there is nothing to explain.

It permits time for contemplating a proper response. The more deterministic a deterrence policy, the greater the pressure to respond quickly if an attack crosses some line, lest the target's credibility be called into question (not only in cyberspace but across the board, as noted above). The excuse that the target is gathering the means and looking for an opportunity may not be credible for a state that has announced a deterrence policy, especially if it is the United States, which is perceived as having the means and having, in advance, explored all the opportunities for retaliation—even in cyberspace. But an instant response may be inappropriate while information is being gathered that validates attribution, assesses the degree of damage, and weighs the various alternatives. If the government deems the attack serious enough, it can strike back. If the government chooses, ultimately, not to respond, all it signals by inaction is that the attack did not cross the red line *at that point and in that context.*

It permits a sub rosa response. The target state may want to strike back but fears sparking an all-out series of exchanges forced upon both governments via public pressure. The sub rosa option allows retaliation but in ways that do not necessarily excite the attacking state's public. Such responses are designed to catch the attention of the attacking state's leaders and let them know that continuation of the aggression would be unwise. Those leaders, acting without pressure from what would otherwise be a population that was injured and aggrieved (from having suffered retaliation), could concede the point without losing face in front of their people. An ambiguous deterrence policy preserves that option; the target state does not have to justify its inaction very strenuously. A deterministic deterrence policy makes such an option difficult to pursue since the apparent lack of response when one was promised will be taken by almost everyone (except the leadership of the attacking state) as no response at all, calling its credibility into question.

THE CHOICE TO RETALIATE UNDER UNCERTAINTY

The costs and benefits of declaring a threshold are strongly related to the choice of whether to retaliate under somewhat ambiguous conditions.[22] To illustrate as much, assume a cyberattack of certain nature but uncertain origin. As far as you, the target, know, the country that you would retaliate against did it with a certain probability; otherwise it did not do it. You could retaliate or not retaliate. If the attackers are innocent and you hold off, then no harm, no foul. If they are guilty and you hit back, then if you believe in retaliation, you did the right thing. However, it you hold off striking a guilty party, you could be seen as a patsy. And if you retaliate against an innocent country, you could be seen as a jerk and have an unnecessary fight on your hands.

You do not need perfect confidence to retaliate, but you have to balance the odds and the costs of being seen as a patsy versus the odds and costs of being seek as a jerk and having a new fight on your hands. Different countries will weigh these odds differently. A Belgium, surrounded on all sides by friends three deep, may fear starting a conflict in error more than it fears being deemed a patsy. It would require very high degrees of confidence before retaliating—or asking NATO to retaliate on its behalf. An Israel, living in a far more hostile neighborhood, may fear for its survival if considered a patsy but figures that its neighbors already deem it a jerk and is anyway locked into a long-term conflict; thus it is more ready to retaliate. Proof in such matters is optional. The United Kingdom threatened to retaliate against Italian submarines because it suspected that such submarines were sinking Republican shipping during the Spanish Civil War. The Italians stopped.[23]

With that in mind, consider the benefits of a declaratory policy. On the one hand, it puts more backbone behind what might otherwise be vague threats. To the extent that threats matter, potential attackers may back off somewhat. They would figure that a country that declares an explicit deterrence policy loses more face if it does not respond after having been attacked. Thus, the target is less likely to shy from retaliation. Further, the odds that others attack are depressed correspondingly, and the odds of suffering a cyberattack go down, at least somewhat.

If every retaliation case were clear-cut—total confidence in attribution and total certainty that an attack crossed (or did not cross) some threshold—then a declaratory policy is a winner. But as soon as ambiguity is introduced, the winnings may evaporate and net losses may result. A country that has put its reputation on the line is one that will suffer more loss to its reputation if an attack of uncertain origin and damage arrives—and the target does nothing. The whole point of a declaratory policy was for the target to put itself in a position where it had to respond: the patsy cost of not responding goes up. Yet it also forces the target to respond under conditions where it might otherwise want to hold off precisely because the impact of being seen as a jerk is too high. In other words, it may have painted itself into a corner.

The target could also choose to buy time in order to remove as much ambiguity as circumstances allow. Here, the trade-off is subtler. As a rule, time brings more certainty: the odds that the putative attacker did it either rise toward one or plummet toward zero. Greater certainty raises the odds that the choice will be the correct one. Conversely, the target has to put up with being deemed a patsy in the interval between when it feels confident enough to retaliate or amasses enough evidence that convinces it to retaliate against another country or hold off retaliation entirely (if the attacker were an unsupported nonstate actor such as ISIL).

As a general rule, the instinct that a rules-based world is safer than one ruled by emotion is a sound basis for policy. But such instinct assumes a world of sufficient black and white. When faced with the gray fog of cyberwar, ambiguity has many attractions. No sane state will harm the United States without fearing some consequences of having angered it. That being so, the absence of an explicit deterrence posture should not be confused with the absence of deterrence. All this suggests the following rule: the determinism of a policy should not exceed the determinism of the domain over which the policy applies.

CHAPTER 25
Punishment and Holding Targets at Risk

The ability to hold targets at risk for punishment is an important part of a deterrence strategy. Without knowing which targets can be put down (and which will stay down), it is difficult to know, much less promise, what damage retaliation can wreak. Since at least World War II, those in the strategic retaliation business have been known to overstate how long enemy infrastructures would be unavailable if destroyed—and cyberspace is a far more difficult environment to make such calculations for.[1] From the retaliator's point of view, the worst outcome would be to huff and puff after the attack that demands reprisal, announce that retaliation would follow, carry it out, and have no one notice.

We start with a question about punishment via cyberspace and then tackle two difficulties: the frequent lack of good targets and the uncertainties of forecasting the effect of retaliation.

PUNISHMENT

Assuming that retaliators can hit what they aim at and miss what they are not aiming at, the choice of punishment *by a return cyberattack* is limited by the availability of targets, constraints on what targets are off-limits, the risks of escalation, the context of the attack, and the character of the attacker.

The leadership of an attacking state cannot be ignored in selecting a punishment. That which deters a leader who wants to avoid loss may not deter one who seeks gain. During the nuclear era, the United States assumed a rational actor that would obviously prefer to avoid a nuclear holocaust. It is less clear how obviously countries wish to avoid suffering a cyberattack—in an environment where attacks are constantly occurring, albeit of lesser size and consequence. It is also unclear what expectations leaders have of how badly a cyberattack can hurt them—and thus how they will compare the actual pain of reprisals to their expectations. All leaders have their unique pressure points and nightmares. Cyberattack threats to what the other side values most are not necessarily what most gets leadership attention and neither may be the response that best reinforces deterrence.

THE LACK OF GOOD TARGETS

Not every country is a good target for a retaliatory cyberattack. If the United States were to retaliate against North Korea's putting the New York Stock Exchange out of commission by attacking in cyberspace, threatening to take down the Pyongyang stock exchange would hardly impress the North Koreans. They neglected to establish a stock exchange in the first place. More to the point, most of the northern part of what used to be called the Hermit Kingdom is off the Internet and has little of importance at risk from cyberattacks.[2]

Countries vary in their susceptibility to cyberattack. The DDOS attacks that knocked out servers in the well-wired nation of Estonia (or "E-stonia," as some of its countrymen like to boast) in May 2007 were greeted with shock. Those against Georgia (August 2008) were greeted with dismay. The January 2009 attacks against Kyrgyzstan hardly made the news. The prospect of retaliating after a cyberattack that came from a target with nothing important to lose is not consoling.

If nothing else, this makes a declaratory policy that restricts everything to cyberspace look weak (without necessarily addressing the problems of a declaratory response that promises violence in return). The results of going ahead with such a policy may be completely successful, from a technical perspective, yet pointless from a strategic one. Retaliation in kind, therefore, makes sense only if there are information systems of value to the attacker at risk. True, as noted, any state with a telephone system, especially a cell phone system, has something at risk, and any state that has purchased a serious turnkey facility to run or make things or to manage records has probably purchased a complex information system in the process of doing so. But those targets are few in number and only provide some leverage.

Matters are more difficult with nonstate actors. Although well-funded groups (think, by comparison, of Aum Shinrikyo circa 1995) could engineer cyberattacks, they, too, rarely have information systems of their own at risk. Jihadists, for instance, tend to skim off established networks or rely on the help of their friends. Unless such groups enjoy quasi-sovereign status somewhere, criminal prosecution (or its extrajudicial equivalent) will have to do. The problem of holding attackers themselves at risk in order to deter them from carrying out cyberattacks is moot if the attackers are operating under a death penalty to begin with—as many jihadist leaders already are. Against such potential attackers (who, fortunately, rarely have serious interest in or much talent at cyberwar), no deterrence policy can be at all persuasive.

It remains to be proven whether *any* retaliation that targets information systems can convince their leaders that the pain avoided by compliance will exceed the pain caused by appearing to yield to *any* retaliation—irrespective of how small the original stakes were.

Finally, the threat of retaliation may be its own worst enemy if it seeks to put something in particular at risk. The more specific the asset the retaliator would publicly hold at risk (for example, China's Three Gorges Dam in exchange for messing with the Hoover Dam), the more likely such an asset would be isolated or receive additional protection. Conversely, if the owner of the asset does not believe that any such attack would have worked and chooses to ignore the warning, it may be vulnerable but not act as if it were deterred. Either way, the threat fails. Note that this is not true of nuclear weapons. If the Soviet Union declared an intent to put Washington, D.C., at especial risk, such knowledge would have been of scarce use in placing the nation's capital out of danger.

Putting together a good cyberattack strike package raises issues that rarely apply to nuclear retaliation. Whatever target is chosen has to be accessible to cyberattack, *and* the damage has to be too serious to be brushed off by the original attacker. The first factor can change from one year (in some cases, one day) to the next. But the second one is also dynamic: systems are replaced all the time, and even when they remain, the importance of the services they provide waxes and wanes thanks to several factors (for example, microwave landing systems become backups, hence less critical, when global positioning systems become more heavily used). Matters become more complex if the response has to be calibrated to produce enough fear but not so much anger that the target counter-retaliates or, worse, escalates. When due account is taken of the time required to compromise a system, it should be clear why cyberattack planners might be perpetually behind the curve. In some cases, there may be *no* systems that are both vulnerable and critical—in part, because reasonable system owners emphasize criticality when choosing which systems to make less accessible or less vulnerable.

But does the retaliator need to know that any *specific* target can be put at risk, if it is confident that there are *enough* targets it can hit whose disruption would make the attacker think twice? A statistical approach to retaliation is less likely to be hobbled by the idiosyncrasies of individual targets that may or may not react to cyberattack threats—but what if the source of variation between the expected and actual is not a matter that can be dismissed as statistical noise but is, instead, systematic? Many of the critical differences among targets—for example, the likelihood that infrastructure owners may be warned, the level of cybersecurity awareness within the general system administrator population, or the spread of certain patches—are general, not particular, discriminators. Mere numbers of targets will not wash out the effects that arise when certain broad events are unpredictable. Furthermore, the broader the range of targets, the greater the possibility of unexpectedly large as well as disappointingly small effects.

A strategy of trying many targets sequentially—to avoid overkill—and waiting until the first success to redeem the promise of retaliation raises other issues. For instance, what is the relationship between the retaliation and any particular attack? If a successful return strike is too long in coming, will it be seen as a retaliatory blow that might be deserved or as aggression that must be answered? Without a declaration, could one be sure that a delayed strike was carried out by the target, or did it claim success for an attack actually carried out for other reasons by some third party? After all, no one target in this world has just one potential attacker.

The last consideration applies to all retaliation but applies with particular force in a new medium. The attacker may simply know little about how harmful a threat to retaliate is, and the potential retaliator may not know how much the target of retaliation fears having its systems interfered with—which touches on the whole point of deterrence in the first place. Perhaps if the retaliation is unexpected or interferes with a system that leaders were assured was impregnable, then it may leave an outsized impression compared to a physical attack whose parameters may be quite familiar ones. To wit, the magic may work. Or it may fail.

THE TEMPTATIONS OF CROSS-DOMAIN DETERRENCE

Although countries might retaliate against a cyberattack with violence, this response cannot blithely be threatened against countries just because the latter have little at risk from cyberspace. If the world really believed that there is no difference between a costly cyberattack that hurt no one and a casualty-inducing kinetic attack of comparable cost (presuming cost-per-life convertors of some sort), then retaliation in kind would mean retaliation *of a similar cost*. A great deal of the controversy over whether the law of armed conflict applies in cyberspace is over the belief that a cyberattack and a kinetic attack are comparable; China, for one, sees them as fundamentally different. Even if countries paid little attention to the *form* of aggression, the equivalence between a nonfatal but catastrophically costly cyberattack and a kinetic attack that could not help but leave casualties is anything but obvious.

The targeted country may also seek relief from cyberattack by carrying out a *kinetic* attack on the attacker's cyberwar corps—but the *tools* of a cyberattack cannot be identified from afar in the same way that the tools of a kinetic attack can be, and so the odds of success would be lower. Alternatively, the target can convince itself that the only way to rid itself of the cyberattack menace is to change the regime that governs the attacking country. If the sole aim of such logic is to minimize the likelihood of future damage to the target country, it can be convincing only by low-balling the cost and risk of war or exaggerating the inconvenience associated with adopting alternative measures to improve cybersecurity by a comparable amount.

A cross-domain response may be viewed by others as an act of aggression, despite the antecedent cyberattack. In so doing, it also raises escalation issues. Others may well ask: Is a cyberattack worth *starting* a war over?

If one believes that a deterrence policy makes sense only if it contributes cost-effectively to the achievement of cybersecurity, one must ask why violence is the best approach to what is normally an engineering problem (of securing information systems). In some cases, such as a response to a North Korean attack, a serious kinetic response could start a war with no small amount of damage to South Korea.[3] Even nuclear weapons aside, the North Koreans have thousands of artillery tubes pointed at Seoul, South Korea. Having fought one Korean War, it is unclear that the United States would welcome a second in response to an attack that would not have taken place if the target systems' defenses were better.

It therefore follows that if other countries have reason to believe that the United States will not *start* what *they* believe is a fresh war in response to a cyberattack, they are unlikely to take the threat of a kinetic punishment with the seriousness that it might otherwise deserve. Even if they are unsure about what the United States actually believes, if they themselves believe in such a firebreak, they may impute similar beliefs to the United States and simply not view such threats as credible.

WILL TARGETS ACTUALLY HIT BACK AT ALL?

The thin history of cyberattacks does not suggest that a cyberattack will necessarily evoke a response. The attacks on Estonia crippled public and major private websites; Estonia complained and tried (fruitlessly[4]) to have NATO declare it an Article V attack so as to trigger NATO's mutual defense measures, but it led to no response.[5] If Georgia had reacted kinetically to the cyberattacks on it in 2008, it would have been difficult to distinguish such reactions from the war Georgia was forced to fight following its simultaneous invasion by Russian forces. Syria did not respond at all to the cyberattack preceding Operation Orchard—or the actual raid itself. Iran did not react kinetically to Stuxnet, even if it created cyberwar cadres to attack two countries (Saudi Arabia and Qatar), neither of which could be plausibly accused of complicity in creating Stuxnet. Similarly, the United States did not respond to attacks by Iran on U.S. e-banking sites.

To be fair, cyberattacks unexploited by kinetic operations are more like raids than wars. In a raid, forces cross borders, wreak mischief, and go home. In a war, they intend to keep what they take or at least turn it over to allies (such as local leaders who will do their bidding). Cyberattacks cannot conquer land or change regimes. In worst-case scenarios, they can disrupt life and maybe break some machines. But they do not persist unless the cost of eradicating them—for instance, by redoing the system attacked or replacing infected machines with uninfected machines—exceeds the cost of tolerating them. Almost all wars tend to be two-sided engagements because the attacked side has no option but to fight or surrender. In a raid, there is a third option: doing nothing (for example, not pursuing the raider for fear of worse)—and not all raids lead to counter-raids. The many U.S. drone strikes have not, so far. China invaded Vietnam in 1979, wreaked damage, caused casualties, and departed believing it taught Vietnam a lesson. Vietnam did not return the favor by invading China. Neither did India in 1962 under similar circumstances. Conversely, Arabs and Israelis traded raids in the first decade after Israel declared independence (1948); Palestinians and Israelis traded attacks over the last three decades as well. Both Koreas sent raiding parties across the thirty-eighth parallel in the years prior to North Korea's 1950 invasion.

The targeted country may also seek relief from cyberattack by carrying out a *kinetic* attack on the attacker's cyberwar corps—but the *tools* of a cyberattack cannot be identified from afar in the same way that the tools of a kinetic attack can be and so the odds of success would be lower.[6]

SUMMARY OBSERVATIONS ON CYBERDETERRENCE

When attacked, it is human nature to want to hit back. And sometimes what the gut wants, the brain should want. A rational aggressor may be inhibited by the fear of consequences, of which future punishment cannot be unimportant. Conversely, the failure to hit back may convince others (including the original attacker) that a country will not defend its values regardless of how it is attacked.

But Cold War analogies that urge the United States to deter cyberattack by threatening retaliation are simplifications.[7] Nuclear deterrence was adopted because nuclear defense was impossible, not just unsatisfactory or costly; it was a second-best answer that assumed that each side believed the other would retaliate when doing so could lead to mutual annihilation.

By contrast, systems are not only capable of being defended, they *are* defended all the time. Furthermore, whereas attribution was largely a non-issue during the Cold War (not until 1964 did the United States have to worry about two hostile nuclear-armed countries), it is a nontrivial issue for a cyberattack. Ambiguity might not stop the show—for many attacks, the attacker will adopt pro forma anonymity if even that—but it can slow it down. Another set of inhibitions arises from the doleful choice between retaliating in kind (when attackers may have less interesting targets and holding even those targets is an iffy proposition) and retaliating using more force and thereby introducing violence into a previously nonviolent contest.

The lesson from this is not that the United States (or any other country, for that matter) should deliberately and openly abjure retaliation. Indeed, even a country that never speaks of retaliation has an implicit deterrence posture if its strength and history suggest that there are limits to how far it can be pushed around. Nevertheless, among the four primary requirements of a successful deterrence policy—credibility, attribution, understood thresholds, and capability—the only one that is *not* in question is U.S. capability (assuming that the attacker has targets at risk from cyberspace). Stuxnet and Snowden are proof of that. This means that the question that CYBERCOM commander Adm. Michael Rogers asked in 2015 has it exactly wrong: bolstering the U.S. capability to carry out cyberattack is the one requirement that *does* not exist among the many that do stand in the way of having cyberdeterrence.[8]

So let us return to our five questions. First, should the United States rely on deterrence? The answer is, clearly not. Strategic deterrence is iffy, at best. Criminal deterrence—which is what nonstate attacks call for—remains explicit in U.S. laws against hacking, but rates of arrest (especially when extradition is needed) and conviction remain disappointingly low. Defense is still necessary and effective in limiting the damage from a first strike (or attacks from nonstate actors). It can also bolster a retaliation threat by shielding a country to some extent from counter-retaliation threats.

Second, should the United States make its deterrence policy explicit and deterministic? The answer is, probably not. Uncertainty of attribution and the difficulty of creating, communicating, and monitoring red lines suggest that a probabilistic, hence implicit, deterrence posture has a lot to recommend itself.

Third, should the United States invest in the ability to carry out strategic retaliation in cyberspace? On the one hand, such a capacity is unlikely to be a cost-effective way of limiting the damage from a cyberattack and might be unwisely used if it existed. On the other hand, if a devastating cyberattack takes place *and* there was no capability to retaliate via *cyberattack*, then the president faces the choice of doing little or using violence. If doing nothing is untenable, then choosing the second option would seem a least-bad option—but still bad enough; hence, the value of having an option in between. Whether a capability developed to carry out *operational* cyberattack (one that would be worthwhile building just for warfighting) can be converted to strategic purpose is an additional question.

Fourth, should the United States have retaliated for attacks of the sort it has already endured from other countries (notably Iran but more recently North Korea)? The many asymmetries between the United States and potential attackers, the risks of escalation, the plethora of other policy instruments at U.S. disposal, and the limited consequences of cyberattacks to date suggest otherwise.[9]

Fifth, should the United States ever retaliate for a cyberattack? Yes; there is very little to be gained by declaring that no possible attack would merit punishment. One cannot guarantee that there will not be times when punishment is the most cost-effective way of limiting the risk to the United States from future cyberattacks.

Much of the case for or against a declaratory deterrence policy rests on whether a first strike in cyberspace would be fatal. Given the uncertainties associated with deterrence, adequate protection may be available from a combination of an implicit deterrence policy (arising from the U.S. history of sometimes going nonlinear) and the ability to take a first strike, ascertain the public's sense of its intolerability, reappraise relationships with the presumed attacker (cyberattacks are clearly unfriendly), and then, if the results are still unsatisfactory, use that incident to anchor a future, more explicit, deterrence policy. The result may be deemed second-strike deterrence, perhaps the least bad alternative where so much uncertainty dominates.

CHAPTER 26
Deterrence by Denial

C an the ability to defend against cyberattacks and thus deny attackers the fruits of their labors dissuade potential attackers from trying and thereby achieve something like what the threat of reprisals aims to do—but without retaliation's problematic features? The answer may depend on how the costs of carrying a cyberattack occur, the psychology of the attackers, and whether it is the cyberattack that is being defeated or the *effect* expected from the cyberattack that is being denied.

Consider, by way of comparison, a war undertaken for conventional purposes: to seize land, overthrow a government, or shape the psychology of power. In contemplating whether to start a fight, a rational state would compare costs and benefits. If the other side is practicing deterrence by punishment, the attacker must consider the damage that its opponent can do to its society beyond those immediate to the battlefield. If the other side is practicing deterrence by denial (which all who defend necessarily do), the attacker must consider the odds of success. Its calculations are colored by the fact that the decision to commit to war means that its military assets are put at risk. To wit, it is costly to wage war, and it is costlier if the other side can destroy one's soldiers and equipment. The odds of success influence the expected gain, and the prospect of losing assets constitutes the expected loss.

Such calculations depend on the relationship between the resources that must be *invested* to be able to mount an attack and the resources that are *expended* to carry out an attack. If expenditures are low (relative to investments), then, having already decided to make the necessary investments, the decision to use them is likely to be influenced more by the prospect of and losses from retaliation and less by the prospect of failing and losing the associated resources expended—since most of the cost of mounting an attack is the cost of being prepared to mount an attack. It is the decision to invest in warfighting capability more than the decision to expend resources in war that remains to be influenced by reducing the prospects of success. Normally, the same kind of information (on the defender's capabilities) that helps tell whether an attack can achieve its goals *also* indicates whether investing in an attack capability to achieve its goals is worthwhile. But the equivalence falls apart if the investment required to *determine* the odds of success is large relative to the investment required to *achieve* success. That understood, the dim prospects for deterrence by denial in cyberspace can now be demonstrated.

WHAT IS BEING DISCOURAGED?

Take a canonical cyberattack—one that starts with a broad scoping of the target, followed by the attempted compromise of the target for the dual purposes of surveillance (looking for particular assets and vulnerabilities) *and* the insertion of malware to get the target system to accept and run the attacker's later commands. These commands, in turn, constitute the attack.

The effort to attack can be divided into three parts. *General investment* (for example, under-standing software vulnerabilities) gives the attacker capabilities against all targets or at least all targets of a particular class (for example, electric power grids). *Specific investment* constitutes the search for particular vulnerabilities in the targeted system and an understanding of the relationships between the target's information system and its operations. *Specific operations* entail the time and effort required to carry out and monitor an attack on particular targets plus whatever assets are used up in (or revealed through) the process of carrying out such operations. If discovery of the exploit used prevents its reuse against this or, worse, any other target—then losing it in the attack, so to speak, has to be included in the cost of carrying out an attack. If a large share of the effort goes into collecting intelligence on the specific target, then the decision to undertake such an effort depends on the likelihood that such an investment will pay off. Unfortunately, the attackers usually must make target-specific investments to discover that the defenses are daunting. If, at that point, the *extra* costs of actually carrying out an attack are modest, the attacker may feel that it has little to lose by trying (apart from revealing the target's vulnerabilities to itself), even if the odds of success are low. If all else fails, hackers will have received live-fire training.

Now assume a target with perfect defenses. The attacker tries over and over, gains nothing every time, concludes that it faces no good prospects of success, and decides not to waste further resources on that target in the future. Here, defense discourages, but is discouragement worth anything? If, having invested in defense (for example, a fortress wall), the defenders make no further effort beyond routine monitoring (for example, patrols along the fortress wall) *whether or not an attack is in progress*, then it need not care what attackers do. Whether or not defense deters is of little value to the defenders. Indeed, the target is better off having adversaries waste their own efforts going down a particular path if the alternative is their redirecting resources into something more dangerous. Such logic does not apply to violent conflict, in which it helps to keep the enemy from starting a fight even if victory is guaranteed because money and blood will have been spilled even with complete victory.

In practice, exactly how costly a failed attempt is to the defender depends on how deep the attackers got. Imagine an attack in which multiple client machines (for example, personal computers) within the organization were infected in the attacker's attempt to penetrate an enclave within the network (for example, industrial machinery). The enclave withstands a breach; the attack has failed in its primary objective. However, this leaves the network's system administrators with the drudgery of discovering all the infected machines and cleaning them up (lest the infected machines be used as a jumping-off point for the next attempt). If the attacker had no hope of breaching the enclave, then it might well have avoided infecting the client machines in the first place—thereby sparing the target the cost of cleaning up the infection. In such a case, defense would have some dissuasive effect.

How would the attacker *know in advance* that its efforts are doomed to failure—or, similarly, how does the target convey as much to the attacker? In physical combat, where the nature and, often, the quantity of the other side's weaponry are visible, the potential attacker can guess the chances of success. Attackers may also convince themselves of their own superiority through immeasurable attributes such as their own superior élan or generalship, but self-deception works only up to a point. As a rough rule, the more stuff the defender can show to the world, the less confident the attacker should be if the odds of success are really low. Of late, the advent of electronic warfare and the rising importance of having tactical intelligence on the other side (for example, to find where they are hiding their assets) suggest the growing uncertainty of such calculations. An attacker might understand what tricks it has itself, but not how well the other side can thwart such tricks or generate its own.

In cyberwar, where a vulnerability discovered is often a vulnerability neutralized, it is not easy to convince others up front that *your* systems will not fail before their tricks. In essence, an attacker can take down a well-tended system only by knowing something about the system, such as a vulnerability, that the defender does not know. The best the other side can do is to demonstrate its ability to defend the system against a known class of attacks and hope that the class is sufficiently encompassing that what remains outside its scope provides little but risk to the attacker (for example, it requires using special forces to penetrate physical barriers). More broadly, the target may have a reputation for defeating the wiles of others. Otherwise, the only way the attacker is going to really know the impenetrability of a target is by trying to penetrate it. If the effort succeeds, the attack is on. Alternatively, if there are multiple barriers protecting the valuable data or controls, then the same problem arises when trying to surmount the next one, especially if there is less available knowledge about the difficulty of surmounting deeper barriers vis-à-vis the surficial ones. If the effort fails, the attacker has to calculate the likelihood that, with N failures, the N-plus-1 effort will be a success. It may use Bayesian logic to convince itself to give up.[1] Or it may reason that having invested so much effort to learn what would not work, the odds of finding what would work on the next attempt *rise* with every failure.[2] The relationship between past failure and future prospects is not straightforward, inasmuch as initial denial may not necessarily deter later attempts.

If an attacker tried to penetrate multiple systems over time (which is typical for cyberespionage), it might predict ultimate failure through, say, successively smaller harvests.[3] But it may, instead, save disruptive or corrupting cyberattacks for when they might do the most good because it fears that wasted attacks may reveal vulnerabilities and stiffen the target's defenses. If so, its opportunity to detect a good defense may be limited. At best, an attacker can conclude that more serious cyberattacks would become harder because its attempts at cyberespionage are becoming harder. However, if the target's defenses are so deep (for example, better backup, adroit monitoring, greater overall resiliency) that they are seen only by attackers who breach the outer layer, then the quality of these defenses may go largely unseen. Being unseen, they are irrelevant to deterrence.

The correspondence between the prospect of failure and the effort devoted to trying is even looser if the investment required to penetrate a system has very little to do with the specific system itself. A great deal of effort on the part of hackers is entailed in finding exploitable vulnerabilities in software (for example, Adobe Flash) used by a large number of potential targets. The attacker may have one hundred comparable targets; perhaps it is interested in compromising only one bank's network as a psychological operation and the target country has multiple banks. Even if any one target decides to mount a perfect defense, this hardly discourages the attack. The attacker's prospective gain from investment goes down by roughly 1 percent. If attacks are effortless once the initial investments are made, the attacker has no reason not to attack such a well-defended target. Indeed, it is hardly worthwhile differentiating the hard targets from the soft targets—just attack them all. Although this sounds contrived, it is a fair characterization of the effort required to recruit bots in order to build botnets. Bot-herders generally spend their resources developing or acquiring vulnerabilities and attack methods such as social engineering tricks; they then trot out their tricks and distribute their malware, such as bad PDF files or corrupted websites, without much regard to who may pick it up. In a watering hole attack, everyone who pulls down the page ingests malware, and some are consequently infected. Although the mass use of safe computing practices may discourage such efforts, the efforts of any one user will not discourage attackers, merely limit an attack's effects on that user. Discouraging *investment* in developing cyberwar capabilities is not the same as discouraging the *use* of such capabilities.

Overall, the greater the role of "generic investment" (for example, looking for zero-day vulnerabilities) compared to target-specific investments (for example, understanding a target's unique failure modes) in building cyberattack capabilities, the less discouragement a good defense will provide to potential attackers. As a general rule, the softer the target set, the more effort will be devoted to general investment in broad-scale attack tools and the less attention will be paid to the particular defenses of any one target. Conversely, the harder the target set, the greater the odds that its vulnerabilities will be unique (intelligence agencies may spend months scoping a high-value target waiting for a flaw to present itself) and the more attention will be paid to target-specific operations. In either case, however, the relationship between initial discouragement and ultimate withdrawal is uncertain.

As noted, the mix between investment and operations in penetrating systems has shifted over time from ninja hackers (circa 1995) getting rapid feedback on whether their efforts were succeeding and thus worthy of continuation to today's toolmakers where most of the commitment precedes contact. *If* initiatives such as that of DARPA to develop self-healing systems work and proliferate among networks, then it may require real-time human intelligence operating in real time to penetrate computers.[4]

The opacity and ambiguity of cyberwar suggest that even the consequences of a perfect defense may not be clear-cut to potential attackers. The attacker's decisionmakers will have little direct knowledge of whether or not attacks by other third-party attackers on the purportedly well-defended target are succeeding; all it can know is that its own efforts enjoy no visible success (yet).

COMPLICATING PSYCHOLOGICAL FACTORS

If the hackers persuade their bosses that goals—for example, hindering the target's ability to make decisions—have been met but are hard to measure, who would know they failed? The hackers themselves may be discouraged, but if the raison d'etre of the cyberwar bureaucracy were at risk from the delivery of bad news, they may hold their tongues. Without bad news, the attacker's decisionmakers have no way of knowing that their investment is futile. Thus, they are not necessarily discouraged from trying again.

Plausible irrationality may also color the effects that good defenses can have on the willingness to attack. A reasonable attacker may presume that, after so many tries and no successes, the prospects of further success are dim. But it is human to believe that the fault may be not in the difficulty of the target but in the failure to make adequate effort. The more people invest in a problem, the more likely they are to press ahead and try to recoup their losses—the certainty that people can recognize and walk away from sunk costs as such is a conceit of economists, not psychologists. The dynamic nature of cyberspace can convince one that targets that seem impregnable today may be vulnerable tomorrow simply because things change all the time, so keep trying.

Several other considerations merit note. Economic theory says that the greater the price of something, the less people will want it: If potato prices rise, people will eat pasta. If the price of success in cyberwar is high, people will find other ways of hurting their enemies. But the size of the relationship depends on the elasticity of demand. A country committed to achieving an effect, and finding it harder but not impossible to do, may elect to throw more resources at trying.

Conversely, even an imperfect defense may persuade attackers to stop cyberattacks altogether. An attacker may reason that an attempt to harm a computer via cyberattacks will lead to the discovery of the attack and may lead the target to discover how the initial penetration was made. If such penetration techniques are discovered, then cyberespionage—which also requires such penetration—becomes that much harder. The attacker may well refrain from cyberattacks in order to maintain its cyberespionage capability. None of this says that defenses cannot dissuade, but such claims need to be viewed carefully.

DISSUADING CYBERATTACK BY DEFEATING ITS STRATEGY

There are many ways to defeat a cyberattacker. The defeat can be proximate: for example, the attack did not penetrate the system, or having penetrated the system, it failed to attain its purposive goal of disruption and/or corruption. Or having achieved its purposive goal, the attacker has failed to extract serious costs because the target is more resilient or capable of recovering faster than the attacker believed. Finally, the cyberattacker can be defeated if its ultimate goals are out of reach: for example, the target's military performance did not suffer or the attacker's coercion strategy failed to deflect the target country from its path.

In that cyberwar is usually instrumental rather than an end in itself, its use can be discouraged if attackers are persuaded that the hoped-for psychological effects on the target are unlikely. Thus, if a cyberattack is meant to keep its target country from intervening elsewhere, the target can signal that it will stick to its policies regardless. If the attacker carries on anyway, it must necessarily hope that other political forces (for example, popular fear of a repeat) may bend the target state's stance.

Ironically, the attitude required to reduce the attacker's expectations that its attack will change the target's policy is the opposite of what conventional strategic thinking would call for. A narrative that says that cyberattacks on, for instance, a country's infrastructure are beneath notice is a very different narrative from one that elevates the importance of cyberattacks in order to justify a violent response. The latter says that an attack has touched a nerve. Affecting insouciance says otherwise. Similarly, policies to hype the threat, the better to make the owners of systems invest in protecting themselves against cyberattack, are inconsistent with downplaying the effects of a cyberattack so as to render them strategically meaningless.

Such logic applies to terrorism as well—hence, the repeated aphorism of cybersecurity expert Bruce Schneier: refuse to be terrorized.[5] The vigorous U.S. response to the September 11 attacks may well have helped raise the profile of violent resistance to the West in general and al Qaeda in particular—which may have been exactly what the terrorists sought in the first place.

CHAPTER 27
Cyberwar Escalation

————●————

onflict in cyberspace can escalate along several paths. It can grow more intensive (striking deeper or lasting longer) or more extensive (striking targets hitherto off limits). Or attacks can jump from cyberspace to physical space.

We know very little about escalation in cyberspace in practice, mostly because very few cyberattacks have taken place. The cyberspace equivalent of Herman Kahn's *On Escalation* does not exist and might not be writable.[1] Few government officials anywhere in the world have defined, much less declared, boundaries between the various distinct levels of cyberwar—perhaps because there is no agreed way to compare cyberattacks in the sense that one act is more heinous or dangerous than another. Presumably, in any conflict, both combatants want less rather than more damage—but not necessarily before they make their point to one another. Both sides also share an interest in keeping control over what breaks out rather than ceding control to fate, the passions of warriors, the intrigues of factions, or the machinations of third parties.[2]

Except for the section below on operational cyberwar, we again assume a conflict in which cyberwar operations are primary and kinetic operations nonexistent or clearly secondary. We then review the purpose and risks of escalation, escalation in operational cyberwar, the logic of tit-for-tat management, the crossover into violence, escalation risks from third parties, and escalation risks from proxy cyberattacks.

WHY ESCALATE?

Escalating to gain military advantage must perforce assume either that what one side does will not affect what the other side tries to do or that even if it does, the initiator will still gain net military advantage (even if only psychologically: do you trust your weapons now that we have shown the ability to compromise them?).[3] As a rule, combatants like to choose the level of combat that most favors them;[4] if these two levels differ, one or the other side may escalate to where the first who would fight at an even higher level gains little advantage but additional pain. In cyberspace, the calculations to escalate have additional elements of complexity arising from the trickiness of predicting BDA. Collecting intelligence permits a guess how vulnerable the other side is. But cyberwarriors are often more aware of the other side's vulnerabilities than of their own (which they would fix if they knew).[5] This makes it easy for one side to argue that it would gain from escalating—and be wrong.

Escalation is also used to signal seriousness. To one's own side, escalation (especially to strategic cyberwar) may signal a country's commitment to one's warfighters by indicating that civilians will gladly share their burden. To the other side, escalation can say, "Cut it out or someone is going to get seriously hurt." Escalation can convey, for instance, that lesser activities (for example, cyberespionage) have reached a point at which the pain is tantamount to that of a cyberattack. Russians call this "escalate to de-escalate." A related purpose is to carry out a contest of pain or perhaps a contest in risk-taking, per Schelling's argument in *Arms and Influence*.[6] Such a strategy presumes escalation dominance—the ability to outmatch one's foe at all levels of escalation.

Last, escalation may be used to test the temper of opponents: How far are they willing to go? How would they react? Are they rational and measured or irrational and erratic? Limiting escalatory moves to cyberspace (not physical space) may limit the pain of getting the wrong answer, but it may also limit its fidelity because it assumes that what holds for the virtual one holds for the physical one—where people *can* get hurt.

The usual stance toward escalation arises from the well-founded sense that war is a negative-sum endeavor. While one side sees tactical advantage in escalating what it does, unless its escalation leads to de-escalation (for example, by frightening the other side into controlling or ceasing its efforts), doing so raises the cost and pain of conflict for both sides. Conversely, escalation management can be good.

ESCALATION AND OPERATIONAL CYBERWAR

Introducing cyberattacks into a conflict may look escalatory, but it should not. It is just another—and nonlethal—way to accomplish the ends for which lethal arms (and some nonlethal arms such as those of electronic warfare) were also designed. But sometimes, an act is judged escalatory based not on what it does but on how it does it. Taking out a bunker with chemical weapons is considered more heinous than doing the same job with high explosives.[7] The Japanese considered the first use of firebombing (March 1945) to be escalatory even though the attack on Dresden, Germany, had already taken place. The use of cruise missiles in Bosnia (1995) was considered escalatory.[8] Although it is unclear whether such sentiments were anything more than sentiments (because neither target could counter-escalate effectively), the broader point stands. However, if opponents feel that introducing cyberattacks opens the door for everyone or that cyberspace weapons are sneaky (in that they work using deception), even though the effects may be modest, their employment might be seen as escalatory. Adversaries may also convince themselves that although the cyberattacks per se were in bounds, their use against military targets portends their use against civilian targets because the latter can be surreptitiously attacked via cyberspace even if kinetic attacks on them would be universally considered off-limits.

Should countries that could attack military systems via cyberspace nevertheless limit its use to avoid escalation? Not necessarily. As a rule, the cost of war is a function of how much (manpower and matériel) is committed to physical combat and what share of that is permanently (rather than temporarily) disabled. Cyberwar does not affect the amount of commitment unless it puts targets in play for physical destruction that would not otherwise have been engaged (for example, because they were not in the actual field of combat). Cyberwar itself is relatively inexpensive compared to physical combat. The fact that cyberwar disables systems using soft kill rather than hard kill does not suggest that its unrestricted use would lead to more of each side's committed forces being killed or destroyed. Nor is cyberwar particularly heinous (compared to, say, chemical warfare). Thus, there is no particular reason to limit its use on the battlefield. Thus, too, one side's holding back from using cyberwar in the hopes that the other side would do likewise is probably not doing itself many favors. There is no ipso facto reason to hold back, and even if there were, the ability of the other side to detect such restraint is limited.

That changes when the range of targets under cyberattack expands beyond the battlefield. One way is by attacking systems linked to a foe's *strategic* command and control. Such escalation may be unintended: many military systems serve both functions (for example, a satellite that senses infrared plumes detects missiles both conventional and nuclear). Whether an inadvertent strike *is* escalatory depends on how the other side reacts. If it believes the attacker went after a nuclear capability in the guise of going after a conventional one, and further infers that such an action was prefatory to a disabling nuclear strike, nuclear escalation may well follow. If it concludes that the blow to its nuclear establishment was unintended or unobservable by the attacker, the results may be unexceptional.

Horizontal escalation is another possibility. A local conflict may be supported by globalized networks that themselves come under cyberattack. The key consideration would be what is in play; just because the attacker deems such targets legitimate does not mean the defender will. It is unclear how the defender may react, largely because cyberattacks have temporary effects—even if some effort has to be made to reverse the effects of such attacks. Reaction in the form of counter-escalation may be more likely if the systems hit are rendered unavailable against third parties (but how common are such circumstances?). Even if the other side responds in kind, the extent of horizontal escalation may still be limited. A bigger problem arises, however, if one side responds to seeing its formerly safe assets at risk from cyberattack by striking the other side's formerly safe assets *kinetically*. Its response may be a way of warning. Or it may infer that those carrying out the cyberattack have put such assets in play for *any* attack. All this is speculative; the history to know whether expanding a conflict in cyberspace leads to its expansion in the physical world has yet to happen.

ESCALATION IN STRATEGIC CYBERWAR

Escalation in the conduct of strategic cyberwar can be discussed in terms of several vectors.[9] One is to threaten regime stability by attacking systems that enable regime control, whether in personal terms (for example, on the bank accounts of the leader or his friends[10]), control terms (for example, police files), or influence terms (for example, state-friendly media). If the adversary is nervous enough about internal stability, then such cyberattacks may signal an interest in regime change, an escalation in goals if not means. Undermining, say, the so-called Great Firewall of China (its system for censoring Internet traffic), the basic trust that citizens have in their government and comparable institutions (via, say, corruption attacks on the financial system), or public confidence in prestige systems may all fall into that category.

Striking civilian systems may be considered escalatory. Such an escalation can proceed from military support systems to dual-use support systems (such as a port serving commercial shipping *and* military logistics) to purely civilian targets (such as a port on an inland body of water that precludes its likely use to support combat)—or it can proceed to such civilian targets directly. Then there are escalation steps even within the category of coercive attacks. Attacks on infrastructure are bad, but attacks that disable or disrupt safety systems (for example, air traffic control) may be worse, and those attacks whose sole purpose is to create civilian casualties (for example, hospital medication monitors) are worse yet. A system may be attacked *with the intent* of persuading civilians to pressure their government into suing for peace. Such attacks are more likely than purely military attacks to be perceived as escalation, particularly if foes read strategic attacks as indications that they can be coerced, which is insulting, not just injurious.

Now step back and ask how serious such escalation may be. What is the worst effect that an unrelenting series of cyberattacks can have on a country? Unfortunately for analysis, no one knows—which has not kept people from forecasting calamity. Much would depend on whether cyberattacks were intended to cause death and destruction. If so, relevant questions may be what machinery can be controlled from attacks originating beyond the factory walls in ways that lead to their destruction, what sort of procedural back-ups exist for disrupted processes, and how quickly countries can either tighten up on security or reduce their dependence on inherently hard-to-secure systems. A country with access to resources in the rest of the world will be more resilient—but such countries are also most dependent on systems in the first place.

THE DIFFICULTIES OF TIT-FOR-TAT MANAGEMENT

In 1980, after running a set of extended prisoner's dilemma contests among political scientists, Robert Axelrod concluded that a tit-for-tat strategy was the optimal one for turn-based interactions.[11] Tit-for-tat strategy is simple: Do not start a fight, but if hit, hit back on the next turn; if not hit, do not hit back. The strategy's extension to escalation is straightforward. Not for nothing do states respond to escalation with escalation of their own in the justified belief that such a strategy is best suited to ensure that no one escalates further. Hence, intrawar deterrence: the threat of counter-escalation to tamp down escalation or escalation threats from already engaged foes (interwar deterrence works against those not fighting). Yet the extension of a tit-for-tat strategy to cyberspace is problematic.

First, long planning times may interfere with reading the results of a tit-for-tat strategy because they impede understanding the relationship between tit and tat. Cyberattacks against specific targets, particularly hard ones, require they be scoped, an exercise that may take months or years. Planning for kinetic attacks tends to be more straightforward, hence quicker, particularly if there is no reason to get the delivery vehicle (for example, a cruise missile) home safely. Easy cyberattack targets are often easy because, being unimportant, they are poorly defended. However, some of the easy targets may be those that were not particularly well guarded because their owners assumed that there was little profit from attacking them; hence, only the really malicious would do so (for instance, hospitals are less security-conscious than banks despite having lives on the line). Thus, attacking them may have all the more shock value for their being psychologically unprepared—but shock value may not be the best help in managing escalation. The most appropriate target system to hit in retaliation may be untouchable; if what remains is sensitive, hitting it may take the struggle up a notch. Thus, it helps for a state to think through its possible target set in advance. It may decide to put certain targets off-limits and therefore not scope them for attack, but if it reverses its prior choice, the clock has to start over again. Long time lags in developing a cyberwar capability may be confused with a lack of response. Iran did not have an immediate capability to respond to Stuxnet; it needed to build up a capability to respond. It took two years before it could carry out retaliatory cyberattacks (for example, the attacks on Saudi Aramco or the DDOS attacks on banks). If the United States effectively retaliates against North Korea for the Sony hack, counter-retaliation (at least in cyberspace) may not be immediate in coming (unless the North Koreans stockpiled attacks against such an eventuality) either—but in the meantime, it may appear that tit-for-tat worked.

Second, the relationships among intent, effect, and perception are far looser in cyberspace than in the physical world. The point of a tit-for-tat strategy is to establish in the foes' mind the correlation between what they did and what was done to them—in hopes that they will not do it again or at least will not escalate. But the reference to the other side's *mind* means that the comparison takes place between their perception of what they did and their perception of what was done to them. Errors in this relationship can arise in many places:

- Your perceptions of what they did may differ from their perceptions (both may differ from reality, but reality actually does not matter in this calculus).
- The effects you wish to produce may differ from the effects they produced because there is no exact equivalent between the two: they have different systems with different vulnerabilities that you may or may not be able to exploit.
- The effects you produce may differ from the effects you meant to produce.
- The effects they think you produced may differ from the effects you *did* produce.[12]

In sum, the relationship between the effects *you* think you produced and the effects *they* think they suffered as a result of tit-for-tat is subject to multiple sources of error. The odds that the right lessons—actions bring calibrated and proportionate reactions—are drawn can be low. This may not matter on the first round, but your perception of how well they learned their lessons may affect what you do on any subsequent rounds. Past the first round, each side must include its estimate of how the other will respond and what further miscalculations ensue. Another way of saying as much is that you will not understand and therefore draw the wrong inferences from their reaction because you do not see all the factors that make them react as they did.

Errors in perception are worse when the system being attacked does not create effects obvious to the public (by way of comparison, a cyberattack that makes the lights go out), or when the system being damaged lacks the kind of performance record to know what a cyberattack has done by comparison. As noted, Iran's line on Stuxnet evolved in the months after the story broke in the *New York Times*. Although announcements would seem secondary to perceptions, they may be the only information that third-party observers, the street, and even those outside the immediate circle of power will get. These disjunctions are not unknown in a kinetic tit-for-tat exchange, but it is hard to think of a kinetic attack (chemical-biological warfare possibly aside) in which the target is so confused about how badly it was damaged.

The problem of BDA may tempt tit-for-tat strategists to try a shotgun approach, hoping for *some* effect. But doing so effectively renounces any precision in escalation management. Although the success of the Stuxnet worm suggests that individual targeting is possible, the attackers were not aiming for a precisely calibrated effect; the more damage, the better. Furthermore, the preparation for the attack was believed to have been a year or two during which there was no reason for Natanz (whose operators probably thought their facility to be safe all along) to suddenly increase its cybersecurity. By contrast, such preparation in the context of a war either presumes a very short war or risks stumbling when the security status of the targeted system shifts from a peacetime to a wartime mode.

The difference between attempt and outcome carries other risks. One side, seeking reprisals, attacks an unexpectedly hard target, fails, and finds itself forced to escalate in kind from a comparable target to an incomparable target in order to wreak the damage that matches what it suffered.

Third, there are no agreed-on redlines in cyberspace. Something that looks to one side like a response in kind may look to the other side as escalation. Figure 27.1 shows what may occur when both parties have thresholds but define them differently. The attacker, in this example the United States, starts by hacking into the target's afloat naval supply facility database in order to scramble its contents. The target takes this as a cyberattack on military support (rather than a weapons system) and responds in what it thinks is like fashion by hacking into the software system that controls Guam's port. The United States takes this to be an attack on the homeland (Guam being a U.S. territory), and it hacks into the software that controls port operations on the target's mainland. The target takes this as an attack on its civilian infrastructure. And so on.

So, *neither* side ever believes that it is the one escalating. Each side is carrying out operations in the zone in which it thinks the other side is already working. Yet between the two, escalation happens. Although similar issues bedevil escalation management in the physical world, with terrorism aside, the United States has no reasonable fear of having its homeland touched by another state.[13] Not so in cyberspace.

Gaining consensus on red lines is hard, especially between two very different combatants. When one side refuses to admit that it might wage cyberwar, even starting such a conversation is hard. A local conflict between the United States and China over Taiwan would take place much closer to China than to the United States. Agreeing that homeland ports are off-limits favors China because the United States would make greater gains more quickly by hobbling Chinese ports than China gains by hobbling, say, the far-more-distant port of San Diego. Or one country may use

What Constitutes Escalation When Each Side Has Different Red Lines?

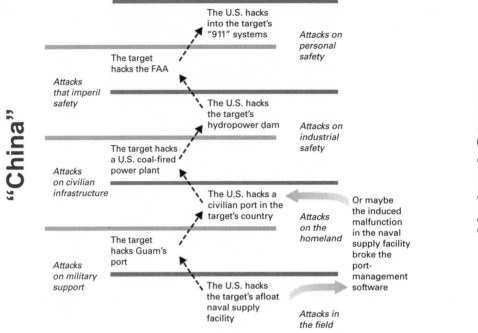

FIGURE 27.1 AN INADVERTENT PATH TO MUTUAL ESCALATION

coal to generate its electricity; the other, hydropower. Both sides agreeing, for safety reasons, not to interfere with dam controls leaves only coal-fired electrical generating capacity at risk. Taking dual-use infrastructures off the table favors countries that use civilian infrastructures for military purposes vis-à-vis those with dedicated military communication lines. Countries that outsource cyberattacks to "patriotic" hackers have an advantage over those that depend on their own employees if the onus against cyberattacks applies only to official cyberwarriors.

Worse is possible if each side maintains deliberately asymmetric red lines. One side might declare that it will escalate if its power grid is touched, while feeling justified in giving itself license to attack the other side's power grid. Thus, an exchange in which both power grids were attacked would appear escalatory to the side with the privileged perspective and may lead to the former's escalation. These asymmetries may arise because one side thinks it can get away with it—either because it deserves to or because it thinks it can bluff the other side accordingly. To appreciate this scenario's plausibility, consider whether the United States should have retaliated against DDOS attacks carried out against U.S. banks by (presumably) Iran. From one perspective, the DDOS attack was hardly an escalatory response to attacks on Iran's most important weapons plant from (what was presumed to be) the United States. From another perspective, the failure of the United States to answer the DDOS attacks means that Iran would attack without penalty.

Without announced boundaries of acceptable behavior, states have to calculate how far they can go without touching the other side's nerves.[14] Similar issues associated with physical attacks might be dealt with through geographical limitations on combat: for example, Northern Watch operations of the 1990s did not extend below Iraq's 36th parallel. Boundaries in cyberspace are harder to define and confine (a reported U.S. strike on a jihadist website supposedly took out 300 servers around the world).[15] Indeed, information system support for combat operations need not be anywhere near the conflict, connectivity permitting; they are more survivable if not. So, a subtle adversary may deliberately outsource such processing to server clouds located in third-party countries in the hopes that the other side will thereby put certain types of attacks on such servers off the table (granted, militaries shy away from entrusting even encrypted critical information to commercial enterprises). Furthermore, it is unclear what kind of attacks would violate neutrality. Would exploiting a flaw in the server's software to corrupt data content count? If the attack on the offshore cloud hurts no other customers, would the offshore country complain—or just drop the contract with the attacked party by arguing that its doing otherwise (now that it knows who the real customer is) would violate neutrality?

The true boundaries have to be logical rather than physical ones. Unfortunately, as Schelling points out, such boundaries will limit the activities of both sides only if they are prenegotiated or obvious (for example, stopping at the river's edge).[16] The nuclear threshold was one such boundary. The distinction between fatal and nonfatal cyberattacks may be another (unless it is hard to link any one casualty to a cyberattack). Otherwise, boundary lines can seem arbitrary and meaningless, and therefore unfair and not credible guides to where the other side will stop when contemplating responses to what the other side does.

If the thresholds are expressed in terms not of categories but of effects (for example, the presence or, even less clearly, the extent of casualties), the problem of intentionality rises: "How was I to know that attacking your systems would put lives at risk? Attacking ours would not have put lives at risk." The same holds for BDA. If a victim is to scream, "Foul!" it must demonstrate not only which systems have been hit but how they were damaged—free BDA for the attackers. Further complications arise for cyberwar carried out against a background of bloody hostilities elsewhere; how does one establish comparability between real and virtual effects?

Accidents and inadvertent cyberattacks only add to the confusion.[17] In figure 27.1, a hypothesized attack on the target's afloat naval supply facility actually corrupted information held by port management software that reconciles civilian and military shipping (and how was the attacker to know that the target's port management software did not do a sanity check on the information coming in from its ships?). Can any combatant count on being able to argue that some effect was an accident that will not be repeated, and that accidents do not justify escalation by the other side? Countries rarely apologize even when wrong, and their victims rarely settle for mere apology, particularly during wartime.[18] More typically in conflict, once a breach has been made, it tends to be exploited with vigor rather than backed away from.[19]

Failures in cyberspace, such as the inability to penetrate a target, tend to be far less obvious to the other side than in failures in the physical world. Thus, a state may attempt escalation and succeed, fail but in such a way as to make no one the wiser, fail in ways that make it obvious only to the target, or fail in ways that are hard to hide. Conversely, one side decides not to escalate, and something on the other side previously considered off-limits fails mysteriously anyway. It could be an accident, a rogue operative, a third-party state, or simply the inability of the target state to distinguish occasional failure from normal operations. So the target responds as if escalation had really taken place.

The difficulty of distinguishing success from failure, however, has a silver lining. If the target state does not want to respond to escalation (perhaps it cannot do so or wants to hold something in reserve), it could announce a response and do nothing further. Faking a kinetic attack is very difficult, but faking a cyberattack is not because nearly everything about it is hidden. Such a stratagem would be the opposite of a sub rosa response, and promised response might claim hard-to-observe effects (such as corruption rather than disruption). An opponent that believes this may well divert resources to calculating which of its information stores or algorithms have been tampered with. What it concludes if it finds something suspicious—for any number of other reasons—is another issue.

Finally, in cyberspace, the intent to react to the other side's escalation by escalating one's own effort cannot necessarily be demonstrated as such. In the Vietnam War, escalation meant adding troops: easy to announce and verify. In cyberspace, neither the quality nor the number of the troops is obvious, nor can they be reliably monitored; indeed, these are usually kept secret. The same goes for the allocation of cyberwarriors between espionage and attack or between this or that theater (since they can generate global effects from home). Meanwhile, as noted, the effects of making a greater effort may be long in coming; finding vulnerabilities is more like an investment, in which throwing more people at finding vulnerabilities produces more vulnerability discoveries—if they exist at all—only after a certain amount of time.[20]

At least in cyberspace it helps that neither side is *yet* locked into a set of automatic escalatory responses. One reason Cold War strategists worried about Berlin was that two armies—each with its standard operating procedures—faced each other almost literally nose-to-nose. An incident started by one side might have resulted in a quick response from opposing forces trained and exercised to respond in a certain way. This could lead to counter-responses from forces with comparable training and standard operating procedures. Because soldiers' lives may be jeopardized by overlooking what the other side does, matters could snowball before cooler heads could prevail. This assumes both sides understood as much. Two sets of cyberwarriors who believe they must automate response to fight "at light speed" could mean that computers have taken matters to a pretty pass faster than humans can react, much less ponder carefully.[21]

With all these uncertainties, successfully *threatening* to retaliate for cyberattacks that cross some threshold will likely require the other side to:

- believe that it will be blamed for attacks deemed escalatory[22]
- believe that the target has the means to carry out the deterrent threat
- believe that the target has the will to carry out the deterrent threat even in the face of threats of counter-reprisals
- believe that if it does *not* cross the threshold, it will *not* face escalation
- feel that its escalation has no compelling *net* military rationale (once retaliation is factored into account)
- not fear losing too much face by complying (which argues for making such a threat implicit or covert)
- believe that the boundaries are well defined, straightforward to monitor, and fair—rather than one-sided, arbitrary, unfounded in customary law, or self-serving.

This is clearly a list of nontrivial length and content. Just as clearly, the success of a tit-for-tat strategy of intrawar deterrence has everything to do with what the other side believes. Thus, those that would adopt such a strategy should have to have a fairly good read of the other side.

ESCALATION INTO KINETIC WARFARE

One of the great risks of escalation in cyberspace is that it may lead to escalation in kinetic space; can one predict under what circumstances that might happen?

First, there may be signals. The more that a country declares that it would respond with all means at its disposal to a sufficiently damaging cyberattack, the greater the loss of face if it does not. The more that a country has explicitly rejected limiting a response to cyberspace, and the more it has embraced the concept of cross-domain deterrence,[23] the greater its odds of crossing from the virtual to the real world.

Second, aggressive action in certain domains seems to strike closer to home than does action in others. The United States and the Soviet Union had many incidents at sea. None of them escalated onto dry land. The United States did not go to war when North Korea captured the USS *Pueblo* in 1968 (nor did it break diplomatic relations with Israel over the sinking of the USS *Liberty* in 1967). Similarly, both sides ran active espionage operations against one another, and, with the possible exception of the furor associated with the Soviet downing of a U-2 aircraft, none of them seriously rippled the boundary between war and peace. U.S. and Soviet aircraft engaged one another during the Korean War without creating a broader crisis. By contrast, there were deeper echoes following incidents involving Army soldiers: for example, the death of Maj. Arthur D. Nicholson Jr. by East Germany in 1985, or the axe murder of 1st Lt. Mark Barrett by North Koreans in 1976. Would a cyberattack on the homeland be considered akin to a naval, air combat, or intelligence incident and thus handled within its own channels? Or would it be considered akin to an army or homeland incident and thus lead to crisis and perhaps the use of force?

Third, the decision to use force—which is, in many cases, tantamount to starting a war—involves answering a set of questions that go beyond the precipitating incident. A rational state would ask itself: What would be gained by going to war? At what price? With what risk? Leaders often persuade themselves that they are going to war because they have no other choice: a world in which they do not go to war would be intolerable. Or they may reason that abjuring war would only postpone conflict, not eliminate its possibility; when war came, outcomes would be worse, perhaps catastrophic.[24] Hence, the question: What would have to be true about a cyberattack to persuade leaders that they had to fight (and risk casualties)? Perhaps the prospect of further cyber-attacks would be deemed intolerable. But Hamlet's "tak[ing] arms against a sea of troubles, and by opposing end them" presupposes that the use of force can end the prospect of cyberattacks. But can they? Given the difficulty of disarming hackers, such a prospect would appear to be dim. If the hackers capable of causing so much trouble left their country, not even occupying it would end their capabilities (although cutting off their financing would slow them down). That leaves, as a rationale for the use of force, the prospect of deterrence. A country punished severely enough for having launched cyberattacks might hesitate before doing it again; onlookers may be similarly dissuaded. But this logic presumes that the attackers understand that it was the cyberattack (and little else) that led to the use of force.

Fourth, under some circumstances, the decision to escalate via cyberspace may signal a disinclination to escalate via kinetic attack. A hopeful adversary (the source of the original cyberattack) may read this positively, ascribing escalation to a desire to look tough before friends, foes, and the voting public, while telling itself that the choice not to respond violently underlines the limits to a confrontation. Conversely, a ruthless adversary may infer the other side's lack of commitment from its failure to escalate to violence. Conversely, if the source of the cyberattack has few assets at risk from cyberspace (as is largely true for North Korea), the target of a cyberattack must choose between not responding and responding with physical force, thereby raising the likelihood of the latter.

In lieu of regime change, escalating from a cyberattack to a kinetic response also crosses a threshold that does not come up when the original provocation and the response were both kinetic. It is unclear whether this threshold is more like a speed bump or a yawning abyss, but it is clearly present. Just as clearly, a cyberattack is less likely to result in a kinetic response than an equivalent kinetic attack would be. However, this raises the question of what constitutes equivalence. Assessing kinetic damage to oneself tends to be a straightforward exercise. Assessing the damage from a cyberattack that leads to the widespread corruption of one's own information systems requires knowing what systems have, in fact, been corrupted (something that, ironically, the attacker may have a better handle on). A target country that has been spooked by a cyberattack into imagining that the real damage is a multiple of the visible damage may well overreact (at least until it realizes over time which of its systems *were* corrupted). In sum, although the risks of violent escalation following a cyberattack are nonzero, they are low, particularly in comparison to a kinetic attack of similar magnitude.

ESCALATION RISKS FROM PROXY CYBERWAR

When two parties face off in cyberspace, the results are complex and hard to forecast, and harder to manage. Adding third parties makes everything harder—and the presence of third parties is often difficult to ascertain accurately because of difficulties in attribution. Attacks by third parties, for instance, might spark escalation in wartime and in ways unavailable in peacetime. For instance, both sides may be exercising self-restraint. A cyberattack from a third party breaches these restraints. Because it is human nature to ascribe evil to one's foes, the target state is more likely to blame its foe for crossing former barriers than to assume a third party carried out the attack. It responds in kind, and its foe does likewise. Both sides escalate when neither intended to do so originally.

How can countries distinguish third-party from adversary attacks—and keep their foes from mistaking third-party attacks for their own attacks? Attribution during a conflict requires some of the same techniques required by attribution in peacetime. In wartime, an attacker's access is both worse and better: worse because there are fewer day-to-day contacts, and better because some of the entry points may come from proximity to military conflict (for example, an enemy UAV transmitter/receiver penetrating the battlefield). Furthermore, the greater volume of attacks in wartime (notably on military forces) creates a larger body of evidence from which to distinguish the adversary's modus operandi from that of third parties.[25] Defenders can choose to distinguish attacks by battlefield foes from others by reasoning that their foes have no interest in wasting their assets, notably their knowledge of the opponents' vulnerabilities, on low-impact attacks; thus, low-impact attacks *pursued through novel means* are ones likely to be carried out by others (who have little to lose if they run out of tricks specific to the target at war).

Can one side prevent third-party attacks from inducing a reaction from the other? Warring parties rarely overflow with mutual trust, and neither side is likely to allow its own warfighters to be monitored so that third-party attacks can be identified by exclusion. Although immunizing a foe's systems from third-party attacks may sound far-fetched, some types of malware do, in fact, keep hosts from being infected by others. Or one side can tell the other what the vulnerabilities are in those systems it would not attack, thus allowing them to be fixed before third parties exploit them. As it is, *finding* such vulnerabilities would require spying on such systems, which itself raises suspicions.

Helpfully, there may be limits to how much mischief third parties can sow. As a rule, third parties must make a larger splash than they do in peacetime to escalate the conflict beyond the level at which it is already being conducted. Because the easy targets will have already been taken offline or hardened early in a war, what remains will be harder and attacking them successfully will require considerable preparation; thus, *early* third-party attacks should rarely rise to escalatory levels.

Cyberattacks by third parties may also not motivate their targets much in wartime, as long as such attacks are no worse than what foes are carrying out. In peacetime, a state that has been attacked in cyberspace and does nothing may need to explain why. In wartime, the same human nature that leads to blaming foes first will help excuse countries in choosing not to retaliate against third parties. They can argue that all attacks are carried out by foes against whom they are doing all they can; thus, a failure to return fire *in cyberspace* would not be seen as cowardly.

Third-party intervention, however, could convert what starts as a well-managed cyberwar (to the extent any cyberwar can be so described) into a free-for-all. To illustrate, consider a reflection into cyberspace of a hypothetical crisis between the United States and Iran. The contest starts with cyberattacks by the United States and Iran on each other. But would Iran stop there? For historical reasons, Iranians are wont to blame the United Kingdom for pretty much everything. Cyberattacks on the United Kingdom could be meant as punishment for real or imagined offenses, but also to discourage possible (more likely, further) UK involvement in what is a two-party struggle. Other potential targets include Sunni Arab states that fear Iran (and that therefore may be inclined to help U.S. kinetic and cyberspace warriors). If Iran follows Saddam Hussein's logic from the first Gulf War, it may target Israel both for its own sake and as a way to goad Israel into doing something that alienates Iran's Sunni Arab foes.

Israel may decide to jump in on its own, anyway. It has already cast a wary eye on President Obama's negotiations with Iran, and the July 2015 treaty may not persuade it to call off further operations against the Iranian nuclear infrastructure. The Gulf States, with similar concerns over what they might see as a squishy ally, could use cyberattacks as Israel would (even if they lack ongoing operations against Iran's nuclear establishment). Such countries have only a few talented hackers, but plenty of cash to buy services from organized crime or suppliers to friendly intelligence agencies.

Russia and China could easily sit out this conflict, but would they? They may recoil at the prospect that a U.S. win would increase its power in Middle East. Russia may help Iran in hopes of a return favor (Iran is also a potentially rich export opportunity). China, for its part, would like to invest its surplus billions in Iran's oil, gas, and mining sectors. Both could want to see the United States tied down in the Middle East so that each can enjoy a freer hand in their respective regions. Thus, any cyberattack that gives Iran an operational advantage will get serious consideration, even if neither country particularly likes Iran's regime (both countries did support the nuclear negotiations). Finally, both may be interested in knowing where the U.S. military is vulnerable to a disruptive cyberattack as well as how it would respond to one. Normally, such an interest would not be pursued given the consequences of getting caught—but what if they bet that any cyberattack occurring in the midst of the military crisis will be attributed to Iran (especially if they adopt enough of Iran's modus operandi)? Finally, both suspect a grateful Iran would be more than willing to supply them intelligence on U.S. forces of the sort that could otherwise have been gained only by being in hostile contact with them. Iran can also lend Russia or China platforms from which to test attacks that can only be launched within range of U.S. RF networks. Iran, in turn, has an interest in playing Russia against China for favors, and each may be unable to avoid competing with the other by demonstrating greater prowess in the precincts of cyberspace. One can easily imagine a cavalcade of cyberattacks, failures, misread results, collateral damage, cascading effects, boasting, accusations, attempts at attribution, retaliation based on such attribution, and counter-retaliation.

What would the United States do with knowledge that Iran is getting help? Perhaps it would be in the U.S. interest to "discover" that Iran had carried out the more sophisticated attacks if such discovery solidifies domestic support for military operations. Perhaps Americans would take cyber-security more seriously if they thought that a middling power such as Iran could carry out such sophisticated cyberattacks.

True, ignoring or downplaying evidence of major power help would hardly discourage such intervention. Yet how badly should the United States want to discourage them? Letting Russia or China attack U.S. forces throws a spotlight on what *they* can do—which can be mined for intelligence value. Unfortunately, as noted, it also gives *them* a fairly good hint about what U.S. forces can do—and so there is intelligence for *them* to mine there. Who learns more quickly (or can deceive others more thoroughly)?

Otherwise, how could powerful third parties be persuaded to stop? First, they may have to be convinced that the United States knows they are up to no good rather than be allowed to believe that the United States is accusing them because it needs someone to blame. Second, they would have to believe that the United States could put sufficient leverage on them, either through sub rosa channels or by taking the case public. If the United States does go public, will third parties deny their participation and argue that the United States is just whining? If their denials do not resonate, will they back down or, conversely, conclude that, having been so accused, in for a dime, in for a dollar? If the latter, would they support Iran more overtly—say, with intelligence or equipment—thereby complicating U.S. efforts?

Incidentally, this scenario should illustrate why horizontal escalation, the successive entry of the uninvolved into a war on one or both sides (or how World War I started), is of lesser concern with wars in cyberspace. The good *and* bad news is that it is difficult to know who is *not* a combatant in cyberspace at any point in time. Furthermore, the entry of others may not matter nearly as much as it does in conventional conflict. Normally, numbers matter a great deal: by joining one side, a country can tip the battle. In cyberspace, arithmetic superiority does not compute so reliably. True, two entities combining their search for vulnerabilities in the same target are likely to be more rather than less efficient, but only if they share their efforts—which is to say, intelligence.[26] The super-secret nature of cyberwar suggests they will do otherwise.

PROXY CYBERATTACKS

The dependence of militaries on information systems may create demands by local combatants to call on global powers for help in hacking their foes. Helping friends without showing up is not new. In the 1980s, the United States fed intelligence to the United Kingdom and Iraq to fight Argentina and Iran, respectively. Thus, many of the questions—for example, how to help while controlling what the recipients do with the information or what they learn about U.S. capabilities from having the information—have probably come up already.

Proxy cyberattacks create especial risks if they touch systems that sit outside the theater of combat. Even if outsiders tacitly agree to bound the violence within borders, information systems are not necessarily built with that tenet in mind. Mischief from outside the theater can affect systems inside the theater and vice versa. Typically, combatants can leverage geography to limit engagements. For instance, Chinese forces were fair game for U.S. forces south but not north of the Yalu River. Russians avoided the Korean theater except for some covert air combat. U.S. forces were not attacked out offshore or beyond the theater. During the First Indochina War, the United States was generous in sending France supplies but not people. In the Vietnam War, although Russian and Chinese "advisers" at North Vietnamese SAM sites were not explicitly off-limits, some U.S. policymakers worried about unintentionally killing them (even as others were disappointed that they escaped harm).

Will proxy cyberwar (or, say, UAVs piloted from Nevada) be considered akin to supplies or to forces? The fact that cyberwar involves people says forces, but the immunity of cyberwarriors sitting out of theater makes it look more like supplies. Local hackers may be trained on and supplied with exploit tools, information on vulnerabilities, and intelligence on targets. After all that, figuratively pulling the trigger is almost an afterthought; should the fact that the trigger-puller is a local combatant necessarily remove the culpability from the country that did everything else to enable a cyberattack?

The separation between local services provided by and out-of-theater systems run by great powers may affect the prospects that cyberattacks may escalate from local systems to global ones. If one side's friend harms the in-theater systems of the other side's friend, will the latter make an issue of it? Can the attacker's friend argue local military necessity? Can the target's friend retort that the attack was really meant to harm it globally under the guise of influencing the local fight? In the end, both powers may need to work out a firebreak, or one may have to step back.

What norms might minimize escalation? One could insist that systems that sit outside the war zone—but not local portals for a global system—are off-limits to cyberattack. But that would raise the question: How much should an attacker be expected to know about how local systems and access points are connected to global systems of the great power friend? Who can map the cloud's boundaries?

Potential asymmetries plague the application of any such norms (as they do for setting red lines). If one side erected a tall wall between local and global, but the other side did not, then attacking the one side's local systems would carry less risk of escalation than attacking the other side's local systems. Why should the latter get a free pass just because of its sloppy architecture? Such asymmetries are compounded by ambiguities in cyberspace. If the citizens of one side's friend depend on capabilities that go haywire if its military is hacked (such systems could easily sit in third countries), and the other side attacks and claims that its attacks were legitimate, will the other side be seen as credible or as opportunistic?

Avoiding escalation in such scenarios might require such great powers to carefully separate their global systems from those sent to theater and require attackers to exercise great caution to ensure that their cyberattacks have precise effects—never easy, even under good circumstances. But it would not hurt for either side to realize that accidents happen, especially in war zones.

CONCLUSIONS

Escalation in cyberspace is likely to be jerky rather than smooth. Herman Kahn's treatment, in which both sides feel their way up an escalation ladder a few steps at a time to see who breaks first, is unlikely to characterize cyberwar (whether it would have characterized nuclear war is untested). What looks to each side like a carefully calibrated climb may, in practice, end up as a set of stalls and jumps. Perhaps there will be only one escalation phase—from unproblematic cyberattacks against military targets to problematic cyberattacks against civilian ones. For instance, take a scenario in which the regional combatant commander makes an urgent request that a SAM site be knocked out. The cyber commander sees no way to get into the SAM site but knows that a "small" attack on the local power supply may have the same effect. The other side finds this "small" attack escalatory. Alternatively, the only attacks that may be deemed seriously escalatory are those that cross the border between instrumental (tactical) and general (strategic) or from legitimate to illegitimate. That, in turn, presupposes norms of what is one and what is the other. No such norms exist or are on the horizon.

At least both sides should understand that responding to the other side's escalation is hardly urgent. Cyberattacks, as noted, cannot disarm another side's ability to respond in kind. The timing of a response ought to be predicated on what it is to accomplish in the context of one's warfighting strategy. Each country should also understand the reaction of the other side (and third parties) to escalation, notably the latter's understanding of cyberwar's ethical norms. In cyberspace, as in other realms of warfare, "the defender frequently does not understand how threatening his behavior, though defensively motivated, may seem to the other side."[27]

CHAPTER 28
Brandishing Cyberattack Capabilities

Brandishing a weapon communicates what one has and suggests that it would be used and how. It is used to shape or at least reinforce other states' estimates of the risks they face by opposing the brandisher. It can be implicit, leaving it to others to determine the implications of its use. Or it can be explicit, with the owner choosing the context, hence the timing, for its signal.[1] This chapter explores ways that cyberwar capabilities can be brandished, obstacles to doing so well, some reasons to do so, some risks involved, and limits on our expectations.

WHAT IS BRANDISHING?

Cyberattack capabilities, to be effective, have to be capabilities against specific systems, and targeted countries vary in what systems they have, how well they have been secured, and how important their secure functioning is to the country's well-being. Brandishing can tell people something they do not know (or at least not know for sure). It can remind leaders of what they know but are not paying attention to—so that they consider such factors front and center when making decisions. It may also be used to remind people of something their leaders know so that the leaders cannot afford to be seen ignoring it. It might induce others to react (and thereby consume their time, resources, energy, and attention) when they would otherwise overlook such capabilities.

With Stuxnet and the Snowden revelations now old news, no one can seriously believe the United States lacks offensive cyberattack capabilities. Perhaps such cyberwar capabilities have already discouraged some mischief.[2] Weapons alone could do this. In 1932 (before Germany had a Luftwaffe), Stanley Baldwin persuaded the British parliament not to intervene too hastily in European affairs by arguing that a serious adversary could use airpower to do great damage to Great Britain: "The bomber will always get through."[3]

Countries brandish to make threats, either specifically ("do this and we will carry out a cyberattack") or generally ("do this, and we will respond—and we can carry out a possible cyberattack"). Or they do so to counter threats, explicit or implicit. It is similar to announcing a capability for ballistic missile defense after the other side has announced a ballistic missile capability—except that cyberwar plays a role more like a weapon aimed at the missile's command and control. Such an announcement may serve to downplay the threat and so assure oneself and allies and thereby weaken the threat's deterrent power. If the underlying threat itself is a counter-deterrent ("if you launch a missile, we will launch one back"), the cyberattack capability can be brandished to reinforce the original deterrent ("yes, but your missile will fail, and so we will ignore your threat"). The credibility of the cyberattack threat will depend on a country's track record in cyberspace coupled with its general reputation at military technology and the likelihood that it would use such capabilities when called on.

YOUR POWER OR THEIR POWERLESSNESS?

Because the potential for cyberattacks arises from the target's vulnerabilities *coupled* with the attacker's ability to exploit them, those who would brandish should first determine whether the point of doing so is to look powerful or to make the other side look powerless. Even if both are useful, it may help to decide what to emphasize.

Looking powerful is the more efficient option. It induces caution in actual or potential opponents. The demonstration does not have to be repeated for each one. Emphasizing one's capabilities can also deflect potential attackers from you to others. Success reflects well on other sources of national power.

But exposing their weaknesses may deter troublesome states by reminding them of their strategic vulnerabilities—particularly if it is their kinetic capabilities that are vulnerable to cyberattack and can therefore be discounted.[4] Such countries can be reminded of how insecure their systems are—and how dependent they are on such insecure systems. Focusing on the other side also deflects accusations of self-promotion ("look at how powerful I am") by shifting the focus toward others—particularly if the source of the demonstration attack can be effectively hidden (or, more likely, ambiguous). After all, a state shown to be vulnerable to one attacker in cyberspace may be presumed vulnerable to others. Even if the country threatens to brandish its own offensive capabilities in response to what others do, its systems will still be vulnerable and perceived as such.

HOW TO BRANDISH CYBERATTACK CAPABILITIES[5]

Marching armies down wide boulevards is a time-honored way for countries to hint at their ability to make war. Cyberwar capabilities, though, resist such demonstrations. Squads of geeks advancing with laptops in their rucksacks somehow do not inspire the same awe. No one doubts what would happen if a nuclear-armed power dropped its big weapon on a city, even though no city has been hit by a nuclear bomb since 1945. The underlying physics work anywhere. But no one knows exactly or even approximately what would happen if a country suffered a full-fledged cyberattack despite the plethora of hostile activity in cyberspace that shows no signs of abating. For one thing, there has never been such a full-fledged attack.

Although demonstrating capability is hard, hard does not mean impossible. The most obvious way of demonstrating that you can hack into someone else's system is to do it and leave a calling card (for example, Kilroy was here). The effect should be obvious to sysadmins, even if not necessarily to the public. But will the calling card be read and transmitted to a country's leadership? If it is simply left for someone to stumble over, the answer may be "no." So, any calling card may itself have to be obvious. Perhaps it can e-mail itself, so to speak, to the sysadmins in the hopes that they will tell the leadership. If the target system is connected to the rest of world—a big if for sensitive systems—it can e-mail itself directly to the target's leadership. That should work (unless the leadership get it into their heads that it was a trick by its own cyberwar proponents to gain more resources). Conversely, if acknowledging a penetration is embarrassing and puts jobs or even (in some countries) lives at risk, such hints may be deliberately ignored. Revealing to the leadership what information has been taken would be simpler, as long as it is clear that such information could *only* have come from penetrating the system.

Second, will the penetration be understood as consequential? If penetration is a one-time event, the target may convince itself that it can prevent a repeat performance. Or the victim may tolerate the attacker's ability to stay on the system precisely because it finds penetration to be less intolerable than the cost of cleaning it up (rare, but not entirely unimaginable) and cannot or will not extrapolate from a simple penetration to the destruction of its digital systems and the process they control.

The impact of the penetration should be higher if the target systems are both critical to the target and thought to be impenetrable (so that any penetration would be impressive). If the target's political power relies on the correct operation of systems that are not only electronically isolated but also hidden, then penetration into lesser systems may leave little impression on the target. Note that penetrating a system and persisting within it require similar skill sets but different technologies. Penetration requires knowledge of vulnerabilities; persistence requires knowing how to hide in dark corners and otherwise evade intrusion and anomaly detection systems.

Third, does the ability to penetrate a computer or network prove the ability to break the broader system built from such components? Bringing systems down requires understanding their failure modes; keeping them down requires being able to insert code into the target networks and system in ways that frustrate *quick* eradication. Attacks on logistics systems may have to last days or weeks before crippling their user base. Attacks on surface-to-air missile systems, however, only have to disable systems for the few minutes that attack aircraft are overhead. Nevertheless, it is unclear how quickly recovery occurs: the history of cyberattacks that require urgent fixes is thin, and documentation from victims of such attacks is even thinner. Perhaps cyberattackers (here and elsewhere) have endeavored to estimate adversary responses by simulating attacks on their own systems and testing their own sysadmins' ability to recover their functionality. Even if so, this still leaves for brandishers the challenge of conveying that their own attacks can keep their systems down for long periods of time. The intended audiences of such a demonstration may be able to determine what flaw allowed such an attack, fix the flaw, and recover some confidence in their own systems. If so, for brandishing to make its mark, cyberattack capabilities must be seen as repeatable.

Furthermore, systems typically targeted by espionage (for example, e-mail networks) are very different from the more hardened systems that run critical infrastructure or war machines. The ability to read files need not imply the ability to write to them, hence alter them, just as the ability to listen to CD recordings on a laptop does not imply the laptop's ability to edit the CD itself. But from a psychological perspective, the difference between penetration and manipulation may not matter so much; if the violation of a system's integrity is shocking and proves that systems cannot keep information—notably personal information—secret, then such distinctions may be lost to leaders. Furthermore, the ability to insert arbitrary instructions into a computer *does* imply the ability to overwrite its hard drive or flood the network that the computer sits on. *Breaking* a system is also a more hostile act, though, than *breaking into* a system.

One way to walk the fine line between demonstrating a capability and using it in such a way as to invite reprisals may be to demonstrate an ability to manipulate the target's system in ways that, if continued or carried out in other contexts, can demonstrably break it. Thus, the demonstrated ability to fog a radar during normal operations implies the ability to do so when the radar is tracking a hostile object. The ability to raise the temperature of someone else's chemical process by one degree may, in some circumstances, imply the ability to raise the temperature to catastrophic levels. Neither are friendly acts, but neither look like acts of war—and yet, they show that acts of war are within one's capability. The usual caveats apply.

A 2012 David Sanger article on Stuxnet was an interesting, perhaps unique, exercise in general brandishing, notably by declaring that the United States was the prime mover of the attack, carried out to ensure that Israel did nothing riskier.[6] Although such revelations admittedly only gave imprimatur to an attribution that was already widely believed, they gave U.S. allies license to own up to pursuing offensive cyberwar programs;[7] by doing so, they made the U.S. development of cyberwar capabilities stand out less.

ESCALATION DOMINANCE AND BRANDISHING

As per Herman Kahn, escalation dominance is the theory that if two sides are at one level of a conflict or confrontation, one side can discourage the other from escalating by showing that the other side cannot win and cannot afford the costs of taking it to a higher level. Escalation dominance, as we demonstrate, requires brandishing in the face of the vast sea of ignorance of what any country can do. Even then, it is unlikely to work well.

For escalation dominance to work at the nuclear level, the other side had to understand what both sides could do (which could reliably be inferred by their weapons inventory), believe that the one side would do it, have similar notions about where the boundaries between levels were, and be able to estimate its tolerance for destruction vis-à-vis the other side's. In practice (notably the Cold War), these conditions were largely met: the relationship between one side's nuclear weapons and the other side's damage was well known; both sides labored hard to make nuclear options credible; weapons, it was believed, tended to sort themselves into tactical and strategic straightforwardly; and whereas different societies might have different pain thresholds, neither side would consider absorbing a nuclear detonation to be painless. The Cold War assumption that the Soviet Union resembled the United States in all four aspects lent credibility to the notion of escalation dominance.

However, when considering escalation dominance in cyberspace, there are other complications, each and all of which lend considerable uncertainty to the workability of escalation dominance in that domain.

First, it is difficult to demonstrate a cyberwar capability by reference to its observable physical characteristics—as nuclear weapons most certainly can.

Second, demonstrating a cyberwar capability in the abstract hardly means proving its effectiveness against the other side's systems, since the defenses of systems vary widely. Granted, a system can be demonstrated to have certain classes of vulnerabilities whose exploitation can permit a broad class of effects (for example, gain remote code execution privileges). But demonstrating *exactly* that usually starts a process that nearly guarantees that such vulnerabilities could be closed by taking them seriously. Those who do not take security faults seriously cannot be coerced easily for precisely that reason. By contrast, nuclear weapons work the same everywhere.

Third, even if one could demonstrate a cyberwar capability against a particular target, it is difficult to predict how long the target would be down. As a very rough rule of thumb, the cost of disruption/corruption is proportional to recovery time. Escalation dominance requires that the other side believe that its recovery time will be long—even though the other side may have a better idea how long recovery would take than the one side does. Granted, destruction is another matter, but in twenty years, a cyberattack has broken something exactly twice (bricking machines is a different class of destruction since no hardware is damaged). No one has yet died. With death and destruction—which is what nuclear weapons do—loss, being permanent, is primary and recovery is secondary.

Fourth, even if one could demonstrate how long another side's systems would be down, this would not necessarily indicate how badly it was hurt—the latter is a function of a society's technical resilience (for example, substitutes for lost functions) and its psychological resilience. Exactly who in the civilian world (for example, which sector) is suffering downtime could affect what level and kind of political pressure could be put on leadership. Part of that calculation by one side would be to understand how decisive political pressure of a particular kind would be on the other side (vis-à-vis one's own side).

Fifth, even if you could demonstrate that your ability to damage and tolerate its damage exceeded its ability to do damage and tolerate your damage, this would not represent escalation dominance unless both sides were confident that the other side would not escalate from cyberspace to the physical world—or unless there was also escalation dominance in the physical world that could and would be brought into play.

Sixth, the already noted difficulties in agreeing where one level leaves off and another begins complicates expressing dominance. One side could believe it can dominate at a particular level of a confrontation only by including attacks that the other side has placed at levels higher or lower. It is a minor consideration but one that cannot be ignored.

It is therefore unclear how a dialogue that established escalation dominance in cyberspace (and solely in cyberspace) would take place. Simply declaring a capability without demonstration proves nothing. But a demonstration would have to be shaped to accommodate the risk that it would itself constitute an attack. How the other side reacts could make such a demonstration self-defeating from the perspective of escalation dominance. The entire point of escalation dominance, after all, is to inhibit the other side from taking action—not goad it into taking action—because it is convinced that it could be outfought at every level of conflict.

A set of declarations in which one side just asserts its ability to dominate cyberwar at multiple levels may do little more than convince the other side to escalate its own rhetoric: for instance, if you threaten a DDOS attack on our banks, we will scramble your bank records. This exchange (however explicit or implicit) would completely blow past the question of dominance at any particular level of conflict and would look more like a contest for who can tell the taller tales. Indeed, it could proceed almost irrespective of what each party was capable of—although how seriously one side would take the other side's claim of being able to do *anything* at a particular level is hard to determine.

COUNTER-BRANDISHING

Now turn the question around to consider counter-brandishing: how might countries deal with the *perception* of their own vulnerability in the face of cyberattack? Much of the discourse on U.S. military intervention in Ukraine, for instance, is sprinkled with fears that Russia would attack the United States with unknown but frightful consequences. Russia's success in Crimea was chalked up in part to its cyberwar capabilities (notwithstanding the tendency to confuse wire-cutting and electronic warfare with cyberattacks). One article noted, "Admiral [James] Stavridis (rt'd) . . . said that Russia's deft use of cyberwarfare . . . was a development that NATO needed to study and factor into its planning."[8] Europeans themselves started counter-hacking drills right after announcing new sanctions on Russia: "Two people with knowledge of a White House review of the effects of further penalties on Russia said April 25 [that] it includes revisiting previous classified exercises in which small numbers of computer experts showed they were able to cripple the U.S. economy in a few days. U.S. officials involved in the review didn't respond to questions about whether the study explores the risk of cyber-counterattacks."[9] Another article warned, "Sanctions will have collateral damage. . . . Russia . . . could enlist its hackers to destabilise American banks and exchanges."[10] Stephen Blank of the American Foreign Policy Council foresaw the possibility of Russia's "opportunistic 'poking around' in the Baltics, which might involve cyberattacks and other forms of 21st-century asymmetric warfare."[11] Richard Clarke warned, "If we move to the heavy sanctions . . . the Russians are going to strike back in some way. . . . What they can do . . . is a cyberattack to get back at us . . . attacking our financial institutions in ways that we'll never be able to prove it was them but we'll suffer the pain."[12] Even the late 2014 hack of JPMorgan Chase, which would normally fit the pattern of cybercrime snugly, was perceived as Russian brandishing: "Some American officials speculate that the breach was intended to send a message to Wall Street and the United States about the vulnerability of the digital network of one of the world's most important banking institutions."[13] As the head of CYBERCOM testified in early 2015: "We believe potential adversaries might be leaving cyber fingerprints on our critical infrastructure partly to convey a message that our homeland is at risk if tensions ever escalate toward military conflict."[14] Similar was the warning that the Syrian Electronic Army "probably will increase its activity if the U.S. launches military strikes on the Middle Eastern nation, a cybersecurity expert [Adam Meyers, vice president of intelligence for CrowdStrike] said Wednesday."[15]

Well-founded self-deterrence is not necessarily bad. Any country pondering actions that may irritate another should make some estimate of what others can do in return. If the cost of intervening in Ukraine is a stock market crash arising from hacking, such considerations cannot be blithely ignored. What makes self-deterrence a problem is when others, notably those of other countries, come to believe what does not merit belief.[16] If such countries hold back from aligning with the United States because they feel themselves threatened or because they fear that the United States will itself shy away from a confrontation at the last minute, then the ability of the United States to act may be unnecessarily constrained.

Should events warrant as much, would there be some useful purpose in daring another country to carry out cyberattacks for the purpose of convincing others (and even oneself) that their threats can be ignored? Three possibilities may result. One is to reveal the bluff; such an outcome permits downplaying or even ignoring further bluster—forcing the bully to up the ante (for example, threaten worse and/or make sure the threat works) or find another trick. Two is that the attack works, but attribution is good—the bully has the advantage of credibility but the disadvantage of opening itself to retaliation (depending on the capability and orneriness of the target vis-à-vis the bully). Three is that the attack works, but attribution is not good enough to put the bully on the spot (or justify retaliation). It probably helps to figure out the odds of the third outcome before calling the bluff.

The wisdom of calling the bluff also depends on the resulting narrative that comes from the attack. The defender—the side making the dare—has three competing interests. First, for foreign consumption, it wants the damage to be nugatory, the better to convince others that the attacker (the side taking the dare) has less in its holster than feared (or advertised). Second, for domestic consumption, it wants the damage to be horrific, the better to convince domestic organizations to take the contingent (as opposed to the day-to-day) threat seriously. Third, for its own purposes, it wants to find out what the attacker has up its sleeve, the better to gauge how much of a threat it really faces, understand the latter's modus operandi, anticipate future lines of attack, and nullify particular exploits that have been demonstrated. Clearly, these are three very contradictory demands.

CAVEATS AND CAUTIONS

Because states may brandish offensive cyberwar capabilities to give teeth to a deterrence policy, its success as a policy option depends on what other countries conclude about the motive for and the timing of such brandishing. A country that could threaten retaliation in cyberspace could use brandishing to give substance to a threat. Absent such a threat, other countries would wonder what the point was of emphasizing its retaliatory capabilities *in that domain*. The answer may be innocent: a bureaucratic process may have reached its conclusion, or a new cyberattack capability may have been deemed mature. Absent such knowledge, others may conclude that more violent responses are off the table—and if they do not particularly fear cyberattack, they may relax and become *less* deterred. The timing of any demonstration may also raise questions, especially if the announcement is not really news (for example, everyone always assumed such capabilities existed). They may ask why the brandisher believed that the point had to be made explicit. Some may therefore view it as a bluff, perhaps putting a brave face on the discovery that cyberattack capabilities are not impressing others (or themselves for that matter).

Brandishing, while creating a narrative about strength, also creates a narrative around the legitimacy of cyberwar. If the demonstration takes place against a live target, it also speaks to the brandisher's intentions vis-à-vis a country that it may not be at war with.

Are the short-terms gains from this sort of brandishing—and its adjunct, intimidation—worth the risk of accelerating the evolution of a particular class of weaponry? In the nuclear race between the United States and the Soviet Union, Nikita Khrushchev would boast that his country could turn out missiles "like sausages." The United States reacted by accelerating its own missile program. By 1961—a year before the Cuban Missile Crisis—the United States knew it had a strategic edge in nuclear delivery systems, notably missiles. Similar perceptions by the Soviets led them to ship missiles to Cuba to adjust the strategic balance. The Soviet reaction to having to back down in Cuba was to accelerate its own programs in order to achieve parity, which it did, thereby setting the stage for Strategic Arms Limitation Talks negotiations. Had neither side flaunted its capabilities, might nuclear parity have been achieved at lower levels? The missile race is hardly unique, as the pre–World War I Anglo-German shipbuilding rivalry demonstrated. Nevertheless, a cyberspace arms race is not the most likely course of events, in part because no one knows what the other side has (and what the other side claims provides only imperfect guidance), and in part because offense is the lesser half of the question; the target's defense is often a better predictor of outcomes.

Finally, a caveat about the potential U.S. use of brandishing. Assume that the United States has convinced others that it can interfere with anyone's military equipment. Then some war breaks out and no (networked digital) equipment falls to cyberattack. Observers may conclude that the United States chose *not* to disrupt the sophisticated systems of one side. If only one side's equipment works, others may see proof that the United States must have played favorites and even blame the United States for atrocities associated with such military equipment. They may not pay attention to counterarguments: for example, we hinted "might" not "would"; some equipment is inaccessible from the outside. Until the hints started flying, no one could imagine that military equipment could be remotely disabled—but afterward, no one can imagine the United States *not* being able to do it.

The current U.S. posture on cyberspace weapons happens to be coy.[17] It stands between our posture on nuclear weapons (terrible—but indispensable in certain very special circumstances) and chemical/biological weapons (too sinful even to contemplate). Although there is no official policy affirming that the United States *would* use cyberattacks in particular situations short of war, there has certainly been no policy that states the contrary. Similarly, the press reported, again without refutation (but incorrectly), that DARPA was working on developing offensive cyberwar capabilities.[18]

CHAPTER 29
Cyberattack in a Nuclear Confrontation

ould the United States brandish its superior cyberwar capability to influence the course of a confrontation with a rogue nuclear state (defined as one with a handful of weapons capable of hitting nearby countries but not the continental United States)? In working the question, we do not *and need not claim* that U.S. cyberattack capabilities can actually confound adversary nuclear capabilities reliably. Few systems are so resistant to cyberwar as nuclear delivery systems because countries pay exceeding attention to their command and control against the day when their regime's survival rests on their being ready for use (or their not going off accidentally). However, the possibility that the United States *could* penetrate the command, control, or operations of nuclear systems cannot be easily disproven either. Iran's leaders undoubtedly thought that their isolating the Natanz centrifuge facility rendered it safe from cyberattack. Then they learned about Stuxnet. The Chinese are also nervous. Thus, what we are asking is whether the *threat* to interfere—not the interference itself—can shape the confrontation.

So, assume that the United States has a robust cyberattack capability from which the rogue state's nuclear arsenal is not *provably* immune (and the U.S. nuclear deterrence capability is deemed sufficiently safe from cyberattack). Although the United States would have more nuclear weapons with longer range, the rogue state is believed to be far more willing to go to the nuclear brink than the United States because it has more at stake (regime survival) and less at stake (the welfare of its people). Also, it may act in ways that are irrational by Western perspectives. Yet the rogue state understands that if it *does* use nuclear weapons, it could face great retaliation.

Now, posit a scenario: the United States faces the choice of acting (for example, crossing some red line) when doing so risks the rogue state releasing a nuclear weapon. Whether the threat is explicit or implicit is secondary. In the face of the threat, there are three possible outcomes: good (the United States goes ahead as if the rogue state could not or would not use nuclear weapons), bad (the United States is deterred from going ahead), or ugly (nuclear weapons are used).[1]

THE BASIC CONFRONTATION

In any confrontation where disaster would result from both sides carrying out their threats, each must ask: Are such threats credible? If one side thinks the other will yield, it pays to stand firm. If it thinks, however, that the other is implacable, it may have no good choice but to, itself, yield. The projection of implacability is beneficial, but the reality of implacability can be suicidal.

Note that the basis for the implacability can also be entirely subjective and not necessarily founded on the facts. Consider this tale: Aaron and Zeke commonly play chicken (Schelling used this metaphor to discuss nuclear confrontations[2]). Invariably, when they played, both turned away before they crashed. One day, a magician, Merlin, shows up with a mysterious paint he applies to Aaron's car. He informs one and all that such paint will allow Aaron to ram any other car without a scratch on his vehicle or himself. So armed, Aaron and Zeke play again. Aaron broadcasts his determination not to swerve. Zeke believes that he is at a great disadvantage, so he swerves and Aaron wins. But Zeke is not convinced that this magic paint lives up to its claims. After some research he confirms his suspicions and, in turn, broadcasts his own findings. But Aaron refuses to believe Zeke. They race again. Zeke knows that both cars would be wiped out in a crash, but he also knows that Aaron is convinced that he and his car can survive a crash. Aaron is implacable. Zeke has to swerve. He is disgusted that Aaron wins based on an illusion, but there it is.

Similarly, if one side is convinced that it will never pay a high price for being implacable, communicates as much, and convinces the other side that it believes it, the other cannot take any comfort from the fact that the first has no technical basis for the belief. The only consideration in the mind of the other side is whether the first party *actually* believes as much, is willing to act accordingly, and can ignore the logic that whispers that no one can possibly act completely confident on the basis of iffy information.[3]

So, in this scenario, a U.S. strategy is to foster the strong impression (whether by saying so, hinting so, or letting others draw their own conclusion) that it believes that the rogue state will not carry out its nuclear threat. Although its confidence may stem from many factors (for example, the rogue state will back down in the face of overwhelming deterrent power), it arises, in part, because the United States *also* drops hints and projects confidence that a flaw, perhaps deliberately induced, somewhere in the other side's nuclear command and control cycle prevents immediate nuclear use. A lesser possibility that can be hinted at is that the command and control is less certain, the weapon is weaker, and/or the delivery system is far less accurate than feared.[4] Although permanently disabling a nuclear command and control system is quite a stretch for cyberwar (even if destroyed, such equipment is far easier to replicate than fissile material is to produce), it is less fantastic to imagine that the United States could delay a weapon's use. A temporary advantage, though, may still give the United States time to cross the red line and thereby carry out a fait accompli. Once the United States has crossed the red line, the onus is on the rogue state to roll it back and reinforce the notion that crossing red lines can have deadly consequences—all the while knowing that nuclear use would also certainly be suicidal at that point. Compulsion is considered much more difficult than deterrence. If the rogue state understands the logic *before* brandishing its own nuclear weapons, it may choose not to ratchet up tensions in advance of the United States crossing red lines.

The success of this strategy requires that the rogue state *believe* that the United States is implacable—based, in part, on its thinking that the United States *believes* it can use cyberattacks to nullify the nuclear threat. It also helps if the rogue state is not completely sure that U.S. confidence is misplaced, although it may work even if the rogue state believes there is no basis for such confidence as long as it understands the United States cannot be convinced otherwise.

Note that this implied or expressed belief in a known flaw is broader than the claim that the United States *caused* the flaw. In many respects, it suffices that the United States knows about the flaw and the rogue state does not (or knows but can do nothing about it over the immediate course of the crisis). The flaw in question could have been created by physical means (for example, saboteurs) or a third party; it could have been sitting there in the design all along. However, a flaw that prevents a nuclear shot is different from a flaw that the United States can exploit to prevent a nuclear shot. The former claim loses credibility if the rogue state can get a shot off, but the latter claim can survive a shot, albeit in weakened form, as argued below.

Although confidence in the ability to frustrate a rogue state's nuclear capability through cyberwar should work like confidence in an effective missile defense, there are important differences. The efficacy of a missile defense system can be publicly demonstrated against an actual missile as sophisticated (for example, armed with comparable penetration aids) as the rogue state's missiles. No such tests are decisive in cyberwar, since cyberwar generally depends on the target system having flaws that its owner is unaware of and that it would fix or route around once made aware—thereby nullifying such an attack. Furthermore, the existence and the basic qualities of a U.S. cyberattack capability can only be surmised—in large part because offensive cyberwar capabilities must be highly classified to remain effective.

Signaling that the rogue state has a flaw in the network elements of its nuclear command and control does not set up a use-it-or-lose-it dilemma for the rogue state—the vulnerability that enabled the flaw to be introduced necessarily preceded the crisis, and, in all likelihood, so did the discovery of the flaw and its exploitation. The rogue state has no ability, hence no incentive, to fire off its weapons in advance of the cyberattack that might disable it because by the time the threat is made, the cyberattack has already happened.

Should the United States extend its advantage by intimating that it would respond to a failed nuclear launch as much as it would to a successful nuclear launch? By so doing, it might further inhibit the rogue state from calling the U.S. bluff since it could not rest behind the assurance that failure would have no greater consequence than not trying. But can the United States retaliate for a failed launch? It is one thing for a nuclear shot to visibly fail; everyone else can read intent. But if a missile fails to launch, can the United States retaliate, especially with nuclear weapons, on the basis of evidence that can only come from cyberspace and thus may be perceived as concocted—even though the retaliatory shot would be anything but concocted?

DISABLING A CAPABILITY VERSUS THWARTING A THREAT

A RAND colleague of mine has surmised: Why bother brandishing a threat that the United States can render a rogue's nuclear command and control inoperable? Why not just render it inoperable? Yes, having a capability is always better; one can actually use it. The risk arises when the rogue state, believing it has working nuclear weapons, puts itself in a position where it has to use them, tries to do so, is frustrated, finds and fixes the problem, and then in the next crisis maneuvers to the point where it has gone too far in its crisis posturing *not* to use them. Conversely, if it thought that it lacked the capability in the first place, it might restrain itself from going out on a limb and could then back down without losing as much face as if it tried and were halted.

Furthermore, having an *unspoken* cyberattack capability will not relieve the pressure on the United States to withdraw from a crisis against a nuclear-armed rogue state. Such pressure may come from internal opposition, allies, or respected interlocutors. It may even come, as discussed below, from the very country that the United States is defending against the rogue state. Even then, having the capability is not useless, even in the public arena. If the knowledge that the foe's nuclear capabilities can be neutralized gives U.S. leadership enough confidence to cross the other side's red line, others may infer that the United States has valid reasons for its confidence even if never revealed. For some, that would be good enough.

The choice between raising doubts about the adversary's nuclear systems in order to win a confrontation and exploiting the adversary's weaknesses to limit the damage from a war may rest on the odds that the rogue state would actually use its weapons. If the odds of use are low (for example, because U.S. implacability is expected to have the desired effect), then hinting is warranted; if the odds of use are high, then silence on what the United States can actually do may be advised, the better to lull the rogue state into assuming its network is functioning (rather than questioning it in ways that ultimately improve its ability to withstand a cyberattack). If the rogue state understands this logic *and* the United States is brandishing its cyberattack capability, it ought to conclude that the United States believes the likelihood of actual use is low because it can, in fact, deter the rogue state. This could reinforce the message that the rogue state's nuclear regime has exploitable flaws—or at least that the United States will act as if this were true.

296 PART IV STRATEGIES

Can brandishing cyberattack capabilities be useful when U.S. steadfastness is *not* a relevant issue? Examples may be precluding a unilateral nuclear shot (for example, a bolt from the blue) or persuading a rogue state not to raise the nuclear ante or otherwise work itself into a position where it felt it had no choice but to use nuclear weapons. Unfortunately, the earlier a rogue state is alerted that its nuclear command and control may have flaws, the more time it has to find and fix them. Although physically breaking such a system would lead to much longer outages, a cyberattack could do so only if the command and control system could break itself or something it was connected to if fed bad instructions. Whether the rogue state can *find* the requisite flaws (that permitted the disabling cyberattack), fix them, and *then* convince itself that there were no other flaws is a different issue. The number of problems in its system is clearly one fewer. If it thought it had only one problem before, it has zero now—so back, with confidence, to the brink. On the one hand, how would it know that it started out with just *one* exploitable flaw? The act of finding one flaw may just be an indication that it had multiple flaws to begin with. Thus, the *expected* number of exploitable flaws could well be greater *after* having eradicated one.[5] Conversely, if it searches and finds no flaw, it may conclude that either the United States was bluffing or that U.S. cyberwarriors were so clever and subtle that the relevant exploit was undetectable even after a painstaking search.[6] Otherwise, is there a point to signaling to a rogue state that its nuclear command and control may have flaws when the rogue state is not under great urgency to use it—as it would be if it tried to stop the United States from crossing a red line?

ROGUE STATE STRATEGIES FOR DISCREDITING THE CYBERWAR BLUFF

Assume the rogue state, having scrubbed its nuclear command and control systems, manages to brush aside all its own doubts about its reliability—despite the difficulty of being certain that the (purportedly all-knowing, all-seeing) U.S. intelligence community does not know something about its nuclear systems that its owner has overlooked (remember Stuxnet) and the knowledge that surprises in cyberspace are surprising in their details, and yet they seem to occur frequently.

If the portrayed basis for U.S. confidence were publicly revealed to be false, the rogue state just may convince itself that the United States *could not and therefore would not* be implacable. Thus, it could signal its own confidence in its nuclear capabilities and thereby hope to dissuade the United States from crossing the aforementioned red line.

But how? One way is to reveal something about its command and control that would indicate that the basis for the U.S. belief is illusory. Against that strategy is the well-founded fear that the more it reveals about its command and control, the more information it gives U.S. (and every other country's) cyberwarriors to work with in pursuit of a *real* flaw. Such revelation may also give useful targeting information to adversary special forces and air forces. The rogue state leaders may also feel that revealing secrets about command and control may tell *internal* audiences (for example, some members of its military) things that its leadership prefer they not know.

The rogue state could also assuage concerns about potential vulnerabilities by shooting a nuclear missile off and having the world watch it detonate. Success would eliminate the possibility that the induced or discovered nuclear command and control flaw is pervasive and endogenous. Furthermore, a failed shot signals a willingness to use such weapons in ways that mere possession does not. A successful shot, though, does not eliminate the possibility that the flaw was of the type that the United States could choose to exploit or not. The United States, after all, could have refused to interfere with the nuclear strike in the belief that a successful launch would not yield serious damage (for example, it was a demonstration shot in the rogue state's territory). This still leaves open the possibility that if the shot *did* matter, the United States could have stopped it. If so, the United States could still maintain its determination to cross whatever red line the rogue state established since it could do so with impunity.

The rogue state, anticipating as much, would have to make its point with a nuclear shot that would generate consequences too weak to merit U.S. nuclear retaliation, but strong enough to exceed what the United States could tolerate with insouciance. Such a test shot could discredit the basis for U.S. confidence (because if it could have stopped the shot, it would have done so). An example might be a nonnuclear warhead atop a nuclear delivery system shot in the direction where detonation, if nuclear, could have killed many. In theory, the United States could not have known that the shot was nonnuclear until detonation. In retort, the United States could suggest that the level of knowledge required to get inside the nuclear command and control cycle is also more than enough to distinguish a nuclear from a conventional shot. All this requires the rogue state to determine the line at which the United States would block a shot, and the line at which it would retaliate devastatingly—and hope there was an interval of daylight between the two (note the parallel to the discussion of the anger-fear interval above—and the possibility that this interval does not exist). Conversely, a demonstration shot gives others reason to question why the rogue state needed a demonstration in the first place (perhaps confirming a basis for rumors of a flaw), uses up at least one missile from what may be a small stockpile, and may not address the suspicion that the exploitable flaw affects nuclear weapons detonation.

Conversely, would it be useful for the United States to persuade the rogue state that it *could* have such control over and above convincing the rogue state that the United States *believes* it does have such control (it helps if the rogue state's leaders were unsure of the details of how their own nuclear command and control systems worked)? If the rogue state's leaders think they might just be firing blanks, they would see themselves as trying to bluff and therefore approach the nuclear-ready crisis with a greater tentativeness. If they fear the United States would detect this tentativeness, then they might reason that the United States would approach the crisis with more confidence—that is, *as if* the rogue state were bluffing. U.S. confidence would preempt rogue state tentativeness. All this means that crossing a red line carries less risk, which, again, puts the rogue state in the position of losing if it backs down—or worse if it launches.

THIRD-PARTY CAVEATS

Although the scenario above features only the rogue state and the United States, few are the scenarios in which the United States alone is at risk from a rogue state's nuclear weapons. More likely is a scenario in which the United States faces a nuclear rogue state while defending a friendly third country. But if the third country is in a position to veto U.S. actions, it can complicate the decision to brandish cyberattack capabilities as a way for the United States to appear implacable. Such countries have many ways to exercise their veto, not least by denying U.S. forces access to their territory. Even if the U.S. military can operate from the sea or distant air bases, third-party objections to pending U.S. actions could undercut the primary U.S. reason for running nuclear risks in the first place.

Even if friendly third parties want to humiliate or even disarm the rogue state more than the United States does, they may well blanch at the cyberwar bluff. First, they and their citizens are likely to be at greater risk, by dint of sitting within range of the rogue state's nuclear systems. Second, they would know less than the United States does about what cyberwar capabilities the United States has and how they might be used. As a result, they may have less confidence that such plans would work.

None of this will pass notice by the rogue state, which may well conclude that it need not stare down the United States if it can scare the third party. Even if the third party would stand with the

United States to present a united front against nuclear blackmail, it would have a harder time projecting the requisite confidence to make a stand, thereby emboldening the rogue state, which figures that its threats are more likely to crack the united front.

The United States may thus need to keep the third party in line if it would leverage its cyberwar capabilities to bolster the allied position in a confrontation. The United States could, for instance, tell its ally: stand fast and play along with our assertion about the fragility of the rogue state's nuclear system with an "or else" attached. A softer option is to convince the third party that the *appearance* of steadfastness would dissuade the rogue nuclear state. Such an argument makes equal sense, though, with or without a cyberwar counter-threat.

The third party's leadership may feel assured by U.S. confidence, but it may also consult its own military officers who have enough daily contact with their U.S. counterparts to gauge exactly how much confidence U.S. commanders really do have in their ability to thwart the rogue's nuclear threat. Or the third party may want some indication that the United States could do what it suggests it can do. What would constitute such evidence, and what would the United States feel comfortable showing the third party?

Any answer beyond "trust me on this" presumes a U.S. policy that is far more open about revealing offensive cyberwar capabilities to other countries (at least those outside the Five Eyes) than it now seems to be. Revelation carries risks. If standing fast requires pro-U.S. forces to project faith in the U.S. ability to nullify a nuclear threat, then those within the allied government that are nervous about taking such a huge risk, skeptics of cyberwar's power, or those predisposed against the United States have every incentive to cast doubt on the proposition. They may be very tempted to leak selective information entrusted by the United States in order to argue that U.S. cyberwar capabilities are overstated (and that therefore pretending otherwise is dangerous). Penetration of third parties by agents of the nuclear rogue cannot be dismissed, either.

Incidentally, a similar logic applies if one replaces the friendly third party by a domestic U.S. constituency (for example, Congress, opinion-makers, the polity). The more prominent a role played by cyberwar capabilities—compared with its retaliatory capabilities—in explaining why the United States is standing fast, the greater the demand to show why such confidence is warranted. It may be in the rogue state's interest, in fact, to argue that cyberwar capabilities are the *primary* basis for U.S. steadfastness in order to pressure the United States to demonstrate what it can do in cyberspace.

So what *can* be shown? If the United States had real-time information on the rogue state's nuclear command and control, the footage might be shown to friends—in hopes that such third parties accept what they are shown. A better demonstration would tweak something in the rogue's nuclear command system that immediately shows up in something that third parties can independently observe—in hopes they accept the fact that the exploit applies to all of the rogue state's nuclear command systems. They may then conclude that the adversary will shy away from confrontation. Thus, at a minimum, the United States would have to share very detailed knowledge about what it knows about the adversary's nuclear command system—and risk revealing sources and methods. But this demonstration may become the basis of its own negation if it leads the rogue state to a successful fix.

The usual caveats apply to such a demonstration. It may all be a bluff. It could fail. It may succeed and simply not be believed. The third party may feel that the rogue nuclear state has work-arounds that would not appear until they had to. And all this rests on the art of the possible in a world in which the rogue nuclear state has every incentive and every means to maintain command and control over its most important military asset.

OTHER CAVEATS

First, those who would brandish cyberattack capabilities ought to understand that fine line between making the rogue doubt its own nuclear capabilities and making the rogue state believe that its neighbors now doubt its own nuclear capabilities. Saddam Hussein did not put on a very convincing show to the United States that Iraq had cleaned itself of weapons of mass destruction. One reason why was that he was nervous about simultaneously assuring his enemy, Iran, of Iraq's state of disarmament. If the rogue believes that it has been disarmed before the eyes of nearby enemies, it may be unexpectedly motivated to prove otherwise, even at the risk of nuclear retaliation by the far-away enemy, the United States.

Second, while nuclear weapons and their delivery systems tend to be analog, and delivery systems a combination of analog and digital, the permissive action links (PALs) that prevent accidental launch of nuclear systems (particularly those of the newer nuclear states) *are* digital. If newer nuclear powers suspect that the United States is trying to thwart weapons use by tampering with the digital components of nuclear command and control systems (analog systems being immune to digital tampering), they may conclude that the United States had found some way to interfere with nuclear command and control *through* these PALs (so that the PALs would prevent a launch even if it were truly ordered). If countries disable these PALs out of fear that they may have been tampered with, the odds of an accidental or inadvertent launch would rise.

Third, establishing such a capability—or even understanding enough about a rogue's nuclear establishment to cast credible hints—generally requires carrying out cyberespionage on it. Spying and not getting caught present a problem. If the rogue state finds evidence of espionage (for example, an American-made implant) during the crisis when the United States wants to create doubt in the rogue state's mind about the integrity of its nuclear command and control, then its doing so may actually help (until the discovery leads to eradication, which then restores the rogue state's confidence). However, if the evidence is discovered during any other crisis (notably a nonnuclear one), then the rogue state might conclude that the United States wants to hobble the rogue state's retaliatory capability prefatory to a first strike.[7] Such conclusions may have very destabilizing effects.

Fourth, tactics that work on rogue states that have few nuclear weapons, fewer delivery systems that can reach the United States, and no cyberwar capabilities of their own may have disastrous results when applied to large nuclear powers with many nuclear weapons, long-range missiles, and their own cyberwar capabilities.

IS THERE MUCH POINT TO DISARMING A TARGET STATE'S NUCLEAR CAPABILITIES?

Even if a cyberattack could temporarily disarm nuclear capabilities, it is unclear what could be achieved by doing so. How sure could hackers be that they were, in fact, disabled? How confident would they be that they saw every path by which nuclear arms could be controlled when there may be several alternative communications paths to the ultimate goal? And even if complete disruption took place, unless the attacker could quickly follow up and destroy the target state's nuclear capacity kinetically (in which case the nuclear standoff alone would have had serious instability characteristics, with or without cyberwar), the target state need only stall for enough time to reestablish command and control over its weapons in order to reestablish deterrence. The window to look for, find, and destroy the target's nuclear capabilities is small, and complete success is required to avoid the risk of a devastating response. Otherwise, if the aggressor tries to carry out operations that would otherwise meet immediate nuclear retaliation, the target state might correctly warn that retaliation, if delayed, is nevertheless coming. Perhaps the aggressor might then reason that retaliation postponed may be retaliation avoided. By then, the prospect of unthinking retaliation that may arise by chance is greatly reduced. Furthermore, by that point, the purpose of retaliation would be compulsion and hence more likely to be resisted by an aggressor who could credibly threaten a counterstrike. To wit, the onus would have been transferred after the initial nuclear strike. But any potential aggressor would be taking a big chance by acting on that logic.

That noted, a *failed* cyberattack could *reveal* one country's intent to disarm another state's ultimate weapon, even if only temporarily. This could alter the target state's view of the attacker's intentions—and *that* might lead to a crisis.

SHOULD TARGETING THE NUCLEAR COMMAND AND CONTROL SYSTEMS OF MAJOR NUCLEAR POWERS BE ABJURED?

Should the United States, Russia, and China foreswear targeting each other's nuclear command and control infrastructure (including indications and warning assets)? Since 1949, the world has managed to maintain the nuclear standoff without a big bang. Those inclined to leave well enough alone could easily answer yes and skip this section.

For the rest, a few considerations merit note. With the invention of cyberwar—which is to say, computers—no country can ignore the possibility, however remote, that their command over nuclear weapons may be wired to fail. This would be true even in a world in which every country pledged not to—because by the time the opportunity for usurpation arises, a usurper would be worried more about its own survival than its reputation for honesty.

As argued, the value of interfering with someone else's command and control only trades immediate for inevitable retaliation. None of the big three nuclear countries can totally disarm the other without taking great casualties from the residual forces whose command and control has not been successfully usurped. Similarly, nuclear blackmail against a country which is then made unsure of its command and control may be stared down until such command and control is restored.

But creating the means to usurp command and control—something that may be inferred if suspicious foreign code is found within nuclear command and control systems—carries huge risks. The victim may easily infer that nuclear war is imminent even if it turns out that it is not (that is, the code was placed there long ago for later use). If a country has declared that such interference will be treated as a nuclear attack, it may find itself forced to act accordingly even if its interests (for example, not being destroyed in a retaliatory strike) would dictate otherwise.

Even discovery without attribution carries risks. As noted, this would discourage the use of PALs—or positive launch control in general. The threat to interfere with continuous command and control (regardless of whether deliberate, accident, human error, or software flaw) may persuade leadership to predelegate nuclear launch control to twitchy weapons commanders. It also might make countries resort to nuclear weapons faster, although, as already noted, use-it-or-lose-it considerations ought not apply when control may have been jeopardized *before* a crisis begins.

Although the risk might seem less if the purpose of penetrating nuclear command and control systems was not to interfere with them but to acquire evidence that they have been used or might be used soon, these risks of getting caught remain. The value of knowing that the "button" has been pushed (even as a missile plume's heat signature can anyway be seen from space) may not merit running the risk. Worse, such "knowledge" may be wrong or misinterpreted, thereby creating some chance that the spying country might react to a launch that did not actually occur[8] (conversely, evidence from a tap may counteract spurious evidence that a launch *was* occurring).

A trickier issue concerns the targeting of systems that command or support both conventional and nuclear systems. The country that chooses not to separate the two risks its nuclear command being confounded by attacks on conventional systems. The country that chooses to attack the combined system must weigh the benefits of interfering with command and control, the odds of being able to do so successfully, and the risks of getting caught. The apparently easy out of targeting just the conventional part of the combined system—if even possible—will not resolve the dilemma. If one side finds rogue code, it may conclude that the other side can and might just want to interfere with the nuclear part of the combined system. This dilemma persists even if the other side wrongly confuses the two parts.

In the face of all these unknowns, the low odds of making cyberwar work, and the risks of getting caught trying to make it work, the case for penetrating adversary nuclear command and control systems is weak. But that does not make the case for a treaty particularly strong. A country that merely advocates for such a treaty may cause others to wonder whether it has figured out how to disable nuclear command and control (and fears being on the receiving end) or has figured out that it could easily be on the receiving end. Both thoughts give others, respectively, fears and hopes in a system where sleeping dogs have lain quietly for decades.

Given the risks associated with getting caught, the *additional* risks that come from being caught after pledging not to try may be both minor and asymmetric. Countries that believe in the rule of law would be far more inhibited than those that do not. Conversely, countries that practice poor OPSEC would or at least should be more inhibited than those that do not.

SUMMARY

Cyberattack capabilities may create opportunities for the United States to bluff rogue nuclear states. The more that the United States projects its belief that it could interfere with a rogue state's nuclear command and control, the more likely a rogue state will understand that it must choose between restraint and annihilation in a canonical crisis, since it will see no possibility that the United States will yield. A secondary benefit may come from injecting doubt into the rogue nuclear state *prior* to crisis. This may inhibit it from going too far down the crisis path to back up from.

If success at a nuclear standoff requires the cooperation of a third-party state (typically at greater risk than the United States would be), such a strategy is more difficult. The third party may demand that the United States prove what it claims, which may be impossible or unwise (consider the greater chances that sensitive information would leak).

Finally, the risks from being caught interfering with the command and control of peer nuclear powers are serious, while the benefits from doing so successfully must be tempered by the realization that success is temporary and will not be forgotten once command and control is restored.

CHAPTER 30
Narratives and Signals

The writer Tom Wolfe once wrote that modern art had "become completely literary: the paintings and other works exist only to illustrate the text."[1] Thus, he maintained, a modern art museum with large paintings and small explanations of them (like classical art museums) was doing it wrong; it should have small paintings and long explanations. Similarly, what is told and believed about a conflict may matter more than outcomes on the ground. So too with cyberwar, which, perhaps more than any other form of combat, is or at least illustrates storytelling.

The narratives of cyberwar do not come prepackaged. Operations in cyberspace lack much precedent to fall back on, and the normal human intuition about how things work in the physical world translates unreliably into cyberspace. Historically, people fought to seize something tangible or to disarm the other side. Cyberattacks cannot directly take anything *away* from others. Alone, cyberattacks can rarely disarm foes. If unaccompanied by physical force, their primary purpose is necessarily coercive (or counter-coercive): an exercise in messaging—but without official words, the message can only be guessed. Because the origins, effects, and sometimes even the existence of cyberattacks are often vague, the nature and ramifications of cyberspace operations beg for explanation.

NARRATIVES TO FACILITATE CRISIS CONTROL

If the first rule of strategy is to ride events and not the reverse, then the first rule of narratives has to be to help ride such events.[2] For instance, if U.S. interests lie in quelling a crisis arising from a cyberattack, then the last thing the leadership needs is to be pressed to greater crisis by hungry media and expedient politicians.

To be sure, sometimes fanning the flames of crisis helps leaders plead convincingly that they must have concessions lest they be overwhelmed by domestic political forces. But there are risks in generating such sentiment only to find it makes reasserting control harder; it may also prevent reaching a modus vivendi with former foes. A posture that plays down the crisis requires not only the right words, but also discipline.

What happens when narratives ignore the need to keep options open may be illustrated by a crisis scenario portrayed in "Cyber Shockwave," the Bipartisan Policy Center's televised simulation of a cyberattack (February 2010).[3] The first instinct of those who played policymakers was to take ownership of the crisis created by a cyberattack—and constantly press for new powers to deal with events. Extraordinary powers, of course, required extraordinary circumstances to justify—which, in turn, facilitated painting the cyberattack in colors vivid enough to highlight the dire threat. An alternative narrative could have placed the responsibility for fixing things on those whose systems were hacked.[4] Stepping back thusly could have colored the crisis differently and bought time for authorities to deal according to their interests with countries that may have supported the attackers.

A NARRATIVE FRAMEWORK FOR CYBERSPACE

Another important narrative element is how countries wish to describe cyberspace itself. Is it a commons or a collection of sovereign entities? Is it a field of cooperation or a field of conflict? Selecting a posture would help explain what rules should govern individual and state behavior in cyberspace—even, perhaps especially, if different rules apply to physical space.[5]

At the risk of excessive abstraction, consider a two-by-two matrix for conveying the essence of cyberspace. Along one axis is the tension between an assertive and an accommodating posture; along the other is the range between optimism and pessimism.

Seeing cyberspace through an assertive optimistic lens would point to a narrative of a commons even if technically cyberspace does not qualify (largely because each part of cyberspace is owned by someone and falls under some country's laws). Like a commons, cyberspace would be seen as something that could be polluted so that people could not trust what flows within. Thus, countries can argue that cyberspace should exist for the unhampered use of all but governed by rules consistent with good values. The posture says that the United States would be prepared to defend the status of cyberspace as such—much as the United Kingdom did for the ocean commons and as the United States is inching toward doing for outer space.[6]

Seeing cyberspace through an accommodating optimistic lens yields a global condominium that fosters agreements that reflect the vastly different values of other countries. Rules are built by consensus and then upheld by all. Because, for instance, most states outlaw computer hacking, presumably all cooperative states will assist one another in suppressing it (traditional espionage aside). U.S. adoption of the condominium narrative means trading off a smaller say in the rules to get more help when enforcing them.

Assertive pessimism yields cyberspace as a field of contention. Sufficient control over cyberspace would be deemed integral to the ability to defend a country (and its allies) against domination by others, just as the power of the United States depends on the ability to control the air. Because the major powers are at peace with one another, and every state has a sovereign space it would control, it is not necessary to emphasize actual conflict. But such a posture puts other nations on notice that the United States does not have to accept, in peacetime, cyberspace rules that might jeopardize its ability to defend itself there.

The fourth posture is pessimistic but accommodating; it concedes that no one country, even the United States, can do much about fundamental risks of cyberspace. Of the four narratives, this one is least likely to be openly voiced—but it may be felt and reflected in a set of policies that hedge against risks.

Each posture has at least some desirable narrative features. The United States may want the help of other nations (condominium) to support U.S. values (commons) in cyberspace while retaining the right to dominate cyberspace if it has to (conflict domain) and conceding that, if it cannot, it has to be prepared to hunker down and protect itself (concession). Nevertheless, picking and sticking to one posture emphasize ideals that countries use as bedrock for positions.

Postures can and should drive narratives. Consider, for instance, how the United States would justify assistance to Estonia and opposition to Russia after a hypothetical repeat and intensification of the 2007 DDOS attack. Viewing cyberspace as a commons leads to arguing that defending cyberspace was everyone's mission regardless of where the attack took place (just as attacks on non-U.S. satellites in geosynchronous orbit are a U.S. concern). Viewing it as a condominium would lead the United States to call on Russia to live up to its own laws and act against the hackers. Viewing it as a conflict domain would support a narrative of Estonia as a NATO ally that must be defended. Finally, viewing it as a conceded space is consistent with the United States helping Estonia recover but overlooking Russia's role.

NARRATIVES AS MORALITY PLAYS

Narratives are also morality plays, in which players assume the guise of good guys. Part of crafting such a narrative requires finding the right role. Should a country, for instance, play the victim, a champion of international norms, or a country that cannot be messed with? And what is the smartest way to portray the attacker: as evil or as a country pursuing its own interests but with too little regard for rules? Do targeted countries own their feckless security behavior and focus on the malign intentions and moral failings of the attacker? If, conversely, the target's leaders wish to deflect attention away from their policies (which may have prompted the attackers) and toward the immediate (but nongovernmental) victim of the cyberattack itself, it may speak of the refusal to take responsibility for private failures and therefore the lack of any reason to yield in the face of further attacks (unless such a narrative may prompt attackers to focus on targets that are clearly a state responsibility).

Sometimes stories of cyberattack can reflect an attacker's overall behavior within which a particular cyberattack is just an element. If, for instance, a cyberattack disrupted some defense or intelligence capability to facilitate a conventional military operation by a country, some might see this as de facto admission that it carried out the attack. However, if the act required preparation that could have started only *prior* to the attack, or the effects of the cyberattack would not have been apparent except to the victim *and* the attacker, then a better case for attribution exists. Would the accused country's reaction help drive the narrative? Maybe not: People and states, once accused, are naturally defensive, whether innocent or not. Even a state's reluctance to open up its records for investigation may prove nothing.

Narratives should justify reactions that countries would take. Because a retaliatory cyberattack cannot disarm foes, it can be justified only by some desired change in a state's behavior (and, helpfully, the behavior of hostile onlookers). Prior military operations by the United States (with rare exceptions such as the 1986 raid on Libya) have been justified by specific operational ends such as waging war or protecting populations (for example, the 1998 Desert Fox campaign against Iraq), but a retaliatory cyberattack cannot use that excuse. Furthermore, a narrative for retaliation needs a story on attribution—which is essentially one of accusation. Accusation is most credible if the narrative offers a plausible motive based on the character of the attacker and what it was trying to achieve. Forensics alone may not carry the narrative, even when professionals find it conclusive. Indeed, if attribution requires forensics, then even the decisionmaking elite will have to trust experts (hence a problem in having the secretive intelligence community represent the nation's cyberwar expertise). The narrative may also have to bridge the gap between retaliation's intentions and its outcomes. If the source of the attack within the country can be determined, retaliation specific to that source may be shaped to communicate rough justice: attacks coming out of universities may be answered by attacks on interests held by a country's intelligentsia.

Unless the accused welcomes the accusation, it can be expected to concoct an alternative narrative, one often built on maligning the accuser.[7] Anticipating the accused's response may help the accuser's narrative. For instance, an attacker's narrative that paints the target as the enemy of the local religion will be reinforced if retaliation is directed against religious institutions (leaving a dilemma if the original attack *did* come out of religious institutions).

The attacker, for its part, can announce its strength or its innocence—but both? It can argue, "We can hit, and we can take hits, and you can do neither." Such a narrative may emphasize the weakness of the target to cyberattack, hinting that states unable to defend their own infrastructures from cyberattack should think twice about starting a fight. The attacker may warn other countries to keep their distance from those foolish enough to place critical data and controls in networks they could not defend. Attacks, whether original or retaliatory, that can be made to look like they came from an ally or service provider (as noted, Iran suspected Russian connivance after Stuxnet) promote a whispered narrative: "Do you trust them?" If they are made to look like insider attacks, a narrative may be: "Can you trust your own forces?"

How well a cyberattack supports a coercive narrative will depend on the audience. A tank may intimidate in a Europe whose narratives of war feature tanks that are deciders. A similar tank may not intimidate in Afghanistan, whose narratives of war picture them as sitting ducks to guerrilla attacks. No cyberattack can yet draw from a well of precedents for its images.

NARRATIVES TO WALK BACK A CRISIS

Those who want to evade consequences following a cyberattack have a difficult narrative job ahead of them. They may be totally innocent. They may be acting within the bounds of what they thought they were allowed to do (for example, national security cyberespionage) only to find that their intentions are misread. The target state may be disinclined to dismiss the incident, accept protestations of innocence, or grant the legitimacy of what the offender did; it may demand the individual attacker offer recompense, or least an apology. So what might the accused say?

We did nothing: China has responded to accusations of EMCE by variously asserting that the accusation is irresponsible, that tracing an attack to a Chinese server proves nothing because third-party attackers can hop through China (and sometimes do), and that China itself is a victim of cyberattacks.[8] Outside of China, this response is regarded as stonewalling and whitewashing. Russia is no better.

Although attribution also tends to get better over time, if accusation leads to crisis, eventual truth may arrive too late. Hence the question: What can countries do to quickly convince others of their innocence (or the legitimacy of their actions)? The target will be understandably reluctant to allow attackers roaming rights in its system to make their cases of innocence, or help the accused make the case for its own innocence—or even reveal what it found on how the attackers operated, particularly if doing so reveals sources and methods.[9]

One strategy to accelerate a peaceful resolution is for the accused to bend toward transparency—such as a fact-finding investigation that others trust (perhaps because the accusers are on board). Inviting accusers to conduct the investigation works best, but countries rarely tolerate their citizens (particularly if employed in its military or intelligence agencies) being questioned by the law enforcement of other countries. One might have thought that the risks of taking positions that would prove embarrassing if wrong might also build confidence in a leader's statements—but some autocrats seem quite content to contradict themselves without embarrassment (see Putin's Crimea statements).

It was a rogue or freelancer: Getting the attacker to stop may require the target to play pretend when evidence of a proscribed systems penetration is sufficiently conclusive. It may let the accused finger eager operatives unaware that their incursions were now out of bounds (spying on critical infrastructure would seem less like pre-attack surveillance if the spies were freelancers rather than government employees). China's central government has pleaded—not implausibly—that its authority over freelancers is looser than it appears from the outside. But this blind eye cannot be turned too often.

Can attackers play the rogue/freelance card without trying to prosecute the guilty? Some governments claim they lack the political power to go after rogue actors: think Hezbollah in Lebanon, or Inter-Services Intelligence in Pakistan. They might add: such rogues hurt us worse than they hurt you, and if we cannot stop them from hurting us, what makes you think we can stop them from hurting you? This argument could backfire, however, if the target country then concludes that it could squeeze the accused country into trying harder.

Issues of command and control will also color the inferences made about other countries. Many foreign government leaders, notably China's, believe that U.S. companies, such as Microsoft, Google, Facebook, and Cisco, are arms of the U.S. government and that their avid and energetic attempts to collect personal information on their customers and feed it to gigantic data-mining machines is just another form of espionage. To most American ears, this claim is preposterous. But Americans, in turn, worry that Huawei, a Chinese manufacturer of telecommunication equipment, acts on behalf of the PLA by inserting eavesdropping code into their routers.[10] After all, its chief executive was a military officer (as are many U.S. CEOs).

Remarks made by those who seem to speak for their government may also stir the pot. When a Chinese general remarked that Los Angeles may be at risk if the United States gets too aggressive over Taiwan or another one suggests that China would go to war to protect Iran, were they not speaking for China itself?[11] Conversely, when a background source in the United States argued that the proper response to a cyberattack may be the aforementioned cruise missile placed down the smokestack of a factory in the attacking country, or a major presidential candidate (Newt Gingrich circa 2012) argued in favor of starting a cyberwar against Iran, are they not speaking for the United States itself?[12]

The "patriotic hacker" excuse is a variant on the rogue case. To wit, cyberattacks were merely the spontaneous and self-coordinated action of citizens rightfully enraged by the actions of the target state. This argument seeks safety in numbers, not only because it takes numbers to generate certain effects (notably from DDOS attacks) but also to point out the unlikelihood of prosecuting people in such large numbers and to hint that the action acquired its legitimacy from the numbers themselves (that is, the action was deserved because the people have so decided).

It was an accident: This narrative holds that bad events in cyberspace should be judged by intentions (that may be legitimate or, as with spying, at least familiar) rather than by results (such as disruption or corruption). Such a case requires evidence that one or perhaps two errors sufficed to yield unfortunate results; no such argument, for instance, could possibly be made for Stuxnet with its four zero-day vulnerabilities. Authorizing incompetent people to carry out operations that risk damage is a legitimate source of the target's grievance. The narrative works better if it leads the accused into proposing norms. As noted, the United States and the Soviet Union experienced many incidents at sea—something that often results when one or both sides play too close to the line and neither communicates its intentions very clearly.[13] But in many cases, what was initially disturbing—the approach of Soviet "fishing trawlers" to U.S. warships for purposes of electronic surveillance—was later accepted as another working day at sea.

This is nothing new: Here, the accused argues that what it did merely extended accepted practices of the physical world into cyberspace—where norms are still in flux. Because analogies from physical space into cyberspace can be drawn in many ways, there will be disagreement over what is permissible. Does the United States, for instance, have the right to establish a virtual embassy in a country in which it has no physical representation, if the attempt to do so violates the state's "sovereign right" to monitor and potentially block communications with its citizens?[14] Does that country, in turn, have a right to block such communications by making such a site inaccessible to anyone (for instance, through DDOS attacks)?

In other cases, the line between assent and tolerance is unclear. There is a great deal of mischief in cyberspace—espionage from China, organized crime winked at by Russia—that the United States and its allies had tolerated because the harm had been modest, attribution was difficult, and the risks of making a fuss were daunting. Likewise, some U.S. behavior (for example, support for the freedom to dissent over the Internet) is tolerated by other states.

Last is the mad intersection between cyberattack, surveillance, circumvention, and intellectual property protection. Many, perhaps most, computers in some countries use bootlegged software.[15] A U.S. corporation introducing a "patch" that disabled such computers might be acting in ways deemed legitimate here and illegitimate there.[16]

A reasonable approach to walking back a crisis is to coolly analyze what the attacker hoped to achieve and could plausibly have achieved. Does it change the boundaries of what is acceptable? Does it make a subsequent military attack easier (and, if so, for how long before the effects wash out)? If the target cannot determine whether any broader objective is enhanced by the action, then it could grant itself the luxury of treating the incident in isolation rather than as a precursor to or a signal of something greater ahead that demands opposition forthwith. It helps if cybersecurity is not seen as a zero-sum game—less as one of two battle fleets lined up against one another and more as one of mutual assistance upon the rough seas.

SIGNALING

Signals differ from narratives in that the former constitute actions meant for the leaders of a country's counterparts—typically, but not exclusively, adversaries—while the latter are meant for public consumption.

Signals are often used to communicate seriousness and capabilities. The United States signaled seriousness to the Soviet Union in 1948, during the Berlin blockade, by sending B-29s to the United Kingdom. In the U.S.-Soviet near-confrontation of the 1973 October War, President Richard Nixon signaled to Soviet leader Leonid Brezhnev by raising the status of U.S. forces to DEFCON 3, "a signal sufficiently clear that it never had to be mentioned in formal messages between the two."[17] During the Sino-Vietnam war, the Chinese air force tried to "to fly as many sorties as possible over the border airspace when the ground assaults started in order to deter the Vietnamese air force from taking action against China."[18] An oft-cited (perhaps apocryphal) tale has the United States reacting to its discovery that Soviet submarine forces were arrayed a little too close to the East Coast by rebasing bombers to Thule, Greenland (hence closer to the Soviet Union). This signaled U.S. displeasure and put the Soviet Union on notice that its actions were observed, interpreted as hostile, and reacted to.

During the early Cold War, U.S.-Soviet state-to-state communications often had to be indirect: the hotline did not exist until 1963. Communicating in public may have led to mutual contests in posturing, complicating mutual accommodation later. But because communications—and surveillance—are now everywhere, why use signals to send the other side's leadership a message only they could see? Perhaps countries signal *because* talk is cheap and, being cheap, may not be taken seriously. Acts—such as stationing forces forward or canceling troop leaves—are more expensive. They convey seriousness that mere words cannot; so does going out on a limb in ways that make retreat difficult. Needless to add, words can help explain signals.

The efficacy of signaling depends on whether it is accepted as such. A state sending a chunk of its fleet to a trouble spot in the nineteenth century was an effective signal in large part because there was warranted confidence that everyone else would regard it so.[19] In cyberspace, there is little basis for such confidence. Unless and until one emerges, there is little reason to believe that such a basis can be arbitrarily created.

In some cases, signals are dog whistles: missed by some, heard by others. A signal whose significance will be missed by the general population but interpreted correctly by the intended audience (such as those who understand the context or the technology) can be useful. It may be even more helpful if it hints at actions when more overt statements may be regarded as a commitment to act. Unfortunately, the greater the subtlety, the higher the odds of misinterpretation.

WHAT CAN WE SAY WITH SIGNALS THAT WOULD COME AS NEWS TO OTHERS?

How can a country tell others something about its policy in cyberspace that others were not aware of? For instance, an investigation in response to a flagrant cybercrime would not signal very much because everyone expects as much. An investigation that conspicuously pulls resources from other investigations would more clearly signal displeasure. An indictment conveys even more displeasure. This leaves it for others to decide whether the action—and the indictment of the PLA officers is a case in point—was taken because of such displeasure, or to signal displeasure. Ironically, the less that people think that it was meant as a signal, the stronger the signal would be; it would be less likely to be taken as show.

Often, the difference between a signal's intent and its effects depends on what others expected beforehand. Leaders will always have some idea, however well- or ill-grounded, of how a state will react to being attacked. In some cases, what a state says ("we stand eight feet tall") may not necessarily discourage attackers ("oh, we thought you were ten feet") more than silence would have.[20]

Might a country gain from broadcasting the various ways in which it has prepared for a confrontation in cyberspace? Could conspicuously mounting better defenses indicate that it expects an attack and it is ready—so ready that attacks on it are likely to be futile, perhaps risky? Good defenses may be interpreted as a rational response to circumstances, such as a newly revealed threat—even if they are actually an incidental response to something hidden (for example, new technology becomes available). Conversely, if the more visible defenses are too burdensome to be maintained easily for long periods, then their continued existence sends a stronger signal.

Might baring teeth be signal enough to ward off cyberattack? As noted, specific cyberattack capabilities cannot be revealed without putting their existence at risk; the same is true for using them, even against third parties. A state could conspicuously hire more hackers for temporary use, but because hackers need some familiarity with the target to be effective, this would not say anything about whatever short-term threat it could pose. A state could also delegate authority downward or authorize hacks-back as a way of signaling that a country was prepared to defend itself even if at risk of escalation.[21]

AMBIGUITY IN SIGNALING

Signals, though, may be read in several ways, in the physical world or cyberspace. Consider, for instance, how others may have reacted to a country's nuclear fallout shelter program:

It is prepared: That is, having taken a cold hard look at the threat, it deems a fallout shelter program appropriate and wants to convey that it can control the losses it might suffer from a nuclear war and hence the degree of coercion that a nuclear threat can produce.

It is scared: Hitherto, it imagined that the odds of an attack were low or that the damage was bearable. It had confidence that its nuclear forces would deter war. Reassessment suggests that earlier confidence was misplaced.

It is on the warpath: As with the previous case, it perceives nuclear conflict as growing more likely, not because it deems the enemy more aggressive or capable but because it has reassessed the necessity of a nuclear confrontation. Building shelters says, "We are about to become aggressive *because* we are better protected."

These three messages are not necessarily mutually exclusive. A state may view the threat from its foes with new alarm, conclude that they are about to start something, and decide to preempt their coercion by accelerating its own capability and baring some teeth.

Now carry over this logic into cyberspace: what might the 2009 establishment of CYBER-COM have conveyed?

It is prepared: Cyberspace is becoming a growing facet of warfare at every level, and it would be prudent to develop defensive and offensive capabilities to ensure that others do not dominate this new domain.

It is scared: The United States is increasingly aware that its own vaunted superiority in conventional conflict—network-centric warfare—may be undermined if its military networks can be attacked by those too weak to match it on the conventional battlefield. Thus, the United States must quickly shore up its defenses and (*pace* Gen. James E. Cartwright) must develop an offensive capability to ensure that no nation attacks the United States in cyberspace with impunity.

It is on the warpath: The United States, home of the information revolution, is extending its wide technological lead over other countries by creating a new form of warfare that can defeat other nations without its even having to show up to fight.

Again, these messages are not mutually exclusive. As with other actions, domestic and each of many foreign audiences may read them differently; even perceptive foreigners misread how the United States works, and vice versa.

The United States has yet to generate a master narrative to accompany the establishment of CYBERCOM, although many top defense and other national security officials have commented on the topic. Perhaps there is no such narrative; much of what goes on within bureaucracies reflects a contest over authority. For example, establishing CYBERCOM preempted moves by the Air Force and potentially other services to lay claim to a new domain. According to former defense secretary Robert Gates, Gen. Keith Alexander deserved a fourth star, and creating CYBERCOM was how to do it.[22] These actions are not meant to convey anything to anybody on the outside. Nevertheless, this will not be the last such action by the United States or any other country that may have others scratching their heads about what the United States "meant by that."[23] Although not every move is part of a narrative, it probably cannot hurt to ponder what others may infer from such actions.

SIGNALING RESOLVE

For years, Japan and China both claimed the Senkaku/Diaoyu Islands. In September 2010, the Japanese arrested a Chinese fisherman for venturing too close to those islands and ramming Japanese vessels. Under Chinese pressure, Japan released the fisherman, but when pressed to apologize, Japan refused. The Chinese were said to be "testing Japan's resolve to back its territorial claims in the East China Sea."[24]

Can resolve about events in cyberspace be usefully signaled? A great deal depends on what a state has claimed as its due in that medium. Countries that draw lines—such as "We will respond to cyberattacks," "We hold certain types of cyberespionage to be a hostile act," "We will not tolerate sites that host malware"—commit themselves to defending such lines if challenged. Otherwise, the lines lose credibility. Conversely, states that draw no lines have less to be resolute about and hence have less to signal.

Is there a cyberspace analogy to placing assets in harm's way—signaling both the readiness to use such assets and the intention to defend them? At first glance, *all* systems are in harm's way, wherever in cyberspace they sit. Perhaps making a system more vulnerable by exposing it to a broader community—such as connecting formerly air-gapped networks—might signal such intent. Yet doing so does not make a system easier to use for military operations (perhaps unless such operations entail bringing the general public into the cause). Furthermore, formerly closed systems are connected all the time, often unknowingly or unthinkingly.

An added complexity in cyberspace is that two states may differ on what constitutes a crossed boundary. One state that sees an intrusion into the business networks of natural gas firms may conclude that the only plausible motive was intelligence preparation of the battlefield prefatory to an attack. The attacker may believe that it was only gathering intelligence for its own use (for example, how such pipelines are managed) and so its actions crossed no boundary. It cannot understand the sharp response its actions evoked. The reverse is also possible: The attacker crosses a boundary. The target is unaware that it did and so fails to respond. The attacker concludes that such boundary claims are not meant to be taken seriously. Unfortunately, even clear lines are easy to cross. Remembering which of your past warnings were followed up by actions and which were not helps in understanding why others who do remember react unhelpfully to new warnings.

Signaling is confounded, paradoxically, by difficulties otherwise associated with collecting indications and warnings of attack. If there is nothing in cyberspace that indicates that an attack is likely within so many hours, then there is nothing that an attacker can use to signal—without outright saying as much—that the target has only so much time before acceding to the attacker's wishes. It is also difficult to convey a small signal. Sending a single ship to a contested area may indicate that the contest is important, but the threat to intervene is limited to the assets on hand. What would connote such limitations with signaling in cyberspace?

The last caution is a general one. If a country carries out objectionable behavior, the victim may respond with something nominal (for example, indict military officers of theirs that it never expects to see in court). If the response is just a signal of displeasure, then the message need not be repeated. If the response was meant to change behaviors and nothing changed, then what started as a signal may become a confrontation; the response may be repeated or more serious steps taken until the behavior does change. The cost of sending a signal may be increased if the other side has a few signals of its own to convey. Whether or not a confrontation is needed, those who signal have to think through whether the signal will be perceived as just a signal or the opening round of a fight.

So signaling, a staple of the Cold War, but hard enough in confrontations with well-defined parameters, may be harder yet in cyberspace. Unfortunately, every move may be read as a signal anyway. It would seem worthwhile to anticipate such inferences and use narratives to align what a country's actions are supposed to convey with what they *do* convey.

CHAPTER 31
Strategic Stability

The quest for strategic stability was a leitmotiv of Cold War thinking. Worries that a first strike from the Soviet Union could disable U.S. nuclear deterrence shaped the U.S. nuclear posture from the late 1950s on and gave rise to a perceived "window of vulnerability" in the late 1970s.[1] Theorists argued that countries in crisis would face an acute prisoner's dilemma whether to strike first and start a nuclear war or hold off with the risk that the other side, thinking similarly, would start a nuclear war and thereby prevail, having gone first. Contemporary arguments for and against building anti-ballistic missiles and agreeing to strategic arms limitations often cited their putative effects on strategic stability. In World War I, the inflexibility of railroad schedules was said to play a role in the alacrity with which both sides mobilized lest they found themselves outgunned on the front at the outset. Nuclear strategists also worried that countries exercising their command and control and indications and warning systems could create a mutually reinforcing cycle that would lead to war.[2] Although nuclear arms have not disappeared, their issues now roll in well-worn, hence comfortable, grooves.

To many, the prospect of cyberwar creates international stability problems in the same way that nuclear weapons did (and still do). Not for nothing did a July 1, 2010, cover story in the *Economist* picture cyberwar as the digital equivalent of the nuclear bomb, a threat to civilization that necessitated international negotiations and prophylactic arms control.[3] But is it so? Do the factors that make nuclear instability an issue apply in cyberspace? Maybe not—but if *strategic stability* includes all possible sources of inadvertent war, then perhaps cyberwar *has* created new ways to stumble into war—not through the interaction of rational actors but through error and misperception on one side exacerbated by hyper-vigilance on the other.[4]

WOULD NUCLEAR DILEMMAS ECHO IN CYBERSPACE?

Unlikely, we would argue.

Nuclear weapons still exist. This alone limits how much strategic instability can arise from cyberspace. Nuclear-armed countries may choose to yield to the demands of others, but they cannot be annihilated or taken over except at a cost to the aggressor far greater than anything cyberwar can promise. Even forcing countries to change their leaders may be off the table. A country that is seriously worried about its survival in the face of nuclear-armed foes can afford to dismiss whatever relative superiority such foes enjoy in cyberspace alone. As argued above, while a cyberattack may, under some circumstances, shape a nuclear confrontation, it does not change its essential nature.

A cyberattack cannot disarm a target state's cyberwarriors. The nuclear era was pervaded by the fear that one side could substantially degrade the other side's retaliatory capability through a first strike. The victimized state would be either completely disarmed or at least so denuded of strike power that it would not credibly strike back without risking the destruction of its cities to no useful strategic end. Each side would be twitchy, perhaps even tempted to jump the gun as clouds gathered.

But if, as argued, cyberwar cannot disarm cyberwarriors, why go after the adversary's cyberwar apparatus first? The country that attacks first, having destroyed little that cannot be quickly reconstituted, is no better off than before, even relative to its foe. Indeed, it may be worse off a week later—by virtue of seeing fewer vulnerabilities left to exploit and by inducing the other side to raise its alert level (thereby favoring security over convenience).

A variant on the destabilizing disarming first strike is a first strike followed by quickly cutting one's own connections to the rest of the world.[5] But not only has the aggressor isolated itself more than any cyberattack could do, but it also has to emerge eventually—whereupon whatever vulnerabilities it has yet to fix are exposed again. When the temporary nature of most cyberattacks is taken into account, this strategy sounds even worse. There is little in this ploy that would convince its potential targets to preempt such a maneuver by going first—although they might respond to its possibility by implanting attacks so that they might be later commanded from within the other side's network, even after the drawbridge is raised.

Cyberwar does not lend itself to alert-reaction cycles. In analyzing a hypothetical U.S.-Soviet confrontation circa 1984, Paul Bracken described how ominous signs could make the other side raise its alert level to make nuclear weapons more readily usable (for example, aircrews would be recalled to base, submarines would launch out to sea).[6] The other side would perceive that its rival was moving closer to striking first and would raise *its* own alert level, prompting the first side to move even closer to striking. Such a dynamic reflects the world of nuclear warfare, in which the only response to a growing threat is to raise the readiness of one's offense, there is a decided first-strike advantage, and many reactions are visible. None of the three apply to cyberwar. A first response to a crisis is likely to be less one of prepping offenses so much as raising defenses (for example, selectively disconnecting systems, disallowing certain services, tightening access controls, or heavily filtering what enters and leaves networks). As noted, there is no first-strike advantage. Finally, few preparatory operations in cyberspace are immediately visible and most of these are used to bolster defenses; invisible operations are unlikely to prompt rapid reactions.

Defenses are not inherently destabilizing. Although greater defenses *might* be interpreted as preparations for a cyberattack, the linkage is relatively weak and could be explained away by a third-party threat,[7] the discovery of a novel threat vector, or simply the belated realization that defenses need to receive proper attention. Many objections to ballistic missile defenses rested on the proposition that a country that had rendered *other countries'* missiles "impotent and obsolete"[8] would therefore be able to attack other nations with impunity; it could lash out whenever it wished. An extension of this argument into cyberspace is that a nation that had perfected the art of defending its systems could hold other countries hostage to its offensive cyberwar capability (assuming, again, that confrontations did not stray into the physical world).

But would it? Confidence in such defenses may be hard to come by. Cyberwar is one surprise after another—inevitably so, because it largely depends on the exploitation of vulnerabilities that the hacker has found and that the defender has not. What would it take to rest assured that one will not be surprised anymore? Rivals could easily conclude that no such confidence is possible in cyberspace. Furthermore, a foe worried enough to yield to coercion may also be concerned enough to make the many trade-offs associated with bolstering its own defenses. It can plausibly hope to reach not perfect defense, but rather a point at which the worst possible damage it can bear from a cyberattack is below the threshold that would force it to concede to aggressors.

A cyberspace arms race would not be visible, hence not destabilizing. Arms races often lead to instability, particularly if one side thinks it will go bankrupt keeping up and therefore contemplates a confrontation to end the wearying drain. In cyberspace, such a race is already on—not between countries but between defense and offense. Even as old vulnerabilities are fixed, new ones keep getting discovered, either in old software or in new software (or as new connections and new applications violate implicit assumptions about security). Such contests would continue even if states had no interest in cyberwar—although the fact that states *are* interested means that they are fueling such contests with money.

Yet the logic that countries must match their rivals' offensive cyberwar capability has little basis. Why? First, as noted, states know little about exactly which weapons their rivals wield—because if they did know, such weapons would be nullified forthwith (at least for systems whose security really mattered). Second, as argued, the best responses to an offensive weapon are defensive measures, not offensive weapons. Third, the whole notion of offense-versus-offense requires that the underlying dynamic of attack and retaliation actually makes sense as a warfighting and war termination strategy. Were that so, deterrence would be primary. But deterrence is a very difficult notion in cyberspace.

It is also unclear how an *offensive* arms race in cyberspace could come close to having a major economic impact. The intellectual skills required to compete in this contest are so specialized that countries will run out of good hackers well before they run out of money to pay them with. A defensive contest *can* be expensive, but even the $80 billion total spent annually on cybersecurity tools is but a few percentage points of the world's spending on arms.

Alas, the same logic suggests arms control would contribute little to strategic stability—apart from the supposition that a country that would sign agreements may be viewed as less of a threat than one that would not. Banning cyberattack weapons requires stretching the concept of *weapon* beyond its bursting point.[9] The requirements of a cyberattack may be separated into knowledge of the target and its vulnerabilities and a capability to translate such knowledge into attack methods that work while evading predetonation detection and deletion. Generally, the first is harder, but knowledge is not per se a weapon in the usual sense. Weaponization is often the simplest part,[10] and once vulnerabilities are found, there are many ways to weaponize that discovery. In other words, not only is verification difficult, but also the rationale for weapon control is weak.

Nor would arms control provide the sort of assurance that nuclear arms control did.[11] If a country is known to lack a nuclear weapons program, others can rest assured that it would take years before having to worry about facing its nuclear weapons in a crisis. The same cannot be said of cyberattack weapons, because nearly everything about specific offensive cyberwar capabilities is hidden—and many capabilities can be acquired quickly from black markets. The knowledge to go from nothing visible to a serious threat does not depend on construction or manufacturing schedules of predictable length. By 2014, Iran and North Korea were recognized as serious cyberwar threats; in 2009, they were rarely seen on the horizon.

MISPERCEPTION AS A SOURCE OF CRISIS

Although the *facts* of cyberwar suggest that strategic instability is not a problem in cyberspace, the *myths* of cyberwar create paths to inadvertent conflict. Uncertainties about allowable behavior, a misunderstanding of defensive preparations, errors in attribution, unwarranted confidence in the other side's *in*ability to attribute, and a misunderstanding of the norms of neutrality can all create problems.[12]

To start with one path, although espionage is not considered a casus belli, cyberespionage might lead to conflict. Perhaps one country gets tired of its systems becoming the playground of another; it may acknowledge the historic legitimacy of espionage but then argue that changes in the *quantity* of espionage—such as how personal information on 22 million Americans may have been sent to China in the OPM hack—are essentially changes in its *quality*, hence its legitimacy. It may have earlier communicated its displeasure, but perhaps too discreetly or subtly to be correctly understood. Alternatively, states sponsoring or condoning such espionage may not believe that such displeasure is credible; they see such outrage as feigned—a departure from norms and a sop to domestic audiences. So systems are penetrated, the target gets really upset and pushes back, and a crisis is on.

A crisis could also arise if hackers err. In the attempt, for instance, to insert a back door to facilitate later entry, the hackers change a system's settings that, unbeknownst to them, causes the target system to fail, perhaps with widespread consequences. Or the hackers play with system settings to see how a system works without realizing how sensitive it is (for example, the aforementioned, albeit false, story of a 2008 power outage in Florida). Finally, spies could leave an implant in critical infrastructure. The target state convinces itself that, maybe because the system targeted by the implant contains no information worth stealing, such an implant can only be considered prefatory to a cyberattack, hence all-out war.

Or one country's defenses may *look like* offensive preparations, and other states may panic when objective circumstances suggest they take a deep breath instead. Such overreaction is more likely if both sides are primed by events in the physical world (for example, terrorist attacks, disputed elections, border spats, or military movements).

Another source of instability may arise when countries infer indications and warning from over-interpreting events (whereas the physical basis for indications and warning of kinetic attack sits on a more solid foundation). As noted, preparations for *eventual* cyberattack are almost indistinguishable from preparations for *imminent* cyberattack. Attacks have to be prepared, perhaps years in advance, and cost only a little to maintain—for instance, to check whether the intelligence is still good and whether the implants are still functioning and accessible. If the number of implants discovered rises precipitously, such an increase could be an indicator of accelerated activity leading to conflict, but it might also be a statistical artifact or an unexpected improvement in the means by which implants can be inserted—or a similar improvement in how well they can be discovered (although forensics experts are getting better at figuring out how long an implant has been in place once discovered). As noted, defensive preparations also make unreliable indications and warning. If nervous leaders thought things through, they might realize that they need not be so eager to respond; everyone with a first-strike potential also has a second-strike potential. But they are not always wise about such matters.[13]

Consider why a state's preparation level might have risen unexpectedly. Perhaps the security folks have just won their bureaucratic argument against the laissez faire folks. Maybe a new energetic CISO just came on board. System administrators could be reacting to a news item, such as discovery of the Stuxnet worm. Maybe some laboratory demonstration revealed how vulnerable the state's key systems were—or, conversely, how easy it would be to secure them if certain new technologies were employed. Or, as with the OPM hack, the installation or test of new defensive software uncovers implants that had been there for months.[14] A new product may have come to market, or the preparations for buying it may have been completed. Yet if others assume that the unexpected activity was all about them—and thus could *only* be undertaken prefatory to attack—it might decide it had to attack first, logic notwithstanding.

In cyberspace, as in the physical world, what is standard operating procedure in one country may be interpreted by another as anything but. Two factors exacerbate the problem in cyberspace. First, because states constantly penetrate one another's networks, they are in a position to observe many things about target countries—but they do not see everything, and what they see is out of context (some valuable information never makes it into computer files). Second, cyberwar is still too new and untested for a universal set of standard operating procedures—much less a well-grounded understanding of another state's standard operating procedures—to have evolved.

Lastly, a crisis can start over nothing at all. Because preparations for cyberattack generally have to be invisible if they are to work efficiently, there is little good evidence that can be offered to prove that one state is *not* starting to attack the other. States may try to assuage fears touched off by otherwise unmemorable incidents by demanding proof that the other side is not starting something. If proof is not forthcoming—and it is unclear what *would* constitute proof—matters could deteriorate.

EXCESSIVE CONFIDENCE IN ATTRIBUTION OR PREEMPTION

Inadvertent crises, such as catalytic conflict,[15] may stem from false attribution. Posit a third party, Yellow, that wants a conflict between Red and Blue. Yellow may have many motivations: (1) Yellow is feeling too much pressure from Red and/or Blue or Yellow seeks revenge on Red and/or Blue, (2) Yellow's friendship would become more valuable for Red or Blue if both were at crossed swords, or (3) if Red and Blue are distracted by one another, Yellow has a freer hand in the rest of the world. So Yellow attacks Red and makes it look as if Blue did it, perhaps by copying Blue's known signatures. If the gambit works, Red and Blue find themselves at odds. But the gambit could fail. Perhaps Yellow revealed its hand; perhaps it lacked access to what Red really knew about Blue's signatures. With failure, it gets blamed not only by Red, but if Red so wishes, also by Blue (which now knows that Yellow is trying to frame it).[16]

Misattribution does not have to be direct. Assume that Red attacks Blue, which turns around and blames Red's friend Orange—a state with better hackers—just because the two are so close and Red is deemed incompetent at the cyber arts. Red, for its part, believes that any and all help it got from Orange was secondary and therefore attacked without considering that such an attack would start a crisis between Orange and Blue. Redirection, as such, is not solely a property of cyberspace, but the problem may be worse in cyberspace because the assistance given between two states is much harder to detect. It need involve only an exchange of people—or just bytes over the wire (in that respect, it resembles intelligence support for military operations).

At least, because disarming hackers is difficult, no country has real reason for preemption—if it understands as much. Some within the U.S. national security community—whose sophistication in these matters is second to none—still believe that counterforce, and thus preemptive counter-force, has its place in cyberspace. Military cultures (such as China's) that place a larger emphasis on stratagems and preemption may see cyberwar as fitting that historic role. The same logic holds for psychological preemption. States, afraid of cyberwar, may reason that cyberattacks (or particularly brazen acts of system penetration) may warn others away from starting a crisis. Compared with violence, cyberattacks are bloodless; attackers may hope that with no one hurt, the target will not find itself forced to call for revenge and thereby set off the crisis that such preemption was meant to head off. This strategy presupposes that a set of attacks can land in a middle ground between those too inconsequential to merit notice and those too consequential to merit absorbing without a response. The middle ground may be nonexistent or too small to hit reliably.

CAN THERE BE A CUBAN MISSILE CRISIS IN CYBERSPACE?

In 1962, the United States and the Soviet Union almost came to nuclear blows after U.S. spy planes discovered Soviet installations of nuclear missiles in Cuba. One can imagine a similar incident taking place after U.S. forensics experts find implants within its critical infrastructure and determine who put them there, and leaders then demand the removal of all the other implants of like nature. The course of such a crisis may pivot on what the other side admits: would it deny everything, or would it use the discovery to brandish its capabilities, talk of those yet to be found, and make threats (for example, to detonate them if something does not happen)?

In the case of Cuba, the Soviets would have preferred denial if the evidence were not so clear; they had to confess. In this hypothetical cyberspace case, confession would fly in the face of twenty years of behavior that no one admits anything. There is as yet no technique of attribution as obviously incriminating as a photograph.

Returning to Cuba, removing missiles from that island would have required using force. The implants in the cyberspace hypothetical would lie in the United States. U.S. system owners can eliminate such implants without seeking permission—but only if they can find them. In some cases, they can do the equivalent of a simultaneous system reboot and clean-out (coupled with actions that work against the ability of trusted *external* machines to reinfect the critical infrastructure). Although such a process would be disruptive, perhaps expensive, it falls far short of what an attack on Cuba would have produced.

In Cuba, the United States had to force the Soviet Union to remove its own missiles—and then validate that this had been done. An equivalent in the hypothetical scenario would be forcing the putative attacker to identify the implants (whereupon they can be readily removed by U.S. system owners) either by signature (whereupon it could be tested for within all possible affected systems) or by location (whereupon these locations would be cleaned up). The attacker in turn might want to see a comparable revelation of the target's implants (just as the Soviets made a quiet quid pro quo deal that had the United States remove its nuclear-tipped Jupiter C missiles from Turkey).

Unfortunately, knowing that these implants had been identified would be difficult—but not necessarily impossible. If other implants were found (without the attacker's knowing as much), then the attacker's honesty could be tested by seeing whether such implants were on the list of those identified. Failure to include them would be prima facie evidence of bad faith—*assuming* that these other implants could be correctly identified as the attacker's (and assuming that the implants did not spread willy-nilly as Stuxnet did). Post hoc threats can also be used: the United States could threaten punishment upon the subsequent discovery of implants placed before the crisis. But that leaves two unknowns (getting the attribution and the implant date correct) plus overcoming the attacker's argument: oops, we forgot (or lost track of) a few.

So although one could imagine a Cuban Missile Crisis in cyberspace, it would and should play out differently and with far lower risks of conflict.

CONCLUSIONS

Does the advent of cyberwar lead to strategic instability? There are no first-strike advantages, the proper reaction to indications and warning of use is defensive rather than offensive (two very separate actions), and arms races in cyberspace are not as meaningful or as damaging as their physical world counterparts. However, countries may react to events out of fear and ignorance, not calculation. What one side finds normal, another finds menacing. A covert move might be discovered and have to be explained. A move with only tactical or commercial implications could be viewed through a strategic lens; agitation follows. Two suspicious states might maneuver to establish their credibility; one begins to obsess that its reputation and resolve have fallen into doubt and must take strong actions to reestablish its capacity to induce caution in others.

Cyberwar is heir to all these risks, and more. It engenders worry, perhaps inordinately so. There is little current track record and no future track record of what it can and cannot do. Attribution is difficult, and the difficulties can tempt some, while the failure to appreciate such difficulties can tempt others. Espionage, crime, and attack look very similar to one another. Nonstate actors can simulate state actors (and vice versa[17]). Everything is done in great secrecy, so what one state does must be inferred and interpreted by others.

Fortunately, mistakes in cyberspace do not have the potential for physical catastrophe that mistakes do in the nuclear arena. Unfortunately, that fact may lead people to ignore the roles of uncertainty and doubt in assessing the risk of inadvertent crisis.

PART V   NORMS

CHAPTER 32
Norms for Cyberspace

N orms can help make cyberspace peaceful, but to date there have been few widely, much less universally, held norms in that medium. Were they even to exist, enforcement would be a problem in peacetime, and a worse one in wartime, in part because who did what to whom can be hard to ascertain. Yet there is growing interest in the topic. Since mid-2010, the fifteen-member UN-chartered Group of Government Experts (GGE), which includes the United States, China, and Russia, has been working on a set of broad principles to govern the behavior of member nations.[1] Bilateral negotiations have also begun with Russia and China over behavior in cyberspace.[2] Accordingly, this chapter examines some potential international norms in terms of their value, advisability, and how well they can be enforced.[3]

NORMS AGAINST HACKING IN GENERAL

In 2000, the author of the "I Love You" virus escaped prosecution because his activities were not illegal in the Philippines. This was corrected within a year.[4] The major countries now outlaw hacking. Yet many countries are reluctant to cooperate with investigations, much less extraditions, for crimes whose victims are overseas, particularly if the hackers work for or on behalf of governments.[5] Russia gets downright self-righteous about protecting criminals in cyberspace.[6] Even when countries would like to cooperate, fighting cybercrime is difficult and expensive; many are unwilling to pay the cost, particularly when it is others that would benefit.[7] Some hackers, like some drug lords, are considered heroes within local communities.

The Convention on Cybercrime (also known as the Budapest Convention) obligates countries to assist investigations into hacking and accept responsibility for bad packets that emanate from their country, be they spam, bit floods, or malware. However, not only are important countries (notably Russia and China) outside the convention, but enforcement inside the convention is not trivial; even NATO's newest members, the countries of eastern Europe, have a hard time keeping the lid on organized cybercrime groups.[8] Observing that such states would not or could not carry out cybercrime investigations themselves is an insult (however merited). In practical terms, how likely is it that they will make an exception for cybercrime when they do not for other crimes?[9] That said, even Russia and China have prosecuted hackers when ignoring them was not in the state's interest.[10]

If countries cannot assist, should they be expected at least to dissociate themselves from criminal or freelance hackers? Condoning hackers who victimize foreigners permits countries to benefit from criminal activity while evading the international condemnation of whatever such hackers do. Perhaps worse is the temptation to privatize the application of military force in cyberspace. Examples include links between the Russian government and the Russian Business Network or between China and both its freelance and "patriotic" hackers. The damage to international comity notwithstanding, countries can corrupt themselves with such alignments, if they find themselves having to overlook other crimes such hackers commit. Freelancers may entangle countries in unwanted crises.

If a state made a good-faith effort to act against freelancers and "patriotic" hackers, victims of such cyberattacks may be more inclined to believe their country's declaration of innocence when attacks emanate from within their borders.

The 1976 Helsinki Accords suggest that even cynically endorsed norms matter. Even though the Soviet Union and its Warsaw Pact allies had little intention of implementing their human rights accords, dissident groups in those countries, such as the Moscow Helsinki Group and Charter 77, insisted that they do so. This insistence played a role in eroding the legitimacy of communist rule. Similarly, countries that declare certain actions in cyberspace to be illegitimate establish a standard to which their acts can be held. National bureaucracies that take official guidance seriously (notably Western ones) will be constantly reminded of this. Even though brazen denial of the obvious is standing practice in many countries, those wishing to assume a roughly consistent narrative for themselves may eventually slouch in the direction in which their words take them.

Norms may also have a demonstration effect. If respected countries sign up, others may be convinced that associating with them requires following along. Many Latin American countries have passed laws to protect personal information because the European Union insisted as much. The more countries that follow such norms, the greater the pressure on the rest to conform. Peer status within the world's communication networks (subject to ITU provisions that make connectivity an inalienable right of countries regardless of their behavior in cyberspace) may also be valuable. Raising the stakes may also encourage other state or nonstate actors to take greater pains to expose such bad behavior on the part of others.

Norms also create a standard by which a country's trustworthiness can be judged. A corporation, for instance, does not need proof before it avoids investing in certain countries; a lack of trust suffices. Countries that need the West more than the West needs them—which is why the rise of China is very important to this calculus—may want to avoid behavior that alienates the West. The rise of cloud computing—outsourcing system functions to servers located in those countries that offer the best package of price, performance, and protection—may reinforce the value to a country of being seen as a good global netizen. Would such business gravitate to servers in countries where rule of law is discretionary?

NORMS ON WHO DID WHAT

Norms that clarify an inherently ambiguous medium may prevent countries from acting badly and getting away with it for lack of proof that they did. Here are some possibilities for facilitating attribution.

Normally, countries use courts to both determine the truth of crimes and mete out punishment for their commission. Western courts have had hundreds of years to understand what constitutes valid evidence. The indictment of the five Chinese hackers in May 2014 might be an example of using courts to determine (culpable) attribution, were it not for the fact that no U.S. trial can start without bringing the accused in front of a judge—something no one expects in this case.

Although attribution works best when the accused accepts the verdict (or at least acts as if the verdict mattered), an accused country is unlikely to accept attribution standards that it would have to abide by unless it sees that the process offers it a net gain applied over all hazards of cyberspace. There are several ways that may be true. First, if one country wants a deal that requires another to refrain from something, it may accept standards as the price for such a deal. Second, countries may agree on standards that are intended to cover third parties, so that if the United States says that, for instance, Iran carried out a cyberattack, it could offer China evidence that the U.S. accusation has merit. China, having accepted a standard attribution methodology, would be obligated to respect that reasoning. China, then, just might understand that a U.S. response to being hacked has a valid basis in fact (even if inappropriate or injurious to peace). To agree, a country would be expected to balance the odds that such rules would be used to bolster accusations against it (which might be reason enough to do less of it), the odds that it might someday use such rules for its own advantage, the harm from refusing to legitimize rules that others find reasonable, and the likelihood that the existence of an impartial judgment process may forestall (what they feel is) a precipitate rush by the United States to retaliate without having to provide requisite public proof of attribution.

The current alternative is leaving matters to intelligence agencies, in large part because today's attribution experts tend to work there. But such communities have the habit of whispering in their leaders' ears and protecting sources and methods (consider the FBI's dilemma in the wake of reports that the key evidence for attributing the Sony attack to North Korea came from taps of North Korean systems).[11] Clearly, trade-offs are involved in making accusations public. If they present evidence to bolster their accusations, they may have to refute the presentation of exculpatory evidence. Evidence, in turn, allows others to infer sources and methods, knowledge that facilitates their future evasion. In such circumstances, revelation cannot be for trivial cause.

There are several approaches to trustworthy attribution mechanisms, but none are obvious winners. A U.S. body of inquiry could be established to focus on fact-finding rather than guilt; in contrast with U.S. courts, this body would allow proceedings in absentia (but not punishment). Such a body could be staffed by representatives of the accuser and the accused. But would each side trust the experts from the other side? From the U.S. perspective, the Chinese or Russians would be considered beholden to their governments and thus unlikely to be given free rein to offer an independent perspective. The Russians and the Chinese may regard (or at least maintain that) U.S. experts as not only equally beholden but also having so much more experience at and tools for making attribution. It would be their show and others would be reduced to spectators.

Shifting from a bilateral to a multilateral forum (one like the IAEA) might assuage some of these concerns (representation from the accuser and the accused would both be diluted), but would Russia or China change their tune if U.S. experts were replaced by experts (many of whom have U.S. ties) from countries considered U.S. friends? In any case, the third party has to be credibly chosen; cyberspace forensics is not a widespread skill, and many of those who have it do have links to domestic or national security agencies. Others may therefore suspect that the investigators are there to spy, not solve crimes.[12]

Other useful precedents include the NTSB and the 1959 Antarctic Treaty, which allows no-warning inspections of facilities. Using an NTSB-like body may allow accused countries to pretend that a cyberattack is accidental or inadvertent, which is diplomatically useful even if it lacks credibility. The NTSB analogy may be pushed one more step. If a foreign aircraft crashes on U.S. soil, the NTSB can compel examination of its maintenance record; is there some useful analogy in cyberspace? The Red Cross may be another model.

A consensus that cyberespionage is *not* a legitimate casus belli may help garner accession to such an arrangement. The same goes for a consensus that distinguishes small cyberattacks appropriate for diplomatic or judicial responses from large ones that might constitute a casus belli. But the thresholds question cannot be avoided. What should they be? How should they be measured? Should large, rich countries be expected to overlook events that would be devastating to small poor ones (the United States can withstand the $100 billion damage of Katrina in ways perhaps no other country can)? Indeed, such a norm would raise the question: What *should* constitute an act of war in cyberspace?

ARMS CONTROL

Arms control frequently arises as a "solution" to war, and those in cyberspace are no exception. But would limiting or banning weapons work?[13] First, although a key purpose of "limiting" arms is to reduce the numbers of weapons (so as to limit how much damage they can do if used), numbers do not matter where duplication is instantaneous. Second, banning attack methods is akin to banishing "how-to" information, which is as feasible as making advanced mathematics illegal. The same holds for banning knowledge about vulnerabilities, which, if nothing else, is a necessary part of the vulnerability-eradication cycle. Third, banning attack code is neither possible nor even desirable: such code has many legitimate purposes, not least of which is in building and, especially, testing defenses against attack from others. Fourth, finding such code is a hopeless quest (finding such coders only somewhat less hopeless).[14] The world's information storage capacity is immense; much of it is legitimately encrypted; and besides, bad code does not emit telltale odors or look funny from far away. If an enforcement entity could search out, read, and decrypt the entire database of the world, it would doubtless find far more interesting material than malware. Exhuming digital information from everyone else's systems is hard enough when the authorities with arrest powers try it; it may be virtually impossible when outsiders try. Fifth, countries are not the only ones with cyberattack weapons.

One might ban writing attack code and then hope that the fear of being betrayed by a whistleblower prevents governments from organizing small groups of elite hackers to engage in banned activities. Alas, if the international community had the manpower and access to reliably enforce norms that way, it could probably enforce a great many other more immediately practical norms (for example, against corruption).

The U.S. Department of Commerce has proposed to ban the export of malware-related software.[15] In mid-2015, it proposed changing the multi-country international arms control regime (Wassenaar) accordingly.[16] These concerns are shared by DoD, whose 2015 strategy states that it "will draw on best-practices to counter the proliferation of destructive malware within the international system."[17] At least this regulation had to define what it is that is being controlled (as opposed to some vague notion of controlling cyberwar arms). Chances are, it will take multiple iterations before the gain from controlling unwanted activities exceeds the loss from inhibiting wanted ones (associated with cybersecurity research and development). The malware market is highly mobile; although black market vendors are difficult to locate for obvious reasons, some of the best gray market vendors are located outside major Western countries such as in Malta (ReVuln) and Thailand (Grugq).

LAW OF ARMED CONFLICT: JUS IN BELLO

The most important basis for developing wartime norms in cyberspace is the law of armed conflict, which is derived from eighteen treaties that the United States is a party to. LOAC is conventionally split into laws that govern what countries can do in war (jus in bello) and the circumstances under which countries can go to war (jus ad bellum).

Although there have been valiant efforts to apply LOAC to cyberspace—notably the Tallinn Manual, discussed below—the *technical* characteristics of cyberwar mean that there is no clean way that the *concepts* of LOAC would work on the other side of the looking glass. Consider deception, proportionality, neutrality, sanctuary—and reversibility, a norm that makes unique sense in cyberspace but not elsewhere.

Deception

LOAC outlaws perfidy and some forms of deception such as false-flagging, disguising combatants as noncombatants, and disguising combat facilities as or locating them within legally protected structures, such as churches or hospitals. This, in part, explains why lawful combatants have to wear uniforms. But not all deception is outlawed; military forces commonly use mock-ups and decoys to draw errant fire and even use false communications to suggest they are in, or heading for, a location different from their true intention. Deception, though, is the sine qua non of cyberwar. If a message sent to a target system announced, "Hey, I'm a cyberattack," it would be easy to filter it out (much as antivirus suites do). Attackers take pains to elude these detection mechanisms by masquerading as legitimate traffic. Deception in the form of honeypots or honeynets is even a standard tool of defense.

Should military systems be forbidden to look like civilian systems in cyberspace? To begin with, the ability to hide works differently in physical space and cyberspace. In the physical world, walls and roofs can mask what goes on inside a building; external indications can belie what goes on inside. In cyberspace, visibility can sometimes go all the way through—but, in many cases, the work of an organization may not be readily guessed by knowing, say, how its networks are managed. Worse, many network management functions—which may be targets of cyberattack—are identical regardless of what system is being managed.

Proportionality

The norm of proportionality is commonly (albeit incorrectly[18]) understood to reflect the feeling that the punishment (retaliation) should fit the crime. Measuring proportionality is not always simple. If Jack hits Joe and Joe has grounds to believe that hitting back just as hard would not deter subsequent attacks by Jack, Joe could conclude that he must hit back much harder to convince Jack to cease. In cyberspace, the problem of attribution strengthens the logic of overmatch: if an attacker can expect to carry out *most* cyberattacks with impunity, then, as General Alexander has argued,[19] the few times attribution is good enough for retaliation may require striking back hard enough to make the *expectation of retaliation* an effective deterrent. That noted, proportionality is prudent if the attacker can counter-retaliate and particularly if escalation is to be avoided. Difficulties in predicting the effects of cyberattacks also complicate proportionality. Physical attacks at least have the "advantage" of being able to call on physics and chemistry to predict their damage. In cyberspace, battle damage may depend on details of the target system that the attacker does not know. The odds that an attack to achieve some minimum effects creates disproportionately harsh ones appear to be higher in cyberspace than in physical space.

Neutrality

In the physical world, belligerents are enjoined from crossing neutral countries to attack one another. Conversely, neutral states that allow attacks to cross their borders put their own neutrality status at risk. In cyberspace, however, neutrals may not be able to distinguish enemy packets from all other traffic crossing their territory. After all, if neutral parties could detect such attacks, the target should have been able to detect them as well; indeed, the target should have a better idea because it knows what systems it has, their sensitive parts, and thus what an adversary armed with intelligence on them would go after. Detection by the target allows filtering out the attacks—thereby rendering detection by neutral countries unnecessary. Finally, if the neutral state *could* scrub *all* malware from transiting traffic (especially if it had powerful decryption technologies others lacked), must it report what it finds, particularly if it would prefer hiding the fact that it filters—much less how it filters? By DoD interpretation, nothing prevents a cyberattack from transiting a third country as long as that country experienced no harmful effects and no attempt was made to establish a "base" in that country.[20]

Regulating cyberwar behavior aimed at neutrals raises unique issues. In the physical world, country A is not enjoined from bombing a dual-use factory supplying military parts located in country B, with which it is at war, even if the factory itself is owned by citizens of neutral country C. Similarly, country A is not enjoined from taking down a server in country B even though it also provides critical services for country C (at one time, China's airline reservation systems sat on U.S. servers). In practice, the interconnections and cross-dependencies among the world's information systems grow harder to trace by the day. The harder they are to trace, the greater the likelihood that any given attack will touch what may be (or looks like) someone else's property.

Sanctuary

Should some slice of global cyberspace be off-limits to all state attackers? If so, what ensures that no sanctuary hosts a function that would be considered a legitimate war target? In some cases, a blind eye would work best. If the United States wants to knock out an overseas website used for terrorist recruiting, a deal may be possible ("we will not blame your country for hosting such a website if you do not blame us for sending bytes into your country to put it out of commission"); more likely, host countries would want to do it themselves or at least have a say in the matter. But would the United States object, for instance, if one party to a quarrel took down a U.S.-based server that was providing essential services, such as port management, to the other party—even if the takedown violates U.S. law (the 1986 Computer Fraud and Abuse Act)? Conversely, does the United States want to make itself a safe haven for websites as long as their owners' home nations are on good terms with the United States? If so, is the United States prepared to act against countries that pursue their enemies by hacking U.S. systems? And if *that* is so, would the United States accept that the right to react to external hackers going after third parties extends to all other states? In the age of the cloud, will anyone actually still know where the data were sitting at the exact time they were erased or corrupted?

Reversibility

Might every cyberattack be required to have an antidote, made available to the target when hostilities cease? Should peace see each side deactivate its implants or identify its implants for the target's deactivation—or should these implants be understood as still useful for cyberespionage, which states normally keep doing even after war ends? An attack that encrypts the only copy of someone's data might be followed by transfer of a decryption key when peace breaks out (think Cryptlocker but without bitcoins). Peace should allow the return of good data to replace corrupted (or erased) data—much as those who lay mines should remember where they put them. Thus, a corruption attack would not be allowed to disturb data unless the true records were stored somewhere else. Reversibility, alas, has practical difficulties. Sometimes offline storage is infeasible if the effort to store precorrupted data locally or send them offsite cues defenders that something is amiss (if data were merely encrypted, this objection would have no force). Conversely, restoration may not be needed; many disruption or even corruption attacks are reversed well before peace breaks out. In many cases, the corrupted or encrypted data (for example, the status of spare parts inventories) had a short half-life in the first place, so restoring prewar data would have little value. Finally, any capability to ease the grief of war may tempt war planners to use tactics and techniques that they might have foregone if the consequences were more serious. The same technologies used in ransomware "could be a way to force an opponent to submit or surrender without a shot being fired and without any equipment being lost on either side . . . [thereby offering] one set of capabilities that can operate in the transition space between diplomacy and military action, as well as more squarely in the military domain."[21]

LAW OF ARMED CONFLICT: JUS AD BELLUM

LOAC allows countries to respond to the hostile acts of other countries in one of two ways. One is by invoking a right to self-defense. Self-defense need not use the same means, counter the actual forces that carried out the original attack, or act right afterward. Although preemption based on a reasonable presumption of hostile intent is allowed, the attack being preempted must be one about to take place. This stricture perforce assumes a time sequence of events for which the concept of "immediate" is meaningful (and thus would probably not cover something such as an implant discovered in a critical system). Conversely, actions taken under the guise of self-defense are not limited to those that disarm the adversary—which, as noted, is pretty much of a nonstarter when it comes to cyberwar. Thus, one country could use force—or its most logical equivalent in cyberspace—to persuade another to "desist" from doing something, but such a country is obligated to say what the other country was supposedly desisted from doing, how it knows the attack was imminent, and why the means used to stop the attack were appropriate to the end. There is no defense for an attacker (or subsequently violated third party) to argue that better defenses could have prevented an attack—in much the same way that a nation that owns precision weapons cannot be prevented from using unguided weapons, even though the risk of collateral damage can be much higher in the latter case. Importantly, advance notice is required when the issue is not immediate self-defense (the latter presumably takes place in one's own territory or under the doctrine of hot pursuit). Making any of these arguments might be a little tricky for cyberspace.

A country can also go to the UN Security Council and convince it that the actions of a particular country constitute a threat to peace. Such a threat need not be an armed attack. Nevertheless, evidence of actual preparations for an "armed attack" would probably be more persuasive. Although the international community could judge whether an act was an "armed attack" after the fact by looking at the attack's consequences rather than its form, doing so requires some judgement about whether a cyberattack would work at all (the odds go down once it is no longer a surprise), much less what damage it might do.

Within the aforementioned GGE, the United States and its friends have contended that the same LOAC that applies in the physical world also applies in the virtual one. In 2013, it looked as if Russia and China had agreed that "international law, and in particular the Charter of the United Nations, is applicable and is essential to maintaining peace and stability and promoting an open, secure, peaceful and accessible ICT [information and communications technology] environment."[22] Since then, both countries have backed away from that belief, arguing that such an agreement could sanction cyberwar and validate a country's right to respond to the threat of cyberwar as it would respond to the threat of physical war.[23]

All this leaves people in the United States asking: What constitutes an act of war?[24] But is that the right question? LOAC, it turns out, does not define the term "act of war." LOAC addresses only what is a legitimate use of force under the right of self-defense. The *conclusion* that something constitutes an act of war is really rhetorical cover for the *decision* to respond to something as if it is an act of war—generally by carrying out some reprisal or going to war. The substitution of decision, which is volitional, for conclusion, which is factual, can be seen as blame-shifting, as if to say: I had no choice but to do *Y* because *X* was an act of war. Indeed, the expression, "I had no choice but" can be understood as a declaration of irresponsibility. Choices always exist—cyberattack is not an invasion, the failure to resist which lays one's country open. So not acting is a choice. Conversely, a country has some serious explaining to do if it responds with war to something in cyberspace that does not clearly look to others like an act of war in physical space. This explanation may be helped by a state having declared a red line in advance, which was then crossed—but not completely and only if others concede that such a red line is legitimate and plausible.

That leads to a revised formulation: a cyberattack can be deemed an act of war if and only if it is in your interest that it be so deemed, and enough others can be convinced that your saying as much is reasonable. The United States deemed the September 11 attacks an act of war by Afghanistan, and NATO understood and supported the U.S. reaction. The latter criterion, however, is an empirical matter: can enough others, in fact, be convinced? Others may reason: we recognize what an act of war is in the physical world, and we are looking for some analogs in cyberspace where X is clearly an act of war, Y is open to interpretation, but Z clearly is not. Unfortunately, when an American expresses that calculus, others may think that the United States is saying it will make war regardless of rules—without considering that such a formulation could also be saying that just because something can be likened to war does not mean that it has to be responded to as if war. After all, one element in determining that a response is not in the U.S. interest is that other nations deem it illegal according to international law and condemn the United States accordingly.

Those who feel that a broad cyberattack is highly unlikely but fret over day-to-day cyberespionage might want to see the latter declared tantamount to an act of war, particularly if its volume and intrusiveness were unprecedented. But what would make cyberespionage cross a threshold below which normal espionage is *not* an act of war? Would it be the volume or the messiness of cyberespionage that would shove it over some red line? Again, how do you specify a threshold? How do you prove it? Need the victim of cyberespionage have to assert and, even harder, have to prove that it never carried out such activities on its own? Since many acts of cyberespionage are never caught or only caught years later, was it espionage or getting caught at espionage that constituted justification for war? And what *is* to be gained from abandoning the long-held consensus that espionage is not a casus belli?

Last is the question of who is a belligerent. The tenet that providing intelligence to a belligerent does not make one a belligerent (for example, the United States provided intelligence to the United Kingdom during the Falklands crisis and to Iraq at war with Iran) could get many countries off the hook when it comes to cyberwar. If the United States carries out a cyberattack against a foe of a U.S. ally, it may be considered a belligerent. But what if the United States did enough R&D to understand the vulnerabilities in the software used by the other side (such as the four zero days in Windows exploited by Stuxnet), carried out enough cyberespionage to determine the systemic vulnerabilities of the other side (such as the role of the PLCs in governing centrifuges in Natanz), and passed them along to an ally in the confident expectation that the ally could figure out how to convert this intelligence into an exploit and deliver it? How much different would that be from handing over the exploit? And, how much different would *that* be from carrying out the attack? At what point does the act of espionage convert over to the responsibility for an attack?

FROM THE TALLINN MANUAL TO LAS VEGAS RULES

Can and ought serious cyberattacks by one side justify a kinetic response by the other? Or should it be a norm that, to paraphrase the *Economist* (admittedly on a different topic), "Nothing can be done with a pencil or a keyboard that warrants a reprisal with a Kalashnikov"?[25]

NATO's Tallinn Manual argues that attacks from cyberspace are no different than kinetic attacks.[26] Countries have the right to respond to them violently in self-defense as long as there is some rough comparability between the damage done by cyberattacks and the intended damage from a kinetic response. Conversely, Las Vegas rules would say: what starts in cyberspace stays in cyberspace. By this tenet, *no* attack that takes place from cyberspace, even if it causes substantial damage, perhaps even death, merits a kinetic response.

The Tallinn Manual is an interpretation of LOAC. Las Vegas rules would be a matter of deliberate policy. Adopting Las Vegas rules would not mean that the Tallinn Manual got LOAC wrong. But the adoption of Las Vegas rules *as policy* would suggest that international security would be better off if the extension of conflict in or from cyberspace to conflict using kinetic weapons were delegitimized, irrespective of its justification in international law.

The word "adoption" necessarily raises the question of who is doing the adopting. Could a country be better off if it renounced without a quid pro quo the option of responding to a cyberattack with violence? If it does so, how confident could it be that others would adopt similar norms? Unfortunately, a solemn agreement among nations to abjure taking cyberspace conflicts into the streets, so to speak, while it builds confidence that others will conform to its norms, does not guarantee they will all behave that way. Countries have been known to break such agreements (or interpret them quite flexibly) if they thought their national security demanded as much, as it might in wartime (which, almost by definition, is when violations would occur). In cyberspace, where proving attribution is usually fraught, a country can deny culpability with considerable plausibility.[27]

Yet a sufficiently widespread agreement (particularly if adopted by the UN or by treaty) that a kinetic response to a cyberattack is an act of aggression would, in and of itself, be a modification of customary international law (to be reflected perhaps in the next version of the Tallinn Manual). Whether tacit norms alone would also alter LOAC is a different issue.

WHAT THE TALLINN MANUAL SAYS

The Tallinn Manual makes three distinctions that apply to this argument:[28]

- The difference among cyberattacks that do not constitute a use of force, do constitute the use of force but are not armed attacks, and are armed attacks (and thereby use force). The manual holds that many cyberattacks—the DDOS on Estonia is given as an example—do not constitute the use of force, much less an armed attack.
- The *lack* of difference between cyberattacks and kinetic attacks that create comparable effects.
- The inclusion of dual-use targets within those that are legitimate targets of force under the "principle of distinction."[29]

Start with rule 9 of the manual: "A State injured by an internationally wrongful act may resort to proportionate countermeasures, including cyber countermeasures, against the responsible State . . . [but only] to induce compliance with international law by the offending State . . . and [once] the internationally wrongful act in question has ceased, the victim-State is no longer entitled to initiate, or to persist in, countermeasures, including cyber countermeasures." Yet actual state practice (customary international law) may vary because "States sometimes appear to be motivated by punitive considerations when resorting to countermeasures, especially when imposed after the other State's violation of international law has ended." Nevertheless, "countermeasures must be 'proportionate' to be lawful" (p. 42).

Although the manual did not hold the DDOS attacks on Estonia to be a use of force, Stuxnet certainly was (p. 47) as "would cyber operations of the same scale and effects" (p. 49) so that "consequences involving physical harm to individuals or property . . . qualify the act as a use of force.

. . . A cyber operation, like any operation, resulting in damage, destruction, injury, or death is highly likely to be considered a use of force" (p. 50).

The manual employs the "use of force" standard to determine whether a state has violated Article 2(4) of the United Nations Charter, consistent with customary international law. By contrast, whether or not a cyberattack is an "armed attack" is determined by whether the target state may respond with its own use of force (p. 52). Its Rule 13 (p. 53) states: "A State that is the target of a cyber-operation that rises to the level of an armed attack may exercise its inherent right of self-defence. Whether a cyber-operation constitutes an armed attack depends on its scale and effects." That noted, "No international cyber incidents have, as of 2012, been unambiguously and publically characterised by the international community as reaching the threshold of an armed attack . . . [even if] a closer case is the 2010 Stuxnet operations" (p. 56). Rule 14 states that "a use of force involving cyber operations undertaken by a State in the exercise of its right of self-defence must be necessary and proportionate." Yet "there is no requirement that the defensive force be of the same nature as that constituting the armed attack. Therefore, a cyber use of force may be resorted to in response to a kinetic armed attack, and vice versa" (p. 60). Indeed, under some circumstances, a state may *preemptively* kill hackers.[30] Furthermore, the level of damage required to start a war via cyberspace need not be particularly large[31] or even the effects produced be intended ones (p. 56).

The effect of any law on what countries do can often be described in terms of the distinctions it holds and those it disregards. The distinctions between attacks on civilian targets and attacks on dual-use targets matter—even if the destruction of all putatively dual-use targets leaves civilians with neither power nor telecommunications.[32] There are serious distinctions that lie in how a country can respond to a destructive attack compared to a disruptive attack (even if the latter is costlier). Consider the attack on Saudi Aramco that rendered thousands of computers useless. Now, what if the Iranian attack damaged only the boot sector(s) of the hard drive, thereby forcing their reformatting (and thereby destroying their data)? The latter might not have been considered physical destruction. Would the two have been so different measured in terms of remediation costs incurred by Saudi Aramco? Only a few of the manual's authors were prepared to argue that "interference with functionality that necessitates data restoration, while not requiring physical replacement of components or reinstallation of the operating system, qualifies as an attack [because] it is the object's loss of usability that constitutes the damage that is necessary to qualify a cyber-operation as an attack" (p. 94). Since war frequently does the first and rarely does the second, the first is well covered by LOAC, and the second is not. In cyberspace, this is an increasingly obsolete difference. A kinetic attack that destroys a database server when the data is backed up is generally less disruptive than a cyberattack that was discovered to have corrupted one of every ten records. If the backup contains the same corruptions, fixing the database would be difficult to impossible.

However, the distinction between a cyberattack and a kinetic attack that causes similar damage does *not* count (nor does anything the target may have done in configuring its system that accidentally permitted the damage from a cyberattack to exceed what the attacker intended). Consider, therefore, a cyberattack that happens to cause a fire in a military facility. Perhaps it generated so much network traffic that it knocked offline the warning system monitor (of whose existence the hackers may have been unaware) that would have otherwise alerted plant officials to a small fire that became a major conflagration. Such a cyberattack could be interpreted as an armed attack, allowing the target to use force against the attacker's dual-use infrastructure.[33] If the Tallinn Manual accurately interprets LOAC for cyberspace, then LOAC, in and of itself, must imply as much. Those who argue that cyberwar is not special and that it can and should obey the rules incumbent for historic domains must perforce agree with such equivalences.

The relevance of the Tallinn Manual is, granted, limited. Cyberattacks create a pattern of loss that may be quite different from what physical attacks cause—one more likely to be measured in terms of lost time rather than broken things, much less hurt people. So what looks like the pattern associated with the use of force is unlikely to be seen in a cyberattack. LOAC does not deal very well with the time-is-money equations. One that broke a $20,000 car might be considered a use of force, but one that caused $2 million worth of extra repair work for sysadmins will not.

But does legality equal wisdom? To wit, is it wise to ignore the *form* in which an attack takes place and focus solely on its *effects* when assessing how to respond? In the United States, whose actions really are dominated by legal concerns, regarding so many alternatives as illegal creates a bias for the remaining operations because they are easier to defend on legal grounds—even if they are not necessarily wise. Many officials reacted to the published reports of NSA activities by averring that because such actions were allowed under U.S. law (and not inconsistent with international norms based on historic espionage) they were therefore acceptable, but that did not automatically make them unobjectionable to observers. Likewise, consider an interpretation of international law that deems a cyberattack on a purely civilian target to be an unwarranted response to a cyberattack on a dual-use facility (for example, a power plant with both civilian and military customers). Policymakers, absent other options, may favor a kinetic response against a military or dual-use facility even if doing so created a greater risk of escalation.

So would wisdom be served by establishing a firebreak between acts in cyberspace and acts in the physical world? By way of analogy, compare a battle that features a very small nuclear weapon (for example, the Army-employed Davy Crockett with a yield comparable to ten tons of dynamite) and one that features a very large conventional weapon (for example, the mother of all bombs, which is comparable to eleven tons of TNT). The primary blast effects would be comparable; ditto, therefore, immediate death and destruction. Yet the former is a nuclear device, which has not been used since 1945; the latter is a conventional device. Even though LOAC sees no difference, no sane strategist would blithely substitute the former for the latter without understanding that such a decision would have consequences. Using a nuclear weapon opens the door to nuclear escalation and billions dead; a war that stays conventional may kill tens of millions (as World War II did), but probably not a billion.

The wisdom of establishing a similar firebreak between cyberattacks and kinetic attacks rests in large part on the warranted belief that the maximum damage from a full-fledged cyberwar is well below the damage from a full-fledged kinetic war. Consider the lack of casualties to date from any cyberattack, the few cyberattacks that have broken anything (two: Stuxnet and the mysterious attack on a Thyssen blast furnace), and the fact that systems could be made a great deal more resistant to cyberattack at the cost of user convenience (for example, by curbing external online access to machinery controls). Arguing that a cyberwar can be as damaging as World War II would require the triumph of imagination over experience and logic. The jump between a cyberattack and a conventional kinetic response therefore lifts one from the domain where none have died to one where tens of millions have. Jumping from cyberspace to the tangible world also shortens the next jump to nuclear war. In sum, escalation control provides a clear argument against exclusive reliance on the Tallinn Manual and in favor of Las Vegas rules that treat cyberspace as a separate venue of conflict.

U.S. declared policy, though, is consistent with Tallinn and not Las Vegas. The "International Strategy for Cyberspace" proclaims a right to self-defense.[34] The "Department of Defense Cyberspace Policy Report" of November 2011 adds, "If directed by the president, DoD will conduct offensive cyber operations in a manner consistent with the policy principles and legal regimes that the department follows for kinetic capabilities, including the law of armed conflict."[35]

VIVA LAS VEGAS

A country can adopt Las Vegas rules for cyberspace unilaterally (without waiting for others) or multilaterally (only if others do). A unilateral declaration makes two statements. First, we will not respond to a cyberattack, in and of itself, with a kinetic attack. Second, we will regard kinetic responses of others to cyberattacks as illegitimate, much as we regard unprovoked kinetic attacks as illegitimate. While the latter statement sounds simple if applied to adversaries, avoiding the taint of hypocrisy demands it be applied to friends as well.[36]

A multilateral declaration among friends (countries unlikely to attack one another in either space) would lend such a proposition greater credibility. But serious application requires that potential adversaries sign up as well. Mutual declarations could have the character of norms rather than treaties given the difficulty of enforcing such declarations on countries at war (which, almost by definition, exists when countries respond kinetically).

Unlike similar declarations mooted for cyberwar—for example, not to do it at all, or at least not going first, or not striking certain targets—it would normally be fairly obvious when countries responded violently and thereby violated such a norm. Ironically, the impetus for norms of behavior in cyberspace is almost opposite of the argument in favor of Las Vegas rules. In the first case, countries are asked to restrain themselves because cyberwar is dangerous. In the second case, countries are asked to restrain themselves not necessarily because cyberwar is dangerous per se, but because cyberwar is considered dangerous by dint of possibly provoking a kinetic response—which really *is* dangerous. The fear of cyberwar may even prompt countries to overreact to a modest cyberattack lest the next cyberattack produce disastrous effects. For them, a kinetic response says: don't even *think* about doing that again. Or both norms can be in effect at the same time: countries should restrain their resort to cyberwar because other countries might react in ways that lead to kinetic war, but such countries can also be trusted to adhere to Las Vegas rules even if the initial cyberattack was particularly damaging or raised popular ire.

Arguments apart from the aforementioned concern about escalation control[37] can also be adduced in favor of Las Vegas rules:

- Attribution may be poor, and mistakes may be made in responding. A response restricted to cyberspace is likely to cause less damage—and is easier to walk back from by both sides—than an unrestricted response.
- Many of the cyberattacks that might be carried out in response would require more time to prepare if the victim of the cyberattack has not scoped out corresponding targets in the attacking country. Countries that pledged to respond only in cyberspace but are pressed to respond by their publics could rationalize their inactivity by pleading that retaliation would take time—and then use such time to ascertain whether the putative cyberattacker was the actual cyberattacker and whether the damage really warranted so much reaction (and also whether popular ire may cool). Kinetic responses do not require that much planning; pressure to respond quickly even though attribution was imperfect would be harder to resist.
- Similarly, the cyberattack may be accidental or inadvertent—or its effects greatly exceeded the attacker's intentions. Although these are not valid excuses under international law, a justification for a response is to affect the attacker's calculus in order to modulate the future threat. If the target ascertains that the future threat is smaller than it would appear based on the initial cyberattack, it may wish to restrain its response. Again, abjuring a quick kinetic response allows time to make such a determination.

- Delegitimizing a kinetic response to a cyberattack makes it difficult for a country to employ a cynical strategy of waiting for some cyberattack to do what it wanted to do all along: use force against one of its foes. Although proportionality norms are supposed to ensure against such behavior, measuring proportionality to the satisfaction of both sides is a lot more problematic than determining whether or not a country responded with force to a cyberattack.

- A similar argument tees off from the ease by which rogue entities (especially those on the government payroll) or third parties can start a catalytic conflict by carrying out a cyberattack, hoping that the target responds kinetically, which then gives license to the original attacker to counter-respond kinetically. If the target state abjures a kinetic response, the initial hacker has less motive to start.

- An attacker that weighs the choice between carrying out a cyberattack and carrying out a cyberattack coupled with a kinetic attack will know that the former will probably not be punished with a kinetic attack while the latter probably will be. Las Vegas rules may persuade the attacker to abjure a kinetic component, a possibility if the cyberattack was deemed a sufficient way to send a message or to take action against a particular actor within the target state.

- Finally, Las Vegas rules will even further delegitimize threats of a nuclear response to a cyberattack.[38]

BUT NOT SO FAST

The case *against* erecting a firewall between a cyberattack and a kinetic response echoes the case *for* deterrence. To wit, any efforts to soften the threat of punishment will weaken the disincentive to carry out cyberattacks. In a world that has yet to see any attacks more serious than Stuxnet, the possibility that a victim of a *more* serious cyberattack will react furiously may have prevented worse. As argued, the United States harvests a great deal of tacit deterrence from its history. Furthermore, certain countries—North Korea and, to some extent, Cuba—have so little dependence on networked systems that a threat to respond in kind to a cyberattack will not be particularly dissuasive, leaving those countries that abjure a violent response to a cyberattack with few deterrence options against such countries (even as it retains other sticks and carrots to influence the attacker). The logic of weakening a deterrence that has, so far, held (admittedly a happy child of many a claimed father) in favor of a policy that may dampen the tit-for-tat aftermath of a catstrophic attack is less than obvious.

Indeed, to return to the nuclear firebreak, note the United States only *now* promises that it "will not use or threaten to use nuclear weapons against non-nuclear weapons states that are party to the NPT [Nuclear Nonproliferation Treaty] and in compliance with their nuclear non-proliferation obligations."[39] Yet it never adopted a no-first-use policy during the Cold War. Indeed, a staple of NATO's defensive posture was the readiness to use nuclear weapons if Warsaw Pact forces crossed into West Germany. This policy was supposed to have the dual effect of deterring a conventional invasion and giving NATO forces a war-breaking option in case deterrence failed. The fact that NATO was serious about the former—it very well could conclude that seeing continental Europe overrun was a worse fate than tempting a global thermonuclear exchange—made the former threat credible; at any rate, no invasion ever ensued. By contrast, a threat to risk kinetic war in order to reduce the odds of a devastating cyberattack is less credible, particularly when many other options exist to reduce the prospect of future damage. There is no cyberwar equivalent to being overrun. Hence, there is less credibility to any threat to start a kinetic war in response to a possible cyberwar—and hence, today's posture provides less deterrence than NATO's more credible Cold War posture did.

Need countries therefore declare that *no* conceivable cyberattack could ever merit a violent response from them? In cases where the consequences of a cyberattack do not threaten the nation's security in and of itself, but reveal the attacker to be heinous and therefore deserving of eradication (think al Qaeda), need nations constrain themselves? Is there some stopping point short of Las Vegas on the way from Tallinn? Granted, ambiguity is hard to express. Consider the following posture statement: we have no intention of responding to a cyberattack with anything outside cyberspace and we do not find doing so legitimate, but we cannot absolutely foreswear such a response against a cyberattack with unimaginably serious but not provably impossible effects. The right landing spot, however, may be painted by a combination of sentiments and silences. The sentiments would be to condemn damaging cyberattacks (of course), but allow a response to take into account means (for example, from which medium the attack came) as well as ends (effects). It would condemn the assumptions that give automatic license to escalate from a cyberattack to a kinetic response. It would question the legitimacy of using a cyberattack as a pretext for violence. But it would never say never.

Countries can also signal as much by conspicuously decoupling strategic cyberwar operations from all other operations, or by conspicuously not putting kinetic forces on higher alert following a cyberattack (that did not presage armed violence). The value of the signal would depend on how others read it. If they believed that the declaring state really did not want a kinetic fight, then the latter's declaring as much tells no one anything. If it believed that the state was prepared for violence but declined to engage in it, it may read the declaration as favoring de-escalation. Conversely, an aggressive leader may infer that kinetic force was abjured because the country's capacity to use kinetic force was unimpressive. Or the refusal to respond with violence may convey that the target country was confident enough in its ability to dominate the proverbial escalation ladder at all rungs of cyberwar intensity and could afford to declare a firebreak in the interests of de-escalation. In the latter case, unless the foe were aggressive, it may conclude that it would be better off settling earlier rather than later, especially if it thought that such confidence suggested that its rival knew something the attacker did not.

WHY NOT LAS VEGAS RULES FOR OUTER SPACE AS WELL?

The rationale for Las Vegas rules would seem to apply to outer space—in some respects, even better. If one country damages another country's satellites and the other country responds in kind, then the worst that can happen is that each will be down a few satellites. The likelihood of anyone on Earth being hurt is very low (small pieces burn up; large pieces have always landed elsewhere). Most infrastructure would survive; cable television would be the big loser, and global positioning system and weather satellites may be spared because they serve friends and foes alike. Such assurances may not apply to a no-holds-barred cyberwar. Responding to either a cyberattack or a space attack with a terrestrial kinetic attack opens the same can of worms. No country has signed up to Las Vegas rules in outer space, however—why might they do so for cyberspace? A five-part answer follows.

First, satellites are indefensible against certain kinetic attacks: a sufficiently desperate attacker could take out a satellite with a very small object placed in an orbit equal to and opposite its target. In low Earth orbit, such weapons would approach the satellite at 36,000 miles per hour—speeds at which paint chips can be damaging—and even at the 13,000 miles per hour that could characterize head-on collisions in geosynchronous orbit, small objects can cause severe damage. Satellites are not armored because serious armor would make them too heavy to loft into orbit. There are as yet no feasible ways to disarm weapons coming at them, if such weapons could even be seen. For this reason, the only defensive strategies have to work through reprisal (including diplomatic or economic measures as well as violent ones). By contrast, cyberspace is eminently defensible—and so a reprisal strategy is less necessary.

Second, because asymmetries in outer space are greater than in cyberspace, a tit-for-tat strategy in space is a losing proposition for many countries, notably the United States, which relies on satellites for command and control of dispersed forces. There are only a handful of countries that have satellites in orbit. By contrast, every country that has a cell phone system enjoys services that could, in theory, be disrupted by cyberattack. Even if only two countries have demonstrated kinetic antisatellite capabilities—the United States in 1985 and 2008 and China in 2007 (Russia may have similar technologies)—any country that can loft a satellite into orbit can launch a satellite killer into a similar orbit if sufficiently motivated. Cyberattack capabilities at fairly low levels are present in (or can be purchased by) many other countries, but it is less clear how widely distributed the capability is to seriously disrupt another country's infrastructure.

Third, some space capabilities are intimately tied to nuclear capabilities. The United States uses Defense Support Program satellites and, soon, Space-Based Infrared System satellites to look for the infrared signatures of nuclear missiles. It uses Milstar and Advanced Extremely High-Frequency satellites to command and control nuclear forces, even in heavy-jamming environments. A tit-for-tat exchange in outer space would put nuclear operations, as currently practiced, in peril (although it is a gross exaggeration to say that countries would be disarmed). Russia has similar early warning and strategic communications satellites. Allowing countries to target nuclear command and control is a recipe for destabilization, something to be avoided in the nuclear arena.

Fourth, kinetic attacks on satellites have the potential to generate so much debris in orbit that the lifetimes of all the other satellites in orbit could be reduced, not only temporarily, but for the hundreds or thousands of years it takes for the debris to fall out of the atmosphere—or until a usable space debris cleanup capability is invented, whichever comes first. China's 2007 antisatellite test, for instance, threw into orbit roughly 2,300 pieces of debris large enough to be tracked, and countless pieces of debris too small to be tracked but large enough to damage. In early 2013, a Russian spacecraft was reported disabled when struck with one piece of debris (weighing less than a gram),[40] and the International Space Station had to maneuver around other debris.[41] A serious tit-for-tat in outer space risks creating the Kessler Syndrome cascade in which debris destroys satellites, thereby causing even more debris, which breaks more satellites and so on until such orbits are unusable. Consequences this serious may need to be deterred with more than a simple threat to respond in kind.

Fifth, the odds of rogue outer space attack (and hence catalytic reaction thereto) are negligible. Knocking out a satellite requires means that are clearly military and, being fairly large, are very difficult to hide or deny after the fact.

For these reasons, it is possible to look askance at Las Vegas rules in outer space while still arguing that similar rules for cyberspace might make sense.

CONCLUSIONS

Writing norms can be a challenging intellectual exercise in which certain behaviors are deemed reprehensible and defined in ways that distinguish them from acceptable (if unwanted) behavior. But writing is the easy part. Due attention must be paid to whether countries that are able and willing to violate such norms agree. More attention is needed to work out mechanisms that can get violators to concede or at least not contest judgments that such norms have been violated. Indeed, if these mechanisms can be established, existing norms (for example, to abjure EMCE) can be placed on firmer footing and further norms can be generated with confidence that agreement implies compliance.

Can norms for cyberwar be derived from LOAC? If cyberspace is perceived as merely the fifth domain of warfare, then, yes. But if strategy and prudence are allowed to play a role—and if the fact that there is no forced entry in cyberspace is duly appreciated—then an attack carried out in cyberspace may wisely be treated differently than an attack carried out in physical domains. The major reason to limit the response to cyberspace is that the damage from escalation in cyberspace likely tops out well below the level of damage from escalation in the physical world. The minor reason is that difficulties of mounting an instant response in cyberspace (vis-à-vis the physical world) give countries time to reconsider their choices. Although traveling toward Las Vegas rules and fore-swearing violent responses to cyberattack would serve stability, a full-throated adoption would give attacked countries too little capability to deal with truly exceptional (and hence highly unlikely) circumstances. Something just shy of Las Vegas on the way over from Tallinn may be just the place for policy to land.

CHAPTER 33
Sino-American Relations and Norms in Cyberspace

The United States and China are destined to be the world's two largest economies and to have the two most powerful (conventionally armed) militaries. The state of Sino-American relations could spell the difference between peace and strife—not only in the physical world but also in cyberspace. Unfortunately, relations between the two countries have become testy since the beginning of the great recession, *particularly* in cyberspace. The United States complains about Chinese EMCE and is not comfortable with its other cyberespionage (the OPM hack was mentioned at the Sino-U.S. Security and Economic Dialogue). U.S. officials suspect that China is putting itself in a position to disrupt U.S. infrastructure if it has to. Furthermore, the Chinese and the United States take very different positions on Internet freedom.

Both countries, by rights, should get along. Neither lusts to conquer other countries, nor is either trying to impose its ideology on the other. Both are willing to negotiate with one another; both understand that business is business. Nevertheless, cyberspace remains a burr in their relationship—and the bad feelings produced by differences in cyberspace can reduce strategic trust and thereby complicate the resolution of other differences (for example, in the South China Sea).

This chapter traces the potential unfolding of the Sino-American relationship in cyberspace. We pursue two themes. One is the course of interaction between the two, colored by the fact that cyberspace ranks higher on the list of U.S. concerns over China's behavior than it ranks on China's concerns with U.S. behavior. Two is that China and the United States may have fundamentally different concepts of the role played by norms and deterrence (as a way to enforce norms). We introduce a modest proposal for reducing some tensions and conclude with a brief assessment of the September 2015 agreement between President Xi and President Obama.

THE UNITED STATES ADVOCATES ITS NORMS

The best statement of U.S. attitude toward norms in cyberspace remains the 2011 "International Strategy for Cyberspace": "We encourage people all over the world to use digital media to express opinions, share information, monitor elections, expose corruption, and organize social and political movements, and denounce those who harass, unfairly arrest, threaten, or commit violent acts against the people who use these technologies."[1]

Norms, though, sit uneasily with sovereignty because the former tells countries how to behave and the latter says they can ignore such advice. Such a dilemma characterized the U.S. reaction to the Google incident of January 2010: condemning China for worming its way into U.S. systems but advocating principles that would allow Western content to worm its way into China. By contrast, the Chinese (and Russians) believe that it is an act of information warfare to inject *either* unwanted content *or* malicious instructions into a country's infrastructure.

Many statements in the strategy point to China, if not necessarily by name. For instance, when the strategy called for "the same protections . . . [to be applied] to Internet Service Providers and other providers of connectivity, who too often fall victim to legal regimes of intermediary liability that pass the role of censoring legitimate speech down to companies," it was referring to China's practice of devolving the state's censorship role to private ISPs.[2] When it continued, "The United States will continue to make clear the benefits of an Internet that is global in nature, while opposing efforts to splinter this network into national intranets that deprive individuals of content from abroad," it was also referring to life behind China's Great Firewall (even though Iran also suppressed Internet speech at that point). Although there might be a legitimate U.S. interest in avoiding balkanization of the Internet so that U.S. citizens could freely access Chinese content, no one believes this to be the point; it is about foreign access to Western material (or Western services such as Facebook that could be conduits for Western material).

Underneath the strategy's diplomatic niceties is a portrait of a United States grown angry with China's behavior in cyberspace. The basic U.S. "strategy" is simple: We will engage the international community in "frank and urgent dialogue" ("frank" is a giveaway) to build consensus around principles of responsible behavior in cyberspace.[3] Specifically, the United States "will continue to encourage other countries to become parties to the [Budapest] Convention" ("other" meaning China in particular).[4] "Responsible behavior" means that "states must identify and prosecute cybercriminals, to ensure laws and practices deny criminals safe havens, and cooperate with international criminal investigations in a timely manner." This would only need stating, of course, if there were other countries that do not do this. Add to this the strategy's declaration that "states should recognize and act on their responsibility to protect information infrastructures and secure national systems from damage or misuse" (p. 10). If one wonders why an *international* strategy asks states to secure their own information infrastructures, the last word, "misuse," provides the clue. Countries should see to it that hackers operating from national networks do not attack networks of other countries or—in light of China's protests that *others* transit China's poorly secured networks to attack Western targets—ensure that other countries secure their networks so well that such transits cannot happen.

If the Chinese *had* recognized themselves in the portrait painted in the strategy, they might have reacted in one of several ways.[5] They could restate their noninvolvement or convert such protestations into hurt innocence ("why are you picking on me?"). They could jump on the bandwagon, pay lip service to some of the ideals, and then suggest that the real sinners are others (Russia is always convenient). They could show where the United States falls short of its ideals.[6] They could point (more than they already do) to U.S. efforts to assert hegemony in cyberspace. They could portray this as one more indication that the United States is starting a new cold war. Or, in the best of all possible worlds, they could at least act a little sheepish and go with the developing-country excuse. All, in fact, are common staples of Chinese discourse on cyberspace. Instead, a *People's Daily* article blandly declared, "It is worth noting that the United States did not list any target country in its cybersecurity strategy."[7]

The strategy also spoke to the evolving U.S. attitude on self-defense: "Consistent with the United Nations Charter, states have an inherent right to self-defense that may be triggered by certain aggressive acts in cyberspace" (p. 10). The sentiment is made clearer on page 14:

> When warranted, the United States will respond to hostile acts in cyberspace as we would to any other threat to our country. All states possess an inherent right to self-defense, and we recognize that certain hostile acts conducted through cyberspace could compel actions under the commitments we have with our military treaty partners. We reserve the right to use all necessary means—diplomatic, informational, military, and economic—as appropriate and consistent with applicable international law, in order to defend our Nation, our allies, our partners, and our interests. In so doing, we will exhaust all options before military force whenever we can; will carefully weigh the costs and risks of action against the

costs of inaction; and will act in a way that reflects our values and strengthens our legitimacy, seeking broad international support whenever possible.

The hesitation is palpable. We really hate war, it says. We would only do it if "warranted," in pursuit of our "inherent right," because we committed ourselves to "our military treaty partners" (as if a cyberattack on the United States would elicit no response, but one on Estonia would leave us no other choice), and only after we "exhaust all options," "carefully weigh the costs and risks of action," and ensure that it reflects our "values" and garners "broad international support." One can almost hear the year and a half's worth of bureaucratic battles that resulted in such tortuous and tortured prose.

Apparently, however, the Chinese heard *that* paragraph loud and clear, particularly when, shortly after its release, the aforementioned smokestack quote made the press. Here came China's opportunity to shift the discussion from its own sins to the verbal aggression of American policymakers. The result was a wave of condemnation accompanied by avowals that China was not waging cyberwar on the United States. Ironically, when the DoD Cyber Strategy was released in 2015, the international strategy seemed to be the lauded standard from which DoD's document was, to the Chinese, an unfortunate departure.

CAN WE TRADE?

In 2009, the Chinese, concerned with their tarnished reputation after years of accusations, opened up Track II negotiations on cyberspace.[8] The Chinese side was staffed by the Chinese Institute for Contemporary International Relations; its delegation has included a rising number of government officials over time. The U.S. side was headed by the Center for Strategic and International Studies but was staffed across Washington, D.C., think tanks, also with a growing cohort of government officials over time.

From the American side, the messaging was clear and oft-repeated: Chinese EMCE has to stop. It is damaging both directly, in terms of lost intellectual property, and indirectly, in terms of the amount of money that organizations must spend to limit its ravages. Such conduct does not befit a relationship that should be, but could not be, characterized by mutual trust. Americans are fed up with it; indeed, the issue worked its way into the primary and general presidential debates in 2012 and 2016. A bad U.S. reaction would damage U.S.-China relations. The U.S. side wanted China to take its law enforcement responsibilities more seriously and was willing to see a deeper relationship between the FBI and China's Ministry of Public Security to do so. At the very least, the Chinese should own up to the amount of cyberespionage they do. The Chinese, not surprisingly, are very defensive about this accusation—which, to them, is what erodes mutual trust.[9]

Chinese participants voiced several themes. One was the present and future U.S. domination of cyberspace—implying that the United States had less to worry about in that domain than everyone else did.[10] In many ways, China was dependent on U.S. capabilities. Its credit card and airline reservations systems were housed in the United States. Its emergency communications depended on a U.S. corporation. It depended on Microsoft, whose actions in 2008 (when an upgrade made many Chinese screens go dark[11]) and 2012 (when it persuaded a U.S. court to shut down a Chinese website, 3322.org[12]) were not forgotten. It was also convinced that Microsoft (and Google, back when it operated in China) were scooping up vast quantities of personal data on China's netizens, where it could be subpoenaed by (or otherwise transferred to) the U.S. government. It was acutely conscious of its own difficulties in keeping the Internet running both in the face of technical challenges (one noted that seventeen provinces at one point or another had lost DNS services) and the "fact" that the United States controlled all the top-level domains. The Chinese saw no basis for U.S. concerns about supply chain security—except as a guide to how they might themselves manage their own risks arising from what others do.

The Chinese were also struck by the discovery of Stuxnet and the U.S. formation of CYBER-COM, which they argued was proof that the United States wanted to militarize cyberspace, while the lack of a Chinese counterpart was proof of China's peaceful intentions. Such suspicion extended to their (since-abandoned) perception that DHS's CyberStorm exercises were preparations for hunkering down in the face of a U.S.-instigated cyberwar. They were unsure of who to talk to on the U.S. side about incidents in cyberspace.[13] Many different participants spoke of the need for mutual trust, notably that the United States must consider China trustworthy and act correspondingly.[14] China, its representatives argued, should not be accused of crimes in cyberspace. Finally, they were upset over the United States arrogating the right to respond to a cyberattack, in large part because the Chinese did not credit U.S. attribution claims when the Chinese themselves could not do attribution very well.

Although the Chinese understood the U.S. disquiet about China's EMCE, they chose not to address it directly. China's traditional position is that it simply does not spy.[15] To quote Qian Xiaoqian, a vice minister and deputy director of the State Internet Information Office, "Our opposition to all forms of hacking is clear and consistent. . . . Lately people have been cooking up a theory of a Chinese Internet threat, which is just an extension of the old 'China threat' and just as groundless."[16] Chinese foreign minister Wang Yi recently argued, "As a matter of fact, China has suffered from hacking. Every day, China is subject to more than 300 largescale hacking activities, and every month, more than 10,000 Chinese websites are changed by hackers, and 80 percent of the government websites are attacked. We have evidence to show that many of these hacking activities come from the U.S. We cannot say who inside the U.S., but these attacks come from U.S. soil."[17] Since Snowden, these denials have been less vociferous, and most Chinese familiar with the issue no longer routinely deny that they spy on corporations (this when asked what they would ask from the United States in return for stopping the practice).[18] The most recent version of *The Science of Military Strategy*, an authoritative analysis of China's military thinking, refers to China's cyberwar units.[19]

The United States made clear what it wants from China, but what China wants is less clear. The dialogue suggests the following list of their dislikes:

- the NSA collecting data on China
- U.S. corporations collecting data on Chinese citizens and using such data for commercial purposes, as noted[20]
- The possibility of supply-chain attacks (arising from corrupted software and services rather than corrupted hardware, the latter being a U.S. worry)
- U.S. support for Internet freedom (many Chinese think the United States wants to use the Internet to destabilize China and they have equated information warfare via the promotion of "rumors" with disabling cyberattacks)
- U.S. control over ICANN, the Internet Assigned Numbers Authority (IANA), most of the top-level domains, and a routing structure that has most Chinese traffic to the rest of the world routed through the United States
- The militarization of cyberspace as indicated by Stuxnet and the U.S. establishment of CYBERCOM (although they never said so explicitly, the Chinese may fear that the United States is preparing a disabling first-strike capability in cyberspace).

The depth and breadth of these complaints would suggest the possibility of a deal—even if some of these complaints cannot really be addressed by the U.S. government within the framework of the Constitution. Both would likely want to retain their traditional national security espionage.[21] For a trade to work, their desires have to be serious enough to merit confession that they do carry out EMCE and thus have something to trade. Otherwise, China is in the unproductive position of being asked for something (that is, reducing EMCE) without the prospect of getting much in return. But does China really need the United States to curb its own activities badly enough to justify giving up EMCE? It may not, and if the promises that President Xi gave to President Obama in September 2015 are indicative, it did not. Although cyberspace is among the top five issues the United States has with China, it does not make the top ten list of the Chinese side.

ONE DETERRENCE, TWO DETERRENCE, RED DETERRENCE, BLUE DETERRENCE

A more fundamental problem in reconciling U.S. and Chinese views on norms is that the two countries have fundamental differences on the roles of norms and the use of deterrence strategies to ensure that they are followed.[22]

In the United States, deterrence is viewed as a fundamental element of international relations with its rules and reprisals, all underscored by the mathematics of game theory. China also believes in deterrence, but in the service of power relationships rather than norms. Its perspective is no less logical than the U.S. perspective.

Blue deterrence (an archetype approximated by U.S. practice) focuses primarily on stated rules and only secondarily on strength. It assumes an ability to punish (an ability the United States does have) and the willingness to do so in the face of potential counter-reprisals. It also fits a world of peers in which the judgment of states that some behavior has gone too far echoes the imposition of law over an anarchic world system. Crossing a line, like breaking the law, requires punishment if lines are to be respected. Thus, although blue deterrence is generally enforced by the proximate target of the unlawful acts, its enforcement can be extended to acts against allies or even the unaligned (for example, Kuwait in August 1990). The law for one is the law for all. But this love of law ought not be exaggerated, however. One reason that the United States can adopt a law-related approach to deterrence is that it has considerable influence over what the law says (and in extremis, it can always use its exceptionalism to exempt itself). Thus, adherence is contingent rather than absolute.[23]

Red deterrence (an archetype approximated by Chinese practice) is focused on power, which, by definition, is relative. The willingness to respond (that is, credibility) and a precise statement over what actions would compel it to respond (that is, crossed lines) are less important. Red deterrence lives in a world of hierarchy in which countries are of unequal power and patterns of deference reflect power relationships. It is thus very finely attuned to the correlation of forces. It recognizes the attraction of the rule of law—but as an instrumental value, a means to an end. The Chinese recognize that the legitimacy of laws and norms depends on who wrote them—and most of them were generated when China was not in the game. Regardless, the application of law has always and will always be influenced by the distribution of power—indeed, law reflects power. Thus, new power arrangements should be reflected in new norms if not new laws—but not all countries are equally obliged to follow them.

Blue and red deterrence are based on competing perceptions about how countries should behave. The differences need not imply a clash if each side would avoid actions it feels entitled to take but the other objects to. But misunderstanding is more likely if each side thinks the other's complaints lack merit. It is easy for blue to thinks red is cynical for favoring power over rules. It is also easy for red to think that blue is hypocritical for using rules to mask power.

Blue deterrence reflects the U.S. dilemmas of the Cold War and, before that, the lead-up to World War II. The lesson was to seek safety in bright lines and a willingness to back them up. Left to be determined was how countries established and indicated such lines, and what they did to assure their enemies (and friends) that they would, in fact, use nuclear weapons in situations where they threatened (or promised) to.

Red deterrence reflects China's experiences during the century of humiliation (1839 to 1949). China had no effective way of warding off depredations from economically advanced outsiders, whether from Europe, Russia, or Japan. When China drew itself together, its goal was to rebuild national strength and thereby gain control over its own destiny—and, as it grew stronger, generate sufficient respect from abroad to win deference for its own interests.

Deeper roots of the difference in orientation lie in competing conceptions of society. In the U.S. mythos, autonomous individuals are the basic unit of organization. They are free agents, subject only to the constraints arising from their interaction with others. These constraints are codified in law. The state exists to serve individual needs collectively expressed. In China, society and the state rather than the individual are the basic unit of organization. Individuals are granted a certain level of authority over others according to their place. Such relationships are expected to be internalized, and this internalization, in turn, minimizes the explicit use of power to gain conformance.

Blue deterrence aims at stability, as befits a status quo country. Red deterrence aims at hegemony. When weak, the point is to oppose hegemony on general principles. When strong, the point is to be a hegemon oneself, so that its interests are always factored into the choices of others. It was China's foreign minister Yang Jiechi who said in 2010, "China is a big country . . . and other countries are small countries and that is just a fact."[24]

To blue, deterrence is something one has; it exists or it does not. It can exist for everyone at once—in that no country crosses another country's lines. If deterrence falters, those who would maintain it must decide whether to signal their intention to back up their words with deeds. A signal can involve moving forces (for example, ships), but it need not mean using force itself. Blue deterrence, as befits a posture born of law, pays a great deal of attention to making lines clear enough to allow third parties to judge actions relative to such lines. North Korea, by one U.S. narrative, invaded South Korea because the United States (in the person of Dean Acheson) failed to include South Korea within America's Pacific defense perimeter (boundary lines). The lesson was that signaling to others what one will defend minimizes errors of inference.

Red deterrence aims to create an aura of fear, uncertainty, and doubt among other countries. The Chinese entry into the Korean War in 1950 was not necessarily motivated by the fear that the United States would *cross* the Yalu. China did not draw a line on the river saying, "Go no farther but feel free to approach." But the very fearlessness with which U.S. forces *approached* the Yalu may have connoted a lack of respect for China itself. The purpose of the intervention, apart from recovering North Korea, was to demonstrate that China had to be treated with respect. True, the lack of clear lines in red deterrence makes things more complicated for others—but if these others have to consult with red to determine what they do, so much the better. Such consultations indicate a relationship in which the other country is a supplicant in search of guidance. Rather than drawing lines, China typically indicates an increasing irritation with the acts of others if they go too far.[25] In that sense, red deterrence is retrospective, implicit, and analog (the degree of irritation is a function of how far the other side has gone). Blue deterrence aims to be prospective (spelled out in advance), explicit, and digital (one either crosses the line or not).

To red, therefore, deterrence is something one does to remind others of the need for respect. Both China's war against India in 1962 and its invasion of Vietnam in 1979 were used to remind its neighbors of what it could and would do. Its 1996 missile volleys off the northern and southern port cities of Taiwan grew from similar imperatives.

In a crisis, red is wont to highlight the unwillingness of others to accord red its rightful respect. The purpose of war is to demonstrate the basis for such respect ("we told you to respect us; now we will force you to"). For this reason, red must carefully calculate the correlation of forces before it sets out to demonstrate how much respect to demand. By contrast, blue finds the roots of many crises in the inability of others to understand what the lines are or believe that they will be held to account if they are crossed. The purpose of war is to reinforce such intentions ("we told you not to do this, you did this, and now we must use punishment to make the point").

For blue, it is important to keep some punishment capability in reserve, particularly if it wants to maintain some element of deterrence after initial punishment. Thus, punishment has to be calibrated in every case when the other side is expected to survive punishment. For red, calibration is less important because the point of applying power is not for red to modulate the behavior of other countries, but to emphasize red's power, in awe of which other countries are expected to modulate their own behavior.

Blue deterrence treats compulsion as different from deterrence; red deterrence sees them as the same. Blue deterrence limits punishment to sins of commission. If the deterrence works, then no one transgresses. The narrative of compulsion—which requires a country to do something or else face punishment—does not fit the transgression model because no line was crossed. The distinction also recognizes the autonomy of the other side. Those who do not cross the line can argue it was not fear that kept them from doing so; they never had any intention of doing so in the first place. One never knows when others are deterred—only when they are not deterred. Red deterrence is based on deference to another country's will, irrespective of issue. Whether the use of power is to keep another country from stepping forward or making it step backward is secondary. It is the degree to which will can be imposed that matters. In so doing, red grants no purchase to autonomy; indeed, red would prefer that submission be seen by the other country as exactly that.

Blue deterrence easily lends itself to alliances, because the unilateral enforcement of universal laws can be readily extended to multilateral enforcement. Blue can even argue with a straight face that alliances join together equals. Red deterrence does not lend itself to alliances because its world is not one of peers; everyone is either up or down relative to another. Red may have friends and allies, but if red is powerful, the latter are clearly supplicants locked into asymmetric relationships and they are not necessarily allies of one another.

Blue deterrence sees international stability arising from the universal adherence to a set of norms that say what one country can do to another; it is enforced by actions taken against norm violators. Red deterrence finds stability in the universal acknowledgement of a global power hierarchy (also known as a pecking order) that dictates patterns of deference. Both forms of deterrence rely on proscription and the power to enforce it, but blue deterrence emphasizes the proscription while red deterrence emphasizes the power. Both forms of deterrence are self-consistent and compatible with human nature—hence neither is inherently illegitimate.

The blue notion that international stability arises when everyone follows the rules is not the Chinese experience. In the era from the end of the Yuan Dynasty (1368) to the arrival of the Western powers (1839), East Asia was largely at peace under the rubric of Chinese hegemony, universally (even if quite grudgingly) acknowledged in the region.[26] Other countries had only some freedom of action. Europe's history during the period was much more sanguinary and dynamic, even after the Treaty of Westphalia, which supposedly laid down rules for states to follow in their dealings with one another.

Whether or not credibility—the willingness to respond to lines being crossed—is more important than power is complex and context-dependent. Daryl Press's *Calculating Credibility* argued from Cold War examples that credibility is overrated.[27] Countries will accede to others not by looking at whether they *would* do what they threatened to do but whether they *could* do what they threatened to do. A country's willingness to back up a threat had less to do with its leader's character and more to do with its capabilities. As countries' capabilities improve, so does the likelihood they will carry out their threat, irrespective of their character. Communicating credibility matters little. Countries will do what they can, not what they say they will. If so, red deterrence is truer to life than blue deterrence.

WHY RED AND BLUE DETERRENCE MATTER TO CYBERSPACE

Differences between blue and red would be reflected in cyberspace. To illustrate as much, consider hegemony, attribution, escalation, stability, and norms as they may apply in that medium and as reflected in U.S. and Chinese approaches.

Hegemony

China obsesses over cyberspace hegemony. U.S. officials and experts do not think in terms of hegemony but assume that countries, if playing under fair and reasonable rules (the provenance of which is held to be beside the point), will rise to their proper level of power and respect in cyberspace as elsewhere.

Might China someday become a cyberspace hegemon; if so, how? Had the U.S. advantage lain with its inherent national capabilities (for example, education, capital), China's path to hegemony would be straightforward and deemed legitimate by the United States (much as Japan's leadership in automaking is). But the Chinese also believe that the U.S. advantage is an artifact of having invented the relevant technologies—an advantage fairly won but unfairly extended. U.S.-based Internet governance groups such as ICANN (which has done little recently except problematically expand the list of top-level domains), IANA, and, to a lesser extent, the Internet Engineering Task Force (whose influence peaked in the 1980s) are also targets of China's revisionist ire. The United States resists radical changes to these arrangements, reasoning that China's rules would come at the expense of Internet freedom, whose promotion China, in turn, believes to be an element of U.S. hegemony. China is also eager to build direct Asia-to-Europe fiber optic connections so as to avoid sending its traffic across the United States (which the Chinese feel lets traffic be intercepted or blocked). Similarly, it wants to leverage its internal market to promote the proliferation of made-in-China technical standards in order to favor indigenous Chinese companies. China therefore makes determined efforts to displace what it calls the eight "guardian warriors" of U.S. hegemony, most notably Cisco (the other seven being Apple, Google, IBM, Intel, Microsoft, Oracle, and Qualcomm).

Yet as successful as Chinese firms have been in hardware markets (for example, Huawei routers, ZTE handsets, Xiaomi cell phones), they have enjoyed far less success in software. Software leadership requires being able to invent or reinvent new things for computers and devices to do. It also benefits from network effects. Neither work yet to China's advantage. As noted, there may be some relationship between software market position and superiority in cyberwar. But if red becomes the hegemon and expects the sort of deference that hegemons deserve, while blue sees no such hegemony and insists that tried-and-true rules (coupled with technical standards) trump power, problems may arise. Worse, even if China becomes the hegemon in East Asia, being a *regional* hegemon in cyberspace means little. Would that force China to be a global hegemon in cyberspace to maintain its regional hegemony in the physical world?

Attribution

Confidence in attribution is very important for blue deterrence; some even want evidence of guilt beyond a reasonable doubt before meting out punishment. Confidence is less important for red deterrence, which is more concerned about the ability to retaliate and prevail against those it would retaliate against.

Red is more likely to ask itself first, not whether some action crossed a line, but whether it can afford to make an issue of it. Who would come out on top? Conversely, even if victory is unlikely, can it afford not to push back if the insults from being successfully attacked erode the aura of power (China was so embarrassed by how deeply its networks were penetrated that President Xi Jinping decided to personally head China's cybersecurity efforts)? Under such circumstances, red's decision to retaliate would have less to do with getting the attacker right and more to do with recovering its reputation. Red would more likely focus on a pattern of attacks that shifts or indicates a shift in power that therefore must be opposed. Blue might more likely retaliate based solely on one attack, especially one that, if left unpunished, threatens the rule of law in cyberspace. U.S. officials remain frustrated that China resolutely refuses to acknowledge the evidence behind U.S. accusations of malfeasance in cyberspace. In U.S. eyes, China is lawless. In Chinese eyes, forcing an admission is forcing China to concede to U.S. hegemony in cyberspace.

Escalation

Cyberattack escalation management presents many of the same challenges associated with cyberattack prevention. Attribution is a less pressing concern; establishing thresholds, more pressing. For blue deterrence, defining these thresholds is necessary to hold the other side to account. Similarly, the ability and willingness to react quickly when such thresholds are breached are essential lest today's unpunished violation becomes the new normal of "acceptable" cyberattacks.

Red would likely see a real conflict in cyberspace as part of an overall struggle. Red may well want to limit the scope of the conflict. Limiting the scope of strategic cyberattack could be an element of its strategy. But picking a level of conflict that best plays to red's advantage matters more. Worrying about occasional attacks that rise beyond that level matters less; patterns are what count. Red is going to look at average behavior to ensure that the game is being played at its preferred level of intensity. Blue is going to look at worst behavior so as to gain respect for lines that should not be crossed. Red would thus be less likely to use carrots and sticks to regulate the exact nature of blue's cyberattacks. As long as one side is more relaxed about one-off violations of perceived norms, a confrontation between two countries is less likely to result in uncontrolled escalation as each side attempts to match or, worse, over-match the other's violations in order to persuade the other side to limit itself. Such behavior is consistent with the realities of cyberattacks, notably their subordination to other forms of conflict and the challenge of determining which attacks crossed which thresholds with any precision.

Sources of Vulnerability

As noted, many assumed that the United States was uniquely vulnerable to cyberattack because of its *advanced* information technology.[28] In a sense, power was inversely correlated to susceptibility, not positively correlated as one might expect. A single-minded emphasis on relative power in cyberspace tends to obscure this dilemma, and conversations with the Chinese who see their power in cyberspace climbing vis-à-vis the United States suggest that they underplay the prospect of greater vulnerability.[29] Hopes that as the Chinese grow increasingly sophisticated about and deepen their dependence on information technology, they will understand the rationale for U.S. norms may not be realized—if the Chinese feel that their information investments add to their national power and hence the ability to command respect in cyberspace while ignoring their growing vulnerability.[30]

Signaling

Problems may arise if either blue or red tries to read the other's signals without grasping that each looks at matters differently. Blue may read red's acts as breaking rules or establishing different norms; red may see blue trying to force behaviors that, once accepted, mean that blue has again exerted superior power. The indictment of the five PLA officers may have been a signal sent by the United States that U.S. law (China has similar laws) cannot be violated with impunity. The Chinese may have read the indictments as a U.S. attempt to demonstrate its extraterritorial power and thereby violate Chinese sovereignty. China's ending its Track I talks on cybersecurity was its way of pushing back.

The United States wanted China to crack down on North Korea's malicious use of the Internet and thereby signal North Korea that destructive (or at least highly disruptive) attacks on international corporations are unacceptable. But China proved reluctant to press North Korea, perhaps because it sees its hacking as one element in a broader tableau—and because any action it takes on behalf of the United States may look like bowing to U.S. pressure. Blue deterrence sees across countries to evaluate and respond to transgressions, while red deterrence sees across transgressions and focuses on its relationship with specific countries. A large, perhaps dominant, element of the U.S. desire to punish North Korea is to create a precedent for punishing cyberattacks, irrespective of who carried them out (as indicated above). China's resistance may have little to do with condoning cyberattacks and more to do with worries about its neighbor. The dean of foreign policy realism, Henry Kissinger—and in many ways the U.S. diplomat who best understood China and red deterrence—was the one who tried to introduce "linkage" as a way of integrating the multiple elements of the U.S.-Soviet relationship rather than focusing on particular behaviors and applying a global rule for dealing with each. When it comes to other countries: blue particularizes, red generalizes. When it comes to norms of behavior: blue generalizes, red particularizes.

Norms

As a rule, the United States seeks norms to distinguish acceptable cyberespionage (that carried out for national security) from unacceptable cyberespionage (that carried out for commercial purposes) *and* to legitimize the principle that countries may respond to sufficiently damaging cyberattacks (howsoever defined) in kind or even with kinetic force. China's interest in norms is driven by its desire to maintain freedom of action at home and to reduce what it sees as U.S. hegemony in cyberspace. Indications that the Chinese arrested some OPM hackers[31]—despite the fact that such espionage clearly fell within the national security realm[32]—in order to curry favor with the United States suggest norms were far less important than power politics. In China, sovereignty trumps other values (but this does not preclude yielding on some issues to preserve a broader relationship).[33] In theory, blue's adherence to norms should persist even after its immediate advantage from such norms has receded or reversed, while red's adherence to such norms should wither once circumstances shift. That remains to be seen.

Overall

Deterrence between the United States and the Soviet Union was, at least at the nuclear level, based on a rough symmetry of capabilities and mutual understanding of what deterrence meant (notwithstanding post–Cold War material from Soviet archives that show some critical differences). Both sides had a rough idea of what lines not to cross and how each side might respond if they were crossed.

In a world of red and blue deterrence, this may not follow. For blue, line-crossing is an act in and of itself; the failure to note and react to it imperils the rule of law. For red, the line is broad and fuzzy; how it reacts to incursions depends entirely on the context, which, in turn, illuminates the balance of power. Transgressions merit response only if they show that one country's perception of another needs correcting—something that requires understanding the precise context. Granted, context is not absent from blue's calculations: in reacting to Sony, U.S. leaders may have remembered the Las Vegas Sands hack and concluded that something had to be done to bolster the rule of law in cyberspace. Again, red is more likely to link events having to do with the other country but in other media. Blue is more likely to link events having to do with the same medium, but involving other countries. When it comes to punishing North Korea, one sees the commander of CYBERCOM arguing in favor of retaliation because others were watching how we would react to the attack—but one did not see the commander of Pacific Command making the case that such punishment was an essential component of the United States managing North Korea.

A world in which blue and red deterrence both work to their mutual advantage requires that each understand deterrence through the other's eyes. The mental gymnastics are not only difficult but also assume that both sides see the rationale in each other's perspective. Granted, blue must be concerned with power (and the United States assuredly is). Red must communicate its vital interests and how prepared it is to defend them (as China assuredly does). But differences in orientation spell differences in emphasis and hence different international behavior, especially as it affects cyberspace.

As China rises, it will want the United States to acknowledge its status as an actual equal (even as China refuses to treat any third country as *its* equal). The United States may speak of mutual respect but quickly add that such respect is any country's due. Inevitably, some incident will arise that the United States will judge in terms of law and China will judge in terms of power and the respect due to power. The two may well talk past each other, neither able to make its point for being unable to see things as the other does. Such an event could very easily take place in cyberspace.

A MODEST PROPOSAL FOR IMPROVING CYBERSPACE BEHAVIOR

Michael Hayden, former NSA director, said, "Ideas have been raised about forming the cyber equivalent of demilitarized zones for sensitive networks, such as the power grid and financial networks, that would be off-limits to attack from nation states."[34] There are indications from the Chinese that they would be receptive to such a deal using the nonaggression pact in cyberspace that Russia and China inked in 2015 as precedent.[35] Indeed, in late 2015, the UN GGE (which China belongs to) agreed, "A State should not conduct or knowingly support ICT [information and communications technology] activity that intentionally damages or otherwise impairs the use and operation of critical infrastructure."[36] Unfortunately, like any agreement not to engage in certain activities characteristic of war, enforcement by punishment is unlikely to take place while war or warlike activities ensue. At that point, treaties would be less compelling and considerations of escalation control—fuzzy as they are—would likely dominate. Thus, the rules provide little serious inhibition to bad behavior.

Fortunately, because cyberespionage is almost always a prerequisite for cyberattack (DDOS/BGP attacks aside), particularly if implants are used, abjuring *peacetime* cyberespionage can inhibit warlike wartime cyberattacks, at least in the first few weeks and months of conflict (while new entryways into target systems are being sought). Even better, countries that abjured cyberespionage would have a hard time coercing others by threatening immediate cyberattacks on critical infrastructure—without at the same time admitting that their word not to carry out (prefatory) cyberespionage was worthless. Accordingly, if both the United States and China are serious about not attacking critical infrastructure, both would also want to agree to mutually abjure cyberespionage on each other's infrastructure. Many Chinese understand the two to be linked and understand that an agreement not to attack could proscribe intelligence preparation of the battlefield—or anything indistinguishable from it.

Any serious agreement requires a mechanism to find violations: to attribute as well as detect them (detection, though, may require distinguishing malware that drifted into the critical infrastructure from malware deliberately put there). Any detection-and-attribution mechanism must pass three wickets. One is getting it right. Two, more important, is to build a good case for what happened. Three, most important, is to be believed: the accused must accept the results as legitimate and unbiased if not accurate (the process of attribution need not resolve every time as long as it resolves often enough to inhibit cheating). The problem is not merely or even mostly technical but political: What arrangements or processes would persuade a country, notably China, to accept conclusions drawn from evidence (without, at the same time, being so stringent that conclusions can rarely be drawn from evidence)?[37]

Part of the political problem from the Chinese perspective is that the United States catches a much greater share of Chinese spying than the Chinese catch of U.S. government spying—any process that produces similar results may be viewed as simultaneously accurate and deeply biased. The Chinese claim that they are attacked frequently from the United States (which remains, for instance, the leading source of bots and botnet command and control servers) but have forwarded no evidence that the U.S. government has carried out specific hacks or protected hackers who have.[38]

China's ability to detect and attribute cyberespionage from the United States is far lower than the U.S. ability to detect and attribute cyberespionage from China. This is composed of three differences. First, China's OPSEC lags U.S. OPSEC, making Chinese spying easier to detect (part of how one can tell good OPSEC is to see which intrusion sets attributed to each country had gone undetected for more than, say, five years before being eventually detected). Second, China's ability to detect intrusions lags behind the U.S. ability to detect intrusions. Third, China's ability to attribute detected intrusions lags behind the U.S. ability to attribute detected intrusions.[39] As long as all three are true, will the Chinese accept that compliance verification would be even-handed (even if all accusations about Chinese behavior are accurate)? Until the Chinese gain confidence in their own attribution capabilities, they may not even believe that U.S. attribution capabilities are good enough, either.[40] Might the Chinese be more forthcoming if they understood attribution better? If so, would achieving an agreement with China be sufficiently worthwhile to the United States to justify teaching (or sending third parties to teach) China some of its attribution techniques? Would the Chinese then be willing to credit such techniques as evidence of verification?[41] At first glance, this notion appears untenable: countries do not teach others such technology. Yet the United States encourages other countries to adopt PALs for their nuclear weapons so that such weapons are not used accidentally or at the instigation of rogue nuclear warriors. There are also offsetting benefits when foes build enough surveillance capability to let them believe that the United States is adhering to (nuclear) arms deals. Furthermore, helping bring Chinese attribution capabilities closer to those available in the United States does not mean that the United States should be expected to teach others how to *detect* cyberespionage intrusions or how to keep their own penetrations from being *detected* by the United States.

CODA: THE SEPTEMBER AGREEMENT BETWEEN PRESIDENT XI AND PRESIDENT OBAMA

On September 25, 2015, during President Xi's visit to the White House, he and President Obama announced: "The United States and China agree that neither country's government will conduct or knowingly support cyber-enabled theft of intellectual property, including trade secrets or other confidential business information, with the intent of providing competitive advantages to companies or commercial sectors." (They also agreed to "cooperate . . . with requests to investigate cybercrimes . . . [make a] common effort to further identify and promote appropriate norms of state behavior in cyberspace . . . [and] establish a high-level joint dialogue mechanism on fighting cybercrime and related issues."). To wit, the president of China committed his country to recognize and adhere to norms of cyberespionage that disallowed none of what the United States does (commercial cyber-espionage is allowed as long as the results are not given to commercial firms) and forbade much of the Chinese behavior that the United States objects to.

Will this agreement lead to major change?[42] Or will the Chinese continue carrying out EMCE and, in the face of U.S.-provided evidence, continue to deny complicity (or argue that "China is a big country and we cannot know everything that goes on inside it")? No monitoring system was established that both sides agreed to accept the results of (nor, apparently, was there talk on how to set one up). The Chinese government did not lose face with this agreement because it has never officially argued that EMCE is no worse than national security cyberespionage.

Assuming China will throttle EMCE, here are some potential reasons why it may have agreed to do so; they are not necessarily mutually exclusive.

- *U.S. pressure.* Perhaps the Chinese folded under threat of sanctions. Despite having an economy almost as large as that of the United States, the Chinese may have felt themselves in an inferior power position. China's economy is shaky (the Shanghai stock market index deflated substantially in mid-2015 despite government attempts to keep the air in), it lacks the many friends that the United States has that would assist its efforts in a confrontation, its military is still substantially inferior, it fears U.S. hegemony in cyberspace, and it lacks the soft power the United States has. Because the Chinese economy depends more on exports to the United States than vice versa, it could lose more in an all-out trade war. Last, the United States appeared much readier to go to the mat on this issue (with Chinese cyberespionage, what started as injury became insult with the OPM hack). Over the last few years prior to the agreement, the United States had put increasing diplomatic pressure on China but had not yet imposed serious consequences on it.[43] It has been U.S. policy since mid-2012 that top U.S. officials bring up EMCE when meeting their Chinese counterparts.[44] The topic was explicitly introduced during the Obama-Xi Sunnylands summit of mid-2013, following which national security advisor Tom Donilon bore down on this topic in a major speech and Treasury Secretary Jack Lew was dispatched to China, in part to reinforce this point.[45] Both the May 2014 indictment and the April 2015 executive order permitting foreign hackers to be sanctioned suggested a ratcheting up of pressure.[46] One former National Security Council staffer has argued that it was the May 2014 indictments that persuaded China to cut back its EMCE (although, as noted, the FBI reported that the number of EMCE cases had risen by 53 percent between 2013 and 2014).[47] Incidentally, an alternative explanation that President Xi simply wanted to have a successful summit and would say anything to get through it was belied by his repeating the promise to the British prime minister and within the Group of 20 nations.
- *The value of further EMCE to them has become disappointing.* Perhaps the Chinese are just not getting very much out of stealing intellectual property (see the chapter on EMCE for why). As noted, the bill of particulars associated with the indictment of the five PLA officers showed very little intellectual property theft in comparison to the taking of business proprietary data. The United States continues to insist it is being hurt. In any negotiation, it pays to trade away something that the other side values more than you do

as a way of getting it to concede things that really matter to you. Indeed, in the latter half of 2015, China may have concluded that it needed to mend relationships all around, and this concession was part of that pattern.

- *The Chinese wanted to rein in freelancers*, and this deal gives Beijing more authority to do just that (just as the December 2014 climate deal gave Beijing more authority to pressure provincial and county governments to get serious about pollution). Chinese leadership may fear that unconstrained freelance or moonlighting hackers threaten good order. Worse, their hacking skills may come to be used at home against Chinese companies or, even worse, against the central government. Chinese officials may also leverage this agreement to professionalize its own hacking. Several months after the agreement, important cyberespionage responsibilities were transferred from the PLA to the Ministry of State Security. Incidentally, it may be time to retire the notion that the Chinese government favors freelancers because their activities can be denied; apparently they are becoming more trouble than they are worth.

The Chinese believe (if post-summit discussions with two Chinese interlocutors are indicative) that the agreement gives China a breathing space from U.S. threats. The United States, they believe, cannot argue that the Chinese have not kept their word until it finds an objectionable act of EMCE that *started after the agreement* was made. Thus, continued talk of sanctions or other forms of pressure is in bad faith. But it is unclear whether such expectations will be met. Subsequent weeks have featured news stories about which specific Chinese companies would be targeted with sanctions.[48]

CHAPTER 34
Cyberwar: What Is It Good For?

Two scholars who agree on little else, Tomas Rid and John Arquilla, have recently asserted that a world with cyberwar is likely to be less violent than a world without it.[1] Both scholars bring Stuxnet up: had cyberwar not been an option, Natanz would have been targeted not with a worm but with bombs. Stuxnet allowed the problem created by Iran's enrichment program to be addressed without violence. To the extent that Stuxnet is archetypical, cyberwar is good for peace.

But is that always so? Suppose that, without having cyberattack capabilities, planners of another anti-nuclear takedown, Operation Orchard, blanching at the prospect of losing aircraft and having to return home, would have scrubbed the mission. In this case, cyberwar capabilities putatively led to more rather than less violence—especially if Syria had chosen to retaliate (which it did not).

MODELING THE INFLUENCE OF CYBERATTACK OPTIONS

So with all due caveats when assessing an ever-changing form of conflict, we model whether Stuxnet or Operation Orchard is a better guide to understanding whether cyberwar is good for peace. In the model, a country faces a situation. If it lacks a cyberwar capability, it can choose only between doing nothing and using force. If it has a cyberwar option, it can choose among doing nothing, carrying out a cyberattack without the use of force, or using force (with or without an accompanying or prefatory cyberattack). If the country without a cyberwar option would have done nothing, then giving it the option must perforce increase the likelihood of violence: either cyberwar makes violence more attractive or a cyberattack unaccompanied by force increases the risk of violence to the extent that the cyberattack could set off a chain of tit-for-tat that culminates in violence.[2]

We now lay the choices out formally as follows, by positing five states. Two are associated with a world without a cyberattack option: 0 (do nothing) or K (attack kinetically). Three are associated with a world with a cyberattack option: 0 (do nothing), C (carry out a cyberattack but not a violent attack), or V (carry out a violent attack with or without a cyberattack).

In a world without cyberattack options, we define the value, to the deciding country, of doing nothing as zero. If K is preferable to doing nothing (that is, K > 0), the country attacks kinetically; otherwise it does nothing.

In a world with cyberattack options, we define the value of doing nothing also as zero (whether or not the zero of a world with cyberattack options is larger than the zero in a world without cyberattack options is irrelevant; it only matters whether C, K, and V are preferable to doing nothing). If V is preferred to C and 0 both, then the country attacks violently: we can state this condition as VC0 or V0C (depending on whether, absent a violent alternative, a cyberattack is preferable to doing nothing). If neither V nor C is greater than zero, then it does nothing (0VC or 0CV). Finally, if a cyberattack is the best option, we have C0V or CV0. This takes care of all six permutations.

Between C, K, V, and 0, there are twenty-four (4 x 3 x 2 x 1) different permutations. However, we can reduce this to twelve by assuming that V is always preferable to K: the availability of an accompanying cyberattack option, we would argue, never reduces the value of carrying out a kinetic attack (vis-à-vis doing nothing). This might seem obvious were it not for the fact that in a

TABLE 34.1 KINETIC/CYBER PREFERENCES AND OUTCOMES

OPTION	OUTCOME WITHOUT CYBER-WAR OPTION	OUTCOME WITH CYBER-WAR OPTION	ANALYSIS
VKC0, VCK0, VCK0	Kinetic	Violent	In three cases, the cyberwar option makes no difference since a violent kinetic attack is chosen.
0VKC, 0VCK, 0CVK	Nothing	Nothing	In three cases, the cyberwar option makes no difference because the choice is to do nothing.
VC0K, V0KC, V0CK	Nothing	Violent	In three cases, cyberwar enables violence, whereas in its absence nothing would have taken place.
CV0K, C0VK	Nothing	Cyberattack	In two cases, a cyberattack is chosen when the alternative would have been to do nothing.
CVK0	Kinetic	Cyberattack	The cyberattack option is chosen when kinetic would have otherwise been chosen.

world with cyberattack capabilities, the target may also have the ability to counter a kinetic attack with its own cyberattack—for instance, by disabling the targeting radar in the attack aircraft, thereby frustrating its ability to drop its bomb load accurately. Nevertheless, the existence of cyberattack capabilities should favor taking the offense, particularly if the issue is something like a raid rather than a full-fledged conflict. The attacker gets to choose the time and the equipment for the attack; for the defender to forestall or frustrate such an attack by using its own cyberattack may require the attack work at any time and on any piece of the attacking equipment. Furthermore, the attacker is more likely to use mobile assets; the defender is often defending fixed assets, which are more likely to be networked (for example, IADS). Mobile assets are harder than fixed assets to attack through cyberspace because their network configurations are more variable and hence less predictable. Thus, the assumption that V is always preferable to K seems reasonable.

So we are left with twelve permutations; VKC0, VCK0, VK0C, VC0K, V0KC, V0CK, 0VKC, 0VCK, 0CVK, CVK0, CV0K, and C0VK. By way of explanation, take VKC0: a kinetic attack is preferred to doing nothing if a cyberattack option *does* exist (because K exceeds 0) and a violent attack is preferred to doing nothing if a cyberattack option *does not* exist (because V exceeds 0). Table 34.1 lists each option, the preferred course if a cyberattack option exists and the preferred course if no such option exists.

Of the twelve permutations, in a world where cyberattack capabilities exist, either:

- The decision is the same: six permutations.
- An attack takes place, where it otherwise would not have: three permutations.
- A cyberattack takes place, where otherwise nothing would have taken place: two permutations.
- A cyberattack takes place, where otherwise a kinetic attack would have taken place: one permutation.

So, in the six (of twelve) cases where something changes, it changes in the direction of more direct violence three times and in the direction of a higher possibility of retaliatory violence two times—but in the direction of less violence only once. Granted that we have not evaluated the relative odds of each permutation; CVK0 may be more likely than the combination of VC0K, V0KC, V0CK, CV0K, and C0VK. Otherwise, the result contravenes the premise that (if aftereffects are disregarded) cyberwar is good for peace.

A more colloquial way of stating the comparison is to imagine a country whose leaders feel that they have suffered something of an insult and that therefore they had to do something, cyberwar was something, and they therefore had to do cyberwar. Asking why they would choose cyberwar—with all of its uncertain effects—over violent war could elicit the answer that the very uncertainties of cyberwar make it attractive compared to the certainty of death, destruction, and an indefinite commitment to battle. A country can carry out a cyberattack, issue a denial, or walk it back in ways that at least its friends might believe, and thereby escape the onus of having withdrawn if it discontinues carrying out cyberattacks in the face of pressure. It appears attractive because the instrument promises release without risk. The proponents of cyberattack can make many promises for their skills; if their claims are made in a highly classified forum, they may avoid external critique. By contrast, proponents of violent war can be refuted by examples drawn from thousands of years of history. Yet if the optimistic judgment of cyberwarriors is false, the country might have been better off never having that option—especially in circumstances where kinetic attack was deemed far too risky. In essence, if the risks of cyberattack are deliberately misunderstood or suppressed, the option to go ahead may seem entirely too attractive.

If one includes nonstate or rogue state actors in the mix, the case against the peaceful nature of the cyberwar option becomes stronger. For the most part, nonstate actors that specialize in violence lack cyberwar capabilities that they might want to substitute for violence.[3] Conversely, hacker groups rarely resort to significant violence, so there is nothing to substitute for there either. Rogue state hackers are a potential added problem all their own. Some intelligence agencies (for example, Pakistan's Inter-Services Intelligence[4]) pursue courses (seemingly) antithetical to declared state policies. Cyberattacks by rogue operators create a path to conflict that carries a low risk to themselves—whereas they would likely stand down if the only option were kinetic warfare. Indeed, there are good reasons to believe that if, say, Russia wanted to convey its ire at one or another U.S. action, then it could convince itself that the risks to its own well-being were low if it simply empowered its *mafiya* to carry out such attacks on the state's behalf, perhaps in return for winking at other *mafiya* activities taking place within Russia itself. The relationship between the state and moonlighting hackers in China is still unclear even after the Mandiant report, although the more recent agreement between Xi and Obama, as noted, suggests they are on the way out. Again, cyberwar creates new opportunities; it rarely substitutes nonviolent activities for the violent opportunities that already exist.

HOW MUCH CYBERSECURITY DO WE REALLY NEED?

People will put up with adverse circumstances up to their tolerance level; then they react. As long as the level of adverse circumstances does not rise unexpectedly, their willingness to react provides a certain equilibrium. The worse things get, the harder people push back to limit how fast matters will deteriorate. If people do nothing radical to attack the cybersecurity problem, it may be because it is not perceived as warranting radical measures.[5]

This logic might not apply if people underestimate the impact of cyberattacks. But do they? After several years of increasing media coverage, this would be hard to believe. The logic also fails if there are latent cybersecurity threats that, not being seen, elicit no responses. Thus, people respond to cybercrime because it happens every day, but they do not respond to the much larger (albeit *potential*) threat to the critical infrastructure (or to military forces) because it has yet to happen—much as the air threat to U.S. battleships was latent for twenty years until Pearl Harbor (ditto for terrorism in the United States until September 11, 2001).

Otherwise, apart from a truly surprising attack, the degree of concern merited by the threat from cyberspace cannot be greater than the cost of making those architectural changes in systems (for example, air-gapping the power grid) necessary to drive the threat down to levels that can or at least should be tolerated.

Most hackers do what they do to gain information they can convert into money or (if on their government's payroll) some advantage in military or economic competition. These needs did not arise yesterday, nor will they disappear tomorrow. If tomorrow's threat will be similar to today's (particularly after the 2013–14 wave of attacks on retailers and banks is factored into cybersecurity spending), then what passes for optimal tomorrow will be similar to what passes for optimal today.

Conversely, should there arise a sufficiently competent and sufficiently nasty actor, today's preparations may look inadequate in retrospect. In a sense, it is fortunate for the United States that there are two other countries—Israel and South Korea—that already face serious cybersecurity challenges from countries that seek damage for the sake of damage. Looking overseas may provide some sense of what a stressed state of cybersecurity looks like. Unfortunately for the United States, the depth of challenge from enemies of those two countries—Iran and North Korea—is limited. If China or Russia turn seriously bad (unlikely but not utterly impossible), today's cybersecurity effort will seem inadequate. But the solution may not necessarily be to spend more today but to figure out in advance what fundamental trade-offs may be needed between convenience and security under such circumstances. These days, it is not security that people seek to maximize but security taking usability, convenience, and flexibility into account. While this looks like joint maximization, choosing what is to be maximized and what is the constraint will determine which trade-offs are made. How does the burden of proof fall upon advocates of security vis-à-vis advocates of competing system features?

The more fundamental question for U.S. policy is whether it is more important to pursue advantage in cyberspace (for both espionage and attack) or to make cyberspace more secure for everyone. A great deal, of course, depends on the relative importance of having a safer cyberspace vis-à-vis bolstering the U.S. national security advantage (in a post–Cold War era when the existential threat to the United States is greatly reduced). Normally, in such choices, cybersecurity gets lip service, but after every country does its sums, it may realize its efforts can be directly applicable to gaining advantage and only indirectly applicable to improving global cybersecurity. The traditional paradigm was that unilateral disarmament is not to the advantage of any one country. Conversely, because U.S. companies control well over 90 percent of the global market for packaged software, there are trade-offs that the United States—*and no other country*—can entertain. The notion that cybersecurity would obtain were it not for the NSA is baseless. It is not the source of system and software vulnerability (a few minor and highly disputed exceptions aside). But the United States *could* usefully devote comparable resources in the pursuit of global cybersecurity.

Meanwhile, the threat from cyberspace may have already passed its acute phase and settled into its chronic phase, where cybercrime, surveillance, and theft of strategic bits of business proprietary data are worthwhile for hackers to do but cyberattack and the wholesale theft of intellectual property are not. If cyberattacks depend on the element of surprise, then perhaps at some point there will simply be no surprises left (more accurately, generating surprise may get harder and harder).

It may then be that the most important events in cybersecurity in 2014 and 2015 are composed of what did *not* happen. To wit, the Russians did not use cyberattacks in confronting Ukraine. They used electronic warfare, even wire-cutters, against communications systems. They kept on spying and executed desultory DDOS attacks (for example, against Ukraine's parliament).[6] But operational use of cyberwar against defense systems never happened (as 2015 ended) so far as was publicly known. Similarly, neither side had tried to take down the other side's infrastructure using cyberattacks (until December 2015)—and *that* would have been hard to hide. One could adduce many reasons for the dog that did not bite: maybe neither side has the requisite digital targets, or maybe Russia already has good access to Ukraine's infrastructure, or neither wants to escalate—or maybe, just maybe, cyberwar was not cost effective in terms of its contribution to warfighting. In the same vein, the bill of indictment against the five PLA hackers did not (because it could not?) cite the theft of intellectual property (the theft of business proprietary data was cited).[7] It would be nice to believe that the Chinese have concluded that the gains from stealing intellectual property and converting into a competitive product are too meager. Time may tell, although the Xi-Obama agreement may have foretold.

George Santayana famously said that only the dead have seen the end of war. Might the living survive to see the end of cyberwar? As long as there have been computers, there have been hackers who have sought to demonstrate their intelligence if not their maturity by getting such systems to do other than what their designers thought they would do. RAND's Willis Ware wrote cogently about the problem of computer security almost fifty years ago.[8] But until the Internet was open to all, the possibility of system compromise was no more than a one-star problem. To wit, a one-star flag officer or civilian equivalent would have been the appropriate person to staff out all the U.S. government's cybersecurity problems. Then the Internet happened, and people who should have known better willy-nilly connected their secrets and machines to it. This rapidly made insecurity in cyberspace a three-star problem for the U.S. government. Then a three-star problem was hyped into a four-star problem, a standing that it never deserved. Hopes that malware and related methods to usurp command and control over machines may become a thing of the past are not unfounded. If so, that would allow the threat from cyberspace to be downgraded from a three-star problem to something like a two-star problem. Unless the Internet is un-invented, cybersecurity is probably never going to revert to a one-star problem or lower. Nevertheless, even a demotion from three to two stars would be good news.

Acknowledgments

Three types of acknowledgments are in order. First is for my wife, Denise Mazorow, who put up with my mental absence (or, perhaps worse, my distracted presence) while working on the material that became this book.

Second is for my students at Georgetown University, the U.S. Naval Academy, the Columbia University School of International and Public Affairs, and the RAND Pardee Graduate School for whom this material was written and upon some of whom this material was unloaded. The continual engagement improved the contents year by year.

Third is for those who helped me shape the material (many—but not all—are fellow RAND colleagues): Lillian Ablon, Robert Anderson, John Arquilla, Ed Balkovich, Isaac Ben-Israel, Richard Betts, Dan Byman, Larry Cavaiola, Cynthia Cook, Brendan Cunningham, John Davis, Paul Davis, Jim Dobbins, Fredrick Douzet, Bob Elder, Gadi Evron, David Frelinger, Allen Friedman, Kenneth Geers, David Gompert, Colin Gray, Jeff Hagen, Mark Hagerott, Scott Harold, Ryan Henry, Andy Hoehn, Myron Hura, Chris Inglis, Brian Jackson, Stuart Johnson, James Lewis, Peter Liebert, Herb Lin, Roger Molander, Forrest Morgan, James Mulvenon, Jim Quinliven, Greg Rattray, Sasha Romanosky, Rena Rudavsky, Gary Schaub, Lara Schmidt, David Senty, Howard Shatz, Steve Simon, Jerry Sollinger, Mark Sparkman, Paul J. Springer, Donald Stevens, Paul Tortora, Francisco Walter, Henry Willis, Peter Wilson, and John Woodward.

Much of the material in this book was drawn from several RAND reports of which I was either the sole or primary author. *Cyberwar and Cyberdeterrence* (MG-877-AF, 2009) was the source of most of the material in chapters 18, 21, 22, 23, 24, and 25, much of chapters 12 and 25, and some of chapters 3, 4, 7, 13, 14, and 17. Most of the material in chapters 28 and 31 and much of chapters 27, 32, and 33 were derived from *Crisis and Escalation in Cyberspace* (MG-1215-AF, 2013). *Brandishing Cyberattack Capability* (RR-175-OSD, 2013) was the source of most of the material in chapter 30 and much of chapters 16 and 29. Also, *What Should Be Classified* (MG-989-JS, 2010) was the source of much of the material in chapter 8; and *Defender's Dilemma* (RR-1024-JNI, 2015) was the source of some of the material in chapter 11.

Notes

Introduction

1. Martin Libicki, *What Is Information Warfare* (Washington, D.C.: National Defense University Press, 1995).
2. In the years before World War I, there was a saying that in Berlin, they will tell you that the situation is serious but not desperate; in Vienna, they will tell you that it is desperate but not serious.
3. Willis Ware, "Security and Privacy in Computer Systems," P-3544, RAND Corporation, 1967.
4. Clifford Stoll, *The Cuckoo's Egg: Tracking a Spy Through the Maze of Computer Espionage* (New York: Random House, 1989).
5. National Science Foundation, "The Internet," *NSF.gov*, http://www.nsf.gov/od/lpa/nsf50/nsfoutreach/htm/n50_z2/pages_z3/28_pg.htm.
6. Barton Gellman, "Cyberattacks by Al Qaeda Feared: Terrorists at Threshold of Using Internet as Tool of Bloodshed, Experts Say," *Washington Post*, June 27, 2002.
7. Robert Lemos, "Safety: Assessing the Infrastructure Risk," *CNET*, August 28, 2002, http://news.cnet.com/2100-1001-954780.html.
8. Viola Gienger, "U.S. Military Aid to Overseas Allies May Face Cuts, Mullen Says," Bloomberg, June 14, 2011.
9. Alicia Budich, "FBI: Cyber Threat Might Surpass Terror Threat," *Face the Nation*, May 21, 2012, http://www.cbsnews.com/8301-3460_162-57370682/fbi-cyber-threat-might-surpass-terror-threat/.
10. James R. Clapper, "Worldwide Threat Assessment of the U.S. Intelligence Community," Statement before the Senate Select Committee on Intelligence, March 12, 2013, http://www.dni.gov/files/documents/Intelligence%20Reports/2013%20ATA%20SFR%20for%20SSCI%2012%20Mar%202013.pdf.
11. Dana Kerr, "'Cyber 9/11' May Be on Horizon, Homeland Security Chief Warns," *CNET*, January 24, 2013, http://news.cnet.com/8301-1009_3-57565763-83/cyber-9-11-may-be-on-horizon-homeland-security-chief-warns/.
12. Ellen Nakashima, "Foreign Powers Steal Data on Critical U.S. Infrastructure, NSA Chief Says," *Washington Post,* November 20, 2014.
13. Sean Gallagher, "Security Pros Predict 'Major' Cyber Terror Attack this Year," *Ars Technica,* January 4, 2013, http://arstechnica.com/security/2013/01/security-pros-predict-major-cyberterror-attack-this-year/.
14. One of the most sophisticated cyberespionage campaigns was undertaken by Spain; Kaspersky Lab, "Unveiling 'Careto'—The Masked APT," report, 2014, http://kasperskycontenthub.com/wp-content/uploads/sites/43/vlpdfs/unveilingthemask_v1.0.pdf.
15. Michael Riley and Jordan Robertson, "China-Tied Hackers That Hit U.S. Said to Breach United Airlines," Bloomberg, July 29, 2015, http://www.bloomberg.com/news/articles/2015-07-29/china-tied-hackers-that-hit-u-s-said-to-breach-united-airlines; Jordan Robertson and Michael Riley, "American Airlines, Sabre Said to Be Hit in China-Tied Hacks," Bloomberg, August 7, 2015, http://www.bloomberg.com/news/articles/2015-08-07/american-airlines-sabre-said-to-be-hit-in-hacks-backed-by-china; Ellen Nakashima, "Security Firm Finds Link between China and Anthem Hack," *Washington Post*, February 27, 2015; Ellen Nakashima, "With Series of Major Hacks, China Builds Database on Americans," *Washington Post*, June 5, 2015; Stephen Braun, "Official Says Hackers Hit Up to 25,000 Homeland Security Employees," *Washington Post*, August 23, 2014; Ellen Nakashima, "DHS Contractor Suffers Major Computer Breach, Officials Say," *Washington Post,* August 6, 2014; Brian Krebs, "Premera Blue Cross Breach Exposes Financial, Medical Records," *KrebsonSecurity.com,* March 15, 2015, http://krebsonsecurity.com/2015/03/premera-blue-cross-breach-exposes-financial-medical-records/; and Brian Krebs, "Data Breach at Health Insurer Anthem Could Impact Millions," *KrebsonSecurity.com,* February 15, 2015, http://krebsonsecurity.com/2015/02/data-breach-at-health-insurer-anthem-could-impact-millions/.

16. Canadian Audit Committee Network Vantage Point, "Cybersecurity and the Audit Committee," March 27, 2013, http://www.tapestrynetworks.com/initiatives/corporate-governance/north-american-audit-committee-networks/upload/Tapestry_EY_CACN_Vantage_Mar13.pdf.

Chapter 1. Emblematic Attacks

1. According to Kaspersky, the Carnabak group targeted banks in thirty countries, though primarily in Russia, and Kaspersky suspects it obtained about $1 billion. A more detailed, earlier report from Group-IB and Fox-IT claimed all attacks were in Russia and placed the damage in the hundreds of millions. See David Auerbach, "How to Fight the Next $1 Billion Bank Hack," *Slate*, February 18, 2015, http://www.slate.com/articles/technology/safety_net/2015/02/_1_billion_bank_hack_how_to_fight_the_next_one.html.

2. Timothy Lee, "How a Grad Student Trying to Build the First Botnet Brought the Internet to its Knees," *Washington Post,* November 2, 2013. For a more technical analysis, see Eugene Spafford, "The Internet Worm Program: An Analysis," Purdue Technical Report, CSD-TR-823, December 8, 1988, http://spaf.cerias.purdue.edu/tech-reps/823.pdf.

3. Amy Harmon, "Hacking Theft of $10 Million from Citibank Revealed," *Los Angeles Times,* August 19, 1995.

4. For the latter, see Dinei Florencio and Cormac Herley, *Is Everything We Know About Password-Stealing Wrong?* undated Microsoft report, http://research.microsoft.com/pubs/161829/EverythingWeKnow.pdf.

5. See Jason Healey, ed., *A Fierce Domain* (Washington, D.C.: Atlantic Council, 2014), chaps. 2 and 3.

6. See "SANS Intrusion Detection FAQ: What Is Solar Sunrise?" http://www.sans.org/security-resources/idfaq/solar_sunrise.php.

7. Julian Borger, "Pentagon Kept the Lid on Cyberwar in Kosovo," *The Guardian,* November 8, 1999.

8. Michele Masterson, "Love Bug Costs Billions," CNN, May 5, 2000, http://cnnfn.cnn.com/2000/05/05/technology/virus_impact/.

9. Timothy Thomas, "The Internet in China: Civilian and Military Uses," *Information and Security: An International Journal* 7 (2001): pp. 159–73.

10. Carolyn Meinel, "Code Red: Worm Assault on the Web," *Scientific American,* October 28, 2002.

11. This claim (without details) was made by the CIA's Tom Donahue (Thomas Claburn, "CIA Admits Cyberattacks Blacked Out Cities," *Information Week,* January 18, 2008, http://www.informationweek.com/cia-admits-cyberattacks-blacked-out-citi/205901631) and was broadcast with more details by the CBS news show "60 Minutes" ("Cyber War: Sabotaging the System," June 11, 2009, http://www.cbsnews.com/news/cyber-war-sabotaging-the-system-06-11-2009/).

12. Marcelo Soares, "Brazilian Blackout Traced to Sooty Insulators, Not Hackers," *Wired.com*, November 9, 2009, http://www.wired.com/threatlevel/2009/11/brazil_blackout/; see also Kim Zetter, *Countdown to Zero Day* (New York: Crown, 2014), chap. 19, note 1.

13. William J. Lynn III, "Defending a New Domain: The Pentagon's Cyberstrategy," *Foreign Affairs,* September/October 2010.

14. " 'We got into Buckshot Yankee and I asked simple questions like how many computers do we have on the network in various flavors, what's their configuration, and I couldn't get an answer in over a month,' U.S. Strategic Command chief Gen. Kevin Chilton told a conference last May." From Noah Shachtman, "Insiders Doubt 2008 Pentagon Hack Was Foreign Spy Attack," *Wired.com,* August 25, 2010, http://www.wired.com/2010/08/insiders-doubt-2008-pentagon-hack-was-foreign-spy-attack/. That was suspected to be true, years earlier. See C. C. Mann, "The Mole in the Machine," *New York Times Sunday Magazine,* July 25, 1999, 32–35.

15. " 'We had a cyber Pearl Harbor. His name was Edward Snowden,' [defense secretary designate Ashton] Carter said, referring to the former intelligence contractor who exposed inner workings of U.S. espionage and surveillance networks." See Craig Whitlock, "Ashton Carter, Passed Over Before, Gets Picked by Obama to be Defense Secretary," *Washington Post,* December 5, 2014.

16. See https://xkcd.com/1354/ for a quick cogent explanation by Randall Munroe of how Heartbleed worked.

17. For the original and best account, see Brian Krebs, "Sources: Target Investigating Data Breach," *KrebsonSecurity.com,* December 13, 2013, http://krebsonsecurity.com/2013/12/sources-target-investigating-data-breach/.

18. See Dan Goodin, "First Known Hacker-Caused Power Outage Signals Troubling Escalation," *Ars Technica*, January 4, 2015, http://arstechnica.com/security/2016/1/first-known-hacker-caused-power-outage-signals-troubling-escalation/. Similar malware was also found in a computer in the information technology network of Kiev's airport, which, among other functions, hosts the airports air traffic control, but it is unclear to what extent air traffic was at risk; Pavel Polityuk and Alessandra Prentice, "Ukraine Says to Review Cyber Defenses after Airport Targeted from Russia," Reuters, January 18, 2016, http://www.reuters.com/article/us-ukraine-cybersecurity-malware-idUSKCN0UW0R0.

19. The NSA's share of all international cyberespionage can only be guessed at, although if the Snowden revelations are anywhere near accurate, it may be substantial.

20. Nathan Thornburgh, "Inside the Chinese Hack Attack," *Time*, August 25, 2005.

21. Shishir Nagaraja and Ross Anderson, "The Snooping Dragon: Social-Malware Surveillance of the Tibetan Movement," University of Cambridge Computer Laboratory Technical Report 746, March 2009, http://www.cl.cam.ac.uk/techreports/UCAM-CL-TR-746.html. The actual discovery was carried out by the University of Toronto Munk Center's Citizen Laboratories.

22. Ibid., 3, 8.

23. At about the same time, Google decided that it could not tolerate China's censorship and decamped to Hong Kong. The State Department's intervention ended up conflating two issues: Chinese hacking and Chinese censorship.

24. Dan Goodin, "IE Zero-Day Used in Chinese Cyber Assault on 34 Firms," *The Register,* January 14, 2010.

25. McAfee Foundstone Professional Services and McAfee Labs, "Global Energy Cyberattacks: 'Night Dragon,'" white paper, 2011, http://www.mcafee.com/us/resources/white-papers/wp-global-energy-cyberattacks-night-dragon.pdf; see also Dmitri Alperovich, "Revealed: Operation Shady RAT," McAfee white paper, August 3, 2011, http://www.mcafee.com/us/resources/white-papers/wp-operation-shady-rat.pdf.

26. Michael Riley and Sophia Pearson, "China-Based Hackers Target Law Firms to Get Secret Deal Data," Bloomberg, January 31, 2012, http://www.bloomberg.com/news/2012-01-31/china-based-hackers-target-law-firms.html.

27. See Angela Moscaritolo, "RSA Confirms Lockheed Hack Linked to SecurID Breach," *SC Magazine,* June 7, 2011, http://www.scmagazine.com/rsa-confirms-lockheed-hack-linked-to-securid-breach/article/204744/, and Matthew Schwartz, "Lockheed Martin Suffers Massive Cyberattack," *Dark Reading,* May 30, 2011, http://www.darkreading.com/risk-management/lockheed-martin-suffers-massive-cyberattack/d/d-id/1098013.

28. Siobhan Gorman, August Cole, and Yochi Dreazen, "Computer Spies Breach Fighter-Jet Project," *Wall Street Journal,* April 21, 2009.

29. A RAND review of cost overruns on the F-35 project discovered no such reasons. Instead, the need to reduce the weight of the aircraft accounted for multiple costly redesigns. Irving Blickstein et al., *Root Cause Analyses of Nunn-McCurdy Breaches,* vol. I (Santa Monica, Calif.: RAND Corporation, 2011), chap. 4.

30. According to the Mandiant report, the "APT1 [hacker group] maintained access to victim networks for an average of 356 days. The longest time period APT1 maintained access to a victim's network was 1,764 days, or four years and ten months." The length of time that a discovered vulnerability sold on the vulnerability market remains undiscovered by anyone else is roughly that long as well; Nicole Perlroth and David E. Sanger, "Nations Buying as Hackers Sell Flaws in Computer Code," *New York Times,* July 14, 2013. Bilge and Dumitras identified eighteen vulnerabilities exploited in the real world before full disclosure. They lasted an average of 312 days before detection; see Leyla Bilge and Tudor Dumitras, "Before We Knew It: An Empirical Study of Zero-Day Attacks in the Real World," Symantec Corporation, 2012, http://users.ece.cmu.edu/~tdumitra/public_documents/bilge12_zero_day.pdf; Dinesh Theerthagiri, "Zero-Day World," *Symantec .com,* blog, October 30, 2012, http://www.symantec.com/connect/blogs/zero-day-world. See also Stefan Frei, "The Known Unknowns," report, NSS Labs, 2013. The "2014 Verizon Data Breach Investigations Report," http://www.verizonenterprise.com/DBIR/2014/, 41, found that the time to discovery of a cyberespionage attack could be measured in months or years two-thirds of the time. More recently, Fire-Eye's Richard Bejtlich observed, "The median amount of time from an intruder's initial compromise, to the time when a victim learns of a breach, is currently 205 days, as reported in our 2015 M-Trends

report. This number is better than our 229-day count for 2013, and the 243-day count for 2012." Richard Bejtlich, Statement before the U.S. House of Representatives Committee on Energy and Commerce Subcommittee on Oversight and Investigations Understanding the Cyber Threat and Implications for the 21st-Century Economy, March 3, 2015, http://docs.house.gov/meetings/IF/IF02/20150303/103079/HHRG-114-IF02-Wstate-BejtlichR-20150303.pdf.

31. "In 70 percent of cases, someone else, likely the FBI, tells a victim about a serious compromise. Only 30 percent of the time do victims identify intrusions on their own." Bejtlich, Statement before the U.S. House of Representatives.

32. See David Kravets, "FBI Director Says Chinese Hackers Are Like a 'Drunk Burglar,'" *Ars Technica,* October 6, 2014, http://arstechnica.com/tech-policy/2014/10/fbi-director-says-chinese-hackers-are-like-a-drunk-burglar/. Reportedly, President Xi Jinping called for better tradecraft after facing the June 2013 complaints of President Obama at the Sunnylands summit.

33. "What was uncommon here was that they hit all of these companies at once. Frankly, that was not particularly clever. That upped their rate of being caught," says Al Huger, vice president of engineering at Immunet; see Kelly Jackson Higgins, "Flaws in the 'Aurora' Attacks," *Dark Reading,* January 25, 2010, http://www.darkreading.com/attacks-breaches/flaws-in-the-aurora-attacks/d/d-id/1132824.

34. Homeland Security Newswire, "Twelve Chinese Hacker Groups Responsible for Attacks on U.S.," December 16, 2011, http://www.homelandsecuritynewswire.com/dr20111216-twelve-chinese-hacker-groups-responsible-for-attacks-on-u-s. A later estimate talked in terms of twenty groups. Danny Yadron, James Areddy, and Paul Mozur, "Chinese Hacking Is Deep and Diverse, Experts Say," *Wall Street Journal,* May 29, 2014.

35. Mandiant, "APT1: Exposing One of China's Cyber Espionage Units," March 2013, http://intelreport.mandiant.com/Mandiant_APT1_Report.pdf.

36. See also Nicole Perlroth, "2nd China Army Unit Implicated in Online Spying," *New York Times,* June 9, 2014, or Novetta, "Axiom Threat Actor Group Report," 2014, https://www.novetta.com/2014/10/cyber-security-coalition-releases-full-report-on-large-scale-interdiction-of-chinese-state-sponsored-espionage-effort/. Axiom seems to be what Symantec called the Elderwood Project.

37. Justin Lang and Ben Makuch, "New Documents Show Canada Fired Back Diplomatically at China over Hacking," *Vice,* May 29, 2015, https://news.vice.com/article/new-documents-show-canada-fired-back-diplomatically-at-china-over-hacking; "Merkel's China Visit Marred by Hacking Allegations," *Der Spiegel,* August 27, 2007; Robert Marquand and Ben Arnody, "China Emerges as a Leader in Cyberwarfare," *Christian Science Monitor,* September 14, 2007; Cory Bennett, "Japanese Leader Hits Chinese Hacking in Speech to Congress," *The Hill,* April 29, 2015, http://thehill.com/policy/cybersecurity/240480-abe-to-congress-no-free-riders-on-intellectual-property.

38. For instance, Yudhijit Bhattacharjee, "A New Kind of Spy: How China Obtains American Technological Secrets," *The New Yorker,* May 5, 2014, discusses operations against Boeing, and Karen Gullo, "California Man Guilty of Stealing DuPont Trade Secrets," *BusinessWeek,* March 5, 2014, http://www.businessweek.com/news/2014-03-05/california-man-convicted-of-stealing-dupont-trade-secrets-1, discusses operations against DuPont.

39. John F. Gantz et al., "The Dangerous World of Counterfeit and Pirated Software," Microsoft white paper, 2013, http://news.microsoft.com/download/presskits/antipiracy/docs/IDC030513.pdf, argues that bootleg copies are more prone to malware.

40. *Washington Post*, "The OPM Cyberattack Was a Bridge Too Far," editorial, July 5, 2015.

41. Robert Giesler, Remarks, Center for Strategic and International Studies Global Security Forum 2011, June 8, 2011, http://csis.org/files/attachments/110608_gsf_cyber_transcript.pdf.

42. See, for instance, Stephen Blank, "Web War I: Is Europe's First Information War a New Kind of War?" *Comparative Strategy* 27, no. 3 (2008): pp. 227–47. Russia denied that it was responsible, but Russia also refused Estonia's entreaties to help track down the source of the attack. Years later, Sergei Markov, a Russian Duma parliamentarian, boasted of having organized the attack: suggestive, perhaps, but hardly conclusive. See Lucian Constantin, "Two-Year-Old Cyberattack on Estonia Again in the Spotlight," *Softpedia,* March 9, 2009, http://archive.news.softpedia.com/news/Two-Years-Old-Cyberattack-on-Estonia-Again-in-the-Spotlight-106353.shtml. Yet the only person ever convicted of being part of the attack was an Estonian citizen of Russian ethnicity.

43. See Bettina Wassener, "Google Links Web Attacks to Vietnam Mine Dispute," *New York Times*, March 31, 2010. In the wake of government action against WikiLeaks, a group of anonymous users flooded sites associated with denying financial or hosting services to the site, but such attacks involved the actions of hundreds or thousands of willing participants, not bots. See John F. Burns and Ravi Somaiya. "Hackers Attack Those Seen as WikiLeaks Enemies," *New York Times,* December 9, 2010. An example is Game-Over Zeus; see Department of Homeland Security U.S. Computer Emergency Readiness Team, "Alert (TA14–150A) GameOver Zeus P2P Malware," June 2, 2014, https://www.us-cert.gov/ncas/alerts/TA14-150A.

44. Lillian Ablon, Martin C. Libicki, and Andrea Golay, "Markets for Cybercrime Tools and Stolen Data: Hackers' Bazaar," RAND Corporation report RR-610-JNI, 2014.

45. Michael Mimoso, "Hackers Using Brute-Force Attacks to Harvest Wordpress Sites," *Threat Post,* April 15, 2013, http://threatpost.com/hackers-using-brute-force-attacks-harvest-wordpress-sites-041513/77730.

46. Peter Bright, "Spamhaus DDOS Grows to Internet-Threatening Size," *Ars Technica,* March 27, 2013, http://arstechnica.com/security/2013/03/spamhaus-ddos-grows-to-internet-threatening-size/. The attack reached 300 gigabytes/second.

47. Maria Korolov, "DDoS Attack on BBC May Have Been Biggest in History," January 8, 2016, http://www.csoonline.com/article/3020292/cyber-attacks-espionage/ddos-attack-on-bbc-may-have-been-biggest-in-history.html

48. Parmy Olson, "The Largest Cyber Attack in History Has Been Hitting Hong Kong Sites," *Forbes,* November 20, 2104, http://www.forbes.com/sites/parmyolson/2014/11/20/the-largestcyberattack-in-history-has-been-hitting-hong-kong-sites/: "The distributed denial of service (DDoS) attacks have been carried out against independent news site Apple Daily and PopVote, which organized mock chief executive elections for Hong Kong. Now the content delivery network Cloudflare, which protects Apple Daily and PopVote, says the DDoS attacks have been unprecedented in scale, pounding the sites with junk traffic at a remarkable 500 gigabits per second."

49. Dan Goodin, "Meet 'Great Cannon,' the Man-in-the-Middle Weapon China Used on GitHub: Powerful Weapon Could Easily Be Used to Inject Malware Attacks into Traffic," *Ars Technica,* April 10, 2015, http://arstechnica.com/security/2015/04/meet-great-cannon-the-man-in-the-middle-weapon-china-used-on-github/.

50. Mark Bowden, "The Enemy Within," *The Atlantic*, June 2010.

51. Robert Lemos, "A Year Later, DDOS Attacks Still a Major Web Threat," *CNET News*, February 7, 2001, http://www.cnet.com/news/a-year-later-ddos-attacks-still-a-major-web-threat/.

52. In combatting the Spamhaus attack, CloudFlare "relied on Anycast, a routing technique that distributes the same IP address across 23 data centers across the world. . . . When it [the incoming message] bears signatures found in the attack traffic—for example, if it's a 3,000-byte response from an open DNS resolver—it is discarded in the CloudFlare data center. Only Legitimate Web requests are allowed to be forwarded to the Spamhaus data center." Dan Goodin, "How Whitehats Stopped the DDoS Attack that Knocked Spamhaus Offline," *Ars Technica,* March 21, 2013, http://arstechnica.com/security/2013/03/how-whitehats-stopped-the-ddos-attack-that-knocked-spamhaus-offline/.

53. Department of Homeland Security Industrial Control Systems–Cyber Emergency Response Team, "Advisory (ICSA-10-090–01) Mariposa Botnet," March 31, 2010, https://ics-cert.us-cert.gov/advisories/ICSA-10-090-01.

54. Brian Krebs, "Spam Volumes Drop by Two-Thirds After Firm Goes Offline," *Washington Post,* November 12, 2008.

55. Brian Krebs, "Rustok Botnet Flatlined, Spam Volumes Plummet," *KrebsonSecurity.com,* March 11, 2013, http://krebsonsecurity.com/2011/03/rustock-botnet-flatlined-spam-volumes-plummet/. See also Shane Harris, "The Mercenaries," *Slate,* November 12, 2014, http://www.slate.com/articles/technology/future_tense/2014/11/how_corporations_are_adopting_cyber_defense_and_around_legal_barriers_the.2.html, and Jim Finkle, "Microsoft Says Cybercrime Bust Frees 4.7 Million Infected PCs," Reuters, July 10, 2014, http://www.reuters.com/article/2014/07/10/us-cybersecurity-microsoft-idUSKBN0FF2CU20140710.

56. Internet Corporation for Assigned Names and Numbers, "Factsheet: Root Server Attack on 6 February 2007," March 1, 2007, http://www.icann.org/en/news/announcements/announcement-08mar07-en.htm.

57. For an explanation, see Craig Timberg, "The Long Life of a Quick 'Fix,'" *Washington Post*, May 31, 2015.

58. Dan Goodin, "Repeated Attacks Hijack Huge Chunks of Internet Traffic, Researchers Warn Man-in-the-Middle Attacks Divert Data on Scale Never Before Seen in the Wild," *Ars Technica*, November 20, 2013, http://arstechnica.com/security/2013/11/repeated-attacks-hijack-huge-chunks-of-internet-traffic-researchers-warn/.

59. Sean Gallagher, "How an Indonesian ISP Took Down the Mighty Google for 30 Minutes; Internet's Web of Trust Let a Company You Never Heard of Block Your Gmail," *Ars Technica*, November 6 2012, http://arstechnica.com/information-technology/2012/11/how-an-indonesian-isp-took-down-the-mighty-google-for-30-minutes/.

60. Dan Goodin, "Chinese ISP Hijacked U.S. Military, Gov Web Traffic," *The Register*, November 17, 2010.

61. Elinor Mills, "Facebook Detour Through China: Accident or Not?" *CNET*, March 24, 2011, http://news.cnet.com/8301-27080_3-20046338-245.html.

62. Paul Mozur, "China Websites Hit with Disruptions," *Wall Street Journal*, January 21, 2014.

63. Dan Goodin, "Strange Snafu Hijacks UK Nuke Maker's Traffic, Routes It Through Ukraine; Lockheed, Banks, and Helicopter Designer Also Affected by Border Gateway Mishap," *Ars Technica*, March 13, 2015, http://arstechnica.com/security/2015/03/mysterious-snafu-hijacks-uk-nukes-makers-traffic-through-ukraine/.

64. Zetter, *Countdown to Zero Day*, chap. 6, location 1762, and chap. 17, location 6252.

65. David Sanger, "Obama Order Sped Up Wave of Cyberattacks against Iran," *New York Times*, June 1, 2012.

66. Later analysis suggested that this flaw was known to others, such as hacker group Zlob (see Peter Szor, *Duqu—Threat Research and Analysis*, McAfee white paper, https://blogs.mcafee.com/wp-content/uploads/2011/10/Duqu1.pdf, 6) and at least one other person (John Borland, "A Four-Day Dive Into Stuxnet's Heart," *Wired.com*, December 27, 2010, http://www.wired.com/2010/12/a-four-day-dive-into-stuxnets-heart) who opined, "A 7-year-old could exploit this. It's bad news. Of course it turned out that this vulnerability had been known for several years by some people, but no one told me." In "Stuxnet and the Future of Cyber War" (*Survival: Global Politics and Strategy* 53, no. 1 [2011]), James P. Farwell and Rafal Rohozinsk claimed that "Stuxnet used off-the-shelf code and tradecraft. . . . Stuxnet's core capabilities and tradecraft, including the use of multiple zero-day exploits, render it more of a Frankenstein patchwork of existing tradecraft, code and best practices drawn from the global cyber-crime community than the likely product of a dedicated, autonomous, advanced research programme or 'skunk works,'" but this opinion was not widely shared.

67. The 2010 NASDAQ hack, supposedly carried out by the Russians, was said to use two zero days. The attack was disrupted, leaving behind the puzzle of what the hackers were trying to do (early suspicion focused on destruction, but later conclusions pointed more to espionage for the purposes of understanding the exchange's technology). Nor was it clear why they were willing to burn two zero days to do it. Michael Riley, "How the Russian Hackers Stole the Nasdaq," Bloomberg, July 17, 2014, http://www.bloomberg.com/bw/articles/2014-07-17/how-russian-hackers-stole-the-nasdaq.

68. Kim Zetter, "How Digital Detectives Deciphered Stuxnet, the Most Menacing Malware in History," *Wired.com*, July 11, 2011, http://www.wired.com/2011/07/how-digital-detectives-deciphered-stuxnet/all/.

69. Jon R. Lindsay, "Stuxnet and the Limits of Cyber Warfare," *Security Studies* 22, no. 3 (2013).

70. Observations confirmed in a conversation with Ralph Langner, an infrastructure security consultant.

71. There are reports that Stuxnet or something very similar was also launched against North Korea's nuclear establishment but to little effect; Kim Zetter, "The U.S. Tried to Stuxnet North Korea's Nuclear Program," *Wired.com*, May 29, 2015, http://www.wired.com/2015/05/us-tried-stuxnet-north-koreas-nuclear-program/. If true, this would point away from exclusive Israeli possession. It is also unclear what to make of Symantec's failure to find a pattern of infections associated with the sally against North Korea.

72. Tom Espiner, "Siemens Warns Stuxnet Target of Password Risk," *CNET*, July 20, 2010, http://www.cnet.com/news/siemens-warns-stuxnet-targets-of-password-risk/; Bruce Schneier, "Internet Worm Targets SCADA," *Schneier on Security*, July 23, 2010, https://www.schneier.com/blog/archives/2010/07/internet_worm_t.html; and e-mail to author from industrial control security expert Joe Weiss, August 30, 2010.

73. John Markoff, "A Silent Attack, But Not a Subtle One," *New York Times,* September 26, 2010.

74. Myrtus, or myrtle, is "an allusion to the Hebrew word for Esther. The Book of Esther tells the story of a Persian plot against the Jews, who attacked their enemies pre-emptively"; see John Markoff and David Sanger, "In a Computer Worm, a Possible Biblical Clue," *New York Times,* September 29, 2010. "Myrtus" could also stand for "MY Remote Terminal UnitS."

75. Symantec cautioned readers to avoid drawing any attribution conclusions: "Attackers would have the natural desire to implicate another party." See Nicolas Falliere, Liam O. Murchu, and Eric Chien, "W32.Stuxnet Dossier Version 1.4," Symantec report, 2011, https://www.symantec.com/content/en/us/enterprise/media/security_response/whitepapers/w32_stuxnet_dossier.pdf.

76. Christopher Williams, "Israeli Security Chief Celebrates Stuxnet Cyber Attack," *The Telegraph,* February 16, 2011; and William Jacobson, "Did Israel Just Admit to Creating Stuxnet?" *Legal Insurrection*, February 15, 2011, http://legalinsurrection.com/2011/02/did-israel-just-admit-to-creating-stuxnet/.

77. Chris Demchak, "Stuxnet: All Signs Point to Russia," *Cryptocomb.org*, 2010, http://www.cryptocomb.org/Stuxnet_%20All%20Signs%20Point%20to%20Russia.pdf); and Jason Miks, "Was China Behind Stuxnet?" *The Diplomat,* October 21, 2010, http://thediplomat.com/2010/10/was-china-behind-stuxnet/.

78. David Sanger, *Confront and Conceal: Obama's Secret Wars and Surprising Use of American Power* (New York: Crown, 2012).

79. William Broad, John Markoff, and David Sanger, "Israeli Test on Worm Called Crucial in Iran Nuclear Delay," *New York Times,* January 15, 2011.

80. Gregg Keizer, "Iran Arrests 'Spies' After Stuxnet Attacks on Nuclear Program," *Computerworld,* October 2, 2010, http://www.computerworld.com/s/article/9189218/Iran_arrests_spies_after_Stuxnet_attacks_on_nuclear_program.

81. David Albright, Paul Brannan, and Christina Walrond, "Stuxnet Malware and Natanz: Update of ISIS December 22, 2010, Report," International Institute for Science and International Security report, February 15, 2011, http://isis-online.org/isis-reports/detail/stuxnet-malware-and-natanz-update-of-isis-december-22-2010-reportsupa-href1/.

82. Symantec Security Response, "Stuxnet 0.5: The Missing Link," Symantec blog, February 26, 2013, http://www.symantec.com/connect/blogs/stuxnet-05-missing-link.

83. Elinor Mills, "Behind the 'Flame' Malware Spying on Mideast Computers (FAQ)," *CNET,* June 4, 2012, http://www.cnet.com/news/behind-the-flame-malware-spying-on-mideast-computers-faq/.

84. See Kaspersky Lab, "Resource 207: Kaspersky Lab Research Proves that Stuxnet and Flame Developers Are Connected," June 11, 2012, http://www.kaspersky.com/about/news/virus/2012/Resource_207_Kaspersky_Lab_Research_Proves_that_Stuxnet_and_Flame_Developers_are_Connected. See also Ellen Nakashima, Greg Miller, and Julie Tate, "U.S., Israel Developed Flame Computer Virus to Slow Iranian Nuclear Efforts, Officials Say," *Washington Post,* June 19, 2012: "Some U.S. intelligence officials were dismayed that Israel's unilateral incursion led to the discovery of the virus, prompting countermeasures."

85. Kelly Jackson Higgins, "Digital Certificate Authority Hacked, Dozens of Phony Digital Certificates Issued," *Dark Reading,* August 30, 2011, http://www.darkreading.com/attacks-breaches/digital-certificate-authority-hacked-dozens-of-phony-digital-certificates-issued/d/d-id/1136244.

86. Nicole Perlroth, "In Cyberattack on Saudi Firm, U.S. Sees Iran Firing Back," *New York Times,* October 23, 2012. Not everyone was convinced, at least initially; see Michael Riley and Eric Engleman, "Code in Aramco Cyber Attack Indicates Lone Perpetrator," Bloomberg, October 25, 2012, http://www.bloomberg.com/news/articles/2012-10-25/code-in-aramco-cyber-attack-indicates-lone-perpetrator.

87. Thomas Erdbrink, "Facing Cyberattack, Iranian Officials Disconnect Some Oil Terminals From Internet," *New York Times,* April 23, 2012.

88. Nicole Perlroth and Quentin Hardy, "Bank Hacking Was the Work of Iranians, Officials Say," *New York Times,* January 8, 2013.

89. Siobhan Gorman and Danny Yadron, "Iran Hacks Energy Firms, U.S. Says," *Wall Street Journal,* May 23, 2013.

90. Ben Elgin and Michael Riley, "Now at the Sands Casino: An Iranian Hacker in Every Server," *Business Week,* December 11, 2014, http://www.businessweek.com/articles/2014-12-11/iranian-hackers-hit-sheldon-adelsons-sands-casino-in-las-vegas.

91. This followed an earlier attack as reported by Chico Harlan and Ellen Nakashima, "Suspected North Korean Cyberattack on a Bank Raises Fears for S. Korea, Allies," *Washington Post,* August 29, 2011: "After

nearly half of the servers for a South Korean bank crashed one day in April, investigators here found evidence indicating that they were dealing with a new kind of attack from an old rival: North Korea. South Korean officials said that 30 million customers of the Nonghyup agricultural bank were unable to use ATMs or online services for several days and that key data were destroyed, making it the most serious of a series of incidents in recent months."

92. Kim Zetter, "A Cyberattack Has Caused Confirmed Physical Damage for the Second Time Ever," *Wired .com,* January 8, 2015, http://www.wired.com/2015/01/german-steel-mill-hack-destruction/.

93. David Fulghum, "Yugoslavia Successfully Attacked by Computers," *Aviation Week and Space Technology* 151, no. 8 (1999): p. 31.

94. The cyberattacks that Richard Clarke reported as a fact in his book are subsumed under "electronic warfare" techniques in a 2012 *New Yorker* article on the raid; see David Makovsky, "The Silent Strike: How Israel Bombed a Syrian Nuclear Installation and Kept It Secret," *New Yorker,* September 17, 2012. Also see David Sanger and Mark Mazzetti, "Israel Struck Syrian Nuclear Project, Analysts Say," *New York Times,* October 14, 2007.

95. See Ellen Nakashima, "U.S. Cyberweapons Had Been Considered to Disrupt Gaddafi's Air Defenses," *Washington Post,* October 17, 2011.

Chapter 2. Some Basic Principles

1. "Supposed to" derives from what a user wants, what its organization (employer) permits, and what its software allows (for example, that may prevent copying intellectual property).

2. In 1993, a terabyte of information cost $1 million (in retail stores). In 2003, the same terabyte cost $1,000, a doubling time of twelve months in bytes per dollar. In 2014, the same terabyte cost $35, a doubling time of twenty-seven months.

3. Not every instance of cyberwar falls so neatly into these two categories. Stuxnet, designed to cripple Iran's nuclear facilities, was not launched to coerce Iran. It was not a good example of strategic cyberwar so defined. But its purpose was not to facilitate kinetic operations, so it is not a good example of operational cyberwar so defined. It was unique in this way, but also in many others.

4. Michael McConnell, "Mike McConnell on How to Win the Cyber-War We're Losing," *Washington Post,* February 28, 2010.

5. The term *deterrence* is not always defined that way. In this work, it is the discouragement that comes from the threat of punishment. Others include within the definition the discouragement that comes from the threat that the attack will simply fail or will succeed but without results that justify the effort. Note that the word "deterrence" comes from the same root as the word "terror" does.

6. Note the controversy over Aaron Swartz, who committed suicide after having been indicted for violating the Computer Fraud and Abuse Act when he downloaded thousands of documents from JSTOR; John Schwartz, "Internet Activist, a Creator of RSS, Is Dead at 26, Apparently a Suicide," *New York Times,* January 12, 2013.

7. The terms "cybercafé" and "cyberinsurance" are already established and hence are not neologisms. For a plea against the overuse of "cyber," see Danny Yadron and Jennifer Valentino-Devries, "This Article Was Written with the Help of a 'Cyber' Machine," *Wall Street Journal,* March 4, 2015.

8. See, for instance, Craig Timberg, "A Flaw in the Design," *Washington Post,* May 30, 2015.

9. Electronics is by far the most efficient way to build systems, but computers started life as mechanical objects; Babbage's imagined-but-never-built machine would have been constructed exclusively from mechanical parts. In November 1967, a colorful article in *Life* magazine mooted the possibility of making computers from fluids flowing in glass using hydraulic pressure. In the mid-1990s, the Defense Advanced Research Projects Agency put a few million dollars into figuring out whether DNA could be used as the basis for computation.

10. Notwithstanding reports that Verizon inserts super-cookies into the exchanges to better characterize users to advertisers. Thomas Halleck, "Verizon Wireless Tracks Every Website Its Customers Visit with 'Supercookies,' Electronic Frontier Foundation Says," *International Business Times,* November 5, 2014, http://www.ibtimes.com/verizon-wireless-tracks-every-website-its-customers-visit-supercookies-electronic-1719720. The location of the ISP also matters. Some countries believe their citizens have too much access

to the Internet. They censor access to certain sites or block access to certain content. Those in these countries, notably Iran and China, do not see the same websites that others do.

11. My own social security number has probably been gathered in at least four cyberattacks: one on the University of California database (Michelle Meyers, "UC Berkeley Computers Hacked, 160,000 at Risk," *CNET,* May 8, 2009, http://www.cnet.com/news/uc-berkeley-computers-hacked-160000-at-risk/), another on the South Carolina tax records, a third on a health insurer that serves many in the Washington, D.C., area, and a fourth at OPM.

12. Ross Anderson, "Privacy versus Government Surveillance: Where Network Effects Meet Public Choice," paper presented at the Workshop on the Economics of Information Security, 2014, http://weis2014.econ infosec.org/papers/Anderson-WEIS2014.pdf. "Around 15 years ago [1999], many of these networks suddenly started running over IP [Internet protocol], as the technology was becoming universal and was much cheaper. But that meant anyone knowing a sensor's IP address could read it and anyone knowing an actuator's could operate it! This 'oops' moment led to a big push over the past decade to build fancy firewalls to re-perimeterise control networks, with mixed success." Dennis Fisher, "Researchers Find Nearly Two Dozen SCADA Bugs in a Few Hours' Time," *Threat Post,* November 26, 2012, https://threatpost .com/researcher-finds-nearly-two-dozen-scada-bugs-few-hours-time-112612/77242.

13. The 1998 Chernobyl virus attacked the computers' BIOS, making them unrecoverable, but until recently few professional hackers were known to do so. See Graham Cluley, "Memories of the Chernobyl Virus," *Naked Security,* April 26, 2011, https://nakedsecurity.sophos.com/2011/04/26/memories-of-the-chernobyl-virus/. In the last few years, changes in the BIOS associated with Intel chips have made such flashing attacks far more difficult—perhaps impossible.

14. There is a surfeit of published material about computer hacking. The more popular items include Jon Erickson, *Hacking: The Art of Exploitation,* 2nd ed. (San Francisco: No Starch Press, 2008), and Stuart McClure, Joel Scambray, and George Kurtz, *Hacking Exposed: Network Security Secrets and Solutions,* 7th ed. (New York: McGraw-Hill Osborne Media, 2012). See also the History of Computing Project, "Books on Hacking, Hackers and Hacker Ethics: An Annotated Bibliography," May 24, 2006, http://www.thocp .net/reference/hacking/bibliography_hacking.htm.

15. Two minor forms of mischief can be added. Theft of service occurs when hackers run their programs on another computer's processors, store files (for example, pornography or jihadist propaganda) on someone else's system, or ride on another network's capacity. With everything about systems becoming cheaper by the year, few people worried about theft of service until more recently, when malware was developed to use a system's processing (and battery) power to generate Bitcoins (Timothy Lee, "More Bitcoin Malware: This One Uses Your GPU for Mining," *Ars Technica,* August 17, 2011, http://arstechnica.com/tech-policy/ 2011/08/symantec-spots-malware-that-uses-your-gpu-to-mine-bitcoins/). Unauthorized adware (not to be confused with spyware, which leads to data theft) can be annoying but is otherwise harmless.

16. Clay Wilson, "Computer Attack and Cyberterrorism: Vulnerabilities and Policy Issues for Congress," Congressional Research Service, 2005.

17. Emil Protalinski, "U.S. Government Pays $250,000 for iOS Exploit," *ZDNet,* March 25, 2012, http:// www.zdnet.com/blog/security/us-government-pays-250000-for-ios-exploit/11044.

18. Fuzzing is so common that the quality of software can be expressed in terms of the number of fuzzing cycles required to find a flaw in it. Chaouki Bekrar, president of Vupen, observed, "The Firefox zero-day we used today we found it through fuzzing, but it required 60 million test cases. That's a big number . . . that proves Firefox has done a great job fixing flaws; the same for Chrome." Michael Mimoso, "Vupen Cashes in Four Times at Pwn2Own," *Threat Post,* March 12, 2014, http://threatpost .com/vupen-cashes-in-four-times-at-pwn2own/104754.

19. Bruce Schneier brought up this debate in "Should U.S. Hackers Fix Cybersecurity Holes or Exploit Them?" *The Atlantic,* May 19, 2014, http://www.theatlantic.com/technology/archive/2014/05/should-hackers-fix-cybersecurity-holes-or-exploit-them/371197/; Dan Geer revisited it in "Cybersecurity as Realpolitik," his keynote address at BlackHat 2014, http://geer.tinho.net/geer.blackhat.6viii14.txt.

20. Andrew Ozment and Stuart E. Schechter, "Milk or Wine: Does Software Security Improve with Age?" Report, Usenix, 2006, http://www.usenix.org/legacy/event/sec06/tech/full_papers/ozment/ozment .pdf.

21. Which is sometimes true; see Gavin O'Gorman and Geoff McDonald, "The Elderwood Project," Symantec, September 2012, http://www.symantec.com/connect/blogs/elderwood-project.

22. The bug was present as far back as the original release code for Windows 95; Andrea Peterson, "Microsoft Just Squashed a 19-Year-Old Software Bug. How Did It Go Undetected So Long?" *Washington Post*, November 12, 2014.

23. Eric Rescorla, "Is Finding Security Holes a Good Idea?" Paper, RTFM, Inc., 2004, http://www.dtc .umn.edu/weis2004/rescorla.pdf. Later research has established that when a vulnerability is announced, the number of different attacks rises, sometimes by several orders of magnitude; see Leyla Bilge and Tudor Dumitras, "Before We Knew It: An Empirical Study of Zero-Day Attacks in the Real World," Symantec Corporation, 2012, http://users.ece.cmu.edu/~tdumitra/public_documents/bilge12_zero_day.pdf. Heartbleed provides another example of a vulnerability that does not seem to have been exploited before having been discovered; Dennis Fisher, "Research Finds No Large Scale Heartbleed Exploit Attempts Before Vulnerability Disclosure," *Threat Post*, September 9, 2014, http://threatpost.com/research-finds-no-large-scale-heartbleed-exploit-attempts-before-vulnerabilitydisclosure/108161. Yet it was vigorously worked afterward—fortunately, to little serious effect. Bruce Schneier concluded two months after Heartbleed was announced that "in the end, the actual damage was also minimal, although the expense of restoring security was great" (Bruce Schneier, "The Human Side of Heartbleed," *Schneier on Security*, June 4, 2014, https://www.schneier.com/blog/archives/2014/06/the_human_side_.html). The public doxing of the Hacking Team (a seller of exploits) apparently liberated code that was used by North Korea to attack South Korean sites: "N. Korean Hackers Get Access to 'Unbeatable' Tools," *Chosun Ilbo*, July 22, 2015, http://english.chosun.com/site/data/html_dir/2015/07/22/2015072201500.html.

24. See, for instance, Dan Goodin, "Google Squashes Nasty Bugs that Led to Perfect-Storm Account Hijacking: Simple but Elegant Exploit Created High-Impact Threat," *Ars Technica*, November 22, 2013, http://arstechnica.com/security/2013/11/google-squashes-nasty-bugs-that-led-to-perfect-storm-account-hijacking/.

25. CERT Coordination Center and AusCERT, *Windows Intruder Detection Checklist*, Carnegie Mellon University, 2006.

26. The industry average for coding errors is 15,000 to 50,000 errors per million lines of delivered code prior to in-house testing with as few as 100 errors per million lines of code after alpha and beta testing; see Steve McConnell, *Code Complete: A Practical Handbook of Software Construction*, 2nd ed. (Redmond, Wash.: Microsoft Press, 2004). But coding *does* make a difference, and there are efforts under way, for instance, to eradicate one of the most common coding errors: buffer overflows (where overly long inputs end up inserting bytes into the middle of programs to bad effect). See Nicole Perlroth, "Reinventing the Internet to Make It Safer," *New York Times*, December 2, 2014.

27. For example, both Heartbleed and Apple's SSL flaw were absent in earlier versions. Dan Goodin, "Extremely Critical Crypto Flaw in iOS May Also Affect Fully Patched Macs," *Ars Technica*, February 22, 2014, http://arstechnica.com/security/2014/02/extremely-critical-crypto-flaw-in-ios-may-also-affect-fully-patched-macs/.

28. Kaspersky Lab, "Equation Group: The Crown Creator of Cyber-Espionage," February 16, 2015, http://www.kaspersky.com/about/news/virus/2015/equation-group-the-crown-creator-of-cyber-espionage.

29. From "Microsoft Security Intelligence Report 16," July-December 2013: "Win32/Obfuscator, the second most commonly encountered threat in 2H13, is a generic detection for programs that have been modified by malware obfuscation tools. These tools typically use a combination of methods, including encryption, compression, and anti-debugging or anti-emulation techniques, to alter malware programs in an effort to hinder analysis or detection by security products. The output is usually another program that keeps the same functionality as the original program but with different code, data, and geometry."

30. Players roll two dice and add the sum of the die faces to their running score. If neither die shows a snake-eye, they can roll again. If one die shows a snake-eye, the score for that turn reverts to zero, and the dice pass to the next player. If two dice show snake-eyes, the player's total score reverts to zero. Typically, the goal is to get to one hundred first, which is doable within a certain expected number of turns. However, were the goal higher, the number of turns required to get to two hundred is a great multiple of the turns required to get to one hundred because at some point the expected gain from rolling the dice one more

time becomes negative (if A = the additional points gained on the current turn and B = the player's score, then the expected points gained on the next roll of the dice = 8 − 10*A/36 [the odds of rolling one snake-eye] − B/36). If the player has any score over 288, the expected gain in score is negative even at the beginning of the turn. Although no score can be said to be impossible to reach, the number of turns required becomes extremely high after a while.

31. Most hardware cannot be hacked as such, but the BIOS can be electronically rewritten ("flashed"). At one point, someone had developed a (since-fixed) attack that updated a printer's firmware in ways that led to its fuser burning up. See Paul Wagenseil, "Printers Can Be Hacked to Catch Fire," *Scientific American,* November 29, 2011, http://www.scientificamerican.com/article/printers-can-be-hacked-to-catch-fire/.

32. Following a cyberattack, the National Defense University's network was reportedly taken down for an extended period to replace its hardware (see Bill Gertz and Rowan Scarborough, "Inside the Ring: NDU Hacked," *Washington Times,* January 12, 2007). On a compromise of the State Department's computers, see Danny Yadron, "Three Months Later, State Department Hasn't Rooted Out Hackers," *Wall Street Journal,* February 19, 2015.

33. In Robert Axelrod and Rumen Iliev, "Timing of Cyber Conflict," *Proceedings of the National Academy of Sciences of the United States of America* 111, no. 4 (2013).

Chapter 3. How to Compromise a Computer

1. Marissa Reddy Randazzo et al., *Insider Threat Study: Illicit Cyber Activity in the Banking and Finance Sector* (Pittsburgh, Pa.: CERT Coordination Center, Software Engineering Institute, Carnegie Mellon University, 2005).

2. Phil Stewart, "U.S. Overhauling Intelligence Access to Try to Prevent Another Snowden," Reuters, July 18, 2013, http://www.reuters.com/article/2013/07/19/us-usa-security-snowden-intelligence-idUS BRE96H18F20130719.

3. Federal News Radio, "White House Cyber Czar's Goal: 'Kill the Password Dead,' " Federal News Radio, June 18, 2014, http://www.federalnewsradio.com/241/3646015/White-House-cyber-czars-goal-Kill-the-password-dead.

4. Proper use assumes the user initiates the session where the credentials are presented (and that the session itself is protected from machine-in-the-middle attacks). The GameOver Zeus malware presents its marks with a sign-in page that captures both credentials at the same time; Josephine Wolff, "To Catch a Cyberthief," *Slate,* June 3, 2014, http://www.slate.com/articles/technology/technology/2014/06/evgeniy_bogachev_gameover_zeus_cryptolocker_how_the_fbi_shut_down_two_viruses.html.

5. See Martin Libicki et al., *Influences on the Adoption of MFA* (Santa Monica, Calif.: RAND Corporation, 2011), www.rand.org/pubs/technical_reports/TR937.html. By way of caveat, the data set of the study was relatively small and not completely random (an inherent problem of dealing with organizations of heterogeneous size and purpose).

6. The encryption algorithm has to be correctly implemented. A flaw in the SSL algorithm found in iOS products allowed hackers to conduct machine-in-the-middle attacks and thereby steal passwords. See Goodin, "Extremely Critical Crypto Flaw in iOS May Also Affect Fully Patched Macs." However, if the machine in the middle is actually a program that sits in the user's machine, or less typically in the server (in this case, the banking machine), then encryption may be defeated if the program has access to the encryption algorithm and key. Defeating that kind of machine-in-the-middle attack is more difficult. Perhaps for high-value transactions, the user can generate an encrypted message using a device that hackers cannot penetrate because, for instance, everything is hard-wired and not mutable. However, this is really a malware problem.

7. *InfoSecurity,* "DDoS-ers Launch Attacks from Amazon EC2," July 30, 2014, http://www.infosecurity-magazine.com/news/ddos-ers-launch-attacks-from-amazon-ec2/.

8. Other reflectors are the Domain Name System, which can yield an eight-fold amplification, and the Simple Network Management Protocol, which can yield an amplification of 650; Lucian Constantin, "Attackers Use NTP Reflection in Huge DDoS Attack," *Computerworld,* February 11, 2014, http://www.computerworld.com/s/article/9246230/Attackers_use_NTP_reflection_in_huge_DDoS_attack.

9. Dan Goodin, "New DoS Tool Lets a Single PC Bring Down an Apache Server," *Ars Technica,* June 8, 2012, http://arstechnica.com/security/2012/06/apache-killer-dos-tool/.

10. One such attack involved queries to overlapping addresses that permit a single client to occupy a server to the exclusion of all other business. Cisco Security Intelligence Operations, *A Cisco Guide to Defending Against Distributed Denial of Service Attacks* (undated), http://www.cisco.com/web/about/security/ intelligence/guide_ddos_defense.html.

11. See the elegant explanation by Randall Munroe, "Exploits of a Mom," http://xkcd.com/327/.

12. Cyrus Farivar, "Dutch Judge Allows Alleged 'Sophisticated' Russian Hacker to Be Sent to U.S.," *Ars Technica,* January 29, 2015, http://arstechnica.com/tech-policy/2015/01/dutch-judge-allows-alleged-sophisticated-russian-hacker-to-be-sent-to-us/.

13. Robbie Brown, "Hacking of Tax Records Has Put States on Guard," *New York Times,* November 5, 2012.

14. Kevin Poulsen, "Finding a Video Poker Bug Made These Guys Rich—Then Vegas Made Them Pay," *Wired.com*, October 7, 2014, http://www.wired.com/2014/10/cheating-video-poker/.

15. Ross Anderson, "Why Cryptosystems Fail," paper presented at the Association for Computing Machinery Conference on Computer and Communications Security, Fairfax, VA, November 1993, http://www .cl.cam.ac.uk/~rja14/Papers/wcf.pdf.

16. Ron Amadeo, "Adware Vendors Buy Chrome Extensions to Send Ad- and Malware-Filled Updates," *Ars Technica,* January 17, 2014, http://arstechnica.com/security/2014/01/malware-vendors-buy-chrome-extensions-to-send-adware-filled-updates/.

17. Dan Goodin, "Speech Recognition Hack Turns Google Chrome into Advanced Bugging Device," *Ars Technica,* January 22, 2014, http://arstechnica.com/security/2014/01/speech-recognition-hack-turns-google-chrome-into-advanced-bugging-device/.

18. According to Simon Singh, Britain had captured thousands of Enigma machines and distributed them among its former colonies, whose leaders believed that the cipher was as secure as it had seemed to the Germans. The British did nothing to disabuse them of this belief and routinely deciphered their secret communications in the years that followed. Simon Singh, *The Code Book: The Evolution of Secrecy from Mary Queen of Scots to Quantum Cryptography* (New York: Random House, 1999), 187. See also Thomas C. Reed, *At the Abyss: An Insider's History of the Cold War* (San Francisco: Presidio Press, 2005).

19. As a small company, the supplier stood to lose little other legitimate business, and cryptography is an area in which the benefits from corrupting a device are obvious. See Scott Shane and Tom Rowman, "Rigging the Game," *The Baltimore Sun*, December 10, 1995, 1A. For the company's denial, see Scott Shane and Tom Rowman, "Congress Has Tough Time Performing Watchdog Role," *The Baltimore Sun*, December 15, 1995, 23. See also Ludwig de Braeckeleer, "For Years U.S. Eavesdroppers Could Read Encrypted Messages without the Least Difficulty," *The Intelligence Daily*, December 29, 2007.

20. See David Sanger and Thom Shanker, "N.S.A. Devises Radio Pathway into Computers," *New York Times,* January 15, 2014, on the subject of supply-chain attacks vis-à-vis Iran.

21. Sean Gallagher, "Photos of an NSA 'Upgrade' Factory Show Cisco Router Getting Implant," *Ars Technica,* May 14, 2014, http://arstechnica.com/tech-policy/2014/05/photos-of-an-nsa-upgrade-factory-show-cisco-router-getting-implant/.

22. Sally Adee, "The Hunt for the Kill Switch," *IEEE Spectrum*, May 2008, http://spectrum.ieee.org/ semiconductors/design/the-hunt-for-the-kill-switch.

23. David Barboza, "Owner of Chinese Toy Factory Commits Suicide," *New York Times,* August 14, 2007.

24. Note an advertisement for the Apple III computer (http://www.aresluna.org/attached/computerhistory/ ads/international/apple/pics/annual83-someoneplease3), which boldly asked: Will someone please tell me exactly what a personal computer can do? and answered with one hundred examples, a large percentage of which were games.

25. John P. Jumper, "Jumper on Airpower: The Air Combat Command Commander Talks About the Realities of Modern Warfare," *Air Force Magazine* 83 (July 2000): p. 43.

26. See also Steven Bellovin, "Why Even Strong Crypto Wouldn't Protect SSNs Exposed in Anthem Breach," *Ars Technica,* February 5, 2014, http://arstechnica.com/security/2015/02/why-even-strong-crypto-wouldnt-protect-ssns-exposed-in-anthem-breach/.

27. Based on a CrowdStrike presentation at the 2015 RSA conference. See also FireEye, "M-Trends 2015: A View from the Front Lines," Report, 2015, https://www2.fireeye.com/rs/fireye/images/rpt-m-trends-2015.pdf.

28. Internal Revenue Service, "IRS Statement on the 'Get Transcript' Application," news release, May 26, 2015, http://www.irs.gov/uac/Newsroom/IRS-Statement-on-the-Get-Transcript-Application.

29. Internal Revenue Service, "IRS, Industry, States Take New Steps Together to Fight Identity Theft, Protect Taxpayers," news release, June 11, 2015, http://www.irs.gov/uac/Newsroom/IRS-and-Industry-and-States-Take-New-Steps-Together-to-Fight-Identity-Theft-and-Protect-Taxpayers.

30. One such malware was Wirelurker, which infected Macintosh machines to the point where "infected Macs were able to compromise non-jailbroken iPhones and iPads by abusing the trusted iOS pairing relationship and enterprise provisioning, a mechanism that allows businesses to install custom-written apps on employee devices." Dan Goodin, "Active 'WireLurker' iPhone Infection Ushers in New Era for iOS Users," *Ars Technica,* November 6, 2014, http://arstechnica.com/security/2014/11/active-wirelurker-iphone-infection-ushers-in-new-era-for-ios-users/. See also Dan Goodin, "iOS Security Hole Allows Attackers to Poison Already Installed iPhone Apps," *Ars Technica,* November 11, 2014, http://arstechnica.com/security/2014/11/ios-security-hole-allows-attackers-to-poison-already-installed-iphone-apps/, about a hack that also leveraged weaknesses in the enterprise provisioning system. The Masque-D malware worked similarly; see John Leyden, "Got an iPhone or iPad? Look Out for Masque-d Intruders," *The Register,* November 20, 2014. http://www.theregister.co.uk/2014/11/10/ios_masque_attack/.

31. "Privacy Scandal: NSA Can Spy on Smart Phone Data," *Der Spiegel,* September 7, 2013; see also Leyden, "Got an iPhone or iPad?"

32. Indeed, the Macintosh personal computer is judged by technical experts as being, if anything, slightly less secure than its Microsoft-based counterparts (it gets hacked less often but mostly because there are fewer of them, making them a less tempting hacking target); see, for instance Elinor Mills, "In Their Words: Experts Weigh In on Mac vs. PC Security," *CNET,* February 2, 2010, http://www.cnet.com/news/in-their-words-experts-weigh-in-on-mac-vs-pc-security/.

33. In a 2013 report, Symantec claimed that there were 387 documented security holes in iOS in 2012, compared to just 13 for Android. Tom Brewster, "Feeling Smug that Your iPhone Can't Be Hacked? Not So Fast . . . ," *The Guardian,* February 12, 2014. The original source for this is Symantec Corporation, "Internet Security Threat Report 2013," 18, April 2013, http://www.symantec.com/content/en/us/enterprise/other_resources/b-istr_main_report_v18_2012_21291018.en-us.pdf.

34. Alas, not always perfectly: malicious proof-of-concept apps were approved by the Apple Store, which requires all qualifying submissions to treat every other app as untrusted. Dan Goodin, "Serious OS X and iOS Flaws Let Hackers Steal Keychain, 1Password Contents," *Ars Technica,* June 17, 2015, http://arstechnica.com/security/2015/06/serious-os-x-and-ios-flaws-let-hackers-steal-keychain-1password-contents/.

35. The NSA and other intelligence agencies discovered that third-party app stores, many of them poorly secured and some of them for jailbroken devices, are the primary source of apps for many countries; see Sean Gallagher, "There's an App for That: How NSA, Allies Exploit Mobile App Stores; 'Five Eyes' Intelligence Agencies Built Tools to Spot Google, Samsung App Protocols," *Ars Technica,* May 21, 2015, http://arstechnica.com/information-technology/2015/05/theres-an-app-for-that-how-nsa-allies-exploit-mobile-app-stores/.

36. Vanja Svajcer, "Sophos Mobile Security Threat Report," 2014, 3, https://www.sophos.com/en-us/medialibrary/PDFs/other/sophos-mobile-security-threat-report.pdf?la=en.

37. The Google Android platform has comparable security features, but the Android will run apps that do not come from the Google Play store. Almost all Android malware comes from third-party distributors. Emil Protalinski, "F-Secure: Android Accounted for 97% of All Mobile Malware in 2013, But Only 0.1% of Those Were on Google Play," *The Next Web,* March 4, 2014, http://thenextweb.com/google/2014/03/04/f-secure-android-accounted-97-mobile-malware-2013-0-1-google-play/.

38. Ryan Naraine, "After Latest iPhone Hack, Charlie Miller Kicked Out of iOS Dev Program," *ZDNet,* November 8, 2011, http://www.zdnet.com/blog/security/after-latest-iphone-hack-charlie-miller-kicked-out-of-ios-dev-program/9773.

39. Verizon found virtually no iOS or Android malware for phones or iPads in the data it examined from Verizon mobile customers last year; Kim Zetter, "Verizon: Mobile Malware Isn't a Problem," *Wired.com,* April 15, 2015, http://www.wired.com/2015/04/verizon-no-mobile-malware/.

40. Charlie Osborne, "Apple's iOS Blocks Gov't Spying Efforts, Gamma's FinSpy Useless Against iPhone," *ZDNet,* August 12, 2014, http://www.zdnet.com/article/apples-ios-blocks-govt-spying-efforts-gammas-finspy-useless-against-iphone/.

Chapter 4. The Search for Cybersecurity

1. If the system does not face the outside world, then its security needs to pass a simpler test: it has to remain in a safe state despite getting any output that any computer it deals with is allowed to generate (or pass through).

2. Deirdre K. Mulligan and Fred B. Schneider, "Doctrine for Cybersecurity," report, Cornell University, May 15, 2011, https://www.cs.cornell.edu/fbs/publications/publicCybersecDaed.pdf. Software systems today are just too large and complicated to be verified using formal logic. Researchers, assisted by computers, have been able to devise formal proofs for small systems (under ten thousand lines of code), and software producers regularly employ automated checking for relatively simple properties of code and for analyzing specifications.

3. McClure, Scambray, and Kurtz, *Hacking Exposed 7.*

4. The secret resides not in the limitations of the set of printable characters (hexadecimal codes 30 to 7E), but in that the program that receives these characters does little but display (or print) them. Any 3 bytes that use the entire 256-character range of an 8-bit byte can be easily expressed with 4 bytes of printable characters—and if the program that inputs them reacts in a sufficiently complex manner (an SQL injection attack just uses printable characters, after all), then malware may have a host to infect.

5. William Jackson, "Time to Give Up on Java?" *GCN,* August 32, 2012, http://gcn.com/articles/2012/08/31/cyberye-java-time-to-give-up.aspx; see also Brian Krebs, "What You Need to Know about the Java Exploit," *KrebsonSecurity.com,* January 13, 2013, http://krebsonsecurity.com/2013/01/what-you-need-to-know-about-the-java-exploit/, and "Security Fix for Critical Java Flaw Released," *Krebson Security.com,* August 12, 2012, http://krebsonsecurity.com/2012/08/security-fix-for-critical-java-flaw-released/; Zack Whittaker, "Homeland Security Warns to Disable Java Amid Zero-Day Flaw," *ZDNet,* January 11, 2003, http://www.zdnet.com/homeland-security-warns-to-disable-java-amid-zero-day-flaw-7000009713/; Rohit Sethi and David Kennedy, "Debate: Because of Inherent Vulnerabilities, It Is Time to Ditch Java," *SC Magazine,* July 1, 2013, http://www.scmagazine.com/debate-because-of-inherent-vulnerabilities-it-is-time-to-ditch-java/article/298545/; and Michael Horowitz, "The Ugly Side of the Latest Java Updates," *Computerworld,* October 18, 2012, http://www.computerworld.com/article/2473404/application-security/the-ugly-side-of-the-latest-java-updates.html.

6. DHS, notably, made this recommendation; see Nicole Perlroth, "Serious Flaw in Java Software Is Found, Then Patched," *New York Times,* January 13, 2013. Having removed Java from two work PCs and one home PC, I have yet to discover any application that has failed to run, but many corporate applications apparently do need it.

7. Dan Goodin, "As Flash 0day Exploits Reach New Level of Meanness, What Are Users to Do?" *Ars Technica,* February 4, 2015, http://arstechnica.com/security/2015/02/as-flash-0day-exploits-reach-new-level-of-meanness-what-are-users-to-do/. Take what you will from the comments of Adobe security boss Brad Arkin: "Oracle could have saved mountains of cash and bad press if Click-to-Play was enabled before Java was hosed by an armada of zero day vulnerabilities. The simple fix introduced into browsers over the last year stopped the then zero day blitzkrieg in its tracks by forcing users to click a button to enable Java. Finding and fixing bugs isn't the way to go, it's . . . making it harder and more expensive for [attackers] to achieve an outcome." Arkin said organizations should follow suit and stop "patching every vulnerability" and instead focus on increasing the cost of exploitation, frustrating attackers. Darren Pauli, "Adobe CSO Offers Oracle Security Lesson: Go Click-to-Play," *The Register,* October 16, 2014.

8. By 2014, Java had been cleaned to where the *Cisco 2015 Annual Security Report,* http://www.cisco.com/web/offer/gist_ty2_asset/Cisco_2015_ASR.pdf, 11, could state, "The decline in Java exploits can be tied partly to the fact that there were no new zero-day Java exploits disclosed and available for adversaries to take advantage of in 2014." A zero-day vulnerability was discovered in mid-2015, though.

9. Matthew Finifter, Devdatta Akhawe, and David Wagner, "An Empirical Study of Vulnerability Rewards Programs," paper, University of California, Berkeley, undated, https://www.cs.berkeley.edu/~daw/papers/vrp-use13.pdf.

10. Usually, pwn (hacker term for a compromise)-to-own contests manage to break every system attacked, but "Left unscathed [at the 2014 Pwn-to-Own contest] was the highest single prize of the contest, $150,000 for the 'Exploit Unicorn.' This rare beast demanded a specific hack: system-level code execution on a Windows 8.1 x64, in IE 11 x64, with an Enhanced Mitigation Experience Toolkit (EMET) bypass." From Seth Rosenblatt, "All Hacking Eyes on the Prize Money at CanSecWest," *CNET,* March 15, 2014, http://www.cnet.com/news/all-hacking-eyes-on-the-prize-money-at-cansecwest/.

11. The Hacking Team discovered that the Chrome safeguards could be routed around: "A separate vulnerability in Windows, designated as CVE-2015–2387, was more directly linked to Hacking Team. . . . While the exploit results in only an escalation of privileges—and hence earned only a rating of 'important' from Microsoft—it's likely the means by which a separate Hacking Team attack exploiting Adobe Flash was able to bypass the Google Chrome sandbox. By combining the Flash exploit with the one for Windows, Hacking Team was able to break out of the security perimeter and surreptitiously install malware on targeted computers." From Dan Goodin, "MS Kills Critical IE 11 Bug After Exploit Was Shopped to Hacking Team," *Ars Technica,* July 14, 2015, http://arstechnica.com/security/2015/07/ms-kills-critical-ie-11-bug-after-exploit-was-shopped-to-hacking-team/.

12. This will require surmounting what is called the bad USB problem. Roughly half of all USB sticks, however, can be reprogrammed to emulate other USB devices that *can* insert malware into computers. See Dan Goodin, "This Thumb Drive Hacks Computers: 'BadUSB' Exploit Makes Devices Turn 'Evil,'" *Ars Technica,* July 31, 2014, http://arstechnica.com/security/2014/07/this-thumbdrive-hacks-computers-badusb-exploit-makes-devices-turn-evil/, and Andy Greenberg, "Only Half of USB Devices Have an Unpatchable Flaw, But No One Knows Which Half," *Wired.com,* November 12, 2014, http://www.wired.com/2014/11/badusb-only-affects-half-of-usbs/.

13. Peter Singer and Allan Friedman, "The 5 Biggest Cybersecurity Myths, Debunked," *Wired.com,* July 2, 2014, http://www.wired.com/2014/07/debunking-5-major-cyber-security-myths/.

14. Quoting Kevin Kelly, "New Rules for the Economy," *KK.org,* November 19, 2012, http://kk.org/newrules/newrules.

15. From Alfred North Whitehead, *An Introduction to Mathematics* (New York: Henry Holt, 1911), chap. 5.

16. According to Larry Clinton, chief executive of the Internet Security Alliance, "Contrary to popular thought, cyber security is not an [information technology] issue. . . . Obviously it has an enormous IT component to it. But the number-one threat that we have, frankly, isn't technical at all. It's people. They say in the automotive world that the biggest safety feature of any car has always been the nut behind the wheel. It is the same thing with respect to cyber systems. It's the people who are our biggest vulnerability." From Dan Parsons, "Government Still Ironing Out Role in Defending Industry from Cyber Attack," *Defense Daily,* July 15, 2015, http://www.defensedaily.com/government-still-ironing-out-role-in-defending-industry-from-cyber-attack/.

17. Adam Shostack, *Threat Modeling: Designing for Security* (Indianapolis, Ind.: Wiley, 2014), 317.

18. From Marvin Minsky, an artificial intelligence pioneer:

> Take the human vision system, for example. There is no computer today that can look around a room and make a map of what it sees, a feat that even a four-year-old is able to do. We have programs that can recognize faces, that can do some focal vision processing and recognition, but not this higher-order processing. Thus, human distance perception is a great example of a "society of mind." There is a suite of cooperating methods, such as gradients, border detection, haze, occlusion, shadow, focus, brightness, motion, disparity, perspective, convergence, shading knowledge, etc. A computer program typically has one or two ways of doing something; a human brain has dozens of different methods to use.

Renato M. E. Sabbatini, "The Mind, Artificial Intelligence, and Emotions: Interview with Marvin Minsky," undated, http://www.cerebromente.org.br/n07/opiniao/minsky/minsky_i.htm.

19. For a readable explanation, see, for instance, Steven Levy, *Crypto: How the Code Rebels Beat the Government—Saving Privacy in the Digital Age* (New York: Penguin Press, 2001).

20. The prospect that tomorrow's faster computers will permit decryption of what is secure today has persuaded certain intelligence agencies to use 192 or 256 bits (rather than 128 bits) in their symmetric keys.

21. Although the original one-way functions involved prime numbers, there are newer techniques, notably elliptical curve cryptography, that are even more difficult to reverse given the same sized key; see

Nick Sullivan, "A (Relatively Easy to Understand) Primer on Elliptic Curve Cryptography," *Ars Technica,* October 24, 2013, http://arstechnica.com/security/2013/10/a-relatively-easy-to-understand-primer-on-elliptic-curve-cryptography/.

22. Although if a weak hash is chosen, this task is not impossible. The Flame worm broke Microsoft's MD-5 hash to masquerade as a software update; Alex Sotirov, "Analyzing the MD5 Collision in Flame," paper, Trail of Bits, Inc., undated, https://www.trailofbits.com/resources/flame-md5.pdf.

23. DHS Assistant Secretary for Cybersecurity Dr. Andy Ozment testified that encryption would "not have helped in this case [the theft of several million OPM records]" because the attackers had gained valid user credentials to the systems that they attacked, likely through social engineering. And because of the lack of multifactor authentication on these systems, the attackers would have been able to use those credentials at will to access systems from within and potentially even from outside the network. Sean Gallagher, "Encryption 'Would Not Have Helped' at OPM, Says DHS Official," *Ars Technica,* June 16, 2015, http://arstechnica.com/security/2015/06/encryption-would-not-have-helped-at-opm-says-dhs-official/.

24. See, for instance, William R. Cheswick and Steven M. Bellovin, *Firewalls and Internet Security: Repelling the Wily Hacker* (Boston: Addison Wesley, 1994) and edition 5 or earlier editions of the McClure et al. *Hacking Exposed* series.

25. DHS's four largest components are Customs and Border Protection (CBP), Immigration and Customs Enforcement (ICE), the Coast Guard, and the Transportation Security Administration (TSA). CBP and ICE are both border patrol agencies. The Coast Guard protects the maritime border of the United States. Most of TSA's manpower checks passengers, luggage, and other cargo that cross between secured and cleared areas of airports. All four may be said to be in the perimeter defense business.

26. Assuming two million civilian government machines to be protected, the half-billion dollars comes out to $25 per machine per year, which is slightly more than antivirus suites cost in bulk.

27. Ellen Nakashima, "Cyber Defense Effort Is Mixed, Study Finds," *Washington Post,* January 12, 2012.

28. According to Hewlett-Packard, almost half of data breaches are caused by vulnerabilities known about for between two and four years; Hewlett-Packard, "Cyber Risk Report 2015," http://www8.hp.com/us/en/software-solutions/cyber-risk-report-security-vulnerability/.

29. Ed Bott, "The Malware Numbers Game: How Many Viruses Are Out There?" *ZDNet,* April 15, 2012, http://www.zdnet.com/blog/bott/the-malware-numbers-game-how-many-viruses-are-out-there/4783.

30. It is not clear that the NSA has not already built the detection elements of such a firewall; see Charles Savage et al., "Hunting for Hackers, N.S.A. Secretly Expands Internet Spying at U.S. Border," *New York Times,* June 4, 2015.

31. To wit, it would cost more to protect the Departments of Agriculture and Commerce together than separately. An argument could be made for a common defense if infections of one department made infections of the other more common (thus creating a public-goods or negative externality argument). But there is little evidence that one department has privileged connections to the other; both go through the overall Internet to get to one another.

32. Thus, an air-gapping strategy that works against almost everyone else may fail when used against a government agency with the resources to oversee and interfere with global supply chains, as the NSA was rumored to have done with the supply chain feeding Iran's Natanz nuclear reactor; Sanger and Shanker, "N.S.A. Devises Radio Pathway into Computers." A counterstrategy may be random commercial sourcing (for example, purchasing a PC from a random Best Buy store). Gwen Ackerman, "Hackers Can Steal Data Wirelessly from PCs that Aren't Even Online," Bloomberg, November 9, 2014, http://www.bloomberg.com/news/2014-11-19/hackers-can-steal-data-wirelessly-from-pcs-that-aren-t-even-online.html.

33. Nicole Perlroth, "Russian Hackers Targeting Oil and Gas Companies," *New York Times,* June 30, 2014.

34. Kelly Jackson Higgins, "'Energetic' Bear Under the Microscope," *Dark Reading,* July 31, 2014, http://www.darkreading.com/attacks-breaches/energetic-bear-under-the-microscope/d/d-id/1297712.

35. Was Shodan good or bad for cybersecurity? It increased the knowledge of attackers and defenders alike, but many of the more sophisticated hackers (such as Russia and China) may already have had such information. A best guess is that it helped diligent but unsophisticated defenders and lower-tier attackers and hurt the rest.

36. Simultaneity stretches the target's response capabilities. It can create confusion that has people focus in one place (such as downtown Oslo) when the larger concern is elsewhere (a camp on the island of Utoya); Michael Schwirtz, "For Young Campers, Island Turned into Fatal Trap," *New York Times,* July 23, 2011. It can also underline the strength of the attacker and give rise to fears that terrorists are everywhere. Al Qaeda's motif called for a high degree of simultaneity (even before 2001 as illustrated by the simultaneous attacks against U.S. embassies in Kenya and Tanzania).

37. This is more of a problem for disruptive or destructive attacks. The effects of an attack meant to corrupt data tend to play out over a longer period and may not be noticed until the pattern of corruption exceeds what can be explained away as random error.

38. A theoretical variant is to shine light into an infected printer; see the briefing given at BlackHat Europe 2014, October 16–17, 2014, https://www.blackhat.com/eu-14/briefings.html#side-channel-attacks-past-present-and-future.

39. See Dan Goodin, "Meet 'badBIOS,' the Mysterious Mac and PC Malware that Jumps Airgaps," *Ars Technica,* October 31, 2013, http://arstechnica.com/security/2013/10/meet-badbios-the-mysterious-mac-and-pc-malware-that-jumps-airgaps/, for a story about a virus that supposedly could transmit itself via sound waves—a hitherto underappreciated transmission mode—to what was presumed to be but was not actually an uninfected computer. With far less confusion, this feat was duplicated by German scientists with the caveat that both devices have to be within fifty meters of each other and the resulting bandwidth only reached roughly fifty bytes/second. James Vincent, "Scientists Create Computer Virus that Transfers Stolen Data Using Inaudible Sounds," *The Independent,* December 3, 2013.

40. See, for instance, Sam Machkovech, "Hacker Exploits Printer Web Interface to Install, Run Doom," *Ars Technica,* September 15, 2014, http://arstechnica.com/security/2014/09/hacker-exploits-printer-web-interface-to-install-run-doom/, or Mark Piesing, "Hacking Attacks on Printers Still Not Being Taken Seriously," *The Guardian,* July 23, 2012.

41. See Brian Krebs, "Target Hackers Broke in Via HVAC Company," *KrebsonSecurity.com,* February 14, 2014, http://krebsonsecurity.com/2014/02/target-hackers-broke-in-via-hvac-company/.

42. Charles Perrow, *Normal Accidents: Living with High-Risk Technologies* (New York: Basic Books, 1984).

43. For example, Nimmy Reichenberg, "Want Better Security? Assume You've Already Been Hacked," *Security Week,* September 14, 2012, https://www.securityweek.com/want-better-security-assume-youve-already-been-hacked, or Howard Solomon, "Assume Your Network Has Been Hacked, Says Cisco," *IT World Canada,* January 16, 2014, http://www.itworldcanada.com/article/assume-your-network-has-been-hacked-says-cisco/88397.

44. This approach was adopted in the heuristic model discussed in chapter 5 of Martin Libicki, Lillian Ablon, and Tim Webb, *Defender's Dilemma* (Santa Monica, Calif.: RAND Corporation, 2015).

45. Nancy Leveson, *SafeWare: System Safety and Computers* (Reading, Mass.: Addison-Wesley, 1995).

46. Or to quote Giovanni Vigna, a computer scientist at the University of California at Santa Barbara, "Hackers are like water; they always go for the path of least resistance. . . . If you put a plug in place, they will find another crack." Craig Timberg, "A Disaster Foretold—and Ignored," *Washington Post,* June 22, 2015.

47. Ross Anderson and Roger Needham, "Programming Satan's Computer," paper, Cambridge University, 1995, https://www.cl.cam.ac.uk/~rja14/Papers/satan.pdf. See also Ross Anderson, *Security Engineering* (Indianapolis, Ind.: Wiley, 2008).

48. David Hughes, "Brighton Bombing: Daily Telegraph Journalist Recalls," *The Telegraph,* October 11, 2009.

49. For an expanded treatment, see John Davis et al., "A Framework for Programming and Budgeting for Cybersecurity," TL-186-DHS (Santa Monica, Ca.: RAND Corporation, 2015).

50. Department of Homeland Security, "Blueprint for a Secure Cyber Future," report, 2011, http://www.dhs.gov/blueprint-secure-cyber-future.

51. Davis et al., "A Framework for Programming and Budgeting for Cybersecurity."

52. The general strategy-to-task methodology was developed at the RAND Corporation, notably by Lt. Gen. Glenn Kent, USAF (Ret.), and David Thaler. See Glenn A. Kent and David Thaler, "A New Concept for Streamlining Up-Front Planning" (Santa Monica, Calif.: RAND Corporation, 1993), and David Thaler, *Strategies to Tasks: A Framework for Linking Means and Ends* (Santa Monica, Calif.: RAND Corporation, 1993).

53. One criminal hacker group stole 1.2 billion log-in credentials from websites (Lisa Eadicicco, "Hackers in Russia Have Stolen More than a Billion Usernames and Passwords," *Business Insider,* August 5, 2014, http://www.businessinsider.com/russian-hackers-steal-usernames-passwords-2014-8). But were they equally serious losses to all the users whose passwords were compromised or websites that were hit? Many sites use passwords as ways of persuading people to pay for content, but few are so hungry for such content, so bereft of friends (from whom they could borrow passwords), and so down on their luck that they would use a stranger's password.

54. In a survey of over 10,000 U.S. companies, PwC found that while 69 percent of chief executive officers say they are either "concerned" or "very concerned" about cybersecurity issues, only 26 percent have identified which types of data they hold are the most attractive to hackers; Hayley Tsukayama, "Hackers Are Getting Better at Offense. Companies Aren't Getting Better at Defense," *Washington Post,* April 22, 2014.

55. Department of Justice Commission for the Review of FBI Security Programs, "A Review of FBI Security Programs," report, 2002.

56. The specific difficulty cited was that although two groups of agents, one in Minneapolis covering Zacarias Moussaoui and one in Phoenix, both looked at flight schools and saw something anomalous, neither communicated its concern to the other (Romesh Ratnesar et al., "How the FBI Blew the Case," *Time,* June 3, 2002). However, two weeks after September 11, the FBI asserted that it had known terrorists had been enrolled in flight schools but had had no information to indicate that the flight students had been planning suicide hijacking attacks (Steve Fainaru and James V. Grimaldi, "FBI Knew Terrorists Were Using Flight Schools," *Washington Post*, September 23, 2001, A24).

57. Lawrence Gordon and Martin Loeb, "The Economics of Information Security Investment," *ACM Transactions on Information and System Security* 5, no. 4 (2002): pp. 438–57.

58. Martin Libicki, *Conquest in Cyberspace* (Cambridge: Cambridge University Press, 2007), 114.

59. For example, as embodied in the ISO 27000 series or the NIST 800 series, notably 800–53. National Institute for Standards and Technology, Joint Task Force Transformation Initiative, "Security and Privacy Controls for Federal Information Systems and Organizations," report, 2013, http://nvlpubs.nist.gov/nistpubs/SpecialPublications/NIST.SP.800-53r4.pdf.

60. But see Quentin Hardy, "Criminal Software, Government-Grade Protection," *New York Times*, July 26, 2014.

61. See Kashmir Hill, "10 Ways to 'Fix' Cybersecurity," *Forbes,* June 18, 2014, http://www.forbes.com/sites/kashmirhill/2014/06/18/10-ways-to-fix-cybersecurity/. New York State's top financial regulator, Benjamin M. Lawsky, said, "It is abundantly clear that, in many respects, a firm's level of cybersecurity is only as good as the cybersecurity of its vendors." Jessica Silver-Greenberg and Matthew Goldstein, "After JPMorgan Chase Breach, Push to Close Wall St. Security Gaps," *New York Times,* October 21, 2014.

62. Australian Government Department of Defence, "Top 4 Mitigation Strategies to Protect Your ICT System," updated November 2012, http://www.asd.gov.au/publications/csocprotect/top_4_mitigations.htm, and "Strategies to Mitigate Targeted Cyber Intrusions," undated, http://www.asd.gov.au/infosec/top35mitigationstrategies.htm. See also James A. Lewis, "Raising the Bar for Cybersecurity," paper, Center for Strategic and International Studies, 2013, http://csis.org/files/publication/130212_Lewis_RaisingBarCybersecurity.pdf.

Chapter 5. Defending Against Attacks of High and of Broad Consequence

1. Thomas Sancton, "Anatomy of a Hijack," *Time,* June 24, 2001.

2. Such as a similar event described in Tom Clancy's fictional *Debt of Honor* (New York: Putnam, 1994).

3. Binomial distributions (also known as bell curves) can also be generated by coin flips, albeit where the number of flips is fixed and the score is the number of times it lands on heads.

4. See Aaron Clauset, Cosma Rohilla Shalizi, and M. E. J. Newman, "Power-Law Distributions in Empirical Data," *SIAM Review* 51, no. 4 (2009): p. 661.

5. In "Surviving on a Diet of Poisoned Fruit," Center for a New American Security, 2014, http://www.cnas.org/sites/default/files/publications-pdf/CNAS_PoisonedFruit_Danzig_0.pdf, Richard Danzig recommended funding "a data collection consortium that will illuminate the character and magnitude of cyberattacks against the U.S. private sector, using the model of voluntary reporting of near-miss incidents

in aviation." This assumes that near-misses increase the sensitivity to hits—in the face of psychological research that suggests the contrary: Robin Dillon-Merrill, Catherine H. Tinsley, and Matthew A. Cronin, "How Near-Miss Events Amplify or Attenuate Risky Decision Making," *Management Science Articles in Advance*, 2012, http://create.usc.edu/sites/default/files/publications/hownear-misseventsamplifyor attenuateriskydecisionmaking_0.pdf.

6. Federal Aviation Administration, "Accident and Incident Data," updated continuously, http://www.faa. gov/data_research/accident_incident/.

7. Eric Hutchins, Michael J. Cloppert, and Rohan Amin, "Intelligence-Driven Computer Network Defense Informed by Analysis of Adversary Campaigns and Intrusion Kill Chains," report, Lockheed Martin, 2010, http://www.lockheedmartin.com/content/dam/lockheed/data/corporate/documents/ LM-White-Paper-Intel-Driven-Defense.pdf.

8. For simplification purposes, rather than assuming exponential and Poisson distributions for the odds of discovery, we assume linear odds: there are only so many combinations to try. In the first case, the hacker could have tried all in two years, and the average time to success will be one year; in the second case, each of the six can be exhaustively searched in four months.

9. Broad, Markoff, and Sanger, "Israeli Test on Worm Called Crucial in Iran Nuclear Delay."

10. Such efforts remain incomplete because such determinations are difficult. For instance, in 2011, a large blackout in the U.S. Southwest (and northwest Mexico) was allowed to take place because no one's search for a single point of failure detected that the system was vulnerable to the loss of the specific high-voltage line in Arizona that tripped. Federal Energy Regulatory Commission and North American Energy Reliability Corporation, "Arizona-Southern California Outages on September 8, 2011," report, 2011, https:// www.ferc.gov/legal/staff-reports/04-27-2012-ferc-nerc-report.pdf.

11. Robert Lemos, "iOS Weaknesses Allow Attacks Via Trojan Chargers," *Dark Reading*, August 1, 2013, http://www.darkreading.com/mobile/ios-weaknesses-allow-attacks-via-trojan/240159321.

12. "[DHS] advisories concern vulnerabilities in the communication protocol used by power and water utilities to remotely monitor control stations around the country. Using those vulnerabilities, an attacker at a single, unmanned power substation could inflict a widespread power outage." Nicole Perlroth, "Electrical Grid Is Called Vulnerable to a Power Shutdown," *New York Times*, October 18, 2013.

13. For instance, Google's bug bounty program will not pay a reward for "Bugs requiring exceedingly unlikely user interaction. For example, a cross-site scripting flaw that requires the victim to intentionally type in an XSS [cross-site scripting] payload into a search field in Google Maps may have negligible impact in all practical cases." Google, "Google Vulnerability Reward Program (VRP) Rules," undated, http:// www.google.com/about/appsecurity/reward-program/.

14. David Sanger and Steven Erlanger, "Suspicion Falls on Russia as 'Snake' Cyberattacks Target Ukraine's Government," *New York Times*, March 8, 2014. See also the reference to a Russian group's recycling of tools since 2007 from Danny Yadron, "Popular Software Gives Hackers Easy Targets, DOD Official Says," *Wall Street Journal*, October 28, 2014.

15. Dennis Fisher, "Black Energy Malware May Be Exploiting Patched WinCC Flaw," *Threat Post*, December 11, 2014, https://threatpost.com/black-energy-malware-may-be-exploiting-patched-wincc-flaw/109835.

16. Kaspersky Lab, "Regin: A Malicious Platform Capable of Spying on GSM Networks," report, November 24, 2014, http://www.kaspersky.com/about/news/virus/2014/Regin-a-malicious-platform-capable-of-spying-on-GSM-networks.

17. Dan Goodin, "How 'Omnipotent' Hackers Tied to NSA Hid for 14 Years—And Were Found at Last," *Ars Technica*, February 16, 2014, http://arstechnica.com/security/2015/02/how-omnipotent-hackers-tied-to-the-nsa-hid-for-14-years-and-were-found-at-last/.

18. See David Sanger and Nicole Perlroth, "Hackers from China Resume Attacks on U.S. Targets," *New York Times*, May 19, 2013, as well as John Reed, "China's Hackers Are Still at It; Iran's Are Getting Better," *Foreign Policy*, May 21, 2013, https://foreignpolicy.com/2013/05/21/chinas-hackers-are-still-at-it-irans-are-getting-better/, citing Richard Bejtlich; later Mandiant reports suggest that full recovery may have taken closer to a year.

19. A third alternative of having ISPs create well-instrumented honey systems will probably not fool the hackers that are talented and dedicated enough to research their targets thoroughly before the first malware is deployed.

20. For instance, once a threshold number of car owners in a city had installed the Lojack car-theft prevention system, auto theft plummeted as the stolen car trade became too hazardous; Ian Ayres and Steven Levitt, "Measuring Positive Externalities from Unobservable Victim Precaution: An Empirical Analysis of Lojack," National Bureau of Economic Research Working Paper No. W5928, 1998.

21. Kim Zetter, "Prison Computer 'Glitch' Blamed for Opening Cell Doors in Maximum-Security Wing," *Wired.com,* August 16, 2013, http://www.wired.com/2013/08/computer-prison-door-mishap/.

22. See, for instance, Ira Winkler, "6 Failures that Led to Target Hack," *Computerworld,* February 12, 2014, http://www.computerworld.com/article/2487616/cybercrime-hacking/ira-winkler--6-failures-that-led-to-target-hack.html, or Michael Riley et al., "Missed Alarms and 40 Million Stolen Credit Card Numbers: How Target Blew It," Bloomberg, March 13, 2014, http://www.bloomberg.com/bw/articles/2014-03-13/target-missed-alarms-in-epic-hack-of-credit-card-data.

23. Hutchins, Cloppert, and Amin, "Intelligence-Driven Computer Network Defense," 2010.

24. My interpretation of the first page of Anderson, "Why Cryptosystems Fail."

25. Aircraft design (at this point) is highly systematized. The United States has two bureaucracies attending to the problem (the NTSB and Federal Aviation Administration, which oversees aircraft construction), plus a very large buyer (DoD) with its own performance standards. Even by 1950, aircraft makers had consolidated into large organizations that internalized and passed down how to design safe aircraft. Furthermore, by the 1960s, experimentation in passenger aircraft had ended.

26. Tyler Moore and Richard Clayton, "The Consequence of Non-Cooperation in the Fight against Phishing," *Proceedings of the Anti-Phishing Working Group eCrime Researchers Summit,* 2008, 1–14.

27. Christopher Strohm, "Hacker-Threat Sharing Has Companies Waiting Amid Breaches," Bloomberg, April 24, 2014, http://www.bloomberg.com/news/articles/2014-04-24/hacker-threat-sharing-has-companies-waiting-amid-breaches; a Ponemon survey found that about 71 percent of security experts say there should be a better way to share threat intelligence, and 61 percent say doing so could have prevented a cyberattack their company experienced.

Chapter 6. What the Government Can and Cannot Do

1. Barack Obama, "Transcript of President Obama's Jan. 17 Speech on NSA Reforms," *Washington Post,* January 17, 2014.

2. Tom Brewster, "U.S. Cybercrime Laws Being Used to Target Security Researchers," *The Guardian,* May 29, 2014; and Electronic Frontier Foundation, "The Computer Fraud and Abuse Act Hampers Security Research," February 13, 2013, https://www.eff.org/files/filenode/cfaa-security-researchers.pdf. Charlie Miller (who has demonstrated the ease with which certain automobiles can be hacked from afar) "and other researchers are pushing for an exemption to digital copyright laws to protect them while they work. Automakers say they own the computer code in their cars, meaning that researchers could be charged under piracy laws when they download it and make alterations." Craig Timberg, "Hacks on the Highway: Automakers Rush to Add Wireless Features, Leaving Our Cars Open to Hackers," *Washington Post,* July 22, 2015.

3. Especially with a decision by a court in Minnesota (where Target is headquartered); Nicole Perlroth, "Banks' Lawsuits Against Target for Losses Related to Hacking Can Continue," *New York Times,* December 4, 2014.

4. See Hal Varian, "System Reliability and Free-Riding," in *Economics of Information Security,* ed. L. Jean Camp and Stephen Lewis (New York: Springer, 2004), 1–15.

5. Ross Anderson and Shailendra Fuloria, "Security Economics and Critical National Infrastructure," Cambridge University, 2009, http://www.cl.cam.ac.uk/~rja14/Papers/econ-cni09.pdf, 3–5.

6. Bipartisan Policy Center, "Cybersecurity and the North American Electric Grid: New Policy Approaches to Address an Evolving Threat," report, 2014, http://bipartisanpolicy.org/wp-content/uploads/sites/default/files/Cybersecurity%20Electric%20Grid%20BPC.pdf.

7. As President Reagan's former Council of Economic Advisers chairman Martin Feldstein has argued; Martin Feldstein, "Everyone Should Pay for Cyber Defense," *Wall Street Journal,* April 22, 2012.

8. See, for instance, three pieces by Ross Anderson, "Why Cryptosystems Fail;" "Why Information Security is Hard—An Economic Perspective," Cambridge University, 2001, https://www.acsac.org/2001/papers/110.pdf; and "The Economics of Information Security," *Science,* October 27, 2006.

9. Network effects, which pervade the world of information technology, arise when products such as operating systems are embedded in and supported by a rich ecology of compatible upstream and downstream services, which makes it especially hard for challengers to gain a foothold. For instance, those who would contemplate buying an operating system for their computer that is *not* Microsoft Windows (circa 1998) know that they would start off with a smaller choice of compatible applications. Application vendors choosing which operating system to build their products to support would gravitate toward Microsoft Windows because of its large installed base. These two choices reinforce one another. The seminal description of modern network effects is Brian Arthur, "Increasing Returns and the New World of Business," *Harvard Business Review,* July 1996, https://hbr.org/1996/07/increasing-returns-and-the-new-world-of-business.

10. Goods whose qualities are hard to evaluate are subject to lemon economics. Consider two types of used cars: good ones and lemons. The owner, but not the buyer, knows which is which. The buyer's best guess is that whatever he sees is an average car. Owners of good cars, facing skeptical buyers, realize that buyers will not see the quality of what they would offer and therefore not pay the owner what the car is worth; the owner keeps his car off the market. What are left are middling-to-poor cars (because there are no good cars being sold). Buyers know as much and therefore bid as if the cars were middling-to-poor. At that point, average cars do not even get the bids they deserve. They too are withdrawn from the market, and the quality of cars gets worse, causing buyers to bid low, and so on until only lemons are left. From George A. Akerlof, "The Market for 'Lemons': Quality Uncertainty and the Market Mechanism," *Quarterly Journal of Economics* 84, no. 3 (1970): pp. 488–500.

11. Axel Arnbak et al., "Security Collapse in the HTTPS Market: Assessing Legal and Technical Solutions to Secure HTTPS," *Queue* 12, no. 8 (2014): pp. 30–43. See also Dan Goodin, "Sites Certified as Secure Often More Vulnerable to Hacking, Scientists Find," *Ars Technica,* December 4, 2014, http://arstechnica.com/security/2014/12/sites-certified-as-secure-often-morevulnerable-to-hacking-scientists-find/.

12. See Eva Galperin, Seth Schoen, and Peter Eckersley, "A Post Mortem on the Iranian DigiNotar Attack," Electronic Frontier Foundation, September 13, 2011, https://www.eff.org/deeplinks/2011/09/post-mortem-iranian-diginotar-attack; and Peter Bright, "Comodo Hacker: I Hacked DigiNotar Too; Other CAs Breached," *Ars Technica,* September 6, 2011, http://arstechnica.com/security/2011/09/comodo-hacker-i-hacked-diginotar-too-other-cas-breached/.

13. See, for instance, Daniel Geer et al., "Cyber Insecurity: The Cost of Monopoly—How the Dominance of Microsoft's Products Poses a Risk to Security," report, September 27, 2003. http://cryptome.org/cyber insecurity.htm, http://cryptome.org/cyberinsecurity.htm.

14. Eric Raymond, "The Cathedral and the Bazaar," online book, February 18, 2010, http://www.catb.org/esr/writings/cathedral-bazaar/.

15. Lucian Constantin, "Software Applications Have on Average 24 Vulnerabilities Inherited from Buggy Components," *PC World,* June 16, 2015, http://www.pcworld.com/article/2936572/software-applications-have-on-average-24-vulnerabilities-inherited-from-buggy-components.html.

16. The "Core Infrastructure Initiative" was founded with an initial $6 million of funding by the Linux Foundation with backing from major tech giants such as Facebook, Intel, and Microsoft after the Heartbleed saga; Alastair Stevenson, "Heartbleed: Linux Foundation Hires Dynamic Duo to Fix OpenSSL," *V3,* May 30, 2014, http://www.v3.co.uk/v3-uk/news/2347497/heartbleed-linux-foundation-hires-dynamic-duo-to-fix-openssl.

17. Robert McMillan, "The Internet Is Broken, and Shellshock Is Just the Start of our Woes," *Wired.com,* September 29, 2014, http://www.wired.com/2014/09/shellshocked-bash/.

18. Lucian Constantin, "Vulnerabilities Found in More Command-Line Tools, wget and tnftp Get Patches," *PC World,* October 30, 2014, http://www.pcworld.com/article/2841592/vulnerabilities-found-in-more-commandline-tools-wget-and-tnftp-get-patches.html.

19. "Xi Who Must Be Obeyed," *Economist.com,* September 20, 2014, http://www.economist.com/news/leaders/21618780-most-powerful-and-popular-leader-china-has-had-decades-must-use-these-assets-wisely-xi, notes that he "has taken charge of secretive committees responsible for reforming government, overhauling the armed forces, finance and cyber-security."

20. President's Commission on Critical Infrastructure Protection, "Critical Foundations: Protecting America's Infrastructures," 1997, https://fas.org/sgp/library/pccip.pdf.

21. Department of Homeland Security, "The National Strategy to Secure Cyberspace," 2003, https://www.us-cert.gov/sites/default/files/publications/cyberspace_strategy.pdf.

22. The publicly released (unclassified) version can be found at https://www.whitehouse.gov/issues/foreign-policy/cybersecurity/national-initiative.

23. Found in http://www.whitehouse.gov/cyberreview/documents/.

24. The for-comment (September 2002) version of the strategy can be found at http://www.giac.org/paper/gsec/2875/national-strategy-secure-cyberspace-in-depth-review/104847.

25. Barack Obama, "National Strategy for Trusted Identities in Cyberspace," April 2011, http://www.whitehouse.gov/sites/default/files/rss_viewer/NSTICstrategy_041511.pdf; Department of Homeland Security, "National Cyber Incident Response Plan (Interim Version)," September 2010, http://www.federalnewsradio.com/pdfs/NCIRP_Interim_Version_September_2010.pdf.

26. As proposed by Doug Lichtman and Eric Posner, "Holding Internet Service Providers Accountable," 14 *Supreme Court Economics Review* 221 (2006): pp. 233–34.

27. Michael J. Assante in testimony before the Subcommittee on Emerging Threats, Cybersecurity, and Science and Technology, House Committee on Homeland Security, July 21, 2009.

28. In late 2008, malware was found in a popular series of digital picture frames; see Elinor Mills, "Latest Problem Import? Infected Digital Photo Frames," *CNET,* January 8, 2009, http://www.cnet.com/news/latest-problem-import-infected-digital-photo-frames/. This may have been a supply chain attack, but it is possible that the code for the digital picture frame was compiled on a machine that itself had a virus, unbeknownst to those developing the software. The source of faults may range from laziness and cockiness to calculation (as a back door to "repossess" systems when payments fall behind) and malice.

29. First, although such devices need not be made in the country that wants to corrupt them, it makes it much easier to insert malware into them. Second, capturing the queered device and selling it to unsuspecting users does little good if the activation instructions are encrypted by the original attacker.

30. Recent advocates of a government program include Brian Krebs, "The Case for a Compulsory Bug Bounty," *KrebsonSecurity.com,* December 13, 2013, http://krebsonsecurity.com/2013/12/the-case-for-a-compulsory-bug-bounty/; Stefan Frei and Francisco Artes, "International Vulnerability Purchase Program: Why Buying all Vulnerabilities above Black Market Prices is Economically Sound," NSS Labs report, 2013, https://www.nsslabs.com/sites/default/files/public-report/files/International%20Vulnerability%20Purchase%20Program%20%28IVPP%29-1.pdf; Dennis Fisher, "The Case for a Government Bug Bounty Program," *Threat Post,* May 31, 2013, http://www.threatpost.com/the-case-for-a-government-bug-bounty-program; and Dan Geers, cited in Howard Solomon, "U.S. Should Outspend Anyone on Bug Bounties, Black Hat Conference Told," *IT World Canada,* August 7, 2014, http://www.itworldcanada.com/post/u-s-should-outspend-anyone-on-bug-bounties-black-hat-conference-told. See also Sandro Gaycken and Felix Linder, "Zero-Day Governance: An (Inexpensive) Solution to the Cyber-security Problem," 2012, http://www.cyberdialogue.citizenlab.org/wp-content/uploads/2012/2012papers/CyberDialogue2012_gaycken-lindner.pdf, which argues for an intensive publicly funded search for zero days.

31. Google's program, which is considered generous, topped out (in 2013) at a $20,000 reward. Microsoft, which until 2013 offered no bug bounties, has recently stepped in with rewards that could conceivably exceed $100,000; Tony Bradley, "Microsoft Bug Bounty Program Puts Big Bucks on the Line," *Forbes,* June 19, 2013, www.forbes.com/sites/tonybradley/2013/06/19/microsoft-bug-bounty-program-putsbig-bucks-on-the-line/. See also https://bugcrowd.com/list-of-bug-bounty-programs/. By contrast, the price of zero days in some relatively secure software (Chrome, iOS) may reach $250,000; Andy Greenberg, "Shopping for Zero-Days: A Price List for Hackers' Secret Software Exploits," *Forbes,* March 23, 2012, http://www.forbes.com/sites/andygreenberg/2012/03/23/shopping-for-zero-days-an-price-list-for-hackers-secret-software-exploits/. For United Airlines, see "Hackers of the World: United," *Economist,* July 15, 2015, http://www.economist.com/blogs/gulliver/2015/07/airline-security.

32. Conditions may have changed enough since 2005 to invalidate much but not all of the Rescorla argument. Some speculate that future patches to Windows 7/8 can be reverse-engineered to discover vulnerabilities that may also exist in Windows XP, which stopped being maintained after April 2014; see, for instance, Gregg Keizer, "Windows XP Die-Hards Can Slash Attack Risk by Dumping IE," *Computerworld,* May 12, 2014, http://www.computerworld.com/s/article/9248277/

Windows_XP_die_hards_can_slash_attack_risk_by_dumping_IE. Finally, as reported (Andrew Auern-heimer, "Forget Disclosure—Hackers Should Keep Security Holes to Themselves," *Wired.com,* November 29, 2012, http://www.wired.com/2012/11/hacking-choice-and-disclosure/), "researcher Dan Guido reverse-engineered all the major malware toolkits used for mass exploitation (such as Zeus, SpyEye, Clampi, and others) [and concluded that] the so-called whitehats of the world have been playing a role in distributing digital arms. . . . [A]ll of the exploits came from 'Advanced Persistent Threats' (an indus-try term for nation states) or from white hat disclosures . . . Criminals actually 'prefer white hat code,' according to Guido, because it works far more reliably than code provided from underground sources. Many malware authors actually lack the sophistication to alter even existing exploits to increase their effectiveness."

33. Except maybe the companies themselves, their employees, and the latter's friends and relatives. Why pay companies to find vulnerabilities in their own products if the reward structure encourages them to create such vulnerabilities in the first place? Finally, those who sell the vulnerability to the government must promise not to sell it to hackers hoping to exploit it before a patch is released.

34. Dan Guido argues in favor of differentiating the discovery of vulnerabilities in software in which bugs are sparse, hence exhaustible, from the discovery of vulnerabilities in software in which bugs are dense, hence nearly inexhaustible; Dan Guido, "Software Security, Disclosure, and Bug Bounties," *Seclists.org,* November 23, 2014, http://seclists.org/dailydave/2014/q4/50.

35. Software makers have strenuously and successfully opposed mandatory indemnification for poorly per-forming products; see Todd Bishop, "Should Microsoft Be Liable for Bugs?" *Seattle Post-Intelligencer,* Sep-tember 12, 2003; Michael A. Cusumano, "Who Is Liable for Bugs and Security Flaws in Software?" *Communications of the ACM* 47, no. 3 (March 2004); Ira Sager and Jay Greene, "Commentary: The Best Way to Make Software Secure: Liability," *BusinessWeek,* March 18, 2002, http://www.bloomberg.com/bw/stories/2002-03-17/commentary-the-best-way-to-make-software-secure-liability; Bruce Schneier, "Information Security: How Liable Should Vendors Be?" *Computerworld,* October 28, 2004, https://www.schneier.com/essays/archives/2004/10/information_security.html; and Chris Gonsalves, "Security Quandary: Who's Liable?" *eWeek,* February 25, 2002, http://www.eweek.com/c/a/Security/Security-Quandary-Whos-Liable.

36. Presidential Policy Directive 21 defines sixteen sectors, including commercial buildings; Office of the Press Secretary, "Presidential Policy Directive—Critical Infrastructure Security and Resil-ience," news release, February 12, 2013, https://www.whitehouse.gov/the-press-office/2013/02/12/presidential-policy-directive-critical-infrastructure-security-and-resil.

37. "Official: Greatest Cyber Risks to National Security Involve Handful of Sectors," *Inside Cybersecurity,* June 22, 2015, http://insidecybersecurity.com/Cyber-General/Cyber-Public-Content/official-greatest-cyber-risks-to-national-security-involve-handful-of-sectors/menu-id-1089.html.

38. See, for instance, National Institute for Standards and Technology, Joint Task Force Transformation Ini-tiative, "Security and Privacy Controls for Federal Information Systems and Organizations."

39. See Kelly Jackson Higgins, "Underwriters Laboratories to Launch Cyber Security Certification Pro-gram," *Dark Reading,* July 6, 2015, http://www.darkreading.com/endpoint/underwriters-laboratories-to-launch-cyber-security-certification-program/d/d-id/1321202.

40. See, for instance, Cory Bennett, "Demand for Cyber Insurance Skyrockets," *The Hill,* January 15, 2015, http://thehill.com/policy/cybersecurity/229568-skyrocketing-demand-seen-for-cybersecurity-insurance.

41. See Ellen Nakashima, "U.S. Rallied 120 Nations in Response to 2012 Cyberattack on American Banks," *Washington Post,* April 11, 2014.

42. Eric Talbot Jensen, "Computer Attacks on Critical National Infrastructure: A Use of Force Invoking the Right of Self-Defense," *Stanford Journal of International Law* 38 (2002): pp. 207–40, argues the efficacy and essentiality of active defense as a protection mechanism.

43. Assuming the attacker had the foresight to anticipate an attack and arranged signaling methods and alter-native servers that permitted continued operations if the primary server were taken out.

44. Within the Linux community, someone came up with a "friendly" worm whose function was to search the Internet and destroy a known "unfriendly" worm (Bryan Barber, "Cheese Worm: Pros and Cons of

a 'Friendly' Worm," SANS Institute, 2001, http://www.sans.org/reading-room/whitepapers/malicious/cheese-worm-pros-cons-friendly-worm-31). His efforts were not applauded. While it would not be totally impossible for someone to invent a virus that hunts down and disables bots, unsuspecting users whose machines had hosted the bots may consider this to be an attack in and of itself.

45. "Under Australia's iCode program, ISPs redirect Web requests from systems suspected of having bot malware to a website with tools to remove malware. Users discover their system has been 'disconnected' when they try to use their Web browser. The iCode system now is in use by 30 ISPs in Australia, covering 90 percent of Internet users there." See Sean Gallagher, "Is an ISP Code of Conduct the Best Way to Fight Botnets?" *Ars Technica,* September 22, 2011, http://arstechnica.com/business/2011/09/us-government-looks-to-fight-botnets-with-isp-code-of-conduct/.

46. See, for instance, Richard Bejtlich, "Five Reasons 'dot-secure' Will Fail," September 25, 2010, http://taosecurity.blogspot.com/2010/09/five-reasons-dot-secure-will-fail.html.

47. Brian Montopoli, "Obama: Malia Asked, "Did You Plug the Hole Yet, Daddy?" *CBS News,* May 28, 2010, http://www.cbsnews.com/news/obama-malia-asked-did-you-plug-the-hole-yet-daddy/.

48. Chris C. Demchak and Peter Dombrowski, "Rise of a Cybered Westphalian Age," *Strategic Studies Quarterly* 32 (2011): pp. 38–39, http://www.au.af.mil/au/ssq/2011/spring/demchak-dombrowski.pdf, suggests that attempts to hold militaries responsible for protecting national systems from cyberattack may be the rule.

49. But again, the fear factor lives on: "The Islamist militants who have seized almost a third of Iraq and Syria pose the next great cyber threat as terrorist organisations hoard cyber weaponry from underground markets, the chief executive of FireEye has warned." From Hannah Kuchler, "Warning Over Isis Cyber Threat," *Financial Times,* September 18, 2014, http://www.ft.com/intl/cms/s/0/92fb509c-3ee7-11e4-adef-00144feabdc0.html#axzz3Jtl6ZKt7.

50. White House Office of the Press Secretary, "Remarks as Prepared for Delivery by Assistant to the President for Homeland Security and Counterterrorism Lisa O. Monaco: Strengthening our Nation's Cyber Defenses," news release, February 11, 2015, https://www.whitehouse.gov/the-press-office/2015/02/11/remarks-prepared-delivery-assistant-president-homeland-security-and-coun.

51. Steve Ragan, "FireEye Customers Get Liability Shield Thanks to SAFETY Act," *CSO Online,* May 1, 2015, http://www.csoonline.com/article/2916649/disaster-recovery/fireeye-customers-get-liability-shield-thanks-to-safety-act.html.

52. James McGregor, "Why the Best and Brightest in China and the United States Have the Most to Lose from a Cyber-related Conflict Between the Two Countries," *The Atlantic,* April 27, 2013, http://www.theatlantic.com/china/archive/2013/04/is-the-specter-of-a-cyber-cold-war-real/275352/.

53. See, for instance, John P. Abizaid, Rosa Brooks, and Rachel Stohl, "Recommendations and Report of the Task Force on U.S. Drone Policy," Stimson Center, June 2014.

54. See Robert McMillan, "Egypt Goes Dark as Last Internet Company Pulls the Plug," *Computerworld,* January 31, 2011, http://www.computerworld.com/article/2512823/internet/egypt-goes-dark-as-last-internet-company-pulls-the-plug.html.

55. Roughly 38 percent of all computers are infected worldwide (Europol, *EU Serious and Organized Crime Threat Assessment,* 2013, https://www.europol.europa.eu/sites/default/files/publications/socta2013.pdf, 28). The figure for China is approximately 50 percent; Xinhua News Service, "Over 50% of Computers in China Have Infections," *WantChinaTimes,* September 17, 2014, http://www.wantchinatimes.com/news-subclass-cnt.aspx?id=20140917000100&cid=1103&MainCatID=0.

56. See Craig Timberg, Ellen Nakashima, and Danielle Douglas-Gabriel, "Cyberattacks Trigger Talk of 'Hacking Back,'" *Washington Post,* October 9, 2014, and Kevin Coleman, "Returning Cyber Fire," *C⁴ISR*, October 13, 2014, http://www.c4isrnet.com/article/20141013/C4ISRNET18/310130003/Returning-cyber-fire. Also, the Commission on the Theft of American Intellectual Property, led by Dennis C. Blair and Jon M. Huntsman, Jr., recommended "that Congress and the administration authorize aggressive cyber actions against cyber IP thieves. Currently, Internet attacks against hackers for purposes of self-defense are as illegal under U.S. law as the attacks by hackers themselves. . . . [I]f counterattacks against hackers were legal, there are many techniques that companies could employ that would cause severe damage to the capability of those conducting IP theft." The IP Commission, Commission on the

Theft of American Intellectual Property, "The IP Commission Report," 2013, http://www.ipcommission
.org/report/IP_Commission_Report_052213.pdf, 83.

57. Charlie Osborne, "Georgia Turns the Tables on Russian Hacker," *ZDNet,* October 30, 2012, http://
www.zdnet.com/georgia-turns-the-tables-on-russian-hacker-7000006611/. The target planted malware
in a file that the hacker took. The hacker's computer was infected when the file was opened. The computer's webcam then turned on and photographed the presumed hacker.

58. Peter Bright, "Anonymous Speaks: The Inside Story of the HBGary Hack," *Ars Technica,* February 15, 2011,
http://arstechnica.com/tech-policy/2011/02/anonymous-speaks-the-inside-story-of-the-hbgary-hack/.

59. Nate Anderson, "How Georgia Doxed a Russian Hacker (and Why It Matters)," *Ars Technica,* November
2, 2012, http://arstechnica.com/tech-policy/2012/11/how-georgia-doxed-a-russian-hacker-and-why-
it-matters/.

60. The argument here is taken from Martin Libicki, David Senty, and Julia Pollack, *Hackers Wanted: An
Examination of the Cybersecurity Labor Market* (Santa Monica, Calif.: RAND Corporation, 2014), http://
www.rand.org/pubs/research_reports/RR430.html.

61. See Seth Rosenblatt, "Ten-Year-Old Hacker Finds Zero-Day Flaw in Games," *CNET,* August 7, 2011,
http://download.cnet.com/8301-2007_4-20089152-12/10-year-old-hacker-finds-zero-day-flaw-in-
games/. See also Elinor Mills, "Teen Finds Bugs in Google, Facebook, Apple, Microsoft Code," *CNET,*
February 2, 2012, http://www.cnet.com/news/teen-finds-bugs-in-google-facebook-apple-microsoft-
code/, about 15-year-old Cim Stordal, or Gu Liping, "Youngest Chinese Hacker Is a Teenager," *ECNS,*
September 28, 2014, http://www.ecns.cn/2014/09-28/136597.shtml, about 12-year-old Wang Zheng-
yang, who reportedly helped fix around one hundred system bugs.

62. It has been broadly observed that the lone brilliant hacker is not necessarily the best acquisition for a security team. "Officials concede the need for a better, earlier, screening system to identify the right people to
become cyberwarriors. There is at least one element on which both countries [Israel and the United States]
agree. The intellectually arrogant, lone-ranger hacker is not the gold standard for innovative, multifaceted cyberoperations." David Fulghum, "Solitary Genius Trumped by the Socially Adept," *Aviation Week
and Space Technology,* July 30, 2012, http://aviationweek.com/awin/solitary-genius-trumped-socially-
adept, 32.

63. The average number of enrollees per computer science department dropped from four hundred at the
height of the dot-com boom to two hundred in 2007 but has since rebounded to three hundred in
2012 (the latest year surveyed). The number of graduates (which lags the number of enrolled students
by one or two years) peaked at around twenty thousand circa 2002 and then fell to below ten thousand in 2009 before rebounding to just under fifteen thousand in 2013. Production of PhDs (which lags
even further) stayed at nine hundred per year between 1995 and 2003, doubled by 2008, and held that
level before establishing new peaks in 2012. From Hal Salzman, Daniel Kuehn, and Lindsay Lowell,
"Guestworkers in the High-Skill U.S. Labor Market: An Analysis of Supply, Employment and Wage
Trends," Economic Policy Institute Briefing Paper, April 24, 2013, http://www.epi.org/publication/
bp359-guestworkers-high-skill-labor-market-analysis/.

64. Christa Case Bryant, "Israel Accelerates Cybersecurity Know-how as Early as 10th Grade," *Christian Science Monitor,* June 9, 2013.

65. Microsoft, "Microsoft Releases National Survey Findings on How to Inspire the Next Generation of
Doctors, Scientists, Software Developers, and Engineers," September 7, 2011, http://www.microsoft.com/
en-us/news/press/2011/sep11/09-07MSSTEMSurveyPR.aspx.

66. The NSA is sponsoring summer camps. See NSA Central Security Service, "NSA's Cyber Camps Make
Summer School Fun," May 11, 2015, https://www.nsa.gov/public_info/press_room/2015/gencyber_
summer_camps.shtml.

67. Sooraj Shah, "KPMG Scales Down Sponsorship of the Cyber Security Challenge Because of a 'Lack of
Credible Candidates,'" *Computing,* January 15, 2004, http://www.computing.co.uk/ctg/news/2323062/
kpmg-scales-down-sponsorship-of-the-cyber-security-challenge-because-of-a-lack-of-credible-
candidates.

68. Alan Paller and George Boggs, "Why We Need More Troops for Escalating Cyberwar," *USA Today,*
March 28, 2013.

69. Brittany Ballenstedt, "DHS Creates Cyber Internships for Community College Students, Veterans," *Nextgov.com,* April 22, 2013, http://www.nextgov.com/cio-briefing/wired-workplace/2013/04/dhs-creates-cyber-internships-community-college-students-veterans/62680/.

70. Homeland Security Advisory Council, "CyberSkills Task Force Report," 2012, http://www.dhs.gov/sites/default/files/publications/HSAC%20CyberSkills%20Report%20-%20Final.pdf.

71. Scott Applegate, "Leveraging Cyber Militias as a Force Multiplier in Cyber Operations," Strategic Studies Institute, 2012.

72. "The 'surge forces' will be trained by the Defense Department and help defend the energy sector, telecommunications and other so-called critical infrastructure, Defense Principal Cyber Adviser Eric Rosenbach said in remarks prepared for a Senate Armed Forces subcommittee hearing." Aliya Sternstein, "Pentagon: U.S. Cyber Reserve Is in the Works," *Nextgov.com,* April 14, 2015, http://www.nextgov.com/cybersecurity/2015/04/pentagon-us-cyber-reserve-works/110113/. See also Aliya Sternstein, "Pentagon to Recruit Thousands for Cybersecurity Reserve Force," *Defense One,* April 16, 2015, http://www.defenseone.com/technology/2015/04/pentagon-recruit-thousands-cybersecurity-reserve-force/110407/.

Chapter 7. What Should Be Secret

1. This is not the same question as: What criteria predispose U.S. officials to classify information? For that, see Barack Obama, Executive Order 12356, "National Security Information," December 29, 2009, https://www.whitehouse.gov/the-press-office/executive-order-classified-national-security-information.

2. In *Secrecy: The American Experience* (New Haven, Conn.: Yale University Press, 1998), Daniel Patrick Moynihan made a broader argument that keeping too much secret gives rise to popular opinion that government statements may be contradicted by such secrets or that there are "facts," irrespective of how otherwise true, that the government knows about but is not speaking of. For instance, the U.S. government's refusal to release classified material that showed the guilt of Alger Hiss persuaded many on the left that he was railroaded.

3. See chapter 4, "Can the Information Be Controlled by the Government?" in Arvin S. Quist, *Security Classification of Information,* vol. 2: *Principles for Classification of Information,* April 1993, http://www.fas.org/sgp/library/quist2/index.html.

4. Or people could start with very fixed ideas and use new information in the context of these fixed ideas to worsen their information. If Chinese intelligence officials believe that U.S. think tanks take orders from the U.S. government (as per Andrea Peterson, "Chinese Cyberspies Have Hacked Middle East Experts at Major U.S. Think Tanks," *Washington Post,* July 7, 2014), they may mislead themselves if they try to discern where the U.S. government is going by gleaning information from stolen think tank files.

5. "[Kim] Philby's most significant breach [was to] . . . read the agency's secret file on its intelligence assets [and report that] . . . Britain had no spies in the Soviet Union . . . The K.G.B. [refused to believe him] reasoning, [as Ben] Macintyre [the author of a book on Kim Philby] writes, was that 'the Soviet Union was a world power and MI6 was the most feared intelligence organization in the world; it therefore stood to reason that Britain must be spying on the USSR. If Philby said otherwise, then he must be lying.' This time around, the secret betrayed was significant. But its strategic value was still zero, because it is not enough for a secret to be of consequence; it must also be understood by those who receive it to be of consequence. Few secrets meet both conditions." From Malcolm Gladwell, "Trust No One: Kim Philby and the Hazards of Mistrust," *New Yorker,* July 28, 2014.

6. Eric Schmitt, "Air Force Blocks Sites that Posted Secret Cables," *New York Times,* December 14, 2010.

7. Michael Howard, *Strategic Deception in the Second World War* (Cambridge: Cambridge University Press, 1990).

8. As well as the right to be left alone; see Louis D. Brandeis and Samuel D. Warren, "The Right to Privacy," *Harvard Law Review* 4, no. 5 (December 15, 1890): pp. 193–220, http://www.jstor.org/stable/1321160.

9. That the marijuana in question was grown in the defendant's *house* is believed to be the reason that Justice Antonin Scalia, otherwise inclined to give police the benefit of the doubt, ruled for the defendant in a case that involved the use of infrared detection as potentially illegal search. See http://caselaw.lp.findlaw.com/scripts/getcase.pl?court=US&vol=000&invol=99-8508 for a summary of the case, *Kyllo versus United States.*

10. The foundational paper may be Ware's "Security and Privacy in Computer Systems."

11. See, for instance, Martin Libicki et al., *Byting Back: Regaining Information Superiority Against 21st-Century Insurgents* (Santa Monica, Calif.: RAND Corporation, 2007), chap. four, for an early discussion of how much an adept phone company can learn about its users.

12. Paul Saffo, "Americans Will Give Up Their Privacy for Trinkets," quoted in Bob Tedeshi, "Privacy vs. Profits," *ZDNet*, September 18, 2001, http://www.zdnet.com/article/privacy-vs-profits/.

13. Mike Masnick, "Mike Rogers: You Can't Have Your Privacy Violated If You Don't Know About It," *TechDirt,* October 20, 2013, https://www.techdirt.com/articles/20131029/18020225059/mike-rogers-you-cant-have-your-privacy-violated-if-you-dont-know-about-it.shtml.

14. David Brin, *The Transparent Society* (New York: Basic Books, 1998).

15. Dustin Volz, "The NSA Is Listening to Every Phone Call in the Bahamas," *National Journal,* May 19, 2014, http://www.nationaljournal.com/tech/the-nsa-is-listening-to-every-phone-call-in-the-bahamas-20140519.

16. Richard Posner's 1978 essay, "An Economic Theory of Privacy," argues that strong privacy rights enable people to present themselves as they want to be presented rather than as they are—much as used car salesmen want to present their products as better than they are. In that sense, privacy can be tantamount to fraud. See http://object.cato.org/sites/cato.org/files/serials/files/regulation/1978/5/v2n3-4.pdf.

17. Mark Mazzetti and David Sanger, "U.S. Fears Data Stolen by Chinese Hacker Could Identify Spies," *New York Times,* July 24, 2015.

Chapter 8. What Does China's Economically Motivated Cyberespionage Cost the United States?

1. Although the U.S. government has not officially indicated what sanctions it would impose, the Chinese may well view as a sanction certain language in the Fiscal Year 2013 Defense Appropriations Bill that bars federal government purchases of IT equipment "produced, manufactured, or assembled" by entities "owned, directed, or subsidized by the People's Republic of China" unless specifically deemed in the U.S. interest. The same perspective may color China's perception of assurances given by SoftBank and Sprint that, as a condition of their merger, they would not purchase equipment from Huawei for Sprint's network. Michael J. De La Merced, "Sprint and SoftBank Pledge to Forgo Huawei Equipment, Lawmaker Says," *New York Times,* March 28, 2013.

2. Early counter-responses include accusations by Yunnan's Geographical Information Bureau of Surveying and Mapping that Coca-Cola had been "illegally collecting classified information with handheld GPS equipment" (Patti Waldmeir, "Coca-Cola Probed Over Mapping in China," *Financial Times,* March 12, 2013, http://www.ft.com/cms/s/0/f02a6abc-8b21-11e2-b1a4-00144feabdc0.html#axzz2PKL4h06R) and the insistence by China's government-backed media that Apple Corporation extend its warranty policy from one to two years ("Daily Report: Pressured by China, Apple Apologizes for Warranty Policies," *New York Times,* April 2, 2013). In 2014, China's antimonopoly agencies were particularly aggressive in going after U.S. firms (although the relationship of this to various cyberespionage controversies is unclear); Neil Gough, "Western Companies Appear to Push Back Against Chinese Crackdown," *New York Times,* September 3, 2014.

3. Lee Glendinning, "Obama, McCain Computers 'Hacked' During Election Campaign: FBI Discovers Cyberattacks During the Summer Originated in China and Stole Large Amounts of Data," *The Guardian,* November 7, 2008; Nicole Perlroth, "Hackers in China Attacked *The Times* for Last 4 Months," *New York Times,* January 30, 2013. The purpose of the attack allegedly was to penetrate gmail accounts.

4. Re: Telvent, see Brian Krebs, "Chinese Hackers Blamed for Intrusion at Energy Industry Giant Telvent," *KrebsonSecurity.com,* September 12, 2012, krebsonsecurity.com/2012/09/chinese-hackers-blamed-for-intrusion-at-energy-industry-giant-telvent/. Telvent is a Canadian company that makes software to help manage energy pipelines, and the theft of its data could facilitate cyberattacks on pipeline controls.

5. Although the current damage to the U.S. economy is likely to be the primary cost of EMCE, two other effects have been theorized. One is that such information facilitates launching cyberattacks on the U.S. critical infrastructure. Another is that EMCE by China will motivate EMCE by China's victims, which would brutalize international commerce as a whole (see David Brooks, "The Brutality Cascade," *New York Times,* March 4, 2013). The publicly available empirical basis for either assertion remains to be seen.

6. Barack Obama, "Cyberspace Policy Review," May 2009, https://www.whitehouse.gov/assets/documents/Cyberspace_Policy_Review_final.pdf.

7. "The Internet is a tremendous capability," Alexander said, "but it also is an enormous vulnerability." "Our intellectual property here is about $5 trillion," he said. "Of that, approximately $300 billion is stolen over the networks per year." Jim Garamone, "Cybercom Chief Details Cyberspace Defense," *Defense.gov,* September 23, 2010, www.defense.gov/news/newsarticle.aspx?id=60987. According to the *Economist,* "A survey by ASIS International, a security-industry body, estimated the annual value of stolen corporate intellectual property at $300 billion in America." *The Economist,* "Intellectual Property: Can You Keep a Secret?," March 16, 2003, http://www.economist.com/news/business/21573580-patent-idea-you-must-publish-it-many-firms-prefer-secrecy-can-you-keep-secret.

8. Stewart Baker, Natalia Filipiak, and Katrina Timlin, "In the Dark: Crucial Industries Confront Cyberattacks," McAfee and Center for Strategic and International Studies, 2011, http://www.mcafee.com/us/resources/reports/rp-critical-infrastructure-protection.pdf.

9. Lawrence Wright ("The Spymaster," *New Yorker,* January 21, 2008, 8) says, "He [Mike McConnell, Director of National Intelligence] claimed that cyber-theft accounted for as much as a hundred billion dollars in annual losses to the American economy."

10. See, for an estimate of British losses, Detica and the Office of Cybersecurity and Information Assurance in the Cabinet Office, "The Cost of Cybercrime," February 2011, https://www.gov.uk/government/uploads/system/uploads/attachment_data/file/60943/the-cost-of-cyber-crime-full-report.pdf. Mark Zwillinger and Christian Genetski, "Calculating Loss Under the Economic Act of 1996," *George Mason Law Review* 9, no. 323 (2000–2001): pp. 323–55, talked in terms of millions of dollars per incident. Rich Bell et al., "Estimating the Economic Cost of Espionage," May 3, 2010, http://bush.tamu.edu/research/capstones/mpia/Engel_Spring2010.pdf, does no better than give qualitative rather than quantitative estimates.

11. More specifically, it is net GDP. For instance, if the United States produces a million widgets and someone walks away with half of them, the net GDP that year is reduced by the amount of half a million widgets.

12. Martin Grueber et al., "2014 Global R&D Funding Forecast," Battelle, December 2013, http://www.battelle.org/docs/tpp/2014_global_rd_funding_forecast.pdf.

13. If Japanese automobile manufacturing provides a useful precedent, Chinese firms are likely to source somewhat more of their components that go into the U.S.-made products from home bases than U.S. firms do, at least initially. Thus, a larger percentage of the difference between sales price and manufacturing costs is likely to go back to China than would be the case for U.S. firms.

14. Jaime Marquez, "Income and Price Elasticities of Foreign Trade Flows: Econometric Estimation and Analysis of the U.S. Trade Deficit," International Finance Discussion Papers no. 324 (June 1988), http://www.federalreserve.gov/pubs/ifdp/1988/324/ifdp324.pdf.

15. Peter Hooper, Karen Johnson, and Jaime Marquez, "Trade Elasticities of the G-7 Countries," *Princeton Studies in International Economics* no. 87 (August 2000).

16. Josh Bivens, "The Benefits of the Dollar's Decline," Economic Policy Institute, July 24, 2003, http://www.epi.org/publication/briefingpapers_bp140/.

17. As Peter Liebert points out (in correspondence with the author, July 27, 2014), what may be a cheap lunch today may be an expensive lunch tomorrow if the Chinese company can leverage its stolen intellectual property to drive its competitors out of business, become a monopoly, and then charge monopoly rents. In maintaining a monopoly, keeping the cost of entry high is important, and it therefore helps to have something that others do not: for example, a patent, ownership of a resource, a first-mover advantage, or a strong brand identity. Whether stolen intellectual property can be leveraged to create a basis for monopoly remains to be seen.

18. See U.S. Census Bureau, "Trade in Goods with China" (updated continuously), https://www.census.gov/foreign-trade/balance/c5700.html. Incidentally, this represents gross imports, not value added, the true measure of how much prices would rise if the renminbi became more expensive. Apple's iPad is "made in China," although China accounts for no more than 4 percent of the value added. Thus, if the value of the renminbi doubled (and nothing else changed), the $500 iPad would have to rise in price to $520 (to afford Apple the same level of profits), not $1,000; see Tim Worstall, "China Makes Almost

Nothing Out of Apple's iPads and iPhones," *Forbes,* December 24, 2011, http://www.forbes.com/sites/timworstall/2011/12/24/china-makes-almost-nothing-out-of-apples-ipads-and-i/.

19. U.S. Census Bureau and U.S. Bureau of Economic Analysis, "U.S. International Trade in Goods and Services, December 2012," www.bea.gov/newsreleases/international/trade/2013/trad1212.htm.

20. Ibid.: Fuel oil, nonmonetary gold, organic chemicals, petroleum products, chemicals-fertilizers, crude oil, copper, metallurgical grade coal, synthetic rubber-primary, aluminum and alumina, nonferrous metals, natural gas liquids, electric energy, wood supplies, manufactured, chemicals-other, manmade cloth, leather and furs, shingles, molding, wallboard, agricultural industry-unmanufactured, hides and skins, precious metals, gas-natural, cotton, and coals and other fuels.

21. Assume the opposite: that copying technology spares China from having to develop such technologies on its own. Would this come at net cost to the U.S. economy? Again, the United States is not worse off because China saves money. The opposite may, in fact, be true. If the funds that China no longer needed to spend on reinventing the U.S. wheel were freed to invent new wheels, then the United States would likely be better off by dint of the well-understood fact that research and development has broad positive externalities. The Organization for Economic Cooperation and Development reported in late 2014 that Chinese R&D was poised to exceed both U.S. and EU R&D spending by 2019. Organization for Economic Cooperation and Development, *OECD Science, Technology and Industry Outlook 2014,* http://www.oecd.org/science/oecd-science-technology-and-industry-outlook-19991428.htm.

22. David Wessel, "U.S. Keeps Foreign Ph.D.s," *Wall Street Journal,* January 26, 2010.

23. Consider how the U.S. detonation of a nuclear weapon demonstrated that the exploitation of atomic properties could yield a great explosion. Countries looking for bigger weapons immediately learned which technological paths to pursue and which to avoid.

24. From the *Economist,* "Changing Faces," March 23, 2013, http://www.economist.com/news/china/21574024-chinas-new-leaders-have-shuffled-their-foreign-affairs-team-relations-other-big-powers-will: "From Russia's perspective, whereas China was until recently a chief buyer of Russian arms, it has now become a chief competitor—often with copied Russian designs."

25. From the *Economist,* "Intellectual Property: Can You Keep a Secret." Also, human spies can carry out cyberespionage more easily for their being human spies; they may have access to computers or at least know, from observation, what is worth stealing. "Su Bin, the owner of a Chinese aviation technology company with an office in Canada, conspired with two unidentified individuals in China to break into the computer networks of U.S. companies seeking information related to military projects, according to charges unsealed in federal court in Los Angeles." See Bloomberg News, "Chinese Citizen Charged in Plot to Steal U.S. Military Data," *Los Angeles Times,* July 11, 2014.

26. The two clearest cases of technology being transferred into identified Chinese products are the technology of titanium dioxide used in white paint (Dan Levine, "U.S. Businessman Convicted in China Economic Espionage Case," Reuters, March 5, 2014, http://www.reuters.com/article/2014/03/06/us-dupont-china-verdict-idUSBREA2501420140306), and computer controls for wind turbines (Michael Riley and Ashlee Vance, "Inside the Chinese Boom in Corporate Espionage," Bloomberg, March 15, 2012, http://www.bloomberg.com/bw/articles/2012-03-14/inside-the-chinese-boom-in-corporate-espionage). Both were leaked as a result of human contact. There was also a reported hack of an Australian company that resulted in a counterfeit (not just copycat) product, but in that case, several involved were convicted and jailed by the Chinese government; Byron Kaye and Jane Wardell, "Australian Metal Detector Company Counts Cost of Chinese Hacking," Reuters, June 24, 2015, http://www.reuters.com/article/2015/06/25/us-china-cybersecurity-australia-idUSKBN0P42LP20150625.

27. As Peter Liebert also points out, intellectual property in the form of software can, in theory, be used immediately. That noted, only a fraction of stolen intellectual property is in the form of ready-to-use code. Furthermore, as soon as the code has to be changed at all (for example, because it is being used with even slightly different hardware), those who now maintain the stolen code have to understand what it does and why it does it—a nontrivial intellectual exercise if there is no one on the original coding team to consult with. Sometimes it is just easier writing new code from scratch.

28. Mandiant's argument that the PLA was behind ATP-1's EMCE campaign does not prove that there are no freelance groups that serve nongovernment clients. But those in the latter transmission belt are probably

less savvy about operational security than those associated with the transmission belt run by the PLA—and yet there are no leaks from that latter quarter about who gets what copied technology.

29. Kevin Barefoot and Raymond Mataloni, "Operations of U.S. Multinational Companies in the United States and Abroad," *Survey of Current Business*, November 2011, http://www.bea.gov/scb/pdf/2011/11%20 November/1111_mnc.pdf.

30. Because the $668 billion of this paragraph is roughly the same as the $700 billion of the calculations on vulnerable U.S. production.

31. This compares to $31 billion in value added from majority-owned U.S. affiliates in China in 2009.

32. See David Shambaugh, *China Goes Global: The Partial Power* (Oxford: Oxford University Press, 2013), 187, for a discussion of how few world-class brands China has.

33. If half of the value added from both the Chinese and U.S. products is accounted for by, say, European components and local servicing, then a transfer of a dollar's worth of production from the United States to China is associated with only fifty cents' worth of value added.

34. Note that unilateral moves by China to limit imports from U.S. vendors can reduce U.S. exports similarly. Witness, therefore, the impact of China's discomfort over (the Snowden-supplied) evidence of U.S. cyberespionage (Michelle FlorCruz, "China Bans Apple, Cisco Systems from Government Use: Cyber Security Concerns or Market Manipulation?" *IB Times,* February 26, 2015, http://www.ibtimes.com/ china-bans-apple-cisco-systems-government-use-cyber-security-concerns-or-market-1829564. Consider, too, the argument that U.S. accusations of Chinese EMCE may have helped motivate China's reaction to U.S. cyberespionage. Then ask: is losing, say, a billion dollars in export sales worldwide because Chinese EMCE allowed Chinese companies to displace U.S. exports substantially different from losing a billion dollars in export sales because of China's (ostensible) fears that buying U.S. networking products can introduce security concerns?

35. Ellen Nakashima, "U.S. Notified 3,000 Companies in 2013 About Cyberattacks," *Washington Post,* March 24, 2014.

36. Department of Justice, "U.S. Charges Five Chinese Military Hackers for Cyber Espionage Against U.S. Corporations and a Labor Organization for Commercial Advantage," May 19, 2014, http://www.justice. gov/opa/pr/2014/May/14-ag-528.html.

37. Aliya Sternstein, "Report: Joint U.S.-China Aviation Ventures Are More Prone to Cyber Intrusions than U.S. Firms," *NextGov.com,* August 7, 2013, http://www.nextgov.com/cybersecurity/2013/08/ report-joint-us-china-aviation-ventures-are-more-prone-cyber-intrusions-us-firms/68225/. American aerospace firms jointly operated by Chinese companies are nearly two and a half times more at risk of cyberespionage than U.S. enterprises.

38. Markets and Markets, "Cyber Security Market worth $170.21 Billion by 2020," news release, http://www .marketsandmarkets.com/PressReleases/cyber-security.asp; see also Martin Giles, "Defending the Digital Frontier," *Economist,* July 12, 2014, http://www.economist.com/news/special-report/21606416- companies-markets-and-countries-are-increasingly-under-attack-cyber-criminals.

39. The hope that one can measure such losses by looking at what happens to stock prices after cyberattacks have been disclosed is the basis of studies that compare stock prices before and afterward (the general results are that there is an immediate effect that often washes out over time); see Brian Cashell et al., "Congressional Research Service Report for Congress: The Economic Impact of Cyber-Attacks," April 1, 2004, http://fas.org/sgp/crs/misc/RL32331.pdf., but also Alison Smith, "Share Prices Are Rarely Hit by Cyber Attacks," *Financial Times,* October 31, 2013, http://www.ft.com/cms/s/0/348d7f1a-417e-11e3- 9073-00144feabdc0.html#axzz3Dzh1mFF4. However, analysts may want to downgrade the stocks of companies that suffered cyberattacks not only because they are worth less as a result (for example, of having lost intellectual property), but also because a successful cyberattack may be an indicator of management's general fecklessness; this persuades analysts that the management team is likely to make other mistakes in the future.

40. World Trade Organization, "TRIPS Material on the WTO Web Site," http://www.wto.org/english/ tratop_e/trips_e/trips_e.htm.

41. Consider a hypothetical. Assume that China, fearful (however unwarranted) that its investment in U.S. debt might not be paid back following a downturn in relations, pulls back from the U.S. market for

treasuries; interest rates on the U.S. debt consequently rise by one-tenth of one percent. That may not seem like much, but when applied to $13 trillion worth of debt, that interest rate increase would cost taxpayers $13 billion a year. To complete the accounting, China would also lose by adopting a second-best investment strategy (the best being U.S. bills). The gainers would be those who continued to invest in U.S. treasuries (they would gain what U.S. taxpayers lost) and those with alternative investment instruments (whose interest rates would fall as China shifted its investments in their direction).

42. Lindsay also argues for skepticism in evaluating the effect of Chinese EMCE, stating: "One day Chinese cyber operators may look back on 2010–13 much the way German submariners looked back on the 'happy time' of 1940–41—namely, as a brief period rich in easy targets before victims learned how to develop active tracking and countermeasures to protect themselves" (24). In suggesting that all this espionage bought the Chinese a hard-to-digest mess of data, he adds: "the ratio of expenditure on back-end assimilation relative to front-end acquisition increased from 5 percent to 45 percent during the same period" (26). Furthermore: "The Soviet Union's reliance on systematic industrial espionage to catch up with the West provides a cautionary tale: the Soviet system became optimized for imitation rather than innovation and was thus locked into a form of second-place dependency, even as it shortened research and development timelines" (36). See Jon R. Lindsay, "The Impact of China on Cybersecurity: Fiction and Friction," *International Security* 39, no. 3 (Winter 2014/15): pp. 7–47.

Chapter 9. Return to Vendor

1. Brian Fung, "The NSA Hacks Other Countries by Buying Millions of Dollars' Worth of Computer Vulnerabilities," *Washington Post,* August 31, 2013. See also Sean Gallagher, "New NSA Chief Explains Agency Policy on 'Zero-Day' Exploits to Senate," *Ars Technica,* March 13, 2014, http://arstechnica.com/tech-policy/2014/03/new-nsa-chief-explains-agency-policy-on-zero-day-exploits-to-senate/, which asks whether the $25 million paid for specific vulnerabilities/exploits or for a subscription to a service that provided them periodically. See also Liam Tung, "NSA: Our Zero Days Put You at Risk, but We Do What We Like with Them," *ZDNet,* March 13, 2014, http://www.zdnet.com/nsa-our-zero-days-put-you-at-risk-but-we-do-what-we-like-with-them-7000027296/, and Kim Zetter, "Obama: NSA Must Reveal Bugs Like Heartbleed, Unless They Help the NSA," *Wired.com,* March 15, 2014, http://www.wired.com/2014/04/obama-zero-day/.

2. The White House, "Liberty and Security in a Changing World," 2013, 37, https://www.whitehouse.gov/sites/default/files/docs/2013-12-12_rg_final_report.pdf.

3. Ellen Nakashima and Ashkan Soltai, "NSA Shouldn't Keep Phone Database, Review Board Recommends," *Washington Post,* December 18, 2014. It is unclear from this quote, however, *when* such vulnerabilities are disclosed or whether they are disclosed in every case.

4. Michael Daniel, "Heartbleed: Understanding When We Disclose Cyber Vulnerabilities," April 28, 2014, https://www.whitehouse.gov/blog/2014/04/28/heartbleed-understanding-when-we-disclose-cyber-vulnerabilities. Apparently, the policy goes back to 2010.

5. Oddly, similar costs and benefits arise from decisions to *insert* a vulnerability into software without the vendor's knowledge. The government gets an intelligence tool, and users get a product less secure than it could have been. But insertion, if discovered, looks much worse.

6. Discussions of successful intelligence operations are highly classified. If intelligence officers are human, they are more apt to exaggerate rather than understate the value of intelligence they collect. Valuations may vary even for evidence presented in court. Consider how important U.S. phone call metadata may have been to catching terrorists—and how quite different judgments were rendered by Judge William H. Pauley III in New York and Judge Richard J. Leon in Washington within two weeks (Adam Liptak and Michael S. Schmidt, "Judge Upholds N.S.A.'s Bulk Collection of Data on Calls," *New York Times,* December 27, 2013). And this is for a metric that is much more tractable than the question of whether or not the president made better decisions as a result of intelligence.

7. Iran managed to compromise systems in sixteen countries without a single zero-day vulnerability; Dan Goodin, "Critical Networks in U.S., 15 Other Nations, Completely Owned, Possibly by Iran," *Ars Technica,* December 2, 2014, http://arstechnica.com/security/2014/12/critical-networks-in-us-15-nations-completely-owned-by-iran-backed-hackers/.

8. It is possible both for vulnerabilities in old code to deplete *and* for products to have a rising number of vulnerabilities over time thanks to new code and new uses for old code that expose vulnerabilities hitherto latent.

9. Ozment and Schechter, "Milk or Wine: Does Software Security Improve with Age?"

10. Frei, "The Known Unknowns."

11. Zetter, *Countdown to Zero Day*, chap. 12, location 4006.

12. See Finifter, Akhawe, and Wagner, "An Empirical Study of Vulnerability Rewards Programs."

13. Ibid.

14. An average patch time of sixty days is suggested by other research; Muhammad Shahzad, Muhammad Zubair Shafiq, Alex X. Liu, "A Large Scale Exploratory Analysis of Software Vulnerability Life Cycles," https://www.msu.edu/~shafiqmu/files/ICSE2012.pdf.

15. The original article is Robert K. Merton, "Resistance to the Systematic Study of Multiple Discoveries in Science," *European Journal of Sociology* 4 (1963): pp. 237–82.

16. One Chinese hacking group seemed to stockpile several zero days, using one as another was fixed; see O'Gorman and McDonald, "The Elderwood Project."

17. Frei, "The Known Unknowns," 10.

18. Might there be a case for returning vulnerabilities to U.S. companies but not do so for their competitors in order to strengthen the security of U.S. products and thereby make them more competitive? A problem is that the acknowledged return of vulnerabilities may *strengthen* security but *weaken* the public's perception of a product's security. The difficulty of making the real security of a product manifest is a serious market failure as argued in Anderson, "The Economics of Information Security." Given that almost all commercial software comes from U.S. companies and nonprofits, such competition is weak. That noted, the harsh reaction of U.S. cloud service providers to press reports that the NSA had tapped into data moving among their clouds (coupled with efforts by foreign countries to restrict local business to national firms) suggests that Silicon Valley still holds to the words of Intel's founder: "Only the paranoid survive."

19. Gregg Keizer, "China Has a Massive Windows XP Problem: By the Time of XP's Retirement in April, Around 10% of All U.S. Computers Will Be Running the OS; in China, 65% of Companies Will Do So," *Computerworld,* August 7, 2013, http://www.computerworld.com/s/article/9241429/China_has_a_massive_Windows_XP_problem. See http://www.netmarketshare.com/operating-system-market-share.aspx?qprid=10&qpcustomd=0 for the raw data.

20. Amber Hildebrandt and Dave Seglins, "Spy Agencies Target Mobile Phones, App Stores to Implant Spyware," *CBC,* May 21, 2015, http://www.cbc.ca/news/canada/spy-agencies-target-mobile-phones-app-stores-to-implant-spyware-1.3076546.

21. Conversely, in "The NSA Is Not Made of Magic" (*Schneier on Security*, May 21, 2014, https://www.schneier.com/blog/archives/2014/05/the_nsa_is_not_.html), Bruce Schneier argued that the Snowden disclosures reveal that there is no magic in the NSA. Its tools are no better than what one would expect taking into consideration the NSA's large budget and the tools that others use.

22. " 'We don't eliminate nuclear weapons until the Russians do,' one senior intelligence official said recently. 'You are not going to see the Chinese give up on "zero days" just because we do.' Even a senior White House official who was sympathetic to broad reforms after the N.S.A. disclosures said last month, 'I can't imagine the president—any president—entirely giving up a technology that might enable him some day to take a covert action that could avoid a shooting war.' " From David Sanger, "Obama Lets N.S.A. Exploit Some Internet Flaws, Officials Say," *New York Times,* April 12, 2014.

23. Kim Zetter, "U.S. Gov Insists It Doesn't Stockpile Zero-Day Exploits to Hack Enemies," *Wired.com,* November 17, 2014, http://www.wired.com/2014/11/michael-daniel-no-zero-day-stockpile/.

24. It would be refreshing to see top intelligence officials criticize specific software companies for making insecure software—as much as they excoriate Apple and Google for allowing people to encrypt cell phone traffic without the key being retrievable by search warrants.

25. See Peter Swire and Kenesha Ahmand, "Encryption and Globalization," *Columbia Science and Technology Law Review* 23 (2012), for a discussion of "going dark" and the "golden age of surveillance."

Chapter 10. Cybersecurity Futures

1. Ablon, Libicki, and Golay, "Markets for Cybercrime Tools and Stolen Data: Hackers' Bazaar."
2. Gregory D. Koblentz, "Strategic Stability in the Second Nuclear Age," report, Council on Foreign Relations, November 2014, http://www.cfr.org/nonproliferation-arms-control-and-disarmament/strategic-stability-second-nuclear-age/p33809.
3. See, for instance, Anderson, *Security Engineering*, chap. 13, "Nuclear Command and Control."
4. See Ross Anderson and Shailendra Fuloria, "Smart Meter Security: A Survey," September 15, 2011; https://www.cl.cam.ac.uk/~rja14/Papers/JSAC-draft.pdf.
5. A shout-out to Neil Gerhsenfeld's book *When Things Start to Think* (New York: Henry Holt and Co., 1999).
6. See Charles Miller and Chris Valasek, "Adventures in Automotive Networks and Control Units," undated report, *Illmatics.com,* http://illmatics.com/car_hacking.pdf.
7. Ron Ross, a fellow in the National Institute of Standards and Technology's Computer Security Division, has maintained that the Internet of Things is indefensible short of a private-public-university collaboration of the type last seen in response to Sputnik; Sean Lyngaas, "NIST Official: Internet of Things Is Indefensible," *Federal Computer Week,* April 16, 2015, http://fcw.com/articles/2015/04/16/iot-is-indefensible.aspx.
8. Sophie Curtis, "'Red Button' Flaw Leaves Smart TVs Open to Cyber Attack," *The Telegraph,* June 9, 2014.
9. See, for instance, Bruce Schneier, "The Internet of Things Is Wildly Insecure—and Often Unpatchable," *Wired.com,* January 6, 2014, http://www.wired.com/2014/01/theres-no-good-way-to-patch-the-internet-of-things-and-thats-a-huge-problem/.
10. See Andy Greenberg, "Hackers Remotely Kill a Jeep on the Highway—With Me in It," *Wired.com,* July 21, 2015, http://www.wired.com/2015/07/hackers-remotely-kill-jeep-highway/, and Timberg, "Hacks on the Highway."
11. Aaron Kessler, "Fiat Chrysler Issues Recall Over Hacking," *New York Times,* July 24, 2015.
12. See chapter five of Libicki, Ablon, and Webb, *Defender's Dilemma.*
13. According to Daniel Geer, "Where the Science is Taking Us," *Lawfareblog.com,* May 29, 2015, http://www.lawfareblog.com/where-science-taking-us-cybersecurity, nearly a thousand cybersecurity start-ups exist.
14. For example, Danny Yadron, "Symantec Develops New Attack on Cyberhacking," *Wall Street Journal,* May 4, 2014.
15. For an interesting set of articles on the security implications of moving to cloud services, see Bruce Schneier, "Should Companies Do Most of their Computing in the Cloud?" *Schneier on Security,* June 2015, https://www.schneier.com/blog/archives/2015/06/should_companie.html, https://www.schneier.com/blog/archives/2015/06/should_companie_1.html, and https://www.schneier.com/blog/archives/2015/06/should_companie_2.html.
16. Mat Honan, "How Apple and Amazon Security Flaws Led to My Epic Hacking," *Wired.com,* August 6, 2012, http://www.wired.com/2012/08/apple-amazon-mat-honan-hacking/.
17. For instance, Ross Anderson, "Security in Open versus Closed Systems—The Dance of Boltzmann, Coase, and Moore," *Open Source Software: Economics, Law and Policy,* IDEI Presentation, Toulouse, France, June 20–21, 2002, http://www.cl.cam.ac.uk/~rja14/Papers/toulouse.pdf.
18. Mimoso, "Vupen Cashes in Four Times at Pwn2Own."
19. Shostack, *Threat Modeling, Designing for Security,* 177: "Fuzzing will not make your code more secure, it will help you find bugs and as those bugs are fixed, the average time to find the next bug using random input goes up. However, the time for a clever human to find that next bug does not change."
20. "End of the Road for Windows XP," *Economist.com,* April 8, 2014, http://www.economist.com/blogs/babbage/2014/04/difference-engine.
21. Mimoso, "Vupen Cashes in Four Times at Pwn2Own."
22. Rosenblatt, "All Hacking Eyes on the Prize Money at CanSecWest."
23. Robert Lemos, "Suspected Russian "Sandworm" Cyber Spies Targeted NATO, Ukraine," October 14, 2014, *Ars Technica,* http://arstechnica.com/security/2014/10/suspected-russian-sandworm-cyber-spies-targeted-nato-ukraine/.
24. IBM has joined with Apple to get iOS into corporations: Apple, "Apple and IBM Forge Global Partnership to Transform Enterprise Mobility," July 15, 2014, http://www.apple.com/pr/library/2014/

07/15Apple-and-IBM-Forge-Global-Partnership-to-Transform-Enterprise-Mobility.html. On the challenge to iOS8, see Andrew Cunningham, "Explaining iOS 8's Extensions: Opening the Platform while Keeping It Secure," *Ars Technica,* June 8, 2014, http://arstechnica.com/apple/2014/06/explaining-ios-8s-extensions-opening-the-platform-while-keeping-it-secure/.

25. As of March 2014, fully two-thirds of all automated teller machines were on Windows XP; Matt Shuffham and David Henry, "Banks to Be Hit with Microsoft Costs for Running Outdated ATMs," Reuters, March 14, 2014, http://www.reuters.com/article/2014/03/14/us-banks-atms-idUSBREA2D13D20140314.

26. Associated Press, "Former NSA Chief Defends Cybersecurity Venture," *New York Times,* August 5, 2014.

27. Consider, by analogy, the far greater profits to be made by pharmaceutical companies by selling drugs to manage conditions over the long term (for example, statins) rather than by selling drugs that actually cure the condition (for example, antibiotics).

28. "To evade sandbox tools that allow malware to run in a carefully controlled laboratory environment, the malware writes a byte of random data to memory 960 million times. The delay that results can trip up the sandbox tool"; see Dan Goodin, "Super Secretive Malware Wipes Hard Drives to Prevent Analysis," *Ars Technica,* May 4, 2015, http://arstechnica.com/security/2015/05/super-secretive-malware-wipes-hard-drive-to-prevent-analysis/.

29. Arik Hesseldahl, "Malware in Sony Attack Linked to 2013 South Korean Incidents," *Recode,* December 4, 2014, http://recode.net/2014/12/04/malware-in-sony-attack-linked-to-2013-south-korean-incidents/.

30. It is a telling irony that Apple advertised the superior security of its Macintosh computers over PCs in their "I'm a Mac and I'm a PC" series, even though they were comparable from a technical security perspective—but Apple has rarely advertised the superior security of its iOS line of products even though they are far more resistant to malware than its competitors, notably PCs, themselves.

Chapter 11. Operational Cyberwar

1. Where networks are defined broadly to include, say, WiFi and/or Bluetooth connectivity, even (especially) if those who own the equipment do not realize that it comes network-ready.

2. Two nice examples of this Achilles' heel can be found in Eric Larrabee, *Commander in Chief: Franklin Delano Roosevelt, His Lieutenants, and Their War* (Annapolis, Md.: Naval Institute Press, 1987): "Maruyama . . . had worked out an impeccable plan, a simultaneous three-pronged attack on the Marine perimeter [on Guadalcanal] supplemented by air strikes and naval gunfire—in short, more of the same. Like previous Japanese plans, it was too ambitious, too complicated, and too dependent on perfect communications" (296). "The Japanese plan [to invade India] was excellent except for one large gaping flaw: It depended on instant success. . . . If Imphal's capture was delayed, their supply problems would mount geometrically" (557).

3. Richard Betts, *Surprise Attack* (Washington, D.C.: Brookings Institution, 1982), 18.

4. Ibid., 14, argues that in 1973, Egypt was not constrained by the premise that it would not attack until the balance of airpower began to turn in its favor. Instead, it resorted "to reliance on air *defense* to neutralize Israeli air power, rather than to meeting it on its own terms."

5. Ibid., 118.

6. See also James C. Mulvenon, "The PLA and Information Warfare," in *The People's Liberation Army in the Information Age,* ed. James C. Mulvenon and Richard H. Yang (Santa Monica, Calif.: RAND Corporation, 1998), CF-145-CAPP/AF, 175–86.

7. John Pomfret, "U.S.-Japan Ties Should Deepen, Gates Says, Citing Threats from China, N. Korea," *Washington Post,* January 14, 2011.

8. Russell F. Weigley, *The American Way of War: A History of United States Military Strategy and Policy* (New York: Macmillan, 1973).

9. The term "assassin's mace" has also been applied to Chinese hypersonic antiship cruise missiles, antisatellite weapons, and electromagnetic pulses.

10. Chinese military writings call for cyberattacks against the United States to be launched from within the United States (James Mulvenon, "Information Warfare and China's Cyber-Warfare Capabilities," speech at Carnegie Endowment for International Peace, Washington, D.C., February 10, 2011). More important, Chinese authorities believe that the U.S. response would be delayed by bureaucratic squabbling over Titles 18 and 50 of the U.S. Code (law enforcement and intelligence, respectively), not to mention Title 10 (military authorities).

11. In cases such as Flame, in which cryptography is involved, it helps to have available sufficient computing resources; see Dan Goodin, "Crypto Breakthrough Shows Flame Was Designed by World-Class Scientists," *Ars Technica*, June 7, 2012, http://arstechnica.com/security/2012/06/flame-crypto-breakthrough/. However, if all that computer processing *precedes* the development of the malware, then destroying the supercomputing capability afterward makes little difference to the course of that particular malware attack or of future attacks for which the cryptography has already been worked out.

12. In theory, *space supremacy* would mean that one state's space constellation could dominate attempts of other countries to maintain a constellation by knocking their spacecraft from orbit. However, terrestrial weapons can also knock spacecraft from orbit (the first U.S. spacecraft shot down was hit by a missile launched from an F-15; the second, in 2008, was hit by a ship-launched missile).

13. Can one define superiority over the *rest* of cyberspace (what neither side owns)? It may not matter inasmuch as few militaries use the commons of cyberspace to do their serious work (although there is a global Domain Name System, DoD owns the dot-mil domain). Furthermore, every network belongs to someone already. Thus, although one may contemplate two sides competing to control third-party networks, these third parties might actually have a word or two to say about the matter—and they have physical control and authentication in real space on their side.

14. This question may be understood more easily in a domain dominated by force-on-force engagements. By way of hypothetical example, consider a British-German World War I–era battleship rivalry. If Germany has ten battleships, then Britain's buying four battleships to bring its total to twelve may be very worthwhile because it allows Britain to have near-certain odds of preventing a German breakout after a decisive battle (for example, Jutland). By contrast, having but eight battleships would mean that preventing a breakout is unlikely. If Britain had four battleships to begin with, bringing its total to eight would only change the odds of preventing a German breakout from impossible to unlikely. Similarly, if Britain had twelve battleships to begin with, then bringing its total to sixteen would only improve its odds from near-certain to certain. The *marginal* value of having an extra battleship is low if Britain has fewer than eight, high if Britain has between eight and eleven, and again low if Britain has twelve or more. In this example, superiority in capability (as proxied by the number of battleships) is critical to naval success.

15. In the United States, the NSA and CYBERCOM are very closely linked bureaucratically; in China, their counterparts lie in different directorates, and cyberwarriors may be less reliant on their intelligence cohorts—but they may also be that much less effective.

Chapter 12. Organizing a Cyberwar Campaign

1. The relationship between cyberspace and outer space is closer in the Air Force. The service's cyberwarriors work in the 24th Air Force, which sits in Air Force Space Command, the successor organization to the U.S. Space Command.

2. Keith Alexander, "Advance Questions for Lieutenant General Keith Alexander, USA, Nominee for Commander, United States CYBERCOM," statement to the U.S. Senate Committee on Armed Services, April 15, 2010, 21, http://www.armed-services.senate.gov/statemnt/2010/04%20April/Alexander%20 04-15-10.pdf, 14.

3. A colleague has suggested that if regional combatant commanders decide whether to carry out a cyberattack, they might profit from advice from CYBERCOM if the other side retaliates by going after networks that exist only to serve forces outside the region. That noted, the harm from a disruptive, or even a corrupting, attack on a system not followed up by military force (for being outside the theater of combat) would be temporary, hence not particularly helpful to the side that would escalate out of region. The argument that cyber weapons are global because their effects are global is not an argument for CYBERCOM, but an argument against their use without considering the global effects of such attacks. Thus, it is another argument for seeking CYBERCOM's advice.

4. If the risk of escalation is sufficiently salient, perhaps higher authorities (for example, the secretary of defense, the president) should make the final call—but not CYBERCOM.

5. For a discussion of this question, see, for instance, James K. Sanborn, "Cyber Steps Up Its Role on the Battlefield," *Marine Corps Times,* August 24, 2014, http://www.marinecorpstimes.com/article/20140825/ NEWS/308250015/Cyber-steps-up-its-role-battlefield.

6. DARPA's Project X is building graphical user interfaces and related tools to allow military professionals without computer science degrees to defend (and attack?) systems; see, for instance, Sara Sorcher, "An Exclusive Look Inside DARPA's Plan to Visualize Cyberoperations," *Christian Science Monitor,* February 16, 2015. Such efforts raise the question: if such operations can be carried out by (expertly trained) everymen, how long would it be before they can be carried out by computers and thus built into the systems being defended (or, conversely, the attack tools)?

7. Richard Smoke, *War: Controlling Escalation* (Cambridge, Mass.: Harvard University Press, 1977), 147–94.

8. One would imagine that if one country found tanks from another country in its territory, this would be incontrovertible evidence that the other country was either mounting an invasion or deliberately allowing others to mount an invasion from its territory. But on June 13, 2014, three tanks from Russia were found in Ukraine, to which Russia essentially reacted: who, me? Andrew Kramer, "Tanks, of Unknown Origin, Roll into Ukraine," *New York Times,* June 12, 2014.

Chapter 13. Professionalizing Cyberwar

1. See Eric Schlosser, *Command and Control: Nuclear Weapons, the Damascus Accident, and the Illusion of Safety* (New York: Penguin, 2013).

2. Sanger and Shanker, "N.S.A. Devises Radio Pathway into Computers."

3. On the unpredictability of grid performance, see also Paul Hines, Eduardo Cotilla-Sanchez, and Seth Blumsack, "Why It's Hard to Crash the Electric Grid," *Arvix* report, 2010, http://arxiv.org/abs/1002.2268.

4. See Noah Schiffman, "DARPA Attempting the Impossible: Self-Simulation for Defense Training," *Network World,* June 6, 2008, http://www.networkworld.com/article/2344569/security/darpa-attempting-the-impossible--self-simulation-for-defense-training.html, and DARPA, "The National Cyber Range: A National Testbed for Critical Security Research," https://www.whitehouse.gov/files/documents/cyber/DARPA%20-%20NationalCyberRange_FactSheet.pdf.

5. For example, Rachel King, "Stuxnet Infected Chevron's IT Network," *Wall Street Journal,* November 8, 2012.

6. Airlines can be particularly sensitive to glitches; Christopher Drew, "United Airlines Grounds Flights, Citing Computer Problems," *New York Times,* July 8, 2005.

7. In June 2011, the FBI "seized Web-hosting servers from a data facility . . . causing a number of sites to go down or transfer operations to other facilities." See Steven Musil, "FBI Seizes Web Hosting Company's Servers," *CNET,* June 21, 2011, http://news.cnet.com/8301-1009_3-20073102-83/fbi-seizes-web-hosting-companys-servers/.

8. One of several committees specifically mentioned in the *Economist,* "The Power of Xi Jinping," September 20, 2014, http://www.economist.com/news/china/21618882-cult-personality-growing-around-chinas-president-what-will-he-do-his-political; the other three are "overall government reform, finance [and], the overhaul of the armed forces."

9. Mark Clayton, "Exclusive: Cyberattack Leaves Natural Gas Pipelines Vulnerable to Sabotage," *Christian Science Monitor,* February 27, 2013.

10. Ellen Nakashima, "In Cyberwarfare, Rules of Engagement Still Hard to Define," *Washington Post,* March 10, 2013. As one example, the notion of "hot pursuit" arises from both a law enforcement and a military context; see Kevin Coleman, "Cyber Rules of Engagement—Hot Pursuit," *InfoTech,* August 18, 2009, http://it.tmcnet.com/topics/it/articles/62417-cyber-rules-engagement-hot-pursuit.htm. But does it apply in cyberspace? The purpose of hot pursuit qua law enforcement is to arrest someone even after he or she crosses jurisdictional lines, but arresting malware neither eliminates nor inhibits it. From a military perspective, it may also be used to disable or disarm someone, but the same objection applies here. A less absurd perspective is that hot pursuit is appropriate in order to intercept the take from cyberespionage before it disappears as evidence of attribution or lands in the hands of the hackers. Such interception, however, tends to require unauthorized access into third-party servers (Chinese hackers often use Taiwanese servers), and if this becomes generalized practice, it may give rise to effective countermeasures (for example, multiple parallel intermediate servers, encryption of exfiltrated information, rapid delivery cycles).

11. Those who argue for granting systems a "right to self-defense" (à la Isaac Asimov's second law of robotics) may wish to rethink their insistence lest they open a Pandora's box of questions about the humanity of machines.

12. Cheryl Pellerin, "Cybercom Builds Teams for Offense, Defense in Cyberspace," *Defense.gov*, March 12, 2013, http://www.defense.gov/news/newsarticle.aspx?id=119506.

13. See, for instance, Brian McCue, *U Boats in the Bay of Biscay: An Essay in Operations Analysis* (Bloomington, Ind.: Ex Libris, 2008).

Chapter 14. Is Cyberspace a Warfighting Domain?

Epigraph: Michael V. Hayden, "The Future of Things 'Cyber'," *Strategic Studies Quarterly* 5, no. 3 (2011): p. 4, http://www.au.af.mil.proxy.lib.ohio-state.edu/au/ssq/2011/spring/hayden.pdf.

1. The very title of the Joint Chiefs of Staff publication on "Cyberspace Operations," the "guidance" of which is "authoritative," says it all.

2. But see Dorothy E. Denning, "Rethinking the Cyber Domain and Deterrence," in *Joint Force Quarterly* 77 (April 2015).

3. Alas, this is not always true as witnessed by OPM having been attacked twice within a year: David Sanger and Julie Hirschfeld, "Hacking Linked to China Exposes Millions of U.S. Workers," *New York Times,* June 4, 2015.

4. From David Sanger, "NATO Set to Ratify Pledge on Joint Defense in Case of Major Cyberattack," *New York Times,* August 31, 2014. But Mr. Daalder (former U.S. ambassador to NATO) noted that NATO's own ability to defend against computer attacks is "still pretty basic," and it has no ability to execute a "forward defense" that involves going into an adversary's computer systems and shutting down an attack.

5. Banks hit by the aforementioned 2012 DDOS attacks supposedly carried out by Iran invested considerable sums (tens or hundreds of millions of dollars may have been involved) to prevent a recurrence.

6. George W. Bush, "The National Strategy to Secure Cyberspace," draft for comment, President's Critical Infrastructure Protection Board, September 2002.

7. If a network's external conduit is larger than some of its internal circuits, a DDOS attack aimed at such internal circuits can cause routing problems if it is not otherwise filtered out. Yet such attacks are rarely heard of, largely because internal networks using gigabit Ethernet are capacious, and high-bandwidth long-distance connections are expensive. A more likely problem—that two parts of an organization that use the open Internet to make a virtual network may be sundered by a DDOS attack—can be addressed by leasing private circuits that cannot be accessed except through the organization's gateway. See also Clay Wilson, "Botnets, Cybercrime, and Cyberterrorism: Vulnerabilities and Policy Issues for Congress" (Washington, D.C.: Congressional Research Service, January 28, 2008), 25, https://www.fas.org/sgp/crs/terror/RL32114.pdf.

8. Charles W. Williamson III, "Carpet-Bombing in Cyberspace: Why America Needs a Military Botnet," *Armed Forces Journal*, May 2008. See also Stephen W. Korns, "Botnets Outmaneuvered: Georgia's Cyberstrategy Disproves Cyberspace Carpet-Bombing Theory," *Armed Forces Journal*, January 2009.

9. From Joint Chiefs of Staff, Joint Publication 3–12R, "Cyberspace Operations," v: Cyberspace can be described in terms of three layers: physical network, logical network, and cyber-persona.

10. Dan Goodin, "Hacking Team Leak Releases Potent Flash 0day into the Wild," *Ars Technica,* July 7, 2015, http://arstechnica.com/security/2015/07/hacking-team-leak-releases-potent-flash-0day-into-the-wild/.

11. See chapter 4 of Richard Overy, *Why the Allies Won* (New York: Norton, 1995), but for a later, more negative view, see Richard Overy, *The Bombing War* (New York: Penguin, 2013).

12. Bernard Brodie, *The Absolute Weapon: Atomic Power and World Order* (New York: Harcourt, Brace, and Co., 1946), 76.

13. "The cyber threat is serious, with potential consequences similar in some ways to the nuclear threat of the Cold War." From Defense Science Board, "Task Force Report: Resilient Military Systems and the Advanced Cyber Threat," 2013, http://www.acq.osd.mil/dsb/reports/ResilientMilitarySystems.CyberThreat.pdf, ES-1. In early 2013, Secretary of State John Kerry likened the threat posed by foreign hackers to "modern day, 21st-century nuclear weapons"; Gerry Smith, "John Kerry: Foreign Hackers Are '21st Century Nuclear Weapons'," *Huffington Post,* January 24, 2013, http://www.huffingtonpost.com/2013/01/24/john-kerry-hackers_n_2544534.html.

14. "The United States and China held their highest-level military talks in nearly two years on Monday, with a senior Chinese general pledging to work with the United States on cybersecurity because the

consequences of a major cyberattack 'may be as serious as a nuclear bomb.'" Jane Perlez, "U.S. and China Put Focus on Cybersecurity," *New York Times*, April 23, 2013.

15. "[Putin] warned that damage from cyberattacks could be higher than that of conventional weapons." RIA Novosti, "Putin Urges Readiness against Cyber and Outer Space Attacks," *Sputnik News*, July 5, 2013, http://sputniknews.com/russia/20130705/182079750.html.

16. The first strategic initiative of the Department of Defense "Strategy for Operating in Cyberspace" (July 2011) is, "Treat cyberspace as an operational domain to organize, train, and equip so that DoD can take full advantage of cyberspace's potential." Although the strategy never uses "warfighting domain" as such, cyberspace is to be treated no differently than the historic four domains: "As directed by the National Security Strategy, DoD must ensure that it has the necessary capabilities to operate effectively in all domains—air, land, maritime, space, and cyberspace."

Chapter 15. Strategic Implications of Operational Cyberwar

1. When attack code is encrypted, the decryption process may be very slow. Part of Stuxnet was encrypted, but the encryption was later broken. As of mid-August 2012, Kaspersky, a major security firm, was unable to break the encryption in the Gauss malware and issued a public call for assistance. Jeff Goldman, "Kaspersky Seeks Help Decrypting Gauss Malware Payload," *eSecurityPlanet.com*, August 15, 2012, http://www.esecurityplanet.com/malware/kaspersky-seeks-help-decrypting-gauss-malware-payload.html.

2. DoD has institutionalized five information operations conditions (INFOCONs), alert conditions for networks parallel to defense conditions (DEFCONs) for general defense conditions (but necessarily invoked at the same time). The higher INFOCONs can be associated with cyberspace lockdowns. See U.S. Air Force Space Command, Instruction 33-107, "Information Operations Condition (INFOCON) System Procedures," July 3, 2006.

3. See M. Taylor Fravel and Evan S. Medeiros, "China's Search for Assured Retaliation: The Evolution of Chinese Nuclear Strategy and Force Structure," *International Security* 35, no. 2 (Fall 2010): 48–87, and Roger Cliff et al., "Entering the Dragon's Lair: Chinese Anti-access Strategies and Their Implications for the United States" (Santa Monica, Calif.: RAND Corporation, MG-524-AF, 2007).

4. Defense Science Board, "Task Force Report: Resilient Military Systems and the Advanced Cyber Threat."

5. Iran sought to disconnect its Internet from the rest of the world; Christopher Rhoads and Farnaz Fassihi, "Iran Vows to Unplug Internet," *Wall Street Journal*, May 28, 2011. See also press reports on Iran's intention, according to communications and IT minister Reza Taqipour, to roll out an operating system to replace Windows; "Iran to Unveil National OS Soon," *PressTV.ir/Sci-Tech*, January 4, 2011, www.presstv.ir/detail/158534.html.

6. Egypt's strategy in the October 1973 war presupposed that the Israeli army would treat its advance toward the Sinai as yet one more exercise that could be ignored safely. See Chaim Herzog, *The Arab-Israel Wars: War and Peace in the Middle East from the War of Independence Through Lebanon* (New York: Random House, 1982), 233–39.

7. Two caveats merit note. First, what impresses one adversary with its own cyberwar capabilities and strategic objectives may not impress another with different attributes. Second, communicating one's preparedness may impel others to ask, "What is going on that they think they have to say this?"

8. John Mearsheimer, *Conventional Deterrence* (Ithaca, N.Y.: Cornell University Press, 1983).

9. Korns, "Botnets Outmaneuvered: Georgia's Cyberstrategy Disproves Cyberspace Carpet-Bombing Theory."

10. See for instance, David Gompert et al., *Mind the Gap: Promoting a Transatlantic Revolution in Military Affairs* (Washington, D.C.: National Defense University Press, 1999).

11. Sanger, "NATO Set to Ratify Pledge on Joint Defense in Case of Major Cyberattack."

Chapter 16. Stability Implications of Operational Cyberwar

1. A somewhat different perspective comes from Thomas Schelling and Morton Halperin, *Strategy and Arms Control* (Dulles, Va.: Potomac Books, 1975). According to Gregory Koblentz, such conditions include weapons vulnerable to a first strike, weapons that are accident prone, early warning systems with high false alarm rates, unreliable command and control systems, weapons susceptible to obsolescence due to technical breakthroughs, force postures that place a premium on rapid decisionmaking, the delegation of launch authority that complicates the control of weapons during a crisis or war, and/or weapons that rely on surprise for their effectiveness. See Koblentz, "Strategic Stability in the Second Nuclear Age."

2. See Stephen Van Evera, *Causes of War* (Ithaca, N.Y.: Cornell University Press, 1999).

3. For a detailed discussion of the source of offense-dominated thinking, see Erik Gartzke and Jon R. Lindsay, "Weaving Tangled Webs: Offense, Defense, and Deception in Cyberspace," *Security Studies* 24, no. 2 (2015): 316–48. Among the many specific sources that argue that offense is dominant in cyberspace are Jonathan Masters, "Confronting the Cyber Threat," report, Council on Foreign Relations, May 23, 2011, http://www.cfr.org/technology-and-foreign-policy/confronting-cyber-threat/p15577; Richard J. Harknett, John P. Callaghan, and Rudi Kauffman, "Leaving Deterrence Behind: War-Fighting and National Cybersecurity," *Journal of Homeland Security and Emergency Management* 7, no. 1 (November 11, 2010); and Eric Sterner, "Stuxnet and the Pentagon's Cyber Strategy," George C. Marshall Institute, October 13, 2010, http://www.marshall.org/article.php?id=918. Not for nothing has former NSA director Gen. Mike Hayden argued that this is a golden age for surveillance, an activity that, like cyberwar, depends on the ability to penetrate computer systems.

4. From Erik Gartzke, "The Myth of Cyberwar: Bringing War in Cyberspace Back Down to Earth," *International Security* 38, no. 2 (Fall 2013): 41–73: "[S]uppos[ing] that information infrastructures are more readily defended than attacked . . . the balance of power would favor those states that could most effectively orchestrate military command, communications, logistics, and intelligence through the internet or similar types of networks. . . . The standard military answer is that command and control are more critical for the offense, as commanders have more need to directly control their forces in the attack. If so, then perhaps cyber defense dominance is actually destabilizing, because it increases the ability to attack and (slightly) decreases the ability of defenders to prevail."

5. For instance, many influential leaders came to regard warfare as a positive good and an indicator that its "race" was robust in a Social Darwinian sense. In *Strategy: A History* (Oxford: Oxford University Press, 2013), 620, Lawrence Freedman observes that the metaphor, popular in 1914, of war as dueling writ large made the threat of war appear as a challenge that honor required meeting.

6. See Karl P. Mueller et al., *Striking First: Preemptive and Preventive Attack in U.S. National Security Policy* (Santa Monica, Calif.: RAND, MG-403-AF, 2006).

7. See Daniel Kahneman, *Thinking Fast and Slow* (New York: Farrar, Straus and Giroux, 2011).

8. If success is undoubted and the drive to the front is already under way, the fact that war started with a cyberattack is beside the point; the conflict is not inadvertent.

9. This is akin to the reasoning that von Moltke the Younger used to persuade others that Germany's survival depended on going to war before Russia became too powerful to oppose.

10. Richard Ned Lebow, *Nuclear Crisis Management: A Dangerous Illusion* (Ithaca, N.Y.: Cornell University Press, 1987), argues that preemption and the fear of losing control account for two of the primary factors leading to inadvertent conflict in the nuclear realm.

11. See James Lewis, "Hackers Don't Want to Crash Stock Exchanges. They Want to Make Money on Them," *Washington Post,* July 9, 2015, for a discussion of how often people assume hackers are responsible when systems fail on their own.

12. David Sanger and Thom Shanker, "Broad Powers Seen for Obama in Cyberstrikes," *New York Times*, February 3, 2013, and Ellen Nakashima, "Obama Signs Secret Directive to Help Thwart Cyberattacks," *Washington Post*, November 14, 2012.

13. A survey of IT professionals by Ponemon found that the average large organization has to sift through nearly 17,000 malware alerts each week to find the 19 percent that are considered reliable. Security professionals only have time to investigate 4 percent of the warnings; Robert Lemos, "Survey Says Security Products Waste Our Time," *Ars Technica,* January 16, 2015, http://arstechnica.com/security/2015/01/survey-says-security-products-waste-our-time/.

Chapter 17. Strategic Cyberwar

1. Thomas C. Schelling, *Arms and Influence* (New Haven, Conn.: Yale University Press, 1966), 201, has described such a conflict (admittedly at the nuclear level)

> as a war of pure coercion, each side restrained by apprehension of the other's response. It is a war of pure pain; neither gains for the pain it inflicts, but inflicts it to show more pain can come. It would be a war of punishment, of demonstration, of threat, of dare and challenge. Resolution, bravery, and genuine obstinacy would not necessarily win the contest. An enemy's *belief* in one's obstinacy might persuade him to quit. But since recognized obstinacy

would be an advantage, displays or pretenses of obstinacy would be suspect. We are talking about a bargaining process, and no mathematical equation will predict the outcome.

2. Clapper, "Worldwide Threat Assessment of the U.S. Intelligence Community," 1, stated:

> We judge that there is a remote chance of a major cyberattack against U.S. critical infrastructure systems during the next two years that would result in long-term, wide-scale disruption of services, such as a regional power outage. . . . However . . . less advanced but highly motivated actors could access some poorly protected U.S. networks that control core functions, such as power generation, during the next two years, although their ability to leverage that access to cause high-impact, systemic disruptions will probably be limited. At the same time, there is a risk that unsophisticated attacks would have significant outcomes due to unexpected system configurations and mistakes, or that vulnerability at one node might spill over and contaminate other parts of a networked system.

3. Scott Borg has calculated that even a temporary shutdown of the power grid could cost the country $700 billion. See Joel N. Gordes and Michael Mylrea, "A New Security Paradigm Is Needed to Protect Critical U.S. Energy Infrastructure from Cyberwarfare," *Foreign Policy Journal,* September 14, 2009, http://www.foreignpolicyjournal.com/2009/09/14/a-new-security-paradigm-is-needed-to-protect-critical-us-energy-infrastructure-from-cyberwarfare/.

4. Ross Anderson and Shailendra Fuloria, "Smart Meter Security: A Survey," September 15, 2011; https://www.cl.cam.ac.uk/~rja14/Papers/JSAC-draft.pdf.

5. U.S.–Canada Power System Outage Task Force, "Final Report of the August 14, 2003, Blackout in the United States and Canada: Causes and Recommendations," report, 2004, http://energy.gov/sites/prod/files/oeprod/DocumentsandMedia/BlackoutFinal-Web.pdf. See also New York Independent System Operator, "Final Report on the August 14, 2003, Blackout," February 2005. Although the sources of the August 2003 Northeast power outage are well studied, a contrary line of reasoning cites the failure of power managers at First Electric to respond with sufficient alacrity when the first transmission line went down. Their non-responsiveness was due, in part, to the effect that the computer worm MSBlast (also known as Blaster) had on their warning systems (the same company had to shut down the Davis-Bessie nuclear power plant several months earlier due to the effects of the Slammer worm). See Robert Lemos, "MSBlast Now to Blame for Blackout, Report Says," *ZDNet,* April 6, 2004, http://www.zdnet.com/news/msblast-not-to-blame-for-blackout-report-says/135296. See also Bruce Schneier, "Perspective: Internet Worms and Critical Infrastructure," *CNET News,* December 9, 2003, http://www.cnet.com/news/internet-worms-and-critical-infrastructure/; and Dan Verton, "Blaster Worm Linked to Severity of Blackout," *Computerworld.com,* August 29, 2003, http://www.computerworld.com/article/2571068/disaster-recovery/blaster-worm-linked-to-severity-of-blackout.html. By this reasoning, someone interested in shutting down the U.S. power grid need only infect warning systems (which are not necessarily air-gapped in the same way that control systems are) and wait for the inevitable system glitch to yield a regional or national power outage cascade.

6. As reported there, "A Chinese PLA hacker attempting to map Florida Power & Light's computer infrastructure apparently made a mistake. The hacker was probably supposed to be mapping the system for his bosses and just got carried away and had a 'what happens if I pull on this' moment." The hacker triggered a cascade effect, shutting down large portions of the Florida power grid, the security expert said. Shane Harris, "China's Cyber Militia," *National Journal,* May 31, 2008, http://www.nationaljournal.com/magazine/china-s-cyber-militia-20080531. But the report was incorrect; a transmission system element fault was the cause. Florida Reliability Coordinating Council (FRCC) Event Analysis Team, "FRCC System Disturbance and Underfrequency Load Shedding Event Report February 26th, 2008 at 1:09 pm," final report, October 30, 2008.

7. Siobhan Gorman, "Electricity Grid in U.S. Penetrated by Spies," *Wall Street Journal,* April 8, 2009, 1.

8. Gorman and Yadron, "Iran Hacks Energy Firms, U.S. Says."

9. Jian-Wei Wang and Li-Li Rong, "Cascade-based Attack Vulnerability on the U.S. Power Grid," *Safety Science* **47** (2009): 1332–6.

10. Jamie Crawford, "The U.S. Government Thinks China Could Take Down the Power Grid," *CNN.com,* November 21, 2014, http://www.cnn.com/2014/11/20/politics/nsa-china-power-grid/.

11. DHS, "Alert (ICS-ALERT-14-281-01B) Ongoing Sophisticated Malware Campaign Compromising ICS (Update B)," December 10, 2014, https://ics-cert.us-cert.gov/alerts/ICS-ALERT-14-281-01B.

12. Dan Goodin, "This System Will Self Destruct: Crimeware Gets Powerful New Functions," *Ars Technica,* November 4, 2014, http://arstechnica.com/security/2014/11/this-system-will-self-destruct-crimeware-gets-powerful-new-functions/.

13. Ellen Nakashima, "Water-pump Failure in Illinois Wasn't Cyberattack After All," *Washington Post,* November 25, 2011; see also Kim Zetter, "Exclusive: Comedy of Errors Led to False 'Water-Pump Hack' Report," *Wired.com,* November 30, 2011, http://www.wired.com/2011/11/water-pump-hack-mystery-solved/.

14. Elinor Mills, "Hacker Says He Broke into Texas Water Plant, Others," *CNET,* November 18, 2011, http://www.cnet.com/news/hacker-says-he-broke-into-texas-water-plant-others/.

15. Government Accountability Office, "TVA Needs to Address Weaknesses in Control Systems and Networks," report, May 21, 2008, http://www.gao.gov/products/GAO-08-526.

16. See Anderson and Fuloria, "Smart Meter Security: A Survey."

17. Douglas Birch, "U.S.: Cyber Attacks on Utilities, Industries, Rise," *NBC News,* September 29, 2011, http://www.nbcnews.com/id/44724508/ns/technology_and_science-security/t/us-cyber-attacks-utilities-industries-rise/#.VawJS_lViko. See also *Dark Reading,* "U.S. Critical Infrastructure Cyberattack Reports Jump Dramatically: A New Report from ICS-CERT Shows the Number of Reported Incidents Increased from 9 to 198 between 2009 and 2011," June 29, 2012, http://www.darkreading.com/attacks-breaches/us-critical-infrastructure-cyberattack-reports-jump-dramatically/d/d-id/1137957.

18. David Sanger and Eric Schmitt, "Rise Is Seen in Cyberattacks Targeting U.S. Infrastructure," *New York Times,* July 26, 2012. More reliably, in early 2013, NSS Labs released a study that tracked a 600 percent jump in industrial control system vulnerabilities revealed between 2010 and 2012, with 124 security flaws being disclosed; see Danielle Walker, "Losing Control: Critical Infrastructure," *SC Magazine,* March 1, 2013, http://www.scmagazine.com/losing-control-critical-infrastructure/article/280939.

19. Mark Clayton, "Alert: Major Cyber Attack Aimed at Natural Gas Pipeline Companies," *Christian Science Monitor,* May 5, 2012.

20. Wright, "The Spymaster."

21. Shane Harris, "Exclusive: Meet the Fed's First Line of Defense Against Cyber Attacks," *Foreign Policy,* April 29, 2014, http://foreignpolicy.com/2014/04/29/exclusive-meet-the-feds-first-line-of-defense-against-cyber-attacks/.

22. The Conficker worm is a good case of multiple infections being carried out and never activated. It was not until the infection count got into the low millions that an organized attempt was made to stop its spread. John Markoff, "Worm Infects Millions of Computers Worldwide," *New York Times,* January 22, 2009.

23. A further assumption is that the computer can be restored to factory conditions; certain malware can overwrite the computer's BIOS and thereby require more intrusive restoration operations. The so-called Equation group's malware was said to be capable of reflashing the BIOS without crashing the system—a difficult feat. Kim Zetter, "Why Firmware Is So Vulnerable to Hacking, and What Can Be Done About It," *Wired.com,* February 24, 2015, http://www.wired.com/2015/02/firmware-vulnerable-hacking-can-done/.

24. One counterargument is that government-induced regulation forces infrastructure owners into interconnection with third-party providers at multiple levels of what would otherwise be a tightly integrated sector; they must then trust machines they cannot control.

25. Molly K. McKew and Gregory A. Maniatis, "Playing by Putin's Tactics," *Washington Post,* March 9, 2014.

26. Cyberwar was best understood as a subset of electronic warfare but not called out as such; see Joint Chiefs of Staff, Joint Publication 3-13.1, *Joint Doctrine for Command and Control Warfare (C2W)* (Washington, D.C.: The Joint Staff, February 7, 1996).

27. Perlroth, "Hackers in China Attacked *The Times* for Last 4 Months."

28. Associated Press, "Russia Classifies Military Casualties in Peacetime," *New York Times,* May 28, 2015.

29. See Bruce Schneier, "Organizational Doxing," *Schneier on Security,* July 10, 2015, https://www.schneier.com/blog/archives/2015/07/organizational_.html, on the subject of organizational doxing.

30. Of course, if the Internet is already polluted from Russian trolls (Adrian Chen, "The Agency," *New York Times,* June 2, 2015) and China's 50-centers (Sarah Cook, "China's Growing Army of Paid Internet Commentators," *Freedomhouse.org,* October 11, 2011, https://freedomhouse.org/blog/china

%E2%80%99s-growing-army-paid-internet-commentators#.VX2GD_lVikp), the ability to get others to accept these documents as true may be nontrivial.

31. Agence France-Presse, "U.S. Blames Russia for Leak of Undiplomatic Language from Top Official," *The Guardian,* February 6, 2014.

32. Hugh Naylor, "Theft of Saudi Documents Suggests an Iranian Hack," *Washington Post,* June 26, 2015.

33. See the discussion in Patrick Morgan, *Deterrence: A Conceptual Analysis* (Beverly Hills, Calif.: Sage Library of Social Research 40, 1977), 149–204.

34. See, for instance, Leslie Gelb and Richard Betts, *The Irony of Vietnam: The System Worked* (Washington, D.C.: Brookings Institution, 1979) and H. R. McMaster, *Dereliction of Duty: Lyndon Johnson, Robert McNamara, the Joint Chiefs of Staff, and the Lies That Led to Vietnam* (New York: Harper-Collins, 1997).

35. For example, Charles Ikle, *Every War Must End* (New York: Columbia University Press, 1971).

Chapter 18. Cyberwar Threats as Coercion

1. Easier is relative. Countries resist coercion because they do not like to be perceived as capable of being pressured. Yet coercion may be considered just another set of created incentives. The threat "Do X or you will be bitten by the dog" is equivalent to "If you do X, I'll intercede with the dog and persuade it not to bite you." The latter sounds slightly friendlier (a great deal depends on the speaker's relationship to the dog).

2. See, for instance, Schelling, *Arms and Influence,* chapter 3.

3. U.S. Department of Defense, *Department of Defense Cyber Strategy* (Washington, D.C.: Department of Defense, April 2015).

Chapter 19. The Unexpected Asymmetry of Cyberwar

1. See, for instance, the arguments in Adam P. Liff, "Cyberwar: A New 'Absolute Weapon'? The Proliferation of Cyberwarfare Capabilities and Interstate War," *Journal of Strategic Studies* 35, no. 3 (2012): pp. 401–28, and Hannes Ebert and Tim Maurer, "Contested Cyberspace and Rising Powers," *Third World Quarterly* 34, no. 6 (2013): pp. 1054–74.

2. A machine connected via the Internet only by using a virtual private network (VPN) to another system is generally no more vulnerable to cyberattack than the system it is connected to, and often, not even that much if communications along the VPN are well filtered.

3. On July 16, 2015, for instance, Thomas Erdbrink, the *New York Times*'s Tehran correspondent, tweeted that all gasoline stations in the city were down because of a computer glitch; https://twitter.com/ThomasErdbrink/status/621582470715060224.

4. "The World's Greatest Bazaar: Alibaba, a Trailblazing Chinese Internet Giant, Will Soon Go Public," *Economist,* May 21, 2013, http://www.economist.com/news/briefing/21573980-alibaba-trailblazing-chinese-internet-giant-will-soon-go-public-worlds-greatest-bazaar.

5. Countries *do* have an advantage when it comes to attacking systems because they have more practice in recruiting agents, better links to Internet service providers, and more resources for supply-chain attacks (for example, substituting altered components for the real thing).

6. From Neil Munro, "Fear of an Electronic Pearl Harbor," *Washington Post,* July 16, 1995, C3: According to a 1994 study by the Pentagon's top-level Defense Science Board, infowar "technologies and capabilities are largely being developed in an open commercial market and are outside of direct government control. . . . A Third World nation could procure a formidable, modern IW capability virtually off-the-shelf."

7. Ablon, Libicki, and Golay, "Markets for Cybercrime Tools and Stolen Data: Hackers' Bazaar."

8. Gabi Siboni and Sami Kronenfeld, "Developments in Iranian Cyber Warfare, 2013–2014," Institute for National Security Studies Insight no. 536, April 3, 2014, http://www.inss.org.il/index.aspx?id=4538&articleid=6809: "Furthermore, the increasingly close ties between the Iranian cyber system and cyber criminals, hackers, and information security experts, mainly Russians, who are prepared to sell their services for money, contribute to the rapid progress in Iran's cyber warfare program."

9. Since most web-based e-mail is free to customers, they are not, strictly speaking, customers, but winning their favor is critical to winning advertisers, the real paying customers.

10. See, for instance, Bruce Schneier's essay on private surveillance as the cousin of public surveillance: Bruce Schneier, "The Public/Private Surveillance Partnership," *Schneier on Security,* August 5, 2013, https://www.schneier.com/blog/archives/2013/08/the_publicpriva_1.html.

11. If the United States is not directly involved, software companies will have an easier time maintaining their neutrality. When it comes to cyberwar, which (if any) side a Microsoft chooses to favor would make the kind of difference that would exceed what the second-tier countries could contribute to the common fight in, say, World Wars I and II.

12. See also Schneier, "The Human Side of Heartbleed," on the difficulties of figuring out which customers to inform prior to public announcement.

13. This is part of the trade-off entailed in using Google products. As another, for instance, consider how Apple iPhones defaulted to backing up photographs into its iCloud.

14. Back doors in switches allowed hackers to eavesdrop on government officials in Greece; see Vassilis Prevelakis and Diomidis Spinellis, "The Athens Affair: How Some Extremely Smart Hackers Pulled Off the Most Audacious Cell-Network Break-in Ever," *IEEE Spectrum,* June 29, 2007, http://spectrum.ieee.org/telecom/security/the-athens-affair.

15. Dennis Fisher, "RSA Denies NSA Backdoor Payment Allegations," *Threat Post,* December 23, 2013, http://threatpost.com/rsa-denies-nsa-backdoor-payment-allegations/103268

16. Peter Bright, "Report: NSA Paid RSA to Make Flawed Crypto Algorithm the Default," *Ars Technica,* December 20, 2013, http://arstechnica.com/security/2013/12/report-nsa-paid-rsa-to-make-flawed-crypto-algorithm-the-default/.

17. U.S. cloud providers must turn over such data if subject to a legal subpoena; Nick Wingfield, "Judge Rules That Microsoft Must Turn Over Data Stored in Ireland," *New York Times,* July 31, 2014. This regime may not last forever as U.S. firms try to assure foreign customers that their data are protected even from U.S. officials; in such a case, they may volunteer such information (or lean on their business partners to do so).

18. Claire Cain Miller, "Revelations of N.S.A. Spying Cost U.S. Tech Companies," *New York Times,* March 21, 2014. Germany and Brazil are prominent among countries that have contemplated mandating restrictions on the export of data.

19. Microsoft, "Unfinished Business on Government Surveillance Reform," June 4, 2014, http://blogs.technet.com/b/microsoft_on_the_issues/archive/2014/06/04/unfinished-business-on-government-surveillance-reform.aspx; see also the full-page advertisement in the June 5, 2014, *Washington Post,* A20.

20. Nicole Perlroth, "Google Offers New Encryption Tool," *New York Times,* June 3, 2014.

21. National Security Agency, "Security-Enhanced Linux," January 15, 2009, http://www.nsa.gov/research/selinux/.

22. Edward Yourdon, *Decline and Fall of the American Programmer* (New York: Prentice-Hall, 1992).

23. See Steve Lohr, "In 2015, Technology Shifts Accelerate and China Rules, IDC Predicts," *New York Times,* December 2, 2014, and Nathan Freitas, "People Around the World Are Voluntarily Submitting to China's Great Firewall. Why?" *Slate,* January 6, 2015, http://www.slate.com/blogs/future_tense/2015/01/06/tencent_s_wechat_worldwide_internet_users_are_voluntarily_submitting_to.html.

24. Granting that the Snowden accusations are unconfirmed, the NSA never imagined its doings would become public, and the harm from the revelations is still yet to be fully worked out.

25. Yet President Obama's January 2014 speech defending the NSA's practices gave considerable prominence to combating the threat of cyberattack: (1) "our capacity to repel cyber attacks have [sic] been strengthened," (2) "the men and women at the NSA know that if another 9/11 or massive cyber attack occurs, they will be asked by Congress and the media why they failed to connect the dots," (3) "the challenges posed by threats like terrorism and proliferation and cyberattacks are not going away any time soon, " and (4) "we cannot prevent terrorist attacks or cyberthreats without some capability to penetrate digital communications, whether it's to unravel a terrorist plot, to intercept malware that targets a stock exchange, to make sure air traffic control systems are not compromised or to ensure that hackers do not empty your bank accounts." Nevertheless, the anti-terrorism rationale was expanded upon by citing specifics but not the anti-cyberattack rationale.

26. Jon Brodkin, "China Builds Own Phone OS, Aims to Be More Secure than Android or iPhone," *Ars Technica,* January 20, 2014, http://arstechnica.com/information-technology/2014/01/china-builds-own-phone-os-aims-to-be-more-secure-than-android-or-iphone/.

27. Bruce Schneier, "New Al Qaeda Encryption Software," *Schneier on Security*, May 14, 2014, https:// www.schneier.com/blog/archives/2014/05/new_al_qaeda_en_1.html. See also Charlie Osborne, "Terrorist Encryption Tools Nothing More than 'Security Cape' and Gov't Red Flag," *ZDNet.com*, February 17, 2015, http://www.zdnet.com/article/black-flag-ops-exposed-terrorist-security-tools-a-red-flag-to-govt-agencies/.

28. Sean Gallagher, "Heads Up, Dear Leader: Security Hole Found in North Korea's Home-grown OS," *Ars Technica,* January 9, 2015, http://arstechnica.com/information-technology/2015/01/heads-up-dear-leader-security-hole-found-in-north-koreas-home-grown-os/: "However, because Red Star has had so few people with access to it, one of the ironic side effects has been that security holes in the operating system may have gone undetected . . . [allowing] any user to elevate their privileges to those of the system's root account and bypass all those security policies put in place by the North Korean regime."

29. Kaspersky was not commissioned as such but was a member (together with Symantec, Microsoft, Trend Micro, and F-secure, et al.) of the ITU–International Multilateral Partnership Against Cyber Threats initiative.

Chapter 20. Responding to Cyberattack

Epigraph. Robert Gates, "Nuclear Weapons and Deterrence in the 21st Century," address to the Carnegie Endowment for International Peace, October 28, 2008.

1. Tom Espiner, "U.S. Reveals Plans to Hit Back at Cyber Threats," *ZDNet News*, April 2, 2008, http:// news.zdnet.co.uk/security/0,1000000189,39378374,00.htm.

2. See, for instance, Rohan Gunaratna, *Inside Al Qaeda's Global Network of Terror* (New York: Columbia University Press, 2002).

3. North Korea, perhaps, excepted: Nicole Perlroth, "North Korea Linked to Digital Thefts from Global Banks," *New York Times,* May 26, 2016, http://www.nytimes.com/2016/05/27/business/dealbook/north-korea-linked-to-digital-thefts-from-global-banks.html?_r=0.

4. See, for instance, Shachtman, "Insiders Doubt 2008 Pentagon Hack Was Foreign Spy Attack."

5. Reuters, "No Harmful Virus Found in South Korean Nuclear Hack," *New York Times,* December 30, 2014.

6. Chernobyl is a good example; see, for example, Michael D. Lemonick, "The Chernobyl Cover-Up," *Time*, November 13, 1989, and "Protests Grow Over Chernobyl 'Cover-Up'," *New Scientist*, October 28, 1989. China's attempt to build a huge petrochemical complex in Xiamen is another example; see Datong Li, "Xiamen: The Triumph of Public Will?" *openDemocracy*, January 16, 2008.

7. A case for discretion comes from the public's tendency to overestimate the risks of insecurity in cyberspace (witness the Ebola scare circa October 2014). There is considerable agreement that the public is wildly inconsistent in how it reacts to low-probability, high-impact risks.

8. Marie Harf, a State Department spokesperson; Nicole Perlroth and David Sanger, "North Korea Loses its Link to the Internet," *New York Times,* December 22, 2014.

9. One might have thought that the defense would have been hardened before the attack took place, but not necessarily. Attackers may be surprised that they were caught. They may worry that defensive efforts will be noticed and might reveal the operation. Or the attackers may simply not be mindful about the effects of retaliation.

10. See, for instance, Gregg Keizer, "Garden-variety DDoS Attack Knocks North Korea Off the Internet," *Computerworld,* December 23, 2014, http://www.computerworld.com/article/2862652/garden-variety-ddos-attack-knocks-north-korea-off-the-internet.html. Initial U.S. official denials were sufficiently vague to foster the notion that the United States *was* responsible. Later, when restrictions were imposed on named North Korean officials, spokesmen described them as the *first* step in a series, suggesting that the DDOS attacks had not been part of the package; Carol Lee and Jay Solomon, "U.S. Targets North Korea in Retaliation for Sony Hack: New Sanctions Target Individuals Working for Arms Industry," *Wall Street Journal,* January 3, 2015.

11. So, why is nuclear retaliation, with no more of a track record, credible? In a sense, its credibility *has* been questioned. In the late 1970s, nuclear theorists, in fact, worried that the Soviet Union could knock out the U.S. intercontinental ballistic missile force and present a fait accompli that would inhibit a U.S. nuclear

response and reveal retaliation as a hollow threat. Nevertheless, the best answer to that question is that, with the consequences of retaliation so destructive, no one really wanted to test anyone else's credibility.

12. Suing for damages may be accepted as legitimate even after a period of years. Given the ambiguities of cyberspace and the general reluctance to admit which tools the defender uses to understand what happened to its system, the resources spent arguing over what the damages were may exceed the actual level of damages in many cases. A nominal compromise in which a token payment is made may be appropriate but hardly contributes to deterrence.

13. *May* if the evidence required to finger an individual within a state exceeds what is required to assign responsibility to a state. Responsibility can entail sins of omission, as well as commission.

14. A great deal will depend on the particulars and the cogency of the attacker's objections. Not all of them would be specious—the U.S. Constitution, for instance, would prevent foreign investigators from using techniques here that may be routine in their own countries.

15. In September 2013, Vladimir Putin issued a travel warning for Russians whom the United States might indict (for hacking, among other crimes) to avoid countries from which the United States could extradite them; see Mark Johnson, "Russia Issues Travel Warning About U.S., Citing Threat of 'Kidnapping,'" *IB Times,* September 3, 2013, http://www.ibtimes.com/russia-issues-travel-warning-about-us-citing-threat-kidnapping-1402265.

16. Senator John McCain, for instance, had talked of cutting Russia out of the Group of Eight for its growing belligerence in general and its role in the attacks or cyberattacks against Estonia in particular. See Eli Lake, "McCain Backs Tougher Line Against Russia," *The Sun* (New York), March 27, 2008.

17. And even putting cyberespionage as the top item in a U.S.-Chinese summit, as was done in the Sunnylands summit of June 2013, may not be that productive if there is all ask and no offer.

18. But see "What Elephant?" http://www.russian-jokes.com/political_jokes/russian_diplomacy.shtml.

19. Note the following logic from David Sanger, Nicole Perlroth, and Eric Schmitt, "U.S. Asks China to Help Rein In Korean Hackers," *New York Times,* December 20, 2014. For now, the White House appears to have declined to consider what one Defense Department official termed 'a demonstration strike' in cyberspace, which could have included targets such as North Korean military facilities, computer network servers and communications networks. . . . 'There are a lot of constraints on us, because we live in a giant glass house,' said one official involved in the high-level debates. The official said the challenge was to find a mix of actions that 'the North Koreans will notice' but that will not be so public that Mr. Kim's government loses face and feels compelled to respond."

20. According to reporting in the *Epoch Times,* "[a] documentary . . . meant as praise to the wisdom and judgment of Chinese military strategists, and a typical condemnation of the United States as an implacable aggressor in the cyber-realm [contained] fleeting shots of an apparent China-based cyberattack [on a server in Alabama that] somehow made their way into the final cut." Matthew Robertson and Helena Zhu, "Slip-Up in Chinese Military TV Show Reveals More Than Intended: Piece Shows Cyber Warfare Against U.S. Entities," *Epoch Times,* August 21, 2011, updated April 7, 2012, http://www.theepochtimes.com/n2/china-news/slip-up-in-chinese-military-tv-show-reveals-more-than-intended-60619.html. The actual recording made its way to YouTube. See NTD Television, "Chinese State TV Deletes Video Showing Telltale Signs of PLA's [sic]," August 30, 2011, https://www.youtube.com/watch?v=fq_jAfiTz-k.

21. Gelb and Betts, *The Irony of Vietnam: The System Worked.*

22. Iraq and Serbia, for instance, traded information on how to defeat U.S. aircraft and avoid anti-radiation missiles; see David A. Fulghum and William B. Scott, "Pentagon Mum About F-117 Loss," *Aviation Week and Space Technology* 150, no. 14 (April 5, 1999). In 2012, North Korea and Iran signed a technology treaty to help combat "common enemies" in cyberspace; Alastair Stevenson, "Iran and North Korea Sign Technology Treaty to Combat Hostile Malware," *V3,* September 3, 2012, http://www.v3.co.uk/v3-uk/news/2202493/iran-and-north-korea-sign-technology-treaty-to-combat-hostile-malware.

23. Robert Lemos, "'Unprecedented' Cyberattack No Excuse for Sony Breach, Pros Say,"*Ars Technica,* December 9, 2014, http://arstechnica.com/security/2014/12/unprecedented-cyberattack-no-excuse-for-sony-breach-pros-say/, reported Mandiant's claim that the attack that laid Sony low could have defeated 90 percent of all corporate defenses.

24. Or even punish people after the fact. Sony's chief spokesman, Robert Lawson, said, "Lynton [Sony Entertainment's president] has no plans to fire or discipline anyone . . . [based] on the belief that because Sony's assailant was a foreign government, with far more resources than a renegade band of hackers, what happened was unstoppable. The studio simply faced an unfair fight." Peter Elkind, "Inside the Hack of the Century," *Fortune,* July 1, 2015, http://fortune.com/sony-hack-part-1/.

Chapter 21. Deterrence Fundamentals

Epigraph. James Cartwright, Statement on the United States Strategic Command before the House Armed Services Committee, March 21, 2007.

1. Brodie, *The Absolute Weapon: Atomic Power and World Order.*
2. For a good summary of RAND work on the topic, see Austin Long, *Deterrence: From Cold War to Long War* (Santa Monica, Calif.: RAND, 2008).
3. By deterrence we restrict ourselves to the prospect of punishment, "taking the fight to our adversaries."
4. There is a political case for favoring deterrence as a strategy: it shows seriousness about cybersecurity without conceding that achieving cybersecurity requires government regulation of business. The Republican Party in its 2012 platform argued, "The frequency, sophistication, and intensity of cyber-related incidents within the United States have increased steadily over the past decade and will continue to do until it is made clear that a cyberattack against the United States will not be tolerated. The current Administration's cybersecurity policies have failed to curb malicious actions by our adversaries and no wonder, for there is no active deterrence protocol. The current deterrence framework is overly reliant on the development of defensive capabilities and has been unsuccessful in dissuading cyber-related aggression." Republican National Committee, "We Believe in America: Republican Platform 2012," http://www.gop.com/wp-content/uploads/2012/08/2012GOPPlatform.pdf, 41.
5. Accordingly, Admiral Mike Rogers declared at the January 2015 International Conference on Cyber Security: "[The attack on] Sony is important to me because the entire world is watching how we as a nation are going to respond do this. . . . If we don't name names here, it will only encourage others to decide, 'Well this must not be a red line for the United States.'" Sam Frizell, "NSA Director on Sony Hack: 'The Entire World is Watching,'" *Time,* January 8, 2015, http://time.com/3660757/nsa-michael-rogers-sony-hack/.
6. This is not just an American sentiment. From Indrani Bagchi, "China Mounts Cyber Attacks on Indian Sites," *The Times of India,* May 5, 2008, http://timesofindia.indiatimes.com/india/China-mounts-cyber-attacks-on-Indian-sites/articleshow/3010288.cms: "A quiet effort is under way to set up defense mechanisms, but cyberwarfare is yet to become a big component of India's security doctrine. Dedicated teams of officials—all underpaid, of course—are involved in a daily deflection of attacks. But the real gap is that a retaliatory offensive system is yet to be created. And it's not difficult, said sources. Chinese networks are very porous—and India is an acknowledged information technology giant."
7. Conceivably, the government could turn over peacefully in the wake of the poor choices that lead to a cyberwar, although it is more plausible that conflict would initially strengthen the government's political standing. Goading Israel into attacking Lebanon did not seem to harm Hezbollah's status in Lebanon.
8. George Quester argued that the British were deterred from intervening against Hitler in 1938 because they feared the Luftwaffe (whose size they grossly overstated). Once engaged in war, they learned that defenses against air attack were, in fact, possible; as a result, they lost fewer lives during the blitz than many Axis cities did in overnight raids the Allies subsequently conducted. George Quester, *Deterrence Before Hiroshima* (New Brunswick, N.J.: Transaction Books, 1986).
9. Some have argued that it was a mistake not to have retaliated against the (purportedly) Iranian DDOS attacks on major banks in late 2012.
10. Similarly, as Richard Bejtlich (a FireEye strategist) asked, "What makes more sense: expecting the two billion Internet users worldwide to adequately secure their personal information, or reducing the threat posed by the roughly 100 top-tier malware authors?" Richard Bejtlich, "Target Malware Kingpins," *Brookings.edu,* February 2, 2105, http://www.brookings.edu/research/opinions/2015/02/02-cybersecurity-target-malware-kingpins-bejtlich.
11. Defense Science Board, "Task Force Report: Resilient Military Systems and the Advanced Cyber Threat."
12. A more formal definition comes from William Kaufmann, "The Evolution of Deterrence 1945–1958," unpublished RAND research paper, 1958: "Deterrence consists of essentially two basic components:

first, the expressed intention to defend a certain interest; secondly, the demonstrated capability actually to achieve the defense of the interest in question, or to inflict such a cost on the attacker that, even if he should be able to gain his end, it would not seem worth the effort to him."

13. By way of compensation, depletion also applies to the attacker. The undeterred attacker will find it continually harder to hit similar targets because they (indeed, all) harden as they recover from each new attack. Even as the quality of retaliation is depleting, so is the quality of the attack that retaliation was meant to deter.

Chapter 22. The Will to Retaliate

1. Some U.S. strategists argued in the late 1970s that the Soviet Union could plausibly take out the land and air legs of the U.S. triad in a first strike, spare U.S. cities, and leave the United States to choose between strategic inferiority and losing its cities. Conversely, John Mueller argued that the prospect of fighting a large-scale conventional war sufficed to deter the Soviet Union in the Cold War. See John Mueller, *Retreat from Doomsday: The Obsolescence of Major War* (New York: Basic Books, 1989).

2. See Morgan, *Deterrence: A Conceptual Analysis*, esp. 103–26.

3. In this respect, nuclear deterrence differed sharply from conventional deterrence, even in the airpower era. Someone attacked by a bombing raid could assume war had already begun and that this war would be decided by other means, such as ground power. Thus, absent solid information that the air raid was an accident or a one-off event, the case for retaliation was strong. See Quester, *Deterrence Before Hiroshima*, esp. 136–58.

4. Stephen Blank, "Can Information Warfare Be Deterred?" *Defense Analysis* 17, no. 2 (2001): pp. 121–38; and Matthew Campbell, " 'Logic Bomb' Arms Race Panics Russians," *Sunday Times*, November 29, 1998.

5. According to a former NSC staffer, third-party attacks are particularly unpredictable. Because groups outside of government can launch them, such attacks can escalate crises even as governments are trying to defuse them.

6. The DDOS attacks on North Korea in December 2014 may have been an example of pile-on (assuming they were not carried out by the United States); see Cecilia Kang, Drew Harwell, and Brian Fung, "North Korean Web Goes Dark Days after Obama Pledges Response to Sony Hack," *Washington Post*, December 22, 2014.

7. See, for instance, Pavel K. Baev, "Apocalypse a Bit Later: The Meaning of Putin's Nuclear Threats," *Brookings.edu*, April 1, 2015, http://www.brookings.edu/blogs/order-from-chaos/posts/2015/04/01-putin-nuclear-threats-meaning.

8. David Sanger and Nicole Perlroth, "Iran Is Raising Sophistication and Frequency of Cyberattacks, Study Says," *New York Times*, April 15, 2015.

9. Schelling, *Arms and Influence*.

10. As of May 2008, over three thousand Kassam rockets had been launched, and fifteen people had been killed; Israel Ministry of Foreign Affairs, "The Hamas Terror War Against Israel," August 3, 2008, http://mfa.gov.il/MFA/ForeignPolicy/Terrorism/Pages/Missile%20fire%20from%20Gaza%20on%20Israeli%20civilian%20targets%20Aug%202007.aspx.

11. These events took place just before the Bush administration left office but a month or two before the Israeli elections.

12. Unfortunately for the analogy, such credibility tends to be associated with what Kahn labeled Type III or splendid deterrence: the ability to get one's way on nonnuclear matters (for example, a conventional attack in Europe) by threatening nuclear action. Finding an analogy in cyberspace requires identifying issues *below* the cyberwar level, where the threat of escalation to cyberwar could decide the issue in one's favor—a prospect that may be defeated by the many uncertainties and ambiguities of cyberwar.

13. See Nick Farrell, "China's Infrastructure a Doddle to Hack," *Techeye*, April 28, 2011, http://news.techeye.net/security/chinas-infrastructure-a-doddle-to-hack; Steven Mufson and Jia Lynn Yang, "China Accuses Hackers of Internet Disruption; Experts Suspect Error by Government Censors," *Washington Post*, January 22, 2014. See also Gao Yuan, "Nation's Cyberspace 'Vulnerability' Exposed by Attack," *China Daily*, May 1, 2015, http://www.chinadaily.com.cn/china/2015-05/01/content_20593546.htm: "Last year, the center detected more than 1,500 major security flaws from telecom carriers, triple the amount found a

year previously. . . . Shen Yi, a researcher at Fudan University, said China has been on the receiving end of foreign online hacking. 'The country lags far behind the West in building an anti-hacking system. When the worst happens, we cannot find an effective way to defend Internet safety.'" See also "Millions Have Their Data Leaked in China," *Want China Times,* April 23, 2015, http://www.wantchinatimes.com/news-subclass-cnt.aspx?id=20150423000110&cid=1103: "As many as 52.79 million people may have had their information leaked from social security units, others from domicile registration units, disease control departments and hospitals"; Don Reisinger, "China's Internet Hit by DDoS Attack; Sites Down for Hours; The Country's Internet Watchdog Says that the Net Is Back Online for the Country and that It Will Work to Improve Security," *CNET,* August 26, 2013, http://www.cnet.com/news/chinas-internet-hit-by-ddos-attack-sites-down-for-hours/, and Stephen Chen, "Huge Cyberattack on China Was Lone Hacker, Official Claims: Experts Express Doubt after Internet Security Boss Claims Amateur in Qingdao Detained for Huge Strike on Servers," *South China Morning Post,* September 25, 2013, http://www.scmp.com/news/china/article/1317101/huge-cyberattack-done-lone-hacker-official-claims ("the biggest ever cyberattack on Chinese domain servers last month was carried out by a lone hacker, according to a government official responsible for internet security"). See also Rich Zhu, "150m Smartphones Affected by Malware," *Shanghai Daily,* July 10, 2015, http://www.shanghaidaily.com/business/it/150m-smartphones-affected-by-malware/shdaily.shtml.

14. Ian Traynor, "Russia Accused of Unleashing Cyberwar to Disable Estonia," *The Guardian,* May 17, 2007.

15. Sanger, "NATO Set to Ratify Pledge on Joint Defense in Case of Major Cyberattack."

16. It is hard to argue that the Russian cyberattacks on Georgia were meant to test Georgia or facilitate a subsequent kinetic attack on that country. Mostly they were carried out to hinder Georgia's media response to the attack.

Chapter 23. Attribution

1. John Swartz ("Chinese Hackers Seek U.S. Access," *USA Today,* March 12, 2007), spoke with Jody Westby, CEO of Global Cyber Risk: "'The Internet was not designed for security, and there are 243 countries connected to the Internet,' says Westby, who estimates 100 countries are planning infowar capabilities." The article from which the quote comes discussed Chinese cyberespionage against U.S. military computer systems. See also Jon Brodkin, "Government-sponsored Cyberattacks on the Rise, McAfee Says," *Network World,* November 29, 2007, http://www.networkworld.com/article/2289197/lan-wan/government-sponsored-cyberattacks-on-the-rise--mcafee-says.html, and James Lewis, "Cyber Attacks, Real or Imagined, and Cyber War," paper, Center for Strategic and International Studies, July 11, 2011, http://csis.org/publication/cyber-attacks-real-or-imagined-and-cyber-war. The latter states, "At least 5 militaries have advanced cyberattack capabilities, and at least another 30 countries intend to acquire them. These high-end opponents have the resources and skills to overcome most defenses." But the claim that many countries were developing cyberwar capabilities is not new. No fewer than thirty countries are working on infowar techniques, according to a December 1994 report prepared by the National Communication System, the DISA-managed unit charged with ensuring that a core of the nation's information networks remains operational during any crisis; see Munro, "Fear of an Electronic Pearl Harbor."

2. See Steven Kull et al., "Public Opinion in the Islamic World on Terrorism, al Qaeda, and U.S. Policies," University of Maryland, College Park, Program on International Policy Attitudes, 2009, http://www.worldpublicopinion.org/pipa/pdf/feb09/STARTII_Feb09_rpt.pdf, 26.

3. Alan Grayson, "On Syria Vote, Trust, but Verify," *New York Times,* September 6, 2013.

4. Kim Zetter, "The Evidence That North Korea Hacked Sony Is Flimsy," *Wired.com,* December 17, 2014, http://www.wired.com/2014/12/evidence-of-north-korea-hack-is-thin/.

5. Federal Bureau of Investigation, "Update on Sony Investigation," news release, December 17, 2014, http://www.fbi.gov/news/pressrel/press-releases/update-on-sony-investigation.

6. Bruce Schneier, "Attack Attribution in Cyberspace," *Schneier on Security,* January 8, 2015, https://www.schneier.com/blog/archives/2015/01/attack_attribut.html.

7. "In nearly every case, [the Sony hackers known as the Guardians of Peace] used proxy servers to disguise where they were coming from in sending these emails and posting these statements. . . . Several times, either because they forgot or because of a technical problem, they connected directly and we could see

that the IPs they were using . . . were exclusively used by the North Koreans." See also Andy Greenberg, "FBI Director: Sony's 'Sloppy' North Korean Hackers Revealed Their IP Addresses," *Wired.com*, January 7, 2015, http://www.wired.com/2015/01/fbi-director-says-north-korean-hackers-sometimes-failed-use-proxies-sony-hack/.

8. Reuters, "China Suggests U.S. May Have Fabricated Evidence for Cyberattacks," May 29, 2014, http://www.reuters.com/article/2014/05/29/us-china-usa-diplomacy-idUSKBN0E914H20140529.

9. Leon Panetta, "Remarks to the Business Executives for National Security in New York City," October 11, 2012, www.defense.gov/transcripts/transcript.aspx?transcriptid=5136.

10. Stewart Baker, "The Attribution Revolution: Raising the Costs for Hackers and Their Customers," testimony before the Senate Judiciary Committee, May 8, 2013, http://volokh.com/2013/05/08/testifying-on-cybersecurity-before-the-senate-judiciary-committee/.

11. Mark Mazzetti and David Sanger, "Security Leader Says U.S. Would Retaliate Against Cyberattacks," *New York Times,* March 12, 2013.

12. Bruce Schneier, "Did North Korea Really Attack Sony?" *Schneier on Security*, December 24, 2015, https://www.schneier.com/blog/archives/2014/12/did_north_korea.html.

13. The classic story being French president Charles De Gaulle's demurring when Dean Acheson offered to show him classified photos of the Soviet missile sites during the Cuban Missile Crisis, saying, in effect, the word of the president is good enough for me. Alas, those days are history.

14. Office of the National Counterintelligence Executive, "Foreign Spies Stealing U.S. Economic Secrets in Cyberspace: Report to Congress on Foreign Economic Collection and Industrial Espionage, 2009–2011," October 2011, http://www.ncix.gov/publications/reports/fecie_all/Foreign_Economic_Collection_2011.pdf.

15. There is a report that Chinese authorities have made arrests in the case of the OPM hack. Ellen Nakashima, "Chinese Government Has Arrested Hackers It Says Breached OPM Database," *Washington Post*, December 2, 2015.

16. Mandiant, "APT1: Exposing One of China's Cyber Espionage Units."

17. Nagaraja and Anderson, "The Snooping Dragon: Social-malware Surveillance of the Tibetan Movement."

18. Note another benefit that persistence yields to attribution. From Marc Ambinder, "Inside the Black Box: How NSA is Helping Companies Fight Back Against Chinese Hackers," *Foreign Policy,* March 13, 2013: "For years, and in secret, the NSA has also used the cover of some American companies—with their permission—to poke and prod at the hackers, leading them to respond in ways that reveal patterns and allow the United States to figure out, or 'attribute,' the precise origin of attacks."

19. How can one distinguish a replicable bot from a disciplined cadre of humans? The latter may have to show enough human insight in their approach to pass a Turing test. Telling evidence of human behavior may emerge if the site mandates passing an I-am-human-and-not-a-bot (for example, captcha) test. Minor differences in approach between one attack and the next may also indicate the human touch. In 2015, DARPA sponsored a capture-the-flag contested only by machines; Aliya Sternstein, "The Smartest Hackers in the Room (Hint: They're Not the Humans)," *NextGov.com,* March 25, 2015, http://www.nextgov.com/cybersecurity/2015/03/smartest-hackers-room-or-these-are-smartest-hackers-world/108466/, and Defense Advanced Research Projects Agency, "Cyber Grand Challenge," http://www.cybergrandchallenge.com/.

20. It took the pattern of Flame's distribution in the Middle East plus the correlation of its modules and Stuxnet's modules to generate the technical forensics that could link Israel with Stuxnet.

21. Peter Steiner, cartoon, *The New Yorker*, July 5, 1993, p. 61.

22. Internet Protocol version 6 (IPv6) may allow better attribution than IPv4 because it tracks the source of a packet more reliably but far from well enough to put a real dent in the attribution problem. IPv6, the urgent need for which was recognized by the early 1990s, well before the world ran out of address spaces, has yet to be completely implemented, particularly in the United States. Even when it is, the first few versions of any attribution-friendly IP would hardly be spoof proof. One might imagine a future in which Internet packets are reengineered to show some machine-specific identification number, but do not expect it very soon.

23. David A. Wheeler and Gregory N. Larsen, "Techniques for Cyber Attack Attribution," paper, Institute for Defense Analyses, 2003, presents 17 different attribution techniques, but these require very high levels of

cooperation among router owners worldwide and reveal only which machine the attack packets are com-ing from (which may be a bot and hence point only to an infected machine, not to the attacker). Many can be foiled easily if their use is anticipated. Finally, as noted, the correlation between machine and person can be quite low.

24. Consider this from Peter Walker, "American Expats Caught Up in Indian Bomb Blast Inquiry," *The Guardian,* July 29, 2008: "When Indian police investigating bomb blasts which killed 42 people traced an email claiming responsibility to a Mumbai apartment, they ordered an immediate raid. But at the address, rather than seizing militants from the Islamist group which said it carried out the attack, they found a group of puzzled American expats. In a cautionary tale for those still lax with their wireless internet secu-rity, police believe the email about the explosions on Saturday in the west Indian city of Ahmedabad was sent after someone hijacked the network belonging to one of the Americans."

25. Incidentally, North Korea did offer to help with the investigation, an offer that was summarily dis-missed by the United States as insincere. Marc Ferranti, "U.S. Rejects North Korea Offer to Investi-gate Sony Hack, Reaches Out to China," *PC World,* December 20, 2014, http://www.pcworld.com/article/2861992/us-rejects-north-korea-offer-to-investigate-sony-hack-reaches-out-to-china.html.

26. In some countries, what investigators are looking for may not be illegal. In Argentina, a group calling themselves the X-Team hacked into the website of that country's supreme court in April 2002. The trial judge stated that the law in his country covers crime against people, things, and animals but not websites. The group on trial was declared not guilty of breaking into the site. Lourdes Heredia, "Hacking 'Legal' in Argentina," BBC, April 16, 2002, http://news.bbc.co.uk/2/hi/americas/1932191.stm.

27. Roger C. Molander, Andrew S. Riddile, and Peter A. Wilson, *Strategic Information Warfare: A New Face of War* (Santa Monica, Calif.: RAND, 1996).

28. See Michael Riley and Jordan Robertson, "Cyberspace Becomes Second Front in Russia's Clash with NATO," Bloomberg, October 14, 2015, http://www.bloomberg.com/news/articles/2015-10-14/cyberspace-becomes-second-front-in-russia-s-clash-with-nato.

29. Replacing tell-tale words with numbers as a way of identifying files, using standard American keyboards, and working (or at least time-stamping files during) standard American hours can go a long way toward removing the national coloration of cyberattacks—but such habits are the exception rather than the rule. Cybersecurity investigators typically find that communications between the malware in their clients' networks and the malware's command and control centers decline sharply at 6 a.m. on Fridays (eastern time) and resumes at 6 p.m. on Sundays—thereby suggesting what time zone the hackers operated from, but also that they got weekends off, signs of regular employment. For a good assessment of the many ways in which attribution can take place precisely because of lackadaisical operational security, see Tomas Rid and Ben Buchanan, "Attributing Cyber Attacks," *Journal of Strategic Studies* 38, no. 1 (2014). Incidentally, if attribution is carried out using cultural rather than geographical markers, how can, say, ethnic Russian hackers be distinguished from Russia's hackers?

30. If the account in Brian Grow, Keith Epstein, and Chi-Chu Tschang, "The New E-spionage Threat," *BusinessWeek,* April 21, 2008, 32–41, is true, the hackers, supposedly Chinese, who sent a rogue email to a vice president of Booz Allen Hamilton also sent a blind copy to James Mulvenon, whose counter-hacker activities are well known in China. One has to believe that such a look-what-we-can-do side message is the work not of national security professionals but of amateurs, albeit talented ones. Paying freelancers offers only a slight advantage in after-the-fact deniability. But the government has less control over free-lancers than it has over its own staff. The former may use amateurish techniques, may wander from the designated target list, and, worse, may be in the target's pocket and thus eager to implicate when "caught."

31. According to Alexander Klimburg of the Harvard Kennedy School of Government's Belfer Center, there are many examples of Russian hackers "lending" their zero-day hacks to the government for espionage purposes, then using them for crime later; Owen Matthews, "Russia's Greatest Weapon May Be Its Hack-ers," *Newsweek,* May 7, 2015.

32. See Michael Reilly, "How Long Before All-Out Cyberwar?" *New Scientist,* no. 2644 (February 20, 2008): pp. 24–25, and Rose Tang, "China Warns of Massive Hack Attacks," *CNN.com,* May 3, 2001.

33. Ross Anderson, who is by no means a cyberwar hawk, nevertheless argued that "[i]f our air-defense threat in 1987 was mainly the Russian air force, and our cyber defense threat in 2007 is mainly from a small

number of Russian gangs, and they are imposing large costs on U.S. and European Internet users and companies, then state action may be needed now as it was then. Instead of telling us to buy antivirus software, our governments could be putting greater pressure on the Russians to round up and jail their cyber gangsters." See Anderson, *Security Engineering*, 220. Elsewhere, Anderson notes that Russian police "were prodded into arresting the gang responsible" for using botnets to extort money from online bookmakers"; ibid., 198, 640. More recently, Russia cooperated in the takedown of the Simda botnet; Dan Goodin, "Botnet that Enslaved 770,000 PCs Worldwide Comes Crashing Down," *Ars Technica,* April 13, 2015, http://arstechnica.com/security/2015/04/botnet-that-enslaved-770000-pcs-worldwide-comes-crashing-down/.

34. Amos Harel and Avi Issacharoff, *34 Days: Israel, Hezbollah, and the War in Lebanon* (Basingstoke, UK: Palgrave-MacMillan, 2008).

35. Thornburgh, "Inside the Chinese Hack Attack."

36. FireEye, "M-Trends 2015."

37. Electronic Frontier Foundation, "RSA Code-Breaking Contest Again Won by Distributed.Net and Electronic Frontier Foundation (EFF)," press release, January 19, 1999, https://w2.eff.org/Privacy/Crypto/Crypto_misc/DESCracker/HTML/19990119_deschallenge3.html.

38. Much as North Korea has denied hacking Sony but applauded those that did; Choe Sang-Hundec, "North Korea Denies Role in Sony Pictures Hacking," *New York Times,* December 7, 2014. North Korea's use of the word "righteous," incidentally, is largely unprecedented in its public affairs announcements (outside of a religious context and the term "self-righteous," it is unusual in English as well). Its use raises the question of where the word came from. Inasmuch as the sentence referenced by this footnote was previously published in the author's *Brandishing Cyberattack Capability* (Santa Monica, Calif.: RAND, 2013, RR-175) (and that the author's work does circulate in East Asia), the conclusion that the term worked its way from that monograph into North Korea's press release is not totally outlandish. If so, then the North Korean extraction of this word from a paragraph on how to coerce without attribution would seem to provide a curious hint that they did it.

39. The aforementioned U.S. attempt to sotto voce claim credit for Stuxnet at the expense of any credit Israel may claim for itself might insulate Israel from blame (albeit not by much), but it also erodes Israel's ability to boast of its dominance over its hostile neighbors (albeit also not by much).

40. Adam Zagorin, "Can KSM's Confession Be Believed?" *Time,* March 15, 2007, reported the following: "[Khalid Sheikh Mohammed] admitted under previous interrogation that a list of 30 supposed U.S. targets, which he circulated shortly after 9/11, was a lie to exaggerate the scale of al-Qaeda's planning. Terrorism experts say that though there is no doubt Mohammed played a major role in planning 9/11, he's famous among interrogators for his braggadocio. 'He has nothing else in life but to be remembered as a famous terrorist,' says Bruce Riedel, senior fellow at the Saban Center at the Brookings Institution and a 29-year veteran of the Central Intelligence Agency. 'He wants to promote his own importance. It's been a problem since he was captured,' says Riedel, who went on to say he wouldn't be surprised if Mohammed was exaggerating his role in other plots."

41. To illustrate as much, assume the target thinks that the attacker is as likely to be State Y as it is State Z (but does not believe that Y and Z colluded). If it retaliates against one, why not against the other? The only way that could be justified is that if believes that the consequences of hitting an innocent State Y are worse than letting State Z get away with an attack.

42. From *Economist.com,* "The Siege," July 12, 2014, http://www.economist.com/news/leaders/21606831-believing-vladimir-putin-has-surrendered-ukraine-would-be-naive-west-must-keep-up: "[The West] connived in Mr. Putin's pretense that he had not invaded eastern Ukraine—even though in a furtive tricksy way he plainly had—because to say otherwise would have required a drastic response."

43. "We have chosen not to make any official assertions about attribution at this point," said a senior administration official, despite the widely held conviction that Beijing was responsible. The official cited factors including concern that making a public case against China could require exposing details of the United States' own espionage and cyberspace capabilities." Ellen Nakashima, "U.S. Decides Against Publicly Blaming China for Data Hack," *Washington Post,* July 21, 2015.

44. Sean Gallagher, "Iranians Hacked Navy Network for Four Months? Not a Surprise," *Ars Technica,* February 19, 2014, http://arstechnica.com/information-technology/2014/02/iranians-hacked-navy-network-for-4-months-not-a-surprise/.

45. The NSA has steadfastly refused to concede that anything released by Snowden, at least as it pertains to overseas operations, represents reality. In May 2014, the DNI reiterated and reinforced its policy forbidding intelligence community officials from commenting on these revelations in any way: Charlie Savage, "Memo Revisits Policy on Citing Leaked Material, to Some Confusion," *New York Times,* May 9, 2014.

46. One of the five individuals indicted by the Department of Justice in May 2014, a soldier with the nom de hack of UglyGorilla, was cited in the Mandiant report.

47. Several of these firms have been referenced earlier. For the two that have not, see Cylance, "Operational Cleaver," report, December 2014, http://www.cylance.com/assets/Cleaver/Cylance_Operation_Cleaver_Report.pdf, and iSight Partners, "Russian Cyber Espionage Campaign—Sandworm Team," report, October 14, 2015, http://www.washingtonpost.com/r/2010-2019/WashingtonPost/2014/10/14/National-Security/Graphics/briefing2.pdf.

48. From Kim Zetter, "U.S. and British Spies Targeted Antivirus Companies," *Wired.com,* June 22, 2015, http://www.wired.com/2015/06/us-british-spies-targeted-antivirus-companies/: "Any time Kaspersky's antivirus and other security software detects a new infection on the machine of a customer who has opted-in to the program, or encounters a suspicious file, data gets sent automatically to Kaspersky's servers so the company's algorithms and analysts can study and track emerging and existing threats." Also, when software crashes and the operating system asks whether you want to tell Microsoft, one is seeing the latter's surveillance net at work as well.

Chapter 24. What Threshold and Confidence for Response?

1. See, for instance, Jamey Keaten and Sylvie Corbet, "France Sees 19,000 Cyberattacks Since Terror Rampage," *Phys,* January 15, 2015, http://phys.org/news/2015-01-france-cyberdefense-chief-cyberattacks-week.html.

2. Tomas Rid, "Deterrence Beyond the State: The Israel Experience," *Contemporary Security Policy* 33, no. 1 (2012): p. 141.

3. Mark Whitaker and John Wolcott, in "Getting Rid of Kaddafi," *Newsweek,* April 28, 1986, reported that "early polls show overwhelmingly popular enthusiasm for the president's decision to punish Kaddafi and, publicly, administration officials are confident that support will hold up." It is quite another question whether the strike on Libya was proportionate or even wise, given that the Lockerbie incident, which killed more than 200, was almost certainly an act of counter-retaliation.

4. The cost of scrubbing Stuxnet from the hundreds of thousands of systems it wormed its way into may well have been comparable to the cost of Iran having to replace the thousand centrifuges that were the worm's target.

5. Iain Thomson, "South Korea Faces $1Bn Bill after Hackers Raid National ID Database," *The Register,* October 14, 2014, http://www.theregister.co.uk/2014/10/14/south_korea_national_identity_system_hacked/.

6. For instance, if Sony executives were to spend a great deal of money making a film that they knew had no commercial prospects, they could be sued for dereliction of their fiduciary duty to shareholders. Can one imagine a major film studio producing a film that portrayed the assassination of a U.S. media mogul—and not getting sued? Also, the First Amendment only covers what U.S. governments cannot do.

7. The planned movie, *Pyongyang,* was cancelled, almost certainly as a result of threats made manifest by the Sony hack; Aly Weisman, "Steve Carell's North Korea–based Thriller Scrapped after Sony Scandal," *Business Insider,* December 17, 2014, http://www.businessinsider.com/steve-carell-north-korea-movie-cancelled-2014-12.

8. Sony's financial statement for the fourth quarter of 2014 claims only $15 million of loss from investigation and remediation expenses, but another $20 million was expected to be incurred in the first quarter of 2015; Tim Hornyak, "Hack to Cost Sony $35 Million in IT Repairs," *Network World,* February 4, 2015, http://www.networkworld.com/article/2879814/data-center/sony-hack-cost-15-million-but-earnings-unaffected.html.

9. Frank Pallotta, "Sony's 'The Interview' Coming to Netflix," CNN, January 20, 2015, http://money.cnn.com/2015/01/20/media/the-interview-makes-40-million/.

10. David Sanger, "Pentagon Announces New Strategy for Cyberwarfare," *New York Times,* April 23, 2015.

11. See Anthony Capaccio, "Cyber-Armageddon Less Likely than Predicted, Clapper Says," Bloomberg, February 25, 2015, http://www.bloomberg.com/news/articles/2015-02-26/cyber-armageddon-less-likely-

than-smaller-attacks-clapper-says for the quote, and James R. Clapper, "Statement for the Record: World-wide Threat Assessment of the U.S. Intelligence Community," before the Senate Armed Services Committee, February 26, 2015, http://cdn.arstechnica.net/wp-content/uploads/2015/02/Clapper_02-26-15.pdf for the document.

12. One possible example of which is Mark Clayton, "Ukraine Election Narrowly Avoided 'Wanton Destruction' from Hackers," *Christian Science Monitor,* June 17, 2014.

13. Consider the following hypothetical mooted by a DoD official lauding the deterrent effect of resilience: "It alters the cost-benefit analysis if the . . . lights only go out for 15 minutes. Now the bad guys are in a pretty bad position, because they launched an attack on the nation . . . and we know what they were trying to do. And if you're the leader of bad country X, you know it's game on, somebody's coming after you, and the response is probably not just going to be cyber if you went after us in a major way." Jared Serbu, "DoD to Be More Transparent about Strategy to Deter Cyber Attacks," Federal News Radio, October 3, 2014, http://www.federalnewsradio.com/394/3714846/DoD-to-be-more-transparent-about-strategy-to-deter-cyberattacks. Now ask: Would the United States retaliate if it were a complete failure? Conversely, if the attacker knew that total failure would not be retaliated against, the deterrent value of a defense posture that stops the attack entirely is less than the deterrence value of a defense posture that allows the lights to go back on after 15 minutes—which is counterintuitive to say the least.

14. Demetri Sevastopluo, "Chinese Hacked into Pentagon," *FT.com*, September 3, 2007, http://www.ft.com/intl/cms/s/0/9dba9ba2-5a3b-11dc-9bcd-0000779fd2ac.html#axzz3gWdmhe9M.

15. Rogers Boyes, "China Accused of Hacking into Heart of Merkel Administration," *Times Online* (London), August 27, 2007, http://www.thetimes.co.uk/tto/news/world/europe/article2595759.ece; see also *Der Spiegel,* "Merkel's China Visit Marred by Hacking Allegations."

16. Gary S. Becker provides the classic formulation of the position that the odds of punishment rather than its severity reduce criminal activity in "Crime and Punishment: An Economic Approach," *Journal of Political Economy* 76, no. 2 (1968): p. 9: "[A] common generalization by persons with judicial experience is that a change in the probability has a greater effect on the number of offenses than a change in the punishment, although, as far as I can tell, none of the prominent theories shed any light on this relation. For example, Hartley Shawcross ("Crime Does Pay Because We Do Not Back Up the Police," *New York Times Magazine*, June 13, 1965) said, 'Some judges preoccupy themselves with methods of punishment. This is their job. But in preventing crime it is of less significance than they like to think. Certainty of detection is far more important than severity of punishment.'"

17. See Vernon Loeb, "Test of Strength," *Washington Post Magazine*, July 29, 2001. Later revelations by Edward Snowden revealed how routinely this was done.

18. Ellen Nakashima, "U.S. Developing Sanctions Against China over Cyberthefts," *Washington Post,* August 30, 2015.

19. See for instance, Evan Thomas, *Ike's Bluff: President Eisenhower's Secret Battle to Save the World* (New York: Little, Brown and Company, 2012).

20. From Defense Science Board, "Task Force Report: Resilient Military Systems and the Advanced Cyber Threat," 32: "Cyber risk can be managed through the combination of deterrence (up to a nuclear response in the most extreme case) and improved cyber defense."

21. See Michael Johnson and Terrence K. Kelly, "Tailored Deterrence: Strategic Context to Guide Joint Force 2020," *Joint Force Quarterly* 74, no. 3 (July 2014): pp. 22–29.

22. For an example of this exercise carried out with sample numbers, see Libicki, *Cyberdeterrence and Cyberwar*, 183–97 (Appendix B).

23. From Arquilla, "Ethics and Information Warfare," 396, citing Hugh Thomas, *The Spanish Civil War* (New York: Harper and Brothers, 1961).

Chapter 25. Punishment and Holding Targets at Risk

1. For a broader survey, see T. W. Beagle, "Effects-based Targeting: Another Empty Promise?" (thesis, School of Advanced Airpower Studies, Air University, 2000).

2. Notwithstanding indications there is enough internal connectivity for the NSA to carry out cyberespionage against North Korea (especially if no one is to notice); see David Sanger and Martin Fackler, "N.S.A. Breached North Korean Networks Before Sony Attack, Officials Say," *New York Times,* January 19, 2015.

3. President Obama indicated as much when he stated, "No, I don't think it was an act of war. I think it was an act of cyber vandalism that was very costly, very expensive. We take it very seriously. We will respond proportionately." Steve Holland and Doina Chiacu, "Obama Says Sony Hack Not an Act of War," Reuters, December 22, 2014, http://www.reuters.com/article/2014/12/22/us-sony-cybersecurity-usa-idUSKB N0JX1MH20141222; but see also Matt Schiavenza, "Why North Korea Sanctions Are Unlikely to Be Effective," *The Atlantic,* January 3, 2015.

4. Or at least prematurely now that NATO changed its mind on forward defense in late 2014; see also Josephine Wolff, "NATO's Empty Cybersecurity Gesture: Its New Approach to Cyberattacks Misses Some Fundamental Points," *Slate,* September 10, 2014, http://www.slate.com/articles/technology/future_ tense/2014/09/nato_s_statement_on_cyberattacks_misses_some_fundamental_points.html.

5. See Traynor, "Russia Accused of Unleashing Cyberwar to Disable Estonia."

6. The sudden death of Mojtaba Ahmadi, who served as commander of Iran's cyberwar headquarters, has been attributed to assassination; the Iranians deny as much, but that hardly settles the matter. "Iranian Cyberwarfare Commander Shot Dead in Suspected Assassination," *The Telegraph,* October 2, 2013, http://www.telegraph.co.uk/news/worldnews/middleeast/iran/10350285/Iranian-cyber-warfare-commander-shot-dead-in-suspected-assassination.html.

7. McConnell, "Mike McConnell on How to Win the Cyber-War We're Losing."

8. He asked, "How do we increase our capacity on the offensive side to get to that point of deterrence?" Ellen Nakashima, "Cyber Chief: Efforts to Deter Attacks Against the U.S. Are Not Working," *Washington Post,* March 19, 2015.

9. The case for U.S. retaliation against Iran to forestall private vigilantism is like a similarly specious case for the death penalty: to inhibit lynching. Conversely, even though rule of law for cyberspace is a good thing, there is something to be said for not eliminating *all* risks for an attacker against whom the United States is not prepared to retaliate officially.

Chapter 26. Deterrence by Denial

1. In essence: whatever a priori likelihood it assigned to the possibility that the target is impenetrable, every failed attempt eliminates the possibility that the target could be penetrated after 1, then 2, then 3 then . . . *N* attempts, there raising the relative a posteriori likelihood that it truly cannot be penetrated.

2. Here, the a priori assumption is that there *is* a pathway in. Every failure eliminates one failure or maybe a larger class of failures, leaving it more likely that the next try will find the pathway, since the past failures are no longer in the search space.

3. The founder of CrowdStrike has argued that one Chinese cyberespionage group, after having tried and failed multiple times, found software from CrowdStrike on a system it had penetrated and forthwith ceased its efforts; Andrea Shalal, "U.S. Firm CrowdStrike Claims Success in Deterring Chinese Hackers," *Web Culture,* April 14, 2015, http://www.webculture.com/17/Tech%20Top%20News/16/a/19280884/ US_firm_CrowdStrike_claims_success_in_deterring_Chinese_hackers.

4. Willie Jones, "DARPA Seeks Self-Healing Networks," *IEEE Spectrum,* October 25, 2013, http://spectrum.ieee.org/riskfactor/computing/it/darpa-seeks-selfhealing-networks.

5. Bruce Schneier, "Refuse to be Terrorized," *Schneier on Security,* August 24, 2006, https://www.schneier.com/essay-124.html. In fairness, his advice was meant to prevent what he felt were stupid and costly defensive policies vis-à-vis discouraging terrorists, many of whom carry out their attacks not for the effect on the actions of the targets, but to gain status against their rivals.

Chapter 27. Cyberwar Escalation

1. Herman Kahn, *On Escalation: Metaphors and Scenarios* (New York: Praeger, 1965).

2. From Schelling, *Arms and Influence,* 191: "We usually think of having failed if a major war ever occurs. And so it has; but it could fail worse if no effort were made to extend deterrence into war itself."

3. For a richer treatment, see Forrest E. Morgan et al., *Dangerous Thresholds: Managing Escalation in the 21st Century* (Santa Monica, Calif.: RAND Corporation, MG-614-AF, 2008), especially the first few chapters.

4. Albert Wohlstetter and Richard Brody, "Continuing Control as a Requirement for Deterring," in *Managing Nuclear Operations,* ed. Ashton B. Carter, John D. Steinbruner, and Charles A. Zraket (Washington, D.C.: Brookings Institution, 1987), 142–96, posits a hypothetical conflict circa 1985 in which the Soviet

Union attacks NATO's southern flank with nuclear weapons to shatter the alliance. NATO concludes that it lacks a comparably good nuclear target, so it escalates to find its own sweet spot, which, by definition, is a sour spot for the Soviet Union, prompting it to counter-escalate, and so on.

5. One can guess at certain types of vulnerabilities (for example, the likelihood that a user has a compromised machine) statistically, but many of the nastiest attacks do enough damage if they succeed but once.

6. Schelling, *Arms and Influence*.

7. Using means rather than ends as the measuring rod of escalation downplays the possibility that means may be shifted, not to gain an advantage but because prior means have been rendered unavailable. Cyberattacks, for instance, may be used as an attempt to replace effects that electronic warfare previously offered.

8. Morgan et al., *Dangerous Thresholds: Managing Escalation in the 21st Century*.

9. A similar point is made in Kahn, *On Escalation*, 5.

10. Attacks, albeit kinetic ones, on facilities owned by friends of Milosevic may have convinced him that losing his friends was worse than losing Kosovo; see Stephen T. Hosmer, *The Conflict Over Kosovo: Why Milosevic Decided to Settle When He Did* (Santa Monica, Calif.: RAND Corporation, MR-1351-AF, 2001).

11. The problem and the strategy, developed by Anatol Rapaport, are discussed in Robert Axelrod, *The Evolution of Cooperation* (New York: Basic Books, 1984). The term *prisoner's dilemma* describes a situation in which each of two players (prisoners) must choose whether to compete with (by ratting on) or cooperate with (by staying silent about) the other. Each player's individual advantage lies with competing with the other (whether or not the other player competes or cooperates), but both would be better off if they both cooperated.

12. In this and the prior bullet, the disjunction is the same if "the effects you produced" is replaced by "the effects you think you produced." For instance, the attacker or the retaliator may not see the collateral damage that it does.

13. Terrorism constitutes an exception, but one that is limited by virtue of the kind of weapons that can be brought into the United States and close to the target without being detected.

14. Countries may have limited visibility into what their foes consider sensitive. The wider the differences between them, the greater the likelihood that the other side will consider a target especially sensitive even as the attacking side considers it no more sensitive than previously hit targets.

15. Ellen Nakashima, "Dismantling of Saudi–CIA Web Site Illustrates Need for Clearer Cyberwar Policies," *Washington Post*, March 19, 2010.

16. His theory of the focal point was developed in Thomas Schelling, *The Strategy of Conflict* (Cambridge, Mass.: Harvard University Press, 1960), 53–80.

17. But it is not as if they are absent in the physical world, though; see Morgan et al., *Dangerous Thresholds: Managing Escalation in the 21st Century*.

18. Although, as noted, the United States never apologized for downing an Iranian Airbus in 1988, it paid $62 million to settle subsequent claims eight years later. In 1904, the Imperial Russian fleet, thinking that it saw Japanese warships, attacked British fishermen and almost precipitated a war with England. See Gavin Weightman, *Industrial Revolutionaries: The Making of the Modern World 1776–1914* (London: Grove Atlantic, 2009), 342–45.

19. Kahn, *On Escalation*, 127.

20. Stuxnet was estimated to have a gestation of a year, and that may have been *after* the necessary zero-day attacks were discovered.

21. Consider, therefore, the implications of this "observation," from Joseph S. Nye, "Nuclear Lessons for Cyber Security?" *Strategic Studies Quarterly* 5, no. 4 (Winter 2011): 18–38: "Rather than the 30 minutes of nuclear warning and possible launch under attack, today there would be 300 milliseconds between a computer detecting that it was about to be attacked by hostile malware and a preemptive response to disarm the attack."

22. This is a much smaller problem for intrawar deterrence because the usual reason to not respond in peacetime is the fear of starting a war—but if the war has already started, such a fear is limited to the fear of the other side escalating.

23. The quote is, "If you shut down our power grid, maybe we will put a missile down one of your smokestacks." Siobhan Gorman and Julian E. Barnes, "Cyber Combat: Act of War," *Wall Street Journal*, May 31, 2011.

24. Examples may include Wilhelmine Germany facing a steadily strengthening Russia and fearing encirclement, a Japan facing an economically devastating cutoff of raw materials, or an Iraq whose ability to pay war debts was, it claimed, being seriously crimped by Kuwaiti stubbornness about oil markets.

25. If the third party is attacking precisely to create further mischief between adversaries, what prevents it from copying one side's modus operandi as part of the ruse? Alas, little. And if foes can argue that the modus operandi is different than what the attack shows, what prevents them from carrying out attacks that look like those of third parties and then excusing themselves with the same argument?

26. Adding the forces of one to the search agenda for the other, conversely, may not be as efficient as having each partner pursue its own approach separately, *if* a failure in imagination rather than a shortfall of effort better explains why attempts to penetrate an adversary's system falls short.

27. Barry R. Posen, "Inadvertent Nuclear War? Escalation and NATO's Northern Flank," *International Security* 7, no. 2 (Autumn 1982): 33.

Chapter 28. Brandishing Cyberattack Capabilities

1. The explicitness of the threat does not necessarily conform to how openly a capability is declared. It is possible to be very open about having a capability without drawing red lines. With somewhat more difficulty, one can make an explicit threat based on an implied capability.

2. See also Henry Farrell, "The Political Science of Cybersecurity IV: How Edward Snowden Helps U.S. Deterrence," *Washington Post,* March 12, 2014: "Nevertheless, when asked, 'Has the U.S. ever "demonstrated capabilities" in cyberspace in a way that would lead to deterrence of potential adversaries?' General Alexander responded, 'Not in any significant way.'" Alexander, "Advance Questions for Lieutenant General Keith Alexander, USA, Nominee for Commander, United States CYBERCOM."

3. See Quester, *Deterrence Before Hiroshima.* Note that this was roughly fifteen years and many generations of aircraft after the last use of airpower against a sophisticated foe. Yet as the Battle of Britain later proved, once countries faced real bombers, damage was less than feared, and they did not always get through.

4. This may explain why South Korea hinted that it is working on malware to do to North Korea's nuclear capability what Stuxnet did to Iran's; "South Korea to Develop Stuxnet-like Cyberweapons," BBC, February 21, 2014, http://www.bbc.com/news/technology-26287527; see also Joe Boyle, "South Korea's Strange Cyberwar Admission," BBC, March 2, 2014, http://www.bbc.com/news/world-asia-26330816.

5. An early version of the core argument of this section can be found in the author's "Wringing Deterrence from Cyberwar Capabilities," in *Economics and Security: Resourcing National Priorities,* ed. Richmond M. Lloyd, William B. Ruger Chair of National Security Economics Papers no. 5 (Newport, R.I.: Naval War College, May 19–21, 2010), 259–72.

6. Sanger, "Obama Order Sped up Wave of Cyberattacks against Iran."

7. "Pre-emptive cyber strikes against perceived national security threats are a 'civilized option' to neutralize potential attacks, Britain's armed forces minister said Sunday. Nick Harvey made the comment at the Shangri-La Dialogue security summit in Singapore in relation to reports that the U.S. had launched cyberattacks to cripple Iran's nuclear program." Agence France-Presse, "Cyber Strikes a 'Civilized' Option: Britain," *Inquirer,* June 3, 2012, http://technology.inquirer.net/11747/cyber-strikes-a-civilized-option-britain. Britain's stance was supported by Canadian defense minister Peter Gordon MacKay, who likened a preemptive cyber strike to an "insurance policy," warning of the need to be prepared.

8. Michael R. Gordon, "Russia Displays a New Military Prowess in Ukraine's East," *New York Times,* April 21, 2014.

9. Christopher Strohm and Kasia Klimasinska, "Europeans Start Hacking Drills Following Russian Sanction," Bloomberg, April 28, 2014, http://www.bloomberg.com/news/2014-04-28/europeans-start-hacking-drills-following-russian-sanction.html.

10. "Turning Off the Taps: There Is More that Could Be Done to Punish Russia," *Economist,* April 19, 2014, http://www.economist.com/news/briefing/21601051-there-more-could-be-done-punish-russia-turning-taps.

11. "Putin's New Model Army: Money and Reform Have Given Russia Armed Forces It Can Use," *Economist,* May 24, 2014, http://www.economist.com/news/europe/21602743-money-and-reform-have-given-russia-armed-forces-it-can-use-putins-new-model-army.

12. Kathleen Miles, "Security Experts Warn of Possible Russian Cyberattack Against the U.S., Ukraine," *Huffington Post,* April 30, 2014, http://www.huffingtonpost.com/2014/04/30/russian-cyberattack-us-ukraine_n_5237377.html. He had posited that a military intervention to stop Iran's nuclear program would involve "attacks in the United States through cyberattacks from Iran." David Horovitz, "Running Out of Time on Iran, and All Out of Options," *Times of Israel,* June 19, 2013, http://www.timesofisrael.com/running-out-of-time-on-iran-and-all-out-of-options/.

13. Matthew Goldstein, Nicole Perlroth, and David Sanger, "Hackers' Attack Cracked 10 Financial Firms in Major Assault," *New York Times,* October 3, 2014. Those actually arrested for the hack were not from Russia but from Florida and Israel; Matthew Goldstein, "4 Arrested in Schemes Said to Be Tied to JPMorgan Chase Breach," *New York Times,* July 21, 2015.

14. Admiral Michael S. Rogers, commander, CYBERCOM, statement before the House Committee on Armed Services Subcommittee on Emerging Threats and Capabilities, March 4, 2015, 10, referring to his earlier testimony before the House Permanent Select Committee on Intelligence.

15. Jim Puzzanghera, "Expect More Web Hacking If U.S. Strikes Syria: Cybersecurity Expert," *Los Angeles Times,* August 28, 2013.

16. From Joel Brenner, "Nations Everywhere Are Exploiting the Lack of Cybersecurity," *Washington Post,* October 24, 2014: "But in the wake of the attack, the New York Times reported, 'No one could tell the president what he most wanted to know: What was the motive?' An unnamed senior official reportedly said: 'The question kept coming back, "Is this plain old theft, or is [Russian president Vladimir] Putin retaliating?"'" The question implied that the U.S. intelligence community believed that the Russian services could penetrate and perhaps take down a major U.S. bank. Two Israeli citizens and a U.S. citizen were ultimately indicted for the JP Morgan Chase hack. See Liz Moyer, "Prosecutors Announce More Charges in Hacking of JPMorgan Chase," *New York Times,* November 10, 2015. Michael Corkery, Jessica Silver-Greenberg, and David Sanger, "Obama Had Security Fears on JPMorgan Data Breach," *New York Times,* October 8, 2014: "Given that uncertainty, can anyone believe the president's freedom of action has not already been impinged upon by this cyber-operation?"

17. Melissa Lee had asked Deputy Secretary of Defense Lynn outright: "Was the U.S. involved in any way in the development of Stuxnet?" Lynn's response is long enough that an inattentive viewer might not notice that it does not answer the question. "The challenges of Stuxnet, as I said, what it shows you is the difficulty of any, any attribution and it's something that we're still looking at, it's hard to get into any kind of comment on that until we've finished our examination," Lynn replies. "But sir, I'm not asking you if you think another country was involved," Lee presses. "I'm asking you if the U.S. was involved. If the Department of Defense was involved." "And this is not something that we're going to be able to answer at this point," Lynn finally says. Kim Zetter, "Senior Defense Official Caught Hedging on U.S. Involvement in Stuxnet," *Wired.com,* May 26, 2011, http://www.wired.com/threatlevel/2011/05/defense-department-stuxnet/.

18. Ellen Nakashima, "With Plan X, Pentagon Seeks to Spread U.S. Military Might to Cyberspace," *Washington Post,* May 30, 2012. The DARPA announcement of an industry day associated with this program, however, noted, "The Plan X program is explicitly *not* funding . . . cyberweapons generation." However, it is funding command and control suites for offensive cyberwar including the use of virtual reality goggles. Andy Greenberg, "DARPA Turns Oculus into a Weapon for Cyberwar," *Wired.com,* May 23, 2014, http://www.wired.com/2014/05/darpa-is-using-oculus-rift-to-prep-for-cyberwar/.

Chapter 29. Cyberattack in a Nuclear Confrontation

1. For the sake of tractability, our analysis will ignore many of the options and branch points that exist in even the simplest nuclear confrontation of this sort. For instance, if the threat from the nuclear rogue is implicit, it may not be obvious to the United States which act crosses the line. Under such circumstances, the loss of face that the rogue state would experience by not responding with nuclear weapons is weaker. However, if the United States concludes that the implicit threats rang hollow once, it may feel it is home free. If the rogue state wants to preserve its ability to threaten, it may have to find and communicate a second threshold (or, what is more difficult, try to compel the United States to pull back or avoid repetition) and declare an explicit threat. Similarly, there may be multiple thresholds of nuclear use, some of which

may invite all-out retaliation and others not. Options may include, in order of severity: a demonstration shot, a burst that destroys equipment but not people (for example, an electromagnetic pulse shot), an anti-ship/fleet attack, an attack on ground forces, an attack on an allied population center, or finally an attack on U.S. soil.

2. Schelling, *The Strategy of Conflict.*

3. But what if one side's determination to make the other side pay far overwhelms the desire to optimize outcomes? This possibility should not be dismissed lightly. People often punish cheaters even at the expense of their own well-being in a game-like situation. Economists have repeatedly shown as much, notably by watching people play the ultimatum game in which two players interact to decide how to divide a sum of money that is given to them; Martin A. Nowak, Karen M. Page, and Karl Sigmund, "Fairness Versus Reason in the Ultimatum Game," *Science* 289, no. 5485 (September 2000): pp. 1773–75. Indeed, this tendency may be hard-wired from birth; see, for instance, Marco F. H. Schmidt and Jessica A. Sommerville, "Fairness Expectations and Altruistic Sharing in 15-Month-Old Human Infants," *PLOS ONE* 6, no. 10 (October 7, 2011).

4. The nuclear command cycle is used loosely to refer not only to the linkage between the order to launch a nuclear weapon and/or detonate a nuclear device but also to the integrity of instructions that collectively launch the missile and detonate the warhead. Corrupted instructions could lead to a misfire, poor aim, failure to detonate, or premature detonation.

5. This is perfectly consistent with the Bayesian model of inference. Assume that the rogue state believes that the number of exploitable flaws in its system is a variable with the following a priori probability distribution: an 80 percent likelihood that there are zero flaws, a 10 percent likelihood that there is one flaw, and a 10 percent likelihood that there are two flaws. The expected number of flaws is 0.3 (80 percent x 0 + 10 percent x 1 + 10 percent x 2). A flaw is then found and eradicated. This eliminates the possibility that the system was flawless. However, it says nothing about whether the system started out with one flaw or with two flaws—both were equally likely beforehand and equally likely afterward (if anything, finding one strengthens the case for there having been two flaws). So, once a flaw has been eradicated, there *now* is a 50 percent likelihood of there being zero remaining flaws and a 50 percent likelihood of there being one remaining flaw. The expected number of flaws *after discovery and eradication* is 0.5 (50 percent x 0 + 50 percent x 1). Thus, while finding and fixing a flaw reduced the *actual number of flaws* by one, it raised the *expected number of remaining flaws* by 0.2.

6. See the statements of Kaspersky when it was itself hacked: Kaspersky Labs, "Duqu Is Back: Kaspersky Lab Reveals Cyberattack On its Corporate Network that also Hit High Profile Victims in Western Countries, the Middle East and Asia," report, June 10, 2015, http://www.kaspersky.com/about/news/virus/2015/Duqu-is-back. See also Kim Zetter, "Attackers Stole Certificate from Foxconn to Hack Kaspersky with Duqu 2.0," *Wired.com,* June 15, 2015, http://www.wired.com/2015/06/foxconn-hack-kaspersky-duqu-2/.

7. There may, in fact, be no correlation between when an implant was discovered and the context in which it was planted, but an excitable rogue state leadership may assume the worst: that the implant was prefatory to a cyberattack rather than cyberespionage, and that the cyberattack is imminent.

8. David Hoffman, "Cold-War Doctrines Refuse to Die," *Washington Post,* March 15, 1998: A1.

Chapter 30. Narratives and Signals

1. Tom Wolfe, *The Painted Word* (New York: Bantam, 1977).

2. An interesting case of a corporate narrative followed hacker takedown of Sony's PlayStation Network (PSN) using what Sony admitted was a known but apparently unpatched vulnerability; Elinor Mills, "Expert: Sony Attack May Have Been Multipronged," *CNET,* May 18, 2011. Sony took most of a week before it acknowledged that PSN was offline; Erica Ogg, "PlayStation Network Outage: 6 Days and Counting," *CNET,* April 26, 2011. Sony was also initially unable or reluctant to reveal whether credit card or other personal information was taken; the senior director of corporate communications said, "Our efforts to resolve this matter involve re-building our system to further strengthen our network infrastructure. . . . it [is] worth the time necessary to provide the system with additional security." Chris Morris, "Hackers Take Down Sony's PlayStation Network," CNBC, April 25, 2011, http://www.cnbc.com/id/42750388/Hackers_Take_Down_Sony_s_PlayStation_Network. Opinions varied on how

sophisticated the attack was, with observers calling it tantamount to script kiddie work ("as simple as grabbing the tools and going after Sony"), while the corporation characterized it as "a very sophisticated attack." Apologies and offers of compensation followed within two weeks; Erica Ogg, "The PlayStation Network Breach (FAQ)," *CNET*, May 3, 2011, http://news.cnet.com/8301-31021_3-20058950-260 .html. After service was restored, Sony underplayed the incident, with its president observing, "Nobody's system is 100 percent secure. . . . this is a hiccup in the road to a network future." Don Reisinger, "Sony: PSN Difficulties a 'Bump in the Road,'" *CNET*, June 23, 2011, http://news.cnet.com/8301-13506_3-20073659-17/sony-psn-difficulties-a-bump-in-the-road/. When challenged on Sony's slowness in alerting customers, the president added, "There is no precedent for this in people's experience. . . . most reports now seem to indicate that we acted very quickly and very responsibly." Erica Ogg, "Sony: PSN Back, but No System Is 100 Percent Secure," *CNET*, May 17, 2011, http://news.cnet.com/8301-31021_3-20063764-260.html. A month later, it was alleged that Sony had laid off employees in a unit responsible for network security two weeks prior to the attack; Dan Levine, "Sony Laid Off Employees Before Data Breach–Lawsuit," Reuters, June 23, 2011, http://www.reuters.com/article/2011/06/24/sony-breach-lawsuit-idUSN1E75M1Y320110624.

3. See Bipartisan Policy Center, "Cyber ShockWave," c. 2010.

4. Following the wave of cyberattacks in late 2013 that hit retail establishments (notably, but not exclusively, Target), the industry's narrative played up the strength of the threat: "'I think what we've learned . . . is that just having the tools and technology isn't enough in this day and age,' Neiman Marcus Chief Information Officer Michael Kingston told the panel [Senate Judiciary Committee]. 'These attackers again are very, very sophisticated and they've figured out ways around that.'" Alina Selyukh, "U.S. Retailers at Senate Hearing: Hackers Have Upper Hand," Reuters, February 4, 2014, http://www.reuters.com/article/2014/02/04/us-usa-hacking-congress-idUSBREA121I620140204.

5. The U.S. government's "International Strategy for Cyberspace," released on May 16, 2011, specified what values it sought, called on other countries to support it, and reserved its right to carry out self-defense—but it did not argue that cyberspace was a commons. Barack Obama, "International Strategy for Cyberspace: Prosperity, Security, and Openness in a Networked World," Report, May 2011, https://www.whitehouse.gov/sites/default/files/rss_viewer/international_strategy_for_cyberspace.pdf.

6. "Junk Science: Scientists Are Increasingly Worried About the Amount of Debris Orbiting the Earth," *Economist*, August 19, 2010.

7. Even though al Qaeda sought to polarize the Islamic world between it and the United States, Osama bin Laden initially denied complicity in the September 11 attacks, albeit not very strenuously or persistently. See, for example, "Bin Laden Says He Wasn't Behind Attacks," CNN, September 17, 2001, http://edition .cnn.com/2001/US/09/16/inv.binladen.denial/index.html?iref=storysearch.

8. See, for example, Meghan Kelly, "Cyber Criminals Attack U.S. Chamber of Commerce, China Footing the Blame," *VentureBeat*, December 21, 2011, http://venturebeat.com/2011/12/21/china-chamber-of-commerce-hack/: "Chinese officials have routinely denied the cyberspying, insisting that their own country also is a victim of such attacks." See also Lolita C. Baldor, "U.S., China to Cooperate More on Cyber Threat," Associated Press, May 8, 2012, http://www.politico.com/news/stories/0512/76036 .html.

9. During the Cuban Missile Crisis, the United States displayed imagery taken by formerly classified U-2 aircraft, but that was two years after one of them, with its surveillance camera, was captured by the Soviet Union.

10. See, for instance, "Huawei: The Company That Spooked the World," *Economist.com*, August 4, 2012, http://www.economist.com/node/21559929.

11. According to Stephanie Lieggi, "Going Beyond the Stir: The Strategic Realities of China's No-First-Use Policy," Nuclear Threat Initiative, January 1, 2005, http://www.nti.org/analysis/articles/realities-chinas-no-first-use-policy/: "In 1996, the U.S. media reported that a Chinese military officer had, in the presence of former Assistant Secretary of Defense Charles Freeman, threatened to attack U.S. cities with nuclear weapons. Reports on the comments—often attributed to General Xiong Guangkai, although the identity of the Chinese official has never been confirmed by Freeman—often claim that the official threatened nuclear attack against Los Angeles if there were a conflict over Taiwan." Matthew

Robertson, "Chinese Admiral Threatens World War to Protect Iran," *Epoch Times*, December 6, 2011, updated December 22, 2011, http://printarchive.epochtimes.com/a1/en/sg/nnn/2011/12%20December%202011/Issue%20390_13_December%202011/390_A5.pdf, reports, "According to a report in Press TV, a news network owned by the Iranian government, Chinese rear admiral and prominent military commentator Zhang Zhaozhong said, 'China will not hesitate to protect Iran even with a third world war'." Note that the source, *Epoch Times*, is associated with a dissident Chinese group.

12. Jonathan Easley, "Gingrich: 'Wage Real Cyber Warfare' to Take Down Iran's Regime," *The Hill*, November 22, 2011, http://thehill.com/blogs/hillicon-valley/technology/195039-gingrich-wage-real-cyber-warfare-to-destabilize-iran-stop-nuclear-program.

13. See David Frank Winkler, *The Cold War at Sea: High-Seas Confrontation Between the United States and the Soviet Union* (Annapolis, Md.: Naval Institute Press, 2000).

14. This is a reference to U.S. attempts to establish a virtual embassy in Iran; see Kirit Radia, "Iran Blocks U.S. 'Virtual' Embassy Within 12 Hours of Launch," *ABC News*, December 7, 2011, http://abcnews.go.com/blogs/politics/2011/12/iran-blocks-us-virtual-embassy-within-12-hours-of-launch/.

15. According to Owen Fletcher and Jason Dean, "Ballmer Bares China Travails," *Wall Street Journal*, May 26, 2011 http://www.wsj.com/articles/SB10001424052702303654804576347190248544826: "Rampant piracy means Microsoft Corp.'s . . . revenue in China this year will only be about 5% of what it gets in the U.S., even though personal-computer sales in the two countries are almost equal, Chief Executive Steve Ballmer told employees in a meeting here."

16. In 2008, "U.S. information technology (IT) giant Microsoft launched a mechanism to blacken the screens of computers using counterfeit Windows. It's right to attack piracy, but the incident also exposed China's online vulnerability to high-tech intrusion from overseas": Lan Tang, "Let Us Join Hands to Make Internet Safe," *China Daily*, February 7, 2012, http://usa.chinadaily.com.cn/epaper/2012-02/07/content_14551811.htm.

17. Yaacov Bar-Siman-Tov, "The Arab-Israeli War of October 1973," in *Avoiding War: Problems of Crisis Management*, ed. Alexander L. George (Boulder, Colo.: Westview Press, 1991), 356. The Soviet Union did likewise, which was a stronger signal because they had never done it before; see Lebow, *Nuclear Crisis Management: A Dangerous Illusion*.

18. Xiaoming Zhang, "China's 1979 War with Vietnam: A Reassessment," *China Quarterly* 184, (2005): p. 862.

19. Smoke, *War: Controlling Escalation*, 165.

20. Sometimes signaling and operational deception can be antithetical. Chinese operational security just prior to China's intervening in the Korean War (late 1950) reduced the fidelity of its signal that it would not tolerate a UN presence too close to the Chinese border; Richard Ned Lebow, *Between Peace and War: The Nature of International Crisis* (Baltimore, Md.: Johns Hopkins University Press, 1981), 149.

21. Akin to the argument made in Schelling, *The Strategy of Conflict*, 187–204.

22. From Robert Gates, *Duty* (New York: Knopf, 2014), 450.

23. Supposedly, upon hearing of a diplomat's death, another diplomat—possibly Charles Maurice de Talleyrand-Périgord, more likely Prince Klemens Wenzel von Metternich—was supposed to have asked, "I wonder what he meant by that?"

24. Martin Fackler, "Japan Asks China to Pay for Damages," *New York Times*, September 26, 2010.

Chapter 31. Strategic Stability

1. The touchstone article is Albert Wohlstetter, "The Delicate Balance of Terror," *Foreign Affairs* 37, no. 2 (January 1959): pp. 211–23.

2. Although the first-strike issue lent real concern to nuclear stability, once a country had an assured second-strike capability, attackers could never figure out how to start a nuclear war with any guarantee that they were not essentially committing suicide. Thus, in practice, the nuclear standoff became quite stable. There does not seem to be an equivalent formulation for cyberwar.

3. As Gen. Alexander testified (Keith Alexander, "Advance Questions for Lieutenant General Keith Alexander, USA, Nominee for Commander, United States CYBERCOM"), "A consensus has yet to emerge, either on how to characterize the strategic 'instability' or what to do about it."

4. The likelihood of inadvertent conflict is a subject of great debate. Robert Jervis, "Arms Control, Stability, and Causes of War," *Political Science Quarterly* 108, no. 2 (Summer 1993): p. 249, argues, "It is hard to find even a single war that was inadvertent in the sense that, immediately after it started, both sides would have preferred to return to peace on the basis of status quo ante."

5. From Richard Clarke and Robert Knake, *Cyberwar* (New York: Ecco, 2010), 179–218.

6. Paul Bracken, "Strategic War Termination," in Carter, Steinbruner, and Zraket, *Managing Nuclear Operations*, 197–214.

7. In the Cold War, the third-party nuclear threat to the United States was far less consequential than the Soviet nuclear threat. Today's cyberwar environment features three comparably competent states, a larger number of second-tier states, and a serious transnational criminal capability.

8. Ronald Reagan, "Address to the Nation on Defense and National Security," Washington, D.C., March 23, 1983.

9. Yet the conceptualization of something as a weapon has strong appeal as witness the argument that such characterization has real meaning. From Thomas Rid and Peter McBurney, "Cyber Weapons," *RUSI Journal* 157, no. 1 (2012): pp. 6–13:

> The line between what is a cyber-weapon and what is not a cyber-weapon is subtle. But drawing this line is important. For one, it has security consequences. If a tool has no potential to be used as a weapon and to do harm to one or many, it is simply less dangerous. Secondly, drawing this line has political consequences; an unarmed intrusion is politically less explosive than an armed one. Thirdly, the line has legal consequences: identifying something as a weapon means, in principle, that it may be outlawed, and its development, possession, or use may be punishable. . . . But even a highly sophisticated piece of malware that is developed and used for the sole purpose of covertly exfiltrating data from a network or machine is not a weapon.

10. Similarly, no state that has amassed the requisite fissile material has failed to complete all the other weaponization steps on the way to building a nuclear bomb. See Peter D. Zimmerman, "Proliferation: Bronze Medal Technology Is Enough," *Orbis* 38, no. 1 (Winter 1994): p. 67.

11. If there were recognized norms that assured each state that its own infrastructure, for instance, would be safe, each might be more relaxed about investing in offensive and defensive cyberwar capabilities because the consequences of failing to keep up would be correspondingly reduced (for example, neither side would worry about losing electricity). That noted, would such norms really be reassuring given difficulties in verification coupled with cyberwar's normal secrecy and ambiguity?

12. From Lindsay, "The Impact of China on Cybersecurity: Fiction and Friction": "Misperceptions about the coercive potency of cyberwarfare or mistakes in the integration of cyber with other warfighting domains would inject additional uncertainty into such a crisis [involving Japan or Taiwan] and make it more unstable. Chinese ability to manage the complex intelligence and command integration necessary to create predictable (and thus usefully weaponized) effects through cyberspace is questionable, even as Chinese doctrine calls for the early and paralyzing use of cyberattacks."

13. Can implants be hijacked by a third party? If yes, then the process of implantation may be particularly risky in that such a third party may have fewer constraints than the implanters, not least because it may conclude that it can carry out an attack, confident that blame will fall on the implanter, whose modus operandi will be all over the implant. No such hijacking has been revealed, but the NSA has reportedly carried out fourth-party interception by intercepting the take from taps engineered by other parties: Sean Gallagher, "NSA Secretly Hijacked Existing Malware to Spy on N. Korea, Others," *Ars Technica,* January 18, 2015, http://arstechnica.com/information-technology/2015/01/nsa-secretly-hijacked-existing-malware-to-spy-on-n-korea-others/. The defenses against such hijacking are relatively straightforward: for example, requiring a digital signature for any subsequent addition of code, be it for attack or eavesdropping. Alternatively, a hijacker could read the implant and reverse-engineer the executable (assuming it is not encrypted) to produce reusable object code; that noted, implants are usually less interesting than penetration methods, and these penetration methods are not obvious from the implant itself.

14. Damian Paletta and Siobhan Hughes, "U.S. Spy Agencies Join Probe of Personnel-Records Theft: Sales Demonstration May Have Uncovered Government Breach," *Wall Street Journal,* June 10, 2015.

15. See chapter nine in William A. Owens, Kenneth W. Dam, and Herbert S. Lin, eds., *Technology, Policy, Law, and Ethics Regarding U.S. Acquisition and Use of Cyberattack Capabilities* (Washington, D.C.: National Academies Press, 2009).

16. A reputation for being able to attribute attacks should reduce the likelihood of getting attacked by Yellow, but ignoring such attacks may also dissuade Yellow. Meanwhile, good attribution will not keep Yellow from attacking someone and pretending to be you.

17. "TV5 Monde Attack 'by Russia-based Hackers'," BBC, June 9, 2015, http://www.bbc.com/news/world-europe-33072034.

Chapter 32. Norms for Cyberspace

1. John Markoff, "Step Taken to End Impasses Over Cybersecurity Talks," *New York Times,* July 16, 2010. See also Alex Grigsby, "The UN GGE on Cybersecurity: What Is the UN's Role?" April 15, 2015, http://blogs.cfr.org/cyber/2015/04/15/the-un-gge-on-cybersecurity-what-is-the-uns-role/.

2. Brian Grow and Mark Hosenball, "Special Report: In Cyberspy vs. Cyberspy, China Has the Edge," Reuters, April 14, 2011, http://www.reuters.com/article/2011/04/14/china-usa-cyberespionage-idUSN1229719820110414.

3. Many doubt that any significant (non-hortatory) treaty is possible. See, for instance, Jack Goldsmith, "Cybersecurity Treaties: A Skeptical View," Hoover Institution, March 9, 2011, http://www.hoover.org/research/cybersecurity-treaties-skeptical-view; Adam Segal and Matthew Waxman, "Why a Cybersecurity Treaty Is a Pipe Dream," Council on Foreign Relations, October 27, 2011, http://www.cfr.org/cybersecurity/why-cybersecurity-treaty-pipe-dream/p26325; and Kristine Rogers, "Resistance Is Not Futile: The Case Against a Cyber Arms Treaty," paper, Air War College, 2010, http://www.worldcat.org/title/resistance-is-not-futile-the-case-against-a-cyber-arms-treaty/oclc/744691453.

4. Carlo Ito, "A Brief History of Nefarious Internet Hacking in the Philippines," *SourcingTrust*, March 30, 2011, http://sourcingtrustblog.com/2011/03/30/a-brief-history-of-nefarious-internet-hacking-in-the-philippines/.

5. Extraditions are not automatic, even with friendly countries, such as the United Kingdom; see Kim Zetter, "Pentagon Hacker McKinnon Wins 10-Year Extradition Battle," *Wired.com,* October 16, 2012, http://www.wired.com/2012/10/mckinnon-extradition-win/.

6. See, for instance, Nicole Perlroth, "After Arrest of Accused Hacker, Russia Accuses U.S. of Kidnapping," *New York Times*, July 8, 2014.

7. Some argue that such countries as Russia or China could find hackers if they wanted to because they monitor their citizens intensively enough to catch hackers who would not be caught in the West, with its civil liberties. But would Western states be comfortable demanding that such countries find hackers by using methods that their own investigators would not be allowed to use?

8. See, for instance, Yudhijit Bhattacharjee, "How a Remote Town in Romania Has Become Cybercrime Central," *Wired.com,* February 2011, http://www.wired.com/2011/01/ff_hackerville_romania/.

9. Federal Bureau of Investigation, "FBI, Slovenian and Spanish Police Arrest Mariposa Botnet Creator, Operators," news release, July 28, 2010, http://www.fbi.gov/news/pressrel/press-releases/fbi-slovenian-and-spanish-police-arrest-mariposa-botnet-creator-operators.

10. John Leyden, "Russian Bookmaker Hackers Jailed for Eight Years," *The Register,* October 4, 2006, http://www.theregister.co.uk/2006/10/04/russian_bookmaker_hackers_jailed/ (this example may be a singular action, however, because it alone appears in multiple articles), and Keith Bradsher, "China Announces Arrests in Hacking Crackdown," *New York Times*, February 8, 2010. Investigators themselves may technically have to commit crimes to trace bad packets through routers that will not disgorge their contents freely. The Snooping Dragon investigation, no doubt, had to; Nagaraja and Anderson, "The Snooping Dragon: Social-Malware Surveillance of the Tibetan Movement."

11. Sanger and Fackler, "N.S.A. Breached North Korean Networks Before Sony Attack, Officials Say."

12. See, for instance, R. Jeffrey Smith, "U.N. Inspectors or Spies? Iraq Data Can Take Many Paths," *Washington Post*, February 16, 1998.

13. See, for instance, Dorothy Denning, "Obstacles and Options for Cyber Arms Control," presented at Arms Control in Cyberspace Conference, Heinrich Böll Foundation, Berlin, Germany, June

29–30, 2001. But also see Abraham D. Sofaer and Seymour E. Goodman, "A Proposal for an International Convention on Cybercrime and Terrorism," Center for International Security and Cooperation, Stanford University, August 2000, http://fsi.stanford.edu/publications/proposal_for_an_international_convention_on_cyber_crime_and_terrorism_a.

14. Sanger, Perlroth, and Schmitt, "U.S. Asks China to Help Rein In Korean Hackers." By some accounts, what the administration is trying to create is a computer equivalent to the Proliferation Security Initiative, an effort begun in the Bush administration, also aimed squarely at North Korea, to stop the shipment of nuclear materials and other weaponry. But in cyberspace that is a far harder task, since it is easier for the North Koreans to hide the transit of computer code than to hide the transit of a cargo ship carrying missiles.

15. U.S. Bureau of Industry and Security, "Intrusion and Surveillance Items: FAQ," http://www.bis.doc.gov/index.php/policy-guidance/faqs, and "More Details Emerge on Multilateral Export Controls on Cybersecurity Items," December 10, 2013, http://www.exportlawblog.com/archives/category/wassenaar.

16. Nate Cardozo and Eva Galperin, "What Is the U.S. Doing About Wassenaar, and Why Do We Need to Fight It?" Electronic Frontier Foundation, May 28, 2015, https://www.eff.org/deeplinks/2015/05/we-must-fight-proposed-us-wassenaar-implementation; and Michael Mimoso, "Head-Scratching Begins on Proposed Wassenaar Export Control Rules," *ThreatPost,* May 21, 2015, https://threatpost.com/head-scratching-begins-on-proposed-wassenaar-export-control-rules/112959.

17. U.S. Department of Defense, *Department of Defense Cyber Strategy*, 27.

18. The LOAC definition of proportionality is that the type or level of force used should not exceed what it takes to accomplish the mission; see also International Committee of the Red Cross, *The Law of Armed Conflict: Basic Knowledge,* June 2002, https://www.icrc.org/eng/assets/files/other/law1_final.pdf.

19. From Alexander, "Advance Questions for Lieutenant General Keith Alexander, USA, Nominee for Commander, United States CYBERCOM":

> Criminal law models depend on deterrence as well. Legal scholars have argued that crimes that often go unsolved (vandalism, for example) should be punished more harshly to ensure an effective example is offered in the few cases where it's available. Under this model, the U.S. should take swift and effective action in every case in which it can attribute an offensive action to a particular adversary. . . . A commander's right to general self-defense is clearly established in both U.S. and international law. Although this right has not been specifically established by legal precedent to apply to attacks in cyberspace, it is reasonable to assume that returning fire in cyberspace, as long as it complied with law of war principles (for example, proportionality) would be lawful.

Conversely, a study by Jeremy Travis, Bruce Western, and Steve Redburn ("The Growth of Incarceration in the United States," National Research Council, 2014, http://www.nap.edu/catalog/18613/the-growth-of-incarceration-in-the-united-states-exploring-causes) concluded that longer sentences have very little deterrence power; the odds of getting caught were more decisive.

20. Stated thus, "However, merely relaying information through neutral communications infrastructure (provided that the facilities are made available impartially) generally would not constitute a violation of the law of neutrality that belligerent States would have an obligation to refrain from and that a neutral State would have an obligation to prevent." Department of Defense, "DoD Law of War Manual," June 2015, http://www.defense.gov/pubs/Law-of-War-Manual-June-2015.pdf, 1002–3.

21. Patrick Tucker, "NSA Chief: Rules of War Apply to Cyberwar, Too" *Defense One,* April 20, 2015, http://www.defenseone.com/technology/2015/04/nsa-chief-rules-war-apply-cyberwar-too/110572/. The last half of the quote was extracted from Maren Leed, *Offensive Cyber Capabilities at the Operational Level*, report, Center for Strategic and International Studies, 2013, http://csis.org/files/publication/130916_Leed_OffensiveCyberCapabilities_Web.pdf.

22. United Nations Group of Governmental Experts, "Report of the Group of Governmental Experts on Developments in the Field of Information and Telecommunications in the Context of International Security," June 24, 2013, http://www.un.org/ga/search/view_doc.asp?symbol=A/68/98, 8.

23. According to a source interviewed by Politico, "We're very disappointed that, in the final analysis, the sense we've gotten for a year or so from China that it was walking back its commitments that international

law applies [in cyberspace] came to fruition when they proposed to delete all the sections having to do with international law." Joseph Marks, "U.S. Makes New Push for Global Rules in Cyberspace," *Politico,* May 5, 2015, http://www.politico.com/story/2015/05/us-makes-new-push-for-global-rules-in-cyberspace-117632.html.

24. See, for instance, Charles J. Dunlap, Jr., "Perspectives for Cyber Strategists on Law for Cyberwar," *Strategic Studies Quarterly* (Spring 2011): pp. 81–99, or Matthew Waxman, "Cyberattacks and the Use of Force: Back to the Future of Article 2(4)," *Yale Journal of International Law* 36, no. 2 (2011): pp. 421–59.

25. "Terror in Paris," *Economist.com,* January 10, 2015, http://www.economist.com/news/leaders/21638118-islamists-are-assailing-freedom-speech-vilifying-all-islam-wrong-way-counter.

26. Although not NATO doctrine, it was written under NATO auspices. References come from "The 'Tallinn Manual' on the International Law Applicable to Cyber Warfare," prepared by the International Group of Experts at the Invitation of the NATO Cooperative Cyber Defence Centre of Excellence, draft (as of August 21, 2012).

27. If Russia can argue that Syria did not use chemical weapons in 2013 or that its forces never fought in Ukraine in 2014, what inconvenient fact *cannot* be denied?

28. The manual also makes a fourth distinction among cyberattacks: between the destruction of physical objects and those that cause disruption or require substantial remediation costs. Its rule 30 states: "A cyberattack is a cyber operation, whether offensive or defensive, that is reasonably expected to cause injury or death to persons or damage or destruction to objects." It does add that attacks on data that result in injury, death, or damage qualify as an attack.

29. "When a civilian object or facility is used for military ends, it becomes a military objective through the 'use' criterion" (109). All dual-use items are military items.

30. "Consider a situation in which the intelligence service of State A receives incontrovertible information that State B is preparing to launch a cyberattack that will destroy State A's primary oil pipeline within the next two weeks [by] causing the microcontrollers along the pipeline to increase the pressure in the pipeline. . . . Intelligence services have no information on the specific vulnerability to be exploited, thereby preventing effective cyber defence of the microcontrollers. However, they do have information that those involved in conducting the attack will be gathered at a particular location and time. . . . strikes against those individuals would be lawful as proportionate anticipatory self-defence should lesser means be inadequate" (62).

31. "For example, a cyber operation that causes a fire to break out at a small military installation would suffice to initiate an international armed conflict. . . . it would be prudent to treat the threshold of international armed conflict as relatively low" (74).

32. Oddly enough, although attacks on civilians are never allowed, states that suffer *military* damage from a cyberattack are on stronger grounds labeling the action an armed attack than those suffering merely *civilian* damage.

33. As per the manual, if the attacking state can say "sorry, didn't mean to, and won't do it again" fast enough, the target has no right to respond that way. But such a sequence assumes the attacking state can know in time that someone, under color of national command, carried out such an attack and that it suppresses the normal human reluctance to confess to a potential adversary that it did wrong.

34. Obama, "International Strategy for Cyberspace: Prosperity, Security, and Openness in a Networked World."

35. Department of Defense, "Department of Defense Cyberspace Policy Report: A Report to Congress Pursuant to the National Defense Authorization Act for Fiscal Year 2011, Section 934," http://www.defense.gov/home/features/2011/0411_cyberstrategy/docs/NDAA%20Section%20934%20Report_For%20webpage.pdf.

36. In theory one could envision the first (we won't) without the second (but others may) as if to say that we're too good to stoop to that level even if we understand that some benighted souls might—but such reasoning has been rare since President Wilson's short-lived "too proud to fight" declaration (after the sinking of the *Lusitania*).

37. See Waxman, "Cyberattacks and the Use of Force: Back to the Future of Article 2(4)," and Matthew Waxman, "Self-defensive Force Against Cyber Attacks: Legal, Strategic, and Political Dimensions,"

International Law Studies 89 (2013): pp. 109–122, of which the latter argues: "As capabilities proliferate among State and non-State actors to conduct various sorts of malicious, hostile or intelligence-gathering activities in cyberspace, any deterrence value of treating them as armed attacks triggering self-defense rights under Article 51 might be outweighed by the dangers of lowering legal barriers to military force in a wider range of circumstances or conditions. . . . Political decision-makers will have a very difficult time rallying support at home and abroad for military responses to isolated cyberattacks that do not cause significant and publicly discernible damage."

38. See Defense Science Board, "Task Force Report: Resilient Military Systems and the Advanced Cyber Threat"; Elbridge Colby, "Cyberwar and the Nuclear Option," *National Interest,* June 24, 2013, http://nationalinterest.org/commentary/cyberwar-the-nuclear-option-8638; and Richard Clarke and Steven Anderson, "Cyberwar's Threat Does Not Justify a New Policy of Nuclear Deterrence," *Washington Post,* June 6, 2013.

39. Department of Defense, "Nuclear Posture Review Report," April 2010.

40. Melissa Gray, "Chinese Space Debris Hits Russian Satellite, Scientists Say," CNN, March 9, 2013, http://www.cnn.com/2013/03/09/tech/satellite-hit. See also Clark Liat, "Study: Clean Up Space Before Dangerous Debris Collisions Increase," *Wired.com,* April 23, 2013, http://www.wired.co.uk/news/archive/2013-04/23/looming-space-junk-threat.

41. Tariq Malik, "ISS Dodges Space Debris from Chinese Satellite," *Huffington Post,* January 30, 2012, http://www.huffingtonpost.com/2012/01/30/iss-dodges-debris-from-de_n_1241167.html.

Chapter 33. Sino-American Relations and Norms in Cyberspace

1. Obama, "International Strategy for Cyberspace: Prosperity, Security, and Openness in a Networked World."

2. Ibid., 24.

3. Ibid., 13.

4. Ibid., 20.

5. Adam Segal, "Chinese Responses to the International Strategy for Cyberspace," Council on Foreign Relations, May 23, 2011, http://blogs.cfr.org/asia/2011/05/23/chinese-responses-to-the-international-strategy-for-cyberspace/.

6. Note the many calls to assassinate Julian Assange following the WikiLeaks materials provided by Private Manning—and that was *before* the Snowden revelations. Nate Anderson, "Meet the People Who Want Julian Assange 'Whacked'," *Ars Technica,* December 3, 2010, http://arstechnica.com/tech-policy/2010/12/meet-the-people-who-want-julian-assange-whacked/.

7. Yu Xiaoqiu, "U.S. Playing Dangerous Game with 'Cyber Deterrence,'" *People's Daily Online,* July 26, 2013, http://en.people.cn/90001/90780/91343/7452284.html.

8. With the Russians, the United States has entertained more formal negotiations, one product of which has been an agreement on a "hotline" in cyberspace so that incidents potentially involving both countries can be talked over before they become full-fledged crises. Why the difference? Russia and the United States have had over fifty years of formal bilateral negotiations to establish a well-worn sense of how to deal with one another. Such history has yet to be made with China.

9. The notion of "mutual trust," so often repeated in so many contexts, is unclear to Western ears that hold to another (albeit self-contradictory) motto: trust but verify. "'Mutual strategic trust,' in Sino-U.S. relations means that both sides are aware of each other's strategic purposes while holding positive expectations of each other's positions and actions on issues of vital interests. Building mutual strategic trust does not mean China and the U.S. deny the existence of interest conflict and ideological differences that exist between them. On the contrary it means that both sides would strive to reduce the impact of conflicts and differences on bilateral relationships and form long-term healthy interactions based on an agreement that they share more common interests than differences." Qian Yingyi et al., "Building Mutual Trust between China and the U.S.," in *China in the World: A Survey of Chinese Perspectives on Politics and Economics,* ed. Binhong Shao (Leiden: Brill, 2014), 128.

10. In the words of Chinese ambassador to the United States Cui Tiankai: "We want assurance that the United States, as the most powerful and technologically advanced country in the world in information

technology, will not hurt China's interest with this technological advantage. Technologically speaking, the United States is much more powerful than China. The weaker one should be worried about the stronger one, not the other way around." See Isaac Stone Fish, "If You Want Rule of Law, Respect Ours," *Foreign Policy,* November 4, 2014, http://foreignpolicy.com/2014/11/04/if-you-want-rule-of-law-respect-ours/.

11. CBS News, "Microsoft Anti-Piracy Tool Angers Chinese," October 28, 2008, http://www.cbsnews.com/news/microsoft-anti-piracy-tool-angers-chinese/, and Thomas Claburn, "Chinese Hackers Angered by Microsoft's Epic Fail," *Information Week,* October 23, 2008, http://www.informationweek.com/software/operating-systems/chinese-hackers-angered-by-microsofts-epic-fail/d/d-id/1073270.

12. Brian Krebs, "Malware Dragnet Snags Millions of Infected PCs," *KrebsonSecurity.com,* September 12, 2012, http://krebsonsecurity.com/tag/3322-org/.

13. The official answer is the National Cybersecurity and Communications Integration Center, a part of DHS, but it is unclear whether the center can speak for what the NSA or CYBERCOM is or is not doing. When asked the same question about China, China's response was to name three separate players—and these did not include the PLA or the Ministry of Foreign Affairs.

14. For instance, Junqing Zhu, "Commentary: U.S. Wronging of China for Cyber Breaches Harm Mutual Trust," *Xinhua Net,* June 6, 2015, http://news.xinhuanet.com/english/2015-06/06/c_134302843.htm.

15. See also "Admit Nothing and Deny Everything," *Economist.com,* June 8, 2013, http://www.economist.com/news/china/21579044-barack-obama-says-he-ready-talk-xi-jinping-about-chinese-cyberattacks-makes-one.

16. See Christopher Bodeen, "U.S. Says Hacking Undermines China's Interests," *Yahoo.com,* April 9, 2013, http://news.yahoo.com/us-says-hacking-undermines-chinas-interests-093148708.html. See also "Official Urges China–U.S. Trust on Cyber Security," *China Daily,* April 10, 2013, www.chinadaily.com.cn/china/2013-04/10/content_16388107.htm.

17. Kim Murphy, "China Hacking? Beijing Is Also a Victim, Foreign Minister Says in Interview," *Los Angeles Times,* June 23, 2015.

18. They also rarely make the case that economic espionage is morally equivalent to national security espionage, despite expectations to the contrary. According to James A. Lewis, a cybersecurity expert at the Center for Strategic and International Studies, "They say that the topic of economic espionage is 'embarrassing' for them. . . . They say, 'In the U.S., military espionage is heroic and economic espionage is a crime, but in China, the line is not so clear.'" Nicole Perlroth, "Cyberattacks a Topic in Obama Call with New Chinese President," *New York Times,* March 14, 2013. Similar sentiments can be inferred from the following remarks from China's ambassador to the United States: "My American colleagues often tell me that they distinguish between cyber activities for national security or intelligence purposes and cyber activity against commercial secrets. This distinction is a bit artificial. How can you distinguish from activities that will hurt national security without hurting the nation's commercial interests?"

19. Shannon Tiezzi, "China (Finally) Admits to Hacking: An Updated Military Document for the First Time Admits that the Chinese Government Sponsors Offensive Cyber Units," *The Diplomat,* March 18, 2015, http://thediplomat.com/2015/03/china-finally-admits-to-hacking/.

20. The Snowden revelations did not help matters—unless the Chinese took account of how quickly U.S. IT firms were distancing themselves from the NSA, notably by encrypting their e-mail services and the information held by consumers' smart phones.

21. The argument that cyberespionage for national security purposes should be more morally acceptable than EMCE is by no means obvious—trade agreements aside. One might note that EMCE often lowers the market value of its victims while cyberespionage for national security rarely does (sloppy defense firms who therefore lose DoD business perhaps excepted). But such a case privileges those whose activities can and are assigned market values. The United States, in its search for terrorists, has managed to intercept telephone metadata from millions of individuals, but such individuals do not have a market value as such. The case that trade secrets are sacrosanct but personal secrets are not is redolent of the 1980s-era jibe about the neutron bomb being the perfect capitalist weapon because it harmed labor (soldiers) but not capital (military equipment).

22. As often remarked, the word "deterrence" is not native to Chinese. Its closest counterpart is coercion: a mix of deterrence (being punished for sins of commission) and compulsion (being punished for sins of omission). If language follows rather than shapes thought, though, this is an effect, not a cause.

23. For instance, the United States may adhere to a law when its interests are otherwise served because doing so is the price for getting others to adhere to other laws that do not always work in their interests. The United States believes that laws and norms are in force until explicitly changed. China's views are that they reflect the state of power at any one point. Robert Gates, the former secretary of defense, heard from one Chinese diplomat that China had lived with Taiwan arms sales since 1979 "because we were weak. But now we are strong." Gates, *Duty*, 416.

24. "The Dragon's New Teeth," *Economist.com,* April 4, 2012, http://www.economist.com/node/21552193.

25. Paul H. B. Godwin and Alice L. Miller, "China's Forbearance Has Limits: Chinese Threat and Retaliation Signaling and Its Implications for a Sino-American Military Confrontation," China Strategic Perspectives 6 (Washington, D.C.: National Defense University Press, April 2013).

26. See David Kang, *East Asia Before the West: Five Centuries of Trade and Tribute* (New York: Columbia University Press, 2012).

27. Daryl Press, *Calculating Capability* (Ithaca, N.Y.: Cornell University Press, 2007).

28. It was only after Stuxnet that the overwhelming superiority of U.S. offensive capability vis-à-vis most of its foes came into appreciation as a counterbalance to such pessimism.

29. Thanks to David Gompert for this insight.

30. From James Mulvenon and Joe McReynolds, "The Role of Informatization in the People's Liberation Army under Hu Jintao," in *Assessing the People's Liberation Army in the Hu Jintao Era*, ed. Roy Kamphausen, David Lai, and Travis Tanner (Carlisle, Pa.: Strategic Studies Institute, 2014): "Shared vulnerabilities could potentially give rise to shared interests with the United States, opening an additional path by which China may move toward becoming a status quo power in the space and cyber domains" (248).

31. Nakashima, "Chinese Government Has Arrested Hackers It Says Breached OPM Database."

32. Some U.S. intelligence officials recognize as much. From Matthew F. Ferraro, "On the OPM Hack, Don't Let China Off the Hook," *The Diplomat,* July 14, 2015, http://thediplomat.com/2015/07/on-the-opm-hack-dont-let-china-off-the-hook/: "'Don't blame the Chinese for the OPM hack,' former NSA and CIA Director Michael Hayden said, arguing that he 'would not have thought twice' about seizing similar information from China if he had the chance. Director of National Intelligence James Clapper echoed the sentiment, saying at a recent conference, 'You have to kind of salute the Chinese for what they did. . . . If we had the opportunity to do that [to them], I don't think we'd hesitate for a minute.'"

33. For instance, Article 1 of China's 2015 draft cybersecurity laws states (as translated): This law is formulated so as to ensure network security, *to preserve cyberspace sovereignty* [emphasis added], national security and societal public interest, to protect the lawful rights and interests of citizens, legal persons and other organizations, and to promote the healthy development of economic and social informatization. Cybersecurity Law (Draft), July 26, 2015, http://chinalawtranslate.com/cybersecuritydraft/?lang=en.

34. Kim Zetter, "Former NSA Director: Countries Spewing Cyberattacks Should Be Held Responsible," *Wired.com*, July 29, 2010, http://www.wired.com/2010/07/hayden-at-blackhat/.

35. Andrey Ostroukh, "Russia, China Forge Closer Ties with New Economic, Financing Accords: Moscow Turns to Asian Investors to Reduce Reliance on Europe and the U.S. Amid Standoff over Ukraine," *Wall Street Journal,* May 8, 2015, and Sean Lyngaas, "Debating the Sino-Russian Cyber Pact," *Federal Computer Week,* May 12, 2015, http://fcw.com/articles/2015/05/12/russian-chinese-cyber.aspx.

36. United Nations Group of Governmental Experts, "Report of the Group of Governmental Experts on Developments in the Field of Information and Telecommunications in the Context of International Security," July 22, 2015, 2; http://daccess-dds-ny.un.org/doc/UNDOC/GEN/N15/228/35/PDF/N1522835.pdf. See also Alex Grigsby, "The 2015 GGE Report: Breaking New Ground, Ever So Slowly," Council on Foreign Relations Guest Blog, September 8, 2015; http://blogs.cfr.org/cyber/2015/09/08/the-2015-gge-report-breaking-new-ground-ever-so-slowly/.

37. Not all attribution evidence is publicly releasable; see Sanger and Fackler, "N.S.A. Breached North Korean Networks Before Sony Attack, Officials Say." This suggests an unbridgeable difference between the confidence that U.S. officials place in attribution and the confidence felt by a fair-minded individual working from open sources, but unwilling to take the word of U.S. sources at face value.

38. That the United States puts more resources into investigating crimes against itself than crimes against other countries is more plausible, but also universal; it remains, therefore, to distinguish that tendency and stonewalling.

39. In the United States, a large share of detection and intrusions is carried out by private companies (many staffed with former NSA employees). China is only starting to develop its own cybersecurity companies. That noted, it can buy cybersecurity expertise: even if some U.S. companies might refuse Chinese business, cybersecurity companies from beyond the United States (for example, Israel) are available.

40. Those caught spying may believe that they have been fairly caught, but absent their testimony to that effect, China's policymaking community may retain its skepticism.

41. An ancillary benefit is that stronger Chinese attribution capabilities could reduce the chances of a catalytic conflict in which China is attacked by someone masquerading as a U.S. source.

42. Early evidence of continued penetration attempts after the summit ended suggests that China's EMCE did not come to an immediate cold stop; see Paul Mozur, "Cybersecurity Firm Says Chinese Hackers Keep Attacking U.S. Companies," *New York Times*, October 20, 2015.

43. According to Siobhan Gorman, "U.S. Homes In on China Spying," *Wall Street Journal*, December 13, 2011: in late 2011, "U.S. officials met with Chinese counterparts and warned China about the diplomatic consequences of economic spying, according to one person familiar with the meeting."

44. Ellen Nakashima, "Indictment of PLA Hackers Is Part of Broad U.S. Strategy to Curb Chinese Cyberspying," *Washington Post*, May 22, 2014.

45. Mark Landler and David Sanger, "U.S. Demands China Block Cyberattacks and Agree to Rules," *New York Times*, March 12, 2013.

46. The White House, "Executive Order: 'Blocking the Property of Certain Persons Engaging in Significant Malicious Cyber-Enabled Activities,'" news release, April 1, 2015, https://www.whitehouse.gov/the-press-office/2015/04/01/executive-order-blocking-property-certain-persons-engaging-significant-m. The Chinese seemed to take the order as aimed at them, although it also seemed to reflect U.S. sanctions on certain North Koreans following the Sony hack. See also Dustin Volz, "Obama Declares Cyberattacks a 'National Emergency,'" *National Journal*, April 1, 2015, http://www.nationaljournal.com/tech/obama-declares-cyber-attacks-a-national-emergency-20150401.

47. Ellen Nakashima, "Following U.S. Indictments, China Shifts Commercial Hacking Away from Military to Civilian Agency," *Washington Post*, November 30, 2015.

48. Geoff Dyer, Gina Chon, and Hannah Kuchler, "Cyber Tensions Rise as U.S. Says Three Big Chinese Groups Benefited from Hacking," *Financial Times*, October 8, 2015.

Chapter 34. Cyberwar: What Is It Good For?

1. John Arquilla, "Cool War: Could the Age of Cyberwarfare Lead Us to a Brighter Future?" *Foreign Policy*, June 15, 2012, www.foreignpolicy.com/articles/2012/06/15/cool_war; Tomas Rid, "Cyberwar and Peace: Hacking Can Reduce Real-World Violence," *Foreign Affairs*, November-December 2013. Rid also makes a broader point about the related cyberspace capabilities in his book *Cyber War Will Not Take Place* (New York: Oxford, 2013): "Cyberespionage can substitute for using human spies, the latter of which can be caught and harmed. Protest in cyberspace is less likely to lead to violence than protest in the streets." See also Evgeny Morozov, "What Fearmongers Get Wrong About Cyberwarfare," *Slate*, May 28, 2012, http://www.slate.com/articles/technology/future_tense/2012/05/cyberwarfare_what_richard_clarke_and_other_fearmongers_get_wrong_.html.

2. In running the causality chain, one must stop somewhere. Perhaps the failure to have attacked Natanz would have yielded a nuclear Iran and thereby increased the total potential for violence. Or nuclear weapons, by raising the price of mischief, enforce peace (a more plausible argument with Cold War Europe in mind but a less plausible one if one brings up the ongoing India-Pakistan disputes). But by this time, one is debating nuclear weapons, not cyberwar.

3. ISIL is developing some capability for cyberattacks as witnessed by its hack of CENTCOM's Twitter feed (Dan Lamothe, "U.S. Military Social Media Accounts Apparently Hacked by Islamic State Sympathizers," *Washington Post*, January 12, 2015), and its interference with websites associated with the Polish stock exchange (Cory Bennett, "Hackers Breach the Warsaw Stock Exchange," *The Hill*, October 24, 2014, http://thehill.com/policy/cybersecurity/221806-hackers-breach-the-warsaw-stock-exchange). But the purpose of such attacks has been to accentuate (rather than substitute for) the violent deeds of ISIL.

4. For instance, see Declan Walsh, "Whose Side Is Pakistan's ISI Really On?" *The Guardian*, May 12, 2011.

5. The 2014 McAfee–Center for Strategic and International Studies report "Net Losses: Estimating the Global Cost of Cybercrime" (http://csis.org/files/attachments/140609_rp_economic_impact_cybercrime_report.pdf) argues, "If cybercrime and cyberespionage cost more than 2% of GDP, we assume it would prompt much stronger calls for action as companies and societies find the burden unacceptable."
6. Serbu, "DoD to Be More Transparent About Strategy to Deter Cyber Attacks."
7. If, as seems likely, the Chinese hack on OPM (discovered in May 2015) was carried out to feed data mining on federal workers in support of their human espionage recruitment efforts, should we pay more attention to the aggressiveness of their efforts—or to the possibility that they realize that cyberespionage can only take them so far and they need human spies?
8. Ware, "Security and Privacy in Computer Systems."

Bibliography

Books and Monographs

Abizaid, John P., Rosa Brooks, and Rachel Stohl. "Recommendations and Report of the Task Force on U.S. Drone Policy." Washington, D.C.: Stimson Center, June 2014.

Ablon, Lillian, Martin C. Libicki, and Andrea Golay. "Markets for Cybercrime Tools and Stolen Data: Hackers' Bazaar." Santa Monica, Calif.: RAND Corporation, RR-610-JNI, 2014.

Anderson, Ross. *Security Engineering*. Indianapolis, Ind.: Wiley, 2008.

Axelrod, Robert. *The Evolution of Cooperation*. New York: Basic Books, 1984.

Bar-Siman-Tov, Yaacov. "The Arab-Israeli War of October 1973." In *Avoiding War: Problems of Crisis Management*, edited by Alexander L. George. Boulder, Colo.: Westview Press, 1991.

Beagle, T. W. "Effects-based Targeting: Another Empty Promise?" Thesis, School of Advanced Airpower Studies, Air University, June 2000.

Betts, Richard. *Surprise Attack*. Washington, D.C.: Brookings Institution, 1982.

Blickstein, Irving et al. *Root Cause Analyses of Nunn-McCurdy Breaches*. Vol. I. Santa Monica, Calif.: RAND Corporation, 2011.

Brin, David. *The Transparent Society*. New York: Basic Books, 1998.

Brodie, Bernard. *The Absolute Weapon: Atomic Power and World Order*. New York: Harcourt, Brace, and Co., 1946.

Carter, Ashton B., John D. Steinbruner, and Charles A. Zraket, eds. *Managing Nuclear Operations*. Washington, D.C.: Brookings Institution, 1987.

Cheswick, William R., and Steven M. Bellovin. *Firewalls and Internet Security: Repelling the Wily Hacker*. Boston: Addison Wesley, 1994.

Clancy, Tom. *Debt of Honor*. New York: Putnam, 1994.

Clarke, Richard, and Robert Knake. *Cyberwar*. New York: Ecco, 2010.

Cliff, Roger et al. "Entering the Dragon's Lair: Chinese Anti-access Strategies and Their Implications for the United States." Santa Monica, Calif.: RAND Corporation, MG-524-AF, 2007.

Davis, John et al. "Framework for Programming and Budgeting for Cybersecurity." Santa Monica, Calif.: RAND Corporation, TL-186-DHS, 2015.

Erickson, Jon. *Hacking: The Art of Exploitation*. 2nd ed. San Francisco: No Starch Press, 2008.

Freedman, Lawrence. *Strategy: A History*. Oxford: Oxford University Press, 2013.

Gates, Robert. *Duty*. New York: Knopf, 2014.

Gelb, Leslie, and Betts, Richard. *The Irony of Vietnam: The System Worked*. Washington, D.C.: Brookings Institution, 1979.

Gerhsenfeld, Neil. *When Things Start to Think*. New York: Henry Holt and Co., 1999.

Godwin, Paul H. B., and Alice L. Miller. "China's Forbearance Has Limits: Chinese Threat and Retaliation Signaling and Its Implications for a Sino-American Military Confrontation." China Strategic Perspectives 6. Washington, D.C.: National Defense University Press, April 2013.

Gompert, David et al. *Mind the Gap: Promoting a Transatlantic Revolution in Military Affairs*. Washington, D.C.: National Defense University Press, 1999.

Gunaratna, Rohan. *Inside Al Qaeda's Global Network of Terror*. New York: Columbia University Press, 2002.

Harel, Amos, and Avi Issacharoff. *34 Days: Israel, Hezbollah, and the War in Lebanon*. Basingstoke, U.K.: Palgrave-MacMillan, 2008.

Healey, Jason, ed. *A Fierce Domain*. Washington, D.C.: Atlantic Council, 2014.

Herzog, Chaim. *The Arab-Israel Wars: War and Peace in the Middle East from the War of Independence Through Lebanon.* New York: Random House, 1982.

Hosmer, Stephen T. *The Conflict Over Kosovo: Why Milosevic Decided to Settle When He Did.* Santa Monica, Calif.: RAND Corporation, MR-1351-AF, 2001.

Howard, Michael. *Strategic Deception in the Second World War.* Cambridge: Cambridge University Press, 1990.

Ikle, Charles. *Every War Must End.* New York: Columbia University Press, 1971.

International Committee of the Red Cross. *The Law of Armed Conflict: Basic Knowledge.* June 2002. https://www.icrc.org/eng/assets/files/other/law1_final.pdf.

Kahn, Herman. *On Escalation: Metaphors and Scenarios.* New York: Praeger, 1965.

Kahneman, Daniel. *Thinking Fast and Slow.* New York: Farrar, Straus and Giroux, 2011.

Kamphausen, Roy, David Lai, and Travis Tanner, eds. *Assessing the People's Liberation Army in the Hu Jintao Era.* Carlisle, Pa.: Strategic Studies Institute, 2014.

Kang, David. *East Asia Before the West: Five Centuries of Trade and Tribute.* New York: Columbia University Press, 2012.

Kent, Glenn A., and David Thaler. "A New Concept for Streamlining Up-Front Planning." Santa Monica, Calif.: RAND Corporation, 1993.

Larrabee, Eric. *Commander in Chief: Franklin Delano Roosevelt, His Lieutenants, and Their War.* Annapolis, Md.: Naval Institute Press, 1987.

Lebow, Richard Ned. *Between Peace and War: The Nature of International Crisis.* Baltimore: Johns Hopkins University Press, 1981.

———. *Nuclear Crisis Management: A Dangerous Illusion.* Ithaca, N.Y.: Cornell University Press, 1987.

Leveson, Nancy. *SafeWare: System Safety and Computers.* Reading, Mass.: Addison-Wesley, 1995.

Levy, Steven. *Crypto: How the Code Rebels Beat the Government—Saving Privacy in the Digital Age.* New York: Penguin Press, 2001.

Libicki, Martin. *Conquest in Cyberspace.* Cambridge: Cambridge University Press, 2007.

———. *What Is Information Warfare.* Washington, D.C.: National Defense University Press, 1995.

———. *Cyberdeterrence and Cyberwar.* Santa Monica, Calif.: RAND Corporation, 2009.

———. *Brandishing Cyberattack Capability.* Santa Monica, Calif.: RAND Corporation, 2013.

———, David Senty, and Julia Pollack. *Hackers Wanted: An Examination of the Cybersecurity Labor Market.* Santa Monica, Calif.: RAND Corporation, 2014.

———, Lillian Ablon, and Tim Webb. *Defender's Dilemma.* Santa Monica, Calif.: RAND Corporation, 2015.

——— et al. *Byting Back: Regaining Information Superiority Against 21st-Century Insurgents.* Santa Monica, Calif.: RAND Corporation, 2007.

——— et al. *Influences on the Adoption of MFA.* Santa Monica, Calif.: RAND Corporation, 2011.

Long, Austin. *Deterrence: From Cold War to Long War.* Santa Monica, Calif.: RAND Corporation, 2008.

McClure, Stuart, Joel Scambray, and George Kurtz. *Hacking Exposed: Network Security Secrets and Solutions.* 7th ed. New York: McGraw-Hill Osborne Media, 2012.

McConnell, Steve. *Code Complete: A Practical Handbook of Software Construction.* 2nd ed. Redmond, Wash.: Microsoft Press, 2004.

McCue, Brian. *U Boats in the Bay of Biscay: An Essay in Operations Analysis.* Bloomington, Ind.: Ex Libris, 2008.

McMaster, H. R. *Dereliction of Duty: Lyndon Johnson, Robert McNamara, the Joint Chiefs of Staff, and the Lies That Led to Vietnam.* New York: Harper-Collins, 1997.

Mearsheimer, John. *Conventional Deterrence.* Ithaca, N.Y.: Cornell University Press, 1983.

Molander, Roger C., Andrew S. Riddile, and Peter A. Wilson. *Strategic Information Warfare: A New Face of War.* Santa Monica, Calif.: RAND Corporation, 1996.

Morgan, Forrest E. et al. *Dangerous Thresholds: Managing Escalation in the 21st Century.* Santa Monica, Calif.: RAND Corporation, MG-614-AF, 2008.

Morgan, Patrick. *Deterrence: A Conceptual Analysis.* Beverly Hills, Calif.: Sage Library of Social Research, 1977.

Moynihan, Daniel Patrick. *Secrecy: The American Experience.* New Haven, Conn.: Yale University Press, 1998.

Mueller, John. *Retreat from Doomsday: The Obsolescence of Major War.* New York: Basic Books, 1989.

Mueller, Karl P. et al. *Striking First: Preemptive and Preventive Attack in U.S. National Security Policy.* Santa Monica, Calif.: RAND Corporation, MG-403-AF, 2006.

Overy, Richard. *The Bombing War*. New York: Penguin, 2013.

————. *Why the Allies Won*. New York: Norton, 1995.

Owens, William A., Kenneth Dam, and Herbert S. Lin, eds. *Technology, Policy, Law, and Ethics Regarding U.S. Acquisition and Use of Cyberattack Capabilities*. Washington, D.C.: National Academies Press, 2009.

Perrow, Charles. *Normal Accidents: Living with High-Risk Technologies*. New York: Basic Books, 1984.

Pinker, Steven. *The Better Angels of Our Nature*. New York: Viking Books, 2011.

Press, Daryl. *Calculating Capability*. Ithaca, N.Y.: Cornell University Press, 2007.

Qian, Yingyi et al. "Building Mutual Trust between China and the U.S." In *China in the World: A Survey of Chinese Perspectives on Politics and Economics*. Ed. Binhong Shao. Boston: Brill, 2014.

Quester, George. *Deterrence Before Hiroshima*. New Brunswick, N.J.: Transaction Books, 1986.

Quist, Arvin S. *Security Classification of Information*, vol. 2. *Principles for Classification of Information*. April 1993. http://www.fas.org/sgp/library/quist2/index.html.

Reed, Thomas C. *At the Abyss: An Insider's History of the Cold War*. San Francisco: Presidio Press, 2005.

Rid, Tomas. *Cyber War Will Not Take Place*. New York: Oxford, 2013.

Sanger, David. *Confront and Conceal: Obama's Secret Wars and Surprising Use of American Power*. New York: Crown, 2012.

Schelling, Thomas C. *Arms and Influence*. New Haven, Conn.: Yale University Press, 1966.

————. *The Strategy of Conflict*. Cambridge, Mass.: Harvard University Press, 1960.

————, and Morton Halperin. *Strategy and Arms Control*. Dulles, Va.: Potomac Books, 1975.

Schlosser, Eric. *Command and Control: Nuclear Weapons, the Damascus Accident, and the Illusion of Safety*. New York: Penguin, 2013.

Shambaugh, David. *China Goes Global: The Partial Power*. Oxford: Oxford University Press, 2013.

Shostack, Adam. *Threat Modeling: Designing for Security*. Indianapolis, Ind.: Wiley, 2014.

Singh, Simon. *The Code Book: The Evolution of Secrecy from Mary Queen of Scots to Quantum Cryptography*. New York: Random House, 1999.

Smoke, Richard. *War: Controlling Escalation*. Cambridge, Mass.: Harvard University Press, 1997.

Stoll, Clifford. *The Cuckoo's Egg: Tracking a Spy Through the Maze of Computer Espionage*. New York: Random House, 1989.

Thaler, David E. *Strategies to Tasks: A Framework for Linking Means and Ends*. Santa Monica, Calif.: RAND Corporation, 1993.

Thomas, Evan. *Ike's Bluff: President Eisenhower's Secret Battle to Save the World*. New York: Little, Brown and Company, 2012.

Thomas, Hugh. *The Spanish Civil War*. New York: Harper and Brothers, 1961.

Van Evera, Stephen. *Causes of War*. Ithaca, N.Y.: Cornell University Press, 1999.

Varian, Hal. "System Reliability and Free-Riding." In *Economics of Information Security*, edited by L. Jean Camp and Stephen Lewis. New York: Springer, 2004.

Ware, Willis. "Security and Privacy in Computer Systems." Santa Monica, Calif.: RAND Corporation, P-3544, 1967.

Weightman, Gavin. *Industrial Revolutionaries: The Making of the Modern World, 1776–1914*. London: Grove Atlantic, 2009.

Weigley, Russell F. *The American Way of War: A History of United States Military Strategy and Policy*. New York: Macmillan, 1973.

Whitehead, Alfred North. *An Introduction to Mathematics*. New York: Henry Holt, 1911.

Winkler, David Frank. *The Cold War at Sea: High-Seas Confrontation Between the United States and the Soviet Union*. Annapolis, Md.: Naval Institute Press, 2000.

Wolfe, Tom. *The Painted Word*. New York: Bantam, 1977.

Yourdon, Edward. *Decline and Fall of the American Programmer*. New York: Prentice-Hall, 1992.

Zetter, Kim. *Countdown to Zero Day*. New York: Crown, 2014.

Articles, Papers, and Reports

Akerlof, George A. "The Market for 'Lemons': Quality Uncertainty and the Market Mechanism." *Quarterly Journal of Economics* 84, no. 3 (1970): pp. 488–500.

Albright, David, Paul Brannan, and Christina Walrond. "Stuxnet Malware and Natanz: Update of ISIS December 22, 2010, Report." International Institute for Science and International Security, February 15, 2011. http://isis-online.org/isis-reports/detail/stuxnet-malware-and-natanz-update-of-isis-december-22-2010-reportsupa-href1/.

Alperovich, Dmitri. "Revealed: Operation Shady RAT." McAfee white paper, August 3, 2011. http://www.mcafee.com/us/resources/white-papers/wp-operation-shady-rat.pdf.

Anderson, Ross. "Privacy versus Government Surveillance: Where Network Effects Meet Public Choice." Paper presented at the Workshop on the Economics of Information Security, 2014. http://weis2014.econinfosec.org/papers/Anderson-WEIS2014.pdf.

———. "Security in Open versus Closed Systems—The Dance of Boltzmann, Coase, and Moore." *Open Source Software: Economics, Law and Policy*, IDEI Presentation, Toulouse, France, June 20–21, 2002. http://www.cl.cam.ac.uk/~rja14/Papers/toulouse.pdf.

———. "Why Cryptosystems Fail." Paper presented at the Association for Computing Machinery Conference on Computer and Communications Security, Fairfax, VA, November 1993. http://www.cl.cam.ac.uk/~rja14/Papers/wcf.pdf.

———. "Why Information Security is Hard—An Economic Perspective." Cambridge University, 2001. https://www.acsac.org/2001/papers/110.pdf.

———. "The Economics of Information Security." *Science*, October 27, 2006.

———, and Tyler Moore. *Information Security Economics—and Beyond.* Cambridge University, 2007. http://www.cl.cam.ac.uk/~rja14/Papers/econ_crypto.pdf.

———, and Roger Needham. "Programming Satan's Computer." Cambridge University, 1995. https://www.cl.cam.ac.uk/~rja14/papers/satan.pdf.

———, and Shailendra Fuloria. "Security Economics and Critical National Infrastructure." Cambridge University, 2009. http://www.cl.cam.ac.uk/~rja14/Papers/econ-cni09.pdf.

———. "Smart Meter Security: A Survey." Cambridge University, September 15, 2011. https://www.cl.cam.ac.uk/~rja14/Papers/JSAC-draft.pdf.

Arquilla, John. "Ethics and Information Warfare." In *The Changing Role of Information in Warfare,* edited by Zalmay Khalilzad et al. Santa Monica, Calif.: RAND Corporation, MR-1016, 1999.

Arthur, Brian. "Increasing Returns and the New World of Business." *Harvard Business Review,* July 1996. https://hbr.org/1996/07/increasing-returns-and-the-new-world-of-business.

Australian Government Department of Defence. "Strategies to Mitigate Targeted Cyber Intrusions." http://www.asd.gov.au/infosec/top35mitigationstrategies.htm.

———. "Top 4 Mitigation Strategies to Protect Your ICT System." Updated November 2012. http://www.asd.gov.au/publications/csocprotect/top_4_mitigations.htm.

Axelrod, Robert, and Rumen Iliev. "Timing of Cyber Conflict." *Proceedings of the National Academy of Sciences of the United States of America* 111, no. 4 (2013).

Ayres, Ian, and Steven Levitt. "Measuring Positive Externalities from Unobservable Victim Precaution: An Empirical Analysis of Lojack." National Bureau of Economic Research Working Paper No. W5928, 1998.

Baker, Stewart, Natalia Filipiak, and Katrina Timlin. "In the Dark: Crucial Industries Confront Cyberattacks." White paper, McAfee and Center for Strategic and International Studies, 2011. http://www.mcafee.com/us/resources/reports/rp-critical-infrastructure-protection.pdf.

Barefoot, Kevin, and Raymond Mataloni. "Operations of U.S. Multinational Companies in the United States and Abroad." *Survey of Current Business* (November 2011): pp. 29–48. http://www.bea.gov/scb/pdf/2011/11%20November/1111_mnc.pdf.

Becker, Gary S. "Crime and Punishment: An Economic Approach." *Journal of Political Economy* 76, no. 2 (1968).

Bell, Rich et al. "Estimating the Economic Cost of Espionage." Report for CENTRA Technology, May 3, 2010. http://bush.tamu.edu/research/capstones/mpia/Engel_Spring2010.pdf,

Bhattacharjee, Yudhijit. "A New Kind of Spy: How China Obtains American Technological Secrets." *New Yorker,* May 5, 2014.

Bilge, Leyla, and Tudor Dumitras. "Before We Knew It: An Empirical Study of Zero-Day Attacks in the Real World." Symantec Corporation, 2012. http://users.ece.cmu.edu/~tdumitra/public_documents/bilge12_zero_day.pdf.

Bipartisan Policy Center. "Cybersecurity and the North American Electric Grid: New Policy Approaches to Address an Evolving Threat." February 2014. http://bipartisanpolicy.org/wp-content/uploads/sites/default/files/Cybersecurity%20Electric%20Grid%20BPC.pdf.

———. "Cyber ShockWave." February 16, 2010.

Bivens, Josh. "The Benefits of the Dollar's Decline." Economic Policy Institute, July 24, 2003. http://www.epi.org/publication/briefingpapers_bp140/.

Blank, Stephen. "Web War I: Is Europe's First Information War a New Kind of War?" *Comparative Strategy* 27, no. 3 (2008): pp. 227–47.

———. "Can Information Warfare Be Deterred?" *Defense Analysis* 17, no. 2 (2001): pp. 121–38.

Bloomberg News. "Chinese Citizen Charged in Plot to Steal U.S. Military Data." *Los Angeles Times*, July 11, 2014.

Bowden, Mark. "The Enemy Within." *The Atlantic*, June 2010.

Brandeis, Louis D., and Samuel D. Warren. "The Right to Privacy." *Harvard Law Review* 4, no. 5 (December 15, 1890): pp. 193–220. http://www.jstor.org/stable/1321160.

Canadian Audit Committee Network Vantage Point. "Cybersecurity and the Audit Committee." March 27, 2013. http://www.tapestrynetworks.com/initiatives/corporate-governance/north-american-audit-committee-networks/upload/Tapestry_EY_CACN_Vantage_Mar13.pdf.

CERT Coordination Center and AusCERT. "Windows Intruder Detection Checklist." Pittsburgh, Pa.: Carnegie Mellon University, 2006.

Cisco Security Intelligence Operations. *A Cisco Guide to Defending Against Distributed Denial of Service Attacks.* http://www.cisco.com/web/about/security/intelligence/guide_ddos_defense.html.

———. *Cisco 2015 Annual Security Report.* 2015. http://www.cisco.com/web/offer/gist_ty2_asset/Cisco_2015_ASR.pdf.

Clauset, Aaron, Cosma Rohilla Shalizi, and M. E. J. Newman. "Power-Law Distributions in Empirical Data." *SIAM Review* 51, no. 4 (2009): pp. 661–703.

Commission on the Theft of American Intellectual Property. "The IP Commission Report." 2013. http://www.ipcommission.org/report/IP_Commission_Report_052213.pdf.

Cusumano, Michael A. "Who Is Liable for Bugs and Security Flaws in Software?" *Communications of the ACM* 47, no. 3 (March 2004).

Cylance. "Operational Cleaver." Report, December 2014. http://www.cylance.com/assets/Cleaver/Cylance_Operation_Cleaver_Report.pdf.

Danzig, Richard. "Surviving on a Diet of Poisoned Fruit." Center for a New American Security, 2014. http://www.cnas.org/sites/default/files/publications-pdf/CNAS_PoisonedFruit_Danzig_0.pdf.

Demchak, Chris C., and Peter Dombrowski. "Rise of a Cybered Westphalian Age," *Strategic Studies Quarterly* (Spring 2011): pp. 32, 38–39.

Denning, Dorothy. "Obstacles and Options for Cyber Arms Control," paper presented at Arms Control in Cyberspace Conference, Heinrich Böll Foundation, Berlin, Germany, June 29–30, 2001.

Detica and the Office of Cybersecurity and Information Assurance in the Cabinet Office. "The Cost of Cybercrime." Report, February 2011. https://www.gov.uk/government/uploads/system/uploads/attachment_data/file/60943/the-cost-of-cyber-crime-full-report.pdf.

Dunlap, Charles J., Jr. "Perspectives for Cyber Strategists on Law for Cyberwar." *Strategic Studies Quarterly* (Spring 2011): pp. 81–99.

Ebert, Hannes, and Tim Maurer. "Contested Cyberspace and Rising Powers." *Third World Quarterly* 34, no. 6 (2013): pp. 1054–74.

Electricity Consumers Resource Council. "The Economic Impacts of the August 2003 Blackout." Report, February 9, 2004. http://www.elcon.org/Documents/Profiles%20and%20Publications/Economic%20Impacts%20of%20August%202003%20Blackout.pdf.

Europol. *EU Serious and Organized Crime Threat Assessment (Socta 2013).* Report, 2013. https://www.europol.europa.eu/sites/default/files/publications/socta2013.pdf.

Falliere, Nicolas, Liam O. Murchu, and Eric Chien. "W32.Stuxnet Dossier Version 1.4." Report, Symantec, 2011. https://www.symantec.com/content/en/us/enterprise/media/security_response/whitepapers/w32_stuxnet_dossier.pdf.

Farwell, James P., and Rafal Rohozinski. "Stuxnet and the Future of Cyber War." *Survival: Global Politics and Strategy* 53, no. 1 (2011): pp. 23–40.

Finifter, Matthew, Devdatta Akhawe, and David Wagner. "An Empirical Study of Vulnerability Rewards Programs." Paper, University of California, Berkeley, undated. https://www.eecs.berkeley.edu/~daw/papers/vrp-use13.pdf.

FireEye. "M-Trends 2015: A View from the Front Lines." Report, 2015. https://www2.fireeye.com/rs/fireeye/images/rpt-m-trends-2015.pdf.

Florencio, Dinei, and Cormac Herley. *Is Everything We Know About Password-Stealing Wrong?* Report, Microsoft, undated. http://research.microsoft.com/pubs/161829/EverythingWeKnow.pdf.

Florida Reliability Coordinating Council Event Analysis Team. "FRCC System Disturbance and Under-frequency Load Shedding Event Report February 26th, 2008 at 1:09 pm." Final report, Tampa, October 30, 2008.

Fravel, M. Taylor, and Evan S. Medeiros. "China's Search for Assured Retaliation: The Evolution of Chinese Nuclear Strategy and Force Structure." *International Security* 35, no. 2 (Fall 2010): pp. 48–87.

Frei, Stefan. "The Known Unknowns." Report, NSS Labs, 2013.

———, and Francisco Artes. "International Vulnerability Purchase Program: Why Buying All Vulnerabilities above Black Market Prices Is Economically Sound." Report, NSS Labs, 2013. https://www.nsslabs.com/sites/default/files/public-report/files/International%20Vulnerability%20Purchase%20Program%20%28IVPP%29-1.pdf.

Gantz, John F. et al. "The Dangerous World of Counterfeit and Pirated Software." Report, Microsoft, 2013. http://news.microsoft.com/download/presskits/antipiracy/docs/IDC030513.pdf.

Gartzke, Erik. "The Myth of Cyberwar: Bringing War in Cyberspace Back Down to Earth." *International Security* 38, no. 2 (Fall 2013): pp. 41–73.

———, and Jon R. Lindsay. "Weaving Tangled Webs: Offense, Defense, and Deception in Cyberspace." *Security Studies* 24, no. 2 (2015): pp. 316–48.

Geer, Dan. "Cybersecurity as Realpolitik." Speech, 2014. http://geer.tinho.net/geer.blackhat.6viii14.txt.

——— et al. "Cyber Insecurity: The Cost of Monopoly—How the Dominance of Microsoft's Products Poses a Risk to Security." Report, September 27, 2003. http://cryptome.org/cyberinsecurity.htm.

Gladwell, Malcolm. "Trust No One: Kim Philby and the Hazards of Mistrust." *New Yorker,* July 28, 2014.

Gordon, Lawrence, and Martin Loeb. "The Economics of Information Security Investment." *ACM Transactions on Information and System Security* 5, no. 4 (2002): pp. 438–57.

Grigsby, Alex. "The UN GGE on Cybersecurity: What Is the UN's Role?" April 15, 2015. http://blogs.cfr.org/cyber/2015/04/15/the-un-gge-on-cybersecurity-what-is-the-uns-role/.

———. "The 2015 GGE Report: Breaking New Ground, Ever So Slowly." Council on Foreign Relations Guest Blog. September 8, 2015. http://blogs.cfr.org/cyber/2015/09/08/the-2015-gge-report-breaking-new-ground-ever-so-slowly/.

Grueber, Martin et al. "2014 Global R&D Funding Forecast." Battelle, December 2013. http://www.battelle.org/docs/tpp/2014_global_rd_funding_forecast.pdf.

Harknett, Richard J., John P. Callaghan, and Rudi Kauffman. "Leaving Deterrence Behind: War-Fighting and National Cybersecurity." *Journal of Homeland Security and Emergency Management* 7, no. 1 (2010).

Hayden, Michael V. "The Future of Things 'Cyber.'" *Strategic Studies Quarterly* 3, no. 4 (2011).

Hewlett-Packard. "Cyber Risk Report 2015." Report, 2015. http://www8.hp.com/us/en/software-solutions/cyber-risk-report-security-vulnerability/.

Hooper, Peter, Karen Johnson, and Jaime Marquez. "Trade Elasticities of the G-7 Countries." *Princeton Studies in International Economics* no. 87 (2000).

Hutchins, Eric, Michael J. Cloppert, and Rohan Amin. "Intelligence-Driven Computer Network Defense Informed by Analysis of Adversary Campaigns and Intrusion Kill Chains." Report, Lockheed Martin, 2010. http://www.lockheedmartin.com/content/dam/lockheed/data/corporate/documents/LM-White-Paper-Intel-Driven-Defense.pdf.

International Group of Experts at the Invitation of the NATO Cooperative Cyber Defence Centre of Excellence. "The 'Tallinn Manual' on the International Law Applicable to Cyber Warfare." Draft, August 21, 2012.

Internet Corporation for Assigned Names and Numbers. "Factsheet: Root Server Attack on 6 February 2007." Marina del Rey, Calif., March 1, 2007. http://www.icann.org/en/news/announcements/announcement-08mar07-en.htm.

iSight Partners. "Russian Cyber Espionage Campaign–Sandworm Team." Report, October 14, 2015. http://www.washingtonpost.com/r/2010-2019/WashingtonPost/2014/10/14/National-Security/Graphics/briefing2.pdf.

Jervis, Robert. "Arms Control, Stability, and Causes of War." *Political Science Quarterly* 108, no. 2 (Summer 1993).

Johnson, Michael, and Terrence K. Kelly. "Tailored Deterrence: Strategic Context to Guide Joint Force 2020." *Joint Force Quarterly* 74, no. 3 (July 2014): pp. 22–29.

Kaspersky Lab. "Regin: A Malicious Platform Capable of Spying on GSM Networks." Report, November 24, 2014. http://www.kaspersky.com/about/news/virus/2014/Regin-a-malicious-platform-capable-of-spying-on-GSM-networks.

———. "Unveiling 'Careto'—The Masked APT." Report, February 2014. http://kasperskycontenthub.com/wp-content/uploads/sites/43/vlpdfs/unveilingthemask_v1.0.pdf.

———. "Equation Group: The Crown Creator of Cyber-Espionage." Report, February 16, 2015. http://www.kaspersky.com/about/news/virus/2015/equation-group-the-crown-creator-of-cyber-espionage.

———. "Resource 207: Kaspersky Lab Research Proves that Stuxnet and Flame Developers Are Connected." Report, June 11, 2012. http://www.kaspersky.com/about/news/virus/2012/Resource_207_Kaspersky_Lab_Research_Proves_that_Stuxnet_and_Flame_Developers_are_Connected.

———. "Duqu Is Back: Kaspersky Lab Reveals Cyberattack on its Corporate Network that also Hit High Profile Victims in Western Countries, the Middle East and Asia." Report, June 10, 2015. http://www.kaspersky.com/about/news/virus/2015/Duqu-is-back.

Kaufmann, William. "The Evolution of Deterrence 1945–1958." Unpublished RAND research paper, 1958.

Koblentz, Gregory D. "Strategic Stability in the Second Nuclear Age." Report, Council on Foreign Relations, November 2014. http://www.cfr.org/nonproliferation-arms-control-and-disarmament/strategic-stability-second-nuclear-age/p33809.

Korns, Stephen W. "Botnets Outmaneuvered: Georgia's Cyberstrategy Disproves Cyberspace Carpet-Bombing Theory." *Armed Forces Journal* (January 2009).

Kull, Steven et al. "Public Opinion in the Islamic World on Terrorism, al Qaeda, and U.S. Policies." University of Maryland, College Park, Program on International Policy Attitudes, 2009. http://www.worldpublicopinion.org/pipa/pdf/feb09/STARTII_Feb09_rpt.pdf.

Leed, Maren. *Offensive Cyber Capabilities at the Operational Level*. Report, Center for Strategic and International Studies, 2013. http://csis.org/files/publication/130916_Leed_OffensiveCyberCapabilities_Web.pdf.

Lewis, James A. "Raising the Bar for Cybersecurity." Paper, Center for Strategic and International Studies, 2013. http://csis.org/files/publication/130212_Lewis_RaisingBarCybersecurity.pdf.

———. "Cyber Attacks, Real or Imagined, and Cyber War." Paper, Center for Strategic and International Studies, July 11, 2011. http://csis.org/publication/cyber-attacks-real-or-imagined-and-cyber-war.

Libicki, Martin. "Wringing Deterrence from Cyberwar Capabilities." In *Economics and Security: Resourcing National Priorities*, ed. Richmond M. Lloyd. William B. Ruger Chair of National Security Economics Papers No. 5, Naval War College, Newport, R.I., May 19–21, 2010, 259–72.

Lichtman, Doug, and Eric Posner. "Holding Internet Service Providers Accountable." 14 *Supreme Court Economics Review* 221 (2006): pp. 233–34.

Lieggi, Stephanie. "Going Beyond the Stir: The Strategic Realities of China's No-First-Use Policy." Nuclear Threat Initiative, January 1, 2005. http://www.nti.org/analysis/articles/realities-chinas-no-first-use-policy/.

Liff, Adam P. "Cyberwar: A New 'Absolute Weapon'? The Proliferation of Cyberwarfare Capabilities and Interstate War." *Journal of Strategic Studies* 35, no. 3 (2012).

Lindsay, Jon R. "The Impact of China on Cybersecurity: Fiction and Friction." *International Security* 39, no. 3 (Winter 2014/15): pp. 7–47.

———. "Stuxnet and the Limits of Cyber Warfare." *Security Studies* 22, no. 3 (2013).

Lynn III, William J. "Defending a New Domain: The Pentagon's Cyberstrategy." *Foreign Affairs* (September/October 2010).

Makovsky, David. "The Silent Strike: How Israel Bombed a Syrian Nuclear Installation and Kept It Secret." *New Yorker*, September 17, 2012.

Mandiant. "APT1: Exposing One of China's Cyber Espionage Units." Report, March 2013. http://intelreport.mandiant.com/Mandiant_APT1_Report.pdf.

Mann, C. C. "The Mole in the Machine." *New York Times Sunday Magazine*, July 25, 1999, 32–35.

Marquez, Jaime. "Income and Price Elasticities of Foreign Trade Flows: Econometric Estimation and Analysis of the US Trade Deficit." International Finance Discussion Papers no. 324 (June 1988). http://www.federalreserve.gov/pubs/ifdp/1988/324/ifdp324.pdf.

Masters, Jonathan. "Confronting the Cyber Threat." Council on Foreign Relations, May 23, 2011. http://www.cfr.org/technology-and-foreign-policy/confronting-cyber-threat/p15577.

McAfee Foundstone Professional Services and McAfee Labs. "Global Energy Cyberattacks: 'Night Dragon.'" White paper, 2011. http://www.mcafee.com/us/resources/white-papers/wp-global-energy-cyberattacks-night-dragon.pdf.

McAfee–Center for Strategic and International Security. "Net Losses: Estimating the Global Cost of Cybercrime." Report, 2014. http://csis.org/files/attachments/140609_rp_economic_impact_cybercrime_report.pdf.

Merton, Robert K. "Resistance to the Systematic Study of Multiple Discoveries in Science." *European Journal of Sociology* 4 (1963): pp. 237–82.

Microsoft. "Microsoft Releases National Survey Findings on How to Inspire the Next Generation of Doctors, Scientists, Software Developers, and Engineers." Report, September 7, 2011. http://www.microsoft.com/en-us/news/press/2011/sep11/09-07MSSTEMSurveyPR.aspx.

———. "Microsoft Security Intelligence Report 16." Report, July–December 2013.

Miller, Charles, and Chris Valasek. "Adventures in Automotive Networks and Control Units." *Illmatics.com*. Undated report. http://illmatics.com/car_hacking.pdf.

Moore, Tyler, and Richard Clayton. "The Consequence of Non-Cooperation in the Fight against Phishing." *Proceedings of the Anti-Phishing Working Group eCrime Researchers Summit,* 2008, 1–14.

Mulligan, Deirdre K., and Fred B. Schneider. "Doctrine for Cybersecurity." Report, Cornell University, May 15, 2011. https://www.cs.cornell.edu/fbs/publications/publicCybersecDaed.pdf.

Mulvenon, James. "Information Warfare and China's Cyber-Warfare Capabilities." Speech given at Carnegie Endowment for International Peace, Washington, D.C., February 10, 2011.

———. "The PLA and Information Warfare." In *The People's Liberation Army in the Information Age*, edited by James C. Mulvenon and Richard H. Yang. Santa Monica, Calif.: RAND Corporation, 1998, CF-145-CAPP/AF, 175–86.

Nagaraja, Shishir, and Ross Anderson. "The Snooping Dragon: Social-Malware Surveillance of the Tibetan Movement." University of Cambridge Computer Laboratory Technical Report 746, March 2009. http://www.cl.cam.ac.uk/techreports/UCAM-CL-TR-746.html.

New York Independent System Operator. "Final Report on the August 14, 2003, Blackout." Report, February 2005. http://www.nyiso.com/public/webdocs/media_room/press_releases/2005/blackout_rpt_final.pdf.

Novetta. "Axiom Threat Actor Group Report." Report, 2014. https://www.novetta.com/2014/10/cyber-security-coalition-releases-full-report-on-large-scale-interdiction-of-chinese-state-sponsored-espionage-effort/.

Nowak, Martin A., Karen M. Page, and Karl Sigmund. "Fairness Versus Reason in the Ultimatum Game." *Science* 289, no. 5485 (September 2000): pp. 1773–75.

Nye, Joseph S. "Nuclear Lessons for Cyber Security?" *Strategic Studies Quarterly* 5, no. 4 (Winter 2011).

O'Gorman, Gavin, and Geoff McDonald. "The Elderwood Project." Symantec, September 2012. http://www.symantec.com/connect/blogs/elderwood-project.

Organization for Economic Cooperation and Development. *OECD Science, Technology and Industry Outlook 2014.* Report, 2014. http://www.oecd.org/science/oecd-science-technology-and-industry-outlook-19991428.htm.

Ozment, Andrew, and Stuart E. Schechter. "Milk or Wine: Does Software Security Improve with Age?" Report, Usenix, 2006. http://www.usenix.org/legacy/event/sec06/tech/full_papers/ozment/ozment.pdf.

Posen, Barry R. "Inadvertent Nuclear War? Escalation and NATO's Northern Flank." *International Security* 7, no. 2 (Autumn 1982): pp. 28–54.

Posner, Richard. "An Economic Theory of Privacy." Report, Cato Institute, 1978. http://object.cato.org/sites/cato.org/files/serials/files/regulation/1978/5/v2n3-4.pdf.

Raymond, Eric. "The Cathedral and the Bazaar." Online book, February 18, 2010. http://www.catb.org/esr/writings/cathedral-bazaar/.

Rescorla, Eric. "Is Finding Security Holes a Good Idea?" Paper, RTFM, Inc., 2004. http://www.dtc.umn.edu/weis2004/rescorla.pdf.

Rid, Thomas. "Cyberwar and Peace: Hacking Can Reduce Real-World Violence." *Foreign Affairs* (November-December 2013).

———. "Deterrence Beyond the State: The Israel Experience." *Contemporary Security Policy* 33, no. 1 (2012): 124–47.

———, and Peter McBurney. "Cyber Weapons." *RUSI Journal* 157, no. 1 (2012): pp. 6–13.

———, and Ben Buchanan. "Attributing Cyber Attacks." *Journal of Strategic Studies* 38, no. 1 (2014).

Rogers, Kristine. "Resistance is Not Futile: The Case Against a Cyber Arms Treaty." Paper, Air War College, 2010.

Salzman, Hal, Daniel Kuehn, and Lindsay Lowell. "Guestworkers in the High-Skill U.S. Labor Market: An Analysis of Supply, Employment and Wage Trends." Economic Policy Institute Briefing Paper, April 24, 2013. http://www.epi.org/publication/bp359-guestworkers-high-skill-labor-market-analysis/.

SANS. "SANS Intrusion Detection FAQ: What Is Solar Sunrise?" http://www.sans.org/security-resources/idfaq/solar_sunrise.php.

Schmidt, Marco F. H., and Jessica A. Sommerville. "Fairness Expectations and Altruistic Sharing in 15-Month-Old Human Infants." *PLOS ONE* 6, no. 10 (2011).

Shahzad, Muhammad, Muhammad Zubair Shafiq, and Alex X. Lin. "A Large Scale Exploratory Analysis of Software Vulnerability Life Cycles." Proceedings of the 34th International Conference on Software Engineering, 2012, 771–81.

Siboni, Gabi, and Sami Kronenfeld. "Developments in Iranian Cyber Warfare, 2013–2014." Institute for National Security Studies Insight no. 536, April 3, 2014. http://www.inss.org.il/index.aspx?id=4538&articleid=6809.

Sofaer, Abraham D., and Seymour E. Goodman. "A Proposal for an International Convention on Cyber-crime and Terrorism." Center for International Security and Cooperation, Stanford University, August 2000. http://fsi.stanford.edu/publications/proposal_for_an_international_convention_on_cyber_crime_and_terrorism_a.

Sotirov, Alex. "Analyzing the MD5 Collision in Flame." Paper, Trail of Bits, Inc., undated. https://www.trailofbits.com/resources/flame-md5.pdf.

Spafford, Eugene. "The Internet Worm Program: An Analysis." Purdue Technical Report, CSD-TR-823, December 8, 1988. http://spaf.cerias.purdue.edu/tech-reps/823.pdf.

Sterner, Eric. "Stuxnet and the Pentagon's Cyber Strategy." Paper, George C. Marshall Institute, October 13, 2010. http://www.marshall.org/article.php?id=918.

Svajcer, Vanja. "Sophos Mobile Security Threat Report." Report, 2014. https://www.sophos.com/en-us/medialibrary/PDFs/other/sophos-mobile-security-threat-report.pdf?la=en.

Swire, Peter, and Kenesha Ahmand. "Encryption and Globalization." *Columbia Science and Technology Law Review* 23 (2012).

Symantec Corporation. "Internet Security Threat Report 2013," vol. 18. April 2013. http://www.symantec.com/content/en/us/enterprise/other_resources/b-istr_main_report_v18_2012_21291018.en-us.pdf

Symantec Security Response. "Stuxnet 0.5: The Missing Link." Symantec blog, February 26, 2013. http://www.symantec.com/connect/blogs/stuxnet-05-missing-link.

Thomas, Timothy. "The Internet in China: Civilian and Military Uses." *Information and Security: An International Journal* 7 (2001): pp. 159–73.

Travis, Jeremy, Bruce Western, and Steve Redburn, eds. "The Growth of Incarceration in the United States: Exploring Causes and Consequences." National Research Council Report, 2014. http://www.nap.edu/catalog/18613/the-growth-of-incarceration-in-the-united-states-exploring-causes.

United Nations Group of Governmental Experts. "Report of the Group of Governmental Experts on Developments in the Field of Information and Telecommunications in the Context of International Security." Report, June 24, 2013. http://www.un.org/ga/search/view_doc.asp?symbol=A/68/98.group.

———. "Report of the Group of Governmental Experts on Developments in the Field of Information and Telecommunications in the Context of International Security." Report, July 22, 2015. http://daccess-dds-ny.un.org/doc/UNDOC/GEN/N15/228/35/PDF/N1522835.pdf.

Verizon. "2014 Verizon Data Breach Investigations Report." Report, 2014. http://www.verizonenterprise.com/DBIR/2014/.

Wang, Jian-Wei, and Li-Li Rong. "Cascade-based Attack Vulnerability on the U.S. Power Grid." *Safety Science* 47 (2009): pp. 1332–36.

Waxman, Matthew. "Cyberattacks and the Use of Force: Back to the Future of Article 2(4)." *Yale Journal of International Law* 36, no. 2 (2011): pp. 421–59.

———. "Self-defensive Force Against Cyber Attacks: Legal, Strategic, and Political Dimensions." *International Law Studies* 89 (2013).

Wheeler, David A., and Gregory N. Larsen. "Techniques for Cyber Attack Attribution." Paper, Institute for Defense Analyses, October 2003.

Williamson III, Charles W. "Carpet Bombing in Cyberspace: Why America Needs a Military Botnet." *Armed Forces Journal*, May 2008.

Wohlstetter, Albert. "The Delicate Balance of Terror." *Foreign Affairs* 37, no. 2 (1959): pp. 211–23.

World Trade Organization. "TRIPS Material on the WTO Web Site." http://www.wto.org/english/tratop_e/trips_e/trips_e.htm.

Wright, Lawrence. "The Spymaster." *New Yorker*, January 21, 2008, 8.

Zimmerman, Peter D. "Proliferation: Bronze Medal Technology Is Enough." *Orbis* 38, no. 1 (Winter 1994): p. 67.

Zwillinger, Mark, and Christian Genetski. "Calculating Loss Under the Economic Act of 1996." *George Mason Law Review* 9, no. 323 (2000–2001).

U.S. Government Documents, Official Statements, and Congressional Testimony

Alexander, Keith. "Advance Questions for Lieutenant General Keith Alexander, USA, Nominee for Commander, United States CYBERCOM." Statement to the U.S. Senate Committee on Armed Services, April 15, 2010. https://epic.org/privacy/nsa/Alexander_04-15-10.pdf.

Assante, Michael J. Testimony before the Subcommittee on Emerging Threats, Cybersecurity, and Science and Technology, House Committee on Homeland Security, July 21, 2009.

Bejtlich, Richard. Statement before the U.S. House of Representatives Committee on Energy and Commerce Subcommittee on Oversight and Investigations Understanding the Cyber Threat and Implications for the 21st-Century Economy, March 3, 2015. http://docs.house.gov/meetings/IF/IF02/20150303/103079/HHRG-114-IF02-Wstate-BejtlichR-20150303.pdf.

Bureau of Industry and Security. "Intrusion and Surveillance Items: FAQ." http://www.bis.doc.gov/index.php/policy-guidance/faqs.

———. "More Details Emerge on Multilateral Export Controls on Cybersecurity Items." December 10, 2013. http://www.exportlawblog.com/archives/category/wassenaar.

Bush, George W. "The National Strategy to Secure Cyberspace." Draft for comment, President's Critical Infrastructure Protection Board. September 2002.

Canadian Audit Committee Network Vantage Point. "Cybersecurity and the Audit Committee." March 27, 2013. http://www.tapestrynetworks.com/initiatives/corporate-governance/north-american-audit-committee-networks/upload/Tapestry_EY_CACN_Vantage_Mar13.pdf.

Cartwright, James. Statement of the United States Strategic Command before the House Armed Services Committee, March 21, 2007.

Cashell, Brian et al. "Congressional Research Service Report for Congress: The Economic Impact of Cyber-Attacks." April 1, 2004. http://fas.org/sgp/crs/misc/RL32331.pdf.

Census Bureau. "Trade in Goods with China." Updated continuously. https://www.census.gov/foreign-trade/balance/c5700.html.

——— and U.S. Bureau of Economic Analysis. "U.S. International Trade in Goods and Services, December 2012." News release, 2012. http://www.bea.gov/newsreleases/international/trade/2013/trad1212.htm.

Clapper, James R. "Worldwide Threat Assessment of the U.S. Intelligence Community." Statement before the Senate Select Committee on Intelligence, March 12, 2013. http://www.dni.gov/files/documents/Intelligence%20Reports/2013%20ATA%20SFR%20for%20SSCI%2012%20Mar%202013.pdf.

———. "Statement for the Record: Worldwide Threat Assessment of the U.S. Intelligence Community before the Senate Armed Services Committee." February 26, 2015. http://cdn.arstechnica.net/wp-content/uploads/2015/02/Clapper_02-26-15.pdf.

Defense Advanced Research Projects Agency. "The National Cyber Range: A National Testbed for Critical Security Research." https://www.whitehouse.gov/files/documents/cyber/DARPA%20-%20NationalCyberRange_FactSheet.pdf.

———. "Cyber Grand Challenge." http://www.cybergrandchallenge.com/.

Defense Science Board. "Task Force Report: Resilient Military Systems and the Advanced Cyber Threat." 2013. http://www.acq.osd.mil/dsb/reports/ResilientMilitarySystems.CyberThreat.pdf.

Department of Defense. "Department of Defense Cyberspace Policy Report: A Report to Congress Pursuant to the National Defense Authorization Act for Fiscal Year 2011, Section 934." Report, 2011. http://www.defense.gov/home/features/2011/0411_cyberstrategy/docs/NDAA%20Section%20934%20Report_For%20webpage.pdf.

———. "Department of Defense Cyber Strategy." Report, April 2015. http://www.defense.gov/Portals/1/features/2015/0415_cyber-strategy/Final_2015_DoD_CYBER_STRATEGY_for_web.pdf.

———. "DoD Law of War Manual." June 2015. http://www.dod.mil/dodgc/images/law_war_manual15.pdf.

———. "Nuclear Posture Review Report." April 2010.

———. "Strategy for Operating in Cyberspace." July 2011.

Department of Homeland Security. "Blueprint for a Secure Cyber Future." Report, November 2011. http://www.dhs.gov/blueprint-secure-cyber-future.

———. "National Cyber Incident Response Plan (Interim Version)." September 2010. http://www.federalnewsradio.com/pdfs/NCIRP_Interim_Version_September_2010.pdf.

———, Industrial Control Systems–Cyber Emergency Response Team. "Advisory (ICSA-10–090–01) Mariposa Botnet." March 31, 2010. https://ics-cert.us-cert.gov/advisories/ICSA-10-090-01.

———. "Alert (ICS-ALERT-14-281-01B) Ongoing Sophisticated Malware Campaign Compromising ICS (Update B)." December 10, 2014. https://ics-cert.us-cert.gov/alerts/ICS-ALERT-14-281-01B.

———, U.S. Computer Emergency Readiness Team. "Alert (TA14-150A) GameOver Zeus P2P Malware." June 2, 2014. https://www.us-cert.gov/ncas/alerts/TA14-150A.

———. "The National Strategy to Secure Cyberspace." February 2003. https://www.us-cert.gov/sites/default/files/publications/cyberspace_strategy.pdf.

Department of Justice. "U.S. Charges Five Chinese Military Hackers for Cyber Espionage Against U.S. Corporations and a Labor Organization for Commercial Advantage." May 19, 2014. http://www.justice.gov/opa/pr/2014/May/14-ag-528.html.

———. Commission for the Review of FBI Security Programs. "A Review of FBI Security Programs." Report, 2002.

Federal Aviation Administration. "Accident and Incident Data." Updated continuously. http://www.faa.gov/data_research/accident_incident/.

Federal Bureau of Investigation. "FBI, Slovenian and Spanish Police Arrest Mariposa Botnet Creator, Operators." News release, July 28, 2010. http://www.fbi.gov/news/pressrel/press-releases/fbi-slovenian-and-spanish-police-arrest-mariposa-botnet-creator-operators.

————. "Update on Sony Investigation." News release, December 17, 2014. http://www.fbi.gov/news/pressrel/press-releases/update-on-sony-investigation.

Federal Energy Regulatory Commission and North American Energy Reliability Corporation. "Arizona-Southern California Outages on September 8, 2011." Report, 2011. https://www.ferc.gov/legal/staff-reports/04-27-2012-ferc-nerc-report.pdf.

Gates, Robert. "Nuclear Weapons and Deterrence in the 21st Century." Address to the Carnegie Endowment for International Peace, October 28, 2008.

Government Accountability Office. "TVA Needs to Address Weaknesses in Control Systems and Networks." Report, May 21, 2008. http://www.gao.gov/products/GAO-08-526.

Homeland Security Advisory Council. "CyberSkills Task Force Report." October 2012. http://www.dhs.gov/sites/default/files/publications/HSAC%20CyberSkills%20Report%20-%20Final.pdf.

Internal Revenue Service. "IRS Statement on the 'Get Transcript' Application." News release, May 26, 2015. http://www.irs.gov/uac/Newsroom/IRS-Statement-on-the-Get-Transcript-Application.

————. "IRS, Industry, States Take New Steps Together to Fight Identity Theft, Protect Taxpayers." News release, June 11, 2015. http://www.irs.gov/uac/Newsroom/IRS-and-Industry-and-States-Take-New-Steps-Together-to-Fight-Identity-Theft-and-Protect-Taxpayers.

Joint Chiefs of Staff. Joint Publication 3–12R, "Cyberspace Operations." 2013. http://www.dtic.mil/doctrine/new_pubs/jp3_12R.pdf.

————. Joint Publication 3–13.1, *Joint Doctrine for Command and Control Warfare (C2W)*. February 7, 1996. http://www.iwar.org.uk/rma/resources/c4i/jp3_13_1.pdf.

National Institute for Standards and Technology, Joint Task Force Transformation Initiative. "Security and Privacy Controls for Federal Information Systems and Organizations." Report, 2013. http://nvlpubs.nist.gov/nistpubs/SpecialPublications/NIST.SP.800-53r4.pdf.

National Security Agency. "Security-Enhanced Linux." January 15, 2009. http://www.nsa.gov/research/selinux/.

————, Central Security Service. "NSA's Cyber Camps Make Summer School Fun." News release, May 11, 2015. https://www.nsa.gov/public_info/press_room/2015/gencyber_summer_camps.shtml.

National Science Foundation. "The Internet." *NSF.gov.* http://www.nsf.gov/od/lpa/nsf50/nsfoutreach/htm/n50_z2/pages_z3/28_pg.htm.

Obama, Barack. "Transcript of President Obama's Jan. 17 speech on NSA reforms." January 17, 2014. http://www.washingtonpost.com/politics/full-text-of-president-obamas-jan-17-speech-on-nsa-reforms/2014/01/17/fa33590a-7f8c-11e3-9556-4a4bf7bcbd84_story.html.

————. "Cyberspace Policy Review." Report, May 2009. https://www.whitehouse.gov/assets/documents/Cyberspace_Policy_Review_final.pdf.

————. Executive Order 12356, "National Security Information." December 29, 2009. https://www.whitehouse.gov/the-press-office/executive-order-classified-national-security-information.

————. "International Strategy for Cyberspace: Prosperity, Security, and Openness in a Networked World." Report, May 2011. https://www.whitehouse.gov/sites/default/files/rss_viewer/international_strategy_for_cyberspace.pdf.

————. "National Strategy for Trusted Identities in Cyberspace." Report, April 2011. http://www.whitehouse.gov/sites/default/files/rss_viewer/NSTICstrategy_041511.pdf.

Office of the National Counterintelligence Executive. "Foreign Spies Stealing U.S. Economic Secrets in Cyberspace: Report to Congress on Foreign Economic Collection and Industrial Espionage, 2009–2011." Report, October 2011. http://www.ncix.gov/publications/reports/fecie_all/Foreign_Economic_Collection_2011.pdf.

Office of the Press Secretary. "Presidential Policy Directive—Critical Infrastructure Security and Resilience." News release, February 12, 2013. https://www.whitehouse.gov/the-press-office/2013/02/12/presidential-policy-directive-critical-infrastructure-security-and-resil.

Panetta, Leon. "Remarks to the Business Executives for National Security in New York City." October 11, 2012. http://www.defense.gov/transcripts/transcript.aspx?transcriptid=5136.

President's Commission on Critical Infrastructure Protection. "Critical Foundations: Protecting America's Infrastructures." Report, 1997. https://fas.org/sgp/library/pccip.pdf.

Reagan, Ronald. "Address to the Nation on Defense and National Security." Washington, D.C., March 23, 1983.

Republican National Committee. "We Believe in America: Republican Platform 2012." http://www.gop .com/wp-content/uploads/2012/08/2012GOPPlatform.pdf.

Rogers, Michael S. Statement before the House Committee on Armed Services Subcommittee on Emerging Threats and Capabilities, March 4, 2015.

U.S. Air Force Space Command. Instruction 33–107, "Information Operations Condition (INFOCON) System Procedures." July 3, 2006.

U.S.-Canada Power System Outage Task Force. "Final Report of the August 14, 2003 Blackout in the United States and Canada: Causes and Recommendations." Report, April 2004. http://energy.gov/sites/ prod/files/oeprod/DocumentsandMedia/BlackoutFinal-Web.pdf.

White House. "The Comprehensive National Cybersecurity Initiative (publicly released version)." Undated. https://www.whitehouse.gov/issues/foreign-policy/cybersecurity/national-initiative.

———. "Liberty and Security in a Changing World." Report, 2013. https://www.whitehouse.gov/sites/ default/files/docs/2013-12-12_rg_final_report.pdf.

———. Executive Order. "Blocking the Property of Certain Persons Engaging in Significant Malicious Cyber-Enabled Activities." News release, April 1, 2015. https://www.whitehouse.gov/the-press-office/2015/04/01/executive-order-blocking-property-certain-persons-engaging-significant-m.

———, Office of the Press Secretary. "Remarks as Prepared for Delivery by Assistant to the President for Homeland Security and Counterterrorism Lisa O. Monaco: Strengthening our Nation's Cyber Defenses." February 11, 2015. https://www.whitehouse.gov/the-press-office/2015/02/11/ remarks-prepared-delivery-assistant-president-homeland-security-and-coun.

Wilson, Clay. "Botnets, Cybercrime, and Cyberterrorism: Vulnerabilities and Policy Issues for Congress." Washington, D.C.: Congressional Research Service, January 29, 2008, https://www.fas.org/sgp/ crs/terror/RL32114.pdf.

News Reports and Opinion

Ackerman, Gwen. "Hackers Can Steal Data Wirelessly from PCs That Aren't Even Online." Bloomberg, November 9, 2014. http://www.bloomberg.com/news/2014-11-19/hackers-can-steal-data-wirelessly-from-pcs-that-aren-t-even-online.html.

Adee, Sally. "The Hunt for the Kill Switch." IEEE Spectrum, May 2008. http://spectrum.ieee.org/ semiconductors/design/the-hunt-for-the-kill-switch.

Agence France-Presse. "Cyber Strikes a 'Civilized' Option: Britain." Inquirer, June 3, 2012. http://technology .inquirer.net/11747/cyber-strikes-a-civilized-option-britain.

———. "U.S. Blames Russia for Leak of Undiplomatic Language from Top Official." The Guardian, February 6, 2014.

Amadeo, Ron. "Adware Vendors Buy Chrome Extensions to Send Ad- and Malware-filled Updates." Ars Technica, January 17, 2014. http://arstechnica.com/security/2014/01/malware-vendors-buy-chrome-extensions-to-send-adware-filled-updates/.

Ambinder, Marc. "Inside the Black Box: How NSA is Helping Companies Fight Back Against Chinese Hackers." Foreign Policy, March 13, 2013.

Anderson, Nate. "How Georgia Doxed a Russian Hacker (and Why It Matters)." Ars Technica, November 2, 2012. http://arstechnica.com/tech-policy/2012/11/how-georgia-doxed-a-russian-hacker-and-why-it-matters/.

———. "Meet the People Who Want Julian Assange 'Whacked.'" Ars Technica, December 3, 2010. http:// arstechnica.com/tech-policy/2010/12/meet-the-people-who-want-julian-assange-whacked/.

Apple. "Apple and IBM Forge Global Partnership to Transform Enterprise Mobility." July 15, 2014. http:// www.apple.com/pr/library/2014/07/15Apple-and-IBM-Forge-Global-Partnership-to-Transform-Enterprise-Mobility.html.

Applegate, Scott. "Leveraging Cyber Militias as a Force Multiplier in Cyber Operations." In forthcoming Strategic Studies Institute book.

Arnbak, Axel et al. "Security Collapse in the HTTPS Market: Assessing Legal and Technical Solutions to Secure HTTPS." *Queue* 12, no. 8 (2014).

Arquilla, John. "Cool War: Could the Age of Cyberwarfare Lead Us to a Brighter Future?" *Foreign Policy*, June 15, 2012.

Associated Press. "Former NSA Chief Defends Cybersecurity Venture." *New York Times*, August 5, 2014.

———. "Russia Classifies Military Casualties in Peacetime." *New York Times*, May 28, 2015.

———. "U.S., China to Cooperate More on Cyber Threat." *Politico.com*, May 8, 2012. http://www.politico.com/news/stories/0512/76036.html.

Auerbach, David. "How to Fight the Next $1 Billion Bank Hack." *Slate*, February 18, 2015. http://www.slate.com/articles/technology/safety_net/2015/02/_1_billion_bank_hack_how_to_fight_the_next_one.html.

Auernheimer, Andrew. "Forget Disclosure—Hackers Should Keep Security Holes to Themselves." *Wired.com*, November 29, 2012. http://www.wired.com/2012/11/hacking-choice-and-disclosure/.

Baev, Pavel K. "Apocalypse a Bit Later: The Meaning of Putin's Nuclear Threats." *Brookings.edu*, April 1, 2015. http://www.brookings.edu/blogs/order-from-chaos/posts/2015/04/01-putin-nuclear-threats-meaning.

Bagchi, Indrani. "China Mounts Cyber Attacks on Indian Sites." *The Times of India*, May 5, 2008. http://timesofindia.indiatimes.com/india/China-mounts-cyber-attacks-on-Indian-sites/articleshow/3010288.cms.

Baker, Stewart. "The Attribution Revolution: Raising the Costs for Hackers and Their Customers." Testimony Before the Senate Judiciary Committee. May 8, 2013. http://volokh.com/2013/05/08/testifying-on-cybersecurity-before-the-senate-judiciary-committee/.

Ballenstedt, Brittany. "DHS Creates Cyber Internships for Community College Students, Veterans." *Nextgov.com*, April 22, 2013. http://www.nextgov.com/cio-briefing/wired-workplace/2013/04/dhs-creates-cyber-internships-community-college-students-veterans/62680/.

Barber, Bryan. "Cheese Worm: Pros and Cons of a 'Friendly' Worm." SANS Institute, 2001. http://www.sans.org/reading-room/whitepapers/malicious/cheese-worm-pros-cons-friendly-worm-31.

Barboza, David. "Owner of Chinese Toy Factory Commits Suicide." *New York Times*, August 14, 2007.

BBC. "South Korea to Develop Stuxnet-like Cyberweapons." February 21, 2014. http://www.bbc.com/news/technology-26287527.

———. "TV5 Monde attack 'by Russia-based hackers'." June 9, 2015. http://www.bbc.com/news/world-europe-33072034.

Bejtlich, Richard. "Five Reasons 'dot-secure' Will Fail." *TaoSecurity* (blog), September 25, 2010. http://taosecurity.blogspot.com/2010/09/five-reasons-dot-secure-will-fail.html.

———. "Target Malware Kingpins." *Brookings.edu*, February 2, 2015. http://www.brookings.edu/research/opinions/2015/02/02-cybersecurity-target-malware-kingpins-bejtlich.

Bellovin, Steven. "Why Even Strong Crypto Wouldn't Protect SSNs Exposed in Anthem Breach." *Ars Technica*, February 5, 2014. http://arstechnica.com/security/2015/02/why-even-strong-crypto-wouldnt-protect-ssns-exposed-in-anthem-breach/.

Bennett, Cory. "Demand for Cyber Insurance Skyrockets." *TheHill.com*, January 15, 2015. http://thehill.com/policy/cybersecurity/229568-skyrocketing-demand-seen-for-cybersecurity-insurance.

———. "Hackers Breach the Warsaw Stock Exchange." *TheHill.com*, October 24, 2014. http://thehill.com/policy/cybersecurity/221806-hackers-breach-the-warsaw-stock-exchange.

———. "Japanese Leader Hits Chinese Hacking in Speech to Congress." *The Hill.com*, April 29, 2015. http://thehill.com/policy/cybersecurity/240480-abe-to-congress-no-free-riders-on-intellectual-property.

Bergen, Peter, and Tim Maurer. "Cyberwar Hits Ukraine." *CNN.com*, March 7, 2014.

Bhattacharjee, Yudhijit. "How a Remote Town in Romania Has Become Cybercrime Central," *Wired.com*, February 2011. http://www.wired.com/2011/01/ff_hackerville_romania/.

———. "A New Kind of Spy: How China Obtains American Technological Secrets." *The New Yorker*, May 5, 2014.

Birch, Douglas. "U.S.: Cyber Attacks on Utilities, Industries, Rise." *NBCnews.com*, September 29, 2011.

Bishop, Todd. "Should Microsoft Be Liable for Bugs?" *Seattle Post-Intelligencer*, September 12, 2003.

BlackHat Europe 2014. October 16–17, 2014. https://www.blackhat.com/eu-14/briefings.html#side-channel-attacks-past-present-and-future.

Bodeen, Christopher. "U.S. Says Hacking Undermines China's Interests." *Yahoo.com,* April 9, 2013. http://news.yahoo.com/us-says-hacking-undermines-chinas-interests-093148708.html.

Borger, Julian. "Pentagon Kept the Lid on Cyberwar in Kosovo." *The Guardian,* November 8, 1999.

Borland, John. "A Four-Day Dive into Stuxnet's Heart." *Wired.com,* December 27, 2010. http://www.wired.com/2010/12/a-four-day-dive-into-stuxnets-heart.

Bott, Ed. "The Malware Numbers Game: How Many Viruses Are Out There?" *ZDNet.com,* April 15, 2012. http://www.zdnet.com/blog/bott/the-malware-numbers-game-how-many-viruses-are-out-there/4783.

Boyes, Rogers. "China Accused of Hacking into Heart of Merkel Administration." *Times Online* (London), August 27 2007. http://www.thetimes.co.uk/tto/news/world/europe/article2595759.ece.

Boyle, Joe. "South Korea's Strange Cyberwar Admission." *BBC.com,* March 2, 2014. http://www.bbc.com/news/world-asia-26330816.

Bradley, Tony. "Microsoft Bug Bounty Program Puts Big Bucks on the Line." *Forbes.com,* June 19, 2013. http://www.forbes.com/sites/tonybradley/2013/06/19/microsoft-bug-bounty-program-putsbig-bucks-on-the-line/.

Bradsher, Keith. "China Announces Arrests in Hacking Crackdown." *New York Times,* February 8, 2010.

Braun, Stephen. "Official Says Hackers Hit Up to 25,000 Homeland Security Employees." *Washington Post,* August 23, 2014.

Brenner, Joel. "Nations Everywhere Are Exploiting the Lack of Cybersecurity." *Washington Post,* October 24, 2014.

Brewster, Tom. "Feeling Smug that Your iPhone Can't Be Hacked? Not So Fast." *The Guardian,* February 12, 2014.

———. "U.S. Cybercrime Laws Being Used to Target Security Researchers." *The Guardian,* May 29, 2014.

Bright, Peter. "Anonymous Speaks: The Inside Story of the HBGary Hack." *Ars Technica,* February 15, 2011. http://arstechnica.com/tech-policy/2011/02/anonymous-speaks-the-inside-story-of-the-hbgary-hack/.

———. "Comodo Hacker: I Hacked DigiNotar Too; Other CAS Breached." *Ars Technica,* September 6, 2011. http://arstechnica.com/security/2011/09/comodo-hacker-i-hacked-diginotar-too-other-cas-breached/.

———. "Report: NSA Paid RSA to Make Flawed Crypto Algorithm the Default." *Ars Technica,* December 20, 2013. http://arstechnica.com/security/2013/12/report-nsa-paid-rsa-to-make-flawed-crypto-algorithm-the-default/.

———. "Spamhaus DDOS Grows to Internet-Threatening Size." *Ars Technica,* March 27, 2013. http://arstechnica.com/security/2013/03/spamhaus-ddos-grows-to-internet-threatening-size/.

Broad, William, John Markoff, and David Sanger. "Israeli Test on Worm Called Crucial in Iran Nuclear Delay." *New York Times,* January 15, 2011.

Brodkin, Jon. "China Builds Own Phone OS, Aims to Be More Secure than Android or iPhone," *Ars Technica,* January 20, 2014. http://arstechnica.com/information-technology/2014/01/china-builds-own-phone-os-aims-to-be-more-secure-than-android-or-iphone/.

———. "Government-sponsored Cyberattacks on the Rise, McAfee Says." *Network World,* November 29, 2007. http://www.networkworld.com/article/2289197/lan-wan/government-sponsored-cyberattacks-on-the-rise--mcafee-says.html.

Brooks, David. "The Brutality Cascade." *New York Times,* March 4, 2013.

Brown, Robbie. "Hacking of Tax Records Has Put States on Guard." *New York Times,* November 5, 2012.

Bryant, Christa Case. "Israel Accelerates Cybersecurity Know-how as Early as 10th Grade." *Christian Science Monitor,* June 9, 2013.

Budich, Alicia. "FBI: Cyber Threat Might Surpass Terror Threat." *Face the Nation,* February 2, 2012. http://www.cbsnews.com/8301-3460_162-57370682/fbi-cyber-threat-might-surpass-terror-threat/.

Burns, John F., and Ravi Somaiya. "Hackers Attack Those Seen as WikiLeaks Enemies." *New York Times,* December 9, 2010.

Campbell, Matthew. "'Logic Bomb' Arms Race Panics Russians." *Sunday Times,* November 29, 1998.

Capaccio, Anthony. "Cyber-Armageddon Less Likely than Predicted, Clapper Says." Bloomberg, February 25, 2015. http://www.bloomberg.com/news/articles/2015-02-26/cyber-armageddon-less-likely-than-smaller-attacks-clapper-says for the quote.

Cardozo, Nate, and Eva Galperin. "What Is the U.S. Doing About Wassenaar, and Why Do We Need to Fight It?" Electronic Frontier Foundation, May 28, 2015. https://www.eff.org/deeplinks/2015/05/we-must-fight-proposed-us-wassenaar-implementation.

CBS News. "Microsoft Anti-Piracy Tool Angers Chinese." October 28, 2008. http://www.cbsnews.com/news/microsoft-anti-piracy-tool-angers-chinese/.

———. "Cyber War: Sabotaging the System." June 11, 2009. http://www.cbsnews.com/news/cyber-war-sabotaging-the-system-06-11-2009/.

Chen, Adrian. "The Agency." *New York Times,* June 2, 2015.

Chen, Stephen. "Huge Cyberattack on China Was Lone Hacker, Official Claims: Experts Express Doubt after Internet Security Boss Claims Amateur in Qingdao Detained for Huge Strike on Servers." *South China Morning Post,* September 25, 2013. http://www.scmp.com/news/china/article/1317101/huge-cyberattack-done-lone-hacker-official-claims.

China Daily. "Official Urges China–U.S. Trust on Cyber Security." April 10, 2013. www.chinadaily.com.cn/china/2013-04/10/content_16388107.htm.

Cho, Joohee. "'Obvious' North Korea Sank South Korean Ship." *ABC News,* May 19, 2010. http://abcnews.go.com/International/obvious-north-korea-sank-south-korean-ship/story?id=10685652.

Chosun Ilbo. "N. Korean Hackers Get Access to 'Unbeatable' Tools." July 22, 2015. http://english.chosun.com/site/data/html_dir/2015/07/22/2015072201500.html.

Claburn, Thomas. "Chinese Hackers Angered by Microsoft's Epic Fail." *Information Week,* October 23, 2008. http://www.informationweek.com/software/operating-systems/chinese-hackers-angered-by-microsofts-epic-fail/d/d-id/1073270.

———. "CIA Admits Cyberattacks Blacked Out Cities." *Information Week,* January 18, 2008. http://www.informationweek.com/cia-admits-cyberattacks-blacked-out-citi/205901631.

Clarke, Richard, and Steven Anderson. "Cyberwar's Threat Does Not Justify a New Policy of Nuclear Deterrence." *Washington Post,* June 14, 2013.

Clayton, Mark. "Alert: Major Cyber Attack Aimed at Natural Gas Pipeline Companies." *Christian Science Monitor,* May 5, 2012.

———. "Exclusive: Cyberattack Leaves Natural Gas Pipelines Vulnerable to Sabotage." *Christian Science Monitor,* February 27, 2013.

———. "Ukraine Election Narrowly Avoided 'Wanton Destruction' from Hackers." *Christian Science Monitor,* June 17, 2014.

Cluley, Graham. "Memories of the Chernobyl Virus." *Naked Security,* April 26, 2011. https://nakedsecurity.sophos.com/2011/04/26/memories-of-the-chernobyl-virus/.

CNN. "Bin Laden Says He Wasn't Behind Attacks." CNN, September 17, 2001. http://edition.cnn.com/2001/US/09/16/inv.binladen.denial/index.html?iref=storysearch.

Colby, Elbridge. "Cyberwar and the Nuclear Option." *National Interest,* June 24, 2013. http://nationalinterest.org/commentary/cyberwar-the-nuclear-option-8638.

Coleman, Kevin. "Cyber Rules of Engagement—Hot Pursuit." *InfoTech,* August 18, 2009. http://it.tmcnet.com/topics/it/articles/62417-cyber-rules-engagement-hot-pursuit.htm.

———. "Returning Cyber Fire." *C⁴ISR,* October 13, 2014. http://www.c4isrnet.com/article/20141013/C4ISRNET18/310130003/Returning-cyber-fire.

Constantin, Lucian. "Attackers Use NTP Reflection in Huge DDoS Attack." *Computerworld,* February 11, 2014. http://www.computerworld.com/s/article/9246230/Attackers_use_NTP_reflection_in_huge_DDoS_attack.

———. "Software Applications Have on Average 24 Vulnerabilities Inherited from Buggy Components." *PC World,* June 16, 2015. http://www.pcworld.com/article/2936572/software-applications-have-on-average-24-vulnerabilities-inherited-from-buggy-components.html.

———. "Vulnerabilities Found in More Command-Line Tools, wget and tnftp Get Patches." *PC World,* October 30, 2014. http://www.pcworld.com/article/2841592/vulnerabilities-found-in-more-commandline-tools-wget-and-tnftp-get-patches.html.

———. "Two-Year-Old Cyberattack on Estonia Again in the Spotlight." *Softpedia,* March 9, 2009. http://archive.news.softpedia.com/news/Two-Years-Old-Cyberattack-on-Estonia-Again-in-the-Spotlight-106353.shtml.

Cook, Sarah. "China's Growing Army of Paid Internet Commentators." *Freedom House,* October 11, 2011. https://freedomhouse.org/blog/china%E2%80%99s-growing-army-paid-internet-commentators# .VX2GD_lVikp.

Corkery, Michael, Jessica Silver-Greenberg, and David Sanger. "Obama Had Security Fears on JPMorgan Data Breach." *New York Times,* October 8, 2014.

Crawford, Jamie. "The U.S. Government Thinks China Could Take Down the Power Grid." *CNN.com,* November 21, 2014. http://www.cnn.com/2014/11/20/politics/nsa-china-power-grid/.

Cunningham, Andrew. "Explaining iOS 8's Extensions: Opening the Platform while Keeping It Secure." *Ars Technica,* June 8, 2014. http://arstechnica.com/apple/2014/06/explaining-ios-8s-extensions- opening-the-platform-while-keeping-it-secure/.

Curtis, Sophie. "'Red Button' Flaw Leaves Smart TVs Open to Cyber Attack." *The Telegraph,* June 9, 2014. http://www.telegraph.co.uk/technology/internet-security/10887137/Red-button-flaw-leaves- smart-TVs-open-to-cyberattack.html.

Daniel, Michael. "Heartbleed: Understanding When We Disclose Cyber Vulnerabilities." *White House.gov* (blog), April 28, 2014. https://www.whitehouse.gov/blog/2014/04/28/heartbleed-understanding- when-we-disclose-cyber-vulnerabilities.

Dark Reading. "U.S. Critical Infrastructure Cyberattack Reports Jump Dramatically: A New Report from ICS-CERT Shows the Number of Reported Incidents Increased from 9 to 198 between 2009 and 2011." *DarkReading.com,* June 29, 2012. http://www.darkreading.com/attacks-breaches/ us-critical-infrastructure-cyberattack-reports-jump-dramatically/d/d-id/1137957.

de Braeckeleer, Ludwig. "For Years U.S. Eavesdroppers Could Read Encrypted Messages without the Least Difficulty." *The Intelligence Daily,* December 29, 2007.

De La Merced, Michael J. "Sprint and SoftBank Pledge to Forgo Huawei Equipment, Lawmaker Says." *New York Times,* March 28, 2013.

Demchak, Chris. "Stuxnet: All Signs Point to Russia." *Cryptocomb.org,* November 26, 2010. http://www .cryptocomb.org/Stuxnet_%20All%20Signs%20Point%20to%20Russia.pdf.

Denning, Dorothy E. "Rethinking the Cyber Domain and Deterrence." *Joint Force Quarterly* 77 (2nd Quarter 2015).

Der Spiegel. "Merkel's China Visit Marred by Hacking Allegations." August 27, 2007.

———. "Privacy Scandal: NSA Can Spy on Smart Phone Data." September 7, 2013.

Dillon-Merrill, Robin, Catherine H. Tinsley, and Matthew A. Cronin. "How Near-Miss Events Amplify or Attenuate Risky Decision Making." *Management Science Articles in Advance,* 2012. http://create.usc.edu/ sites/default/files/publications/hownear-misseventsamplifyorattenuateriskydecisionmaking_0.pdf.

Drew, Christopher. "United Airlines Grounds Flights, Citing Computer Problems." *New York Times,* July 8, 2015.

Dyer, Geoff, Gina Chon, and Hannah Kuchler. "Cyber Tensions Rise as U.S. Says Three Big Chinese Groups Benefited from Hacking." *Financial Times,* October 8, 2015.

Eadicicco, Lisa. "Hackers in Russia Have Stolen More than a Billion Usernames and Passwords." *Business Insider,* August 5, 2014. http://www.businessinsider.com/russian-hackers-steal-usernames-passwords-2014-8.

Easley, Jonathan. "Gingrich: 'Wage Real Cyber Warfare' to Take Down Iran's Regime." *The Hill,* November 22, 2011. http://thehill.com/blogs/hillicon-valley/technology/195039-gingrich-wage-real- cyber-warfare-to-destabilize-iran-stop-nuclear-program.

Economist. "Putin's New Model Army: Money and Reform Have Given Russia Armed Forces It Can Use." *Economist.com,* May 24, 2014. http://www.economist.com/news/europe/21602743-money-and- reform-have-given-russia-armed-forces-it-can-use-putins-new-model-army.

———. "End of the Road for Windows XP." *Economist.com,* April 8, 2014. http://www.economist.com/ blogs/babbage/2014/04/difference-engine.

———. "The Dragon's New Teeth." *Economist.com,* April 4, 2012. http://www.economist.com/ node/21552193.

———. "Hackers of the World: United." *Economist.com,* July 15, 2015. http://www.economist.com/blogs/ gulliver/2015/07/airline-security.

———. "Admit Nothing and Deny Everything." *Economist.com*, June 8, 2013. http://www.economist.com/news/china/21579044-barack-obama-says-he-ready-talk-xi-jinping-about-chinese-cyberattacks-makes-one.

———. "The Power of Xi Jinping." *Economist.com*, September 20, 2014. http://www.economist.com/news/china/21618882-cult-personality-growing-around-chinas-president-what-will-he-do-his-political.

———. "The Siege." *Economist.com*, July 12, 2014. http://www.economist.com/news/leaders/21606831-believing-vladimir-putin-has-surrendered-ukraine-would-be-naive-west-must-keep-up.

———. "The World's Greatest Bazaar: Alibaba, a Trailblazing Chinese Internet Giant, Will Soon Go Public." *Economist.com*, May 21, 2013. http://www.economist.com/news/briefing/21573980-alibaba-trailblazing-chinese-internet-giant-will-soon-go-public-worlds-greatest-bazaar.

———. "Turning Off the Taps: There Is More that Could Be Done to Punish Russia." *Economist.com*, April 19, 2014. http://www.economist.com/news/briefing/21601051-there-more-could-be-done-punish-russia-turning-taps.

———. "Changing Faces." *Economist.com*, March 23, 2013. http://www.economist.com/news/china/21574024-chinas-new-leaders-have-shuffled-their-foreign-affairs-team-relations-other-big-powers-will.

———. "Huawei: The Company that Spooked the World." *Economist.com*, August 4, 2012. http://www.economist.com/node/21559929.

———. "Intellectual Property: Can You Keep a Secret." *Economist.com*, March 16, 2003. http://www.economist.com/news/business/21573580-patent-idea-you-must-publish-it-many-firms-prefer-secrecy-can-you-keep-secret.

———. "Terror in Paris." *Economist.com*, January 10, 2015. http://www.economist.com/news/leaders/21638118-islamists-are-assailing-freedom-speech-vilifying-all-islam-wrong-way-counter.

———. "Xi Who Must Be Obeyed." *Economist.com*, September 20, 2014. http://www.economist.com/news/leaders/21618780-most-powerful-and-popular-leader-china-has-had-decades-must-use-these-assets-wisely-xi.

Electronic Frontier Foundation. "RSA Code-Breaking Contest Again Won by Distributed.Net and Electronic Frontier Foundation (EFF)." Press release, January 19, 1999. https://w2.eff.org/Privacy/Crypto/Crypto_misc/DESCracker/HTML/19990119_deschallenge3.html.

———. "The Computer Fraud and Abuse Act Hampers Security Research." February 13, 2013. https://www.eff.org/files/filenode/cfaa-security-researchers.pdf.

Elgin, Ben, and Michael Riley. "Now at the Sands Casino: An Iranian Hacker in Every Server." *Business Week,* December 11, 2014. http://www.businessweek.com/articles/2014-12-11/iranian-hackers-hit-sheldon-adelsons-sands-casino-in-las-vegas.

Elkind, Peter. "Inside the Hack of the Century." *Fortune,* July 1, 2015. http://fortune.com/sony-hack-part-1/.

Erdbrink, Thomas. "Facing Cyberattack, Iranian Officials Disconnect Some Oil Terminals From Internet." *New York Times,* April 23, 2012.

———. Twitter update. July 16, 2015. https://twitter.com/ThomasErdbrink/status/621582470715060224.

Espiner, Tom. "Siemens Warns Stuxnet Target of Password Risk." *CNET.com,* July 20, 2010. http://www.cnet.com/news/siemens-warns-stuxnet-targets-of-password-risk/.

———. "U.S. Reveals Plans to Hit Back at Cyber Threats." *ZDNet News,* April 2, 2008a. http://news.zdnet.co.uk/security/0,1000000189,39378374,00.htm.

Fackler, Martin. "Japan Asks China to Pay for Damages." *New York Times,* September 26, 2010.

Fainaru, Steve, and Grimaldi, James V. "FBI Knew Terrorists Were Using Flight Schools." *Washington Post,* September 23, 2001, A24.

Farivar, Cyrus. "Dutch Judge Allows Alleged 'Sophisticated' Russian Hacker to Be Sent to U.S." *Ars Technica,* January 29, 2015. http://arstechnica.com/tech-policy/2015/01/dutch-judge-allows-alleged-sophisticated-russian-hacker-to-be-sent-to-us/.

Farrell, Henry. "The Political Science of Cybersecurity IV: How Edward Snowden Helps U.S. Deterrence." *Washington Post,* March 12, 2014.

Farrell, Nick. "China's Infrastructure a Doddle to Hack." *Tech Eye,* April 28, 2011. http://news.techeye.net/security/chinas-infrastructure-a-doddle-to-hack.

Federal News Radio. "White House Cyber Czar's Goal: 'Kill the Password Dead.'" June 18, 2014. http://www
.federalnewsradio.com/241/3646015/White-House-cyber-czars-goal-Kill-the-password-dead.

Feldstein, Martin. "Everyone Should Pay for Cyber Defense." *Wall Street Journal*, April 22, 2012.

Ferranti, Marc. "U.S. Rejects North Korea Offer to Investigate Sony Hack, Reaches Out to China." *PC World*,
December 20, 2014. http://www.pcworld.com/article/2861992/us-rejects-north-korea-offer-
to-investigate-sony-hack-reaches-out-to-china.html.

Ferraro, Matthew F. "On the OPM Hack, Don't Let China Off the Hook." *The Diplomat*, July 14, 2015.
http://thediplomat.com/2015/07/on-the-opm-hack-dont-let-china-off-the-hook/.

Finkle, Jim. "Microsoft Says Cybercrime Bust Frees 4.7 Million Infected PCs." Reuters, July 10, 2014. http://
www.reuters.com/article/2014/07/10/us-cybersecurity-microsoft-idUSKBN0FF2CU20140710.

Fish, Isaac Stone. "If You Want Rule of Law, Respect Ours." *Foreign Policy*, November 4, 2014.

Fisher, Dennis. "Research Finds No Large Scale Heartbleed Exploit Attempts Before Vulnerability Disclosure." *Threat Post*, September 9, 2014. http://threatpost.com/research-finds-no-large-scale-
heartbleed-exploit-attempts-before-vulnerabilitydisclosure/108161.

———. "Researchers Find Nearly Two Dozen SCADA Bugs in a Few Hours' Time." *Threat Post*, November 26, 2012. https://threatpost.com/researcher-finds-nearly-two-dozen-scada-bugs-few-hours-
time-112612/77242.

———. "RSA Denies NSA Backdoor Payment Allegations." *Threat Post*, December 23, 2013. http://threatpost
.com/rsa-denies-nsa-backdoor-payment-allegations/103268.

———. "The Case for a Government Bug Bounty Program." *Threat Post*, May 31, 2013. http://www.threatpost
.com/the-case-for-a-government-bug-bounty-program.

———. "Black Energy Malware May Be Exploiting Patched WinCC Flaw." *Threat Post*, December 11, 2014.
https://threatpost.com/black-energy-malware-may-be-exploiting-patched-wincc-flaw/109835.

Fletcher, Owen, and Jason Dean. "Ballmer Bares China Travails." *Wall Street Journal*, May 26, 2011.

FlorCruz, Michelle. "China Bans Apple, Cisco Systems from Government Use: Cyber Security Concerns or
Market Manipulation?" *IB Times*, February 26, 2015. http://www.ibtimes.com/china-bans-apple-
cisco-systems-government-use-cyber-security-concerns-or-market-1829564.

Freitas, Nathan. "People Around the World Are Voluntarily Submitting to China's Great Firewall. Why?"
Slate, January 6, 2015. http://www.slate.com/blogs/future_tense/2015/01/06/tencent_s_wechat_
worldwide_internet_users_are_voluntarily_submitting_to.html.

Frizell, Sam. "NSA Director on Sony Hack: 'The Entire World Is Watching.'" *Time*, January 8, 2015.

Fulghum, David A. "Solitary Genius Trumped by the Socially Adept." *Aviation Week and Space Technology*,
July 30, 2012.

——— and William B. Scott. "Pentagon Mum About F-117 Loss." *Aviation Week and Space Technology* 150,
no. 14, April 5, 1999.

———. "Yugoslavia Successfully Attacked by Computers." *Aviation Week and Space Technology* 151, no. 8,
1999.

Fung, Brian. "The NSA Hacks Other Countries by Buying Millions of Dollars' Worth of Computer Vulnerabilities." *Washington Post*, August 31, 2013.

Gallagher, Sean. "NSA Secretly Hijacked Existing Malware to Spy on N. Korea, Others." *Ars Technica*, January 18, 2015. http://arstechnica.com/information-technology/2015/01/nsa-secretly-hijacked-
existing-malware-to-spy-on-n-korea-others/.

———. "Encryption 'Would Not Have Helped' at OPM, Says DHS Official." *Ars Technica*, June 16, 2015. http://
arstechnica.com/security/2015/06/encryption-would-not-have-helped-at-opm-says-dhs-official/.

———. "Heads Up, Dear Leader: Security Hole Found in North Korea's Home-grown OS." *Ars Technica*,
January 9, 2015. http://arstechnica.com/information-technology/2015/01/heads-up-dear-leader-
security-hole-found-in-north-koreas-home-grown-os/.

———. "Iranians Hacked Navy Network for Four Months? Not a Surprise." *Ars Technica*, February 19, 2014.
http://arstechnica.com/information-technology/2014/02/iranians-hacked-navy-network-for-4-
months-not-a-surprise/.

———. "Is an ISP Code of Conduct the Best Way to Fight Botnets?" *Ars Technica*, September 22, 2011. http://
arstechnica.com/business/2011/09/us-government-looks-to-fight-botnets-with-isp-code-of-conduct/.

———. "New NSA Chief Explains Agency Policy on 'Zero-day' Exploits to Senate." *Ars Technica*, March 13, 2014. http://arstechnica.com/tech-policy/2014/03/new-nsa-chief-explains-agency-policy-on-zero-day-exploits-to-senate/.

———. "Photos of an NSA 'Upgrade' Factory Show Cisco Router Getting Implant." *Ars Technica*, May 14, 2014. http://arstechnica.com/tech-policy/2014/05/photos-of-an-nsa-upgrade-factory-show-cisco-router-getting-implant/.

———. "There's an App for That: How NSA, Allies Exploit Mobile App Stores; 'Five Eyes' Intelligence Agencies Built Tools to Spot Google, Samsung App Protocols." *Ars Technica*, May 21, 2015. http://arstechnica.com/information-technology/2015/05/theres-an-app-for-that-how-nsa-allies-exploit-mobile-app-stores/.

———. "Tor Network's Ranks of Relay Servers Cut Because of Heartbleed Bug." *Ars Technica*, April 17, 2014. http://arstechnica.com/security/2014/04/tor-networks-ranks-of-relay-servers-cut-because-of-heartbleed-bug/.

———. "How an Indonesian ISP Took Down the Mighty Google for 30 Minutes; Internet's Web of Trust Let a Company You Never Heard of Block Your Gmail." *Ars Technica*, November 6, 2012. http://arstechnica.com/information-technology/2012/11/how-an-indonesian-isp-took-down-the-mighty-google-for-30-minutes/.

———. "Security Pros Predict 'Major' Cyber Terror Attack this Year." *Ars Technica*, January 4, 2013. http://arstechnica.com/security/2013/01/security-pros-predict-major-cyberterror-attack-this-year/.

Galperin, Eva, Seth Schoen, and Peter Eckersley. "A Post Mortem on the Iranian DigiNotar Attack." The Electronic Frontier Foundation, September 13, 2011. https://www.eff.org/deeplinks/2011/09/post-mortem-iranian-diginotar-attack.

Garamone, Jim. "Cybercom Chief Details Cyberspace Defense." *Defense.gov,* September 23, 2010. www.defense.gov/news/newsarticle.aspx?id=60987.

Gaycken, Sandro, and Felix Linder. "Zero-Day Governance: An (Inexpensive) Solution to the Cyber-security Problem." University of Toronto CyberDialogue 2012, March 2012. http://www.cyberdialogue.citizenlab.org/wp-content/uploads/2012/2012papers/CyberDialogue2012_gaycken-lindner.pdf.

Geer, Daniel. "Where the Science is Taking Us." *Lawfareblog.com,* May 29, 2015. http://www.lawfareblog.com/where-science-taking-us-cybersecurity.

Gellman, Barton. "Cyberattacks by Al Qaeda Feared: Terrorists at Threshold of Using Internet as Tool of Bloodshed, Experts Say." *Washington Post,* June 27, 2002.

Gertz, Bill, and Rowan Scarborough. "Inside the Ring: NDU Hacked." *Washington Times,* January 12, 2007.

Gienger, Viola. "U.S. Military Aid to Overseas Allies May Face Cuts, Mullen Says." Bloomberg, June 14, 2011. http://www.bloomberg.com/news/2011-06-13/pentagon-aid-to-foreign-militaries-may-face-cuts-mullen-says.html.

Giesler, Robert. Remarks, Center for Strategic and International Studies Global Security Forum 2011, June 8, 2011. http://csis.org/files/attachments/110608_gsf_cyber_transcript.pdf.

Giles, Martin. "Defending the Digital Frontier." *Economist,* July 12, 2014. http://www.economist.com/news/special-report/21606416-companies-markets-and-countries-are-increasingly-under-attack-cyber-criminals.

Glendinning, Lee. "Obama, McCain Computers 'Hacked' During Election Campaign: FBI Discovers Cyber-attacks During the Summer Originated in China and Stole Large Amounts of Data." *The Guardian,* November 7, 2008.

Goldman, Jeff. "Kaspersky Seeks Help Decrypting Gauss Malware Payload." *eSecurityPlanet.com,* August 15, 2012. http://www.esecurityplanet.com/malware/kaspersky-seeks-help-decrypting-gauss-malware-payload.html.

Goldsmith, Jack. "Cybersecurity Treaties: A Skeptical View." Hoover Institution, March 9, 2011. http://www.hoover.org/research/cybersecurity-treaties-skeptical-view.

Goldstein, Matthew. "U.S. Extends Investigation of JPMorgan Chase Hacking." *New York Times,* July 28, 2015.

———. "4 Arrested in Schemes Said to be Tied to JPMorgan Chase Breach." *New York Times,* July 21, 2015.

———, Nicole Perlroth, and David Sanger. "Hackers' Attack Cracked 10 Financial Firms in Major Assault." *New York Times,* October 3, 2014.

Gonsalves, Chris. "Security Quandary: Who's Liable?" *eWeek*, February 25, 2002. http://www.eweek.com/c/a/Security/Security-Quandary-Whos-Liable.

Goodin, Dan. "Active 'WireLurker' iPhone Infection Ushers in New Era for iOS Users." *Ars Technica*, November 6, 2014. http://arstechnica.com/security/2014/11/active-wirelurker-iphone-infection-ushers-in-new-era-for-ios-users/.

———. "Botnet that Enslaved 770,000 PCs Worldwide Comes Crashing Down." *Ars Technica*, April 13, 2015. http://arstechnica.com/security/2015/04/botnet-that-enslaved-770000-pcs-worldwide-comes-crashing-down/.

———. "Critical Networks in U.S, 15 Other Nations, Completely Owned, Possibly by Iran." *Ars Technica*, December 2, 2014. http://arstechnica.com/security/2014/12/critical-networks-in-us-15-nations-completely-owned-by-iran-backed-hackers/.

———. "Extremely Critical Crypto Flaw in iOS May Also Affect Fully Patched Macs." *Ars Technica*, February 22, 2014. http://arstechnica.com/security/2014/02/extremely-critical-crypto-flaw-in-ios-may-also-affect-fully-patched-macs/.

———. "Google Squashes Nasty Bugs that Led to Perfect-Storm Account Hijacking: Simple but Elegant Exploit Created High-Impact Threat." *Ars Technica*, November 22, 2013. http://arstechnica.com/security/2013/11/google-squashes-nasty-bugs-that-led-to-perfect-storm-account-hijacking/.

———. "Hacking Team Leak Releases Potent Flash 0day into the Wild." *Ars Technica*, July 7, 2015. http://arstechnica.com/security/2015/07/hacking-team-leak-releases-potent-flash-0day-into-the-wild/.

———. "How 'Omnipotent' Hackers Tied to NSA Hid for 14 Years—And Were Found at Last." *Ars Technica*, February 16, 2014. http://arstechnica.com/security/2015/02/how-omnipotent-hackers-tied-to-the-nsa-hid-for-14-years-and-were-found-at-last/.

———. "How Whitehats Stopped the DDoS Attack that Knocked Spamhaus Offline." *Ars Technica*, March 21, 2013. http://arstechnica.com/security/2013/03/how-whitehats-stopped-the-ddos-attack-that-knocked-spamhaus-offline/.

———. "IE Zero-Day Used in Chinese Cyber Assault on 34 Firms." *The Register*, January 14, 2010. http://www.theregister.co.uk/2010/01/14/cyber_assault_followup/.

———. "iOS Security Hole Allows Attackers to Poison Already Installed iPhone Apps." *Ars Technica*, November 11, 2014. http://arstechnica.com/security/2014/11/ios-security-hole-allows-attackers-to-poison-already-installed-iphone-apps/.

———. "Meet 'badBIOS,' the Mysterious Mac and PC Malware that Jumps Airgaps." *Ars Technica*, October 31, 2013. http://arstechnica.com/security/2013/10/meet-badbios-the-mysterious-mac-and-pc-malware-that-jumps-airgaps/.

———. "MS Kills Critical IE 11 Bug after Exploit Was Shopped to Hacking Team." *Ars Technica*, July 14, 2015. http://arstechnica.com/security/2015/07/ms-kills-critical-ie-11-bug-after-exploit-was-shopped-to-hacking-team/.

———. "Serious OS X and iOS Flaws Let Hackers Steal Keychain, 1Password contents." *Ars Technica*, June 17, 2015. http://arstechnica.com/security/2015/06/serious-os-x-and-ios-flaws-let-hackers-steal-keychain-1password-contents/.

———. "Sites Certified as Secure Often More Vulnerable to Hacking, Scientists Find." *Ars Technica*, December 4, 2014. http://arstechnica.com/security/2014/12/sites-certified-as-secure-often-morevulnerable-to-hacking-scientists-find/.

———. "Speech Recognition Hack Turns Google Chrome into Advanced Bugging Device." *Ars Technica*, January 22, 2014. http://arstechnica.com/security/2014/01/speech-recognition-hack-turns-google-chrome-into-advanced-bugging-device/.

———. "This System Will Self Destruct: Crimeware Gets Powerful New Functions." *Ars Technica*, November 4, 2014. http://arstechnica.com/security/2014/11/this-system-will-self-destruct-crimeware-gets-powerful-new-functions/.

———. "This Thumb Drive Hacks Computers: 'BadUSB' Exploit Makes Devices Turn 'Evil.'" *Ars Technica*, July 31, 2014. http://arstechnica.com/security/2014/07/this-thumbdrive-hacks-computers-badusb-exploit-makes-devices-turn-evil/.

———. "As Flash 0day Exploits Reach New Level of Meanness, What Are Users to Do?" *Ars Technica*, February 4, 2015. http://arstechnica.com/security/2015/02/as-flash-0day-exploits-reach-new-level-of-meanness-what-are-users-to-do/.

————. "Chinese ISP Hijacked U.S. Military, Gov Web Traffic." *The Register,* November 17, 2010. http://www.theregister.co.uk/2010/11/17/bgp_hijacking_report/.

————. "Crypto Breakthrough Shows Flame Was Designed by World-Class Scientists." *Ars Technica*, June 7, 2012. http://arstechnica.com/security/2012/06/flame-crypto-breakthrough/.

————. "First Known Hacker-Caused Power Outage Signals Troubling Escalation." *Ars Technica*, January 4, 2015. http://arstechnica.com/security/2016/1/first-known-hacker-caused-power-outage-signals-troubling-escalation/.

————. "Meet 'Great Cannon,' the Man-in-the-Middle Weapon China Used on GitHub: Powerful Weapon Could Easily Be Used to Inject Malware Attacks into Traffic." *Ars Technica,* April 10, 2015. http://arstechnica.com/security/2015/04/meet-great-cannon-the-man-in-the-middle-weapon-china-used-on-github/.

————. "New DoS Tool Lets a Single PC Bring Down an Apache Server." *Ars Technica,* June 8, 2012. http://arstechnica.com/security/2012/06/apache-killer-dos-tool/.

————. "Repeated Attacks Hijack Huge Chunks of Internet Traffic, Researchers Warn Man-in-the-Middle Attacks Divert Data on Scale Never Before Seen in the Wild." *Ars Technica,* November 20, 2013. http://arstechnica.com/security/2013/11/repeated-attacks-hijack-huge-chunks-of-internet-traffic-researchers-warn/.

————. "Strange Snafu Hijacks UK Nuke Maker's Traffic, Routes It Through Ukraine; Lockheed, Banks, and Helicopter Designer Also Affected by Border Gateway Mishap." *Ars Technica,* March 13, 2015. http://arstechnica.com/security/2015/03/mysterious-snafu-hijacks-uk-nukes-makers-traffic-through-ukraine/.

————. "Super Secretive Malware Wipes Hard Drive to Prevent Analysis." *Ars Technica,* May 4, 2015. http://arstechnica.com/security/2015/05/super-secretive-malware-wipes-hard-drive-to-prevent-analysis/.

Google. "Google Vulnerability Reward Program (VRP) Rules." Undated. http://www.google.com/about/appsecurity/reward-program/.

Gordes, Joel N., and Michael Mylrea. "A New Security Paradigm Is Needed to Protect Critical U.S. Energy Infrastructure from Cyberwarfare." *Foreign Policy Journal,* September 14, 2009. http://www.foreignpolicyjournal.com/2009/09/14/a-new-security-paradigm-is-needed-to-protect-critical-us-energy-infrastructure-from-cyberwarfare/.

Gordon, Michael R. "Russia Displays a New Military Prowess in Ukraine's East." *New York Times,* April 21, 2014.

Gorman, Siobhan. "Electricity Grid in U.S. Penetrated by Spies." *Wall Street Journal,* April 8, 2009.

————. "U.S. Homes In on China Spying." *Wall Street Journal,* December 13, 2011.

————, August Cole, and Yochi Dreazen. "Computer Spies Breach Fighter-Jet Project." *Wall Street Journal,* April 21, 2009.

————, and Julian E. Barnes. "Cyber Combat: Act of War." *Wall Street Journal,* May 31, 2011.

————, and Danny Yadron. "Iran Hacks Energy Firms, U.S. Says." *Wall Street Journal,* May 23, 2013.

Gough, Neil. "Western Companies Appear to Push Back Against Chinese Crackdown." *New York Times,* September 3, 2014.

Government of China. Cybersecurity Law (Draft). July 26, 2015. http://chinalawtranslate.com/cybersecurity draft/?lang=en.

Gray, Melissa. "Chinese Space Debris Hits Russian Satellite, Scientists Say." CNN, March 9, 2013. http://www.cnn.com/2013/03/09/tech/satellite-hit.

Grayson, Alan. "On Syria Vote, Trust, but Verify." *New York Times,* September 6, 2013.

Greenberg, Andy. "DARPA turns Oculus into a Weapon for Cyberwar." *Wired.com,* May 23, 2014. http://www.wired.com/2014/05/darpa-is-using-oculus-rift-to-prep-for-cyberwar/.

————. "FBI Director: Sony's 'Sloppy' North Korean Hackers Revealed Their IP Addresses." *Wired.com,* January 7, 2015. http://www.wired.com/2015/01/fbi-director-says-north-korean-hackers-sometimes-failed-use-proxies-sony-hack/.

————. "Hackers Remotely Kill a Jeep on the Highway—With Me In It." *Wired.com,* July 21, 2015. http://www.wired.com/2015/07/hackers-remotely-kill-jeep-highway/.

————. "Only Half of USB Devices Have an Unpatchable Flaw, But No One Knows Which Half." *Wired.com,* November 12, 2014. http://www.wired.com/2014/11/badusb-only-affects-half-of-usbs/.

———. "Shopping for Zero-Days: A Price List for Hackers' Secret Software Exploits." *Forbes,* March 23, 2012. http://www.forbes.com/sites/andygreenberg/2012/03/23/shopping-for-zero-days-an-price-list-for-hackers-secret-software-exploits/.

Grow, Brian, and Mark Hosenball. "Special Report: In Cyberspy vs. Cyberspy, China Has the Edge." Reuters, April 14, 2011. http://www.reuters.com/article/2011/04/14/china-usa-cyberespionage-idUSN1229719820110414.

———, Keith Epstein, and Chi-Chu Tschang. "The New E-spionage Threat." *BusinessWeek*, April 21, 2008, 32–41.

Gu Liping. "Youngest Chinese Hacker Is a Teenager." *Ecns.com,* September 28, 2014. http://www.ecns.cn/2014/09-28/136597.shtml.

Guido, Dan. "Software Security, Disclosure, and Bug Bounties." *Seclists.org,* November 23, 2014. http://seclists.org/dailydave/2014/q4/50.

Gullo, Karen. "California Man Guilty of Stealing DuPont Trade Secrets." *Business Week,* March 5, 2014. http://www.businessweek.com/news/2014-03-05/california-man-convicted-of-stealing-dupont-trade-secrets-1.

Halleck, Thomas. "Verizon Wireless Tracks Every Website Its Customers Visit with 'Supercookies,' Electronic Frontier Foundation Says." *International Business Times,* November 5, 2014. http://www.ibtimes.com/verizon-wireless-tracks-every-website-its-customers-visit-supercookies-electronic-1719720.

Hardy, Quentin. "Criminal Software, Government-Grade Protection." *New York Times,* July 26, 2014.

Harlan, Chico, and Ellen Nakashima. "Suspected North Korean Cyberattack on a Bank Raises Fears for S. Korea, Allies." *Washington Post,* August 29, 2011.

Harmon, Amy. "Hacking Theft of $10 Million from Citibank Revealed." *Los Angeles Times,* August 19, 1995.

Harris, Shane. "Exclusive: Meet the Fed's First Line of Defense Against Cyber Attacks." *Foreign Policy,* April 29, 2014. http://foreignpolicy.com/2014/04/29/exclusive-meet-the-feds-first-line-of-defense-against-cyber-attacks/.

———. "China's Cyber Militia." *National Journal,* May 31, 2008. http://www.nationaljournal.com/magazine/china-s-cyber-militia-20080531.

———. "The Mercenaries." *Slate,* November 12, 2014. http://www.slate.com/articles/technology/future_tense/2014/11/how_corporations_are_adopting_cyber_defense_and_around_legal_barriers_the.2.html.

Heredia, Lourdes. "Hacking 'Legal' in Argentina." BBC, April 16, 2002. http://news.bbc.co.uk/2/hi/americas/1932191.stm.

Hesseldahl, Arik. "Malware in Sony Attack Linked to 2013 South Korean Incidents." *Recode,* December 4, 2014. http://recode.net/2014/12/04/malware-in-sony-attack-linked-to-2013-south-korean-incidents/.

Hildebrandt, Amber, and Dave Seglins. "Spy Agencies Target Mobile Phones, App Stores to Implant Spyware." *CBC,* May 21, 2015. http://www.cbc.ca/news/canada/spy-agencies-target-mobile-phones-app-stores-to-implant-spyware-1.3076546.

Hill, Kashmir. "10 Ways to 'Fix' Cybersecurity." *Forbes,* June 18, 2014. http://www.forbes.com/sites/kashmir hill/2014/06/18/10-ways-to-fix-cybersecurity/.

Hines, Paul, Eduardo Cotilla-Sanchez, and Seth Blumsack. "Why It's Hard to Crash the Electric Grid." *Arxiv,* October 2010. http://arxiv.org/abs/1002.2268.

History of Computing Project. "Books on Hacking, Hackers and Hacker Ethics: An Annotated Bibliography." May 24, 2006. http://www.thocp.net/reference/hacking/bibliography_hacking.htm.

Hoffman, David. "Cold-War Doctrines Refuse to Die." *Washington Post,* March 15, 1998.

Holland, Steve, and Doina Chiacu. "Obama Says Sony Hack Not an Act of War." Reuters, December 22, 2014. http://www.reuters.com/article/2014/12/22/us-sony-cybersecurity-usa-idUSKBN0JX1MH20141222.

Homeland Security Newswire. "Twelve Chinese Hacker Groups Responsible for Attacks on U.S." News release, December 16, 2011. http://www.homelandsecuritynewswire.com/dr20111216-twelve-chinese-hacker-groups-responsible-for-attacks-on-u-s.

Honan, Mat. "How Apple and Amazon Security Flaws Led to My Epic Hacking." *Wired.com,* August 6, 2012. http://www.wired.com/2012/08/apple-amazon-mat-honan-hacking/.

Hornyak, Tim. "Hack to Cost Sony $35 Million in IT Repairs." *Network World,* February 4, 2015. http://www.networkworld.com/article/2879814/data-center/sony-hack-cost-15-million-but-earnings-unaffected.html.

Horovitz, David. "Running Out of Time on Iran, and All Out of Options." *Times of Israel,* June 19, 2013. http://www.timesofisrael.com/running-out-of-time-on-iran-and-all-out-of-options/.

Horowitz, Michael. "The Ugly Side of the Latest Java Updates." *Computerworld,* October 18, 2012. http://www.computerworld.com/article/2473404/application-security/the-ugly-side-of-the-latest-java-updates.html.

Hughes, David. "Brighton Bombing: Daily Telegraph Journalist Recalls." *The Telegraph,* October 11, 2009. http://www.telegraph.co.uk/news/politics/6300215/Brighton-bombing-Daily-Telegraph-journalist-recalls.html.

InfoSecurity. "DDoS-ers Launch Attacks from Amazon EC2." *InfoSecurity,* July 30, 2014. http://www.infosecurity-magazine.com/news/ddos-ers-launch-attacks-from-amazon-ec2/.

Inside Cybersecurity. "Official: Greatest Cyber Risks to National Security Involve Handful of Sectors." *Inside Cybersecurity,* June 22, 2015. http://insidecybersecurity.com/Cyber-General/Cyber-Public-Content/official-greatest-cyber-risks-to-national-security-involve-handful-of-sectors/menu-id-1089.html.

Israel Ministry of Foreign Affairs. "The Hamas Terror War Against Israel." Web site, August 3, 2008. http://mfa.gov.il/MFA/ForeignPolicy/Terrorism/Pages/Missile%20fire%20from%20Gaza%20on%20Israeli%20civilian%20targets%20Aug%202007.aspx.

Ito, Carlo. "A Brief History of Nefarious Internet Hacking in the Philippines." *SourcingTrust,* March 30, 2011. http://sourcingtrustblog.com/2011/03/30/a-brief-history-of-nefarious-internet-hacking-in-the-philippines/.

Jackson Higgins, Kelly. "'Energetic' Bear Under the Microscope." *Dark Reading,* July 31, 2014. http://www.darkreading.com/attacks-breaches/energetic-bear-under-the-microscope/d/d-id/1297712.

———. "Underwriters Laboratories to Launch Cyber Security Certification Program." *Dark Reading,* July 6, 2015. http://www.darkreading.com/endpoint/underwriters-laboratories-to-launch-cyber-security-certification-program/d/d-id/1321202.

———. "Flaws in the 'Aurora' Attacks." *Dark Reading,* January 25, 2010. http://www.darkreading.com/attacks-breaches/flaws-in-the-aurora-attacks/d/d-id/1132824?

———. "Digital Certificate Authority Hacked, Dozens of Phony Digital Certificates Issued." *Dark Reading,* August 30, 2011. http://www.darkreading.com/attacks-breaches/digital-certificate-authority-hacked-dozens-of-phony-digital-certificates-issued/d/d-id/1136244?.

Jackson, William. "Time to Give Up on Java?" *GCN,* August 32, 2012. http://gcn.com/articles/2012/08/31/cyberye-java-time-to-give-up.aspx.

Jacobson, William. "Did Israel Just Admit to Creating Stuxnet?" *Legal Insurrection,* February 15, 2011. http://legalinsurrection.com/2011/02/did-israel-just-admit-to-creating-stuxnet/.

Jensen, Eric Talbot. "Computer Attacks on Critical National Infrastructure: A Use of Force Invoking the Right of Self-Defense." *Stanford Journal of International Law* 38 (2002): 207–40.

Johnson, Mark. "Russia Issues Travel Warning About U.S., Citing Threat of 'Kidnapping.'" *IBTimes,* September 3, 2013. http://www.ibtimes.com/russia-issues-travel-warning-about-us-citing-threat-kidnapping-1402265.

Jones, Willie. "DARPA Seeks Self-Healing Networks." *IEEE Spectrum,* October 25, 2013. http://spectrum.ieee.org/riskfactor/computing/it/darpa-seeks-selfhealing-networks.

Jumper, John P. "Jumper on Airpower: The Air Combat Command Commander Talks About the Realities of Modern Warfare." *Air Force Magazine* 83 (July 2000): 41–43.

Kang, Cecilia, Drew Harwell, and Brian Fung. "North Korean Web Goes Dark Days after Obama Pledges Response to Sony Hack." *Washington Post,* December 22, 2014.

Kaye, Byron, and Jane Wardell. "Australian Metal Detector Company Counts Cost of Chinese Hacking." *Reuters,* June 24, 2015. http://www.reuters.com/article/2015/06/25/us-china-cybersecurity-australia-idUSKBN0P42LP20150625.

Keaten, Jamey, and Sylvie Corbet. "France Sees 19,000 Cyberattacks Since Terror Rampage." *Phys,* January 15, 2015. http://phys.org/news/2015-01-france-cyberdefense-chief-cyberattacks-week.html.

Keizer, Gregg. "China Has a Massive Windows XP Problem: By the Time of XP's Retirement in April, Around 10% of All U.S. Computers Will Be Running the OS; in China, 65% of Companies Will Do So." *Computerworld,* August 7, 2013. http://www.computerworld.com/s/article/9241429/China_has_a_massive_Windows_XP_problem.

———. "Garden-variety DDoS Attack Knocks North Korea Off the Internet." *Computerworld,* December 23, 2014. http://www.computerworld.com/article/2862652/garden-variety-ddos-attack-knocks-north-korea-off-the-internet.html.

———. "Iran Arrests 'Spies' After Stuxnet Attacks on Nuclear Program." *Computerworld,* October 2, 2010. http://www.computerworld.com/s/article/9189218/Iran_arrests_spies_after_Stuxnet_attacks_on_nuclear_program.

———. "Windows XP Die-Hards Can Slash Attack Risk by Dumping IE." *Computerworld,* May 12, 2014. http://www.computerworld.com/s/article/9248277/Windows_XP_die_hards_can_slash_attack_risk_by_dumping_IE.

Kelly, Kevin. "New Rules for the Economy." *KK.org* (blog), November 19, 2012. http://kk.org/newrules/.

Kelly, Meghan. "Cyber Criminals Attack U.S. Chamber of Commerce, China Footing the Blame." *VentureBeat,* December 21, 2011.http://venturebeat.com/2011/12/21/china-chamber-of-commerce-hack/.

Kerr, Dana. " 'Cyber 9/11' May Be on Horizon, Homeland Security Chief Warns." *CNET,* January 24, 2013. http://news.cnet.com/8301-1009_3-57565763–83/cyber-9-11-may-be-on-horizon-homeland-security-chief-warns/.

Kessler, Aaron. "Fiat Chrysler Issues Recall Over Hacking." *New York Times,* July 24, 2015.

King, Rachel. "Stuxnet Infected Chevron's IT Network." *Wall Street Journal,* November 8, 2012.

Kramer, Andrew. "Tanks, of Unknown Origin, Roll into Ukraine." *New York Times,* June 12, 2014.

Kravets, David. "FBI Director Says Chinese Hackers Are Like a 'Drunk Burglar.'" *Ars Technica,* October 6, 2014. http://arstechnica.com/tech-policy/2014/10/fbi-director-says-chinese-hackers-are-like-a-drunk-burglar/.

Krebs, Brian. "Chinese Hackers Blamed for Intrusion at Energy Industry Giant Telvent," *KrebsonSecurity.com,* September 12, 2012. http://krebsonsecurity.com/2012/09/chinese-hackers-blamed-for-intrusion-at-energy-industry-giant-telvent/.

———. "Data Breach at Health Insurer Anthem Could Impact Millions." *KrebsonSecurity.com,* February 15, 2015. http://krebsonsecurity.com/2015/02/data-breach-at-health-insurer-anthem-could-impact-millions/.

———. "In Home Depot Breach, Investigation Focuses on Self-Checkout Lanes." *KrebsonSecurity.com,* September 14, 2014. http://krebsonsecurity.com/tag/target-data-breach/.

———. "Premera Blue Cross Breach Exposes Financial, Medical Records." *KrebsonSecurity.com,* March 15, 2015. http://krebsonsecurity.com/2015/03/premera-blue-cross-breach-exposes-financial-medical-records/.

———. "Target Hackers Broke in Via HVAC Company." *KrebsonSecurity.com,* February 14, 2014. http://krebsonsecurity.com/2014/02/target-hackers-broke-in-via-hvac-company/.

———. "Malware Dragnet Snags Millions of Infected PCs." *KrebsonSecurity.com,* September 12, 2012. http://krebsonsecurity.com/tag/3322-org/.

———. "Rustok Botnet Flatlined, Spam Volumes Plummet." *KrebsonSecurity.com,* March 11, 2013. http://krebsonsecurity.com/2011/03/rustock-botnet-flatlined-spam-volumes-plummet/.

———. "Security Fix for Critical Java Flaw Released." *KrebsonSecurity.com,* August 12, 2012. http://krebsonsecurity.com/2012/08/security-fix-for-critical-java-flaw-released/.

———. "Spam Volumes Drop by Two-Thirds After Firm Goes Offline." *Washington Post,* November 12, 2008.

———. "The Case for a Compulsory Bug Bounty." *KrebsonSecurity.com,* December 13, 2013. http://krebsonsecurity.com/2013/12/the-case-for-a-compulsory-bug-bounty/.

———. "What You Need to Know about the Java Exploit." *Krebs on Security,* January 13, 2013. http://krebsonsecurity.com/2013/01/what-you-need-to-know-about-the-java-exploit/.

Kuchler, Hannah. "Warning Over ISIS Cyber Threat." *Financial Times,* September 18, 2014. http://www.ft.com/intl/cms/s/0/92fb509c-3ee7-11e4-adef-00144feabdc0.html#axzz3Jtl6ZKt7.

Lake, Eli. "McCain Backs Tougher Line Against Russia." *The Sun* (New York), March 27, 2008.

Lamothe, Dan. "U.S. Military Social Media Accounts Apparently Hacked by Islamic State Sympathizers." *Washington Post,* January 12, 2015.

Landler, Mark, and Sanger, David. "U.S. Demands China Block Cyberattacks and Agree to Rules." *New York Times,* March 12, 2013.

Lang, Justin, and Ben Makuch. "New Documents Show Canada Fired Back Diplomatically at China over Hacking." *Vice,* May 29, 2015. https://news.vice.com/article/new-documents-show-canada-fired-back-diplomatically-at-china-over-hacking.

Lee, Carol, and Jay Solomon. "U.S. Targets North Korea in Retaliation for Sony Hack: New Lee Sanctions Target Individuals Working for Arms Industry." *Wall Street Journal,* January 3, 2015.

Lee, Timothy. "How a Grad Student Trying to Build the First Botnet Brought the Internet to its Knees." *Washington Post,* November 2, 2013.

———. "More Bitcoin Malware: This One Uses Your GPU for Mining." *Ars Technica,* August 17, 2011. http://arstechnica.com/tech-policy/2011/08/symantec-spots-malware-that-uses-your-gpu-to-mine-bit-coins/.

Lemonick, Michael D. "The Chernobyl Cover-Up." *Time,* November 13, 1989.

Lemos, Robert. "'Unprecedented' Cyberattack No Excuse for Sony Breach, Pros Say." *Ars Technica,* December 9, 2014. http://arstechnica.com/security/2014/12/unprecedented-cyberattack-no-excuse-for-sony-breach-pros-say/.

———. "MSBlast Not to Blame for Blackout, Report Says." *ZDNet,* April 6, 2004. http://www.zdnet.com/news/msblast-not-to-blame-for-blackout-report-says/135296.

———. "Safety: Assessing the Infrastructure Risk." *CNET,* August 26, 2002. http://news.cnet.com/2100-1001-954780.html.

———. "Survey Says Security Products Waste Our Time." *Ars Technica,* January 16, 2015. http://arstechnica.com/security/2015/01/survey-says-security-products-waste-our-time/.

———. "Suspected Russian 'Sandworm' Cyber Spies Targeted NATO, Ukraine." *Ars Technica,* October 14, 2014. http://arstechnica.com/security/2014/10/suspected-russian-sandworm-cyber-spies-targeted-nato-ukraine/.

———. "A Year Later, DDOS Attacks Still a Major Web Threat." *CNET News,* February 7, 2001. http://www.cnet.com/news/a-year-later-ddos-attacks-still-a-major-web-threat/.

———. "iOS Weaknesses Allow Attacks Via Trojan Chargers." *Dark Reading,* August 1, 2013. http://www.darkreading.com/mobile/ios-weaknesses-allow-attacks-via-trojan/240159321.

Levine, Dan. "U.S. Businessman Convicted in China Economic Espionage Case." Reuters, March 5, 2014. http://www.reuters.com/article/2014/03/06/us-dupont-china-verdict-idUSBREA2501420140306.

———. "Sony Laid Off Employees Before Data Breach–Lawsuit." Reuters, June 23, 2011. http://www.reuters.com/article/2011/06/24/sony-breach-lawsuit-idUSN1E75M1Y320110624.

Lewis, James. "Hackers Don't Want to Crash Stock Exchanges. They Want to Make Money on Them." *Washington Post,* July 9, 2015.

Leyden, John. "Got an iPhone or iPad? Look Out for Masque-d Intruders." *The Register,* November 20, 2014. http://www.theregister.co.uk/2014/11/10/ios_masque_attack/.

———. "Russian Bookmaker Hackers Jailed for Eight Years." *The Register,* October 4, 2006. http://www.theregister.co.uk/2006/10/04/russian_bookmaker_hackers_jailed/.

Li, Datong. "Xiamen: The Triumph of Public Will?" *openDemocracy,* January 16, 2008.

Liat, Clark. "Study: Clean Up Space Before Dangerous Debris Collisions Increase." *Wired.com,* April 23, 2013. http://www.wired.co.uk/news/archive/2013-04/23/looming-space-junk-threat.

Liptak, Adam, and Michael S. Schmidt. "Judge Upholds N.S.A.'s Bulk Collection of Data on Calls." *New York Times,* December 27, 2013.

Loeb, Vernon. "Test of Strength." *Washington Post Magazine,* July 29, 2001.

Lohr, Steve. "In 2015, Technology Shifts Accelerate and China Rules, IDC Predicts." *New York Times,* December 2, 2014.

Lyngaas, Sean. "Debating the Sino-Russian cyber pact." *Federal Computer Week,* May 12, 2015. http://fcw.com/articles/2015/05/12/russian-chinese-cyber.aspx.

——. "NIST Official: Internet of Things Is Indefensible." *Federal Computer Week,* April 16, 2015. http://fcw.com/articles/2015/04/16/iot-is-indefensible.aspx.

Machkovech, Sam. "Hacker Exploits Printer Web Interface to Install, Run Doom." *Ars Technica,* September 15, 2014. http://arstechnica.com/security/2014/09/hacker-exploits-printer-web-interface-to-install-run-doom/.

Malik, Tariq. "ISS Dodges Space Debris from Chinese Satellite." *Huffington Post,* January 30, 2012. http://www.huffingtonpost.com/2012/01/30/iss-dodges-debris-from-de_n_1241167.html.

MarketsandMarkets.com. "Cyber Security Market Worth $170.21 Billion by 2020." http://www.marketsandmarkets.com/PressReleases/cyber-security.asp.

Markoff, John. "Worm Infects Millions of Computers Worldwide." *New York Times,* January 22, 2009.

——. "A Silent Attack, But Not a Subtle One." *New York Times,* September 26, 2010.

——. "Step Taken to End Impasse Over Cybersecurity Talks." *New York Times,* July 16, 2010.

——, and David Sanger. "In a Computer Worm, a Possible Biblical Clue." *New York Times,* September 29, 2010.

Marks, Joseph. "U.S. Makes New Push for Global Rules in Cyberspace." *Politico,* May 5, 2015. http://www.politico.com/story/2015/05/us-makes-new-push-for-global-rules-in-cyberspace-117632.html.

Marquand, Robert, and Ben Arnody. "China Emerges as a Leader in Cyberwarfare." *Christian Science Monitor,* September 14, 2007.

Masnick, Mike. "Mike Rogers: You Can't Have Your Privacy Violated If You Don't Know About It." *Tech Dirt,* October 20, 2013. https://www.techdirt.com/articles/20131029/18020225059/mike-rogers-you-cant-have-your-privacy-violated-if-you-dont-know-about-it.shtml.

Masterson, Michelle. "Love Bug Costs Billions." CNN, May 5, 2000. http://cnnfn.cnn.com/2000/05/05/technology/virus_impact/.

Matthews, Owen. "Russia's Greatest Weapon May Be Its Hackers." *Newsweek,* May 7, 2015.

Mazzetti, Mark, and David Sanger. "Security Leader Says U.S. Would Retaliate Against Cyberattacks." *New York Times,* March 12, 2013.

——. "U.S. Fears Data Stolen by Chinese Hacker Could Identify Spies." *New York Times,* July 24, 2015.

McConnell, Michael. "Mike McConnell on How to Win the Cyber-war We're Losing." *Washington Post,* February 28, 2010.

McGregor, James. "Why the Best and Brightest in China and the United States Have the Most to Lose from a Cyber-related Conflict Between the Two Countries." *The Atlantic,* April 27, 2013. http://www.theatlantic.com/china/archive/2013/04/is-the-specter-of-a-cyber-cold-war-real/275352/.

McKew, Molly K., and Maniatis, Gregory A. "Playing by Putin's Tactics." *Washington Post,* March 9, 2014.

McMillan, Robert. "The Internet Is Broken, and Shellshock is Just the Start of Our Woes." *Wired.com,* September 29, 2014. http://www.wired.com/2014/09/shellshocked-bash/.

——. "Egypt Goes Dark as Last Internet Company Pulls the Plug." *Computerworld,* January 31, 2011. http://www.computerworld.com/article/2512823/internet/egypt-goes-dark-as-last-internet-company-pulls-the-plug.html.

Meinel, Carolyn. "Code Red: Worm Assault on the Web." *Scientific American,* October 28, 2002.

Meserve, Jeanne. "Sources: Staged Cyber Attack Reveals Vulnerability in Grid." CNN, September 26, 2007. http://www.cnn.com/2007/US/09/26/power.at.risk/index.html?iref=topnews.

Meyers, Michelle. "UC Berkeley Computers Hacked, 160,000 at Risk." *CNET,* May 8, 2009. http://www.cnet.com/news/uc-berkeley-computers-hacked-160000-at-risk/.

Microsoft. "Unfinished Business on Government Surveillance Reform." June 4, 2014. http://blogs.technet.com/b/microsoft_on_the_issues/archive/2014/06/04/unfinished-business-on-government-surveillance-reform.aspx.

Miks, Jason. "Was China Behind Stuxnet?" *The Diplomat,* October 21, 2010. http://thediplomat.com/2010/10/was-china-behind-stuxnet/.

Miles, Kathleen. "Security Experts Warn of Possible Russian Cyberattack Against the U.S., Ukraine." *Huffington Post,* April 30, 2014. http://www.huffingtonpost.com/2014/04/30/russian-cyberattack-us-ukraine_n_5237377.html.

Miller, Claire Cain. "Revelations of N.S.A. Spying Cost U.S. Tech Companies." *New York Times,* March 21, 2014.

Miller, Greg, and Sari Horwitz. "Justice Dept. Targets General in Leak Probe." *Washington Post,* June 27, 2013.

Mills, Elinor. "Behind the 'Flame' Malware Spying on Mideast Computers (FAQ)." *CNET,* June 4, 2012. http://www.cnet.com/news/behind-the-flame-malware-spying-on-mideast-computers-faq/.

———. "Hacker Says He Broke into Texas Water Plant, Others." *CNET,* November 18, 2011. Http://www.cnet.com/news/hacker-says-he-broke-into-texas-water-plant-others/.

———. "Latest Problem Import? Infected Digital Photo Frames." *CNET,* January 8, 2009. http://www.cnet.com/news/latest-problem-import-infected-digital-photo-frames/.

———. "Teen Finds Bugs in Google, Facebook, Apple, Microsoft Code." *CNET,* February 2, 2012. http://www.cnet.com/news/teen-finds-bugs-in-google-facebook-apple-microsoft-code/.

———. "Expert: Sony Attack May Have Been Multipronged." *CNET,* May 18, 2011. http://news.cnet.com/8301-27080_3-20063789-245.html.

———. "Facebook Detour Through China: Accident or Not?" *CNET,* March 24, 2011. http://news.cnet.com/8301-27080_3-20046338-245.html.

———. "In Their Words: Experts Weigh In on Mac vs. PC Security." *CNET,* February 2, 2010. http://www.cnet.com/news/in-their-words-experts-weigh-in-on-mac-vs-pc-security/.

Mimoso, Michael. "Head-Scratching Begins on Proposed Wassenaar Export Control Rules." *Threat Post,* May 21, 2015. https://threatpost.com/head-scratching-begins-on-proposed-wassenaar-export-control-rules/112959.

———. "Hackers Using Brute-Force Attacks to Harvest Wordpress Sites." *Threat Post,* April 15, 2013. http://threatpost.com/hackers-using-brute-force-attacks-harvest-wordpress-sites-041513/77730.

———. "Vupen Cashes in Four Times at Pwn2Own." *Threat Post,* March 12, 2014. http://threatpost.com/vupen-cashes-in-four-times-at-pwn2own/104754.

Montopoli, Brian. "Obama: Malia Asked "Did You Plug the Hole Yet, Daddy?" *CBS News,* May 28, 2010. http://www.cbsnews.com/news/obama-malia-asked-did-you-plug-the-hole-yet-daddy/.

Morozov, Evgeny. "What Fearmongers Get Wrong About Cyberwarfare." *Slate,* May 28, 2012. http://www.slate.com/articles/technology/future_tense/2012/05/cyberwarfare_what_richard_clarke_and_other_fearmongers_get_wrong_.html.

Morris, Chris. "Hackers Take Down Sony's PlayStation Network." CNBC, April 25, 2011. http://www.cnbc.com/id/42750388/Hackers_Take_Down_Sony_s_PlayStation_Network.

Moscaritolo, Angela. "RSA Confirms Lockheed Hack Linked to SecurID Breach." *SC Magazine,* June 7, 2011. http://www.scmagazine.com/rsa-confirms-lockheed-hack-linked-to-securid-breach/article/204744/.

Moyer, Liz. "Prosecutors Announce More Charges in Hacking of JPMorgan Chase." *New York Times,* November 10, 2015.

Mozur, Paul. "China Websites Hit with Disruptions." *Wall Street Journal,* January 21, 2014.

———. "Cybersecurity Firm Says Chinese Hackers Keep Attacking U.S. Companies." *New York Times,* October 20, 2015.

Mufson, Steven, and Jia Lynn Yang. "China Accuses Hackers of Internet Disruption; Experts Suspect Error by Government Censors." *Washington Post,* January 22, 2014.

Munro, Neil. "Fear of an Electronic Pearl Harbor." *Washington Post,* July 16, 1995.

Munroe, Randall. "Exploits of a Mom." Comic. http://xkcd.com/327/.

———. "Heartbleed Explanation." Comic. https://xkcd.com/1354/.

Murphy, Kim. "China Hacking? Beijing Is Also a Victim, Foreign Minister Says in Interview." *Los Angeles Times,* June 23, 2015.

Musil, Steven. "FBI Seizes Web Hosting Company's Servers." *CNET,* June 21, 2011. http://news.cnet.com/8301-1009_3-20073102-83/fbi-seizes-web-hosting-companys-servers/.

Nakashima, Ellen. "Cyber Chief: Efforts to Deter Attacks Against the U.S. Are Not Working." *Washington Post,* March 19, 2015.

———. "Cyber Defense Effort Is Mixed, Study Finds." *Washington Post,* January 12, 2012.

———. "DHS Contractor Suffers Major Computer Breach, Officials Say." *Washington Post,* August 6, 2014.

———. "Foreign Powers Steal Data on Critical U.S. Infrastructure, NSA Chief Says." *Washington Post,* November 20, 2014.

————. "In Cyberwarfare, Rules of Engagement Still Hard to Define." *Washington Post,* March 10, 2013.

————. "U.S. Decides Against Publicly Blaming China for Data Hack." *Washington Post,* July 21, 2015.

————. "U.S. Developing Sanctions Against China Over Cyberthefts." *Washington Post,* August 30, 2015.

————. "U.S. Notified 3,000 Companies in 2013 About Cyberattacks." *Washington Post,* March 24, 2014.

————. "Water-pump Failure in Illinois Wasn't Cyberattack After All." *Washington Post,* November 25, 2011.

————. "Obama Signs Secret Directive to Help Thwart Cyberattacks." *Washington Post,* November 14, 2012.

————. "Dismantling of Saudi-CIA Web Site Illustrates Need for Clearer Cyberwar Policies." *Washington Post,* March 19, 2010.

————. "Indictment of PLA Hackers Is Part of Broad U.S. Strategy to Curb Chinese Cyberspying." *Washington Post,* May 22, 2014.

————. "Security Firm Finds Link between China and Anthem Hack." *Washington Post,* February 27, 2015.

————. "U.S. Cyberweapons Had Been Considered to Disrupt Gaddafi's Air Defenses." *Washington Post,* October 17, 2011.

————. "U.S. Rallied 120 Nations in Response to 2012 Cyberattack on American Banks." *Washington Post,* April 11, 2014.

————. "With Plan X, Pentagon Seeks to Spread U.S. Military Might to Cyberspace." *Washington Post,* May 30, 2012.

————. "With Series of Major Hacks, China Builds Database on Americans." *Washington Post,* June 5, 2015.

————. "Following U.S. Indictments, China Shifts Commercial Hacking Away from Military to Civilian Agency." *Washington Post,* November 30, 2015.

————. "Chinese Government Has Arrested Hackers It Says Breached OPM Database." *Washington Post,* December 2, 2015.

————, and Ashkan Soltani. "NSA Shouldn't Keep Phone Database, Review Board Recommends." *Washington Post,* December 18, 2014.

————, Greg Miller, and Julie Tate. "U.S., Israel Developed Flame Computer Virus to Slow Iranian Nuclear Efforts, Officials Say." *Washington Post,* June 19, 2012.

Naraine, Ryan. "After Latest iPhone Hack, Charlie Miller Kicked Out of iOS Dev Program." *ZDNet,* November 8, 2011. http://www.zdnet.com/blog/security/after-latest-iphone-hack-charlie-miller-kicked-out-of-ios-dev-program/9773.

Naylor, Hugh. "Theft of Saudi Documents Suggests an Iranian Hack." *Washington Post,* June 26, 2015.

Net Market Share. "Desktop Operating System Market Share." Updates continuously. http://www.netmarketshare.com/operating-system-market-share.aspx?qprid=10&qpcustomd=0

New Scientist. "Protests Grow Over Chernobyl 'Cover-Up.'" *New Scientist,* no. 1688, October 28, 1989.

New York Times. "Daily Report: Pressured by China, Apple Apologizes for Warranty Policies." April 2, 2013. http://bits.blogs.nytimes.com/2013/04/02/daily-report-pressured-by-china-apple-apologizes-for-warranty-policies/.

NTD Television. "Chinese State TV Deletes Video Showing Telltale Signs of PLA's Hacking Effort." August 30, 2011. https://www.youtube.com/watch?v=fq_jAfiTz-k.

Ogg, Erica. "PlayStation Network Outage: 6 Days and Counting." *CNET,* April 26, 2011. http://news.cnet.com/8301-31021_3-20057493-260.html.

————. "Sony: PSN Back, but No System Is 100 Percent Secure." *CNET,* May 17, 2011. http://news.cnet.com/8301-31021_3-20063764-260.html.

————. "The PlayStation Network Breach (FAQ)." *CNET,* May 3, 2011. http://news.cnet.com/8301-31021_3-20058950-260.html.

Olson, Parmy. "The Largest Cyber Attack in History Has Been Hitting Hong Kong Sites." *Forbes,* November 20, 2104. http://www.forbes.com/sites/parmyolson/2014/11/20/the-largestcyberattack-in-history-has-been-hitting-hong-kong-sites/.

Osborne, Charlie. "Apple's iOS Blocks Gov't Spying Efforts, Gamma's FinSpy Useless Against iPhone." *ZDNet,* August 12, 2014. http://www.zdnet.com/article/apples-ios-blocks-govt-spying-efforts-gammas-finspy-useless-against-iphone/.

————. "Georgia Turns the Tables on Russian Hacker." *ZDNet,* October 30, 2012. http://www.zdnet.com/georgia-turns-the-tables-on-russian-hacker-7000006611/.

———. "Terrorist Encryption Tools Nothing More than 'Security Cape' and Gov't Red Flag." *ZDNet,* February 17, 2015. http://www.zdnet.com/article/black-flag-ops-exposed-terrorist-security-tools-a-red-flag-to-govt-agencies/.

Ostroukh, Andrey. "Russia, China Forge Closer Ties with New Economic, Financing Accords: Moscow Turns to Asian Investors to Reduce Reliance on Europe and the U.S. amid Standoff over Ukraine." *Wall Street Journal,* May 8, 2015.

Paletta, Damian, and Siobhan Hughes. "U.S. Spy Agencies Join Probe of Personnel-Records Theft: Sales Demonstration May Have Uncovered Government Breach." *Wall Street Journal,* June 10, 2015.

Paller, Alan and George Boggs. "Why We Need More Troops for Escalating Cyberwar." *USA Today,* March 28, 2013.

Pallotta, Frank. "Sony's 'The Interview' Coming to Netflix." CNN, January 20, 2015. http://money.cnn.com/2015/01/20/media/the-interview-makes-40-million/.

Parsons, Dan. "Government Still Ironing Out Role in Defending Industry from Cyber Attack." *Defense Daily,* July 15, 2015. http://www.defensedaily.com/government-still-ironing-out-role-in-defending-industry-from-cyber-attack/.

Pauli, Darren. "Adobe CSO Offers Oracle Security Lesson: Go Click-to-Play." *The Register,* October 16, 2014. http://www.theregister.co.uk/2014/10/16/adobe_clicktoplay_would_have_avoided_java_zeroday_masscare/.

Pellerin, Cheryl. "Cybercom Builds Teams for Offense, Defense in Cyberspace." *Defense.gov,* March 12, 2013. http://www.defense.gov/news/newsarticle.aspx?id=119506.

Perlez, Jane. "U.S. and China Put Focus on Cybersecurity." *New York Times,* April 23, 2013.

Perlroth, Nicole. "After Arrest of Accused Hacker, Russia Accuses U.S. of Kidnapping." *New York Times,* July 8, 2014.

———. "Banks' Lawsuits Against Target for Losses Related to Hacking Can Continue." *New York Times,* December 4, 2014.

———. "Cyberattacks a Topic in Obama Call with New Chinese President." *New York Times,* March 14, 2013.

———. "Electrical Grid is Called Vulnerable to a Power Shutdown." *New York Times,* October 18, 2013.

———. "Hackers in China Attacked *The Times* for Last 4 Months." *New York Times,* January 30, 2013.

———. "In Cyberattack on Saudi Firm, U.S. Sees Iran Firing Back." *New York Times,* October 23, 2012.

———. "Reinventing the Internet to Make It Safer." *New York Times,* December 2, 2014.

———. "Russian Hackers Targeting Oil and Gas Companies." *New York Times,* June 30, 2014.

———. "2nd China Army Unit Implicated in Online Spying." *New York Times,* June 9, 2014.

———. "Serious Flaw in Java Software Is Found, Then Patched." *New York Times,* January 13, 2013.

———. "Google Offers New Encryption Tool." *New York Times,* June 3, 2014.

———, and Quentin Hardy. "Bank Hacking Was the Work of Iranians, Officials Say." *New York Times,* January 8, 2013.

———, and David Sanger. "Nations Buying as Hackers Sell Flaws in Computer Code." *New York Times,* July 14, 2013.

———, and David Sanger. "North Korea Loses its Link to the Internet." *New York Times,* December 22, 2014.

Peterson, Andrea. "Chinese Cyberspies Have Hacked Middle East Experts at Major U.S. Think Tanks." *Washington Post,* July 7, 2014.

———. "Microsoft Just Squashed a 19-year-old Software Bug. How Did It Go Undetected So Long?" *Washington Post,* November 12, 2014.

Piesing, Mark. "Hacking Attacks on Printers Still Not Being Taken Seriously." *The Guardian,* July 23, 2012.

Polityuk, Pavel and Alessandra Prentice. "Ukraine Says to Review Cyber Defenses after Airport Targeted from Russia." Reuters, January 18, 2016. http://www.reuters.com/article/us-ukraine-cybersecurity-malware-idUSKCN0UW0R0

Pomfret, John. "U.S.-Japan Ties Should Deepen, Gates Says, Citing Threats from China, N. Korea." *Washington Post,* January 14, 2011.

Poulsen, Kevin. "Finding a Video Poker Bug Made These Guys Rich—Then Vegas Made Them Pay." *Wired .com,* October 7, 2014. http://www.wired.com/2014/10/cheating-video-poker/.

PressTV.ir/Sci-Tech. "Iran to Unveil National OS Soon." *PressTV,* January 4, 2011. http://www.presstv.ir/detail/158534.html.

Prevelakis, Vassilis, and Diomidis Spinellis. "The Athens Affair: How Some Extremely Smart Hackers Pulled Off the Most Audacious Cell-Network Break-in Ever." *IEEE Spectrum.org,* June 29, 2007. http://spectrum.ieee.org/telecom/security/the-athens-affair.

Protalinski, Emil. "F-Secure: Android Accounted for 97% of All Mobile Malware in 2013, But Only 0.1% of Those Were on Google Play." *The Next Web,* March 4, 2014. http://thenextweb.com/google/2014/03/04/f-secure-android-accounted-97-mobile-malware-2013-0-1-google-play/.

———. "U.S. Government Pays $250,000 for iOS Exploit." *ZDNet,* March 25, 2012. http://www.zdnet.com/blog/security/us-government-pays-250000-for-ios-exploit/11044.

Puzzanghera, Jim. "Expect More Web Hacking If U.S. Strikes Syria: Cybersecurity Expert." *Los Angeles Times,* August 28, 2013.

Radia, Kirit. "Iran Blocks U.S. 'Virtual' Embassy Within 12 Hours of Launch." *ABC News,* December 7, 2011. http://abcnews.go.com/blogs/politics/2011/12/iran-blocks-us-virtual-embassy-within-12-hours-of-launch/.

Ragan, Steve. "FireEye Customers Get Liability Shield Thanks to SAFETY Act." *CSO Online,* May 1, 2015. http://www.csoonline.com/article/2916649/disaster-recovery/fireeye-customers-get-liability-shield-thanks-to-safety-act.html.

Randazzo, Marissa Reddy et al. *Insider Threat Study: Illicit Cyber Activity in the Banking and Finance Sector.* Pittsburgh, Pa.: CERT Coordination Center, Software Engineering Institute, Carnegie Mellon University, June 2005.

Ratnesar, Romesh et al. "How the FBI Blew the Case." *Time,* June 3, 2002

Reed, John. "China's Hackers Are Still at It; Iran's Are Getting Better." *Foreign Policy,* May 21, 2013. https://foreignpolicy.com/2013/05/21/chinas-hackers-are-still-at-it-irans-are-getting-better/.

Reichenberg, Nimmy. "Want Better Security? Assume You've Already Been Hacked." *Security Week,* September 14, 2012. https://www.securityweek.com/want-better-security-assume-youve-already-been-hacked.

Reilly, Michael. "How Long Before All-Out Cyberwar?" *New Scientist,* no. 2644 (February 20, 2008): 24–25.

Reisinger, Don. "China's Internet Hit by DDoS Attack; Sites Down for Hours: The Country's Internet Watchdog Says that the Net Is Back Online for the Country and that It Will Work to Improve Security." *CNET,* August 26, 2013. http://www.cnet.com/news/chinas-internet-hit-by-ddos-attack-sites-down-for-hours/.

———. "Sony: PSN Difficulties a 'Bump in the Road.'" *CNET,* June 23, 2011. http://news.cnet.com/8301-13506_3-20073659-17/sony-psn-difficulties-a-bump-in-the-road/.

Reuters. "China Suggests U.S. May Have Fabricated Evidence for Cyberattacks." May 29, 2014. http://www.reuters.com/article/2014/05/29/us-china-usa-diplomacy-idUSKBN0E914H20140529.

———. "No Harmful Virus Found in South Korean Nuclear Hack." *New York Times,* December 30, 2014.

Rhoads, Christopher, and Farnaz Fassihi. "Iran Vows to Unplug Internet." *Wall Street Journal,* May 28, 2011.

RIA Novosti. "Putin Urges Readiness against Cyber and Outer Space Attacks." *Sputnik News,* July 5, 2013. http://sputniknews.com/russia/20130705/182079750.html.

Riley, Michael. "NSA Said to Have Used Heartbleed Bug, Exposing Consumers." Bloomberg, April 12, 2014. http://www.bloomberg.com/news/articles/2014-04-11/nsa-said-to-have-used-heartbleed-bug-exposing-consumers.

———. "How the Russian Hackers Stole the Nasdaq." Bloomberg, July 17, 2014. http://www.bloomberg.com/bw/articles/2014-07-17/how-russian-hackers-stole-the-nasdaq.

———, and Eric Engleman. "Code in Aramco Cyber Attack Indicates Lone Perpetrator." Bloomberg, October 25, 2012. http://www.bloomberg.com/news/articles/2012-10-25/code-in-aramco-cyber-attack-indicates-lone-perpetrator.

———, and Sophia Pearson. "China-Based Hackers Target Law Firms to Get Secret Deal Data." Bloomberg, January 31, 2012. http://www.bloomberg.com/news/2012-01-31/china-based-hackers-target-law-firms.html.

———, and Jordan Robertson. "China-Tied Hackers That Hit U.S. Said to Breach United Airlines." Bloomberg, July 29, 2015. http://www.bloomberg.com/news/articles/2015-07-29/china-tied-hackers-that-hit-u-s-said-to-breach-united-airlines.

———. "Cyberspace Becomes Second Front in Russia's Clash with NATO." Bloomberg October 14, 2015. http://www.bloomberg.com/news/articles/2015-10-14/cyberspace-becomes-second-front-in-russia-s-clash-with-nato.

———, and Ashlee Vance. "Inside the Chinese Boom in Corporate Espionage." Bloomberg, March 15, 2012. http://www.bloomberg.com/bw/articles/2012-03-14/inside-the-chinese-boom-in-corporate-espionage.

——— et al. "Missed Alarms and 40 Million Stolen Credit Card Numbers: How Target Blew It." Bloomberg, March 13, 2014.http://www.bloomberg.com/bw/articles/2014-03-13/target-missed-alarms-in-epic-hack-of-credit-card-data.

Roberts, Dexter. "Chinese Hackers Like a 'Drunk Burglar,' 'Kicking Down the Door,' Says FBI Director." *Business Week,* October 6, 2014. http://www.businessweek.com/articles/2014-10-06/fbi-chief-james-comey-lambasts-chinese-hackers.

Robertson, Jordan and Michael Riley. "American Airlines, Sabre Said to Be Hit in China-Tied Hacks." Bloomberg, August 7, 2015. http://www.bloomberg.com/news/articles/2015-08-07/american-airlines-sabre-said-to-be-hit-in-hacks-backed-by-china.

Robertson, Matthew. "Chinese Admiral Threatens World War to Protect Iran." *Epoch Times*, December 6, 2011, updated December 22, 2011. http://printarchive.epochtimes.com/a1/en/sg/nnn/2011/12%20December%202011/Issue%20390_13_December%202011/390_A5.pdf.

———, and Helena Zhu. "Slip-Up in Chinese Military TV Show Reveals More than Intended: Piece Shows Cyber Warfare Against U.S. Entities." *Epoch Times*, August 21, 2011, updated April 7, 2012. http://www.theepochtimes.com/n2/china-news/slip-up-in-chinese-military-tv-show-reveals-more-than-intended-60619.html.

Rosenblatt, Seth. "All Hacking Eyes on the Prize Money at CanSecWest." *CNET,* March 15, 2014. http://www.cnet.com/news/all-hacking-eyes-on-the-prize-money-at-cansecwest/.

———. "Ten-Year-Old Hacker Finds Zero-Day Flaw in Games." *CNET,* August 7, 2011. http://download.cnet.com/8301-2007_4-20089152-12/10-year-old-hacker-finds-zero-day-flaw-in-games/.

Sabbatini, Renato M. E. "The Mind, Artificial Intelligence, and Emotions: Interview with Marvin Minsky." Undated. http://www.cerebromente.org.br/n07/opiniao/minsky/minsky_i.htm.

Sager, Ira, and Jay Greene. "Commentary: The Best Way to Make Software Secure: Liability." *BusinessWeek,* March 18, 2002. http://www.bloomberg.com/bw/stories/2002-03-17/commentary-the-best-way-to-make-software-secure-liability.

Sanborn, James K. "Cyber Steps Up Its Role on the Battlefield." *Marine Corps Times,* August 24, 2014. http://www.marinecorpstimes.com/article/20140825/NEWS/308250015/Cyber-steps-up-its-role-battlefield.

Sancton, Thomas. "Anatomy of a Hijack." *Time,* June 24, 2001.

Sanger, David. "NATO Set to Ratify Pledge on Joint Defense in Case of Major Cyberattack." *New York Times,* August 31, 2014.

———. "Obama Lets N.S.A. Exploit Some Internet Flaws, Officials Say." *New York Times,* April 12, 2014.

———. "Document Reveals Growth of Cyberwarfare between the United States and Iran." *New York Times,* February 22, 2015.

———. "Obama Order Sped up Wave of Cyberattacks against Iran." *New York Times,* June 1, 2012.

———. "Pentagon Announces New Strategy for Cyberwarfare." *New York Times,* April 23, 2015.

———, and Steven Erlanger. "Suspicion Falls on Russia as 'Snake' Cyberattacks Target Ukraine's Government." *New York Times,* March 8, 2014.

———, and Martin Fackler. "N.S.A. Breached North Korean Networks Before Sony Attack, Officials Say." *New York Times,* January 19, 2015.

———, and Julie Hirschfeld. "Hacking Linked to China Exposes Millions of U.S. Workers." *New York Times,* June 4, 2015.

———, and John Markoff. "After Google's Stand on China, U.S. Treads Lightly." *New York Times,* January 14, 2010.

———, and Mark Mazzetti. "Israel Struck Syrian Nuclear Project, Analysts Say." *New York Times,* October 14, 2007.

————, and Nicole Perlroth. "Iran Is Raising Sophistication and Frequency of Cyberattacks, Study Says." *New York Times,* April 15, 2015.

————, and Nicole Perlroth. "Hackers from China Resume Attacks on U.S. Targets." *New York Times,* May 19, 2013.

————, and Eric Schmitt. "Rise Is Seen in Cyberattacks Targeting U.S. Infrastructure." *New York Times,* July 26, 2012.

————, and Thom Shanker. "Broad Powers Seen for Obama in Cyberstrikes." *New York Times,* February 3, 2013.

————, and Thom Shanker. "N.S.A. Devises Radio Pathway into Computers." *New York Times,* January 15, 2014.

————, Nicole Perlroth, and Eric Schmitt. "U.S. Asks China to Help Rein In Korean Hackers." *New York Times,* December 20, 2014.

Sang-Hundec, Choe. "North Korea Denies Role in Sony Pictures Hacking." *New York Times,* December 7, 2014.

Savage, Charlie. "Memo Revisits Policy on Citing Leaked Material, to Some Confusion." *New York Times,* May 9, 2014.

———— et al. "Hunting for Hackers, N.S.A. Secretly Expands Internet Spying at U.S. Border." *New York Times,* June 4, 2015.

Schiavenza, Matt. "Why North Korea Sanctions Are Unlikely to Be Effective." *The Atlantic,* January 3, 2015.

Schiffman, Noah. "DARPA Attempting the Impossible: Self-Simulation for Defense Training." *Network World,* June 6, 2008. http://www.networkworld.com/article/2344569/security/darpa-attempting-the-impossible--self-simulation-for-defense-training.html.

Schmitt, Eric. "Air Force Blocks Sites that Posted Secret Cables." *New York Times,* December 14, 2010.

Schneier, Bruce. "The NSA Is Not Made of Magic." *Schneier on Security,* May 21, 2014. https://www.schneier.com/blog/archives/2014/05/the_nsa_is_not_.html.

————. "New Al Qaeda Encryption Software." *Schneier on Security,* May 14, 2014. https://www.schneier.com/blog/archives/2014/05/new_al_qaeda_en_1.html.

————. "The Human Side of Heartbleed." *Schneier on Security,* June 4, 2014. https://www.schneier.com/blog/archives/2014/06/the_human_side_.html.

————. "The Internet of Things Is Wildly Insecure—and Often Unpatchable." *Wired.com,* January 6, 2014. http://www.wired.com/2014/01/theres-no-good-way-to-patch-the-internet-of-things-and-thats-a-huge-problem/.

————. "The Public/Private Surveillance Partnership." *Schneier on Security,* August 5, 2013. https://www.schneier.com/blog/archives/2013/08/the_publicpriva_1.html.

————. "Attack Attribution in Cyberspace." *Schneier on Security,* January 8, 2015. https://www.schneier.com/blog/archives/2015/01/attack_attribut.html.

————. "Did North Korea Really Attack Sony?" *Schneier on Security,* December 24, 2014. https://www.schneier.com/blog/archives/2014/12/did_north_korea.html.

————. "Information Security: How Liable Should Vendors Be?" *Computerworld,* October 28, 2004. https://www.schneier.com/essays/archives/2004/10/information_security.html.

————. "Internet Worm Targets SCADA." *Schneier on Security,* July 23, 2010. https://www.schneier.com/blog/archives/2010/07/internet_worm_t.html.

————. "Organizational Doxing." *Schneier on Security,* July 10, 2015. https://www.schneier.com/blog/archives/2015/07/organizational_.html.

————. "Perspective: Internet Worms and Critical Infrastructure." *CNET News,* December 9, 2003. http://www.cnet.com/news/internet-worms-and-critical-infrastructure/.

————. "Refuse to be Terrorized." *Schneier on Security,* August 24, 2006. https://www.schneier.com/essay-124.html.

————. "Should Companies Do Most of Their Computing in the Cloud?" *Schneier on Security,* June 2016. https://www.schneier.com/blog/archives/2015/06/should_companie.html, https://www.schneier.com/blog/archives/2015/06/should_companie_1.html, and https://www.schneier.com/blog/archives/2015/06/should_companie_2.html.

———. "Should U.S. Hackers Fix Cybersecurity Holes or Exploit Them?" *The Atlantic,* May 19, 2014. http://www.theatlantic.com/technology/archive/2014/05/should-hackers-fix-cybersecurity-holes-or-exploit-them/371197/.

Schwartz, John. "Internet Activist, a Creator of RSS, Is Dead at 26, Apparently a Suicide." *New York Times,* January 12, 2013.

Schwartz, Matthew. "Lockheed Martin Suffers Massive Cyberattack." *Dark Reading,* May 30, 2011. http://www.darkreading.com/risk-management/lockheed-martin-suffers-massive-cyberattack/d/d-id/1098013.

Schwirtz, Michael. "For Young Campers, Island Turned into Fatal Trap." *New York Times,* July 23, 2011.

Segal, Adam. "Chinese Responses to the International Strategy for Cyberspace." Council on Foreign Relations, May 23, 2011. http://blogs.cfr.org/asia/2011/05/23/chinese-responses-to-the-international-strategy-for-cyberspace/.

———, and Matthew Waxman. "Why a Cybersecurity Treaty Is a Pipe Dream." Council on Foreign Relations, October 27, 2011. http://www.cfr.org/cybersecurity/why-cybersecurity-treaty-pipe-dream/p26325.

Selyukh, Alina. "U.S. Retailers at Senate Hearing: Hackers Have Upper Hand." Reuters, February 4, 2014. http://www.reuters.com/article/2014/02/04/us-usa-hacking-congress-idUSBREA121I620140204.

Serbu, Jared. "DoD to Be More Transparent about Strategy to Deter Cyber Attacks." Federal News Radio, October 3, 2014. http://www.federalnewsradio.com/394/3714846/DoD-to-be-more-transparent-about-strategy-to-deter-cyberattack.

Sethi, Rohit, and David Kennedy. "Debate: Because of Inherent Vulnerabilities, It Is Time to Ditch Java." *SC Magazine,* July 1, 2013. http://www.scmagazine.com/debate-because-of-inherent-vulnerabilities-it-is-time-to-ditch-java/article/298545/.

Sevastopluo, Demetri. "Chinese Hacked into Pentagon." *FT.com,* September 3, 2007. http://www.ft.com/intl/cms/s/0/9dba9ba2-5a3b-11dc-9bcd-0000779fd2ac.html#axzz3gWdmhe9M.

Shachtman, Noah. "Insiders Doubt 2008 Pentagon Hack Was Foreign Spy Attack." *Wired.com,* August 25, 2010. http://www.wired.com/2010/08/insiders-doubt-2008-pentagon-hack-was-foreign-spy-attack/.

Shah, Sooraj. "KPMG scales down sponsorship of the Cyber Security Challenge because of a 'lack of credible candidates.'" *Computing,* January 15, 2004. http://www.computing.co.uk/ctg/news/2323062/kpmg-scales-down-sponsorship-of-the-cyber-security-challenge-because-of-a-lack-of-credible-candidates.

Shalal, Andrea. "U.S. Firm CrowdStrike Claims Success in Deterring Chinese Hackers." *Web Culture,* April 14, 2015. http://www.webculture.com/17/Tech%20Top%20News/16/a/19280884/US_firm_CrowdStrike_claims_success_in_deterring_Chinese_hackers.

Shane, Scott, and Tom Rowman. "Rigging the Game." *Baltimore Sun,* December 10, 1995.

———. "Congress Has Tough Time Performing Watchdog Role." *Baltimore Sun,* December 15, 1995.

Shawcross, Hartley. "Crime Does Pay Because We Do Not Back Up the Police." *New York Times Magazine,* June 13, 1965.

Shear, Michael and Scott Shane. "White House Weighs Sanctions After Second Breach of a Computer System." *New York Times,* June 12, 2015.

Shuffham, Matt, and David Henry. "Banks to Be Hit with Microsoft Costs for Running Outdated ATMs." Reuters, March 14, 2014. http://www.reuters.com/article/2014/03/14/us-banks-atms-idUSBREA2D13D20140314.

Silver-Greenberg, Jessica, and Matthew Goldstein. "After JPMorgan Chase Breach, Push to Close Wall St. Security Gaps." *New York Times,* October 21, 2014.

Singer, Peter and Allan Friedman. "The 5 Biggest Cybersecurity Myths, Debunked." *Wired.com,* July 2, 2014. http://www.wired.com/2014/07/debunking-5-major-cyber-security-myths/.

Smith, Alison. "Share Prices Are Rarely Hit by Cyber Attacks." *Financial Times,* October 31, 2013. http://www.ft.com/cms/s/0/348d7f1a-417e-11e3-9073-00144feabdc0.html#axzz3Dzh1mFF4.

Smith, Gerry. "John Kerry: Foreign Hackers Are '21st Century Nuclear Weapons.'" *Huffington Post,* January 24, 2013. http://www.huffingtonpost.com/2013/01/24/john-kerry-hackers_n_2544534.html.

Smith, R. Jeffrey. "U.N. Inspectors or Spies? Iraq Data Can Take Many Paths." *Washington Post,* February 16, 1998.

Soares, Marcelo. "Brazilian Blackout Traced to Sooty Insulators, Not Hackers." *Wired.com,* November 9, 2009. http://www.wired.com/threatlevel/2009/11/brazil_blackout/.

Solomon, Howard. "Assume Your Network Has Been Hacked, Says Cisco." *IT World Canada,* January 16, 2014. http://www.itworldcanada.com/article/assume-your-network-has-been-hacked-says-cisco/88397.

———. "U.S. Should Outspend Anyone on Bug Bounties, Black Hat Conference Told." *IT World Canada,* August 7, 2014. http://www.itworldcanada.com/post/u-s-should-outspend-anyone-on-bug-bounties-black-hat-conference-told.

Sorcher, Sara. "An Exclusive Look Inside DARPA's Plan to Visualize Cyberoperations." *Christian Science Monitor,* February 16, 2015.

Steiner, Peter. Cartoon. *The New Yorker,* July 5, 1993.

Sternstein, Aliya. "The Smartest Hackers in the Room (Hint: They're Not the Humans)." *NextGov.com,* March 25, 2015. http://www.nextgov.com/cybersecurity/2015/03/smartest-hackers-room-or-these-are-smartest-hackers-world/108466/.

———. "Report: Joint U.S.-China Aviation Ventures Are More Prone to Cyber Intrusions than U.S. Firms." *NextGov.com,* August 7, 2013. http://www.nextgov.com/cybersecurity/2013/08/report-joint-us-china-aviation-ventures-are-more-prone-cyber-intrusions-us-firms/68225/.

———. "Pentagon: U.S. Cyber Reserve Is in the Works." *NextGov.com,* April 14, 2015._http://www.nextgov .com/cybersecurity/2015/04/pentagon-us-cyber-reserve-works/110113/.

———. "Pentagon to Recruit Thousands for Cybersecurity Reserve Force." *Defense One,* April 16, 2015. http://www.defenseone.com/technology/2015/04/pentagon-recruit-thousands-cybersecurity-reserve-force/110407/.

Stevenson, Alastair. "Iran and North Korea Sign Technology Treaty to Combat Hostile Malware." *V3,* September 3, 2012. http://www.v3.co.uk/v3-uk/news/2202493/iran-and-north-korea-sign-technology-treaty-to-combat-hostile-malware.

———. "Heartbleed: Linux Foundation Hires Dynamic Duo to Fix OpenSSL." *V3,* May 30, 2014. http://www .v3.co.uk/v3-uk/news/2347497/heartbleed-linux-foundation-hires-dynamic-duo-to-fix-openssl.

Stewart, Phil. "U.S. Overhauling Intelligence Access to Try to Prevent Another Snowden." Reuters, July 18, 2013. http://www.reuters.com/article/2013/07/19/us-usa-security-snowden-intelligence-idUSBRE96H18F20130719.

Stone, Andrea. "Many in Islamic World Doubt Arabs Behind 9/11." *USA Today,* February 27, 2002.

Strohm, Christopher. "Hacker-Threat Sharing Has Companies Waiting Amid Breaches." Bloomberg, April 24, 2014. http://www.bloomberg.com/news/articles/2014-04-24/hacker-threat-sharing-has-companies-waiting-amid-breaches.

———, and Kasia Klimasinska. "Europeans Start Hacking Drills Following Russian Sanction." Bloomberg, April 28, 2014. http://www.bloomberg.com/news/2014-04-28/europeans-start-hacking-drills-following-russian-sanction.html.

Sullivan, Nick. "A (Relatively Easy to Understand) Primer on Elliptic Curve Cryptography." *Ars Technica,* October 24, 2013. http://arstechnica.com/security/2013/10/a-relatively-easy-to-understand-primer-on-elliptic-curve-cryptography/.

Swartz, John. "Chinese Hackers Seek U.S. Access." *USAToday,* March 12, 2007.

Szor, Peter. *Duqu—Threat Research and Analysis.* White paper. McAfee, undated. https://blogs.mcafee.com/wp-content/uploads/2011/10/Duqu1.pdf.

Tang, Lan. "Let Us Join Hands to Make Internet Safe." *China Daily,* February 7, 2012. http://usa.chinadaily .com.cn/epaper/2012-02/07/content_14551811.htm.

Tang, Rose. "China Warns of Massive Hack Attacks." *CNN.com,* May 3, 2001. http://www.cnn.com/2001/WORLD/asiapcf/east/05/03/china.hack/.

Tedeshi, Bob. "Privacy vs. Profits." *ZDNet,* September 18, 2001. http://www.zdnet.com/article/privacy-vs-profits/.

Telegraph. "Iranian Cyberwarfare Commander Shot Dead in Suspected Assassination." October 2, 2013. http://www.telegraph.co.uk/news/worldnews/middleeast/iran/10350285/Iranian-cyber-warfare-commander-shot-dead-in-suspected-assassination.html.

Theerthagiri, Dinesh. "Zero-Day World." *Symantec.com*, October 30, 2012. http://www.symantec.com/connect/blogs/zero-day-world.

Thomson, Iain. "South Korea Faces $1Bn Bill after Hackers Raid National ID Database." *The Register,* October 14, 2014. http://www.theregister.co.uk/2014/10/14/south_korea_national_identity_system_hacked/.

Thornburgh, Nathan. "Inside the Chinese Hack Attack." *Time*, August 25, 2005.

Tiezzi, Shannon. "China (Finally) Admits to Hacking: An Updated Military Document for the First Time Admits that the Chinese Government Sponsors Offensive Cyber Units." *The Diplomat,* March 18, 2015. http://thediplomat.com/2015/03/china-finally-admits-to-hacking/.

Timberg, Craig. "A Flaw in the Design." *Washington Post,* May 30, 2015.

———. "The Long Life of a Quick 'Fix.'" *Washington Post,* May 31, 2015.

———. "A Disaster Foretold—and Ignored." *Washington Post,* June 22, 2015.

———. "Hacks on the Highway: Automakers Rush to Add Wireless Features, Leaving Our Cars Open to Hackers." *Washington Post,* July 22, 2015.

———, Ellen Nakashima, and Danielle Douglas-Gabriel. "Cyberattacks Trigger Talk of 'Hacking Back.'" *Washington Post,* October 9, 2014.

Traynor, Ian. "Russia Accused of Unleashing Cyberwar to Disable Estonia." *The Guardian,* May 17, 2007.

Tsukayama, Hayley. "Hackers Are Getting Better at Offense. Companies Aren't Getting Better at Defense." *Washington Post,* April 22, 2014.

Tucker, Patrick. "NSA Chief: Rules of War Apply to Cyberwar, Too." *Defense One,* April 20, 2015. http://www.defenseone.com/technology/2015/04/nsa-chief-rules-war-apply-cyberwar-too/110572/.

Tung, Liam. "NSA: Our Zero Days Put You at Risk, But We Do What We Like with Them." *ZDNet,* March 13, 2014. http://www.zdnet.com/nsa-our-zero-days-put-you-at-risk-but-we-do-what-we-like-with-them-7000027296/.

Verton, Dan. "Blaster Worm Linked to Severity of Blackout." *Computerworld*, August 29, 2003. http://www.computerworld.com/article/2571068/disaster-recovery/blaster-worm-linked-to-severity-of-blackout.html.

Vincent, James. "Scientists Create Computer Virus that Transfers Stolen Data Using Inaudible Sounds." *The Independent,* December 3, 2013. http://www.independent.co.uk/life-style/gadgets-and-tech/scientists-create-computer-virus-that-transfers-stolen-data-using-inaudible-sounds-8980674.html.

Volz, Dustin. "The NSA Is Listening to Every Phone Call in the Bahamas." *National Journal,* May 19, 2014. http://www.nationaljournal.com/tech/the-nsa-is-listening-to-every-phone-call-in-the-bahamas-20140519.

———. "Obama Declares Cyberattacks a 'National Emergency.'" *National Journal,* April 1, 2015. http://www.nationaljournal.com/tech/obama-declares-cyber-attacks-a-national-emergency-20150401.

Wagenseil, Paul. "Printers Can Be Hacked to Catch Fire." *Scientific American,* November 29, 2011. http://www.scientificamerican.com/article/printers-can-be-hacked-to-catch-fire/.

Waldmeir, Patti. "Coca-Cola Probed Over Mapping in China." *Financial Times,* March 12, 2013. http://www.ft.com/cms/s/0/f02a6abc-8b21-11e2-b1a4-00144feabdc0.html#axzz2PKL4h06R.

Walker, Danielle. "Losing Control: Critical Infrastructure." *SC Magazine,* March 1, 2013. http://www.scmagazine.com/losing-control-critical-infrastructure/article/280939.

Walker, Peter. "American Expats Caught Up in Indian Bomb Blast Inquiry." *The Guardian,* July 29, 2008.

Walsh, Declan. "Whose Side is Pakistan's ISI Really On?" *The Guardian,* May 12, 2011.

Want China Times. "Millions Have Their Data Leaked in China." April 23, 2015. http://www.wantchinatimes.com/news-subclass-cnt.aspx?id=20150423000110&cid=1103.

Washington Post. "The OPM Cyberattack Was a Bridge Too Far." *Washington Post*, editorial, July 5, 2015.

Wassener, Bettina. "Google Links Web Attacks to Vietnam Mine Dispute." *New York Times*, March 31, 2010.

Weisman, Aly. "Steve Carell's North Korea–based Thriller Scrapped after Sony Scandal." *Business Insider,* December 17, 2014. http://www.businessinsider.com/steve-carell-north-korea-movie-cancelled-2014-12.

Wessel, David. "U.S. Keeps Foreign Ph.Ds." *Wall Street Journal*, January 26, 2010.

Whitaker, Mark and John Wolcott. "Getting Rid of Kaddafi," *Newsweek,* April 28, 1986.

Whitlock, Craig. "Ashton Carter, Passed Over Before, Gets Picked by Obama to Be Defense Secretary." *Washington Post,* December 5, 2014.

Whittaker, Zack. "Homeland Security Warns to Disable Java Amid Zero-Day Flaw." *ZDNet,* January 11, 2003. http://www.zdnet.com/homeland-security-warns-to-disable-java-amid-zero-day-flaw-700000 9713/.

Williams, Christopher. "Israeli Security Chief Celebrates Stuxnet Cyber Attack." *The Telegraph,* February 16, 2011.

Wingfield, Nick. "Judge Rules that Microsoft Must Turn Over Data Stored in Ireland." *New York Times,* July 31, 2014.

Winkler, Ira. "6 Failures that Led to Target Hack." *Computerworld,* February 12, 2014. http://www .computerworld.com/article/2487616/cybercrime-hacking/ira-winkler--6-failures-that-led-to-target-hack.html.

Wolff, Josephine. "To Catch a Cyberthief." *Slate,* June 3, 2014. http://www.slate.com/articles/technology/technology/2014/06/evgeniy_bogachev_gameover_zeus_cryptolocker_how_the_fbi_shut_down_two_viruses.html.

———. "NATO's Empty Cybersecurity Gesture: Its New Approach to Cyberattacks Misses Some Fundamental Points." *Slate,* September 10, 2014. http://www.slate.com/articles/technology/future_tense/2014/09/nato_s_statement_on_cyberattacks_misses_some_fundamental_points.html.

Worstall, Tim. "China Makes Almost Nothing Out of Apple's iPads and iPhones." *Forbes,* December 24, 2011. http://www.forbes.com/sites/timworstall/2011/12/24/china-makes-almost-nothing-out-of-apples-ipads-and-i/.

Xinhua News Service. "Over 50% of Computers in China Have Infections." *Want China Times,* September 17, 2014. http://www.wantchinatimes.com/news-subclass-cnt.aspx?id=20140917000100&cid= 1103&MainCatID=0.

Yadron, Danny. "Symantec Develops New Attack on Cyberhacking." *Wall Street Journal,* May 4, 2014. http://online.wsj.com/news/articles/SB10001424052702303417104579542144023585057.

———. "Popular Software Gives Hackers Easy Targets, DOD Official Says." *Wall Street Journal,* October 28, 2014.

———. "Three Months Later, State Department Hasn't Rooted Out Hackers." *Wall Street Journal,* February 19, 2015.

———, James Areddy, and Paul Mozur. "Chinese Hacking Is Deep and Diverse, Experts Say." *Wall Street Journal,* May 29, 2014.

———, and Jennifer Valentino-Devries. "This Article Was Written with the Help of a 'Cyber' Machine." *Wall Street Journal,* March 4, 2015.

Yu, Xiaoqiu. "U.S. Playing Dangerous Game with 'Cyber Deterrence.'" *People's Daily Online,* July 26, 2013. http://en.people.cn/90001/90780/91343/7452284.html.

Yuan, Gao. "Nation's Cyberspace 'Vulnerability' Exposed by Attack." *China Daily,* May 1, 2015. http://www .chinadaily.com.cn/china/2015-05/01/content_20593546.htm.

Zagorin, Adam. "Can KSM's Confession Be Believed?" *Time,* March 15, 2007.

Zetter, Kim. "Former NSA Director: Countries Spewing Cyberattacks Should Be Held Responsible." *Wired .com,* July 29, 2010. http://www.wired.com/2010/07/hayden-at-blackhat/.

———. "Senior Defense Official Caught Hedging on U.S. Involvement in Stuxnet." *Wired.com,* May 26, 2011. http://www.wired.com/threatlevel/2011/05/defense-department-stuxnet/.

———. "How Digital Detectives Deciphered Stuxnet, the Most Menacing Malware in History." *Wired.com,* July 11, 2011. http://www.wired.com/2011/07/how-digital-detectives-deciphered-stuxnet/all/.

———. "Exclusive: Comedy of Errors Led to False 'Water-Pump Hack' Report." *Wired.com,* November 30, 2011. http://www.wired.com/2011/11/water-pump-hack-mystery-solved/.

———. "Pentagon Hacker McKinnon Wins 10-Year Extradition Battle." *Wired.com,* October 16, 2012. http://www.wired.com/2012/10/mckinnon-extradition-win/.

———. "Prison Computer 'Glitch' Blamed for Opening Cell Doors in Maximum-Security Wing." *Wired .com,* August 16, 2013. http://www.wired.com/2013/08/computer-prison-door-mishap/.

———. "Obama: NSA Must Reveal Bugs Like Heartbleed, Unless They Help the NSA." *Wired.com*, March 15, 2014. http://www.wired.com/2014/04/obama-zero-day/.

———. "U.S. Gov Insists It Doesn't Stockpile Zero-Day Exploits to Hack Enemies." *Wired.com*, November 17, 2014. http://www.wired.com/2014/11/michael-daniel-no-zero-day-stockpile/.

———. "The Evidence That North Korea Hacked Sony Is Flimsy." *Wired.com*, December 17, 2014. http://www.wired.com/2014/12/evidence-of-north-korea-hack-is-thin/.

———. "A Cyberattack Has Caused Confirmed Physical Damage for the Second Time Ever." *Wired.com*, January 8, 2015. http://www.wired.com/2015/01/german-steel-mill-hack-destruction/.

———. "Why Firmware Is So Vulnerable to Hacking, and What Can Be Done About It." *Wired.com*, February 24, 2015. http://www.wired.com/2015/02/firmware-vulnerable-hacking-can-done/.

———. "Verizon: Mobile Malware Isn't a Problem." *Wired.com*, April 15, 2015. http://www.wired.com/2015/04/verizon-no-mobile-malware/.

———. "The U.S. Tried to Stuxnet North Korea's Nuclear Program." *Wired.com*, May 29, 2015. http://www.wired.com/2015/05/us-tried-stuxnet-north-koreas-nuclear-program/.

———. "Attackers Stole Certificate from Foxconn to Hack Kaspersky with Duqu 2.0." *Wired.com*, June 15, 2015. http://www.wired.com/2015/06/foxconn-hack-kaspersky-duqu-2/.

———. "U.S. and British Spies Targeted Antivirus Companies." *Wired.com*, June 22, 2015. http://www.wired.com/2015/06/us-british-spies-targeted-antivirus-companies/.

Zhang, Xiaoming. "China's 1979 War with Vietnam: A Reassessment." *China Quarterly* 184 (2005): 851–874.

Zhu, Junqing. "Commentary: U.S. Wronging of China for Cyber Breaches Harms Mutual Trust." *XinhuaNet*, June 6, 2015. http://news.xinhuanet.com/english/2015-06/06/c_134302843.htm.

Zhu, Rich. "150m Smartphones Affected by Malware." *Shanghai Daily*, July 10, 2015. http://www.shanghaidaily.com/business/it/150m-smartphones-affected-by-malware/shdaily.shtml.

Index

Aaron, Zeke, and magic paint, 293–94
account hijacking, 32–33
address space layout randomization (ASLR), 39, 43
Adobe products: Acrobat, 41; cybersecurity and vulnerabilities in, 41, 42, 72; Flash, 39, 41, 42, 72, 270, 367n11; opinions about, 39; Postscript, 41; purpose of, 42; vulnerabilities in and patches for, 23, 125
Advanced Encryption Standard (AES), National Institute for Standards and Technology (NIST), 45, 46
advanced persistent threat (APT): concept and purpose of, 5, 9; detection of, 10–11, 356n31; incidents and emblematic attacks, 6, 9–10; malware and, 37; notification of from outside, 11, 356n31; reverse-engineering codes for, 374–75n32; time between compromise and discovery, 10–11, 355–56n30
affinity cards, 95–96
Agent.BTZ worm, 8
agoras and castles, 27–28
Air Force, U.S., 163, 387n1
aircraft: avionic redundancies, 29; knowledge about and safety of, 67, 68, 371n25
air-gapping: concept and purpose of, 49; critical infrastructure and cybersecurity, 49–50; cybersecurity role of, 49–50, 128, 368n32, 369n39; infection of air-gapped systems, 8; Iranian nuclear centrifuges facility, 15; mandate for, 76–77; SIPRnet, 8
Akamai, 12, 34, 160, 177
Alaskan oil pipeline Aurora incident, 6, 14, 59
Alcoa, 112
Alexander, Keith, 100, 145, 189, 309, 380n7
Allegheny Technologies Incorporated, 112
alliance defense in cyberspace, 176–78
Amazon and Amazon Web Services, 34, 97, 124, 206
American Airlines, 2
Anderson, Ross, 35, 67, 71, 402–3n33
Android, 39, 39–40, 40, 365n35, 365n37, 365n39
Anonymous, 84, 120, 230
Anthem, 2
antivirus software, 47–48, 125–26, 250, 368n26, 404n48
Apache, 115–16, 205–6

Apple: Apple III advertisement, 364n24; apps for devices from, 39, 365nn34–35; China warranty policy demands, 379n2; guardian warrior status of, 340; iCloud default, 395n13; jailbreaking devices, 39; market share of, 40; security of Macs and prevalence of hacking, 365; security of Microsoft machines compared to, 39, 365nn32–33; SSL vulnerability, 124, 362n27; terrorist iPhone, help breaking into, 205. *See also* iOS; smart phones/iPhones
APT1 (Comment Group), 63, 64, 69, 355–56n30, 371n18, 381–82n28
Aramco attack, 6, 18, 231, 252, 265, 276, 327
Argentina hacker trial, 402n26
Arms and Influence (Schelling), 273
art and art museums, 302
Assange, Julian, 417n6
asynchronous transfer mode (ATM) communications, 21
attachments, 9, 22, 26
attribution: ambiguous, 247–48, 328, 403nn41–42; capabilities for, 344, 420n41; confession and self-attribution, 246–47, 403nn38–40; confidence in, 240–42, 248–50, 315, 316, 340–41, 344, 401n13, 419n37, 420nn39–41; convincing evidence of, 238–40; correctness of, importance of, 238; delayed, 214; deterrence and, 199–200, 225–28, 235–37, 238, 240–41, 250, 340–41; difficulty of, 242–43, 401–2nn22–26; disclosure of attacks and decisions about, 213–14, 215; ease of, factors in, 241–42, 401n18; easy-to-attribute attacks, 228; evidence for, decisions about revelation of, 248–50, 403n43, 404nn45–48; forensic technology to determine, 240–41; government and freelance hackers, 243–46, 250, 305–6, 402nn30–31, 402–403n33; jurisdictional conflicts and, 214; methods by which attribution is made, 240, 344; national coloration of attacks, 198, 243, 250, 402n29; norms on, 318–19; policy of and strategy for, 226–28; proof of, standards for, 238; retaliation and, 250; sophistication of code and, 241–42; strategic stability and false attribution, 315, 316, 414n16; third-party attacks and confusion about, 230
Aurora Alaskan oil pump incident, 6, 14, 59

About the Author

Martin C. Libicki is a distinguished visiting professor at the U.S. Naval Academy and a senior management scientist at the RAND Corporation. His work involves the national security implications of information technology, notably as it involves cybersecurity and cyberwar. He has a PhD from the University of California, Berkeley, and an undergraduate degree from MIT.